Very Practical Ethics

Very Practical Ethics

Engaging Everyday Moral Questions

DAVID BENATAR

OXFORD
UNIVERSITY PRESS

Oxford University Press is a department of the University of Oxford.
It furthers the University's objective of excellence in research, scholarship,
and education by publishing worldwide. Oxford is a registered trade mark of
Oxford University Press in the UK and in certain other countries.

Published in the United States of America by Oxford University Press
198 Madison Avenue, New York, NY 10016, United States of America.

© Oxford University Press 2024

All rights reserved. No part of this publication may be reproduced, stored in
a retrieval system, or transmitted, in any form or by any means, without the
prior permission in writing of Oxford University Press, or as expressly permitted
by law, by license or under terms agreed with the appropriate reprographics
rights organization. Inquiries concerning reproduction outside the scope of the
above should be sent to the Rights Department, Oxford University Press, at the
address above.

You must not circulate this work in any other form
and you must impose this same condition on any acquirer

Library of Congress Cataloging-in-Publication Data
Names: Benatar, David, author.
Title: Very practical ethics : engaging everyday moral questions / David Benatar.
Description: 1. | New York, NY, United States of America : Oxford University Press, [2024]
Identifiers: LCCN 2024013826 | ISBN 9780197780800 (paperback) |
ISBN 9780197780794 (hardback) | ISBN 9780197780824 (epub) |
ISBN 9780197780831 (ebook)
Subjects: LCSH: Applied ethics.
Classification: LCC BJ1031 .B45 2024 | DDC 170—dc23/eng/20240604
LC record available at https://lccn.loc.gov/2024013826

DOI: 10.1093/9780197780831.001.0001

Paperback printed by Marquis Book Printing, Canada
Hardback printed by Bridgeport National Bindery, Inc., United States of America

To Jess
Very practical and ethical (and more)

Contents

Preface	xiii
1. Introduction	1
Quotidian ethics	1
The content and structure of this book—and a guide to readers	2
Methodology	7
Rejecting relativism	7
More plausible competing normative theories	10
The method of practical ethics	12
Right and wrong	13
The scope of morality	17
Manners and morals	19
The scope of duty	21
Ethics, not religion or law	24
Very practical ethics	26
2. Sex	28
Some common errors	29
Sexual practices and sexual orientation	31
The significance view and the casual view	33
Promiscuity (and premarital sex)	34
Marital sex	36
Paedophilia	37
Bestiality and necrophilia	39
Rape	40
Extramarital sex	41
Masturbation	43
Choosing between the significance and casual views	44
The reproductive view and the anti-reproductive view	50
Homosexuality, etc.	52
Incest	56
Conclusion	58
3. Environment	63
Global warming, climate change, and resultant harms	64
Denialism	68
Non-identity	71
Causal inefficacy?	73

Do individuals have a duty not to emit?	78
A lesser duty	80
Objections	88
What is the extent of an individual's duty?	90
Lowering one's carbon footprint	93
Low emissions reductions	93
Diet	94
Driving	96
Flying	98
Procreation	100
What is one's duty?	106
A political duty	107
Conclusion	110

4. Smoking — 112
Smoking alone	114
Harm to others	117
Is the risk increment too negligible?	119
The case of cars	122
Offence to others	124
Two kinds of offence	124
Distinguishing the two kinds of offence	127
What kind of offence does smoking cause others?	131
Abstaining when others do not?	133
Electronic cigarettes	134
Consent	137
Ifs and butts	138
Appendix—Driving and smoking	141

5. Giving Aid — 145
Peter Singer's argument	146
Reliability of the premises	149
Demanding conclusion	156
Voluntary servitude	159
Insurance	163
Restitution	165
Conclusions	168

6. Consuming Animals — 171
Death and suffering	171
Chickens	172
Pigs	173
Cattle	174
Sheep and goats	175
Aquatic animals	176

Speciesism	176
Moral equality?	181
Costs and benefits	184
Utilitarianism	190
Rights theory	191
Contractarianism	197
Causal inefficacy?	202
General Carnivore's last stand	208
Religious arguments	208
'Eating meat benefits animals'	210
'More animals are killed in feeding vegans'	211
Exceptions?	213
A practical postscript	216
7. Language	**218**
Conventions and morality	219
The words in question	221
Group slurs	223
Use and mention	223
Use and use	229
Group names	236
Sexist language	239
The feminist critique	239
'Man'	241
Compounds of 'man'	242
'He'	244
Preferred pronouns	248
Impertinences	251
Should the convention be changed?	253
The (limited) force of convention	254
Inconsistencies	255
Complexities	258
Responding to the 'casual critique'	258
Speciesist language	259
Insults and slurs	260
Companion animals	262
Animal pronouns	263
Profanity	264
Responding to (perceived) breaches of language ethics	267
Conclusion	269
8. Humour	**270**
Problematic categories of humour	270
Non-contextual criticisms	272
Contextual criticisms	277

Common mistakes in humour ethics	280
The benefits are ignored	280
Contextual considerations are oversimplified	282
Offence is given too much weight	284
Judging jokes	285
Conclusion	286

9. Bullshit — 288

What is bullshit?	289
The prevalence and dangers of bullshit	293
Responding to bullshit	296
Tolerating bullshit	297
Challenging bullshit	300
Producing bullshit	304
Conclusion	309

10. Forgiveness — 310

Some cases	311
What is forgiveness?	312
Who can forgive?	313
Which negative attitudes and feelings?	314
Spectrum or threshold?	315
What forgiveness is not	317
Pharmaceuticals and forgetting	318
Justification	319
Excuse	319
Condoning	320
Mercy	321
Reconciliation	322
Performatives and behaviour	322
Alteration of the normative situation	323
To forgive or not to forgive?	327
Negative reactive attitudes and feelings	329
Repentance	330
Forgiving the unrepentant?	333
Is it ever wrong not to forgive?	338
Taking back forgiveness	339
When (not) to say 'I forgive you'	340
Who may forgive?	341
Conclusion	343

11. Conclusion — 345

Causal inefficacy	346
How demanding is duty?	349
The paradox of desert	353

Introducing the paradox	354
Application of the paradox	356
Implications for the extent of duty	359
Offence	362
What is offence?	363
Evaluating offence	365
Applications	366
Non-quotidian views about quotidian ethics	367
Uncommon views	367
The unreliability of many common views	372
Human fallibility	373
Moral knowledge and moral action	374
Judging others	375
A concluding, but not a final word	377
Notes	379
Bibliography	419
Index	435

Preface

Practical ethics is an area of philosophical inquiry devoted to the study of practical moral problems. Not all such problems are *equally* practical. The problems examined in this book are among those that are, in important senses, more practical than others.

They are moral problems confronting ordinary individuals in their everyday lives. Such problems are to be distinguished from those that are faced by people in their professional roles or in their public positions, and from those pertaining to law or public policy. They are also to be distinguished from problems that ordinary individuals might face only rarely.

Partly because the problems in this book are faced by so many people, and so often, they have much greater practicality. They are also more practical because anybody reaching conclusions about them can, at least in principle, immediately act upon those conclusions. By contrast, reaching conclusions about what the law or public policy should be is practically far removed from implementing those decisions.

The main title of this book is intended both to highlight the relevance of the issues that are discussed in the book and to differentiate it from at least three or four earlier books that have all been entitled *Practical Ethics*.[1] The subtitle further clarifies the book's focus on everyday ethical issues.

Regrettably, such issues, albeit with some exceptions, have historically received relatively little attention by philosophers and philosophy teachers.[2] That has begun to change. *Very Practical Ethics* is intended as a further step in addressing this neglect.

In the Introduction that follows this Preface, I say much more about the content of the book, and something about its structure. I also provide a guide to readers, who, I hope, will include students of philosophy,[3] and non-philosophers, in addition to professional philosophers. Having such a broad readership in mind requires presenting some concepts for novices that are unnecessary for those already well versed in philosophy. My guide to readers indicates which (subsequent) parts of the Introduction might be skipped by those who require no introduction to such concepts, and who wish to move directly to the substantive topics.

Although this is a book of very practical ethics, it is not a 'how-to (be moral)' book. There are *some* clear conclusions that can be reached—such as 'do not eat meat' and 'do not smoke in the presence of those who are not themselves smoking'. However, the conclusions are not always that straightforward. Sometimes the evidence and arguments do not generate a definitive conclusion. This, I shall argue, is true of sexual ethics. In other cases, while the weight of evidence and argument support one of competing conclusions, that conclusion is general rather than particular. For example, the conclusion that one has a duty to limit one's carbon emissions, even when coupled with general principles governing such reduction, leaves open the question whether some specific emissions are morally prohibited or morally permitted.

Turning from substance to style, there are two practices that should be explained. First, I avoid the common academic convention of referring to people by their surnames only. In polite society one does not usually address or even refer to people in this way if they are in one's presence. I do not see why that should change if they are not in one's presence. Thus, I prefer to use both first and last name, or title and last name.[4]

Second, I put all references to racial categories, such as 'black' and 'white', in scare quotes. (The exceptions are where I am quoting others who have not done so.) I do so in order to signal just how problematic these categories are. They are dubious categories and have a vicious history.[5] While there are some who think that the same categories must now be used in order to rectify the legacy of that history, this view underestimates just how problematic continued use of these categories is. Somebody who recommended that I drop the scare quotes, was willing to 'grant that the categories have fuzzy boundaries, and that race is socially constructed', but said that in 'many respects . . . the categories are not all that vague. Barak Obama is Black. Rachel Dolezal is not'.

I do not deny that there are clear cases, but there are many more contested cases than this comment suggests. Barack Obama, for example, given his 'white' mother, would be regarded, in the South African context, as 'Coloured' rather than 'African' (and thus not 'black' in the narrower sense in which that word is used in what is arguably still the world's most racially obsessed country). While Barack Obama is not South African, the point is that the same person would be classified in different ways in different places, which tells us something about the categories. For a further example, consider that there have been some contexts in which (even Ashkenazi) Jews have *not* been regarded as 'white', and other contexts in which they *are* regarded as 'white'.[6]

Given the spectrum of racial features, and the oddity and arbitrariness of racial classifications, there are millions, of people who are unclear cases, even when some people think that they are clear. That is precisely what I am trying to emphasize. There is some value in keeping the absurdity and danger of such classifications front and centre.[7] Those who doubt this, should ask whether they would be similarly happy to use terms like 'mulatto', 'quadroon', and 'octoroon', all racial classifications once in use in the United States,[8] without scare quotes.

The only chapter in this book that was, prior to some minor revisions, previously published, is the chapter on humour. That paper first appeared under the title 'Taking Humour (Ethics) Seriously, but Not Too Seriously', in the *Journal of Practical Ethics*, Vol. 2, No. 1, June 2014, pp. 24–43.

Some sections within other chapters draw on other previously published work, but are generally written afresh. One of the central ideas in Chapter 2 draws on 'Two Views of Sexual Ethics: Promiscuity, Paedophilia and Rape', in *Public Affairs Quarterly*, Vol. 16, No. 3, July 2002, pp. 191–201, although it is developed *much* further in this book. That chapter also presents related ideas first published in 'Homosexuality, bestiality, and necrophilia', in *Palgrave Handbook of Sexual Ethics*, edited by David Boonin (Cham, Switzerland: Palgrave Macmillan, 2022), pp. 223–31.

In Chapter 7, some of the material on group slurs is adapted from 'The New Blasphemy', *Politicsweb*, 30 March 2021.[9] Parts of the section on sexist language are drawn from 'Sexist Language: Alternatives to the Alternatives', in *Public Affairs Quarterly*, Vol. 19, No. 1, January 2005, pp. 1–9, and some ideas on impertinences were first presented in 'A First Name Basis?', *Think*, Vol. 10, No. 29, Autumn 2011, pp. 51–57. The section, in the Conclusion, about the paradox of desert, is adapted from "The Paradox of Desert," in *Journal of Applied Philosophy*, doi: 10.1111/japp.12721.

I am struck by the large number of people whom some other authors thank for contributions to their work. By contrast, I have received input from only a few people, which heightens my appreciation for the role they played in helping me polish the manuscript. David Boonin provided numerous helpful comments on the entire manuscript. Two other (but anonymous) reviewers for Oxford University Press also read the whole manuscript and provided helpful feedback. Jessica du Toit's astute input led me to make some clarifications to Chapters 1, 6, and 10. Dale Jamieson kindly read Chapter 3 and made valuable suggestions. Travis Rebello provided some research assistance, primarily for Chapter 4. Todd Shackelford, with the assistance of Austin Jeffery and Jennifer Vonk, provided some sources on unusual sexual practices among non-human animals (for Chapter 2). Larry Bloom and, separately, those who attended a Philosophical Briefings seminar at Western University in London, Ontario, discussed my thoughts on the paradox of desert. It was while on sabbatical at the Rotman Institute of Philosophy at Western University that I completed this book.

Finally, some more personal acknowledgements. I have now taken early retirement from the University of Cape Town, and left South Africa. This is thus a good opportunity to extend my thanks to the University of Cape Town Philosophy Department's administrative staff, with whom I worked, especially during my long tenure as head of department. While they did not make *direct* contributions to this book or to my earlier ones, their superlative skills and attitudes provided the kind of support that enabled me to continue doing my academic work. I am immensely appreciative.

As always, I am grateful to my family not only for their interest in, and support of, my work but also for being the exemplary people they are.

1
Introduction

The ethics of everyday life may sound mundane. However, while it is most certainly, and appropriately, mundane in the sense of being rooted in the material world, it is not mundane in a second sense—dull, or lacking interest. Ethical questions about our daily lives are, or at least should be, of great interest to us all.

Moreover, many of the specific views I shall defend about everyday ethical issues are far from commonplace. That does not mean that they are either extreme or *needlessly* provocative. Instead, ordinary thinking about everyday ethics, much like ordinary thinking about other ethical questions, is often mired in convention and oversimplification. Any attempt to think freshly, with nuance, and without an ideological agenda, is likely to lead not only to unusual views about each particular question, but also to an unusual *constellation* of views about the different questions.

Quotidian ethics

Practical ethics is the area of philosophy devoted to asking and responding to practical moral questions. It is distinguished from other areas of moral philosophy, which focus on more theoretical questions, such as (i) those concerning the nature of morality (the domain of metaethics), and (ii) what makes some actions morally right and others morally wrong, or which character traits are virtues, and which are vices (the subject matter of normative ethical theory).

Most work in practical ethics has been focused on moral questions concerning law and public policy, or professional ethics, or other 'big' (sometimes life-and-death questions). Such questions include whether abortion, capital punishment, human cloning, affirmative action, or limiting immigration are morally permissible or should be legally permissible. They also include questions about the fiduciary duties of professionals and elected and other public officials.

The subject of this book is different. It is concerned with the ethical problems that confront ordinary people in their everyday lives. By 'ordinary people' I refer to people acting in their individual capacities rather than in a professional or other positional capacity. By 'everyday lives' I mean the kinds of questions that pervade the lives of ordinary people, rather than ones that they might encounter only rarely in a life. Thus, ordinary people may very occasionally face the decision whether to have an abortion, whether to take their own lives or to assist the suicide of others. However, these are (hopefully) rare decisions and thus fall beyond the scope of what I have called 'quotidian ethics'[1] (from the Old French 'cotidien' and the Latin 'quotidianus', meaning 'every day').[2]

Obviously, there can be no precise boundary to the area of inquiry designated by the term 'quotidian ethics'. What proportion of 'ordinary people' must face a moral issue, and just how often must they face it, in order for it to count as a quotidian ethical issue? There can be no precise answers to these questions, but there is nonetheless some value in identifying quotidian ethics as an interesting subset of practical ethical questions.

The content and structure of this book—and a guide to readers

There are more topics in quotidian ethics than could possibly be included in a book of reasonable length.[3] However, the book does cover a wide range of topics: sex, forgiveness, consuming animals, helping those in need, smoking in the presence of non-smokers, humour, bullshit, language, and what duties we have with regard to preserving the environment and avoiding global warming.

More specifically, given the quotidian ethics theme of the book, I shall examine those facets of these topics that have relevance to ordinary people in everyday life. Thus, for example, some ethical issues pertaining to the environment relate to which public policies, laws, and international agreements should be put in place to prevent further global warming and to protect the environment in other ways. However, these are not the *quotidian* ethical questions. The quotidian ethical questions are instead about the nature and extent of the *individual's* duties regarding the environment, in either the presence or the absence of appropriate policies, laws, and international treaties. Something similar might be said about the difference between whether smoking in the presence of non-smokers should be *legally* permitted, and the question, either in the presence or absence of such a law, whether it is *morally* permissible to do so.

Some of the issues covered in this book are matters of life and death. They impact on whether somebody, human or animal, will live or die. Others are less momentous. Some might wonder why one would include the relatively unimportant issues at all. Indeed, Peter Singer cited the relative unimportance of sexual morality as one reason for excluding a discussion of that topic from his book, *Practical Ethics*. I do not follow that lead. Merely because an issue is *relatively* unimportant, does not mean that it has *no* importance. Those who doubt this should imagine what life would be like if we attended only to life-and-death issues, and paid no attention to all the others. This would be a world without civility, without respect for privacy, without consideration for people's dignity, and a world even more laden with bullshit than ours already is. Even if these failings do not kill, they can make life miserable. It would typically not be as miserable as absolute poverty, but it would nonetheless be miserable, sometimes with life-threatening effects.

Peter Singer offers a second reason for excluding sexual morality from his *Practical Ethics*. He says, correctly, that ethics 'is not primarily about sex', and that we should not understand 'morality as a system of nasty puritanical prohibitions, mainly designed to stop people from having fun'.[4] He is correct too that decisions 'about sex may involve considerations of honesty, concern for others, prudence, avoidance of harm to others and so on, but the same could be said of decisions about driving a car'.[5] That, in my view, is not a (decisive) reason to *exclude* a discussion of sex, but is rather a reason also to *include* a discussion of car use. (Car use raises a range of ethical issues. While no single chapter of this book is devoted to car use, those issues are raised in the course of other chapters—the chapter on the environment and the one about smoking.)

A third reason for including sex is that, unlike among academics, at least in the western world, who may disproportionately hold the view that sex is not, in itself, especially laden with ethical import, this is not a view shared by the vast majority of humanity. It is thus worth inquiring whether the view that prevails in western universities is correct, or whether there might be something to be said for the view held by most people.

The mixture of topics covered in this book and their varied importance raises a question about the order in which to present them. There is no obvious order in which they must appear. The trouble with presenting the less weighty issues first is that some readers might see them as relatively unimportant and then not read further. The risk of presenting the life-and-death issues first is that the other issues might then seem like an anticlimax. Alternating between more and less momentous topics would also be odd, because some topics are more closely related to one another than to others. This is true of the three topics I cover that are matters of life and death—the environment, consuming animals, and giving aid.

Although the chapters have to be sequenced in one particular order in this book, I have attempted, as far as possible, to write each chapter in a way that it can stand alone, rather than resting on or building on earlier chapters. This means that, generally, *the chapters may be read in any order the reader prefers*, rather than specifically in the order they appear in this book. Perhaps the clearest, but still a limited, exception, is that in the chapter on consuming animals I explicitly refer to the earlier chapter on the environment. This is because there is a problem that is common to both those topics and there is a need to point to similarities and differences between the manifestation of that problem in the two topics. Notwithstanding that reference, however, it is still possible to read those two chapters in a different order from that in which they appear.

Given the necessity of choosing an order for the chapters' appearance in this book, I begin with sex. My jovial pretext for doing so, is that there is a sense in which all our moral problems begin with (procreative) sex. Without procreative sex none of us would have existed to confront the moral issues that face us. (Even if you were the product of artificial or assisted reproduction, the same is not true of all your ancestors, whose existences were a necessary condition for yours.)[6]

The chapter on sex is followed by one on the environment. The increasingly urgent environmental problem—global warming and resultant climate change—is partly a product of the sheer number of people there now are. The other factor driving the problem is the volume of greenhouse gases that is being emitted. No individual can solve this problem. Nevertheless, there are important questions to be asked about what individuals should do, especially in the absence of national and international cooperative schemes designed to satisfactorily resolve the problem.

The next chapter is concerned with smoking—specifically tobacco products rather than marijuana or other such substances. While some attention is devoted to the ethics of smoking when others are not affected by the smoke, the bulk of the chapter asks whether smokers may smoke in the presence of non-smokers. Readers in some parts of the world may respond that the answer to this question is *obviously* negative. In doing so, they may forget just how recent and geographically limited that response is. There are still many places where people think nothing of smoking in indoor public places. Even where smoking in the presence of non-smokers has become much less acceptable, it is often still the case that smokers will smoke in crowded outdoor spaces and thoroughfares, as well as 'in the privacy' of their own homes and cars, even though they share these spaces with, respectively, non-smoking members of the public, and non-smoking members of their family.

The smoking question is also interesting because it highlights one context in which offence—a particular kind of offence—*is* a good reason for desisting from the offending practice. It is helpful to distinguish this kind of offence from other kinds, which carry much less moral weight.

Although smoking (whether or not in the presence of non-smokers) does have some (relatively small) impact on global warming, that is not the focus of this chapter. Thus, there are some connections between the environment chapter and the one on smoking. Between them, these two chapters also consider the ethics of driving. The environment chapter focuses on the environmental impact of driving, while the smoking chapter compares the risks posed by smoking in the presence of non-smokers with the risks drivers pose to others.

Following the chapter on smoking is one on the extent of an individual's duty to assist those in dire need. It focuses on giving aid to the world's absolute poor, but similar questions sometimes arise for other forms of human and animal suffering.

Animals are the subject of the following chapter, but here the focus is not on positive duties to alleviate animal suffering and prevent animal death. Rather, I consider whether we have negative duties to desist from killing animals, and from purchasing or eating their flesh and other products.

The next chapter shifts from momentous life-and-death issues to three chapters related to communication, the first of which is about language. The shift may seem jarring, but there may be something instructive in such a response. Curiously, many people today, judging by their expressed outrage, seem much more concerned about perceived breaches of language—and humour—ethics than they are by killing and eating animals, or allowing impoverished people to die. That lop-sidedness suggests a distorted ethical perspective. However, this does not mean that the ethics of language is unworthy of consideration. The fact that so much store is placed on it, gives additional reason to explore it and to debunk some of the views people hold about it. This is the longest chapter in the book. However, it is divided into subsidiary topics, and readers may read selectively (but not without some cost).

The eighth chapter is about humour. It includes some jokes. (There are more jokes in other chapters, although those are generally relegated to the notes for more studious readers.) Although the humour chapter is about a light-hearted matter, the discussion of the ethics of humour is serious.

Although bullshit, in its technical philosophical senses, is typically a linguistic practice, it raises a unique set of issues that are covered in the following chapter. Hitherto, most of the limited philosophical discussion of bullshit, has been about its ontology—what it is. I survey those views, but the focus of this chapter is on whether it is morally permissible to bullshit, and on what, if anything, we should do about the bullshit of others. Much of what is said in this chapter also applies to phenomena such as deception, disingenuousness, and the use of pretexts (to the extent that these are not merely variant forms of bullshit).

The final substantive chapter (before the Conclusion) is about forgiveness. The ethical questions about forgiveness—when, if ever, one may, must, or must not forgive—apply to breaches of ethics in all the previous chapters, as well as to any other moral breaches. Although forgiveness is something we do, it is, I argue, something that is fundamentally done in the head, even if that then has behavioural manifestations. In this way, forgiveness is unlike the other topics covered, all of which apply to actions, including verbal actions.

In the Conclusion, I examine some recurring issues, and undertake some comparative work, looking at similarities and differences between the different contexts in which those issues arise. In the process, I show how the same line of reasoning can lead to somewhat different conclusions in the different contexts.

In the remainder of this Introduction, I shall outline some other introductory matters. Not all readers will need to read all of what I have to say in these remarks. In the next section, I render explicit the methodology that I use to grapple with practical ethical questions. Those who already have some familiarity with practical ethics could skip this section, although some of them may nonetheless be interested in my explicit rendering of the methodology.

In the following section, I discern different senses in which the word 'right' and 'wrong' are used. This too will be of less interest to seasoned philosophers, but should be very helpful to those who are new to academic thinking about ethics.

I then turn, in the next section, to examining the scope of morality. Here I am interested in what falls within the domain of morality, and what falls beyond it. This is not a question about what is morally right and what is morally wrong, but rather about what matters can be subject to moral evaluation. In the section that follows, I look more specifically at the relationship between morals and manners, and ask to what extent manners are, and are not, part of morality. These questions are more contested, and therefore interest in them should not be restricted to beginners.

The same is true of what I say next, about the scope of *duty*. This is to be distinguished from the question about the scope of *morality*. Once we know the domain of morality, there can be competing views about how extensive or demanding our duties are within that domain.

In the penultimate section of the introduction, I speak about the relationship between ethics and, respectively, religion and law. Because non-philosophers regularly confuse these, reading this section will be important for those new to the academic study of ethics.

In the final section, I say something about why the study of quotidian ethical issues constitutes *very* practical ethics.

Methodology

Asking an ethical question is easy enough. One can simply ask whether some or other action may or may not be performed.[7] However, how does one go about *answering* an ethical question?

Rejecting relativism

Some people, usually non-philosophers, think—or at least *say* they think—that ethics is 'all relative'. According to such a relativistic view, whether an action is morally permissible depends entirely on whether the person performing the action, or the culture or society in which the action is performed, thinks that the action is morally permissible. If such a view were correct, then practical ethics would be a set of exclusively empirical questions. It would amount to determining what an individual's, a culture's, or a society's views about different practices actually are. Doing that, might be less straightforward than it appears. This is because people sometimes say one thing but think another, either because they are dishonest or because they do not truly know their own views. It is also unclear how we are meant to determine what a society or culture 'thinks'. Even if it is what a majority of people in a culture or society thinks, how do we determine the parameters of a culture or society, or what most of its members think? Not everybody responds to surveys. Should we accept the dictum that, in determining what somebody or some group thinks, 'actions speak louder than words', such that we may then be guided by observable actions rather than self-reports of opinions? Even then, there will often be challenges in determining what most people do.

We may set these problems aside, because there is a deep flaw in the view that ethics is relative in the sense of being determined entirely by the views either of the individual performing an action or of the culture or society in which the action is performed. This flaw is a familiar one to philosophers, but one that is lost on many, but certainly not all, non-philosophers. If what is right depends on what an individual, culture, or society thinks, then there are (almost?) no limits on what can be morally permissible. If an individual or culture thinks, as many have, that torturing heretics, executing homosexuals, enslaving people, or engaging in genocide, are morally permissible, then we have no basis for morally condemning such actions when they are performed by those people or cultures who think that they are permissible.

It is hard to believe that a commitment to such implications would survive a true 'test of faith'. Such a test would involve the relativist being subjected to some highly aversive treatment—torture or rape, for example—that the tester believes to be permissibly inflicted on relativists. How many relativists would restrict their objections to such treatment to those of the form 'please stop, I don't like this'? How many of them would desist from adding objections of the kind: 'Please stop, what you are doing is *wrong*'? There is a way to answer that question, namely by applying the test to all relativists. However, it would surely be unethical to conduct such tests, and thus we are restricted to imagining what their results would be. That is not hard to do. There would likely be a few highly committed holdouts. The rest, if we know anything about human nature, would likely venture moral objection.

There is another way of expressing the flaw in moral relativism. According to this view, it is impossible for people to be mistaken in their moral judgements. If, according to this view, somebody or some culture *thinks* that an action is right (or wrong) then it actually is right (or wrong) for them. That is an astounding view to hold. If people can be mistaken about almost everything else, then it would be surprising if they could not be mistaken in their moral judgements. Yet that is precisely what moral relativists would have us believe.

One reason why many people are attracted to moral relativism is that they fail to distinguish it from what is called descriptive relativism. The latter is the view that there is moral disagreement, between individuals and between groups. Descriptive relativism is clearly true. There *is* moral disagreement, although there might not be quite as much as people think. The point is that the fact of moral disagreement does not mean that all the disagreeing parties are correct in holding their respective views.

While moral disagreement is not the same as disagreement about empirical matters, understanding the logical distinction between what somebody thinks and whether they are correct, can be illustrated by empirical disagreement. While people may disagree, for example, about whether there is anthropogenic (that is, human-caused) climate change, it does not follow that everybody is correct. Views may differ, but to the extent that these views are incompatible with one another, at least some of the competing views must be wrong.

As difficult as it sometimes is to prove, or convince people, which empirical views are correct, it is admittedly even more difficult to prove, or convince people, which ethical views are correct. However, that does not mean that everybody is right.

The rejection of relativism does not entail the view that local circumstances or even local views do not count. In other words, one can think that the context makes a difference to what we ought to do. Whether, for example, one may make a noise, might well depend, at least in part, on whether there is anybody in the vicinity who will be disturbed by that noise. Even an individual's or a culture's views can make a difference to whether an action is right or wrong. If, for example, one has a (defeasible) moral duty to treat people respectfully, what one should and should not do might then depend, in part, on what, in a particular context, is regarded as respectful or disrespectful. Those who reject relativism can—and should—recognize this. The rejection of relativism is the rejection of the view that what is thought to be morally right or wrong is *decisive* in determining what is right or wrong.

More plausible competing normative theories

Many of those who reject moral relativism may (nonetheless) treat practical ethics as *applied ethics*, a term that is often treated as synonymous with practical ethics, but which, technically, is not identical. Talk of *applied* ethics suggests that something is being applied to something. A common interpretation of this is that normative ethical theory is being applied to practical questions. Normative relativism is one possible, but unpromising, normative theory. However, there are other, more plausible theories, over which philosophers are more evenly divided.

For example, consequentialists are of the view that the right action is determined not by any intrinsic feature of the action but rather entirely by its consequences. While some consequentialists think that we are obligated only to produce consequences that are 'good enough', the so-called satisficers, many others, the 'maximizers', think that the right action is the one that produces the *best* consequences. They can be divided over the question of 'best for whom?'. Normative egoists think that our focus should be on 'best for the person performing the action'. More plausibly, utilitarians think that the right action is the one that produces the best consequences overall, taking all affected beings into account.

While consequentialists can disagree about what kinds of consequences are good, there is an intuitive plausibility to the idea that once one has identified what is good, it is better to produce more rather than less of it.

Nevertheless, consequentialism has been subjected to some important objections. Most fundamentally, because it treats consequences as decisive in evaluating actions, it must hold that the end always justifies the means. That view is far from obviously true, and it is unsurprising that there are others who think that the end does not *always* justify the means—that some actions are morally impermissible even if they will produce the best consequences. The suggestion here is that it is wrong to steal, torture, or kill innocent people even if the consequences of doing so are better than the consequences of all alternative actions.

The view that the end does not always justify means is often characterized as 'deontology'. That term, which is much less transparent than 'consequentialism' is, can be used in narrower and broader senses. In the narrower sense it refers to so-called duty-based views (where the duty in question is not a consequentialist duty, but rather a duty to perform or not perform certain actions based, at least partially, on their intrinsic nature). In the broader sense, the term 'deontology' can *also* be used to refer to so-called rights-based views.[8] Deontological views are arguably even more diverse than consequentialist ones, perhaps because one way of characterizing them is simply as a negation of the consequentialist view that the end *always* justifies the means.

Thus understood, deontological views are *not* necessarily committed to rejecting the relevance of consequences to moral deliberation. They are committed only to rejecting the idea that the consequences are the decisive moral consideration. Such a view is congenial to those who fear that consequentialists would either deny rights to individuals or would override those rights too readily.

The problem for deontology arises when the consequences of not violating a right are sufficiently extreme that it begins to look unreasonable to refuse to perform an intrinsically bad action when that is the only way to avoid catastrophe. While many people think that it would be wrong, for example, to kill one person to save two, or even five, or ten, it is much harder to defend the view that it is wrong to kill one person if that is necessary to save thousands, or tens of thousands, or hundreds of thousands of people. For this reason, some deontologists agree that while we may not usually infringe the rights of people, we may do so if that is necessary to avert catastrophic outcomes.[9] The challenge for them is to provide an explanation for this, that is consistent with deontology, and that does not instead collapse into some form of consequentialism.

Despite the differences between consequentialists and deontologists, they both seek to answer the same question: 'What should I do?' Other moral theorists think that we should be primarily concerned with a different question: 'What kind of person should I be?' These virtue theorists are primarily interested in what character traits one should have, to what extent one should have them, and in what combination.

This is not to say that virtue theorists are uninterested in what we do. They just think that what we should do is derivative from the kinds of people we should be. For consequentialists and deontologists, the derivation works in the opposite direction. They are fundamentally interested in what we should do (and not do), and then derive from this a view about what sort of person one should be. For example, according to utilitarians, one should be the kind of person disposed to act in ways that maximize utility.

The method of practical ethics

The purpose of briefly mentioning these normative theoretical disagreements is not to explore them, and *a fortiori*, not to resolve them. Indeed, the point to be made is that these disagreements are ongoing, and that any approach to practical moral problems that amounts to applying one or other theory to the practical issues is going to face a problem. That problem is that those who do not accept the theory, will reject the idea that the way to answer the practical question is by applying that theory.

That is why, in grappling with practical moral problems, it is better to bypass normative ethical theories as much as possible. This is less problematic than it may seem to those with firm normative theoretical commitments. This is because the most plausible versions of any of the most competitive theories are likely to agree on the right course of action in most cases, even if they do so for different reasons. There will be extreme situations in which adherents of different normative ethical theories may diverge, but these are not likely to be typical quotidian ethical cases.

Even if, and when, they diverge regarding quotidian ethical issues, it is best not to assume one of the competing theories, but rather to attempt to grapple directly with the practical issue. This is the case, not only because there is theoretical disagreement that is not resolved by application of a theory, but also because grappling with the practical problem can inform theory.

If we avoid the application of theory implied by the term 'applied ethics' and seek instead to do 'practical ethics', we need some other method for engaging the practical moral problems. The method that I and others use is rarely rendered explicit, but it can be.[10] In broad outline, the method is to proceed from the most reliable relevant premises, by way of appropriate inferences to the conclusions that follow. This process has four components. These are not four separate stages, but rather four interwoven features.

The first of these is *conceptual analysis*. Maximum clarity is required, both to understand whatever question is posed and to answer it as well as possible. Language contains ambiguities. Further confusion is generated by its sloppy use. Good arguments require the elimination of such problems. Thus, one crucial component of our method is to analyse what the question and key terms mean. If the precise question is not understood, then whatever answer one provides will be unreliable. Both in the question and in the answer, the relevant sense of ambiguous terms must be made explicit, words must be used precisely, and key concepts must be explained.

The second feature is what we might call *empirical data-referencing*. When reflecting on practical moral problems, the relevant facts about the world are crucially important. Sometimes the relevant facts are clearly apparent. More often they require careful study. Answering empirical questions is not the task of philosophers but rather of (natural and social) scientists. Although philosophers (as philosophers) do not generate empirical data they must draw on scientific findings. They must do so honestly and critically. Cherry-picking data to suit one's preferences puts the epistemic cart before the evidentiary horse. At the same time, not all data are equally reliable and thus some discernment is required. Even then, the exercise of that discernment should not be guided by what would serve one's preconceptions.

The third feature is *normative testing*. Although good answers to practical moral questions are reliant on the facts, they are not determined by the facts. Moral arguments also embody normative claims.[11] Good moral arguments will start with the most basic, reliable normative assumptions and argue for more contested moral claims from there. Normative claims are tested by a variety of standards. They must comply with logical standards (more about which I shall say below). Other tests include their explanatory power, and their attentiveness (but not their servility) to moral intuitions. (Whether the method of thought-experiment complies with these standards is a matter of some dispute.)

The final feature of the methodology is *logical thinking*. The laws of logic are really the laws of thought. They require, among other things, consistency, drawing appropriate inferences and avoiding inappropriate ones, and eschewing irrelevancies (such as *ad hominem* attacks). The requirements of logic must be met in analysing concepts, testing norms, applying these to empirical data, and making the inferences that generate one's conclusions.

Right and wrong

Discussions of practical ethics will inevitably be replete with references to 'right' and 'wrong'. However, neither of those terms are unambiguous, with 'right' being even more ambiguous than 'wrong'. Some clarification of the different senses of these terms is thus required.

Obviously, there are *non-moral* senses of both 'right' and 'wrong'. If, for example, one asks a child what '2 + 2' equals, and the child answers 'four', then we can say that the answer is right (or correct), but we make no moral claim in doing so. Similarly, if the child answers 'five', and we respond that the answer is 'wrong' we are not thereby passing any moral judgement. We mean only that the answer is mathematically incorrect.

Even if we set aside non-moral senses of 'right' or 'wrong', these words remain ambiguous. (See Figure 1.1.)

One sense of 'right' is 'required'. An action is morally required if we *must* perform it—or, put another way, if it would be morally wrong not to perform it. However, 'right' might also mean 'permissible'. An action that is morally permissible is one that one *may* perform if one so chooses, but which one is *not obligated* to perform. In other words, while it is wrong not to perform required actions, it is not wrong to desist from performing permitted actions.

There is *a* sense, albeit a different one, in which a morally required action is also a kind of morally permissible action. That is to say, it is not impermissible to perform morally required actions. However, there is a reason why we do and should distinguish between morally required and morally permissible actions. Unlike (other) permissible actions, it *is* morally wrong not to perform a morally required action. Morally required actions lack the discretionary element that characterizes paradigmatic permissible actions.

When the word 'right' is used as an adjective (or even as an adverb), it is most commonly used in one of these two senses. However, there is a third adjectival sense (or related adverbial sense), which might be captured as 'morally preferable', 'morally praiseworthy', 'morally desirable', or 'supererogatory'[12]—doing something good that is beyond the requirements of duty. It should be most clear why 'right' in this sense differs from 'required'. Such actions are, by definition, more than one is required to do. It may be less clear how this category differs from 'permissible'. This is because, like (other)

Right	Wrong
1. Required (Must)	~1. Prohibited (Must not)
2. Permissible (May: Neither 1 nor ~1/~2)	~2. Impermissible (May not)
3. Supererogatory (Better)	~3. Deficient (Better not)
4. A right	4. A right violation

Figure 1.1 Morally right and morally wrong.

permissible actions, supererogatory actions are permissible rather than required. However, unlike other permissible actions, which have no positive moral value, supererogatory actions do secure 'moral credit'. Playing chess may be (merely) permissible, but it typically has no positive moral value. By contrast, to the extent that spending all one's spare time helping the poor is not a moral requirement, it does nonetheless have positive moral value.

The word 'wrong' is less ambiguous than 'right', for the simple reason that 'wrong' is, in one sense, the opposite of both of the first two senses of 'right'. The opposite of a morally required action, that is, an action one *must* perform, is a morally prohibited action, an action one *must not* perform. The opposite of a morally permissible action, an action one *may* perform, is a morally impermissible one, an action one *may not* perform. However, there is no difference between a morally prohibited action and a morally impermissible one. Both are actions that one 'may not' or 'must not' perform.

However, there is a different sense of 'wrong' that contrasts with the third sense of 'right'. According to this sense an action is 'wrong' if, while not morally prohibited, it would be better not to do. This is admittedly a sense used more rarely, but it does seem to have at least some application. Perhaps, for example, your refusal to forgive a particular person for a particular wrong is not prohibited, but nonetheless has some negative moral value. It would be morally better to forgive, and it is morally worse that you do not.

These three senses of 'right' and 'wrong' can be conceived of as existing on a spectrum. There are two ways of representing that spectrum, as illustrated in Figure 1.2.

The difference between those two representations is that (a) represents supererogatory actions as ones that are *beyond* the requirements of duty, which is what supererogation is. Here, there is a spectrum ranging from prohibited to merely deficient, to neutral-permitted, to required, and finally to beyond that which is required. That is one reasonable way of capturing the

(a)	Prohibited	Deficient	Permitted	Required	Supererogatory

(b)	Prohibited	Permitted				Required
		Deficient (Negative value)	Neutral (Neither positive nor negative value)	Supererogatory (Positive value)		

Figure 1.2 Right and wrong on a spectrum.

different categories. Another reasonable way is illustrated in (b), where supererogatory actions are (again correctly) represented, along with morally deficient actions, as a species of permitted action—that is action that is neither required nor strictly prohibited.

Figure 1.2 may well be an oversimplification in the following way. It suggests that the boundaries between the different categories are sharp. In fact, they are more plausibly thought of as being fuzzy. Where exactly does duty end and supererogation begin? How morally deficient must an action be for it to be prohibited? Similarly, when does an action veer from having strictly neutral moral value into being either marginally deficient or marginally positive? These are contested matters, and not only in the substantial ways that will be elaborated below. Even those with broad theoretical agreement about the scope of duty, can disagree about whether some actions are prohibited rather than merely deficient, and about whether some actions are required or instead supererogatory. For this reason, it is best to see the boundaries between the different categories as fuzzy and imprecise.

All the foregoing senses of 'right' and 'wrong' are adjectival (or adverbial) senses. 'Right' also functions as an abstract noun—'a right'. Talk of rights is now widespread not only in moral, but also in political and legal discourse. However, this was not always the case. Talk of rights was once relatively rare (and before that, almost entirely absent). It is now so pervasive that some people seem to think that no other moral vocabulary is necessary. For those people, all and only those actions that violate rights are morally wrong. That is a mistake.[13] We need a wide variety of concepts to capture the various nuances of morality. While rights have correlative duties, we still need the distinct concept of duty, both to fully understand those rights that have correlative duties, but also to identify duties that are not correlated to rights. In addition to rights and duties, we need to be able to talk about supererogation, virtue, and vice, for example. Those who recognize that there is more to morality than merely rights, can still recognize that one way in which something can be wrong is that it violates a right.

In contrast to those who want to reduce all moral discourse to the language of rights, there are others who think that we should reject all talk of moral rights on the grounds that there simply are no such things. This critique seems to be grounded in the mistake of reifying rights—presuming that those who appeal to them think that they exist as a kind of *thing*. That, however, is a very uncharitable reading of what is meant by 'a right'. Speaking about a right is not like the proposition that there are such beings as (real rather than fictional) unicorns. Instead, to say that somebody has 'a right' is to say that they have a claim, privilege (or liberty), power, or immunity.[14] A moral (or even a legal) claim, for example, is not an object but rather a shorthand for speaking about moral (or legal) relationships.

Although we can speak about 'a wrong', that phrase is not perfectly parallel to 'a right'. As an abstract noun, 'a right' is something that somebody *has*. By contrast, 'a wrong' is something that is done (in the broad sense that can include omissions). Although this looks like another abstract noun, it is actually a nominalized adjective. If a wrong$_{adjective}$ action$_{noun}$ is performed, we say that the action$_{noun}$ is a wrong$_{nominalized\ adjective}$.

The scope of morality

The distinction between different senses of 'right' and 'wrong' is helpful for understanding competing views about the nature or scope of morality. Some people have a minimalist view of morality, according to which it ranges over only:

(a) actions (or omissions), that
(b) affect non-consenting others; and
(c) are either prohibited, permitted, or required.

Some such views further restrict the scope of (b) to actions that *harm* others, but other views might also include at least actions that either *offend* or *wrong* others even without harming them. What counts as a harm or a wrong can also be either more or less minimalist. For example, according to one conception of harm, a person can only be harmed if there is a negative effect on their mind or body (whether or not they are aware of the effect). Other conceptions of harm allow the possibility that one can be harmed even in the absence of such an effect. They might allow, for example, the possibility of posthumous harm, when a negative effect on mind and body is no longer possible.

Any view that limits morality to (a), (b), and (c), thereby excludes evaluation of the following from the scope of morality:

(a') beliefs, desires, intentions, or character traits, for example.

(b') even actions (and omissions) that affect only oneself or *consenting* others; and

(c') even actions (and omissions) that are right or wrong in the third sense enumerated above and in Figure 1.1.

While the most minimalist views of morality might impose all these restrictions, minimalism, like maximalism, is a matter of degree. A view about morality's scope can be more or less minimalist, or more or less maximalist. There is thus a spectrum of possible views.

What view should we take about the scope of morality? There is likely no definitive argument for any of the views on such a spectrum. For example, those who adopt minimalist views can simply insist that everything beyond (a), (b), and (c) above, falls beyond the scope of morality. However, there is a case to be made for thinking that this is an impoverished view of morality.

This is because these minimalist views seem inconsistent with the view that morality concerns how we 'ought' and 'ought not' not to live (where 'to live' can include both what we do and what kind of people we are). It is difficult to think of a good reason why the way in which we ought and ought not to live should be restricted in the way in which minimalist views of morality suggest. How we ought to live can include judgements not only about what is prohibited, required, or permitted, but also about what is better or worse to do.

The case for a more extensive view of the scope of morality can only be made if one recognizes that not all aspects of morality have equal force. For example, it is, all things being equal, more important to avoid that which is prohibited than either (i) to avoid that which is merely deficient or (ii) to do that which is supererogatory. (The 'all things being equal' clause is important because duties to avoid inflicting very minor harms might be less important than a supererogatory action that prevents great harms.) Because such priorities are widely recognized by those adopting more maximalist views of morality's scope, this condition is not a difficult one to meet.

Perhaps it will be suggested that nobody really holds the kinds of minimalist views of morality's scope that I have described. To the extent that that is true, we are all agreed on the view I am suggesting that we ought to accept. However, it is not clear to me that we do all agree.

For example, in the realm of sexual ethics, we often hear sceptics arguing that harmless bestiality with a willing animal, consensual necrophilia,[15] as well as contracepted sex between adult siblings, for example, cannot be wrong because they do not harm (non-consenting) parties. Such arguments seem to assume the sort of minimalist view of morality's scope that I have described, because they are interested only in harm to non-consenting beings. This is not to say that more maximalist views of morality *must* condemn such practices. (That is something to be discussed in the chapter on sex.) The point is merely that more maximalist views of morality's scope must look at more than whether an action harms a non-consenting party.

Manners and morals

One area where questions about the scope of morality arise is the relationship between manners and morals (or, in other words, between etiquette and ethics).[16] Although there are conceptual differences between manners and morals, no sharp line can be drawn between them and there is certainly significant overlap, as illustrated in Figure 1.3, and explained below.

It may well be impossible to provide a set of necessary and sufficient conditions to distinguish manners and morals (or etiquette and ethics). Nevertheless, at least two generalizations may be made:

First, manners or etiquette are more essentially connected to convention than morality is. This is not to deny that convention may play *some* role in morality, but this will be most pronounced where morality overlaps with manners. Nor is it to deny that there are some people who see morality as

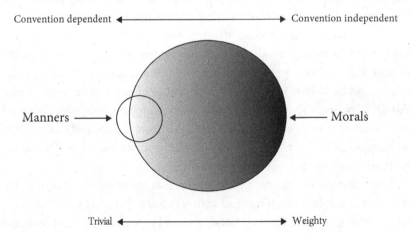

Figure 1.3 Manners and morals.

entirely a matter of convention. However, morality does not *have* to be understood in such a way, whereas it is very difficult to make sense of etiquette that is divorced from social conventions. The idea of a practice constituting good manners but having no connection to—and, *a fortiori*—being at odds with convention, involves a misunderstanding of what etiquette is.

Second, where manners do not overlap with the requirements of morality, they are typically more trivial matters than those within the scope of morality. It is also less clear in such cases that we really *must* do what the convention requires. A plausible example is the appropriate piece of cutlery with which one should eat one's peas. While this can easily be seen to be a matter of etiquette, it strains credulity to think that a matter as trivial as this could, at least routinely, be a matter of morality. Those who take ignorance about, or violation of cutlery conventions to constitute a moral breach, even a minor one, are mistaken.

A prohibition on murder, by contrast, is clearly a prohibition of morality, but to describe it as (also) bad manners would sound like a trivialization of the prohibition. Even when manners do overlap with (rather than contradict) morality, they tend to be less momentous than those aspects of morality that clearly do not overlap with good manners. For example, swearing at somebody (without good cause), is arguably both rude and immoral, but clearly not as immoral as murder, which is well beyond the scope of manners.

What both manners and morals have in common is that both require one to consider other people. Where manners do not overlap with morals, the consideration is for expectations generated entirely by the social convention. Eating one's peas with the wrong piece of cutlery offends only because the convention dictates that the piece of cutlery one used is wrong.

Where manners and morals overlap, the convention gives contextual substance to a more general ethical principle. For example, morality might require that we treat people with respect. What counts as respect, however, might be heavily influenced by convention. For example, respecting a mosque—or, more specifically, its Muslim worshippers—requires taking off one's shoes when one enters. However, respecting a church and its Christian worshippers would typically require that one keep one's shoes *on*. 'No shoes, no (Christian) service'.

While convention can sometimes give substance to moral requirements, it cannot override them. If it is bad manners not to bring a human sacrifice when visiting an Aztec temple, morality would indeed require bad manners in such a case. Such cases, where good manners are in conflict with morality, are not depicted in Figure 1.3.

The scope of duty

Minimalist and maximalist views of the scope of *morality*, are not to be confused with minimalist and maximalist views of the scope of our *duty*. The scope of morality concerns what is subject to moral evaluation. Does it include only our duties and permissions, or does it also include, for example, supererogation and the avoidance of that which, although not strictly prohibited, is morally deficient? By contrast, the scope of *duty* concerns how extensive one aspect of morality—namely, our duty—is.

The scope of *duty* needs to be distinguished from the scope of *a duty*. The latter is technically distinct from a duty's strength. Duties can have either a broader or a narrower scope.[17] For example, a duty to save people from catastrophe might be a duty to save just a few such people or it might be a duty to save very many such people. The former duty has a more limited scope than the latter. Duties can also vary in their *strength*—that is, how readily they can be overridden by other moral considerations. The stronger a duty is, the less easily it can be outweighed. The scope and strength of a duty are not unconnected. The wider the scope, the more likely the outer bands of a duty's scope are overridable.

The scope or extent of a person's duty (in general) is a function of the scope and strength of individual duties. In other words, how demanding *duty* is, depends on how extensive and how strong each of a person's *duties* are.

Some views, most notably maximizing versions of consequentialism expand the scope of duty—both what we have a duty to do and what we have a duty not to do—thereby reducing the scope of the permitted and arguably eliminating the supererogatory. This is because maximizing consequentialist views require us to perform that action, of all the possible actions, that will produce the *greatest* amount of good. All other actions are prohibited. While some prohibited actions are worse than others, all are prohibited. The category of morally deficient actions collapses into the category of prohibited ones. The only scope for permissions is where more than one possible action will maximize the good. We then have moral permission to choose between those (typically relatively limited) options. Supererogation is technically

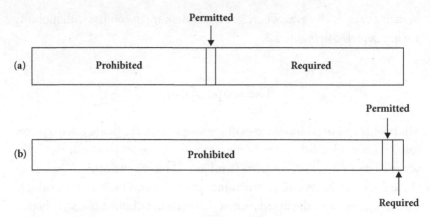

Figure 1.4 The scope of duty: Maximizing consequentialism.

obliterated because we are required to do the best. There can be no going beyond *that* duty.[18] This is illustrated in Figure 1.4.

Here again there are two ways of representing the relationships between the (remaining) senses of 'right' and 'wrong'. Version (a) represents how much of the spectrum is consumed by duty—both prohibition and requirement. This version represents how much is required of us, both positively and negatively. Because maximizing views both require much and prohibit much, each of these categories is represented as being substantial. That is an entirely reasonable representation. However, version (b) is also reasonable. Instead of representing how much is required of us, it (roughly) represents the proportion of possible actions that fall into each category. Most actions— all the sub-optimum ones—are prohibited. A very small number of possible actions—often only one—is required. Similarly, at most only a few options are permitted, and then only when more than one action will maximize good outcomes.

How demanding duty is—or may be taken to be—is the subject of considerable debate. The maximizing consequentialist view that we have extensive duties, is not shared by everybody. Satisficing consequentialists, who think that our duty is not always to produce the *best* possible consequences but rather to produce *good enough* consequences, clearly have a less demanding view of what duty requires.

Those who think that we have no natural positive duties arguably have an even less demanding view. The concept of 'natural positive duties' requires some explanation. Positive duties are duties to *do* things, and negative duties are duties *not* to do certain things. Natural duties are those duties that do not arise from our voluntary undertakings and actions. We have them on account of our nature (as moral agents) and, where they are owed to a being, also on account of that being's nature. A duty not to torture sentient beings would be a compelling candidate for a natural duty. You have such a duty not because, for example, you promised not to torture. Instead, you have the duty because of how it will feel to the tortured being and because you, as a moral agent, have moral responsibility.

There are those who think that we have no positive natural duties. It is possible to hold such a view and yet think that we do have positive duties arising from our promises or our negligence, for example.[19] Because positive duties require considerable time and effort to fulfil, denying that we have any *natural* positive duties creates a substantial degree of discretion, thus rendering many more actions permissible, in all three senses of permissible—neutral, supererogatory, and deficient. Two possible representations of this are offered in Figure 1.5. (The differences between version (a) and version (b) are the same as the differences between (a) and (b) in Figure 1.2.)

All things being equal, positive duties are more demanding than negative ones. This is because duties to do things require time and effort. By contrast, negative duties can be fulfilled by doing nothing.[20] When you do nothing—sitting in a chair, or lying in your bed, for example—you are simultaneously fulfilling billions of negative duties to billions of beings not to kill them, not to unreasonably limit their liberty, and not to assault them, for example.

This does not mean that the costs of fulfilling negative duties are *never* great. If for example, you have a duty not to betray somebody who will be

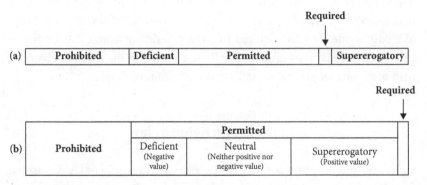

Figure 1.5 The scope of duty: No positive natural duties.

killed if you violate that duty, but you will be killed if you do not betray that person, then the price you pay for fulfilling your negative duty is a very steep one indeed. There might be disagreement about whether you still have a duty not to betray somebody when the costs to you are that high. The point is that *if* you do have a duty in that circumstance, the cost of fulfilling it can be very serious. In any event, such cases are not quotidian, at least in non-extreme circumstances. It may become quotidian in totalitarian societies, but such societies are not the circumstances for which this book is written.[21]

That said, in quotidian contexts there are frequently less extreme but nonetheless substantial costs to be paid for fulfilling even negative duties. Just how much of a cost people can be required to bear in fulfilment of a purported duty is a question that recurs in almost all the topics covered in this book. How does one respond to that question, as well as to the question about what positive duties we have? The general approach is to weigh up competing considerations in a bid to determine what it is reasonable to expect of people in different circumstances.

When we do that, it is unlikely that positions at the extremes are going to be supportable. For example, those who deny that we have *any* positive natural duties are committed to saying that we have no duty at all to save a life even when we can do so easily and without cost. In other words, they are committed to the view that we have no natural duty of 'easy rescue'. Weighing the strong interest of the person in being saved and the, at most, very weak interest of the potential saviour in not saving, it is difficult to conclude that it is reasonable for the potential saviour to have *no* duty to save. However, the more burdensome the saving becomes, the less reasonable it is to think that morality requires the potential saviour to save.

The general point here applies not only to saving lives but also to other issues. For example, just how much of a cost is one morally required to pay in desisting from bullshit, or in calling out the bullshit of others? How much of a cost is one morally required to pay by desisting from contributing to carbon emissions? Such questions will be engaged in the relevant chapters, with some further general remarks in the concluding chapter.

Ethics, not religion or law

Some non-philosophers confuse ethics with either religion or law. Consider, first, the confusion between ethics and religion. Religions typically have views on ethical questions, but it would be a mistake to think that we need to look no further than religion to answer ethical questions.

First, and most obviously, religiously based ethical views would have no force for those, atheists, who reject the foundational assumptions of theistic religion. Second, even theists can and do disagree about ethical questions. Some of these disagreements are between different religions. Others are disagreements between different denominations within a religion. There are even disagreements between individuals within a given denomination.

While some of the disagreements are synchronous, others are diachronous—different members of the same religion have different ethical views at different historical times. For example, slavery or child marriage might have been accepted by Jews, Christians, and Muslims centuries ago, but are not accepted by *many* adherents of those religions today.[22] What has changed? Not the texts that were, and are still, taken as authoritative! What has changed are the interpretations or applications of those texts. Very often what explains the change in interpretation or application is a change of ethical view. Child marriage or slavery come to be viewed as unethical. The religious traditions and the interpretations that underly them, change accordingly. In other words, the texts do not logically precede the ethical view in the way that is usually assumed. Instead, the texts are viewed through a particular ethical prism, that can change over time, leading to different interpretations, or at least different practices.

What this shows is that even theists and other religious people cannot abrogate the need for thinking about what is and is not ethical. Religion does not provide a mechanism for short-circuiting such deliberations.

The relationship between ethics and law is more complicated, primarily on account of jurisprudential debates about the nature of law. There are those, namely legal positivists, who draw a clear conceptual distinction between morality and law. On this view, laws can be immoral and yet be laws.

Opponents of legal positivism, known as natural law legal theorists, think that morality must play at least some role in determining what the law is. They disagree among themselves about just what that role is. In its most extreme form, meeting the conditions of morality is a necessary (but not a sufficient) condition for something to count as a law. An immoral 'law' is no law at all. Other natural law legal theorists defend a weaker connection between law and morality.

These differences should not obscure the fact that neither legal positivists nor natural law theorists can avoid ethical deliberation. For legal positivists, ethical inquiry is necessary to undertake a moral evaluation of law, and to determine what morality requires of us. For natural law theorists, ethical inquiry is necessary, to some or other extent, either to determine what the law is or to determine the moral authority of law.

There are other differences between law and morality. Most importantly, morality does not have the (sharp) teeth that law has. There may sometimes be repercussions to the wrongdoer for moral wrongdoing, usually when there is social recognition of the wrong. (When a society is mistaken about the requirements of morality, as they often are, there can be negative repercussions for those who act *rightly*.) Sometimes the repercussions of violating social standards can be very significant. However, unless morality is enshrined in law, those repercussions, all else being equal, will be a pale shade of the repercussions for violating the law.[23] That does not mean, of course, that acting morally is less important than acting within the bounds of the law.

That law has teeth is one of a few reasons why law should not range over all of morality. For example, using the coercive power of the law to enforce morality's minutiae would be inappropriate. There are often even good reasons not to employ the coercive power of the law to enforce more important features of morality, not least because doing so might be counterproductive or dangerous, all things considered.

Very practical ethics

While law and morality are neither the same nor coextensive, law (or 'law', according to some natural law views) can be evaluated morally. There is, however, a crucial difference between morally evaluating laws or public policies and morally evaluating the actions of individuals.

If one establishes that a law or public policy is morally or otherwise defective, it is not at all easy for an ordinary person to bring about a change in that law or policy. Unless you are an absolute monarch, a dictator, or some other autocrat, you cannot simply change law or policy. To bring about legal or policy change you need to work through the complex processes that need to be followed. So much of this depends on others, on procedures, and on power structures, that the task is immensely difficult or impossible (at least for the foreseeable future).

The situation is different if one is evaluating the actions of individuals, at least with regard to the actions of one individual—oneself. If one changes one's mind about what is right or wrong, one can more readily change one's conduct accordingly.

This is an oversimplification, because morally defective law or policy frequently imposes a penalty for doing the right thing. In such cases, altering one's behaviour is not so easy. If, for example, it is morally permissible to tell a joke but the law prohibits telling such a joke, one can tell it only at the significant potential cost to oneself of violating the law.

However, there are many other cases and ways in which a change of moral view can be implemented by the individual person. This is especially (but not only) so when the correct moral view restricts actions rather than permits or requires them. If you decide that telling certain jokes, using certain words, bullshitting, emitting a particular volume of greenhouse gases, eating animals, smoking in the presence of non-smokers, or forgiving somebody under some set of conditions, is wrong, you can desist, and you can generally do so immediately.

There are also occasions in which a conclusion that some action by an individual is permitted or required can be implemented by an individual person, and again often immediately. If, for example, you decided that you should be giving away more to those in dire need, you could do so. If you concluded that you should be more forgiving, you could act on that without obtaining the agreement of others.

There may be psychological hurdles in the way of either desisting from actions that are wrong or performing actions that are right. However, those are your own internal hurdles to overcome. They do not require negotiating the complex processes of generating legal or policy changes.

This is one way in which quotidian ethics is not merely practical ethics, but is instead *very* practical ethics. What to do or not do, is very much more in the hands of an individual person than what a law or policy should prohibit, permit, or require. Because quotidian ethical issues are not only ones confronting ordinary people, but also ones that those people face in their everyday lives, they are questions that arise fairly *frequently*. That is another way in which quotidian ethics is very practical ethics.

2
Sex

There was a time—a time that has not passed in sexually more conservative places—when sex had an outsized connection with morality in many people's minds. Even in those places where this is thought no longer to be the case, we immediately know what is meant if somebody is referred to as having 'loose morals'. In such cases, reference is not being made to the person's deficit of honesty, generosity, humility, tolerance, justness, or compassion, for example. Instead, reference is being made to their deviance from a highly restrictive sexual code.

It is indeed a mistake to think that morality is inseparable from puritanical views of sex. This is not to deny that there is an ethics of sex—that is, that some sexual behaviour is morally wrong, while other sexual behaviour is morally permissible. One does not have to be puritanical to condemn rape, for example. Those who reject sexual puritanism need only deny that morality should be preoccupied with sex, or that sex must be subjected to the most conservative restrictions.

However, it is also a mistake to think that where there has been a major liberalization in views about sex, this has resulted in all taboos about sex being overthrown. Instead, it *altered* the practices (and number of practices) regarded as taboo. Premarital sex, promiscuity, and homosexuality are now widely accepted—even celebrated—in many places. Adultery, for good reason, is still thought to be wrong, but a much more lenient view is taken towards it. Yet there remain sexual practices that elicit all the horror and opprobrium (and more) that premarital sex, promiscuity, and homosexuality once did, and still do in sexually conservative societies. These still-taboo practices include paedophilia, bestiality, and necrophilia.[1]

Rape (like sexual assault more generally) is a curious case in that the most sexually conservative societies condemn some instances but are very indulgent of other instances. More specifically such societies tend to condone rape (and sexual assault) by the most powerful men, especially of the wives, sisters, and daughters of the disempowered and of outsiders. They also tend to condone the rape by all men of their *own* wives, while condemning other rapes (and sexual assaults) to varying degrees. Rape is often also condoned in sexually more liberalized societies, but arguably less so. Marital rape has at least been recognized and sometimes criminalized, and many powerful men are now being held to account for rape and sexual assault to an extent that was not previously the case. Thus, rape and sexual assault may be more condemned in sexually liberalized societies than in sexually conservative ones. To this extent, a sexual revolution has caused a realignment of moral judgements about sex rather than merely a restriction of negative judgements.

On the face of it, this cluster of views—accepting premarital sex, promiscuity, and homosexuality, but regarding rape, paedophilia, bestiality, and necrophilia as morally wrong, or even heinous—seems perfectly defensible, at least to many people. However, if we probe these matters, we find that this precise constellation of views is hard to justify. Something has to give. What exactly it is that has to give, depends in part on what view of sexual ethics one takes. In turn, what view of sexual ethics one takes, depends in part on what judgements about sexual ethics one is prepared to let go.

Some common errors

One problem is that many judgements about sexual ethics and the justifications offered for those judgements are characterized by some fundamental errors. For example, many people's judgements about sex are based on whether they are repulsed by the sexual practice in question. This explains much opposition not only to necrophilia and bestiality but also to homosexuality.

However, whether or not these practices are morally permissible, disgust is a very unreliable indicator of whether a sexual (or other) practice is morally acceptable. Disgust, just like attraction, is an aesthetic response and one that varies considerably between people. People with different sexual orientations are attracted to and repulsed by different things. One's own disgust response to a sexual activity of a particular kind is no more reliable an indicator of what is ethical than somebody else's arousal regarding the same kind of activity. This is not to deny that sometimes disgust is apt and attraction inapt (and vice versa). However, it is then incumbent on us to provide an explanation for the aptness or inaptness of our response. The disgust one feels is not sufficient to demonstrate the wrongfulness of the action that disgusts one.

Another common mistake in sexual ethics and in practical ethics more generally is to claim that an action is wrong on account of its purported unnaturalness. There tend to be two kinds of problem with such claims. First, it is often difficult to make sense of the claim that the condemned action is unnatural. Second, and more important, it is not clear why an action, even if unnatural, is thereby wrong.

One possible interpretation of the claim that certain sexual practices are unnatural is that they violate the law of nature. However, this rests on a misunderstanding of what a law of nature is.[2] Laws of nature differ from social laws in important ways. Whereas the latter are prescriptive, the former are descriptive. That is to say, laws of nature simply describe the way nature works. They do not say anything about what should be done. It follows that whereas social laws can be violated, it is impossible to violate a natural law. One cannot, for example, violate the law of gravity. You can ignore it, but you do so at your peril. No sexual practices that are physically possible violate any natural laws.

Another interpretation of the claim that certain sexual practices are unnatural is that they do not occur in nature. However, there is a sense in which anything humans do is natural, given that we are part of nature. Perhaps, then, the claim is that the condemned sexual practices do not occur in the non-human natural world. That claim is, at least very often, false. Promiscuity,[3] homosexuality,[4] paedophilia,[5] interspecies sex,[6] and even some necrophilia,[7] are found in the animal kingdom.

Even if some sexual practices did not occur in the non-human natural world, it would be hard to see why that would make them wrong. Scientific medicine including treatments for cancer, as well as organ transplants, do not occur in the non-human natural world, yet that does not make them wrong. If we cannot infer wrongfulness from unnaturalness there, then we also cannot do so in the case of sexual practices.

A further common error in thinking about the ethics of sex is to suggest that we need only look to God's word to determine which practices are morally acceptable and which are not. Such an approach obviously rests on the controversial assumption that God exists. Accordingly, it will have no force against those who reject that assumption. Given that it is much easier to argue for the wrongfulness of some sexual practices (such as rape) and the permissibility of others (such as much consensual marital sex) than it is to argue for the existence of God, even theists should seek arguments that do not rest on controversial premises.

Appeals to God's word will not even convince all theists. First, theists might disagree about which scripture correctly captures God's word. Even when they agree on the text, they may disagree about the correct interpretation of it. (For example, does sex between a married man and a single woman constitute adultery, if we understand 'adultery' as it is in the decalogue?[8] Some religious people would answer affirmatively, but those following the original interpretation would have to answer negatively.[9])

Even if there were agreement on the interpretation, there would be a further question whether the prohibition (or permission) were still operative. For example, many theists who accept the Bible as the word of God do not believe that the prohibition on sex with (or while) a menstruant woman[10] is still operative. By contrast, many theists do not believe that the earlier implicit biblical permission for polygamy and for what today would count as paedophilia, are still operative.

Finally, even when there is agreement that a prohibition (or permission) is still operative, there can be disagreement about whether the prohibition is a moral or non-moral one. For example, even those who still follow the biblical proscription against eating leaven on Passover,[11] do not believe that it is *immoral* to eat leaven during this festival. Instead, it is a ritual prohibition. What then is the status of various sexual prohibitions? We cannot assume that they are moral rather than ritualistic.

The underlying point is that even theists interpret religious texts through a moral prism. Given that there can be no reference to God's word without interpretation, and given that interpretation is morally informed, even theists have reason to think about sexual ethics in deciding how to interpret a scripture.

Sexual practices and sexual orientation

Sexual *practices* should not be confused with sexual *orientation*. Sexual practices are the sexual activities in which beings engage. Sexual orientations consist in what one finds sexually attractive or arousing. While orientation and practice are often congruent, they are not always so. For example, many people with a homosexual orientation have married and had sex with people of the opposite sex (often because of social pressures). Similarly, people who are attracted to members of the opposite sex sometimes engage in homosexual sexual activity (in prisons, for example, where the amount of homosexual activity outstrips the number of homosexually oriented people). Somebody might be attracted to children, animals, or corpses, or to people of the same or opposite sex, without ever acting on those desires.

Sexual behaviour tends to be more controversial than sexual orientation. Among the possible explanations for this is that sexual orientation, unlike sexual behaviour, might be thought to be beyond a person's control. Sexual orientation is indeed not something one typically chooses. However, that does not mean that it is immune to ethical evaluation. Having a pyromaniacal disposition may well be something one does not choose. Accordingly, we might not *blame* a pyromaniac for having those dispositions. Nevertheless, we might view those dispositions as undesirable—the sort of dispositions we should curtail, counter, or cure, if possible. Other unchosen attributes—such as one's skin colour[12]—are ethically neutral. Thus, we cannot tell merely because an attribute is unchosen, whether we should have a negative, positive, or neutral attitude towards it.

Sexual practices are more within our control. However, sexual dispositions can be potent, and it can take great amounts of self-control to desist from acting on them. This is no less true of those with unusual orientations than it is of those with more usual orientations. Indeed, it may even be more difficult for some of those with unusual orientations who, whether for moral or prudential reasons, must *always* desist from acting on their orientations. Sexual drives also vary in intensity from person to person. If we assume that such variation is to be found across orientations, then there are some homosexuals, paedophiles, zoophiles, and necrophiles who, for prudential or moral reasons, can never fulfil their desires. That is a lot to ask of somebody. Whether it is something we *should* ask of them depends on whether the actions that would fulfil those desires are always morally impermissible. That is a good reason to focus on the evaluation of sexual practices rather than of orientations (even though the evaluation of sexual practices will have implications for our evaluation of orientations).

Given that homosexuality is now much more commonly accepted than it was before, discussion of homosexual practices can be delayed in order to consider first those sexual practices that are still widely reviled. To that end, it helps to distinguish between two competing views of sexual ethics—two views that also shed light on other contested sexual practices.

The significance view and the casual view

The first of these views is that for sex to be morally acceptable, it must be an expression of mutual romantic[13] love. It must, in other words, signify feelings of affection that are commensurate with the intimacy of the sexual activity. On this view a sexual union can be acceptable only if it reflects the reciprocal romantic love and affection of the parties to that union. We might call this the *significance view* (or, alternatively, the *love view* or *romantic view*) of sex, because it requires sex to signify romantic love in order for it to be permissible.

To clarify, the significance view stipulates a necessary condition for the moral permissibility of sex. It is not a sufficient condition. In other words, while sex *must*, according to the significance view, meet the significance condition in order to be morally permissible, it is not necessarily *enough* that it meet that condition. Other conditions may also need to be met. If, for example, Romeo and Juliet's sex is an expression of their mutual romantic love, but Romeo is married to Romina, and Juliet to Julio, then Romeo and Juliet's sex may be in breach of other ethical requirements.

According to an alternative to the significance view, sex need not have any romantic significance in order to be morally permissible. We might call this the *casual view*. Sexual pleasure, according to this view, is morally like any other pleasure and may be enjoyed subject only to the usual sorts of moral constraints. A gastronomic delight, obtained via theft, would be morally impermissible, but where no general moral principle (such as a prohibition on theft) applies, there can be no fault with engaging in gourmet pleasures. Having meals with a string of strangers or mere acquaintances is not condemnable as 'casual gastronomy', 'eating around', or 'culinary promiscuity'. Similarly, according to the casual view, erotic pleasures may permissibly be obtained from sex with strangers or mere acquaintances. There need not be any love or affection. (Nor, for that matter, need there always be pleasure. Just as a meal or a theatre performance might not be pleasurable and is not for that reason morally impermissible, so sex is not, nor ought, always to be pleasurable.)

Both the significance view and the casual view are moral claims about when people *may* (morally permissibly) engage in sex. They are not descriptive claims about when people *do* engage in sex. Clearly both kinds of sex *do* occur. Sometimes sex does reflect love, and sometimes it does not.

The significance view, as a moral view, could take one of two alternative forms from the one presented thus far. Instead of stipulating 'the expression of mutual romantic love' as a necessary condition for sex being morally *permissible*, it could make either one of two claims:

a. While there is no moral requirement that sex must be the expression of mutual romantic love, sex that does express mutual romantic love is morally better than sex that does not.
b. While there is no moral prohibition against sex that is not an expression of mutual romantic love, such sex is morally defective, and it would be better to avoid it.

The contrasting casual view would be the view that:

a. Sex that is an expression of mutual romantic love is morally no better than sex that is not an expression of such love.
b. Sex that is not an expression of mutual romantic love is morally no worse than sex that is.

While these are possible alternative versions of the significance and casual views, they are arguably not the most common versions. Most people who think that sex ought to be significant, think that sex without such significance is morally *impermissible* and not merely either defective or less ideal. Similarly, most of those who adopt the casual view would not concede either that casual sex is morally deficient or that significant sex is morally better.

Thus, while we can keep the alternative versions in mind, for the sake of not complicating matters even more than they already are, we should focus, at least initially, on the version of the significance and casual views that was first presented.

Promiscuity (and premarital sex)

A sexually promiscuous person is somebody who is casual about sex—somebody for whom sex is not (or need not be) laden with romantic significance. (Promiscuity is obviously a matter of degree, and sex need not even be *tinged* with romantic significance for the most promiscuous people.) This is not to say that the sexually promiscuous will have sex with simply anybody. Even the promiscuous can exercise some discretion in their choice of sexual partners just as the gastronomically 'promiscuous' may be discriminating in the sort of people with whom they may wish to dine. The sexually promiscuous person is not one who is entirely undiscriminating about sexual partners, but rather somebody for whom romantic attachments are not a relevant consideration in choosing a sexual partner. It is thus clear why promiscuity is frowned upon by advocates of the significance view of sex. The promiscuous person treats as insignificant that which ought to be significant. The advocate of the casual view, by contrast, will see nothing wrong with promiscuity.

Some premarital sex is promiscuous. To the extent that it is, advocates of the significance view will frown on it, while advocates of the casual view will not. However, not all premarital sex is promiscuous. Some people have sex before getting married but with too few people for their sex to count as promiscuous. If that sex is not an expression of mutual romantic love, then it will nonetheless fail to meet the permissibility condition of the significance view, but obviously will be unproblematic from the perspective of the casual view.

Some non-promiscuous premarital sex is an expression of mutual romantic love. This does meet the significance condition, as it has been stated thus far. Thus, the significance view *per se* does not have to frown on *all* premarital sex. However, there are versions of the significance view that require the mutual romantic love to be *exclusive* in the sense that each party sexually expresses romantic love only with one another. Usually that exclusivity condition will be dyadic—that is, restricted to two partners. There is no categorical bar to a version that allowed *ménages à trois* (or even *quatre*). However, because in the real world it would be unusual for three or four people to have three- or four-way mutual romantic love, it is much less likely that the significance view's conditions would be met for threesomes and foursomes. There would also be plenty of scope for self-deception about the number of people for whom one could feel and sexually express such love, resulting in the significance view cautioning against the more crowded copulations. (A similar rationale, *mutatis mutandis*, may be used to rule out polygamy or to radically restrict the number of permissible spouses.)

Some versions of the significance view would require a firm *commitment* to the romantic and resultant sexual exclusivity. Insofar as the required commitment is that signalled by an official marriage ceremony, the augmented significance + commitment view would disapprove of all premarital sex in the pre-ceremonial sense of 'premarital'. However, to the extent that a commitment can be present even in the absence of a marital *ceremony*—that is 'unofficially'—then even the significance + commitment view would not disapprove of all pre-ceremonial sex, so long as it was not also pre-commitment sex.[14]

There are some, but not decisive, reasons for those who already endorse the significance view, to augment it with an exclusivity requirement to which the parties make either an unofficial or official commitment. First, the exclusivity requirement could be seen as an extension of the significance requirement. To love somebody in the strongest romantic way is to love them in a way that one does not love others. Parental love for children does not seem to lessen with additional children in the way that romantic love for a partner does with additional partners.[15] Second, given the propensity for self-deception—convincing oneself that sex is not mere lust but the expression of (exclusive) romantic love—a mutual commitment is a good safeguard for ensuring that the significance condition is met. Finally, an official commitment (in the form of marriage) will be an even stronger safeguard than an unofficial commitment.

Marital sex

The multiply augmented version of the significance view that requires marriage in order for sex to be morally permissible does not imply that all (consensual) sex within marriage is morally permissible. After all, there are loveless marriages. Some are loveless from the start and others become loveless. While the parties to the marriage may have made a commitment to one another, the sex that they have, assuming that it is not also a sexless marriage, is not an expression of mutual romantic love.

The casual view, of course, permits marital sex that is not the expression of mutual romantic love. One other view that could also permit loveless marital sex is a *marriage view*, which permits all (consensual) marital sex and prohibits all non-marital sex. However, it is not clear why sex is morally permissible only within marriage if the marriage requirement is not an extension of the significance view. Moreover, the marriage view has other problematic implications, as will become apparent later.

In the interim, the implications of both the significance and casual views for a variety of other sexual practices need to be considered. The choice to engage in some of these practices is quotidian, but the choice to engage is others is not, at least for most people. For example, innumerable people never even consider engaging in bestiality, or necrophilia. However, the implications of the significance and casual views for even these practices need to be investigated for the purposes of understanding what these views entail. That, in turn, is necessary, for determining whether either of these views should be invoked in determining the morality of more quotidian sexual practices.

Paedophilia

The significance view has an explanation why paedophilia is *always* wrong. Children, it could be argued, are unable to appreciate the full significance that sexual activity should have. Adherents of the significance view are not obliged to take all paedophilia to be wrong. They might think that children (beyond a certain age) *can* understand the full significance of sex. I am thus claiming only that the significance view has a way of arguing that paedophilia is wrong, not that it must argue in that way.

To claim that children are unable to appreciate the full significance of sexual activity is not to suggest that children are asexual beings, but rather that they may lack the capacity to understand how sex expresses a certain kind of love. Having sex with a child is thus to treat the child as a mere means to attaining erotic pleasure without consideration of the mental states of which the provision of that pleasure should be an expression. Even if the child is sexually aroused, that arousal is not an expression of the requisite sorts of feelings. If the child is beyond infancy, the experience, in addition to being objectifying, may be deeply bewildering and traumatizing.

Unlike the significance view, the casual view seems to lack the theoretical resources to rule out *all* paedophilia. If sex is morally just like other (pleasurable) activities and bears no special significance, why may it not be enjoyed with children? One common answer is that sex (with an adult[16]) can be harmful to a child. In the most extreme cases, including those involving physical force or those in which an adult copulates with a very small child, physical damage to the child can result. But clearly not all paedophilic acts are of this kind. Many, perhaps most, paedophilic acts are non-penetrative and do not employ physical force.

Psychological harm is probably more common than physical damage. It is not clear, however, as a number of authors writing on this topic have noted, to what extent that harm is the result of the sexual encounter itself and to what extent it is the result of the secrecy and taboo that surrounds that sexual activity.[17] Insofar as a thorough embracing of the casual view of sex would eliminate those harms, the defender of this view cannot appeal to them in forming a principled objection to sexual interaction between adults and children. Because a society in which there were no taboos on paedophilia would avoid harm resulting from taboos on such activities and would simultaneously be inclusive of the paedophile's sexual orientation, it has everything to recommend it for defenders of the casual view.[18] At the most, advocates of this view can say that the current psychological harms impose temporary[19] moral constraints on sex with those children who given their unfortunate puritanical upbringing or circumstances would experience psychological trauma. Even such children may not be damaged by every kind of sexual interaction with an adult. For example, there is reason to believe that where the child is a willing participant that the harm is either significantly attenuated or absent.[20]

Here it might be objected that although a child may sometimes appear to be a willing participant in sexual conduct with an adult, it is impossible for a child to give genuine consent to sexual activity.[21] For this reason, it might be argued, it is always wrong to engage in sexual relations with a child. Now, while this claim is entirely plausible on the significance view of sexual ethics, one is hard-pressed to explain how it is compatible with the casual view. What is it about sex, so understood, that a child is unable to consent to it? On this view, sex need carry no special significance and thus there is nothing that a child needs to understand in order to enter into a permissible sexual encounter. In response, it might be suggested that what a child needs to understand are the possible health risks associated with (casual) sex.

That response, however, will not suffice to rule out all that those opposed to paedophilia wish to rule out. First, some sexual activities—most especially the non-invasive ones—do not carry significant health risks. Second, where children themselves are not thought competent to evaluate the risks of an activity, it is usually thought that a parent or guardian may, within certain risk limits, make the assessment on the child's behalf. Thus, a parent may decide to give a child a taste of alcohol, allow a child to read certain kinds of books, or permit a child to participate in a sport that carries risks. If sex need be no more significant than other such activities, it is hard to see why its risks (especially when, as a result of safe sex, these are relatively small), and not those of the other activities (even when the latter are greater), constitute grounds for categorically excluding children and invalidating the consent which they or their parents give.

There is another consent-related objection that might be raised against paedophilia.[22] It might be argued that given the differences between adults and children, it is not possible for an adult and a child to understand one another's motives for wanting to have sex. The mutual unintelligibility of their motives makes it impossible for each party to know even roughly what the encounter means to the other and the absence of this information compromises the validity of the consent.

Although this objection, like the previous one, is thoroughly plausible according to the significance view, it lacks force if we adopt the casual view. Notice that the absence of mutual intelligibility of motives is not thought to be an objection to those activities with children, such as playing a game, that are not thought to carry the significance attributed to sex by the significance view. A child might be quite oblivious that the adult is playing the game only to give the child pleasure and that the adult may even be losing the game on purpose, in order to enhance the child's pleasure or to build the child's sense of self-esteem. Yet, this is not thought to constitute grounds for invalidating a child's ability to consent to game playing with adults. The need for some mutual intelligibility of motive arises only if sex must be significant.

Nor is it evident, on the casual view (unless it is coupled with a child-liberationist position),[23] why children need consent at all. If a parent may pressure or force a child into participating in a sport (perhaps on grounds of 'character-building'), or into going to the opera (on grounds of 'learning to appreciate the arts'), why may a parent not coerce or pressure a child into sex? If the casual view is correct, a parent may reasonably believe that treating sex as one does other aspects of life forestalls neurosis in the child and that gaining sexual experience while young is an advantage. If the evidence were sufficiently inconclusive that reasonable people could disagree about whether children really did benefit from an early sexual start, then those defenders of the casual view who also accept paternalism towards children, would have to allow parents to decide for their children.

Bestiality and necrophilia

As with paedophilia, the significance view has the capacity to rule out all bestiality and necrophilia, which is different from saying that the significance view *must* rule out all instances of these practices. If it is thought that non-human animals are not capable of understanding the (human) significance of sex, then sexual activity between a human and a non-human animal cannot be the expression of mutual romantic love. Similarly, it could be argued that there can be no mutuality in sexual activity with a (human) corpse, at least if one accepts a version of the significance view that requires the mutuality to be synchronous. Even if the erstwhile person donated his or her body for necrophilic purposes, there can be no synchronic mutual romantic love expressed through the sex. If the mutuality must be synchronous, then the significance view can rule out all necrophilia. (It would then also need to rule out sex within a mutual romantic relationship if one partner gives advance consent to sexual intercourse while she or he is sleeping, or once he or she becomes mentally incompetent.)

The casual view of sex cannot categorically oppose either bestiality or necrophilia. It can condemn bestiality that is harmful to animals, and it can denounce necrophilia in cases in which the person whose corpse is used did not give consent before death. There is even scope for disapproving of those instances of both practices that pose significant health risks. However, this is not sufficient to rule out all instances of bestiality and necrophilia. Animals are not always harmed by sexual activity with them. Living people can give consent to the use of their later dead bodies by necrophiles. Finally, there are forms of sexual contact that need not pose a health risk to the zoophile or necrophile, or via them to others.

Rape

Advocates of both the significance and casual views of sex can explain why rape (of adults) is wrong. Whether or not interference with a child's freedom is justified, few people think that it is acceptable to interfere with the freedom of adults by, for example, forcing them to take up sport, go to the opera, or eat something (irrespective of whether it would be good for them). Those who accept this, even if they have the casual view of sexual ethics, have grounds for finding rape (of adults) morally defective. To rape people is to force them to do something that they do not want to do. Rape is an unwarranted interference with a person's body and freedom.

This does not mean that the significance and casual views have the same implications for rape. The significance view is able to provide an explanation why rape is a *special* kind of wrong. According to the significance view, raping people—forcing them to have sex—is not like forcing them to engage in other activities, such as going to the opera or to dinner. It is to compel a person to engage in an activity that should be an expression of deep affection. To forcibly strip it of that significance is to treat a vitally important component of sexual activity as though it had no special significance (and perhaps as a mere trifle). It thus expresses extreme indifference to the deepest aspects of the person whose body is used for the rapist's gratification.

The problem, for the defenders of the casual view is that rape need be no more serious an interference than would be forcing somebody to eat something, for example. Thus, although the casual view can explain why rape is wrong, it cannot explain why it is a special kind of wrong.

One qualification needs to be added. Perhaps a proponent of the casual view could recognize that rape is especially wrong when the victim does not share the casual view—that is, for those victims who believe (mistakenly, according to the casual view) that sex ought to be significant. A suitable analogy would be that of forcing somebody to eat a pork sausage. The seriousness of such an interference would be much greater if the person on whom one forced this meal were a vegetarian (or a Jew or a Muslim) than if he were not. A particular violation of somebody's freedom can be either more or less significant, depending on that person's attitudes.

Although some may be willing to accept that rape is especially wrong only when committed against somebody who holds the significance view of sex, many would not. Many feminists, for example, have argued for the irrelevance, in rape trials, of a woman's sexual history. But if the casual view is correct, then her sexual history would be evidence—although not conclusive evidence—of her view of sexual ethics. This in turn would be relevant to determining how great a harm the rape was (but not to *whether* it was rape and thus to whether it was a wrongful harm). Raping somebody for whom sex has as little significance (of the sort under consideration) as eating an orange,[24] would be like forcing somebody to eat an orange. Raping somebody for whom sex is deeply significant would be much worse. Although a significance view of sex might also allow such distinctions between the severity of different rapes, it can at least explain why rape of *anybody* is more serious than forcing somebody to eat an orange.

Extramarital sex

The disagreement between the significance and casual views has some relevance to extramarital sex, but only some. Both views can explain why adultery is wrong. If parties to a marriage have made an undertaking of sexual exclusivity, as is usually the case, then the adulterer is breaking a promise that they made (and the extramarital partner is enabling that promise-breaking[25]). If it is wrong to break a promise, then it is wrong to break this promise. That is sufficient to make adultery wrong on both the significance and casual views.

The significance view, unlike the casual view, can explain why breaking a promise of sexual exclusivity is worse than breaking a promise to go see a particular film with one person because one goes to watch it with somebody else instead. Breaking more important promises is worse than breaking less important ones, and the significance view can explain why a promise of sexual exclusivity is a particularly important promise.

In addition, it matters to the significance view, but not to the casual view, whether the extramarital sex is an expression of mutual romantic love. If it is not, then that is a further problem. According to the simplest significance view this additional problem does not relate to the adulterous feature of the extramarital sex. If the significance view is augmented to include an official commitment via marriage, then there is an additional problem related to the adulterous feature.

Because so much extramarital sex is a breach of promise, it is often (although not always) also accompanied by deception. The adulterous member of the marital couple (and sometimes also the person with whom he or she is having an affair) hides the fact that the promise is being or has been broken. Sometimes this is via overt lying, sometimes by evasive language and behaviour, and sometimes merely by failing to disclose the adulterous relationship. Not every failure to disclose is an instance of deception. However, when one has made an undertaking of sexual exclusivity and this undertaking has been breached, one typically owes a disclosure of that fact. In such cases, the failure of the defaulting promiser to disclose does constitute a kind of deception. That too is wrong.

Extramarital sex does not constitute promise-breaking if the marriage is an 'open' one. Marriages can be open to varying degrees. An entirely open marriage is one in which either no undertaking of sexual exclusivity is made or where the parties to the marriage have released one another from the duties previously generated by such an undertaking. Partially open marriages include those where one party but not the other undertakes sexual exclusivity or is released from such an undertaking. Other partially open marriages are those in which some, but not unlimited, extramarital sexual activity is allowed for one or both parties.[26]

To the extent that somebody is not violating an obligation of sexual exclusivity, their extramarital sex cannot be faulted on this basis. There would also be much less reason to deceive anybody about engaging in such sexual activity. This is not to say that there would never be any reason to deceive. Perhaps one is in an open marriage, but one knows that one's spouse would react badly to news of one's dalliances. One might then deceive despite not breaking a promise. In such cases the deception may be wrong even though the extramarital sex is not. (Perhaps the understanding is that while extramarital sexual activity is permitted, it must be disclosed to the spouse.) However, in general there is less incentive to deceive when a marriage is open.

Is there anything wrong with extramarital sex when the marriage itself is open to such sex? Put another way, is there anything wrong with open marriages? The casual view must answer these questions in the negative. If sex is morally no different from any other pleasurable activity, then just as one is free to have meals and listen to music with people other than one's spouse, one is free to engage in sexual activity with people other than one's spouse.

The significance view, by contrast, must render entirely open marriages impermissible. If there are no restrictions on the number of extramarital partners with whom one may have sexual contact, then some of that sex will fall foul of the significance requirement. However, the significance view need not frown on all extramarital sexual activity. If, for example, a marriage was partially open, allowing perhaps a single extramarital partner, then it would be possible for at least some versions of the significance view— versions that do not require complete sexual exclusivity between only two people—to permit a partially open marriage of this kind. However, significance views, unlike casual views, would render substantially and completely open marriages morally impermissible. Significance views would not allow the range of sexual activity that such marriages would permit.

Masturbation

It is clear that masturbation does not fall foul of the casual view of sex. Diogenes the Cynic encapsulates this view when he said, in reference to his own public masturbation, 'if only I could stop being hungry by rubbing my belly too'.[27]

It is much less clear whether the significance view must take a particular view of masturbation, at least if we understand this term, as it often is understood, to refer to the manual stimulation of one's *own* genitals for sexual gratification.[28] One possibility is that because masturbation is not an expression of mutual romantic love, advocates of the significance view should view it as morally impermissible. However, an alternative view is that because (or when) masturbation does not involve two (or more) parties, the mutual requirement is inapplicable.

One possible response to this is to still require the expression of romantic love. However, it must be a rare masturbator who pleasures themself as an expression of auto-romantic love[29] (if the idea of *romantic* love for self is even coherent). Another possible response to the inapplicability of the *mutuality* requirement is to add the inapplicability of the *romantic* requirement, and thus to regard the significance view as being silent on the question of masturbation. In other words, we might think that the significance view only applies to sexual activity between two or more beings. (However, if a corpse is not a 'being' then the significance view would then also be silent on necrophilia.)

Choosing between the significance and casual views

Is there any way of choosing between the significance and casual views of sex? Some might take the foregoing reflections to speak in favour of or against one of the views. Those who are convinced that promiscuity is morally permissible may be inclined to think that the casual view must be correct because it supports this judgement. They may be willing to accept its implications for other sexual practices.[30] Others, who believe that paedophilia, bestiality, and necrophilia are wrong, and that rape is a special kind of evil that is unlike other violations of a person's body or autonomy, may think that the significance view is correct given that it can support these judgements.

There are other factors that are also relevant to evaluating each of these views of sexual ethics. Consider first those who speak in favour of the significance view. This view fits well with judgements most people make about forms of intimacy that, although not sexual practices themselves, are not unrelated to the intimacies of sex: (1) casually sharing news of one's venereal disease (a) with a mere acquaintance, or (b) with one's spouse or other close family member; (2) Undressing (a) in the street, or (b) in front of one's spouse in the privacy of one's bedroom. Very few people would feel exactly the same about (a) as about (b) in either of these examples. This would suggest that most people think that intimacies are appropriately shared only with those to whom one is close, even if they disagree about just how close one must be in order to share a certain level of intimacy. The significance view seems to capture an important psychological feature about humans. Although descriptive psychological claims do not entail normative judgements, any moral view that attempted to deny immutable psychological traits characteristic of all (or almost all) humans would be defective.

But are these psychological traits really universal or are they rather cultural products, found only among some peoples? There are examples of societies that are much less restrictive about sex (including sex with children) than western societies, just as there are societies in which there are many more taboos pertaining to food and eating than there are in most western societies. It is too easy to assume that the way one's own society feels about sex and food is the way all societies do. If so, and if others are better off for their more open views of sex, then the defender of the casual view may have a message of sexual liberation that would be worth heeding.[31] This is not to say that it would be an easy matter (even for an individual, let alone a whole society) to abandon the significance view and thoroughly embrace the casual view. But if the casual view is the preferable one, then even if it would be difficult to adopt, it would nonetheless be a view to which people ought to strive. One way to do this would be to rear children with the casual view.

Whether viewing sex as significant is characteristic of all humanity or only of certain human cultures is clearly an empirical issue that psychologists, anthropologists, and others would be best suited to determining. Moreover, it is not clear whether even the relevant evidence is (yet) available for even these disciplinary experts to advise. Thus, disconcertingly, we may currently be unable to settle this question.

Hybrids of the two views may be possible. For instance, it may be thought that sex is not quite like other pleasures, but that it also need not be linked to the deepest forms of romantic love. On one such view, it might be sufficient that one *like*[32] (rather than love) somebody in order, for example, to copulate. However, no such mixed view would resolve our problem. Any view that took a sufficiently light view of sex that would justify promiscuity would have difficulty ruling out all paedophilia or bestiality, or classifying rape as the *special* wrong it is often thought to be.

Nor do I think that a non-hybrid intermediate view will be able to drive a moral wedge between promiscuity, on the one hand, and rape, paedophilia, bestiality, and necrophilia on the other. Such an intermediate view would (as the casual view does) deny that sex must be an expression of romantic affection, but (in common with the significance view) deny that sex is like other pleasures. Although one obviously cannot anticipate every possible way in which such a view might be developed, it is hard to imagine how any version could, in the requisite way, distinguish promiscuity from rape and paedophilia. Consider two versions of an allegedly intermediate view that have been proposed.

The first of these[33] is that although sex need not be an expression of romantic affection, it is unlike other pleasures in that it is intimate or private. The latter part of this claim might be understood as being either descriptive or normative. The descriptive claim is that most people prefer to engage in sex (i) with intimates[34] or (ii) away from the view of others. The normative claim is that people *ought* to engage in sex only (i) with intimates or (ii) away from the view of others. If the basis for (some or other of) these claims is that sex is or ought to be a deep expression of a romantic affection, then the view under discussion is either support for, or a disguised version of, the significance view rather than an alternative intermediate view.

It is hard to think of other reasons why sex is morally permissible only *between intimates*, but perhaps there is some such reason why sex is or ought to be *private*. If there is, then there would be an intermediate view between the significance and casual views. But what would be wrong, on this intermediate view, with *private* sex between an adult and a willing child or animal? What would be wrong with private sex with a corpse, if the person whose corpse it is had given consent in advance of death? And why would coerced private sex be worse than other kinds of coerced activities in private? There is reason to suspect that any plausible answer to these questions would have to appeal to the normative significance of sex as an expression of affection, and any such appeal could not lead to a special condemnation of rape and all paedophilia, bestiality, and necrophilia without also implying a condemnation of promiscuity.

The second version of an allegedly non-hybrid intermediate view that has been suggested is that sex is unlike other pleasures because it is 'personally involving ([that is,] psycho-dynamically complex)' in ways that other pleasures are not.[35] However, it seems that any interpretation of the view that sex is personally involving would be, or would lend support to, a significance view of sex. It would surely be inappropriate to engage in personally involving behaviours with those (such as mere acquaintances) with whom personal involvement (at the relevantly complex or deep level) is not really possible. If that is so, then it is hard to see how the second non-hybrid intermediate view can succeed in driving a wedge between promiscuity on the one hand, and rape and paedophilia, bestiality, and necrophilia on the other.

One other possibility is an alternative to both the significance and casual views that is neither a hybrid of the two nor intermediate between them. One such suggestion, offered by Fiona Woollard, is that it is not the significance of sex that counts but rather the significance of sexual *autonomy* and *integrity*.[36] Put another way, for sex to be morally permissible it must be respectful of sexual autonomy and integrity. How serious a wrong is, need not depend (only) on the importance of the activity. The importance of control over that activity matters. Given that sexual autonomy (as well as sexual integrity) is especially important, such violations are more serious than violations of some (but not all) other forms of autonomy.

If sexual autonomy is of special importance, then this would explain why rape is especially wrong. But why, if we reject the significance view, is sexual autonomy an especially important form of autonomy? Fiona Woollard suggests that it is because the 'sexual is both rooted in one of the most primitive and most powerful bodily urges and able to implicate a huge variety of complex human attitudes'.[37]

She acknowledges that the same is true of the gastronomic, and thinks that it would not be a problem for the sexual liberal to concede that rape is no worse than force-feeding, so long as we appreciate just how bad force-feeding is.[38] This is hard to believe. As bad as it is to force something like an orange into somebody's mouth, it must surely be worse, for example, to force a penis into a mouth, vagina, or anus.

Nevertheless, Professor Woollard does attempt to show why interferences with sexual autonomy may be worse than interferences with gastronomic autonomy. She says the 'sexual seems to be primarily interpersonal in a way that eating is not' and that 'sexual encounters seem to have more significant implications for others' attitudes to us as embodied beings'.[39] Yet she denies that this implies that 'any sex that is not interpersonal is therefore bad'.[40] (By 'sex that is not interpersonal' she seems to mean sex that does not meet the significance condition.) This, she says, is because sex 'that is not interpersonal may simply lack implications for a person's attitudes toward other persons as embodied beings. Lacking implications is not the same as implying bad attitudes'.[41] Moreover, she says, 'non-interpersonal sex can express good attitudes toward *oneself* as an embodied being'.[42]

This seems like an unpromising line of argument. First, even if eating is not primarily interpersonal, force-feeding somebody certainly is. It (usually) expresses a very bad attitude towards the person force-fed.[43] Overriding people's autonomy generally, even though not always, implies a bad attitude towards that person. However, perhaps the claim is that, for reasons not explained, overriding autonomy pertaining to a primarily interpersonal activity is worse than overriding forms of autonomy that do not pertain to primarily interpersonal activities.

The problem with this is that sex is not the only primitive and powerful urge that is primarily interpersonal. Power is another. Sometimes people want power as a means to sex, but sometimes they want sex as a means to power (and want power as a means to other things). Ultimately, both power and sex are, from an evolutionary perspective, means to enhancing fitness. It is thus unsurprising that power is a primitive and powerful urge. It is also primarily interpersonal because to have power is to have it over or relative to other people. The presence or absence of power and the relative levels of power also 'implicate a huge variety of complex human attitudes'. Thus, if sexual autonomy is special because sex is 'both rooted in one of the most primitive and most powerful bodily urges and able to implicate a huge variety of complex human attitudes'[44] then all autonomy is special because power shares all those same features.

Even if we restrict our attention to sex, there are problems for Professor Woollard's argument. Bestiality, necrophilia, and paedophilia need not imply any bad attitudes towards the animal, corpse, or child with whom there is sexual activity. In at least some of these cases, most plausibly bestiality and paedophilia, there may even imply positive attitudes. The zoophile and paedophile may love the animal or child with whom they have sex. They may also express good attitudes towards themselves by gratifying themselves.

Animals, children, and corpses are, of course, not autonomous, and thus an argument grounded in the wrong of violating autonomy is unlikely to be able to rule out such sex with them. If there is no autonomy, then there is no autonomy to violate. This is why Professor Woollard also makes reference to 'sexual integrity'. She does so in reference to paedophilia.[45] 'Sexual integrity' is a vague concept, but she understands it to involve 'the absence of sexual violation' and she says that sexual violation 'includes, but may not be limited to, sex without appropriate consent'.[46]

The problem with this is that it begs the question. *Why* is sex without consent a violation if the being is incapable of giving consent and if consent from such a being is not required for numerous other activities? The significance view of sex can explain this. The casual view cannot. Saying that sexual integrity is important also does not provide the required explanation. Everybody can agree that sexual integrity is good, especially if one understands it as the absence of sexual violation. However, one may not simply stipulate that the absence of consent constitutes a sexual violation when that is exactly what is in question. Parents routinely make decisions on behalf of their children and are thought to be permitted to do so, on condition that these decisions are not (seriously) harmful to the children.

It is true that some of these other decisions are unavoidable. If one does not feed a child because one cannot obtain his or her full consent, the child will die. Food is thus necessary in a way in which sex is not. However, not all food is necessary and thus the force of the necessity argument soon runs out. Is it a violation of one's children's gastronomic integrity to give them candy floss, an ice cream, a biscuit, or a chocolate? Is it a violation of one's children's recreational integrity to take them to the ballet, theatre, cinema, or sports match? Why should sex be different—if the significance view is mistaken?

The above conclusions should obviously be extremely troubling to those who approve of promiscuity but who abhor paedophilia, bestiality, necrophilia, and rape. The foregoing deliberations show, however, that this should provide little cause for self-satisfaction on the part of those who condemn promiscuity along with rape and all paedophilia, bestiality, and necrophilia. Their moral judgements about *these* practices may be consistent but it remains an open question whether they are consistently right or consistently wrong. Which it is, will depend on which of the rival views of sexual ethics is best, and the significance view is not without difficulty even to those who advocate it.

For example, it seems to prohibit sex between married people who have ceased loving one another or who, perhaps on account of an arranged marriage, do not (yet?) love one another. This is at odds with the views of many sexual conservatives, who do not oppose sex within marriage even if it is a loveless marriage. The marriage view—the view that all and only (consensual) sex within marriage is permissible—cannot be a refuge for sexual conservatives, for while it prohibits promiscuity, and premarital and extramarital sex, it provides no reason why people should not be allowed to marry and then have sex with children, animals, and corpses. Nor can the marriage view be combined with the significance view, precisely because they have contradictory positions on loveless marital sex. Moreover, there is no rationale within the marriage view for coupling it with the significance view.

By contrast, there *is*, as noted earlier, a possible basis for extending the significance view to include a marital requirement. If the significance view is extended to include an official (marital) undertaking of sexual exclusivity, then it can rule out marriage with children and animals, for example. However, this is a version of the significance view rather than a version of what I have called the marriage view.

Some versions of the significance view would also permit bigamy or limited polygamy, as well as some *partially* open marriages. While there are many sexual conservatives who support bigamy and limited polygamy, there are many others who do not. Moreover, many of those sexual conservatives who endorse polygamy permit more spouses than a reasonable interpretation of the significance view could allow. Until all these matters are resolved, adherents of both the significance view and the casual view have cause for unease.

The reproductive view and the anti-reproductive view

The significance view and the marriage view each stipulate a necessary condition for sexual ethics—conditions that the casual view rejects. There are two other views that stipulate other necessary conditions for sex to be morally permissible. According to the *reproductive view* of sexual ethics, sex must have procreative potential in order to be morally permissible. The *anti-reproductive view* of sexual ethics maintains that for sex to be morally permissible it must *not* be procreative (at least in the sense that one takes reasonable precautions to prevent procreation[47]).

Neither of these views is a competitor to the significance, marriage, or casual views. The distinction between the reproductive and anti-reproductive views cuts across the distinction between the significance, marriage, and casual views. It is thus possible for either the reproductive or anti-reproductive view to be coupled with either the significance, marriage, or casual view. When it is the significance or the marriage view that is added to either the reproductive or the anti-reproductive view, then the combined view imposes two necessary conditions for sex to be morally permissible—either (a) the expression of mutual romantic love or (b) the marital context, and either (c) the presence or absence of (d) procreative potential.

Although neither the significance nor the marriage nor the casual view is in competition with the reproductive and anti-reproductive views, there is another view that *is* in competition with the latter two views. This is a reproductively neutral view, according to which it makes no moral difference whether sex is reproductive or not. This view, like the casual view, rejects the imposition of a necessary condition that a competing view demands. Thus, if the significance view or marriage view is combined with the neutral view about reproduction, then only one necessary condition is imposed.

The various possible combinations and their combined conditions are presented in Figure 2.1.

The anti-reproductive view is that of anti-natalists, who maintain that it is wrong to bring new sentient beings into existence. There are different possible routes to the anti-natalist view, but the ones leading to the most extensive version—namely, that *all* procreation is wrong—are based on arguments that there is nothing to be gained and much to suffer by being brought into existence. Anti-natalists need have no objection to sex. Indeed, they might think that it can be one means of making life less bad for those who have already come into existence. However, given their opposition to procreation, anti-natalists think that those having sex must take suitable precautions to prevent sex leading to procreation. There is much to be said in defence of the anti-natalist view—indeed so much that the arguments, advanced elsewhere,[48] cannot be rehearsed here.

	Reproductive view	Anti-reproductive view	Reproductively neutral view
Significance view	Sex must be significant and reproductive	Sex must be significant and not reproductive	Sex must be significant
Marriage view	Sex must be marital and reproductive	Sex must be marital and non-reproductive	Sex must be marital
Casual view	Sex must be reproductive	Sex must not be reproductive	Sex need not be significant, reproductive, or non-reproductive

Figure 2.1 Possible combinations of sexual ethics views.

Homosexuality, etc.

The reproductive view is more popular (but not, I suggest, more plausible) than the anti-reproductive view. The reproductive view rules out sex between people of the same sex, and sex with animals, prepubescent children, or corpses. While the latter implications have wide appeal, the implication for homosexual actions appeals to sexual conservatives (of a certain kind). Unfortunately for them, the view would also seem to rule out sex between married people who have no chance of reproducing (at least through sex) on account of menopause or hysterectomy, for example.[49]

They sometimes make valiant attempts to permit sterile marital sex on the grounds that it is the *kind* of sex—between human adults of the opposite sex—that is procreative even if it is not procreative in these particular cases. However, one problem with this is that it is not clear why the reproductive view should apply to kinds of sex rather than to instances of it. Of course, one can never tell whether a specific instance *will* result in procreation, but one can tell whether a particular instance has a *chance* of being procreative. Even if the reproductive view should apply to kinds of sexual activity, it is not clear why the relevant kind is 'penile-vaginal intercourse' rather than 'penile-vaginal intercourse between fertile people'.

The more fundamental problem is that unlike the significance view, for which one readily sees a rationale even if one does not accept it, it is difficult to see why sex must be reproductive in order to be morally permissible.

Some arguments for the reproductive view are versions of the argument that a sexual practice is wrong because it is unnatural. One such argument is that those engaging in non-reproductive sex are using their genitalia for the wrong purpose. In attributing a purpose to the genitalia, those advancing this argument are assuming that there is a purposive agent who had assigned a purpose to the genitalia. If that agent is the person whose genitalia they are, then that person can attribute any purpose to them, including the purpose of bringing pleasure.

Thus, if the argument about the wrong purposes is to work, the purposes must be an agent other than the person whose genitalia they are. Theoretically, the most plausible candidate for such an agent is God. If God created humans and endowed their genitalia with procreative purpose then, the argument goes, humans who use their genitalia for non-procreative purposes are using them in the wrong way. There are at least three problems with this argument.

First, it rests on the controversial assumption of God's existence. Second, even if one accepts that assumption, it is unclear why we must also assume that God did not endow the genitalia with multiple purposes. Those who think that God created the genitalia for particular purposes must surely think that these include not only procreation but also urination. If they have two purposes, there is no obvious reason to think that they might not also have a third—sexual pleasure. Third, even if God did not endow the genitalia with the purpose of providing pleasure, it is not clear why it is wrong for humans to use their genitalia for pleasurable purposes. Nobody thinks that wearing glasses is wrong because it puts the ears and nose to the purpose of supporting the glasses. Yet we have no more reason for thinking that God intended this purpose than we have for thinking that he intended the genitalia to serve pleasurable purposes. Indeed, we may even have *less* reason for thinking that God intended us to use our ears and noses to support glasses, given that humans have likely derived pleasure from sex for as long as there have been humans, whereas glasses are a relatively new invention.

There is a variant on this argument that avoids appeal to purposes. According to this variant the various parts of our bodies have functions (as distinct from purposes). The function of the heart is to pump blood around the body, the function of the ears is auditory sensation, and the function of legs and feet is locomotion. In attributing a function, one need not assume that we were created by a deity. Functions are compatible with purposes, but they do not presuppose them. We can tell something's function from what it does without having to postulate whether a purposive agent created it to function in that way.

On one interpretation of 'function', the genitalia may well have multiple functions. After all what they do includes procreation, urination, and pleasure. However, there is an account of function that may be seen to shorten this list. According to this view something's functions are 'those of its effects that explain its existence'.[50] Elucidating this, Michael Levin notes that the function of sharks' teeth is to tear flesh because the tearing of flesh is what explains why sharks have teeth. He notes that sharks' teeth might also have the effect of impressing aquarium visitors, but that does not explain why sharks have teeth. Similarly, what explains the existence of the genitalia is their procreative effects. (The urological features are explained by the urinary effects, but the external urinary organs need not have been different in males and females had it not been for the procreative function.) Although the genitals can produce pleasure, that pleasure is not what explains the existence of the genitals. Instead, the pleasure is explained by its contribution to procreation. If sex were not pleasurable, there would be much less of it, and thus much less procreation. In other words, instead of the pleasure explaining the existence of the genitals, it is procreation that explains the existence of the pleasure from the genitals.

Michael Levin employs this understanding of function in an argument that homosexuality is unnatural and abnormal. He does *not* argue that homosexuality is therefore immoral. However, he thinks that it is undesirable, and that its undesirability has moral implications. The undesirability, he says, stems from the fact that homosexuals (unlike heterosexuals and bisexuals) negate the evolutionary function of their genitalia.

To negate the evolutionary function of a body part is to use it in a way that does not allow the proper evolutionary function. The person who wears glasses may be using the ears and nose in ways unrelated to their evolutionary function. However, because wearing glasses does not prevent the nose and ears from being used in keeping with their evolutionary functions, wearing glasses does not *negate* those functions.

Professor Levin argues, however, that those whose only sexual activity is homosexual are like somebody who is so devoted to playing 'Old MacDonald' on his teeth that he never uses them for biting and chewing food. His teeth *could* be used for chewing, but since he never uses them in this way, he negates their evolutionary function. We should expect that those who negated the evolutionary function of their teeth in this way would, on average, do less well and thus be less happy than those who did not. Professor Levin says that we should expect a similar reduction in happiness by those who negate the evolutionary function of other body parts, including the genitalia. He says that homosexuality 'is likely to cause unhappiness because it leaves unfulfilled an innate and innately rewarding desire'.[51]

However, there is a problem here. It is clear why people who never use their teeth for chewing will likely fare less well than those who do use their teeth in accordance with their natural function. They will have a restricted range of food and thus of nutrition. Adequate nutrition is essential to wellbeing. The causal explanation is clear. The same is not true of homosexuals who never use their genitals in accordance with their natural functions. More specifically, what is the 'innate and innately rewarding desire' that is left unfulfilled? If it is the desire for sexual satisfaction, then the claim seems clearly false. Homosexuals derive sexual satisfaction from sex with people of the same sex. It is heterosexual sex that would not fulfil their sexual desires.

Perhaps, then, the desire is for parenthood. However, homosexuals *can* fulfil that desire. One means to this is adoption, at least when adoption is possible. If the 'innate and innately rewarding desire' is not for parenthood in the sense of rearing children, but instead for parenthood in the sense of producing biological offspring, then adoption will not fulfil the desire. However, lesbians can still choose to procreate through donor sperm and artificial insemination. In the case of homosexual men, it is not clear how such a desire could be innately fulfilling. (Michael Levin, like so many opponents of homosexuality, focuses on male homosexuals even though he thinks that his arguments also apply to lesbians.) Women can gain fulfilment from procreation (as distinct from sex) because there is typically something that it feels like for a woman to gestate a child.[52] However, procreation (again, as distinct from sex) does not feel like anything to a man. Men can procreate without knowing whether they have, and they can think that they have procreated without their having done so. Given that procreation cannot be an 'innately fulfilling desire' for men, and that it can be fulfilled by not only heterosexual but also homosexual women, it does not seem as though that could be the desire that Michael Levin had in mind.[53]

Furthermore, some homosexuals, just like some heterosexuals, may not want to have children. Alternatively, they might want to have children but believe, with good anti-natalist cause, that it would be wrong to bring children into existence. Some things that would make one happier are also things that one may not do. (The rapist, for example, may have an 'innate and innately rewarding desire' to have sex with people irrespective of whether they want to have sex with him. It does not follow that he is morally entitled to have sex with all those people.)

Michael Levin's argument concerns homosexuality, but the same argument could also be advanced against exclusive bestiality and necrophilia.[54] More generally, it is quite common for sexual conservatives of a certain kind to lump homosexuality together with bestiality and necrophilia. They tend to offer a *reductio ad absurdum*. For example, they suggest that if a state permits homosexual activity, then it should also permit such practices as bestiality and necrophilia;[55] and given that the latter two should not be permitted, neither should homosexuality. Sometimes they offer a similar argument regarding the morality of these practices: if homosexual activity is morally permissible then bestiality and necrophilia must also be morally permissible; but given that the latter two kinds of activity are not permissible it cannot be the case that homosexual activity is permissible.

This sort of argument impresses sexual conservatives more than it should, but it is also taken less seriously by sexual progressives than they should take it. In other words, it is taken more seriously than it should by those who advance the argument, but less seriously than it should by those to whom it is directed. This curious asymmetry is because many (although not all) sexual conservatives tend to combine a reproductive view with a significance view of sex, whereas many (but again not all) sexual progressives tend to combine a reproductively neutral view with a casual view of sex. The upshot of this is that sexual conservatives often have all the resources needed to distinguish homosexuality from both bestiality and necrophilia. Homosexual sex can meet the significance condition, whereas sex with animals and corpses cannot. However, if one rejects the significance view, as sexual progressives tend to do, then one does not have that resource to distinguish homosexuality from bestiality and necrophilia.[56]

Nor can other arguments be employed to show that bestiality and necrophilia are wrong in all cases. Some other version of an argument from unnaturalness will not work for reasons considered earlier. Similarly doomed is an appeal to the disgust that many people feel about bestiality and necrophilia. Those who defend a casual view will not be able to appeal to biblical proscriptions on bestiality, both because of the usual problems with such an appeal, but also because this would be at odds with the casual view.

Incest

The reproductive view has mixed implications for incest.[57] On the one hand, it rules out all those instances of incest that are non-reproductive. These include cases involving infertile (for example, pre-pubescent or post-menopausal) family members. However, it rules out those cases not because they are incestuous but rather because they are not reproductive.

On the other hand, the reproductive view, would, in principle, permit those cases of incest that do have procreative potential—such as penile-vaginal intercourse between fertile siblings. It is true that the very incestuous sexual activities that have procreative potential also carry elevated risk for the resultant offspring. However, that would provide good grounds for taking procreative incestuous sex to be morally wrong only if the risk is *sufficiently* elevated, and if the harm that is being risked is sufficiently serious. It is unlikely that *all* cases of procreative incestuous sex would meet those conditions (if one rejects anti-natalism).

Even when the risk and harm are sufficiently great, what would be making such instances of incest wrong is not their failure to meet the procreative criterion. Instead, it would be the fact that when it does meet that criterion it is harmful, or at least imposes significant risk of serious harm. Thus, the wrongfulness would be on the basis of the harm of procreating rather than on the basis of not procreating.

Other views of sexual ethics will rule out even fewer instances of incest. All views can rule out those incestuous practices that will impose significant risks of severe harms, but none of the views, except the procreative view, can rule out non-procreative incest. This is true of the anti-procreative view, and of the view that is neutral on the question of procreation.

Similarly, it should be clear that the casual view cannot rule out incest that will not produce offspring. If siblings may have a meal together and attend a concert together, there is no reason, according to the casual view, why they should not have sex with one another, assuming that they take adequate contraceptive precaution (or abort if that is an option).

Even the significance view, which rules out many more instances of sex than the casual view, cannot rule out all non-procreative incest. This is because it is possible, even if unusual, for siblings or other close relatives to have mutual romantic love and for sex between them to be an expression of this. Variants of the significance view that add further conditions might well reduce the allowable instances of incest (as they reduce the allowable instances of any other sexual activity), but none of them can rule out as much incestuous sex as the reproductive view. Incestuous relationships can be exclusive. They can occur within the context of an unofficial commitment. If marriages between close relatives are permitted, they can even occur within the context of an official marital commitment. In the last of these cases, some incest could also be permitted under the marriage view. (If there is no moral problem with incest, then there is no reason why incestuous marriages should not be permitted.)

Given the foregoing it is unsurprising that it is notoriously difficult to justify the view that all incest is wrong. When asked to justify why they think that consensual contracepted sex between adult siblings is wrong, most people flail around for an answer, but produce nothing compelling.[58] It is very likely that the general aversion to incest is a psychological product of our evolution. An aversion to incest would have been selected on account of its protection against producing unhealthy offspring. The point, however, is that our aversion does not neatly track the instances where incest is likely to have this effect. The aversion spills over and also operates in response to benign incest. The general aversion may be apt, but there are some instances in which it is without justification.

Conclusion

No view of sexual ethics is devoid of difficulties (if by 'difficulty' we mean being at odds with some judgements of many of those people who are sympathetic to the view). For example, the casual view and the neutral view about procreation seem to permit too much. The anti-reproductive view permits all sex, as long as it is not procreative. For many people even this is too permissive. The significance view, in disallowing some marital sex, seems to prohibit too much. Yet it permits some incest, which most advocates of the significance view (like most people more generally) would claim is impermissible. The reproductive view permits some polygamy and some sex with young adolescents.

The various views of sexual ethics, what they sometimes permit and what they (almost) always prohibit is summarized in Figure 2.2.

In the face of these difficulties, some people might be willing to bite whichever bullets must be bitten in order to accept the view they take to be correct. Thus, some advocates of the casual view might be willing to accept that some instances of paedophilia, bestiality, and necrophilia are morally permissible. Such a position is consistent, but it is not obviously correct. Perhaps sex *is* different from other activities.

Everybody has to bite the incest bullet (although the reproductive view can rule out more incest than the other views). As no view supports the wrongfulness of all incest, that seems like a bullet we should all bite, especially since the reproductive view has difficulties of its own. These include opposition to both homosexuality and masturbation. Although those implications will seem entirely reasonable to some, there is much to be said for the opposite view. The reproductive view is also at odds with the anti-reproductive view. That incompatibility will not trouble anybody other than anti-natalists, but those who are untroubled should consider this: If you are opposed to incest that could result in a child because of the great risk of imposing a harm on the resultant child, then remember that *each and every* child produced by any couple stands a one hundred percent chance of suffering serious harm, including death. The serious harms will not always be congenital in the usual sense of that term—that is, present from birth—but they are an inevitable

	Promiscuity	Premarital sex	Marital sex	Extra-Marital sex	Polygamy	Paedophilia	Bestiality/ Necrophilia	Homo-sexuality	Incest	Mastur-bation
Significance View	✗	✓ (if the expression of mutual love)	✓ (if the expression of mutual love)	✓ (if the expression of mutual love)	✓ (but limited number of spouses)	✗ (unless child can understand significance)	✗	✓ (if the expression of mutual love)	✓ (if the expression of mutual love)	✗ (or N/A?)
+ exclusivity	✗	✓ (with only one partner)	✓	✗	✗	✗ (unless child only partner)	✗	✓	✓	✗ (or N/A?)
+ unofficial commitment	✗	✓ (only with unofficial commitment)	N/A	✗	N/A	✗ (unless unofficial commitment made)	✗	✓	✓	✗ (or N/A?)
+ official commitment	✗	✗	✓	✗	✓	✗ (unless married)	✗	✓	✓	✗ (or N/A?)
Marriage View	✗	✗	✓	✗ (In open marriage)	✓	✓ (if married)	✓ (if married)	✓ (if married)	✓ (if married)	✗ (or N/A?)
Casual View	✓	✓	✓	✓	✓	✓	✗	✓	✓/✗	✓
Reproductive View	✓ (if reproductive)	✓ (if reproductive)	✓ (if reproductive)	✓ (if reproductive)	✓ (if reproductive)	✗ (unless post-puberty)	✓	✗	✓	✗
Anti-Reproductive View	✓ (if not reproductive)	✓ (if not reproductive)	✓ (if not reproductive)	✓ (if not reproductive)	✓ (if not reproductive)	✓ (if not reproductive)	✓	✓	✓ (if not reproductive)	✓
Neutral View	✓	✓	✓	✓	✓	✓	✓	✓	✓	✓

Figure 2.2 The implications of different views of sexual ethics.

1. Where a view prohibits all (or almost all) instances of a practice, this is marked with an ✗. (Exceptions are in parentheses).
2. Where a view can permit a practice, this is marked with a ✓. (Conditions in parentheses.)
3. Given the exceptions to the prohibitions and the conditions for the permissions, there is a judgment call in whether to mark a particular block with an ✗ or a ✓.
4. Where the variants of the significance view include cumulative conditions (in the left most column) then the parenthetical comments under the relevant practices are also cumulative.
5. Where two consistent views – see Figure 2.1 for the possibilities – are combined then a practice must meet the conditions of both views in order to be permissible. In other words, there must be a tick in each of the relevant blocks in Figure 2.2. If there is a cross in even one box, then the practice is prohibited on the combined view.

consequence of being brought into existence. There is thus some wisdom in the quip that life is a terminal disease that, except in the case of artificial and assisted reproduction, is sexually transmitted.

This thought should at least unsettle those who hold the view that in most cases it makes no difference whether sex is reproductive or not.[59] More difficult is the choice between the significance and casual view. (The marriage view has very little to recommend it. What is it about marriage that has morally transformative power independent of a significance condition?)

It is unsatisfying to be left without a clear answer to the question whether we should be favouring the significance view or the casual view. What makes this uncertainty still more disconcerting is that the choices are not within some narrow band on a spectrum of possibilities. Instead, they are towards different extremities of that spectrum. We must adopt either a substantially (but not entirely) conservative position or a sexual libertine position (restricted only by the anti-reproductive requirement, I suggest). The substantially conservative view prohibits all casual sex but not homosexual sex between those homosexuals who love one another. The libertine position, by contrast, permits all (non-procreative) sex, subject to the usual ethical constraints, including not lying, cheating, stealing, and harming.

In the absence of a convincing argument for either the significance or the casual view of sexual ethics, the appropriate response is either a tentative theoretical choice, coupled with a clear acknowledgement that it is tentative, or alternatively agnosticism.

Agnosticism about the correct view of sex, like agnosticism on any other issue, is not to be confused with indifference. One may care deeply about an issue while realizing that the available evidence is insufficient to make a judgement on it. Caring deeply, however, should not stand in the way of a dispassionate assessment of the evidence. There is a great danger that in matters pertaining to current sexual taboos, clear thinking will be in short supply.

The agnostic conclusion is a deeply unsatisfying one. It is even more frustrating for those who wonder what they should do in practice. That a conclusion is frustrating does not mean that it is not the correct one to reach. Sometimes the evidence is insufficient to reach a definitive conclusion. However, the question remains: How should we respond, practically, to this uncertainty?

The first thing to notice is that, for many people and many practices, we do not need to have settled on one of the views of sexual ethics to know what we may do. For example, advocates of both views can agree that there is no way to distinguish heterosexual from homosexual sex. Neither falls foul of the casual view, and both can regularly meet the conditions of the significance view. In such cases, the more general agnosticism does not imply agnosticism about this.

Other practices will violate the requirements of the significance view, but many of them will be moot for those many humans who are not considering paedophilia, bestiality, or necrophilia. There would thus be nothing inconsistent about engaging in casual sex while desisting from these other practices. However, those who, in their promiscuous practice, follow the casual view, would have no grounds for criticizing those who *do* engage in those instances of paedophilia, bestiality, and necrophilia that do not violate independent moral prohibitions (such as a prohibition against wrongfully harming). If you want to 'put *out*' casually, you may also have to 'put *up*' with a greater range of practices.

But what about the choice between engaging in and avoiding casual sex? Those inclined to the significance view are likely to note that sex that meets the significance condition is also acceptable according to the casual view, and thus a precautionary principle suggests that one should, in the face of uncertainty, follow the significance view. If one follows that view in practice, and it turns out that the casual view is correct, one will not have done anything wrong. By contrast, if one engages in casual sex and it turns out that the significance view is correct, then one would have done something wrong.

The problem with this response is that there are costs other than the risk of doing wrong, and these include the foregoing of pleasures that might be morally innocent. This may lead those who are inclined towards the casual view to suggest that we need to consider the probability that the casual view is mistaken and weigh that up against the costs of foregoing the hedonic benefits of the casual view.

Even if the casual view is mistaken, it may matter *how* mistaken it is. Is sex in the absence of mutual romantic love *prohibited*, or is it instead either morally *defective* or merely *less than ideal*? My focus was on versions of the significance and casual views that disagreed in prohibiting or permitting casual sex. This was because those are the most common versions of the significance and casual views. However, it is quite possible that one of the alternative interpretations of the significance view is more plausible. Perhaps, sex that fails the significance condition is not morally impermissible, but instead either morally defective or merely less than morally ideal.[60] If either of those alternatives is correct, then the lesser moral costs would make the risk of harmless wrongdoing more readily overridable.

The difficulty is determining just how we quantify the various probabilities and moral costs. Given these difficulties, it is quite possible that reasonable people could disagree about these matters. While reasoning about ethics can sometimes bring us to more definitive conclusions, that is not always the case. Sometimes, it can narrow the range of reasonable views but not to the point that only one view is left standing. That, at least for now, seems to be true of the disagreement between advocates of the significance and casual views of sex.

3
Environment

In a formulation that is memorable both for its brevity and its profanity, Jonathan Franzen has said that the story of our environmental problem 'can be told in fewer than a hundred and forty characters: We're taking carbon that used to be sequestered and putting it in the atmosphere, and unless we stop we're fucked'.[1]

To be sure, something is lost in the succinctness of this formulation. Some of what is lost are further scientific details, but more important for our purposes is that the summary glosses over important moral dimensions to the problem. The 'we' who will suffer the consequences of carbon emissions is not co-extensive (although it does overlap) with the 'we' who are causing the bulk of those emissions. The problem is thus not merely a prudential one.[2] Emitters are harming not only themselves but also other humans, both present and future, and both spatially proximate and distant. Emitters are also harming members of many other species around the globe. We are doing all this by altering the global environment through our emissions.

This, as one writer has suggested contra Ecclesiastes, is 'something new under the sun'.[3] For the vast majority of human history, any impact that members of our species had on the natural environment was a local impact. Pollution, for example, was almost exclusively local. Even if some effects were felt somewhat further afield, the effects were not global. This changed, not because local pollution stopped, but rather because it became supplemented by the more momentous problem of global pollution.[4] The start of this change can be dated to the beginning of the Industrial Revolution, when humans began releasing previously sequestered carbon into the atmosphere. Initially the effects—global warming and the consequent climate change—were limited, but they have increased exponentially, with resultant harms.

What, if anything, ought we to do about this? The 'we' is again ambiguous—and multiply so. 'We' can refer to our species collectively, to human groupings of various sizes (such as countries, groups of countries, such as the European Union, or corporations), or to individuals. In the last of these, the question would be better formulated as: 'What, if anything, ought

I (rather than "we") to do about problems regarding the natural environment?' It is this question that falls within the domain of quotidian ethics. It is not a question about what treaties, public policy, or law ought to be adopted in response to the problem. Instead, it is an ethical question that confronts each individual in daily life.

To be precise, it may not confront *every* single individual. There are many people, typically among the world's most disadvantaged, who are such low emitters that they are not candidates for a duty to reduce their emissions. Their emissions are involuntarily low. The question confronts those individuals who are emitting at an unsustainable level—that is, at a level that is not universalizable without serious adverse effects. This is not to say that low-level emitters do not have other environmental duties, most importantly (but not only) duties not to pollute their local environment.[5] My focus here will be on the problem of global warming and climate change. However, some attention will also be given to other environmental issues.

Although there are some people who attribute moral status to ecosystems themselves (including the global ecosystem), one does not have to accept that controversial view in order to think that one can have duties concerning the environment. This is because sentient beings—humans and other animals—can be adversely affected by changes in the natural environment. One's duties *concerning* the natural environment can thus be derivative from the duties one owes *to* the sentient beings who are and will be dependent on that environment.

Even with this recognition, any argument for the view that individuals have duties concerning the environment is not straightforward. The complexity is partly empirical and partly moral. Indeed, at least some of the moral complexity rests on the empirical complexity. Consider, first, some further empirical details.

Global warming, climate change, and resultant harms

All life on earth is carbon-based. That is to say, carbon is the main component of all life on our planet. Carbon is essential to life in other ways too. Carbon dioxide (CO_2)—the combination of a carbon atom with two oxygen atoms—is necessary for photosynthesis. Without photosynthesis, there would be no plants, and thus no herbivores, and thus no omnivores and carnivores.[6] Moreover, via the process of photosynthesis, plants emit oxygen—a substance without which aerobic organisms, such as ourselves, would die.

There are natural cycles of carbon. In the so-called fast cycles, carbon moves between the atmosphere (both air and water), plants, and animals. Put another way, the fast cycle takes place within the 'biosphere', at least if we use this term to refer to the sphere of earth where the majority of life exists.[7] For example, a carbon atom may move from the air to a plant, entering stomata on the latter as part of a CO_2 molecule. The plant then uses it to photosynthesize. That carbon atom could then enter an animal which ingests the plant or part thereof. That animal may then exhale the carbon atom, releasing it back into the atmosphere. From there it could be carried to the ocean, where it forms part of a bicarbonate. It may then enter marine algae, which is then eaten by a marine animal. And so on for millions of years.[8]

In the 'slow' cycle, carbon moves between the biosphere and other parts of the earth, such as sediment and rock. For example, some carbon entering the ocean comes to form part of calcium carbonate in shell-building organisms. When those organisms die and sink to the sea floor they can eventually turn to rock. Carbon can be returned to the atmosphere via volcanos and rock weathering. This cycle is slow because it can take millions of years for a particular carbon atom to complete one such cycle.[9]

The fast and slow cycles interact because when carbon does move from rock to biosphere it can then become part of a fast cycle. Similarly, carbon in a fast cycle can get trapped into a slow cycle.

These cycles have, for about ten thousand years, resulted in fairly stable levels of CO_2 in the atmosphere.[10] That changed when humans started burning fossil fuels. These fuels are sources of carbon that had been sequestered for millions of years until they were accessed through mining and drilling. When burned they contribute CO_2 to the atmosphere. Another major anthropogenic source of CO_2 is cement production.[11] The problem of CO_2 emissions is compounded by deforestation, either by logging or burning. Burning trees emits CO_2, but more importantly destroying trees removes a significant CO_2 sink, given the role that trees play in removing CO_2 from the atmosphere.

A proportion of anthropogenic carbon emissions is naturally reabsorbed from the atmosphere (through the cycles described above). However, because the carbon emissions for which humans are responsible exceed the natural carbon sinks,[12] there is a steady accumulation of CO_2 in the atmosphere. The cumulative result is that atmospheric CO_2 levels have been rising, and at an increasing rate. At the beginning of the Industrial Revolution the atmospheric CO_2 level was about 280 parts per million (ppm). As of August 2023, it is over 419 ppm.[13] This is 'almost certainly' higher than it has been for at least four million years.[14]

Carbon dioxide is a 'greenhouse gas' because it plays an important role in creating the 'greenhouse effect', namely increasing the earth's temperature. It is not the only greenhouse gas, or even the most potent one. Other anthropogenic greenhouse gases include methane and nitrous oxide, which respectively absorb eleven times and 270 times more heat than CO_2 does.[15] However, CO_2 is emitted in so much greater quantities that it is regularly used as the benchmark for greenhouse gas emissions. This is why the 'carbon footprint' is so often spoken about.

This footprint is, however, only part (albeit the major part) of the greenhouse gas footprint. Sometimes the latter is expressed as a carbon dioxide equivalent (CO_2e) because the emission of other greenhouse cases is 'expressed in terms of the amount of carbon dioxide that would have the same impact'.[16] The 'carbon footprint', even when expressed as a CO_2e, is itself only part of a person's ecological footprint, which includes the use not only of greenhouse gases but also other resources, such as food, water, and building materials.

The increase in atmospheric CO_2 has caused and continues to cause global warming. Global warming is not identical with climate change, but the former does cause the latter, which in turn can trigger feedback loops that exacerbate further global warming and thus further climate change. Thus far the global temperature has increased by a little over 1 degree centigrade since 1870.[17] It is projected to increase a further 1 to 4 degrees (depending in large part on what we do).[18] (Others suggest that the increase may be as much as 7 degrees.[19])

These may seem like very small differences in temperature. However, a degree or two difference in global temperature can have very significant climatic effects. For example, during the coldest period of the last ice age, earth's 'globally averaged temperature was "only" about 5°C colder'[20] than it is now. Part of the reason why minor differences in global temperatures can make such a difference is that these are global *averages*. At particular points on earth, especially but not only near the poles, the temperature variance can be much greater. For example, Verkhoyansk, a Siberian town, reached a record temperature of 38 degrees centigrade in 2020, over 18 degrees above the average for June.[21]

Global warming brings about climate change in a variety of ways. For example, one consequence of a warmer environment is the melting of polar ice sheets.[22] This, in turn, results in rising sea levels. The expansion of water as it warms also contributes to rising sea levels. Warmer air and water also fuel tropical cyclones (which include hurricanes and typhoons). Warmer surface water generates more water vapour, and warmer air holds more water vapour. Cyclones thus carry more water, increasing their precipitation. When these are combined with higher sea levels, surges are greater and cause more coastal flooding.[23] The strength of monsoons is also expected to increase with global warming, given that land will heat more than sea in summer, and the differential temperature between land and sea is the driver of monsoons.[24]

One possible consequence of more intense storms is less precipitation at other times or places, resulting in droughts.[25] Meanwhile, coastal aquifers are vulnerable to salination by rising sea levels.[26] Another consequence of global warming is an increase in heat waves.[27] As oceans absorb more CO_2, including anthropogenic CO_2, they become more acidic.[28]

It is 'virtually certain' that global warming will lead to a reduction of the permafrost.[29] That could possibly cause the release of methane beneath the permafrost, which would in turn accelerate global warming.[30]

Climate changes can be expected to cause various harms. Rising sea levels could cause the displacement of people living in low-level coastal areas. Currently more than 10% of humanity lives in such areas. By 2060, according to one calculation, between 879 million and 949 million people could be living in low-lying coastal zones.[31] Those negatively affected will be disproportionately people in developing countries, because such countries will be less able to mitigate the effects of climate change. There may be serious political implications of large-scale population migrations, especially if these are across international borders.

Low-lying island states, such as the Marshall Islands, the Maldives, Anguilla, Tuvalu, and Kiribati, that rise only a few meters above sea level, are already witnessing the threat of rising sea level and may well become uninhabitable. These states have relatively small populations, but their migrations, forced by climate change, will be a serious dislocation for such people, as it will be for others forced to leave their homes and perhaps their countries.

Although some humans will be able to adapt to climate changes, if not by migration then through technological and other adaptations, this will not be the case for all people. Some people's quality of life will deteriorate, and some will die as a result of the climate changes. One common cause is likely to be heatstroke.[32] Other possibilities include diseases whose vectors are insects and microbes that thrive in warmer, moister climates.[33] Reduced water security as a result of climate changes may result in many people using less hygienic water sources, which could result in an increase in water-borne infectious diseases.[34] Existing health problems are also expected to be exacerbated.[35] While there would likely be fewer cold-related deaths, it seems that this benefit would, at least in the long run,[36] if not already now,[37] be more than offset by the deaths caused by global warming.[38]

Disease and death are also the fates that await many animals of other species. They will die as their habitat becomes unhabitable—either through rising sea levels, melting ice sheets, acidification of the seas, or warmer aquatic or hotter terrestrial habitats.

Rising planetary temperature is also expected to have effects on food production. There is currently 'medium confidence' that some of these effects will be good in some places.[39] For example, higher concentrations of atmospheric CO_2 may serve as a fertilizer, stimulating growth of some plant species. However, this is more likely to be in places that currently have more temperate weather. The effects of global warming are likely to be negative in the tropical and subtropical zones, which also tend to be poorer.[40] It has also been suggested that increased CO_2 may impact negatively on the nutritional quality of some crops 'by increasing levels of carbohydrates, such as glucose, while decreasing the levels of important nutrients such as protein, iron, and zinc'.[41]

There is thus a long and a complex causal chain, from greenhouse gas emissions to global warming to climate change to harms (and possibly some benefits) to humans and animals, with feedback loops from global warming and climate change to increased greenhouse gas emissions. This is summarized in Figure 3.1.

Denialism

Of course, there are those who deny one or other component of the foregoing account. Some deny that global temperatures are increasing. Others concede that there is global warming, but deny it leads to the kinds of climate change stated. Yet others concede both global warming and climate change, but deny that either are anthropogenic. Those who deny that global warming

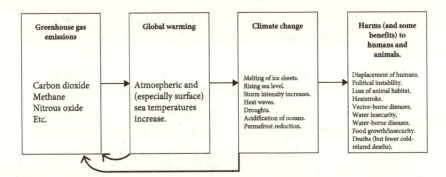

Figure 3.1 From greenhouse gases to harming masses.

is anthropogenic argue that the recorded warming is part of the usual natural flux of warmer and cooler periods. Finally, there are those who concede that the warming is anthropogenic, but who deny that it will cause significant harm. This, they say, is because humans will be able to adapt to the new circumstances. They often forget about the non-human animals.

This is not the place, and I am not the person, to present a comprehensive argument against such denialism. That is a task for climate scientists. Those who are not climate scientists and who cannot evaluate the evidence for themselves might wonder whom they should believe. There are a few reasons which, when combined, give the non-scientist good grounds for believing that humans *are* responsible for the recent sharp increase in atmospheric CO_2, and for the resultant global warming which is already causing some harm and which can be expected to cause still more.

First, the overwhelming majority of climate scientists are convinced by the evidence for climate change caused by anthropogenic global warming. By 'overwhelming majority', I do not mean 70% or even 80%. Well in excess of 90%—probably around 97%—of climate scientists hold this view.[42] That is an extraordinarily high level of consensus, especially considering that the dissenters have substantially less expertise and prominence.[43]

Granted, scientists—even a majority of them—can be mistaken. However, that mere possibility does not provide non-experts with grounds for thinking that the majority of climate scientists *are* mistaken in this this case. This is precisely because non-experts are not experts—they are unable to evaluate the evidence themselves. There are many situations in which non-experts are therefore left at sea, epistemically. These are situations in which the experts are divided among themselves. However, climate change is not one of those situations. The extraordinary high level of agreement among the experts gives lay people good reason for accepting their conclusions as a working assumption.

The Intergovernmental Panel on Climate Change (IPCC), in its various reports, has been very careful in reaching conclusions and indicates its evolving level of confidence in particular conclusions. For example, it differentiates between 'limited', 'medium', and 'robust' evidence for a conclusion, between 'low', 'medium', and 'high' levels of agreement, and 'very low', 'low', 'medium', 'high', and 'very high' levels of confidence in a conclusion.[44] There are clearly particular claims in which the scientists have less confidence, and it is unlikely that there is no error in the consensus view. However, it is also unlikely that the broad conclusions are false.

In its Fifth Assessment Report, the IPCC noted that the 'evidence for human influence on the climate system has grown since the IPCC Fourth Assessment Report' and that it 'is *extremely likely* that more than half of the observed increase in global average surface temperature from 1951 to 2010 was caused by the anthropogenic increase in GHG [greenhouse gas] concentrations and other anthropogenic forcings together'.[45] This report also concluded that '[m]ultiple lines of evidence indicate a strong, consistent, almost linear relationship between cumulative CO_2 emissions and projected global temperature change to the year 2100'.[46] In its Sixth Assessment report it said that anthropogenic 'climate change is unequivocal and ongoing'.[47]

By contrast, there is good reason to doubt the dissenters. Many of them have had links to those, such as fossil fuel companies, with powerful vested interests in obfuscating the dangers of anthropogenic global warming and climate change. It is a common practice for companies with such vested interests to 'manufacture doubt' about powerful research that yields conclusions that are bad for their business.[48]

Individuals, even if they have no connection with such companies, can also have vested interests in denying anthropogenic global warming and climate change. If humans are causing the planet to warm and the climate to change, then humans are also the cause of the harms that result from these developments. That raises questions about whether individuals have duties to reduce the emissions that begin this (admittedly complex) causal chain. One way to block such questions is simply to deny the factual claims which they presuppose. This is an unfortunate response to such questions, precisely because the facts are so clear and cannot reasonably be denied.

Non-identity

Another argument against individuals having moral duties to reduce their greenhouse gas emissions has the aura of a philosophical technicality. It may appear, at least to non-philosophers, to be a splitting of hairs. However, it must nonetheless be considered seriously. According to this argument, it is possible that people will suffer and die as a result of anthropogenic climate change without it being the case that those people will be *harmed* by the emissions that bring about the climate change. How could this be the case? More specifically, how could it be that some humans, through their greenhouse gas emissions, bring about the suffering and death of others without it being the case that the former have harmed the latter?

The argument that no harm is done depends on two claims—one metaphysical and one conceptual. The metaphysical claim is that the identity of people is highly sensitive to circumstances. Each one of us was formed from the union of a sperm and an ovum. If a different sperm and ovum had fused, then a different person would have resulted. However, precisely which sperm and ovum fuse is the result of a confluence of highly contingent circumstances, including the birth of one's own parents, their meeting, and their copulating at the time they did. If copulation had been a month earlier or later it would have been a different ovum, and if it had been a day or even a minute earlier or later it could well have been a different sperm.

The implication of this is that which future people are brought into existence will depend on whether greener policies are adopted or whether we continue with 'business as usual'. Which of these options are adopted will affect the identity of the future people who will either have better or worse lives.

The problem is that if we continue with the current emissions practices, the future people who suffer as a result, will not be the same people who would exist if we were instead to adopt greener policies. Although the future people in the green scenario would have better lives, they are not better *for* the people who exist in the high emissions future. In other words, either the people in the high emissions future exist with their poor quality of life or they do not exist at all. Because existing with the worse quality of life is not worse *for them* than the alternative, they are not harmed. This problem is depicted, in greatly simplified form, in Figure 3.2.

This brings us to the conceptual claim—that to harm somebody is to make him or her worse off than he or she *would otherwise have been*. This is an influential and widely accepted conception of harm. However, it seems to

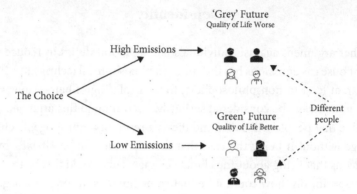

Figure 3.2 The Non-Identity Problem: Worse without being worse for anybody.

require that somebody exist in both of two alternatives in order for them to be worse off in one alternative than they would otherwise have been in the other.

The implication of the metaphysical and conceptual claims is that we do not harm future people by failing to adopt greener policies. If failing to adopt such policies does not harm anybody then, according to the argument, we can have no duty, based on the interests of future people, to adopt such policies.[49]

There is much that could be said in response to this argument. For example, one might deny that it is a necessary condition for somebody's being harmed that they are made worse off. Alternatively, one might deny that a person must exist in both of two alternative scenarios in order for that person to be worse off.[50]

However, for present purposes it need only be noted that the argument can be *bypassed* to a sufficient degree. That is to say, even if the non-identity argument shows that some future people who suffer as a result of one's emissions will not be harmed by those emissions, there are at least some people in the future who will be harmed by those emissions, even on the postulated account of 'harm'.

First, whereas the argument has greater application to the adoption of climate-related *policies* and *laws*, it applies in a more limited way to the climate-related practices of *individuals*. This is because the identity of many of those future people who will be affected by one's contribution to global warming and climate change does not depend on one's choices. They will exist whether or not the individual has a greater or a smaller carbon footprint.[51] This is because one individual's emission practices are unlikely, especially for the foreseeable future, to affect which offspring are produced by *other* people. (Similarly, an individual's emissions are unlikely to impact on the identity of many future non-human animals.)

By contrast, we can easily see how an individual's emission practices could affect the identity of his or her *own* children. If you do not fly, for example, you might end up meeting and procreating with a different person than if you did fly.

Second, even if we set aside future people, there are many already existent people—especially but not only the younger ones—who stand to be affected depending on the quantity of anthropogenic greenhouse gases emitted between now and the later period of their lives.[52] These people stand to be harmed or benefited in the stated standard sense, and thus their interests could be the basis for environment-related duties. Thus, even if the non-identity problem cannot be resolved, it cannot be employed to argue against individuals having duties to diminish their carbon footprint.[53]

Causal inefficacy?

There is a more serious challenge to the idea that individuals have duties to reduce their greenhouse gas emissions. Any individual, contemplating whether or not to desist from going for a drive or from taking an aeroplane trip could wonder whether their emission omission would make any difference. Global warming and its effects are not caused by a single drive in a car or even by the heavier carbon footprint of an individual taking a commercial flight. Global warming is caused by millions of such actions. If an individual desists while almost everybody else persists, no harm is prevented. According to this causal inefficacy argument—sometimes also known as the argument from inconsequentialism—one cannot be morally required to desist when one's omission will make no difference.[54]

The causal inefficacy argument is not an argument against coordinated reductions of greenhouse gas emissions. If a government or international body introduces (and enforces) policies or laws that reduce such emissions, those policies and laws are not causally inefficacious. This is because they govern a vast number of actions (or omissions) and the aggregation of these *does* make a difference. Indeed, international agreements—if they are sufficiently far-reaching and adhered to—are the best ways of addressing the problem. The quotidian ethical question confronting the individual arises largely because international agreements and national laws are woefully inadequate in their scope and adherence. The question is: What should I do, given that my country, and all countries collectively, are not doing as much as they should be doing? The causal inefficacy problem is raised as a reason for answering that the individual has no duties to desist from activities that increase emissions.

The claim that each individual makes no difference to climate change seems to result from what Derek Parfit called a 'mistake of moral mathematics'.[55] If a collection of actions makes a difference then it cannot be the case that each one of those actions makes no difference. This is because the sum of any number of zeros is zero. We know that the sum of emissions by all individuals does not make zero difference. To the contrary, it makes a massive difference. Thus, each individual's emissions cannot make zero difference. The difference that each individual makes may be imperceptible or insignificant, but it is not zero.

If the argument from 'causal *inefficacy*' or 'inconsequentialism' is taken literally to mean that the actions of individuals have *no* effect or consequences, then it may be in error, depending in part on what we mean by having 'no effect'. A more charitable interpretation of the argument is that the emissions of individuals are inconsequential in the sense of being insignificant or imperceptible rather than absent. If that is the correct interpretation (or version) of the argument, it would be less ambiguous to refer to it as the argument from *insignificant* or *imperceptible* difference.

Another way of explaining the mistake is to distinguish between two interpretations of the claim that my emissions as an individual 'make no difference':

a. Climate change and its resultant harms will occur whether or not I emit.
b. My emissions do not contribute to climate change and thus to the resultant harms.

The first of these claims is true, but the second, which is not implied by the first, may well be false. In other words, my emissions as an individual make no difference in the first sense: global warming and climate change will occur whether or not I emit. However, my emissions as an individual do make a difference in the second sense: I contribute to global warming and climate change.[56]

Some people may wonder how an action could contribute to some outcome if that outcome would occur even if the action were not performed. The clearest cases are those in which an outcome is overdetermined. Imagine, for example, that you are a member of a firing squad. If you do not fire a lethal shot at the condemned prisoner, then other members of the firing squad will still do so. Your firing a lethal shot makes no difference to the outcome. The prisoner will die whether or not you shoot. However, you have certainly contributed to his death in firing what would be, all by itself, a lethal shot. It would be disingenuous to say that you played no role in bringing about his death.

Obviously, cases like this differ from the climate change case in one important way. In the firing squad case, your action is *sufficient* to bring about the death of the prisoner. That is not the case with climate change. No individual's actions are sufficient to bring about climate change. However, there can be more than one kind of way in which an individual's action makes no difference in the first sense but does make a difference in the second sense. Climate change is a good example of one such alternative way.

Whenever an individual engages in an action that results in the emission of previously sequestered carbon, that individual is adding carbon to the atmosphere. It is true, as I noted above, that some of that carbon will be taken into a slow carbon cycle and thus prove harmless. However, because there is a limit to how much carbon can be taken into carbon sinks, the addition to the atmosphere of even that carbon which is subsequently sunk, means that other carbon will not be sunk. Thus, either directly or indirectly, all carbon emitted into the atmosphere from previously sequestered carbon sources adds to the cumulation of carbon to the atmosphere. That cumulation contributes to global warming, which contributes to climate change, which causes the resultant harms.

This is not to say that the relationship between one's emissions and the resultant harms is linear. The world is too complicated for the relationship to be such. Even the relationship between emissions and global warming (the first two adjacent blocks in Figure 3.1) is not strictly linear, at least if one takes a sufficiently granular view. For example, there are seasonal shifts in atmospheric CO_2 levels, more markedly in the Northern Hemisphere than in the Southern one. The CO_2 levels drop in spring and summer, and rise in autumn and winter. However, the annual average level has been on an upward trajectory since more precise measurements began in the late 1950s.[57]

The relationship between emissions and climate change (the first and third blocks in Figure 3.1) is still more complex, mainly on account of there being an intermediary factor—global warming. While increased global warming produces more climate change, thresholds or tipping points play a bigger role in the causal chain connecting global warming to climate change than they do in the connection between emissions and global warming. Most complex of the relationships in Figure 3.1, is the relationship between emissions and the harms to humans and animals that provide the basis for the moral concern—that is between the first and final blocks in Figure 3.1. The intermediate factors and feedback loops account for the increased complexity of the relationship. A causal relationship between an action and an outcome does not have to be linear in order for the former to be a contribution to the latter.

A further complexity is added by a relationship that is not depicted in Figure 3.1. The first block in that figure represents greenhouse gas emissions rather than the actions that cause them. In some cases, such as driving one's own car, the connection between the action and the emission is direct. As you drive, your car emits greenhouse gases. However, there are other activities to which a carbon footprint is attributed but which are linked to emissions in a more complex way. In such cases the link between the activity and the eventual harm is even more complicated, as reflected in Figure 3.3.

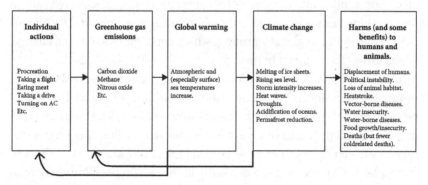

Figure 3.3 From individual actions to harming masses.

Consider, for example, somebody who is contemplating whether to purchase a ticket on a commercial flight (or to take a flight with a ticket purchased by somebody else). Whether or not that person buys a ticket, the flight will proceed. It may thus appear as though the purchase of the ticket makes no difference to emissions. However, purchasing a plane ticket does constitute a contribution to emissions, although indirectly. Purchases add to demand, albeit imperceptibly. It is true that not every ticket purchase leads to additional flights. However, each purchase does add to demand in two ways. First, at various thresholds, increased demand does lead to new flights and to additional emissions.

This does leave open the possibility that some air ticket purchases may be part of a series that never reaches the next threshold that triggers a new flight. Even in such cases, there is a second very indirect way in which purchasing a ticket contributes to demand. Each individual who purchases a ticket contributes to preserving the social acceptance of air ticket purchases. The more people purchasing air tickets the more such purchases are normalized. To be sure, any individual purchase contributes only a miniscule amount to such social norms but, as noted earlier, there is a difference between no contribution and an imperceptible one.

I have argued that one can 'contribute to climate change' through some action, even when climate change would occur irrespective of whether one performed that action. One contributes, in the relevant sense, when one's action has some (even if only imperceptible) effect. I have just described some such effects. Other actions may literally have *no* effect. Such actions do not 'contribute', in the relevant sense, to climate change. However, because it is very difficult, if not impossible, to tell the difference between an action that makes no difference and one that makes only an imperceptible one, it difficult to state definitively, at least in practice, that any particular action will have no effect.

Making a contribution to a bad outcome, in the sense specified, is sufficient for one to have a moral reason to desist from the action that makes that contribution. To the extent that one cannot tell whether a given instance of the kind of action that contributes to bad outcomes, does actually contribute, one also has a moral reason to desist from the action. However, whether or not one accepts this claim, having a *moral* reason needs to be distinguished, from having a moral *obligation*. Having a moral reason to abstain from an emission is not sufficient to generate an obligation to abstain. This is because there may be other reasons not to abstain from an emission. To determine whether somebody has a moral obligation one has to consider all morally relevant reasons (which could include prudential ones) and weigh them. That weighing could be done in the ways that various kinds of consequentialists would, but it need not be. Deontologists and others, can also weigh reasons.

When we do weigh up the reasons, we should reach the conclusion, I shall argue, that individuals do have a duty, albeit a limited one, to reduce their emissions. I shall not consider a virtue theory approach to the question, but those who do, may very well reach conclusions that have the same practical effect about what each individual ought to do.[58]

Do individuals have a duty not to emit?

A cartoon by Stan Eales shows two men standing in front of a 'Friends of the Earth' sign. They are looking at another man, hanging by the neck from a rope, with an overturned chair beneath him—evidently a suicide. The caption reads: 'He appears to have drastically reduced his carbon dioxide emissions.'[59]

Coming from a cartoonist who is described as having been 'green long before it became fashionable',[60] this cartoon is self-deprecatory. However, it may also embody a subtle response to those opponents of environmentalism who allege that it implies that we should not breathe, and that suicide is thus an implication of those seeking carbon neutrality.[61] Concerns about CO_2 emissions have no such implications. As indicated earlier, there are natural cycles of carbon, in which CO_2 emissions are approximately balanced by CO_2 intakes. For example, while we humans exhale CO_2, plants take in CO_2 and emit oxygen, which we inhale.

Thus, there is no collective duty and *a fortiori* no individual duty to abstain from *all* CO_2 emissions. That is neither possible[62] nor necessary, nor desirable. The problem is not the emission of CO_2 *per se*. Instead, the problem is the emission of previously sequestered CO_2 at the *rate* at which humans are emitting it.[63] The earth's CO_2-modulating mechanisms cannot keep up with our collective and cumulative emissions,[64] but they could compensate for a much lower rate of emissions.

What this means is that even *some* anthropogenic emissions from sequestered[65] carbon would be unproblematic, at least for the foreseeable future. Our immediate collective duty is thus *radically* to reduce (rather than entirely eliminate) emissions from fossil fuels. If that is our collective duty, what is my duty as an individual?

That question would be relatively easy to answer if we had a satisfactory cooperative scheme—adequate in scope and adherence, as well as fair—for reducing emissions to acceptable levels. The answer then, would be to comply with the scheme and not to be a free-rider, to the extent that free-riding were even possible. (If there were an appropriate scheme in place, the choice architecture would likely be very different, often obviating the possibility of free-riders. For example, if the electricity grid were fed only with renewable energy, my using extra electricity would not involve additional emissions from fossil fuels.)

The difficult question arises when, as is now the case, there is either no cooperative scheme or only an inadequate one. Is an individual duty-bound to reduce his or her emissions when most others are either not doing so or not doing so to the requisite degree? Opinion is divided.

Some are of the view that each one of us has responsibility for his or her own contribution to the problem and that we have extensive duties to reduce that contribution, whether or not others are similarly reducing theirs.[66] According to this view, we (sentient inhabitants of earth) are headed towards catastrophe, and the complacency of others is neither an excuse nor a justification for one's own inaction. Each individual has a duty not to emit more than is strictly necessary.[67] According to a variant view, the duty is to reduce emissions to a 'sustainable' level—that is, to a level that if all other people acted likewise the catastrophe would be averted.[68]

Others take a different view. They may recognize the dangers of global warming and climate change resulting from anthropogenic greenhouse gas emissions, but argue that no individual can have a duty to desist from emitting if most others are emitting with abandon. One cannot have a duty to desist from emitting if one's doing so will not prevent, or even lessen, the catastrophic outcome.[69]

To use and adapt a Neronian metaphor, both views are opposed to fiddling while the earth burns. Those who adopt the first view, employ this metaphor in its traditional sense, to mean that we should not live as though everything were normal when we are heading to catastrophe. Those who adopt the second view could deploy the metaphor in a novel way, to mean that we are not required to attend to the trifles which will not prevent the catastrophe. On this view, our focus should be on what will actually avert the catastrophe.

A lesser duty

As is often (but not always) the case with contrasting views, both of these views contain an element of truth. While there is something to be said for each view, there is also something to be said against each of them. The balance of considerations, I shall argue, supports an intermediate view. In brief, this is the view that while each individual *does* have a duty to reduce his or her emissions even if others are not doing so, the scope of this duty is more limited than it would be if everybody were restricting their omissions to sustainable levels.

That view might initially appear strange. If other people are emitting more than they should be, it might be thought that I would have a more demanding (rather than a less demanding) duty. In other words, I should limit my emissions more than I would be required to if everybody else were limiting their emissions. Thus, some argument will be required in order to defend the view that the individual's duty is more limited when others are not joining the effort. The prior task, however, is to argue that there is a duty at all to reduce one's emissions. There are a few considerations that support the claim that there is such a duty.

First, I argued earlier that there is a *reason* to reduce one's emissions and thus one's contribution to global warming. There being such a reason, while not sufficient to conclude that there is a *duty* to reduce, is one consideration in support of such a duty.

A second consideration is that denying a duty to reduce emissions is likely to make the already serious problem still worse. If individuals have *no* duty to reduce their emissions, they have *carte blanche* to continue their emissions unabated, or even to increase them. Over a lifetime this will make a bigger difference than will be made by a single emission or its omission. The lifetime aggregation of a single individual's emissions will likely still make only an insignificant difference to the outcome. Nevertheless, it will be an exacerbation of the problem. If, however, we do have duties as individuals to reduce our emissions, then even though many other people will ignore the claim that they have a duty, others will act on it. An aggregation of those reductions will mitigate the problem, even though it will not solve it.

A third but related consideration is that the more people who accept a duty to restrict their emissions, the more others are likely to do likewise, thus enhancing the mitigation of the problem. Each person sets an example for others.

Those who emit without restriction, encourage others, through their example, to do likewise. Indeed, the argument against a duty to restrict one's emissions begins with the claim that others are not restricting their emissions, and then employs this to deny that anybody else has a duty to restrict their emissions.

However, the influence can work in the opposite direction too. If one reduces one's own emissions, even while others fail to do so, one can serve as an example to others to do likewise. It also renders one more credible as a supporter, if not an advocate, of policies and laws that limit emissions. Such exemplative behaviour, both in itself and in its influence on others, can aggregate to greater significance.

Expressing the second and third considerations another way, we might say that both the postulate that individuals do have a duty to limit their emissions and the postulate that they have no such duty, can alter the outcome. Given how much is at stake—global catastrophe—there is a powerful consideration in favour of the first of these postulates.

However, there are also a number of reasons for thinking that the duty is more limited than it would be if (almost) everybody else were limiting their emissions. First, the most intuitive way of arriving at the opposite conclusion—namely that each individual has a duty to emit no more than his or her sustainable share—does not in fact generate that conclusion. Instead, as I shall now argue, it supports mine.

As noted above, it is 'a mistake of moral mathematics'[70] to fail to distinguish between an action making an imperceptible difference to an outcome and the action making no difference at all. In the case of harms brought about collectively, it is a mistake to think that each action makes no difference. To correct this mistake, Jonathan Glover recommends what he calls the 'principle of divisibility', namely 'that the harm done in such cases should be assessed as a fraction of a discriminable unit, rather than as zero'.[71] To illustrate the problem that results from rejecting this principle, he offers the following example:

> Suppose a village contains 100 unarmed tribesmen eating their lunch. 100 hungry armed bandits descend on the village and each bandit at gunpoint takes one tribesman's lunch and eats it. The bandits then go off, each one having done a discriminable amount of harm to a single tribesman. Next week, the bandits are tempted to do the same thing again, but are troubled by new-found doubts about the morality of such a raid. Their doubts are

put to rest by one of their number who does not believe in the principle of divisibility. They then raid the village, tie up the tribesmen, and look at their lunch. As expected, each bowl of food contains 100 baked beans. The pleasure derived from one baked bean is below the discriminable threshold. Instead of each bandit eating a single plateful as last week, each takes one bean from each plate. They leave after eating all the beans, pleased to have done no harm.[72]

Professor Glover suggests that if we reject the principle of divisibility, then we reach the conclusion that it makes a moral difference whether each bandit steals one bowl from one villager or whether each bandit steals one bean from the bowl of each one of the villagers. Because it actually makes no moral difference which of these *modi operandi* the bandits follow, we should *accept* the principle of divisibility.

The principle of divisibility is offered as a way of determining how much harm each individual does in cases of collectively produced harms with contributing causes that are indiscernible. There *can* be (but there is not always) a difference between how much harm one causes and the extent of one's moral responsibility. Put another way, causal responsibility is not identical with moral responsibility.[73] Nevertheless, it is natural to think that each bandit in the above case is morally responsible for the harm he causes, which in aggregate is the same irrespective of whether each bandit steals one bowl or 1% of each of one hundred bowls. It may seem that emitters are similarly responsible for their share of emissions and should desist from emissions that exceed their *fair* share.[74]

However, the case of the bandits (as it is presented), differs in two ways from the case of global warming and climate change.[75] First, and most importantly, in the case of the bandits they are the only parties responsible for the raid and theft. For example, nobody else is responsible by, for example, having ordered the theft or having threatened the bandits with harm if they did not steal the beans.

In the climate change case, by contrast, the emitters are not the only people responsible for the emissions. For example, the energy infrastructures within which millions of individuals operate are not infrastructures of their own choice. Indeed, many of them would much prefer an alternative, greener energy infrastructure. Even if we have a duty to advance infrastructural changes—something that will be discussed towards the end of this chapter—we do not have the same control over the infrastructure as we do over our own actions.

There are many reasons beyond the individual's control why the more polluting infrastructure remains in place. This is partly attributable to the cost of changing the infrastructure. Earlier generations made choices or were constrained by their technological options, and these are now costly to change. Even when change could be implemented cost-effectively, there are powerful vested corporate and other interests in continuing to use fossil fuels. Those protecting those vested interests bear a share of the responsibility. The same applies to those politicians who have the *de jure* power to make some changes but choose not to do so, sometimes because they fear backlash from a segment of the voters. The voters whose backlash they fear also bear some responsibility.

Faced with your inability as an individual to change the energy infrastructure, you have some control over how much you draw on it, but very few people can detach themselves entirely from it. In some circumstances, if you are to use electricity at all, you may have no realistic choice but to draw electricity from a grid that is powered by the burning of fossil fuels. Similarly, unless you produce all your own food, you may have no choice but to purchase foods that have been transported using fossil fuel energy (even short distances) to the shop from which you purchase them. You can minimize your carbon footprint though your choice of which foods to buy, but you cannot entirely avoid the food supply chain and its associated energy infrastructure.

If you have no realistic choice but to draw on energy largely produced through the burning of fossil fuels, then those who are responsible for the power grid being fed by such power rather than by solar or hydro power, for example, bear some of the responsibility to reduce your emissions.

In other words, we should not ignore the very important role played by other parties who, beyond their own personal emissions, are also responsible for the infrastructure that enables high emissions. Ignoring that responsibility would surely be a mistake. You, as an individual, may not be responsible for all the emissions you cause because some of your emissions are also the responsibility of those who have enabled the problematic energy infrastructure.

If, in a modified case of Professor Glover's beans, somebody created an unavoidable infrastructure whereby some people, pursuing their own personal activities, would indirectly deprive villagers of their beans, those engaged in those personal activities would not bear the full responsibility for the villagers being deprived of their beans. This is compatible with thinking that they would bear *some* responsibility.

This line of thought is able to explain why an individual ought to emit less when a satisfactory cooperative scheme for addressing the problem of emissions is introduced. Any practicable cooperative scheme will have to be one that alters the energy infrastructure to make it more sustainable. To the extent that the choice architecture makes it that much easier not to emit, the lower one's emissions should be.

The second difference between the case of the bandits and the case of global warming is that in both variants of the bandit case, each bandit bears an *equal* share of responsibility for what they collectively do. It does not matter which of the two theft methodologies they employ. (Granted, the methodology in the second case is *proposed* by only one of their number. However, it is, I stipulate, willingly *accepted* by all of them, which is why they are all equally responsible for it.[76]) The case of global warming, by contrast, is more complicated. People emit (and have emitted) different amounts. As a result, their shares of responsibility are unequal, even if they are proportionate to their emissions. When we add the responsibilities that others have for preserving the emissions infrastructure, the precise share of the individual emitters must be further adjusted. How exactly that is to be done is not clear.

Perhaps it will be objected that this first argument for a lesser duty (mistakenly) assumes that the moral responsibility of one person must be diminished by the moral responsibility of another. However, the argument makes no such general assumption. It is true that there do seem to be some cases in which more than one person can be fully responsible. The clearest such cases are cases of overdetermination. Consider the firing squad again. If the bullet from each member of the firing squad is sufficient to kill the prisoner, each member is aware of this and is acting freely, then it may well be that each member of the firing squad bears full responsibility for the death of the prisoner.[77]

It does not follow from cases such as this that the responsibility of others cannot *sometimes* diminish one's own. I have argued that that is exactly what happens with responsibility for carbon emissions. However, even if one rejects this argument there are three further considerations which, when taken together, also lead to the conclusion that an individual's duty is limited.

The first of these additional considerations is that when an individual performs an act that results in emissions, those emissions are typically a miniscule part of the global problem. Taking a ride in one's car, although it contributes to atmospheric levels of CO_2, contributes in only a vanishingly small way. The effect on global warming is even more minute and indirect. Its role in bringing about the harms that result from global warming is infinitesimal. In other words, the action that causes the emission is not actually harming, but rather merely contributing in an extraordinarily indirect and minor way to a harm.

The second consideration is that desisting from some particular emissions is not without cost—typically to the person who desists, but sometimes also to others. Sometimes the cost is minor, such as foregoing the pleasure of a joy ride. However, if, as in this case, the emissions are also relatively low, it may *sometimes* be reasonable to take such a ride, especially if one is cutting one's emissions more significantly elsewhere. In other words, it is entirely reasonable to expect people to forego that pleasure sometimes, and even often, in order to reduce emissions. It becomes less plausible to suggest that they must *always* forego that pleasure, given that doing so will not avert the bad outcome.

On other occasions, the costs of not emitting are immense. If, for example, you need coronary artery bypass surgery, which evidently has a carbon footprint of about 1.1 tonnes CO_2 (tCO_2),[78] you surely cannot be required to forgo it for environmental reasons.

Nor do personal costs need to reach that level in order for relatively high emissions to be warranted on some occasions. If, for example, you live far enough from beloved family members (such as your parents or siblings) that you cannot see them without taking a flight, *always* forgoing the flight carries significant psychological and emotional costs. Similarly, if your work requires that you drive, you can avoid those emissions only at the cost of your job. If you do not have an alternative job prospect, you can avoid the travel emissions only at the cost of being unemployed.

A third consideration is that the problem of insignificant difference arises precisely because there are so many people emitting. It might be thought that this consideration supports a more extensive rather than a limited duty: if everybody else is emitting as much as they are, then my duty to desist from emitting is even more extensive. However, for reasons I shall explain, that is not the correct conclusion to draw.

Instead, the point is that if there were many fewer people driving and flying, for example, then one's own driving and flying would not be contributing to (dangerous) global warming or to climate change. There are different scenarios in which there would be many fewer people driving and flying. These include the scenario in which the world's human population were much smaller than it currently is, and the scenario in which cars and flying were less available than they are now. (Both of these scenarios were once actual.) In other words, the problem arises as activities that generate emissions are scaled up.

Contrast this with actions that would clearly be wrong on the small scale, and whose connection with harm becomes obscured when they are scaled up. Imagine, for example, that you enjoy sipping human tears. You 'own' a slave, whom you regularly flog in order to generate the tears that you savour. This would clearly be wrong. Imagine, however, that many others also develop the taste for tears and an industry develops in which millions of slaves are kept on tear farms, where they are flogged, and their tears harvested. The tears are then sold in shops. You now do not need to 'own' a slave or to flog one in order to sip human tears.

You and others notice that given the industrial nature of tear farming, no individual's purchase of a vial or tears, let alone the consumption of commercially produced tears, makes anything more than an insignificant difference to the amount of suffering endured by the slaves. When you stand in the shop's aisle of tears, the slaves whose tears are on the shelves have already been flogged. Whether you purchase tears will not undo the pain they have already endured. You might wonder whether your purchase might contribute to future demand. However, the supply manager's orders are not so sensitive to purchases that your purchase of a few vials will likely make a difference to the size of the next order.

In this case it seems that your duty to desist from purchasing tears is as strong as it would be if you were harvesting the tears yourself. You have a duty not to flog the slave yourself, and you have a duty not to pay another individual to do the flogging and tear collection for you. The immorality of procuring and consuming slave tears is not magically undone by industrializing the scale of the operation. In the context of industrialization your duty is not limited merely to reducing the volume of tears you consume. You should not consume tears at all.

Emissions are not like this case. They are *globally* harmless when they are on a small scale. (Some emissions can pollute on the local scale, which I shall discuss later.) They become catastrophic on the large scale. Your actions by themselves are not problematic. They become problematic only because so many others are doing likewise. That collectively generated problem ultimately requires a collectively generated solution. You have a duty to reduce your emissions. However, given the considerations I have listed, it would be unfair to impose as extensive a duty on you as you would have if everybody else were pulling their weight.

To see why this would be unfair, consider the flip side, namely the case of the free-rider (sometimes known as a free-loader). A free-rider is somebody who benefits from others' adherence to a cooperative scheme but does not himself bear the burden of such adherence. There are many examples, but the most literal one is somebody who does not pay the fare for public transportation—he or she rides free—while the system of public transportation is maintained by all those who do pay their fare, namely the fare-riders. The free-rider benefits without paying his or her share of the costs.

If almost everybody else is paying their fair share of the costs, then the free-rider's failure to pay his share does not lead to the cooperative scheme's failure. In other words, any cooperative scheme can withstand a certain amount of free-riding. However, that does not create an entitlement for some people to free-ride. Even though the free-rider's action makes only an insignificant difference to the scheme, it is *unfair*, and thus wrong, for him to free-ride. What this suggests is that it is not only whether one makes a difference to the outcome that counts morally but also whether being excused or required is fair or unfair.[79]

Against the background of an absent or inadequate cooperative scheme to reduce emissions, it is unfair to impose an extensive requirement on the conscientious while almost everybody else ignores their own responsibility and proceeds unchecked. Why should one person (or a few people) bear the full cost of a fair share when the overwhelming majority of others are not, and the few who are bearing full cost will not prevent the feared outcome? Expecting somebody to be a rare-fare-rider is, like free-riding, unfair.

These considerations about the free-rider and the rare-fare-rider are encapsulated in Figure 3.4.

	Free-Riding	Rare-Fare-Riding
Background	Most people are bearing their fair share	Most people are not bearing their fair share
Cooperative Scheme	Functional	Absent
Outcome	Free-rider makes no significant difference to the functionality of the cooperative scheme	Rare-fare-rider makes no significant difference to generating a cooperative scheme
Fairness	Unfair to excuse the free-rider	Unfair to require the rare-fare-rider
Duty	A perfect duty not to free-ride remains	No perfect duty to be a rare-fare-rider

Figure 3.4 The free-rider and the rare-fare-rider.

Objections

The foregoing argument might elicit either of two objections, each from a different direction. First, it might be objected that one *does* have a full duty even if nobody else is fulfilling theirs. Merely because others are flouting their duties, does not mean that you have a lesser duty.

Of course, it is sometimes true that one has a (full) duty even though others are flouting their duties.[80] The question is whether that is true in the case at hand—environmental duties. I have given reasons for thinking that one does not. Whatever residual force the objection has, may derive from the public transportation case, where it might be thought that you must *always* pay your fare even if others are never paying theirs.

Perhaps this is thought to be the case because one is, after all, deriving the benefit of the ride. That is certainly a relevant consideration, but to better see how much of a duty that generates, it may help to get a clearer picture of the kind of scenario the rare-fare-rider inhabits. One possibility is that the public transportation has hitherto been run as a free service. The government has recently decided to fund the system's continuing functioning from fares. The government (notionally) introduces a fare, but almost nobody is paying, and the government does (almost) nothing to enforce fare payment.

Thus, while *existence* of the public transportation system (and even its funding *via taxes*), is attributable to a (state-mediated) cooperative scheme, there is no effective cooperative scheme for funding that system *via fares*.

The law requiring fare payment is a dead letter law—or perhaps, more accurately, a stillborn law. Perhaps intuitions differ about the extent of one's duty in in this case, but it is certainly not unreasonable think that you do not have a perfect duty to pay *every* time you walk through the space where the turnstile would have been. Almost nobody else is swiping their fare card. It is not fair to expect you to do so under these circumstances.

The second objection to the argument about free-riders and rare-fare-riders comes from the opposite side. According to this objection, my argument suggests that there may not be even *any* duty to be a rare-fare-rider. If almost nobody else is bearing *any* cost, how can an individual be required to bear even some of the costs?

This objection also has *some* force. If the only consideration were the fairness between free-riders and rare-fare-riders, then the conclusion should certainly be that there is no duty on the few individuals who would comply. However, there *are* other considerations, including fairness to 'non-riders', who are not gaining any benefit but who are bearing some of the cost. In the public transportation case, these are people who pay taxes that support the public transportation but who do not use it, perhaps because they walk or cycle instead.

In the environmental case, the non-riders are those with very low emissions but who will pay a steep price from global warming and climate change—typically the world's most disadvantaged people. The unfairness to the non-riders in the environmental case is much greater than in the public transportation case, given the much greater cost. This is why it is likely that the objection that there are not even lesser duties has less force in the environmental case than it does in the public transportation case.

The argument for there being (only) lesser duties regarding greenhouse gas emissions, is that this conclusion balances considerations in favour of there being full duties and in favour of there being no duties at all. Therefore, those who accept the conclusion that there are (only) lesser duties are not committed to rejecting the considerations that favour there being no duties. Such considerations can be recognized. However, if one *also* recognizes the considerations that pull one towards a full duty, one can recognize that the best way to balance these considerations is to conclude that there are duties but only lesser ones. Even if one thinks that the balance of considerations does not yield this conclusion in the case of rare-fare-riders on public transportation, it arguably still produces that conclusion in the environmental case, given the stronger countervailing considerations in the latter case.

What is the extent of an individual's duty?

If the argument so far is correct, then individuals with a large carbon footprint have a duty to reduce their emissions, but that duty is limited if most others are not also reducing their emissions. While there is a duty to reduce emissions, the duty does not require that the individual reduce his or her emissions all the way to a sustainable level (where 'a sustainable level' means a level at which everybody could be emitting likewise without serious adverse effects). What is that level, and how far off is it from the current level of emissions?

At present, people's carbon footprints are of very different sizes. Some of this difference is within given countries, but more noticeably it is between countries. Luxembourg has the highest annual per capita CO_2 emissions—38 tonnes (38 tCO_2). Qatar, at 25 tCO_2 is the second highest. Rwanda has the lowest—0.1 tCO_2. China is the country with the largest overall CO_2 emissions, but given its massive population size, its consumption per capita is 'only' 6.3 tonnes per person. The per capita emissions for the United States are 18 tCO_2. For Canada and Australia they are, respectively, 16 tCO_2, and 15 tCO_2. Japan's are 10 tCO_2 and the United Kingdom per capita carbon footprint is 8 tCO_2.[81]

How do these amounts compare to an equal sustainable share? To answer this question, we have to consider three factors—how much CO_2 (from previously sequestered sources) has already been emitted, how much global warming we can 'afford', and how much more emission can be afforded before we reach 'unaffordable' warming. The Intergovernmental Panel on Climate Change has said that in order to keep the likelihood of global warming beneath a 2°C increase over the global temperature in about 1870, the cumulative emissions should not exceed about 2900 gigatonnes CO_2 ($GtCO_2$).[82] As of January 2021, the cumulative emissions were 2333 $GtCO_2$.[83] That left only 567 $GtCO_2$.

We cannot simply divide this amount by the then current human population (about 7.8 billion people). If we did that, then each currently existing person would have a share of 72.2 tonnes for the remainder of their lives. That would be more than most people of advanced age would need, but would exceed current consumption patterns of younger people in higher emitting countries. More importantly, it would make no allowance for new people—or very little allowance if the surplus not used by old people were then allocated to a new generation. That is not a sustainable allocation.

To avoid hitting the much-feared 2°C temperature increase, we would need to reduce the per capita emissions to 2.1 tCO_2e by 2050.[84] That is approximately the upper limit of what an equal share would be if a global (or near global) cooperative scheme were adopted. It is the *upper* limit because this level of emission does not *guarantee* that a 2°C increase will not occur. It only makes it likely that it will not occur. Moreover, it would be better if the average global temperature did not increase even by 2°, given the climate change and harms that have already resulted even from a 1° increase. Finally, the upper limit on an *equal* sustainable share might be higher than the upper limit on a *fair* sustainable share. If, for example, one factors in past emissions, one might well conclude that those who benefited from higher emissions before should have a smaller share (for a period) if that were necessary to counter the disadvantage of historic low-emitters.

Contrasting these figures with current per capita CO_2 (rather than the greater CO_2-*equivalent*) emissions in advanced economies is sobering, and highlights the futility of thinking that even the goal of 2.1 tCO_2e can be attained (by 2050) without a global cooperative scheme. Countries that currently emit around 2.1 tCO_2 per capita (which is less than 2.1 tCO_2e) include: Brazil (2.3 tCO_2); Indonesia, Vietnam, Albania, and Armenia (all at 2.2 tCO_2); Colombia (2.1 tCO_2); Peru (2.0 tCO_2); Bolivia (1.9 tCO_2); Morocco (1.9 tCO_2); India (1.7 tCO_2); Paraguay (1.7 tCO_2); and Sri Lanka (1.6 tCO_2).[85] It is difficult to imagine much wealthier countries voluntarily reducing their emissions to such levels, at least without major infrastructural change. It is probably not reasonable to expect individuals in those societies to reduce their personal emissions to these levels—given the personal costs combined with the fact that it will not change the outcome.

Even if my duty does not require me to reduce my emissions to the sustainable level, its extent remains unclear. This is because 'reduce' is a term covering a wide spectrum of diminutions—from the very minor to the drastic. What more can be said about the extent to which each one of us should reduce personal emissions? It is unlikely that one could provide a formula to indicate the required level of reduction, because this is not a matter that lends itself to that kind of precision. Put another way, it is hard to know where duty ends, and supererogation begins. Nevertheless, it is possible to set some parameters and enumerate some relevant factors.

First, the considerations in favour of there being a duty to reduce emissions suggest that the duty requires significantly more than a minimal reduction off a high base of emissions. If you are a big emitter, you are not fulfilling your duty if you merely do some recycling or take a few fewer joy rides.

Second, it does not follow that reducing 'until it hurts' is a good gauge of the extent of one's duty. This is because this standard depends too much on idiosyncrasies. Some people, given their consumerist predilections, might 'hurt' too easily while others, given their lesser appetite for carbon-emitting goods, might only hurt below the level to which they are duty-bound to reduce.

Third, how much one is required to reduce will depend, in part, on one's starting point. All other things being equal, the more voluminous one's baseline emissions, the more one is obligated to reduce them. By contrast, if one's baseline emissions are low, one will have either no duty to reduce emissions or only a limited one. This is because, all things being equal (again), the closer one is to the level of emissions that one is permitted, the less one has to reduce in order to reach that level.

Fourth, all else is not always equal. Sometimes the reason, or part of the reason, why a given individual has a higher carbon footprint, is attributable to the infrastructure within which that individual is embedded. Some people have lower greenhouse gas emissions because they live in a society whose energy is more dependent on fossil fuels that cause higher emissions. To the extent that such individuals cannot as easily reach the lower emission levels of individuals living in societies with greener energy arrangements is also the extent to which they are less obliged to do so.

Fifth, this point about costs can be generalized. The greater the cost of a reduction to an individual the less that individual is required to make it, again all else being equal. The same reduction can have different costs for different people. If, for example, you live in an environment that is either very hot or very cold, giving up either air-conditioning or heating will come at a greater cost than it would for somebody living in a place with a more temperate climate. (That said, giving up air-conditioning or heating is to be distinguished from using them less. The latter may be required even when the former is not. This is because both air-conditioning and heating can be—and routinely are—used excessively. For example, emissions can be reduced by adding a layer of clothing instead of turning up the thermostat a few degrees further.)

Finally, the better the cooperative scheme that is in place, the greater one's duty to keep one's emissions down. Such reductions will likely come at lower cost to the individual because effective cooperative schemes will bring more benefits without high level emissions. The upshot of this is that the costs of reduction to the individual will be lower.

The fact that the extent of limited duty cannot be more precisely indicated gives rise to a problem—that individuals will take the duty to be more limited than it actually is. There is significant incentive and scope for individuals to rationalize that their rate of carbon emissions is compatible with the extent of their duties. That is a real problem. Each of us should be alert to the incentive we have to rationalize our own actions, and each of us should endeavour to compensate for the inclination to rationalize.

That might be an unsatisfying and not entirely successful response to the problem arising from an inability to specify the extent of our duties more precisely. However, we should resist a more definitive 'solution' to this problem—namely, to pretend that a precise specification would be an accurate one. The gain of precision would be a loss of truth.

Lowering one's carbon footprint

An individual's carbon footprint consists not only of that person's direct emissions but also of his or her indirect emissions. Direct emissions occur when, for example, one drives one's car, uses a gas stove, or burns wood or coal. Indirect emissions are added to one's carbon footprint when, for example, one uses electricity that was generated by burning fossil fuels, or when one is a passenger in a commercial aircraft. In these latter cases, others are directly generating the emissions, but they are doing so on behalf of the individuals who utilize the electricity or reap the benefit of the flight. Lowering one's carbon footprint can be achieved by reducing either direct or indirect emissions or both.

Low emissions reductions

When many people think of living 'greener' they think of activities such as replacing incandescent lightbulbs with energy efficient lighting, turning off lights when they are not in use, recycling of paper, plastic, glass, metal, and other items, using reusable shopping bags, washing clothes in cold water and then hanging them to dry rather than using a drying machine. These changes do all diminish one's carbon footprint, but they are *relatively* low impact in comparison with other changes one can make.

For example, switching to energy efficient bulbs saves less than 0.2 tCO$_2$e per year. Washing clothes in cold water, hang drying them, and recycling, each saves between 0.2 tCO$_2$e and 0.8 tCO$_2$e each year, relative to the alternatives of washing in warm water, machine drying, and not recycling.[86] You would have to use about 19 685 disposable plastic bottles in order to equal the carbon footprint (1.63 tCO$_2$e) of a return economy flight from New York to London.[87] Using one disposable plastic bag from a supermarket instead of reusable bag has a carbon footprint of 10 grammes CO$_2$ (gCO$_2$e).[88] One would have to use 163 000 such disposable bags in order to equal the carbon footprint of a return flight of the same distance[89] Complicating matters still further is that using reusable bags does not necessarily have a lesser carbon footprint. Given that each such bag has a greater carbon footprint than thin plastic bags, if one accumulates more reusable bags than one needs, and consequently reuses each one less frequently, the net negative impact can be greater.[90]

This does not mean that the lower impact changes are not worth making. Some of them are very easy to make. Easy changes are more likely to be adopted by a larger number of people, with the aggregative effect being significant. The ease with which we can make these changes should not obscure the cooperative framework that enables this. There have to be energy saving bulbs readily available in order for one to be able to buy them without difficulty. There has to be a recycling infrastructure in order for an individual to be able to recycle. There was once no such infrastructure. It now exists in many places, although some people have questioned whether all recycling is worth the trouble and expense.[91] It is financially more worthwhile recycling some materials than others.[92]

Diet

There are more significant ways for individuals to reduce their emissions. Shifting to an entirely plant-based diet is one widely known example. Why such a shift reduces emissions is explained by two factors. The first of these is the inefficiency of growing crops to feed agricultural animals that are later eaten by humans. One exacerbating by-product of this, is that vast amounts of forest and jungle have been cleared for producing feed for animals who will be later be eaten. That deforestation removes one of the word's key carbon sinks.[93]

The second factor is the large quantity of methane produced by ruminant animals (such as cattle, sheep, and goats). It should thus come as no surprise that meat contributes 56.6% of all greenhouse gases produced in an average diet. Dairy contributes a further 18.3%.[94]

One study in the United Kingdom investigated the daily greenhouse case emissions of six different diets, each with an average of 2000 kilocalories per day. The findings can be found in Figure 3.5.[95]

Meat consumption obviously varies considerably between people. Low meat-eaters make only marginal reductions annually by shifting to an entirely plant-based diet. However, there are many high meat-eaters. United Kingdom adults between the ages of 19 and 64 were found, on average, to consume 110 grams of meat per day.[96] Switching from a high-meat diet to a vegan diet would reduce one's emissions by 1.5 tCO_2e per year—about the same as one return economy flight between London and New York. It is noteworthy that the annual carbon footprint of high meat-eating, exceeds the 2050 goal of 2.1 tCO_2e for all emissions per capita needed to prevent a 2°C temperature increase. Even vegans use about half that aspirational allowance on their nutritional requirements alone, highlighting just how elusive the eventual 2.1 tCO_2e per capita goal currently is.

Diet	Defined as	Mean dietary greenhouse gas emissions	
		Daily	Annually
High meat-eaters	≥100 grams per day	7.19 $kgCO_2e$	2.6 tCO_2e
Medium meat-eaters	50–99 grams per day	5.63 $kgCO_2e$	2.1 tCO_2e
Low meat-eaters	<50 grams per day	4.67 $kgCO_2e$	1.7 tCO_2e
Fish-eaters		3.91 $kgCO_2e$	1.4 tCO_2e
Vegetarians		3.81 $kgCO_2e$	1.3 tCO_2e
Vegans		2.89 $kgCO_2e$	1.1 tCO_2e

Figure 3.5 Dietary greenhouse gas emissions.

Driving

Another domain in which individuals can make a significant difference to the volume of their emissions is driving. Emissions obviously differ from car to car, depending in part on car size (which is generally getting larger[97] rather than smaller) and car age. Different driving circumstances also make a difference. This makes it difficult to compare data on the average emissions. According to one UK source, that figure for cars with an internal combustion engine is about 165 gCO_2 per kilometre.[98] According to one US source, it is about 250 gCO_2 per kilometre.[99] If, intermediate between these figures, we assume a rate of 200 gCO_2/km then the annual emissions for various average distances travelled can be found in Figure 3.6.[100]

Thus, from an emissions perspective, driving 14 000 kilometres per year in a car with an internal combustion engine is a little worse than eating a high meat diet for the same period. (Eating meat is much worse from other perspectives, which are discussed in the chapter on consuming animals. These provide independent reasons for desisting entirely from, rather than merely reducing, meat consumption.) Driving 10 000 kilometres per year is nearly as environmentally bad as eating a medium-meat diet, and driving 8000 kilometres is about as environmentally bad as eating a low-meat diet. Driving 4000 kilometres per year makes less of an emissions impact than a vegan diet. However, one's car emissions are *in addition* to what one eats. Moreover, while everybody has to eat, not everybody has to drive.

The conventional wisdom is that: (i) a hybrid vehicle (that operates on both fuel and electricity) has lower emissions than a car with an internal combustion engine; (ii) an electric car has lower emissions than a hybrid;

Distance per year (Km)	Country with this average	Annual emissions
14 000	United States of America	2.8 tCO_2
10 000	Australia	2 tCO_2
8 500	Canada	1.7 tCO_2
7 000	Sweden	1.4 tCO_2
6 250	Italy	1.25 tCO_2
4 000	Japan	0.8 tCO_2

Figure 3.6 Annual driving emissions for representative distances.

and (iii) living car-free offers the greatest reduction in greenhouse case emissions. The truth is more complicated.

Whether electric cars reduce greenhouse gas emissions depends on the context. Electric cars require greater greenhouse gas emissions during manufacture than do cars with an internal combustion engine. If we average these emissions costs over the usual life of a car, then according to one calculation they amount to 70 gCO_2e per kilometre for an electric car.[101] By contrast, the carbon emissions involved in manufacturing a petrol or diesel powered car are only 40 gCO_2e per kilometre.[102] (Obviously, the further a car drives over its lifetime, the lower the average per kilometre emission attributable to production, but batteries, like other car parts, have a limited lifespan.[103])

In principle, the greater emissions involved in manufacturing an electric car can be massively outweighed by the reduced emissions from operating it. However, whether this actually happens depends on how the electricity that is used to power the electric car is generated.[104] If it is generated through the burning of fossil fuels, then one has greater manufacturing emissions but no reduction in emissions from operating the electric car. If, however, the electricity grid is powered, either substantially or entirely, without generating emissions, then switching to an electric car does significantly reduce one's emissions.

This is not to say that an electric car can have *no* environmental benefit even when it is powered by a fossil fuelled grid. Car pollution is typically not only global but also local. Cars emit many pollutants other than CO_2. These include nitrogen oxides and particulate matter. Smog, containing such substances, can accumulate when a large number of cars in an urban area all emit exhaust fumes. In the concentrations found in many urban areas, this can be detrimental to health. Because electric cars have no tailpipe emissions, they do not contribute to local smog. Depending on how the electricity that powers them is produced, they may have an indirect emissions impact, but there is some advantage to the local environment if the pollution is taking place further away from human habitation. Those considering switching to an electric car need to know if they are only helping reduce local pollution or whether they are also contributing to slowing global warming and climate change.

This requires specific knowledge about one's local power grid. The answer to the question 'How green is my grid?' varies from country to country, but can also vary from region to region within a country. In Paraguay and Iceland, for example, all the greenhouse gas emissions of electric cars are those that result from manufacture. The electrical power on which such cars operate involves no emissions. Operating an electric car in Sweden or Brazil, involves only minimal emissions beyond those resulting from manufacture.[105] In France and Canada 'electric cars can halve emissions'[106] relative to a regular car. In Italy, Japan, Germany, and the United Kingdom, 'electric cars match the best hybrids'.[107] If you live in India, South Africa, Australia, Indonesia or China, then owning and driving an electric car would 'produce emissions comparable to normal petrol vehicles'.[108]

Car buyers also need to be aware of the difference between advertised emissions data, typically from the laboratory, and the higher emissions that usually occur on roads in the real world.[109] Because the difference is largely attributable to operating variables, the discrepancy is relevant to those whose car operation, either directly or indirectly, is dependent on the burning of fossil fuels.

In principle, living car-free will result in even lower emissions than a green-powered electric car. However, whether it does in practice, depends on what one does as a result of living without a car. Walking or cycling adds no previously sequestered carbon to the atmosphere. Using public transport could add a little or none, depending on how that transport is powered. However, that is still typically better than a private vehicle. If one routinely uses taxis then that would amount to little reduction in emissions. One will simply have outsourced one's private emissions.

Flying

Aviation is responsible for only 1.9% of all greenhouse gas emissions.[110] However, greenhouse gases do not account for aviation's full (3.5%) contribution to global warming.[111] One important reason for this is that aircraft's emissions are largely at altitude, where they cause more damage. Airlines contribute a slightly larger share (7%) of all greenhouse gases emitted *through transportation*, compared with the 41% contributed by passenger cars.[112] The proportion attributable to airlines is so small mainly because so many more people drive than fly. Flying has *much* greater emissions per capita than driving.

Just how great those emissions are depends on the distance travelled and the class of seat one purchases. Because business and first class seats have more space, their share of the aircraft's emissions is proportionally greater. Figure 3.7 contains some examples of emissions for various return flights.[113]

Some complexities are lost in the above. For example, although shorter flights emit less than longer flights, they do not emit less *per kilometre*. This is for two reasons.[114] First, take-off requires more energy than cruising. Because shorter flights have fewer cruise kilometres, the higher emissions of their take-off are distributed over the fewer kilometres of the trip. Second, aircraft that are less fuel efficient are often used for the shorter distances.

Disturbingly, none of the emissions in Figure 3.7 are counted in the per capita emissions of individual countries (some examples of which were provided earlier). Whereas the emissions of domestic flights are counted in national emission counts, the emissions of international flights are not attributable to any country.[115] One upshot of this is that the official emissions levels of especially wealthier countries are an understatement of the actual emissions. (Another consequence is that countries have less incentive to reduce these emissions.) A more accurate—and fairer—representation would attribute the emissions from international flights (a) to the countries in which the aircraft were registered, (b) in equal share to the countries between which the flights takes place, or (c) proportionally, to the residence or nationality of the passengers.

Trains are generally much more carbon efficient than aeroplanes. However, except over short distances, the door-to-door travel time is considerably longer. In some regions (such as Europe) train infrastructure is far better than in others (such as Africa), and train travel is obviously impossible for trips across oceans. (In Figure 3.7, only the trip from Berlin to Stockholm

From	To	Economy	Business	First class
London	Sydney	4.97 tCO_2e	14.41 tCO_2e	19.88 tCO_2e
New York	Melbourne	4.65 tCO_2e	13.47 tCO_2e	18.58 tCO_2e
Auckland	Vancouver	3.17 tCO_2e	9.18 tCO_2e	12.66 tCO_2e
Cape Town	Amsterdam	2.71 tCO_2e	7.87 tCO_2e	10.85 tCO_2e
Tokyo	Moscow	2.09 tCO_2e	6.06 tCO_2e	8.35 tCO_2e
Washington DC	Paris	1.72 tCO_2e	5.00 tCO_2e	6.90 tCO_2e
Athens	Nairobi	1.27 tCO_2e	3.68 tCO_2e	5.08 tCO_2e
Los Angeles	Toronto	0.89 tCO_2e	2.59 tCO_2e	3.57 tCO_2e
Denver	Mexico City	0.65 tCO_2e	1.90 tCO_2e	2.62 tCO_2e
Berlin	Stockholm	0.23 tCO_2e	0.68 tCO_2e	0.93 tCO_2e

Figure 3.7 Flight emissions for return trips.

could reasonably be made by train, although that would take at least thirteen hours.) Given that there are currently no low-carbon commercial flight options and that these are unlikely to be introduced anytime soon,[116] the choices that individuals currently face and are likely to face for the foreseeable future are: to fly, to fly less, or not to fly at all.

Some people might think that purchasing carbon offsets is yet another option. In theory it is, but in practice there are serious concerns. A carbon offset is a measure taken to counter the effect of a carbon emission. If, for example, one takes a flight, but purchases an offset to fund the planting (or preservation) of trees that will absorb that amount of carbon, then one has made a 'net zero' carbon emission.

The main problems with offsets are structural. One pertains to what is known technically as 'additionality'. What this means is that for one's offset to be effective, it must be the case that the offset is not something that would have happened otherwise. That is to say, the offset intervention must be added to what would otherwise have happened, in order to compensate for the emissions. Would the forest one pays to have preserved, have been preserved anyway? Would the trees that are planted, have been planted anyway? If so, then there is no real offset.[117]

Even when a carbon remover is added, there are concerns about how long it will remain in place. Will it remain as long as the carbon that is emitted by the flight for which the offset was purchased? If not, then there is only a partial offset.[118]

Purchasing carbon offsets may make people feel better about their emissions, but we do not have robust grounds for thinking that they do in fact offset the emissions for which they are thought to compensate.

Procreation

Very probably, the single biggest decision one can take to reduce emissions is one that is rarely mentioned,[119] namely to avoid having a child—or an additional child. Of course, procreation involves no direct greenhouse gas emissions (even though it does result in the 'emission' of a new carbon-based baby). The greenhouse gas emissions that result from procreation are indirect. We should not be concerned here with those relatively trivial emissions associated with the increased nutritional needs of a pregnant woman. The emissions about which we should be concerned are those that one's offspring will inevitably generate.

There have been highly variable estimates of the carbon footprint made by producing a single child. Some variability is to be expected, given that the children produced will, just as existing people do, contribute varying quantities of greenhouse gases in the course of their lives. Thus, one suggestion has been that the carbon cost of having a child depends on whether he or she will be carbon-conscious, average, or a high emitter, which have been estimated, respectively as 100 tCO_2, 373 tCO_2, and 2000 tCO_2.[120]

The first two estimates seem far too optimistic. Consider the carbon-conscious progeny first. Of course, there are people who each contribute less than 100 tCO_2 over the course of their lives, but almost all of these are people who *cannot* rather than *will not* emit more. In other words, their low emissions are not the result of carbon consciousness. Instead, they are the result of living in deprived circumstances.

How much carbon emission is compatible with being 'carbon conscious'? Even if we adopt the extreme standard of 2.1 tCO_2 per annum, we get a total of 168 tCO_2 over the course of a 80-year lifespan. However, given the current challenges of meeting the 2.1 tCO_2 standard in wealthier countries, that is probably too demanding a standard for individuals within such countries. In the United States, where the current per capita level of emissions is 18 tCO_2 per year, an annual 10 tCO_2 would plausibly count as carbon conscious. That adds up to 800 tCO_2 over the course of a life of eighty years. This is the equivalent of 172 return flights between New York and Melbourne, or more than twice a year from cradle to grave.[121] That is for one child. If one has two or three or four children, the impact is considerably greater.

In other countries, with greener infrastructures and where the current per capita annual emissions are lower, a carbon conscious person could reasonably emit less. For example, perhaps a carbon conscious person in the United Kingdom, where the per capita footprint is 8 tCO_2, could reduce this in the foreseeable future to 6 tCO_2 or even 5 tCO_2. That amounts to 400 tCO_2 over a life of 80 years.

The estimate of 373 tCO_2 emissions for the average child brought into existence (in the developed world) also seems unduly optimistic. If we assume a life-span of 80 years, that amounts to 4.66 tCO_2 per person per year. If we regard the per capita emissions as 'average', then this figure exceeds the current average in the eighty-six countries at the top of the per capita emissions list.[122] It would be more accurate to treat the per capita emissions level of the country in which the child will live as the emissions level of an 'average' emitter one would bring into existence.

In contrast to the foregoing undue optimism, the high-emitter estimate of 2000 tCO_2 for an 80-year life is more reasonable,[123] although the *average* person in Luxembourg and Qatar emits a lot more. Thus the high emitters in those countries emit more.

There is an important distinction to be drawn between:

a. The emissions that result from a person's existence; and
b. The emissions for which a parent of that person is responsible.

Some people make the mistake of assuming that these are equivalent. They think that each parent's carbon footprint is increased by the full complement of greenhouse gas emissions made by each of their children.[124] If your (biological) child[125] will emit 373 tCO_2 then that full amount is added to your carbon footprint.

Others have suggested that because it takes two to procreate,[126] only 50% of one's child's emissions should be added to the carbon footprint of each parent.[127] Procreation is indeed usually an activity for which two people are jointly responsible. There are exceptions. For example, if a woman is raped and has no access to safe abortion then the rapist bears full responsibility for bringing the child into existence. If a woman steals a man's sperm and inseminates herself then she bears full responsibility for bringing the child into existence.[128] Such exceptions aside, it may well be reasonable to split progeny's greenhouse gas emissions equally between the two parents. That would be consistent with how a person's driving emissions are calculated. If she drives alone, she is fully responsible for all the emissions, but if she carpools with one other person then only half of the trip's emissions are added to her carbon tally, with the other half being attributed to her passenger.

It has also been suggested that procreators' responsibility for emissions does not end with their children. If their children also have children, then each grandparent is responsible for 25% of each of the grandchildren's emissions.[129] In principle, this could be extended to subsequent generations, although the further in the future the more uncertain we should be about the level of emissions that will then occur. We do not currently know whether per capita emissions will remain the same, increase, or decrease in the coming decades and, a *fortiori*, in the further future. Moreover, the more generationally remote one's descendants the smaller the share of their emissions that will be added to an ancestor's carbon footprint.

On these assumptions, having a child can add an immense volume of emissions to a procreator's carbon footprint. In the United States, for example, if emissions remain constant, then having a child would add 9441 tCO_2. If per capita annual emissions were reduced to 0.5 tCO_2 by 2100 then a procreator's offspring would add 'only' 562 tCO_2 to her carbon footprint. If, by contrast, annual per capita emissions were to increase linearly 1.5 times until 2100, then the carbon footprint would increase by a whopping 12 730 tCO_2.[130]

These attributions of responsibility are open to challenge. If, for example, two parents are together responsible for all of their child's life-long emissions then either that offspring:

a. bears *no* responsibility for any of his or her own emissions (because all the responsibility is borne by the parents); or
b. bears at least some responsibility, but this is a case in which the responsibility of some people (the offspring) does not diminish the responsibility of others (the parents).

The first of these options leads to absurdity. If the person brought into existence bears no responsibility for his or her emissions because all the responsibility lies with his or her parents, then it is also true that the parents are not responsible for these emissions because responsibility for them lies with their own parents. However, their own parents are also not responsible for precisely the same reason, and so forth.

The second option may not lead to absurdity, but it is nonetheless liable to an objection—namely that responsibility for emissions is not like the responsibility of each member of the firing squad discussed earlier. In other words, while it is sometimes the case that one individual's responsibility does not diminish the responsibility of another, that is not the case with responsibility for emissions.

There can be reasonable disagreements about the details of parcelling out responsibility for offspring's emissions, but an outline of a plausible broad structure can be provided. It would contain the following elements:

1. The parents together bear full responsibility—usually 50% each—for all of each offspring's emissions until the age of majority.

2. Thereafter the parents together bear responsibility—again, usually 50% each—for all of each offspring's 'subsistence emissions' while the offspring bears responsibility for his or her 'luxury emissions'.[131]
3. The implication of this is that the parents are not responsible for their own lifetime subsistence emissions, as well as any of their emissions until they reached majority. This responsibility would lie with their own parents.

The reasons for the above should be obvious, but they can be spelled out. Nobody is responsible for his or her own subsistence emissions because these are the basic emissions required to sustain oneself (in a given environment). Short of suicide or unreasonable deprivation, one has no choice but to make those emissions. Because these emissions are essential to the life that one's parents started (obviously without one's consent), they together bear full responsibility for them.

Until one reaches the age of majority, one's parents are also responsible for all one's other emissions. This is because, as a minor, one is not (fully) responsible for one's actions and because one typically has much less scope to act on one's decisions even when one can make them. For example, a minor might 'decide' to install solar panels on the roof of the family home but the minor is unable to implement that decision without parental agreement.

In other words, nobody can be responsible for those of their own emissions that are the responsibility of their parents. While creating a child might be part of the luxury carbon footprint of the procreators, a component of the offspring's emissions constitutes the subsistence carbon footprint of the offspring.

This is all obviously an oversimplification. First, responsibility for one's actions is not something that suddenly arises fully formed on one's eighteenth birthday (or any other day). As an infant, one lacks all responsibility, but one gradually becomes more responsible in the course of one's childhood and adolescence.

Second, many people do not suddenly enjoy full independence when they reach the age of majority. For example, they may continue to live under their parents' roof and to be educated at their parents' expense.

Third, although there is a conceptual difference between subsistence and luxury emissions, there is no bright line separating those either. Some amount of food is a necessity, but that does not mean that any nutrition beyond survival amounts to a luxury. Bare survival is not where necessity ends. Well-being requires more nutrition than mere survival does. Yet much eating goes beyond the requirements of well-being, and there are levels of consumption beyond which eating is detrimental to well-being. More complex assignments of responsibility might take such complexities into account, but the more nuanced they are, the more scope there is for disagreement about the nuances.

Another detail around which there is likely to be disagreement is whether procreators bear any responsibility for the emissions of their grandchildren and great-grandchildren. If so, how much? Would this lead to some emissions being the responsibility of both parents and grandparents—a kind of double counting of responsibility? There might not be a problem with this particular double counting. However, if there is, then the responsibility of the parents would be diminished by the more limited extent to which the grandparents are responsible. It is clear that procreators bear some *causal* responsibility for the existence of their grandchildren. Had the grandparents not reproduced then there would have been no grandchild. However, this is not sufficient to say that the grandparents bear *moral* responsibility for the grandchildren's emissions.

An argument against their having moral responsibility might point to the fact that parents are not held morally responsible for the actions of their adult offspring. If procreation is one of the actions of those adult offspring, then the grandparents are not responsible for that action or for the emissions that result. On the other hand, when one procreates one knows that one is creating a being who stands a high chance of procreating. Perhaps there is some moral responsibility for the more distant effects of such dangerous actions.

We do not need to settle this debate. Even without attributing the emissions of grandchildren and subsequent generations to their ancestors, producing a child adds a significant amount to a procreator's carbon footprint—namely, 50% of a lifetime of subsistence emissions and 50% of all emissions during a childhood. No other ordinary action of an individual has a carbon emission impact of that magnitude.

There is a further environmental problem with procreation. Not only does it add to emissions it also reduces every other person's permissible *share* of emissions. The more people there are, the smaller must be each individual's share of emissions in order to avoid a particular level of global warming and climate change. In other words, a procreating couple not only adds massively to their own luxury emissions they also add more claimants to a share of emissions.[132]

What is one's duty?

If my earlier argument is correct, then each of us has a duty to limit his or her greenhouse gas emissions. To the extent that a cooperative scheme to effect the required reductions is absent, one's individual duty is limited. What does this imply for each of the kinds of emissions just discussed? More specifically:

a. Are any of these kinds of emissions categorically prohibited?
b. Must one reduce emissions in every category (such as diet, driving, flying, and procreating), or is it sufficient that one reduce one's emissions overall?

Based on the environmental considerations alone, I do not think that my argument implies an affirmative answer to the first question. Consider procreation first. Given both the miniscule contribution that producing a single child makes to the total problem and the significant costs to potential procreators of desisting entirely from procreation, I do not think that a couple has a duty to desist from having any children on the basis of environmental considerations.[133] However, there is an environmental duty to *limit* the number of children one has, not least because the costs to the parents of not having an additional child diminish the more children they already have.

If producing a child is not always wrong on environmental grounds, then it is hard to see how actions that produce much lower emissions can always be wrong. In other words, if we do not have a strict environmental duty to desist from having even one child, how could we have a strict duty never to fly or drive, for example? Perhaps it will be replied that having children is a more important project than flying or driving and thus that the lesser emissions are offset by the lesser importance. However, it is difficult to see how that claim must always be true. If, for example, one cannot have a reunion with a close relative without taking a flight then taking that flight can be very important to that person (and the relative). The fewer such reunions there are the more important each reunion is. Even if such reunions are not quite as important as having a child, they also involve significantly lower emissions.

There are other (that is, non-environmental) arguments that support a strict moral duty not to procreate.[134] These arguments focus on the serious harm done through procreation to those who are brought into existence. There are also non-environmental arguments that support a duty not to eat animals.[135] These arguments focus on the serious harm done to animals. The environmental arguments, although not decisive in themselves, add weight to the conclusions of these independent arguments not to eat meat or procreate. Given these other arguments, we should desist entirely from procreating and from eating meat, but not primarily for environmental reasons.

How should we answer the second question—whether one must reduce emissions in every category or whether it is sufficient to reduce one's emissions overall? One's duty is to reduce one's emissions overall. This would likely involve cutting one's emissions in each category, but not necessarily to the same extent. Each individual has some discretion about how to fulfil the duty of limiting emissions. If, for example, one has a taste for some high-emission activities, one will have to cut emissions more elsewhere in order to fulfil one's duty. If one is emitting relatively little overall, then one might have greater latitude to engage in an emissions-producing activity, on condition that this activity does not entirely (or even significantly) offset all the emissions savings in another area.

Moreover, the project of reducing emissions may sometimes involve a trade-off between different emissions. If, for example, driving to a destination would involve fewer emissions than taking a short flight, and assuming that the trip is sufficiently significant to justify some emissions, one's duty might be fulfilled by driving rather than flying.

A political duty

While it is important for individuals to cut their emissions, the problem of global warming and climate change can only be solved or seriously mitigated through collective action, especially at the national and international levels. Laws and energy infrastructures have to change within countries, and binding, far-reaching environmental agreements have to be made between countries. Do individuals have a duty, through political activism, to contribute to bringing about such collective action?

Some have gone so far as to say that this is the only duty we have regarding global warming. According to this view, cutting one's own emissions may have some symbolic value, but it will do nothing to solve the problem. Instead, we should be focused on achieving a collective response.

Whether one views such a political duty as an addition or as an alternative to a duty to reduce one's emissions, it is likely to invite the causal inefficacy objection that is also levelled against an individual having a duty to restrict his emissions. If one expends effort trying to bring about political change regarding the environment, one's efforts will make either miniscule difference if the outcome is eventually achieved, or no difference if it the outcome is not achieved. If one's political efforts fail, then the effort would be even more wasted than they would be if one gave up car travel, for example. At least in the latter case one is making some, even if only an imperceptible difference—there is slightly less CO_2 in the atmosphere as a result of one's not driving. If one's work for political change fails, the efforts would have been entirely wasted.

Those who think that there is a duty to engage in political activism regarding global warming could respond to this objection in some of the same ways as one could respond to the causal inefficacy argument against an individual's duty to reduce emissions. If such a response were unsuccessful there would still be another reason not to think that everybody has a duty to engage in political activism about global warming. Temperaments and abilities differ, and not everybody is suited to political activism. Even if everybody has a duty to help confront a problem, it is not the case that everybody has to help in the same way. Not every doctor has to be a surgeon and not every member of the military has to be a combat soldier. Similarly, not every citizen has to be a political activist.

There are two political duties concerning global warming—both more basic and less demanding than the duty to engage in political activism—that could more plausibly be attributed to everybody. These are both duties to support the establishment of collective environmental action, but in a more limited sense of 'support'. In this more limited sense, 'support' means much less than engaging in political activism.

The first and more basic of these duties is negative. It is a duty not to stand in the way of changes that will minimize or counter global warming. For example, if your political representative in the legislature (such as your constituency's member of parliament or your district's congresswoman) has proposed or supported appropriate environmental legislation, you have a duty not to contribute to his or her paying a price for that at the next election. That would include a duty not to vote against them on account of their support for the appropriate environmental action.

The second duty is positive but in a minimalist way. It too does not require political activism, but only the minimal political activity of voting for proposals, in referenda, for example, that would mitigate or counter global warming (and other environmental problems).

There are a few reasons why these two duties can more plausibly be attributed to everybody than can the duty to engage in political environmental activism. First, they are not as closely linked to temperament and aptitude as is a (purported) duty to engage in political activism. Voting is something for which almost everybody has aptitude, and that, in democracies, almost everybody can do. Of course, there are people who are uninclined to vote. Moreover, not everybody who votes, votes wisely. These may be the results of temperamental and aptitude differences. However, the minimal activity of voting at infrequent elections or referenda does not require a very particular temperament and requires only the most minimal aptitude. Moreover, the duty tells one *how* one should vote. In referenda on environmental policies this would be a duty to vote in favour of a collaborative scheme to ward off a global tragedy. In elections, it would be a duty not to vote against candidates on account of their support of such policies. (The duty does not preclude one voting against them for other reasons if these other reasons are sufficient to outweigh their support for appropriate environmental legislation.)

Second, both these duties require so much less of anybody than does a duty to engage in political activism. The claim here is obviously not that one can be morally required to do something only if what one is required to do is minimal. Instead, the point is that given both the causal insignificance of an individual's action and the fact that, because there is no cooperative scheme in place, most others are not doing likewise, it is difficult to say that the individual has a duty to act if his doing so will require much of him. It is much more reasonable to attribute a duty to the individual under the above conditions, if it does not involve a major cost to him or her.

Obviously, we can imagine scenarios in which a duty to vote would be costly to an individual. This would happen, for example, in jurisdictions where there are frequent referenda. However, the extent to which voting becomes costly is also the extent to which one would be less obliged to vote in *every* referendum. Even when referenda or elections are held only every few years, the duty to vote could be defeated by other considerations. One is not

A duty to support collective action to reduce global warming?	
1. A duty to engage in political activism supporting the establishment of such action.	✗
2. A duty not to oppose the establishment of such action.	✓
3. A duty not to 'punish' those who work for the establishment of such action.	✓
4. A duty not to free-ride when a collective action scheme has been established.	✓

Figure 3.8 What duties are there to support collective action to reduce global warming?

required to postpone one's urgent surgery because a referendum happens to have been scheduled for that day, even if an advance or postal vote is not possible.

The political duties discussed so far are those that support the *establishment* of collective action schemes. Once a cooperative scheme is in place, then one has a duty of adherence—that is a duty not to be a free-rider. One's compliance may make only minimal difference and it may require a significant cost to oneself. However, given that almost everybody else is doing their part and that an aggregation of those insignificant parts is what secures the overall good, it would be unfair and thus wrong to be a defaulter.

The foregoing discussion of our duties to 'support' collective action to reduce global warming is summarized in Figure 3.8.

Conclusion

Although this chapter has been concerned with the duties that individuals have concerning the environment, its focus has been on greenhouse gas emissions and the adverse consequences of these. These are the most serious and urgent environmental problems, and they are of global proportions. However, they are not the only environmental problems.

Some of the ways of reducing emissions carry dangers of their own. Nuclear power is one important example. Some nuclear waste can remain radioactive for thousands of years, giving rise to problems of very long-term safe storage.[136] Nuclear reactors also pose risks. They are now much safer than they once were, but nuclear accidents and incidents do occur. Relatively few people have died thus far as a result of these, but that could change. In many cases thus far there were no fatalities, in some cases there were just a few. In the worst cases, hundreds or more died. The explosion and subsequent meltdown at Chernobyl in 1986, was the worst case, with a few hundred thousand people displaced, many adverse health sequelae, and about 4000 people estimated to have died, mostly as a consequence of cancer.[137]

Even these deaths and other harms are likely to be dwarfed by the death and misery expected to be caused by global warming. That is one reason why I have focused on greenhouse gases. Another is that individuals typically have less control over the decision whether to build nuclear reactors than they do over their own (especially direct but also some indirect) emissions.

There are other forms of pollution that are very much more within an individual's control. These include littering, not cleaning up after one's companion animal has defecated in a public place,[138] relieving oneself in a public place, noise pollution, and water pollution. These forms of pollution, while lacking the momentousness of greenhouse gas emissions, are nonetheless significant. They make a big difference to the daily lives of people. We inhabit not only a global environment but also a local one. Walking through litter-strewn, faeces-dotted, cacophonous streets, parks, and beaches, is unpleasant, and sometimes antithetical to physical and psychological health. Polluted rivers, lakes, and seas pose health risks both to humans and to animals. Moreover, avoiding such forms of pollution is often much easier than lowering one's emissions. You can relatively easily put your garbage in a trash can, pick up after your companion animal, use a toilet, keep your music volume down and your car exhaust muffler functional. These are courtesies that should be much more common than they are.

4
Smoking

Smoking has been both glorified and vilified. Given the now well-recognized dangers of smoking, the latter is not hard to understand. Tobacco is a harmful, addictive substance. It is now well established that smoking causes cancer—most commonly lung cancer but also carcinomas of the mouth, larynx, oesophagus, stomach, pancreas, kidney, bladder, ureter, and cervix.[1] Cancer is not the only disease caused by smoking. There is also sufficient evidence to infer a causal relationship[2] with, among other conditions, coronary artery disease,[3] stroke,[4] abdominal aortic aneurysm,[5] chronic obstructive pulmonary disease (COPD),[6] 'neovascular and atrophic forms of age-related macular degeneration' (or tobacco amblyopia),[7] periodontitis,[8] ectopic pregnancy,[9] and erectile dysfunction.[10] Smokers are at greater risk of tuberculosis, and smoking exacerbates asthma.[11] Smoking tends to result in diminished overall health and increased risk for mortality in both men and women.[12]

Smoking is also a financially costly activity. While it brings some pleasure, especially to those addicted to it, it is an acquired taste. The body is naturally resistant to smoke inhalation. Those learning to smoke have to overcome the impulse to cough.

Thus, tobacco is a harmful, expensive drug that is initially unpleasant to inhale. It would be hard to understand why smoking such a substance has become as prevalent as it has, if it were not for tobacco's addictive properties and the glorification of smoking. Smoking has been presented and often perceived as glamorous and sophisticated. In advertisements and film, smokers are rugged men or sultry women.[13] For children it has the allure of being an adult activity, but also something rebellious for children. It is what the 'cool kids' do.

It is little wonder, therefore, that anti-smoking campaigns have sought to remove the glamour—for example, images of young, beautiful, athletic people enjoying cigarettes—and even replacing them with horrific images of diseased body parts and dire warnings. Many countries have also introduced various restrictions on smoking. In an increasing number of jurisdictions, it is banned in offices and other indoor places, sometimes even including restaurants and bars. Many campuses are now smoke-free zones. Smoking has also been banned in airplanes and, except for designated smoking lounges, in airports too. There are prohibitions on selling cigarettes to minors, while adults who purchase them must pay hefty ('sin') taxes on these products.

This has all contributed to smoking becoming less popular in the developed world, where most of the anti-smoking measures have been introduced. While the prevalence of smoking is increasing elsewhere, in those places where smoking has been restricted smokers are often indignant about the restrictions. They feel as though they have been banished to the periphery to enjoy their cigarettes, and that they are, in a way, viewed as second-class denizens.

The ethics of regulating tobacco through legal and policy restrictions on its production, marketing, sale, purchase and use, is *not* the subject of this chapter. Instead, I am interested in a different set of ethical questions—those confronting the (potential) smoker, rather than the legislator or regulator. Primary among these is the question: When, if ever, may a smoker smoke in the presence of non-smokers? In asking this question we might assume a situation in which it is in fact legal, at least in some circumstances, to smoke in their presence. (In one's own home, albeit in the presence of non-smoking family members, is one prominent example.) Our question then is whether it is morally permissible to take advantage of that legal freedom—a legal freedom that may or may not be warranted.

It is not necessary to make the assumption of legal permissibility. It is possible to ask whether one may smoke in the presence of non-smokers if the law prohibits this. However, this question is complicated by the legal prohibition. Assuming that there is some—even if defeasible—reason to obey the law, and specifically a law of this kind, then an additional moral consideration against smoking is introduced if smoking is legally prohibited. The way to remove this potentially confounding variable is to consider the scenario in which smoking is not legally prohibited or restricted. If, as I shall argue, smokers ought not to smoke in the presence of (non-consenting[14]) non-smokers even when they are legally permitted to do so, then *a fortiori* they should not do so when the law also prohibits it.

My central question is whether smokers may smoke in the presence of non-smokers. However, it is worth noting that, in addition, one could ask whether one smoker may smoke in the presence of other smokers. Here we need to consider two possible scenarios:

1. The smoker in whose presence another smoker is smoking, is *not* smoking in the given context.
2. The smoker in whose presence another smoker is smoking, *is* smoking in the given context.

We should (generally[15]) treat cases of the first kind in the same way as we treat smokers smoking in the presence of non-smokers. The smoker is a non-smoker in that context (and may even be desisting from smoking in that context precisely so as not impose his smoking on others). In many of these cases, the person considering smoking may not know whether those not smoking in the context do or do not smoke elsewhere.

In cases of the second kind, two or more smokers are all imposing their smoking on other smokers. Given that each of those smokers is imposing his or her smoke on another smoker, he or she could reasonably be seen to be waiving, or at least weakening, his or her own claim against the other smoker not to smoke in his or her presence. If you impose your smoke on others, you have either no complaint or a much weaker complaint when they impose their smoke on you. Although it is possible to make fine distinctions between impositions of different kinds and varying intensity, and these may sometimes apply to different kinds of smoking, I shall not be examining these matters.

Smoking alone

Although my primary question is whether smokers may smoke in the presence of non-smokers, there may be another ethical question that we should consider first—namely, whether one should smoke at all. Suggesting that this is an ethical question is not uncontroversial. According to some people ethical questions arise only when one's conduct can affect others. Actions that affect only oneself, this view maintains, can have prudential but not moral value or disvalue.

One response to this restrictive view of the domain of ethics is to question it.[16] If ethics is devoted to questions about how we should live, then there seems to be no reason why actions that affect only oneself should fall outside the domain of ethics. How we should live includes acting in ways that do not affect others. Indeed, most ethical theories do not exclude such actions from the realm of ethics. These actions can affect how much good is produced, even if only for oneself, and thus are of interest to consequentialists. Many deontologists think that we can have moral duties to ourselves. Because some actions that affect only oneself are virtuous and others are vicious, virtue theorists would also not exclude such actions from the domain of ethics.

There is a second possible response to those who think that whether one should smoke at all is not an ethical question. This is to note that even if the domain of ethics is restricted to actions that affect others, and even if there are some actions that affect only oneself, smoking is almost never such an action. This is true even when one does not smoke in the presence of others.

Smoking, whether or not in the presence of others, contributes, even though imperceptibly, to environmental problems. Those environmental problems affect others. For example, the production, transportation, and smoking of cigarettes contribute nearly 84 million tCO_2e emissions annually.[17] Tobacco production also contributes to deforestation. Nearly 5% of overall deforestation in tobacco-growing countries in the developing world is attributable to tobacco production.[18] Obviously, the contribution of any single smoker to environmental problems is miniscule. Indeed, the individual smoker's contribution, via smoking, to climate change is typically even smaller than flying or even driving, for example. Yet, it does have *some* effect on others.[19]

Smokers who smoke alone can affect others in much more noticeable ways. Most people, including smokers, have close relationships with other people. Those others are thus invested in one's life and well-being. When one's life is threatened or one's health impaired by smoking, then others are indeed affected.

The claim here is *not* that we should always put the interests of others ahead of our own. Nor is it even the claim that it is wrong to smoke alone because others will be adversely affected if one becomes sick and dies. Instead, it is the claim that insofar as others are affected by one's private smoking, smoking is not an *exclusively* self-regarding act, even if it is a *primarily* self-regarding act. (A *primarily* self-regarding act is an act that affects primarily oneself even though it may also affect others in very limited ways. An *exclusively* self-regarding act is an act that affects only oneself.) Thus, whether smokers should smoke at all remains an ethical question even if ethics *is* limited to acts that can affect others. It is a separate, but ethical question, how much weight one should give to the interests of others.

When asking whether one should smoke at all, it is helpful to distinguish between (i) those who have not yet started smoking and (ii) those who are already smokers and who may be considering whether to quit smoking. The ethical question for those who have not yet begun smoking can be answered more easily. This is because it is very difficult to see how one's own interests could be served by becoming addicted to an expensive and dangerous drug. Nor are the (just) interests of others generally served by one's becoming a smoker.[20] Thus, there is a happy congruence between one's own interests and the personal interests of others. There is no good reason to take up smoking and very good reason not to take it up.

The situation of those who already smoke is somewhat more complicated. There are clearly some very good reasons for quitting smoking. The risk of adverse health effects reduces significantly when one ceases smoking. The longer since one ceased smoking the greater the decrease in risk.[21] Those who begin smoking as young adults but stop before they are 40 'avoid more than 90% of the excess risk during their next few decades of life, as compared with those who continue to smoke, and even those who stop at 50 years of age avoid more than half the excess risk'.[22]

While there are these and other very important benefits to ceasing smoking, those who already smoke can have *some* reasons to continue doing so. Breaking an addiction is not easy. It may be especially difficult against the backdrop of other challenges in a person's life. These do not seem like very strong considerations, but it is not always obvious that they are outweighed by the reasons to give up smoking, especially if the decision to continue smoking is only a temporary one which could be revisited at a more opportune time. Similarly, an older light-smoker who has been lucky enough to avoid serious harm to her health, might reasonably decide that the pleasure derived from smoking one cigarette a day is worth the now modest risks. There are thus at least some circumstances in which, all things considered, it is not obviously wrong for a smoker to continue smoking.

However, smokers should be aware that their addiction is likely to lead to rationalizations for continued smoking. Smokers will think that continued smoking is reasonable more often than it actually is. They should thus not be too confident in their own judgements that continued smoking is reasonable.

Harm to others

Arguably the more important ethical issue pertaining to smoking is whether smokers may smoke in the presence of non-smokers.[23] There are two broad kinds of argument that are advanced in support of a negative answer. The first of these is rooted in the *harm* that a smoker does (or risks doing) to the non-smoker in causing the latter to become a passive smoker. The second kind of argument is grounded in the *offence* caused to the passive smoker.

It is often thought that the harm argument is the much stronger argument. It certainly has considerable force. However, at least in some circumstances, it faces challenges to which the offence argument is immune. That may seem surprising, but it should become less so when different kind of offence arguments are distinguished. However, I begin by considering the harm argument.

There are two kinds of cigarette smoke. Mainstream smoke is that which the smoker inhales through the cigarette. Some of this is then exhaled. Sidestream smoke is that which comes from the burning end of the cigarette. Sidestream smoke is intrinsically more dangerous than mainstream smoke. It contains higher levels of known carcinogens than mainstream smoke. This is because it is not filtered (as mainstream smoke is in filtered cigarettes).[24] However, sidestream smoke is typically diluted in a larger volume of air, which is why passive smoking is not as dangerous as active smoking.

Nevertheless, there are significant risks associated with passive smoking. While 'there is no safe level of exposure to tobacco smoke',[25] the risks increase with increased exposure. For example, non-smoking spouses of smokers have an increased risk of lung cancer. For female non-smoking spouses, that increased risk is around 20%, and for male non-smoking spouses it is approximately 30%.[26] Non-smokers exposed to the smoke of co-workers have a 12%–19% increased chance of lung cancer.[27] Passive smoking also increases the risk of coronary heart disease by 25%–35%,[28] and the risk of stroke by about 20%–30%.[29]

These risk increments are only a fraction of the increased risk to the smokers themselves. For example, lifelong smokers have a 300% to 500% increased risk (above baseline) of developing many cancers. The increased risk of lung cancer is even higher—a monstrous 1400% to 2900% increase.[30]

Nevertheless, the increased risks to passive smokers are not negligible. They are also much higher than risks that are deemed sufficiently high to necessitate governmental regulation of (other) air pollutants, of carcinogens in foods, and of mortality risks from nuclear reactor accidents.[31]

It follows that even if morality need be no more sensitive to risks than the law should be, the risks of passive smoking should not be imposed on (non-consenting) non-smokers. The case for not imposing the risks of passive smoking would be even stronger if it is the case, as it may well be, that morality should be even more risk averse than the law needs to be.

Foetuses constitute a distinctive risk category. They do not inhale second-hand smoke. However, they are passive smokers of another kind if their mothers smoke—and even if their non-smoking mothers are exposed to the smoke of others.[32] Foetal exposure to cigarette toxins is via the placenta. For example, women who smoke during the early stages of pregnancy put their child at greater risk of being born prematurely with low birthweight,[33] cleft lips and palates,[34] and reduced lung function.[35] Infants whose mothers smoked during and after pregnancy are at greater risk of sudden infant death syndrome.[36]

One does not need to attribute moral status to foetuses themselves in order to be concerned about these particular risks.[37] Given that the children and adults who develop from the foetuses are harmed, the foetuses do not also need to count morally in order for the harm to matter.

Thus far, I have been speaking about the harms that passive smoking does to *humans*. However, companion animals can also be harmed by second-hand smoke. This is true of dogs, cats, birds, mice, guinea pigs, and fish.[38] Given that these animals are morally considerable,[39] the others in the presence of whom smokers should not smoke include companion animals.

According to the harm argument against smoking in the presence of non-smokers, smoking significantly elevates the risks of disease in non-smokers and actually causes harm to some of them. To the significant extent that we are not morally entitled to harm others, or to put others at (significant) risk of serious harm, smokers ought to desist from smoking in the presence of non-smokers. There would be some exceptional cases, in which a smoker might be morally entitled to smoke in the presence of a non-smoker. For example, if a non-smoker willingly entered a designated smoking area, the smoker's entitlement to smoke would not incinerate. Subject to such exceptions, the harm argument seems straightforward and forceful, but it does face some challenges.

Is the risk increment too negligible?

The first challenge to the harm argument denies that smoking in the presence of non-smokers always imposes a serious risk of serious harm. Sometimes, according to this challenge, smoking in the presence of non-smokers makes no significant difference to the non-smokers' risk of harm.

To better understand this challenge, we should distinguish between two broad kinds of scenario. The first is where a smoker repeatedly exposes the same person or people to cigarette smoke over an extended period. This is typically the case when a smoker smokes in the presence of those with whom she lives or works.

The second scenario is where a smoker exposes different people to her smoke on different occasions. If, for example, somebody smokes in a restaurant or on a train, she exposes other diners in the restaurant or travellers on the train to the smoke. If, as is often the case, those people will never again share a carriage with or be in the same restaurant as *this* smoker, then their exposure to this particular smoker's smoke is limited. This is not to deny that the passive smokers bear the cumulative risk of exposure to multiple different smokers in the same restaurant or train at the same time, as well as in different times and places. It is to say only that the increased risk each smoker poses to each non-smoker is minimal.

Does it make a moral difference whether cumulative risks are the product of a single smoker or of innumerable different smokers? It certainly cannot make a difference if one is determining whether and how to regulate smoking. This is because the aggregative effects of particular kinds of actions is clearly relevant to what laws and policies we should have. Laws are not made to govern only one action, by one person, at one time. Instead, their scope ranges over sets of actions of a particular kind. It does not matter whether those actions are of a single person or multiple people.

The harder question is the one that confronts not the legislator but rather the individual smoker: Does it make a difference whether the cumulative risks imposed on others are the result of my smoking or of the smoking of innumerable smokers including me? Those who think that it does make a difference argue that in the latter case, my smoking has only a negligible impact on the non-smokers who happen to be in my vicinity when I smoke.

Of course, there is a sense in which the same is also true of any given cigarette I smoke in the presence of a family member or co-worker. That individual cigarette is going to have only a minimal effect on the family or co-workers. One difference, though, is that when the cumulative risk is a product of *my* smoking, the individual cigarette is part of a pattern of my own behaviour. Even *if* my one cigarette can be excused because it causes only an indiscernible and minimal increase in risk, my pattern of smoking in the presence of family and co-workers cannot be so excused because it does cause a significant increase in risk. By contrast, when the cumulative risk results from innumerable different smokers, of which I am only one, then the aggregative risk for any individual is not a product of my own pattern of behaviour. Some people think that when my smoking does not significantly elevate anybody's risk of harm, I am not morally obliged to desist from smoking. This is the 'causal inefficacy' argument (again[40]). There is reason to reject it.

Although the smoker makes only a minimal difference to the risk levels of the non-smoker who is transiently in his presence, a minimal difference is not the same as no difference at all. This should not be a controversial claim. Those who nonetheless dispute it should consider that if each of the individual smokers who smoked in the presence of a non-smoker over the course of the latter's life, made no difference to the risks incurred by the non-smoker, then the non-smoker's risk of disease from repeated exposure to second-hand smoke would not elevate at all. Yet, we know that the risk does elevate significantly. The risks to an individual rise irrespective of whether the second-hand smoke comes from the cigarettes of one person or of hundreds of different people. The individual smoker is thus making *some* contribution to the risk levels of the non-smoker, even if it is a minimal contribution.

If one is making *some* contribution to increasing a person's risk, we should recognize it and treat it as such. A minimal contribution to increased risk matters (at least) minimally rather than not at all. The smoker might respond that if it matters *only* minimally, then it should be morally permissible for the smoker to smoke in the presence of those who are only briefly in his presence. After all, there are many occasions in which our actions minimally increase the risks of others. It seems unreasonable to think that every time an action would have this effect, we ought to desist from the action.

However, in determining whether we may impose some minimal risk of harm on others, we need to know, *inter alia*, what good might be gained from doing so—or what good might be lost by not doing so. Although smoking may cause only a minimal increment in risk for those transiently in the smoker's presence, not much if anything is gained by smoking in their presence, and not much is lost by not doing so. In other words, one inflicts a minimal risk on others in smoking in their presence. That minimal risk provides at least a minimal reason against smoking in their presence, and that minimal reason is not outweighed by reasons in favour of smoking in the presence of the non-smokers.

This may sound like a utilitarian calculation, but it need not be. In determining whether the smoker has a right to smoke in the presence of non-smokers, the deontologist might need to consider the interests of both the smoker and the non-smoker. Just as it is said that my right to swing my arm ends at the tip of your nose, so it might be the case that the smoker's right to smoke the cigarette ends at the tip of the non-smoker's nose. Given that the smoker has no control over the smoke once it leaves the cigarettes or he exhales it, his right to smoke would be limited to *places* where the fumes would not be inhaled by others.

The non-smoker does not have to be harmed for there to be such a limitation on the smoker's rights. Consider the case of the person who plucks a single hair from the head of a person he transiently encounters. That is the one and only hair that the plucker ever plucks from that person's head. It would be a stretch to say that this plucker significantly *harms* the plucked (although he might contribute to harm if thousands of other pluckers also pluck one hair from the same person's head), yet the plucker might still *wrong* the plucked.

This argument is strengthened if the plucker knows—or should know—that he is not the only plucker, and that the series of pluckings will leave the plucked either bald or balding. (To the extent that the plucker is in the same situation as the smoker, he knows or should know that his plucking is part of a series of pluckings.)

Perhaps it will be suggested that the plucker is not analogous to the smoker because the plucker literally touches part of the plucked's body. If that is the concern, then imagine an intermediate case in which smoking a single cigarette in somebody's presence causes one of their hairs to fall out. Here again we might deny that a harm has been done and yet agree that somebody has been wronged (for it surely does not matter whether one causes the hair to fall out by plucking it or by exposing it to a chemical). But if one wrongs somebody by needlessly emitting a chemical that causes a hair to fall out, then one wrongs somebody by needlessly emitting a toxic chemical that lodges in somebody's lungs.

To emphasize, we cannot ignore the fact that the risk imposed by the single smoker is not the total smoking risk imposed on the non-smoker. If each smoker transiently smoking in the presence of any given non-smoker can justify his smoking by the fact that he makes only a minimal difference to the non-smoker's risk, the effect is a significantly increased risk for the non-smoker. There must be something wrong with the reasoning that results in this. If nobody is wronging the non-smoker by smoking in his presence, how does it come to be that he incurs a significantly elevated risk as a result of exposure to all that smoke? Even if it were the case that no smoker *wrongs the non-smoker*, they all *do wrong* in contributing needlessly to that significantly elevated risk.

The case of cars

There is a second, and lesser, challenge that might be advanced by those seeking to defend smoking in the presence of non-smokers. Those who advance this challenge might note that there are other activities that also impose risks on others and sometimes harm them, and yet it seems unreasonable to say that we ought always to desist from such activities. If we are not required to desist from other activities, we should similarly not be required to desist from smoking in the presence of non-smokers.

The foremost example of a comparable activity is driving a motor vehicle. If we think that driving is sometimes morally permissible despite the risks it imposes on others, should we not concede that smoking in the presence of non-smokers may similarly be permissible?

This argument, at least as it applies to driving, assumes that drivers impose risks on non-drivers that are at least as great as the risks that smokers impose on non-smokers when smoking in their presence. Is this assumption true? The answer to this question is far from clear, not least because of a dearth of comparable data. However, some informed estimates are possible. These suggest, but do not prove, that the assumption is false. Because many readers will prefer to avoid entering this empirical thicket, the basis for this conclusion has been relegated to an appendix to this chapter.

None of this is to deny the real harms done by driving. Nor is it to suggest that the risks to others of our vehicle use should not influence how much we drive, and under what conditions.[41] It is only to say that the risks imposed by a smoker on non-smokers in whose presence he smokes, are greater than those imposed by a driver on those not using cars.

There are other important differences between smoking and driving. First, driving often has important benefits to the driver and to others, that smoking lacks. Indeed, driving is sometimes even a necessity. For example, one may need to get to work or to purchase groceries. Sometimes this is possible on foot, bicycle, or via public transport (which can also pose risks to pedestrians and cyclists), but sometimes it is not. Even when it is, it might take much longer, be less effective, and sometimes be riskier. By contrast, smoking lacks this kind of value to the smoker. This is not to deny the relief pleasures that smoking brings to the smoker. However, the smoker would certainly have been better off not having become a smoker and will usually be better off if she could quit.

A second important difference between smoking and driving is that insofar as smoking has some value to the smoker, it can be obtained without smoking in the presence of non-smokers. It may be easier to light up whenever and wherever one wants, but it is possible to derive the pleasures of smoking without doing so in the presence of others. Given the smoker's desire to smoke and the non-smoker's interest in not inhaling smoke, the smoker's fulfilling her desire away from the non-smoker is the most reasonable way to respond to that conflict. This is true even when the inconvenience to smokers is quite considerable, as it is on long distance flights when they must go many hours before being able to light up away from non-smokers.

The much more considerable benefits of some driving, by contrast, cannot be derived unless, in any important sense, one drives 'in the presence of non-drivers'. Of course, I am not here recommending driving on pavements and lawns. Instead, I am saying that driving even on roads is, in an important sense, driving in the presence of non-drivers. Pedestrian and cycle paths are often adjacent to and intersect with roads. Pollution from cars spreads to neighbouring areas. Contributions to global warming and climate change affect the planet. One cannot eliminate these risks without ceasing to drive.

There are ways to *minimize* the risks to others—including minimizing how much one drives, driving a vehicle with lower emissions, adhering to the speed limit, obeying traffic signals, and not driving under the influence of alcohol. These are the restrictions that drivers must accept and within which they must act. However, there is no such thing as not driving in the presence of non-drivers if by 'not driving in the presence of non-drivers' one means in a way that can have as little affect at all on non-drivers as smoking alone has on non-smokers.[42]

These considerations support the view that while one should limit how much one drives, one should *entirely* avoid smoking in the presence of (non-consenting) non-smokers. However, the case against smoking in the presence of non-smokers is not limited to the 'harm to others' argument. There is also an offence argument. Although an argument grounded in the harm done to non-smokers may initially seem like a much stronger argument than one grounded in the offence caused to non-smokers, the latter argument is much stronger than it initially appears to be.

Offence to others

One reason why an offence argument may initially appear unpromising, lies in the very word 'offence'. It is a term with broad application, and some actions that cause offence are not thereby (even *prima facie*) wrong to perform. Consider a variety of examples (which are summarized in Figure 4.1 below).

Two kinds of offence

1. Some people are offended at the sight of a man or boy wearing earrings, yet that offended response does not show that it is wrong for male humans to wear earrings. It is more reasonable to think that the offended should desist from taking offence if they can, or that they should live with the offence if they cannot overcome that feeling.
2. If others find one's harmless and non-intrusive religious practices to be offensive, one is not therefore under a moral obligation to desist from practising them. There may be disagreement about whether the religious practices are indeed harmless and non-intrusive. If they are harmful or intrusive then *that* would be the reason to desist from them. The mere fact that people take offence is not what generates a duty to desist.
3. If some people are offended by the sight of two homosexuals holding hands or embracing in public, this does not morally obligate homosexuals to desist.
4. Expressing unpopular opinions can also offend, but the fact that they offend is not sufficient to render their expression morally wrong.

Sometimes unpopular opinions are unpopular because they are either false or immoral. In such cases, one does have a moral (even though not necessarily a legal) duty to desist from uttering those views. Even then, the duty is grounded not in the unpopularity of the view, but instead in its falsity or immorality. After all, there are many opinions that are unpopular precisely because they are either true or moral, and are falsely construed as the opposite.
5. Perhaps your naming your dog 'King Charles' is offensive to your royalist neighbours. (Your motivation may not even be flippancy. Perhaps he is a King Charles Spaniel, and you think that the name is apt.) It may be prudent or generous for you to respect your neighbours' sensibilities, but it really does not seem as though you have a moral obligation to do so.

Contrast these with other cases of offence in which the offending party *does* seem to have a moral obligation to desist from the actions that cause offence:

6. You are smoking at a party. Ash trays have not been provided. You decide to tap the ash off the end of your cigarette into the punch bowl. Your fellow partygoers may or may not notice the ash in the bowl (before they dish up some punch for themselves). If they do not, they may imbibe the ash-laced punch, either then tasting the ash or swallowing it without consent. If they do notice the ash while it is still in the bowl, they will either have to forgo the punch or, if they are either brave or desperate, fish out the ash before dishing up a helping for themselves.
7. You are at another party. You have just partaken of some *hors d'oeuvres* which have left your fingers sticky. You are in conversation with somebody who is drinking water. You dip your fingers into her glass to clean your fingers.
8. You make much noise in public places by, for example, modifying your car exhaust to raise the decibels, or blaring your car music as you drive (especially, although not only, through a residential area at 02h00).
9. For your entertainment, you release an ammonium sulphide stink bomb in your philosophy class.
10. Saliva is accumulating in your mouth, and you spit it onto the pavement. Swallowing is not your thing. Alternatively, you have finished

chewing your gum and you stick it under the classroom desk in front of you.

Some may wonder whether 'offence' is the most accurate way to refer to the negative states caused by actions 6 to 10. They might argue that 'offence' is best reserved for actions such 1 to 5, and that we need a different term to refer to the negative states caused by actions 6 to 10. One possibility is 'nuisance'. However, Joel Feinberg thinks that 'nuisance' has 'unavoidable suggestions of triviality',[43] which leads him to distinguish between 'offensive nuisance', the lesser category, and 'profound offense', the more severe category.[44]

Other options are 'annoyance' and 'irritation'.[45] 'Annoyance' seems inadequate because it is quite natural to say that the negative response some people have to actions in the left-hand column of Figure 4.1 is one of annoyance. 'Irritation' is a good way of describing the response to some of the actions in the right-hand column—those where gustatory or olfactory irritants are operative. However, there are other actions in the right-hand column, such as dipping one's fingers in another's drink, spitting saliva, and gum deposits— that are not well described as (physical) irritants. If 'irritants' is expanded to include psychological ones, then it would be applied to actions in the left-hand column too.

In the absence of clear terminology to differentiate the negative responses to actions in each column, it seems reasonable to preserve the broader term, 'offence', and to recognize that there are the two kinds of offence I have delineated.

Does not provide grounds to desist	Provides grounds to desist
1. Males wearing earrings	6. Putting one's ash in the punch bowl
2. Practising an unpopular religion	7. Dipping one's fingers in another's drink
3. Homosexuals' public affection	8. Making a noise in public places
4. Expressing unpopular opinions	9. Releasing stink bombs in public places
5. Naming one's dog 'King Charles'	10. Spitting on the ground/depositing gum

Figure 4.1 Two kinds of offence.

Distinguishing the two kinds of offence

Is there a principled way to distinguish those cases in which people performing actions that cause offence have (at least presumptively) a duty not to perform those actions, from those cases in which people performing actions that cause offence may continue to engage in the offending conduct? There can be no formula but, as Joel Feinberg noted in a different context, there are various relevant considerations:[46]

a. The more *intrusive* an action the more reason, all other things being equal, the person performing that action has to desist from it.
b. Relatedly, the easier it is for the offended person to *avoid* the offending conduct without undue cost, the less reason, all other things being equal, the person performing the action has to desist from it.
c. The more *important* the offending action is to the person performing it, and the fewer the *alternative* opportunities, the less reason there is, all things being equal, for the person engaging in the offending conduct to desist from it.
d. Considerations a, b, and c can also be bundled by asking whether the offending action is primarily self-regarding or substantially other-regarding. (A *primarily* self-regarding act, it was noted earlier, is an act that affects primarily oneself even though it may also affect others in very limited ways. A substantially other-regarding act is an act that has a significant impact on others.) The greater the extent to which an offending action is primarily self-regarding, the less reason, all things being equal, the actor has to desist from it. By contrast, the greater the extent to which an offending action is substantially other-regarding, the more reason, all things being equal, the actor has to desist from it.[47]
e. The greater *social value* of the offending conduct, the less moral reason, all things being equal, the actor has to desist from it.
f. All things being equal, to the extent to which the person performing the offending action is doing this *in order to* cause offence,[48] there is moral reason for that person to desist. All things are not equal when, for example, that offence is deserved.

The application of these considerations should not be mechanical. Not all of them are relevant in all cases, and some are weightier than others. However, weighing them up in a reasoned way, shows why we should indeed reach the conclusion that those performing actions 1 to 5 need not desist from them despite any offence they may cause, whereas those considering actions 6 to 10 should desist on account of the offence they are likely to cause.

Males wearing earrings do not intrude upon others. Anybody who is offended by the sight can avert their eyes. It is thus easy to avoid the offence without undue cost. Moreover, wearing earrings is of some importance to those who wear them. The importance lies in wearing them in public (as opposed to only in restricted environments in which they will not offend). How we dress and whether and how we adorn ourselves is important to people. It is typically not *as* important as their religious, political, or moral commitments, but it is nonetheless of some importance. It does not have much social value, at least not directly, and there is thus not this further consideration in its favour, but no such further consideration is necessary, given that it is a primarily self-regarding action. If there were a particular male who were wearing earrings in order to offend (his conservative father, for example), then the wearing of earrings itself would be concomitantly less important to him and there would be more moral reason to desist (unless the offence was deserved).

Harmless, non-intrusive religious practices are, by definition, not intrusive. Thus, even if performed in public, they are easily avoidable by, and without undue cost to, those who are offended by them. Moreover, religious practices tend to be very important to those who undertake them. Those religious practices that cause offence are unlikely to be ones with great social value, although there is (indirect) social value in people performing religious practices that are important to them. These are primarily self-regarding actions and there is little reason for the person practising them to desist if they cause offence.

Ordinary displays of affection by homosexuals (like those of heterosexuals) are not intrusive. One might see two people holding hands or embracing, but one can easily avert one's eyes if that makes one uncomfortable. Although it is true that people could reserve their handholding and embracing for the private realm, for many people it is important to be able to express their affection without this constraint. There is no great social value in this expression, although there is in people feeling free to give such expression. Perhaps there are some people who display this affection precisely to offend, but such cases are surely the exception.

The expression of opinions that give offence is often not intrusive. (It becomes intrusive if it is done in particular ways—such as heckling—but then it is the method rather than the content that is intrusive.) Those who are offended by an opinion, can stop reading or listening to it. Even when they cannot easily evade exposure to the opinion, there is often great social value in their being exposed to these ideas, as John Stuart Mill argued.[49] If the offensive ideas are true (or even only partially true), then their expression can lead to falsehoods being replaced by truth. However, there is often social value even in the expression of mistaken views, both because our understanding of the truth can be refined by its encounter with falsehood and because in testing truthful ideas against alternatives we have more reason to be confident in the views we take to be true. In being tested against falsehood, they (in the words of John Stuart Mill) cease to be 'dead dogma' and become 'living truth'.[50] The expression of unpopular ideas is important not only socially but also to the people expressing them. Freely expressing one's opinions is very important to many people.

What people name their companion animals typically matters much less to them than expressing their opinions or practising their religion. Nor does one's naming of one's companion animals have significant social value. Nevertheless, it has *some* personal importance, and naming one's companion animals does not intrude in a significant way on other people. One's neighbours and others might occasionally hear one calling one's companion animal's name, but if that counts as an intrusion at all, it is a miniscule and typically infrequent one.[51] Setting aside the possibility that the animal himself may have some interest in what he is named,[52] naming one's companion animals is not a significantly other-regarding action. Thus, assuming that one is not naming out of malice,[53] the fact that some people may be offended by a particular name does not provide one with a moral reason to desist.

The other offence-causing examples I have provided are different. Putting one's ash in the punch bowl is intrusive in a way in which the previous actions are not. If the other partygoers do not notice the ash in the bowl they might inadvertently put it in their mouths or even ingest it. In this way, one's action transgresses the bodily boundary. Nor are all bodily intrusions equal. Oral intrusion may not be *the* most serious, but it is among the more serious and is typically more severe than intrusions upon somebody's visual sense. Indeed, the latter are intrusions in a metaphorical rather than a literal sense. If the other partygoers do notice the ash in the bowl before they partake of the punch, then they can avoid this intrusion, but only at the cost of foregoing the punch.[54] It is important to you, the smoker, to get rid of your ash, but you can do this without polluting the punch bowl. It may take you a little more effort, but that is what is required to avoid the significantly other-regarding action of depositing your ash in the punch.

Similar considerations apply to your washing your fingers in your conversational companion's water. That person's drink is her drink. It is not (also) your finger bowl. You are intruding upon her personal space in non-insignificant way. It may be important to you to clean your fingers, but it is at least as important to the other person that you not do that in her drinking water. Although she could go get another glass of water, if somebody has to take their leave, it should be you, to wash your fingers, rather than her to get more water. Dipping your fingers in her drink is not a primarily self-regarding action. Nor does it have any social value. While the intent may not be malicious, the action does display a disregard for the reasonable claims of others.

The same is true of making unnecessary noise in public places. Noise may not be literally intrusive in the way that transgressing the oral boundary is, but it is also more serious than hearing the expression of ideas you find offensive. The latter can be ignored in a way in which noise cannot be. It is a serious intrusion. Just how serious it is, depends on a number of considerations, including the volume of the noise, its duration, and when and where it occurs. Sometimes those who are offended by noise can avoid it without unreasonable cost. You need not go to the rock concert if you do not like loud music, given that loud music is part of what a rock concert is. However, if your neighbour has rock music blaring at 02h00 while you are trying to sleep, you cannot easily avoid it. Moving to a new home is too much to ask of you. Playing his music that loud may be important to him, but he can do it another time of day or, better still, use headphones. The creation of noise is thus a substantially other-regarding action—of a negative rather than positive kind.

Some of these considerations also apply to releasing an ammonium sulphide stink bomb in your philosophy class. Olfactory intrusion, even if not quite as intimate as oral intrusion, is nonetheless a serious intrusion, especially if the scent is malodorous as it is in this case. (In order to smell something, particles from that which is smelled must make contact with the olfactory receptors in one's nose.) Those not wishing to smell the odour can move to another location but sometimes, as in the case at hand, this comes at unreasonable cost. Others should not have to leave class in order to avoid the intrusions of your stink bombs. Perhaps you are motivated by maliciousness, but that is not required in order for you to desist. It is sufficient that your socially useless activity is substantially other-regarding, even if it also serves some trivial interest of yours. You are not entitled to get your entertainment from intruding on others in this way.

Saliva on the sidewalk and gum under a public desk are not as intrusive as ingested ash. The saliva, even if not also the gum, is likely to be less intrusive than some noise. Nevertheless, they are both pollutants. Many people would much rather not step in other people's gob,[55] and almost everybody would rather not find their fingers touching well-masticated gum, even if it had long since dried out. Those who spit their saliva onto the floor or who deposit their chewed gum under public desks may have some interest in doing so, but they have alternative opportunities to do that. Your own saliva really can be swallowed. You are doing it often, even if you do not realize it. If you really do not wish to do that on a given occasion, then carry a tissue or handkerchief into which you can expectorate. The same applies to your chewed gum. Public spaces are not your garbage bins or wash basins. Spitting and depositing your gum in public places is not a primarily self-regarding action even if is not as substantially other-regarding as some of the others.

The spitting example may be more controversial than some of the others.[56] However, it does not matter, in thinking about smoking, whether some people think that there is nothing wrong with spitting on the ground. What matters is how they justify that claim. If, for example, they do so by arguing that saliva on public paths is not intrusive or that it is easily avoidable by those who do not like to encounter it, then they agree about which considerations are relevant and disagree only about how intrusive or avoidable pavement-disposed mucous is.

What kind of offence does smoking cause others?

A smoker's smoke could, in principle, offend not only non-smokers but also other smokers. For example, a cigarette smoker might be offended by cigar smoke or pipe smoke. However, for two reasons, I shall focus on offence to non-smokers. First, as noted earlier, when a smoker imposes his smoke on other smokers, he arguably gives up, or at least considerably weakens, the claim he has against others not to engage in similar behaviour. Second, smoking offending smokers is, in practice, much less common than smoking offending non-smokers.

Smoking in the presence of non-smokers clearly falls into the category of offence that provides those causing the offence with moral reason to desist from the offence-causing action. This is so, even though smokers are almost never smoking in order to cause offence to non-smokers.

Smoking in the presence of non-smokers intrudes upon the latter in literal ways. The smoke enters the non-smoker's body—mainly via nose and mouth, but also the eyes. It is malodorous, and it irritates eyes and airways. (Smokers often forget just how obnoxious cigarette smoke is, because they have inured themselves through their repeated exposure to it.)

The unpleasantness of cigarette smoke to non-smokers is largely an ordinary physiological response. This enhances its intrusiveness and reduces the ability of the offended person to ignore it. It is like the taste of ash, the sound of noise, or the smell of ammonium sulphide. It is not psychologically mediated as are offence at the sight of males wearing earrings, unpopular religious practices or homosexuals embracing, or hearing unpopular opinions or your neighbour's dog being called 'King Charles'. (It is true that some of the offences in the right-hand column of Figure 4.1 are also psychologically mediated, but they are in in the right-hand column despite, rather than because of, that feature.)

Non-smokers can avoid the unpleasantness of smokers' smoke only by avoiding all the places in which smokers smoke. If smokers smoke in homes, offices, shops, restaurants, buses, trains, stations, cinemas, theatres, hotels, and even entrances to buildings, then non-smokers have to withdraw from all these places in order to avoid smoke to which they do not wish to be exposed. That imposes significant costs on non-smokers.

We can grant that smoking is important to smokers, mainly because they will suffer nicotine withdrawal without cigarettes (or without some other source of nicotine such as gum or a patch). However, smokers can avoid that unpleasantness without having to give up smoking. They can do so by smoking, but not in the presence of non-smokers. Granted, this involves some inconvenience—and sometimes this inconvenience is not inconsiderable. Smokers who are considering the interests of non-smokers cannot light up whenever and wherever they want. They must go outside or to a designated area—or wait for the aeroplane in which they are travelling to land, and they can get to a smoking area. That is an inconvenience, but the convenience of smokers is not enough to justify the more serious intrusions of smoke on non-smokers. It is also not the only inconvenience people need to incur in order to avoid intruding on others. For example, instead of voiding your bladder or bowels in the street when the urge arises, you appropriately seek out a toilet even if at some inconvenience to yourself. (Many people would prefer to inconvenience themselves in *this* way, but there are some who would prefer the instant relief.)

Not only is smoking in the presence of non-smokers significantly other-regarding (in a negative way) it also has no social value. It is not like the expression of unpopular ideas. Many would go further and claim that smoking has *negative* social value. Some of this is an aggregation of the negative health effects on smokers and passive smokers.[57]

Some of the economic costs may be better candidates for *social* disvalue, but the net effect of these is more contested. Smoking-related illness results in work absences, with the consequent negative impact on the economy. Yet smokers also contribute to the national purse though the hefty taxes that are often imposed on cigarettes. Smoking-related illness also results in healthcare costs, not all of which are borne by the person for whom the healthcare is provided. Instead, those costs are covered either by public resources or by private insurance to which others are contributing. However, there is conflicting evidence whether the higher annual medical costs for smokers are offset by the additional years of medical costs for non-smokers.[58]

Fortunately, we do not need resolution on these economic questions. Even if the earlier deaths of smokers (and passive smokers) amounts to a healthcare saving, that would no more be a consideration in favour of smoking in the presence of non-smokers than the healthcare savings from suicide or murder would be a consideration in favour of those practices. Healthcare does cost, but when it lengthens life of good quality or improves the quality of what remains, then it is worth the cost. Reducing costs by reducing quality and quantity of life is not the sort of saving that amounts to a (net) social good. Creating healthcare needs that then require healthcare resources is also not a social good. In fact, it is a form of wastage. It is far better to spend those resources on conditions we cannot prevent.

Abstaining when others do not?

In deciding to abstain from smoking in the presence of non-smokers, does it make a difference whether other smokers are already smoking in the presence of the same non-smokers? In cases where nobody else is smoking in their presence, one's own smoking is likely to cause offence. However, if other smokers are already smoking, it might be argued that the offensive smoke and odours are already present. According to this argument, there is a much bigger difference between nobody smoking and one person smoking than there is between one person and two people smoking in the presence of non-smokers. There is then even less difference between, say, twenty people smoking and twenty-one people smoking in the presence of non-smokers.

There is *some* truth in this. However, other things are also true. First, each additional smoker will make some difference. Second, how much difference that is will depend on numerous factors, including the size of the space within which they are smoking, the quality of the ventilation, and the number of people present.[59] Third, it is unlikely that there is steady and continuous diminishing marginal disutility. For example, some point may be reached where an additional smoker creates a tipping point to a literally unbearable atmosphere. Fourth, smokers are going to be prone to rationalize about these matters, which will make their judgements unreliable. Fifth, if one is not entitled to smoke in the presence of non-smokers, one cannot gain such an entitlement simply because other unentitled people are acting as though they were entitled.

Finally, there are interactive effects. If one smoker is smoking in the presence of non-smokers and another smoker excuses himself to smoke elsewhere, that *could* sometimes (even though it often would not) have a positive effect on those smoking without regard to the non-smokers.[60] Similarly, if the second smoker lights up in the presence of the non-smokers, that might encourage a third, fourth and fifth smoker to do so too.

Putting these considerations together, the strong presumption should be against smoking in the presence of non-smokers even if other smokers are already smoking. There might be exceptional cases, but smokers' identification of these is unlikely to be reliable. The presumption against smoking is further strengthened to the extent that the harm argument has force. Each additional cigarette adds to the risk even if it does not always add to the offence.

Electronic cigarettes

The (age standardized) prevalence of tobacco smoking has decreased from about 20.6% of the world's population aged fifteen or older in 2000 to 20.2%

in 2015.[61] The smoking of electronic cigarettes, however, has been increasing rapidly since they were first marketed (in China) in 2004. By 2016 there were about 35 million adults smoking electronic cigarettes.[62] This is still vastly overshadowed by the number of tobacco smokers, of whom there are over a billion. Nevertheless, it is worth briefly considering whether the ethics of using electronic cigarettes differs from the ethics of smoking conventional cigarettes.

Electronic cigarettes, sometimes known as e-cigarettes,[63] are touted as much less dangerous than regular cigarettes. They do contain toxic substances (such as cadmium, nickel, lead, and toluene), but at much lower levels than regular cigarettes.[64] They also include some substances such as vegetable glycerin, propylene glycol, as well as many flavourings that are considered safe as food additives but whose safety as an inhalant is unknown.[65] One review of the health effects of electronic cigarettes concludes that at 'present, it is impossible to reach a consensus on the safety of e-cigarettes except perhaps to say that they may be safer than conventional cigarettes but are also likely to pose risks to health that are not present when neither product is used'.[66]

There are two obstacles to overcoming this uncertainty. The first is time. Electronic cigarettes have simply not been around long enough to know what the long-term effects in humans are. More difficult, however, is the highly variable content of electronic cigarette liquids and aerosols, the fact that their listed contents often do not include all the actual contents,[67] the difference made by the specifics of the heating element, the temperature reached, and features of the wick.[68] In other words, there are many confounding variables.

Thus, whereas the earlier uncertainty about the risks of smoking tobacco has long since been eliminated, the same is not true of electronic cigarettes. In the face of this uncertainty, a non-smoker, considering only her own interests, should not begin using electronic cigarettes. There is nothing to be gained and there is a possibility of at least some harm. The case for not starting is strengthened if the electronic cigarette contains nicotine, as the majority do.[69] Indeed, given the labelling inaccuracies already mentioned, electronic cigarettes can have nicotine content without this reflecting on the list of contents. The amount of nicotine is also not always accurately stated.[70]

While nicotine is less dangerous than other contents of traditional cigarettes, it is a powerfully addictive substance and the main reason why smokers become dependent on tobacco. Thus, smokers of electronic cigarettes with nicotine content are likely to become addicted to such cigarettes. There is also the possibility that the addiction might lead some of them to smoking tobacco, the dangers of which are known and immense. In other words, electronic cigarettes might serve as a gateway to tobacco smoking.

The situation may be different for those who already smoke. If electronic cigarette smoking is less dangerous than smoking tobacco, but still provides nicotine on which the smoker is dependent, it seems that the smoker would do well to shift to electronic cigarettes. His nicotine needs will be met but with lower risk. Such a course of action assumes that electronic cigarette smoking is indeed less dangerous. We do not know that that is the case, but given what we currently know, it is not an unreasonable assumption at present.

The case for shifting from tobacco to electronic cigarettes would be strengthened if electronic cigarettes can help smokers to cease (or reduce) smoking. However, there is thus far no clear evidence of the efficacy of electronic cigarettes as a method of quitting—or of their efficacy compared to other methods for quitting, such as nicotine patches.[71] It is even possible that electronic cigarette smokers may be *less* likely to quit. This was the finding of one meta-analysis,[72] although it has been suggested that this analysis suffered from methodological problems that cannot be avoided until a 'passel of high quality, large-scale randomised trials assessing e-cigarettes in various clinical populations' have been conducted.[73]

Given the uncertainty about the health effects of electronic cigarettes on those smoking them, it should not be surprising that we still do not know enough about the health effects on non-smokers in whose presence e-cigarettes are smoked. (There is no side-stream smoke from electronic cigarettes. All the smoke is mainstream smoke exhaled by the smoker.)

There have been *some* studies. These have reached different conclusions about the level of nicotine exposure in passive e-cigarette smoking. For example, one study found that 'emissions of nicotine from e-cigarettes were significantly lower than those of tobacco cigarettes',[74] but another found that the metabolites of nicotine were present at similar levels in the blood of those passively exposed to tobacco smoke and those passively exposed to e-cigarette vapours.[75]

The limited research thus far suggests that although e-cigarette vapours contain some toxic substances, they do so at much lower levels than tobacco smoke.[76] However, the World Health Organization concludes that it is 'nevertheless reasonable to assume that the increased concentration of toxicants from SHA [second-hand aerosol] over background levels poses an increased risk for the health of all bystanders'.[77] Whether the levels of risk that electronic cigarette smokers impose on the non-smokers around them are sufficient to provide a harm-related reason to desist, remains to be seen. Much more research needs to be done. In the interim, it seems reasonable that electronic cigarette smokers should err on the side of caution and desist from even electronic smoking in the presence of non-smokers.

However, even those smokers who reject this precautionary harm argument, should desist from smoking electronic cigarettes in the presence of non-smokers for offence-related reasons. Electronic cigarettes produce great plumes of smoke—even more than cigarettes—as well as odours that may be unpleasant to non-smokers. The smoke and odours are intrusive and may even be irritants. They are not easy to avoid if the smoker is smoking in places where non-smokers need to be. Although the electronic smoking may be important to the smoker—perhaps even as a means of quitting—there are opportunities for this that do not intrude on non-smokers. If there is any social value in electronic smoking, it is likely to lie in reducing the amount of tobacco smoking. However, here again the social benefit can be derived without the electronic smoking taking place in the presence of non-smokers.

Consent

In principle, both the harm and offence arguments against smoking in the presence of non-smokers are at least weakened if the non-smoker is competent and gives informed consent to the smoker to smoke in his or her presence. This is because although the non-smoker may still be harmed or offended by the smoke, there is at least one sense in which he is not *wronged* if he gives consent—namely, his rights are not violated. If one thinks that we have duties to ourselves, then it may be wrong for the non-smoker to give such consent, in just the same way that the smoker might be faulted for taking up smoking. On some accounts it may even be wrong for the smoker to exploit the consent that the non-smoker should not have given. However, if it is wrong, it is much less wrong than smoking in the presence of non-smokers who have not consented.

While there are some instances of genuine consent, there are many obstacles to smokers obtaining it from non-smokers. First, it obviously cannot be obtained from children. They lack the capacity to give consent.

Second, even in the case of many adults, the smoker cannot be confident that the consent he seeks from the non-smoker would be genuine consent. Where there are power differentials—employer-employee, manager-worker, teacher-student, employer-applicant, and so forth—the person with greater power cannot be confident that any agreement obtained from the less powerful party constitutes real consent. The weaker party may not feel free to withhold consent even if the more powerful party would accept such withholding[78] and not penalize the weaker party. Even when there are not obvious power differentials, non-smokers may often feel pressured into agreeing to smokers smoking in their presence. This may take the form of peer pressure. Alternatively, it may be thought impolite to refuse a request from a smoker to be allowed to smoke. Therefore, requesting and obtaining 'consent' is often insufficient.

For this reason, it is typically better not even to request consent. In other circumstances, a smoker might say: 'Please excuse me for taking my leave, but because I do not want you to be unwillingly exposed to my cigarette smoke, I am going to smoke outside'. That approach would give the non-smoker much more scope to withhold consent—by simply allowing the smoker to leave. However, it would also allow a genuinely consenting non-smoker to respond: 'I really don't mind if you want to remain here and have your cigarette in my presence'.

A third problem is that obtaining consent is often practically impossible when there is a large and changing group of people who would be exposed to the smoke. Sometimes there are simply too many people to elicit consent effectively from them all. In public places where people are coming and going, there is no static group of people whose consent one can seek before smoking. Before a cigarette or sequence of cigarettes were finished, some new people, whose consent one will not have obtained, will have moved into the affected space.

Ifs and butts

There is nothing to be gained from starting to smoke. Becoming a smoker is to one's own detriment. For those who do become smokers, it is usually in their overall interest to cease smoking, and sooner rather than later.

However, a smoker can have a *pro tanto* interest in smoking. That interest conflicts not only with his or her own overall interest but also with the interests of non-smokers in whose presence the smoker might smoke. The way to avoid these unnecessary conflicts is not to become a smoker in the first place. However, once the conflicts exist, priority should be given to the interests of non-smokers. In other words: if one has not started smoking, do not start; if one has started, try to stop; and if one cannot stop, or stop yet, then prioritize the interests of non-smokers.

The latter involves not smoking in their presence and even not fouling spaces (such as hotel rooms) that non-smokers may later occupy.[79] In some parts of the world, smokers have either developed these sensitivities or been required by legislation or regulations to act as though they had them. One effect of rules barring smoking within buildings (other than private homes), is that smoking has shifted to just outside the entrances of these buildings. (Where entire campuses are smoke-free, the smoking shifts to just outside the entrances to the campus.) The upshot of this is that non-smokers often have to walk the gauntlet of smokers in order to enter and exit the area where smoking is prohibited. While this is not as bad as smoke-laden indoor areas, non-smokers are still subjected to some risk and offence.

This problem can also apply to newer generation restrictions that bar smoking within a specified distance from the entrance to buildings. Smokers often then congregate at that point. This does not quite lead to an infinite regress because some spaces more distant from building entrances are not ones through non-smokers need to pass. There—and in designated smoking spaces—is where smokers should go if they want to smoke. These more distant and designated spaces do not include city sidewalks where others are regularly passing. Non-smokers need to use those pavements and should not have to do so at the cost of passing through plumes of offensive smoke.

For those who smoke, there are ethical requirements beyond desisting from smoking in the presence of non-smokers. The most important of these pertain to fire and litter. Fire is the less common but the more dangerous. Many household fires are started because of the careless use of smoking materials, mainly cigarettes. Such careless use includes 'leaving a lit cigarette unattended, smoking in bed or smoking while under the influence of alcohol, illicit drugs or medication.'[80] Similarly, careless disposal of still smouldering cigarette butts outdoors can and sometimes does cause wildfires, even where smoking accounts for only a small proportion of wildfires.[81] These are all cases in which there would be 'no fire without a smoke' (as distinct from the adage that there is 'no smoke without a fire').

Such fires can and do result in the deaths of people and animals, and the destruction of homes and other property. Indeed, smoking 'is the leading cause of residential or total fire death in all eight countries with available statistics' and 'is a leading cause of fires in many more countries'.[82] Even in residential fires, the victims include not only the smokers themselves but also other members of the household. Young children and the elderly being disproportionately affected.[83] When a smoker's careless discarding of a cigarette causes a wildfire, the web of victims extends much further afield. Given the dangers and the simple precautions that can prevent them, smokers ought to exercise the caution required to avoid starting fires with their cigarettes and other smoking material.

Even when negligently discarded cigarette butts do not cause fires, they do constitute litter. About six trillion cigarettes are produced globally each year. The vast majority of those are filtered. The filter is made of cellulose-acetate, a plastic product that is not biodegradable. It is photodegradable. Ultraviolet rays break it down into smaller pieces, but the component pieces never disappear.[84] Not all cigarette butts (which include the filter) are negligently discarded. Some are placed in appropriate receptacles (and will end up in landfill).[85] However, there are millions of butts tossed to streets, gutters, sidewalks, lawns, bushes and elsewhere. (Bans on indoor smoking might partially explain why so many cigarettes are discarded outdoors.[86]) Much of this makes its way into drains, rivers, and then lakes, seas, and oceans.

We obviously cannot know exactly how many butts are littered each year, but it is clear that the number is staggering. According to Ocean Conservancy's 2018 report on the International Coastal Cleanup, cigarette butts were the most commonly collected item (ahead of food wrappers, plastic beverage bottles, plastic bottle caps, plastic bags, straws and stirrers, and everything else). Enough cigarette butts were collected to line the distance of five marathons.[87] Nor is this an aberration in a single year. Cigarette butts consistently occupy the number-one position and constitute about a third of all items collected.[88]

All this suggests that a vast number of smokers are disposing of their cigarette butts inappropriately. On the quite plausible assumption that the earth is not a giant trash can, they ought not to be doing that. The same goes for 'collateral litter', such as cigarette packaging, matches, and disposable lighters.[89]

Smokers of electronic cigarettes also need to exercise caution. Cases of (accidental and intentional) ingestion of electronic cigarette fluid, especially by young children, have become more common.[90] The severity of the deleterious effects depends on the amount ingested and the weight of the person ingesting, but death is one possible outcome.[91]

The ubiquity of cigarette ends is just one indication that we are unlikely to see the end of cigarettes—and of smoking more generally—any time soon. While tobacco was long used in the Americas before the arrival of Europeans, it was only after the latter's arrival in the so-called New World that tobacco smoking spread to other parts of the globe and was popularized. One of the early European opponents of smoking was King James I of England, a man much better known for the Bible translation that bears his name, than for his 'A Counterblaste to Tobacco'. In the latter he described smoking as 'a custom loathsome to the eye, hateful to the nose, harmful to the brain, dangerous to the lungs, and in the black stinking fume thereof, nearest resembling the horrible Stygian smoke of the Pit that is bottomless'.[92] That assessment, at least, has stood the test of time.

Appendix—Driving and smoking

Does driving cause as much (risk of) harm to non-drivers as smoking does to non-smokers? To the best of my knowledge, there are no comparable data that would enable us to answer this question with any confidence.

The absence of data is attributable to many factors. These include the absence of a common denominator. In what follows, I shall compare the number of cigarettes smoked to number of kilometres driven. That seems like a fair comparison, but even if it is, it is not obviously the only fair comparison.

There are other reasons too for the dearth of comparable data. For example, while there are approximate data for the number of cigarettes smoked, there are large data gaps in the number of kilometres driven globally. We have these data for some countries but not for others. Moreover, while there is detailed information about the risks of smoking to non-smokers, perhaps because these do, with a given denominator, vary less in different countries, the extant data on risk of driving to non-drivers specifically, is limited. This is especially true for the risk of morbidity (rather than mortality). Despite these limitations, some comparisons can be made.

Vehicles raise the risks for, and cause harm to, others in two broad ways—most obviously and directly via road accidents, but also via environmental degradation. The latter includes both local and global effects—pollution of local air, and a contribution towards global climate change. We should consider each of these and compare them with the risks and harms imposed by smoking in the presence of non-smokers.

Consider road accidents first. There are currently about 1.3 million deaths from road accidents per year, but that total figure tells us very little about the magnitude of the risk. The best measure is the number of deaths per billion kilometres driven. Unfortunately, those data are not available for the entire world, but they are available for twenty-two countries. We would expect the death rates to be lower in these mainly developed countries than they would be in poorer countries,[93] but they do reflect the risks of most of those who are reading this.

The rate of deaths per billion kilometres travelled varies by country, but (for the countries for which data are available) most are within the range of 3 (Norway) and 7.3 (United States). However, the rates for two outliers, the Czech Republic and Korea are, respectively, 11.5 and 13.8.[94] Some of these deaths are of people who had assumed the risks of driving. Thus, not all road accident deaths are analogous to smokers imposing risks on non-smokers. Nevertheless, a large proportion of road accident deaths are of pedestrians and cyclists,[95] who are among those who can most plausibly be said to have had the risks imposed on them by drivers.

How does this compare with deaths from passive smoking? Currently about 5.7 trillion[96] cigarettes are smoked globally per year and there are approximately 884 000 passive-smoking related deaths per year.[97] That amounts to about 155 passive-smoking related deaths per billion cigarettes smoked.[98] Not all cigarettes are smoked in the presence of non-smokers. Thus, the rate of deaths from passive smoking per billion cigarettes smoked in the presence of non-smokers must actually be higher.

The rate of deaths from car accidents is thus much lower than the rate of deaths from passive smoking. However, car accidents do not only cause death. Indeed, many more victims of vehicular accidents are seriously injured than are killed. Whereas there are 1.3 million road accident deaths per year, there are about 53 million serious injuries from motor vehicle accidents.[99]

Just as road accidents cause not only death but also injury, passive smoking causes not only death but also disease. However, here it is very difficult, if not impossible, to find reliable comparative data. That leaves an important gap in our understanding of the relative risk to others of injury and disease.

What about environmental and consequent health impact of driving, and how does this compare with passive smoking? Non-smoking spouses of smokers inhale the equivalent of between 0.36 and 2.79 cigarettes per day.[100] We know that motor vehicles produce known toxic substances, including carbon monoxide, nitrogen oxide, sulphur dioxide, benzene, and lead as well as particulate matter. However, this is diluted in a greater volume of air than second-hand smoke is indoors. Nevertheless, the sheer number of cars typically pollutes even vast expanses of air. The aggregated emissions from motor vehicles have a major impact on the burden of disease,[101] as do other sources of air pollution. The levels of pollution vary from place to place. Urban areas are worse than rural ones, and some cities and countries are worse than others.

Exposure to the average air pollution in the United States has been calculated[102] as the equivalent of smoking 0.4 cigarettes per day. In the European Union, the pollution is equivalent to smoking 1.6 cigarettes per day. In China the average is 2.4, but in Beijing it is 4. On a bad day in Beijing, it is 25. To see the relevance of these equivalences to the relative risks inflicted on others by smoking and by driving a car, we need to note the following. First, average air pollution is a function not only of vehicular pollution but also of industrial and other pollution.[103] Thus, not all of the above air pollution is the result of driving. Second, the air pollution required to produce the above equivalences is generated by millions of kilometres driven.

Clearly much uncertainty remains, which means that no confident conclusion may be reached. Nevertheless, it seems that the net result of the available evidence, summarized in Figure 4.2, is that the risks imposed on a non-smoker is an enclosed space are often greater than those imposed

	Passive Smoking	Driving	
Deaths from passive smoking	155 per billion cigarettes[i]	3 to ±13 per billion km[ii]	Accident fatalities
Disease from passive smoking	No reliable comparative data.		Accident injuries
Non-smoking spouse's passive smoking equivalent to actively smoking:	0.36 to 2.79 cigarettes per day[iii]	cigarettes per day[iv]: 0.4 (USA average) 1.6 (EU average) 2.4 (China average)	Inhaling air pollution equivalent to smoking:

i. Per billion cigarettes smoked, not per billion cigarettes smoked in the presence of non-smoker. Thus, the actual rate of deaths per billion cigarettes smoked in the presence of non-smokers is higher.

ii. Accident fatality rates are likely higher for developing countries for which data on fatalities per billion km is not available. But fatalities include drivers and others who are not analogous to passive smokers.

iii. Based on 1.07 hours of exposure per day, typically to the smoke of a single smoker.

iv. Aggregated from millions of km travelled by different cars. Some of this air pollution is not from vehicles.

Figure 4.2 Imposed risks from cigarettes and cars.

by a single driver through his or her vehicular emissions. The same is true through the more indirect affects that driving has on the global environment. The aggregation of millions of kilometres driven has significant destructive effects, but the contribution of any individual driving is unlikely to be greater than the harm done to passive smokers in an enclosed space.

5
Giving Aid

A life of extreme poverty is terrible. It is not called *grinding* poverty for nothing. The hardship is pervasive and unrelenting. It intrudes into every aspect of the afflicted lives. Hunger gnaws chronically, only occasionally satisfied (and then often only partially). The associated malnutrition corrodes health and, in the case of children, stunts growth and development. Access to clean water for drinking and cleaning is limited and often time-consuming. In these conditions disease ravages. The extreme poor are also more susceptible to the elements. They have inadequate, if any shelter, and thus have little protection against the wind, rain, cold, and heat. They are also hit worse by unusual natural disasters such as droughts, floods, and earthquakes. In addition, they are less able to secure themselves against the threats of criminality. Their greater vulnerability to disease, disaster, and delinquency is compounded by their lesser access to medical care. Extreme poverty cramps, cripples, and kills.

About a billion people—approximately one in eight people in the world—currently live in such poverty.[1] At least a further 4.4 billion people are poor by the standards of the developed world.[2] Their lives are typically not as bad as those of the bottom billion but, to varying degrees, they suffer some of the hardships associated with poverty and run the risk of slipping (back) into poverty.

What do the world's more affluent owe to the world's poorest people? There are at least two interpretations of this question. One might be asking what affluent *countries* (and international organizations) owe to the world's poor. Alternatively, one might be asking what affluent *individuals* owe to the world's poor. It is very likely that the problem of global poverty, like the problem of climate change, can be solved only by states (and international organizations) and not by individuals.[3] However, as long as extreme poverty persists (perhaps because states have not done what they should do), affluent individuals confront the question of what they, as individuals, must do about the problem.[4]

By 'affluent' individuals, I mean everybody who has the resources to help the poor to some degree. This includes not only the billionaires but also other high-income people (defined as living on more than $50 per person per day),[5] and at least those of the upper-middle-income people who approximate that level of resources. By this standard, the affluent likely include all those who are reading this.

There are those who think that although it is commendable to give assistance, we affluent people have no duties, in the strict sense, towards the poor.[6] However, even those who think that there is no 'stringent duty' to rescue the poor, typically think that we have *some* duty, albeit a limited one, to provide aid.[7] It would be highly implausible to think that if one could save a person's life without any cost to oneself or others, that one would have no duty to save that life.

There is thus widespread agreement that we affluent people do have some duties to the world's poor. The disagreement is about how extensive those duties are. There are some who think that the duties of the affluent towards the poor are so extensive that we ought to give away most of what we have—that we do wrong in failing to do so.

There are two broad kinds of argument for the view that affluent individuals have extensive duties to the world's poor. One is grounded in the needs of the poor and on our ability to help. On this view, the suffering of the poor, combined with our ability to relieve some of it, forms the basis for our duty. Another kind of argument grounds our duty in our involvement, often unwittingly (and typically indirectly), in causing or benefiting from the suffering of the global poor. According to this view, our duty is one of compensation for our own complicity in, or benefit from their plight. My focus will be on a famous example of the former kind of argument, although I shall also consider a compensation argument. Both these arguments, if sound, have substantial implications for how we should lead our lives.

Peter Singer's argument

Peter Singer asks us to imagine a scenario in which, while you are on your way to work, you notice a young child drowning in a pond. Nobody else is around. You could easily save the child without any risk to yourself. You would ruin your shoes, muddy your clothes and be late for work. Must you save the child, or may you allow the child to drown while you hurry on to work with your clothes undamaged? Most people, he says, think that it would be wrong to allow the child to drown.

Peter Singer utilizes this case in slightly different ways.[8] Sometimes he begins his argument with it,[9] and then provides a principle that he says explains the judgement we make in this case. On other occasions, he first presents that principle and then cites the case as an application of the principle.[10] Either way, the principle constitutes the first premise of an argument of his which has the following form:[11]

1. If we can prevent something bad from happening, without sacrificing anything of comparable moral importance, we ought to do it.
2. Extreme poverty is bad.
3. There is some extreme poverty we can prevent without sacrificing anything of comparable moral significance.
4. Therefore, we ought to prevent some extreme poverty.

The conclusion of this argument may seem modest, but that is only because the word 'some' is so vague, referring, as it does, to anything between (but not including) 'none' and 'all'. In fact, the conclusion claims that one ought to prevent as much extreme poverty as one can without sacrificing anything of comparable moral significance. The extent of one's duty thus depends on which sacrifices are and which are not of 'comparable significance'.

Peter Singer purposefully leaves the concept of 'comparable significance' unspecified because he wants the principle that constitutes the first premise of the argument to have as broad appeal as possible. More specifically, he wants this principle to appeal not only to utilitarians such as himself, but also to others. Thus, a deontologist, for example, might regard the violation of a right—or, at least certain rights—as being of comparable significance, in which case the principle would not require us to prevent that poverty which could only be prevented by violating rights.

According to Peter Singer, the principle is nonetheless a very demanding one because there are serious limits on what could plausibly be thought of as being of a moral importance comparable to extreme poverty. It seems that the principle does not require one to give away so much that one is reduced to extreme poverty oneself. This is because the extreme poverty of one person is comparable with that of another. One is entitled to meet one's own basic needs. Furthermore, perhaps some 'luxuries' are permitted if they really are needed to preserve one's capacity to generate the income needed to continue meeting one's needs and to continue giving. On this basis one would be permitted to purchase an alarm clock, but only the cheapest effective one, if that is necessary to wake up and get to work on time. If an inexpensive, reliable car is needed to get to work and one cannot live closer to work or find other, at least equally lucrative employment closer to home, that too could be justified. A personal computer may well be necessary, at least for many kinds of work.

However, at least according to Peter Singer, the principle requires one to give away everything beyond what is required to keep oneself from extreme poverty and to facilitate one's continued giving. The principle would prohibit spending money on lavish foods; any beverage other than water; a swanky car; more clothes or a bigger house than one strictly needs; theatre or cinema tickets; art, music, and home entertainment technology and subscriptions; private education for one's children; and holidays that cost anything, to name but a few of the common luxuries in which most affluent people indulge.

Although Peter Singer acknowledges that utilitarians must accept that the principle has *all* these implications, he says that those who are not utilitarians must, 'if they subscribe to the principle of universalizability, accept that at least *some* of these things are of far less moral significance than the extreme poverty that could be prevented by the money they cost'.[12] It is possible to see how Aristotelians could reach a less demanding conclusion than utilitarians, because to flourish presumably requires considerably more than merely meeting one's own basic needs. However, it is not clear why Peter Singer thinks that deontologists could plausibly say that *anything* on the above list is of comparable moral significance. Thus, he may be underestimating how extensive the principle's application is for some non-utilitarians. While deontologists could, consistent with the principle, refuse to violate rights to prevent extreme poverty, the principle does *appear* to require them to sacrifice all the same luxuries.

Peter Singer recognizes that his conclusion is a demanding one.[13] The danger of such a demanding conclusion is that many people may view it as unattainable and see no reason to give any more than the paltry amounts most people give. Thus, for pragmatic reasons, he offers a 'fall-back' position on how much affluent people should contribute. In some of his earlier work on this topic, he suggested a tithe[14]—10%—but more recently has proposed a sliding scale, beginning at 5% but increasing depending on how much one earns.[15] The fall-back position is a way of avoiding 'the best becoming the enemy of the good'. It is more demanding than common practice, but not so demanding as to appear unattainable to the vast majority of affluent people. It is thus more likely to get people to give more.[16]

It does, of course, make a difference whether giving a tithe or the relevant amount on the sliding scale is the full extent of one's duty or whether it is nothing but a good start. Peter Singer thinks it is the latter. Given that I am interested in the full extent of our duties, I shall set aside his pragmatics in this chapter, and shall assess the argument for his more demanding conclusion.

Reliability of the premises

Peter Singer's basic argument has three premises. Of these, the second—that extreme poverty is bad—is incontrovertible. The other premises, however, have been subjected to criticism.

The third premise has two components. It claims both that (i) there is some extreme poverty we can prevent; and (ii) that we can do so without sacrificing something of comparable moral significance. Some critics have noted that it is far from clear that each charitable contribution we make meets both these conditions. Given the administrative costs of running aid organizations, the inevitable wastage at various points in the chain, the amount of aid money that is spent in the aid-providing countries in order to transport the aid, the corruption in countries in which the aid is delivered, and so forth, it might well be that much of what one contributes does not do any good at all.[17] Even when it does do some good, one cannot discount the possibility that it also comes at a significant moral cost. Perhaps, for example, some poor people are fed, but this comes at the cost of keeping them under the control of militias that control access to the aid, or a country becomes aid-dependent.[18]

These are complex, partly empirical matters that cannot be resolved here. However, these issues are sufficiently weighty that there is an important disanalogy between saving a child drowning in front of one and contributing to an aid agency with the aim of saving a distant poor person's life. In the former, one's ability to save a life through one's sacrifice is far clearer than it is in the latter. That said, it does not have to be the case that charitable contributions *generally* prevent some extreme poverty without sacrificing something of comparable moral significance. Peter Singer's argument requires only that there be *some* charities (or at least one[19]) that meet these conditions—and that we can be reasonably confident that they meet the conditions.

The latter, epistemic requirement may be harder to meet than one might think. The negative effects are often downstream and not readily discernible. Even when they are discernible to aid agencies, such agencies have vested interests in these not becoming more widely known. Organizations such as Give Well[20] make it easier than it once was to make more informed decisions, but the complexity of the issues, the way the possible risks can change over time, and the limits of social science means that reasonable doubts will often remain. However, I shall set these concerns aside here and will instead focus on the first premise, even though I shall return later to a complication with the third premise.

What reason do we have to accept the first premise? Here it might be thought to make a difference what role the drowning child analogy plays in Peter Singer's argument. If the purpose of the analogy is to harness an intuition that is then used to generate the first premise, then it might seem as though the analogy provides some reason to accept the premise. The problem with this, however, is that an alternative analogy—a much better analogy for world hunger—would harness a different intuition and could generate a principle that leads to a much less demanding conclusion.

Instead of a child drowning in a pond, imagine a sea seething with drowning people.[21] Those closer to the shore are attempting to get to dry land, but many of them are prevented from doing so by some people on the shore who are pelting them with projectiles. Others on the shore are throwing children into the sea. Many of those in the sea, who find brief respite on tiny islands that appear at low tide are copulating and producing new children who, when the tide rises again, begin to drown. (We shall have to imagine a gestation period of only a few hours.) Now imagine that this is not a freak event occurring on a single day, but one that occurs every day for one's entire life. Finally, imagine that there are many people on the beach who are not exacerbating the situation, but that only a few of them are helping to alleviate it.

The additional features of this case are necessary to reflect the extended duration of the problem, the number of people in need, the fact that their plight is often caused or exacerbated by proximate agents, that the needy themselves are creating more need through procreation, and that one is not the only person who could help (insofar as trying to save people will be successful).

In such a situation, how much should you do to reduce this tragedy? I doubt that most people's intuitions would support an answer that is nearly as demanding as Peter Singer's. Intuitively one would have to do something, perhaps even quite a lot, to help, but it would not be wrong if one failed to devote to life-saving every waking minute that was not required for ensuring one's own subsistence and continued capacity for life-saving.

If we were asked what principle explained our judgement in this perennial-mass-drowning case, it would be something like: 'If you can contribute to reducing a massive ongoing tragedy without undue moral or personal sacrifice, you should do so'.[22] Such a principle would not require you to do anything immoral in pursuit of minimizing the tragedy. Nor would it require you to abandon entirely your own life projects, although it would require some, perhaps even considerable, sacrifice. Such a principle would lead to a conclusion much less demanding than Peter Singer's (ideal, even if not his pragmatic, fall-back) conclusion.

For this reason, his drowning child analogy is more charitably interpreted *not* as generating the first premise of his argument, but instead as a clear application of the principle that that premise embodies. However, if that is the case, then we must recognize that the analogy does not justify his principle. The fact that the principle produces an intuitive result when applied to this case does not, by itself, show that the principle is correct. If the same principle produces counter-intuitive results when applied to other cases, then there are also considerations against it.

The principle does indeed produce counter-intuitive results, and not only with regard to relieving the condition of the world's absolute poor. First, some have suggested that the principle is incompatible with people's having rights. If you have a right to your property, for example, then, according to the objection, it cannot be the case that you *must* give (most of) it away.[23] Similarly, if you must give away (most of) what you have then you cannot have a right to your property.

Peter Singer's response is that even if we have a *right* to retain our property it may still be the case that we *ought* to give much of it to the poor. This response is compelling if the claim is that while we should have a *legal* right to retain our property, we ought, morally, still to give much of it away. However, the response is much less plausible (although not absurd) if the claim is that while we have a *moral* right to retain our property,[24] we also have a strict moral duty to give away (much of) what we have. If one has a strict moral duty to give X away, then one cannot have a moral entitlement to keep it.

That, many people think, is incompatible with a moral right to X, which implies that one does have a moral entitlement to X.

This implication, if it is one, is arguably most disturbing in the case of a right to, or over one's body (irrespective of whether one views such rights as a form of property right). However, the point does not have to be made with reference to rights. For example, most of us could donate a kidney to save somebody's life without, it seems, our having to sacrifice anything of comparable significance.[25] Thus, according to Peter Singer's principle, we are morally required to give up a kidney under such circumstances. This is at odds with ordinary views, according to which donating a kidney is morally *heroic* rather than morally *required*. It may be morally excellent to donate a kidney, but it is not wrong to keep both one's kidneys.

Peter Singer seems willing to give up the ordinary view and accept the implication that we each ought to donate our second kidney to save a life. He cites, with apparent approval, the case of Zell Kravinsky, who (in addition to giving away millions of dollars also) donated one of his kidneys to save the life of a stranger.[26] However, if his principle has the implication of denying our rights to and over our bodies then it is a much more controversial principle than Peter Singer purports it to be. Its appeal may be restricted to utilitarians, for whom rights can be impediments to maximizing utility.

Another counter-intuitive implication of Peter Singer's principle is that it does not recognize any moral difference between (i) relieving harms one is (at least partly) responsible for having caused; and (ii) relieving harms one has *no* responsibility for having caused. The principle is concerned only with whether one can prevent something bad and makes no mention of whether the bad one can prevent is something one bears some responsibility for having brought about. In other words, the principle requires the same level of sacrifice irrespective of whether one is responsible for having caused the harm one is relieving. Yet, it intuitively seems as though we have more extensive duties to those we have (wrongfully) harmed than to those we have not. This is different from the claim that we owe *nothing* to those we have not harmed.[27]

Consider two drivers. The first chances upon a pedestrian who has been knocked over by a hit-and-run. The second (negligently) knocks over a pedestrian himself. Arguably, both drivers have a duty to stop, provide some immediate assistance, and to call an ambulance. Yet it seems that the second driver's duties are considerably more expansive. They might include paying for medical expenses, and compensating for lost earnings during the recovery period. This would be true even if the accident victim were comfortably able to pay his or her own medical expenses and could afford not to earn for a while. Although the victim can bear these costs, it is unreasonable for the driver who knocked this person over to expect the victim to bear them. The same is not true of the driver who chances upon an accident victim. Even though this driver should also provide some immediate assistance, he can expect the injured pedestrian to bear the costs of medical treatment. Even if the pedestrian could not afford those costs, the driver cannot be expected to bear these all himself. In other words, while both drivers may have duties of rescue, only one driver—the one who was responsible for having caused the injury—also has duties of compensation.

Utilitarians may well want to reject the idea that we have more extensive duties to those we harm. Indeed, utilitarians characteristically think that we are as responsible for our omissions as we are for our actions. We are thus, on their view, as culpable for failing to help those in serious need whom we have not harmed as we are for the harm that we do to others.[28] However, if Peter Singer's principle requires us to embrace this view of responsibility, including the implication that the two drivers have the same, equally demanding set of obligations, then it may well be that the principle is not as broadly accepted as it needs to be, to constitute an uncontroversial premise in the argument. Peter Singer specifically aimed to show that the principle need not appeal only to utilitarians.[29] If, upon scrutiny, the principle does, after all, have limited appeal, then the conclusion it helps generate is less secure.

There is another locus of responsibility that Peter Singer's principle does not recognize as having moral relevance. This is the *victim's* responsibility for his or her situation. More specifically, it fails to recognize any moral difference between (i) relieving harms for which the victim is not responsible; and (ii) relieving harms for which the victim *is* responsible. The principle is concerned only with whether one can prevent something bad without comparable cost, and makes no mention of whether the bad that one can prevent is the responsibility of the person one could help. Yet, it intuitively seems as though individuals may not have as extensive duties to those who have brought some evil on themselves. One could think that the *state* has an extensive duty even to such people, without being committed to thinking that individuals have the same duty.

Consider a serial drunk driver who eventually ploughs his car into a concrete wall, badly injuring himself. After you call an ambulance, he receives emergency treatment that saves his life. However, unless he receives expensive surgery, he will be paraplegic for the remainder of his life. You could pay for the surgery without sacrificing anything of comparable moral importance. Are you obliged to pay for the surgery? Many people who think that you should save the drowning child would deny that you are also obliged to save the drunk driver from paralysis. Given that Peter Singer's principle implies that you *should* pay for the surgery,[30] it may be, for this reason too, that it is not as broadly accepted as it needs to be to constitute an uncontroversial premise in the argument.

Recognizing this problem does not require one to think that the poor are responsible for their situation. The problem rests on no such dubious claim.[31] The point is that the principle used to argue for extensive duties to the world's poor also commits one to extensive duties to those who *are* responsible for their condition. That suggests a problem with the principle.

We should conclude from the foregoing considerations that the first premise of Peter Singer's argument does not have the broad appeal it may at first appear to have. It is, in fact, a deeply controversial premise, and thus hardly a secure footing for his argument.

Those who reject the first premise in favour of a more restricted alternative will reach a much less demanding conclusion than Peter Singer does. As I indicated earlier, if we sought a principle to apply to the perennial-mass-drowning case, it would be something like: 'If you can contribute to reducing a massive ongoing tragedy without undue moral or personal sacrifice, you should do so'.

But what if we sought a principle to apply to isolated rescue cases that one might encounter, such as Peter Singer's drowning child? One possibility, adapted from a suggestion by John Arthur, is: 'If we can prevent something bad from happening *to an innocent* without sacrificing anything of *substantial* importance, we should do it'.[32]

There are two differences between these rules. First, whereas Peter Singer's rule speaks of 'preventing something bad from happening', John Arthur's rule adds 'to an innocent'. This addition addresses the problem presented by cases where the person to whom something bad will happen (or is happening) is responsible for this condition. A victim's responsibility for his or her own need could factor into John Arthur's principle because those who are responsible for their condition would not be innocent in the relevant sense. This is not to say that we should never save those who are responsible for their condition. John Arthur's principle does not preclude saving such people. It merely has nothing to say about such cases.

There is also an important difference between Peter Singer's 'comparable (moral) importance' and John Arthur's 'substantial importance'. The former involves a *comparison* between the bad one could prevent and the sacrifice that would be required to prevent that bad, whereas the latter focuses only on the importance of what one would need to sacrifice. The former is also considerably more demanding. Although it does not require sacrifices that are 'equivalent' to, or even 'nearly as bad as', the bad that could be prevented, one would be required to make any sacrifice that fell short of 'nearly as bad', because such a sacrifice would not compare, even approximately, with the bad that could be prevented. The 'substantial importance' formulation requires much less. If a sacrifice is not comparable to the bad that it could avert it would not be required if it was nonetheless a sacrifice of 'substantial importance'.

This is depicted in Figure 5.1, which compares Peter Singer's and John Arthur's respective principles, and more specifically the difference between 'comparable significance' and 'substantial significance'.

In Figure 5.1, the height of each bar is indicative of how bad something is. A is the serious harm one can prevent—perhaps somebody dying from starvation. B is a sacrifice that, while not *equal* to A, is nonetheless *comparable* to it. This sacrifice is thus *not* required according to Peter Singer's rule. The sacrifice reflected in C is not comparable and thus *is* required by Professor Singer's rule. However, because C is (plausibly) a sacrifice of 'substantial significance', it is not required by John Arthur's principle. Sacrifice D

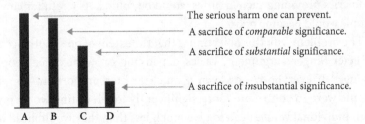

Figure 5.1 Comparing Peter Singer's and John Arthur's rules.

is (plausibly) a sacrifice of 'insubstantial significance', and thus is required by John Arthur's principle.

The counter-intuitive implications of Peter Singer's principle are largely avoided by the revised John Arthur principle. Of course, the latter would require *some* sacrifice of material resources, with the upshot that one did not have an all-things-considered (moral) right to those resources, but this is much less controversial than the claim that one does not have an all-things-considered right to *most* of one's property. However, it would *not* require one to give most of what one has, because that would be a substantial sacrifice. It would certainly not require one to donate a kidney, although doing so would be praiseworthy. Because one's general duties to those in need would be limited, there would be plenty of scope for additional duties to those for whose plight one bears some responsibility.

We may conclude, therefore, that one reasonable response to Peter Singer's argument is to deny the first premise of that argument. If it is replaced with a more reasonable principle, we shall still be required to contribute to relieving suffering, but the extent of that duty will be much more limited.

Demanding conclusion

However, let us set the premises of the argument aside for the moment, in order to consider the conclusion of Peter Singer's argument. A common objection to that conclusion is that it has unacceptable implications. This is taken as evidence that it must be mistaken (either because at least one of the premises is false or because there is a mistaken inference to the conclusion, at least as he understands the conclusion).

His conclusion does not always have the implications it is thought to have. For example, some argue that if everybody were to give up all their luxuries to contribute to the world's poor, the economy would collapse, because entire industries providing such luxuries would be ruined. As a result, many more people would become poor.

The problem with this objection is that the extent of one's duty, according to Peter Singer's argument, varies depending on what other people are giving.[33] If everybody—or even a much greater proportion—of affluent people were to contribute more significantly to alleviating world poverty, each individual would need to give much less than they would need to give if only a small proportion of people are contributing to this cause. On either scenario, the luxury industries and economy need not collapse. If most or all affluent people were giving their fair share to alleviate poverty, then they would still have plenty left over for luxuries. However, if most affluent people are not helping the poor to any significant extent, then the few who do give away all their spare resources need not worry that their contributing so much would lead to the collapse of the luxury industries and thus the economy.

However, there are genuine implications of Peter Singer's conclusion that are very plausibly thought to be unacceptable. Most importantly, his conclusion, at least as he understands it, requires considerable self-sacrifice. As we saw, this includes non-vital organs, such as a second kidney, if one can thereby save a life. Nor do the demands end here, at least for utilitarians. One might be able to save *five* lives by donating *all* one's vital organs (before one's own need for them had been exhausted). This would come at the cost of one's own life, but is the loss of one life of comparable importance to the loss of five lives? All things being equal, utilitarians would have to answer this question in the negative. Of, course, all things are often not equal. If, for example, those who one would save are not likely, in aggregate, to do more ongoing good than one could do if one did not sacrifice one's own life on this occasion, then the utilitarian would not require one to donate one's organs in that situation.

Even if we concede that the sacrifice will often be of comparable (or greater) moral significance, there may be circumstances in which a utilitarian acting on Peter Singer's principle will be required, literally, to sacrifice her own life to save the lives of others. The greater the number of other lives one can save through one's own death, the more likely it is that according to the utilitarian one is required, all things considered, to make that sacrifice. Similarly, the younger those one could save are, and the older one is, the more likely, all else being equal, that one would be morally required to sacrifice one's own life. (All else would not equal in the transplant case if one's organs were now too old.)

Non-utilitarians may be able to resist this conclusion by treating the sacrifice of one's own life as of comparable significance to the bad one prevents for any one of the individuals one would otherwise be able to save, and by refusing to aggregate lives. However, even though the conclusion may not bind them to sacrificing their biological life, it seems to require them, as it requires utilitarians, to sacrifice their lives in a figurative sense. To a very considerable extent one is required to give up one's own projects and pleasures, for unless these involve preventing very bad things from happening, forgoing them does not amount to a sacrifice of comparable moral importance.

Hobbies, sport, reading, gastronomy, theatre, and cinema all consume resources, whether financial or temporal or both. *Some* recreation may be necessary to keep one productive, but Peter Singer's conclusion would limit this to the minimum necessary. One's recreation would be restricted to the least amount of the least costly recreation required to generate the most possible resources for good causes.

Nor is it merely recreational activities that are expansively regulated by Peter Singer's conclusion. For many affluent people one of their biggest and most enduring projects is their work or profession. The lucky ones gain some satisfaction from their vocation. As this yields resources with which one can help those in need, one need not necessarily forsake such satisfaction. That is, unless one could generate more resources by switching professions. Even if such a switch reduced one's professional satisfaction, it may nonetheless be required because professional satisfaction is not *per se* of comparable importance to a life, at least according to Peter Singer's demanding standards.

Of course, if one would be so thoroughly unhappy in some alternative profession that one would be unable to keep at it, and thus unable to continue generating resources, then switching to that profession might indeed be a sacrifice of comparable importance. However, there would be an imperative to choose the most lucrative tolerable line of work. To opt for a less lucrative but more satisfying career option is to fail to prevent something very bad (the deaths one can prevent with additional resources) from happening, even though the sacrifice (greater professional satisfaction) would not be of comparable moral importance. In short, Peter Singer's conclusion imposes very stringent restrictions on which professions one might pursue.

Another important project for many people is producing and rearing children. Rearing children in the developed world costs an immense amount— between around two hundred thousand and three hundred thousand dollars for the period from birth to age eighteen. Of course, costs do not end then. Tertiary education, in particular, is especially expensive. If affluent people were to forgo becoming parents, they would have plenty of additional disposal income to contribute towards saving the world's poor.[34] Forgoing having children is a sacrifice. However, if one accepts Peter Singer's demanding standards, the importance of the sacrifice is not *comparable* to the bad that the sacrifice aims to prevent. Peter Singer himself does not recognize this, but it may nonetheless be what his demanding standards commit him to recognizing,[35] especially given the further environmental costs that procreation has.[36] (I happen to think that procreation is morally wrong, but not for the reasons Peter Singer's argument would suggest.)[37]

Voluntary servitude

It is often said that the conclusion of Peter Singer's argument (as distinct from his fall-back position) is 'excessively demanding'. That may be an understatement. It requires one to give up all personal projects and pleasures except insofar as these do not detract, even indirectly, from relieving as much of the world's bountiful misery as one is personally able to relieve. Those who comply with the conclusion enter ('voluntary') servitude. Their lives are devoted, at least beyond their own biological survival, to serving the basic ends of others. They may derive some, even immense satisfaction from such a life, but that is incidental. They are in ('voluntary') servitude. Of course, the servitude is voluntary only in the sense that nobody is literally forcing them into it. However, there is an important sense in which, on Peter Singer's argument, the servitude is *not* voluntary—namely, it is morally required. One can refuse the servitude but only on pain of violating one's purported moral duties. If they are to act in accordance with their duties, they *must* become servants.

Herein lies a possible response to Peter Singer's conclusion, at least for non-utilitarians. According to this response, one can accept all the argument's premises, but deny that these entail so demanding a conclusion. One can say this if a life of servitude compares in moral importance to extreme poverty. To live such a life is to reduce oneself to near subsistence level and to give up everything that enriches life—including various sensory pleasures, appreciation of the arts, intellectual stimulation, and the experience of visiting other parts of the world. Living a life of servitude involves choosing the career that will generate the most possible resources for others, rather than the one that will bring oneself satisfaction (or surplus resources). It also involves forgoing having children so that one can devote the resources that would be used to rear them to instead save the offspring of others who are procreating apace.

The suggestion is not that a life without luxuries is as bad as a life without the basics, or that a life without professional satisfaction or children is as bad as dying. After all, the first premise of Peter Singer's argument is not: 'If we can prevent something bad from happening, without sacrificing anything *(nearly? as) bad*, we ought to do it'. Instead, the premise is: 'If we can prevent something bad from happening, without sacrificing *anything of comparable moral importance*, we ought to do it'. Perhaps for utilitarians, the latter reduces to the former, but the latter formulation was specifically chosen to broaden the principle's appeal. Thus, there must be at least some scope for thinking that two fates might not be as bad as one another, while thinking that subjecting oneself to the less bad fate in order to spare somebody else from the other, is nonetheless a sacrifice of comparable moral importance. A sacrifice of 'comparable moral importance' may be a sacrifice that one cannot morally be asked to make.

Given the inevitable imprecision here, we should not expect to be able to prove definitively that a life of servitude is (or is not) of 'comparable moral importance'. However, there are some considerations that lend support to the view that it is.

First, Peter Singer allows that non-utilitarians could treat rights violations as being of 'comparable moral importance'. Even if we think that minor rights violations, such as small thefts here and there, do not compare in moral importance to death, one could think that stealing the vast bulk of somebody's resources, thereby leaving them with enough to meet only their basic needs, would amount to a sufficiently serious rights violation. Similarly forcing somebody into servitude—making them work, providing them with the basics in return, but using the bulk of the resources they generate for use by others—is a plausible candidate for a serious rights violation.

There is a difference, of course, between having most of one's property taken from one and giving the same amount of one's property away. There is similarly a difference between being forced into servitude and voluntarily entering into it. However, even if, in each comparison, the former is worse than the latter, the differential badness is reduced if morality really does oblige (that is, 'force') one to give away much of what one has and to enter servitude. Therefore, there is some reason for non-utilitarians to think that the sacrifices are of comparable moral importance.

Second, imagine a world in which extreme poverty had ended. In this improved world (almost) all humans have their basic needs met. However, a billion or so people have no more than that. They subsist in servitude, often doing work from which they derive no satisfaction. While they are entitled to share life with a (willing) partner, they are not allowed the resources that would enable them to rear children. They have few if any luxuries. Peter Singer would very likely, and appropriately, take the condition of these people to be a bad. It would surely not be as bad as extreme poverty, but it nonetheless would be sufficiently bad that we would be called upon to alleviate it if we could do so without sacrificing anything of comparable moral importance. If this condition is just one level up from extreme poverty, then a sacrifice that reduces one to this level may well be of '*comparable* moral importance' even though it is not of '*equivalent* moral importance'.

Those who think that reducing ourselves to servitude is a comparable moral cost will reach a conclusion about our duties that is less demanding than Peter Singer's. According to this view, his argument does not prohibit all luxuries. One is permitted to live significantly above subsistence levels. Moreover, it will sometimes favour more expensive luxuries over some less expensive ones, namely if the more expensive ones are also more important ones. For example, a trip abroad to reunite with close family is costlier than a bottle of champagne, but forgoing the former will likely be a greater sacrifice than the latter.[38]

Peter Singer explicitly rejects a version of the view I have outlined here, albeit one that does not identify a life lived in accordance with the full extent of his conclusion as a life of voluntary servitude.[39] His response is to say that although a 'rich and varied life ... may be the most desirable form of life for a human being in a world of plenty, it is wrong to assume that it remains a good life in a world in which buying luxuries for oneself means accepting the continued avoidable suffering of others'.[40] He provides the analogy of a doctor who encounters hundreds of injured victims of a train crash, and says that it would be wrong for the doctor to treat fifty of the patients and then head to the opera on the grounds that the opera is part of an enriched life. We, he says, are all in the situation of the doctor.

One major problem with this response is that, in fact, we are not in the situation of the doctor. The doctor is facing an emergency that will pass. Giving up the opera on this single occasion is not an immense personal sacrifice. We are instead in the situation of those beholding, every single day of their lives, a sea filled with drowning people, and we are being asked (if we accept Peter Singer's view about the full extent of our duties) to devote all our lives to the service to others. Following this view, we may serve ourselves only to the extent that this does not detract from serving others and, in the case of the non-utilitarian, in order to meet our basic needs.[41]

This is why there is a problem with *generalizing* the application of the principle that constitutes the first premise of Peter Singer's argument. Even if it is reasonable in individual cases or in temporary emergencies to require people to make significant sacrifices to prevent greater evils, it may not be reasonable to require people to make such sacrifices all the time.[42] A sacrifice made in an individual situation (such as a child drowning in a pond) or in a temporary emergency (such as attending to multiple injured victims of a train accident) may not be sacrifices comparable in moral importance to the ills they are preventing. Yet, when the same sacrifices are required all the time, they do become comparable because they crowd out any opportunity to lead one's own life in keeping one's own preferences.

What we have here is a kind of moral sorites problem. A regular (that is, non-moral) sorites problem arises in the following way:

1. A million grains of sand amount to a heap of sand.
2. A heap of sand minus a grain of sand remains a heap (because the difference between a heap and no heap is not a single grain).

If we iterate 2. enough times we are led to the conclusion that a single grain of sand is a heap of sand. But that conclusion is absurd, for a single grain of sand is not a heap of sand.

There are various ways in which philosophers have sought to solve this problem. What is clear, however, is that there *is* a problem to solve. Removing one grain does not a non-heap make, but if one removes enough grains one no longer has a heap. Similarly, in the moral case. There may be no sharp line on the spectrum of sacrifices demarcating when a modest sacrifice we are required to make becomes an extensive sacrifice that we are not required to make, but that does not mean that there is no difference between the former and the latter.

Thus, the premises of Peter Singer's argument may all be true without their leading to a conclusion as demanding as he presumes. This would be because the third premise may be false if we assume the extensive scope of 'some' that he presumes, and yet may be true if we assume a more restrictive scope. In other words, there is 'some' extreme poverty that we can prevent without sacrificing anything of comparable moral significance, but not as much as Peter Singer thinks. This is because preventing the amount of extreme poverty he thinks we can prevent, *would* require sacrifices of comparable significance. If the scope of 'some' in the third premise is limited, then it must be limited to the same degree in the conclusion.

The plausibility of the servitude argument diminishes the further one moves away from the subsistence level. The more luxurious one's life, the less plausible it is to say that sacrificing some of the sumptuousness would be of comparable moral importance to extreme poverty. It will be very difficult to determine precisely where one's duty ends, and supererogation begins. The servitude argument thus provides not only a less demanding but also a less precise conclusion about the extent of our duties than Peter Singer's argument does. That, however, may be a strength. It may well be that the extent of our duties is much more vague than extreme conclusions (on both sides of the spectrum) would suggest.

Insurance

Even if one thinks that reducing oneself to servitude is not a sacrifice of comparable importance to extreme poverty, it may still be the case that one does not have to help the poor as much as Peter Singer thinks—*yet*!

According to Peter Singer's argument, we have a duty to prevent extreme poverty only if we can do so without sacrificing something of comparable moral importance. If servitude does not count as a sacrifice of comparable moral importance, then other fates that might later befall one may well meet the condition.

For example, one might well someday require life-saving medical or surgical therapy. In some parts of the world, but not others, the state will cover the costs of such therapy. Where it does, the likelihood that it will continue to cover those costs in the future may vary from jurisdiction to jurisdiction. Otherwise, one might be dependent on health insurance. Purchasing such insurance would likely be permissible under Peter Singer's conclusion. However, health insurance often does not cover all needs. Moreover, those who can now purchase insurance can quickly lose the ability to do so if they lose their jobs, a phenomenon that is far from unknown. Without a job, many people can no longer generate resources to cover their other basic needs. Some of them live in states that provide adequate unemployment benefits, but many people cannot count on the state to help them if they no longer have an income. Their basic needs will then be unmet.

In other words, those who can meet their basic needs now may require substantial resources to meet those needs later if some unfortunate fate (such as illness or loss of job) befalls them (or, less often, if the state in which they live, becomes a failing or failed state). If those resources have been given away then the extreme poverty those resources (hopefully) prevented, will have involved a sacrifice of comparable moral importance. This suggests that one would be entitled, even according to Peter Singer's argument, to save considerable amounts as personal insurance against unfortunate fates. We might call this the 'personal insurance proviso'—or, perhaps, the 'Unlockean proviso', namely that one should give only to the extent that 'there is enough, and as good, left for oneself'.[43]

How much Peter Singer's argument would permit one to save would depend on multiple factors. These would include the level of state health and unemployment insurance, the reliability of the state to continue providing such support, the reliability of the state to protect one more generally, one's job vulnerability, and the number of one's dependents. In addition, there is a question about what the appropriate level of risk aversion is. In other words, just how cautious is one entitled to be in planning for future possible calamities?

However, in all cases, invoking the 'personal insurance proviso' to justify giving less now to prevent or alleviate extreme poverty, is not a license for living a more luxurious life. The savings that this proviso permits within the framework of Peter Singer's argument are justified only insofar as they insure against sacrifices whose importance is comparable to extreme poverty. It is a license to save resources to ward off catastrophes rather than to spend those resources on luxuries. Typically, one would save and invest as an insurance against future misfortune, but with a provision in one's will that the resources be used, upon one's death, to prevent bad. That is, at least, if one leaves no dependents. If one does, then there may be a case for keeping the resources in trust in case these are needed to rescue the dependents from catastrophe.

Some might worry that this intergenerational transfer could be justified *ad infinitum* and thus a delay in charitably giving would end up as never giving. However, there are a few considerations that militate against such an implementation of the personal insurance proviso. First, to the extent that Peter Singer's argument does require voluntary servitude, it requires the world's affluent to desist from procreating (until absolute poverty has been eradicated). Thus, any affluent person acting strictly in accord with that interpretation of Peter Singer's argument, should not have children and thus subsequent offspring in the further future. Instead, the conscientious and consistent adherent of the hyper-demanding conclusion of Professor Singer's argument, may have a surviving spouse, or siblings, but no progeny. They might sometimes have adopted children. However, because the resources to rear even adopted children could probably do more good saving others, most genuine adherents of Peter Singer's view would not even have adopted children. This limits the temporal horizon.[44]

Second, control over the resources one leaves in one's estate erodes with time after one's death. Even trusts can be depleted, or the terms of the trusts overturned. Thus, even if one had violated the anti-procreative implications of the hyper-demanding conclusion, and had children, the argument would discourage saving for too far into one's post-mortem future.

Third, and relatedly, is the discount rate. The further in the future some bad will occur, the less sure we can be that it will occur at all, or that the resources one bequeaths would prevent it. It becomes harder and harder to justify holding resources to prevent some future harm to one's progeny. In any event, beyond one's grandchildren or possibly great-grandchildren, one's offspring are as strangers to one and thus withholding resources to save them rather than other strangers, but ones whose lives overlap with one's own, will be harder to justify.

Perhaps some extreme altruists will employ the discount rate to ward off the personal insurance proviso. In other words, they might argue that instead of saving resources for the mere possibility of saving oneself later, we should spend it now to save lives we know are currently endangered. They might also argue that one is not warranted in saving one's own life if the resources required to do so could be used to save many other lives. This, they might say, is to give excessive weight to one's own life—that is, to value one's life more than the lives of others.

Utilitarians may indeed embrace such conclusions. However, insofar as the premises of Peter Singer's argument really can be accepted not only by utilitarians but also by non-utilitarians, his argument cannot commit everybody to such conclusions. The argument must allow a non-utilitarian to save his own life later even if, with the same resources, he could save the lives of a greater number of others sooner.

Restitution

In criticizing the first premise of Peter Singer's argument, I noted that it made no distinction between (i) relieving harms one is (at least partly) responsible for having caused; and (ii) relieving harms one has *no* responsibility for having caused. This, I said, is a problem because our duties are more extensive in the former case than they are in the latter.

Peter Singer's argument does not assume that the world's affluent bear any responsibility for global poverty. His argument is predicated only on the needs of the poor and the ability of (relatively) rich individuals to meet some of those needs. However, there is a different, but not incompatible, kind of argument in support of duties to aid the world's poor. This kind of argument is based on the claim that the world's affluent *are* partly responsible for global poverty—and that they benefit from the plight of the poor. The affluent thus owe compensation to the poor.[45]

In support of this conclusion, it is noted that the current global economic and political order is stacked in favour of the affluent, developed world. This is unsurprising, given the superior bargaining power of the richer countries in the negotiations that lead to international agreements.[46] The global order also props up corrupt and oppressive dictators and oligarchies by selling them weapons and allowing them to borrow money and sell national resources, all of which are used to further subjugate their people.[47]

Of course, most individuals in affluent countries are not directly or wittingly involved in such practices. However, their governments and some of the agents acting on behalf, or with the consent of their governments are directly and knowingly involved. Those agents are negotiating and reaching agreements, they are selling arms, approving loans, and so forth. The suggestion is that individual members of these countries are complicit in the actions of those who act on their behalf.

This last claim is not uncontroversial. Is an individual really complicit in everything his or her government does? What if that individual voted *against* the government? What if he or she, despite voting *for* the governing party (on a balance of considerations), does not support those of its policies or positions that result in exacerbating the problems of poorer countries? These are hardly unusual scenarios. Very often one votes for a candidate or party only because the alternative is worse.

For these reasons, it may well be that 'responsibility for' or 'complicity' in the actions of one's state is not as strong a basis for individuals' duties as are other factors. For example, benefiting from injustice can ground a duty to compensate, even if one benefited unwillingly and was appalled by and in no way complicit in the injustice. Imagine, for example, that a criminal routinely makes deposits into your bank account and sends anonymous notes to advise you that the deposits are from the sale of goods stolen in a particular neighbourhood. You are not responsible for those thefts, or for the deposits into your account (which, I presume, you cannot stop), but you are a beneficiary, albeit an unwilling one. That you are a beneficiary of injustice is sufficient to think that you should compensate for those unjust credits, perhaps by contributing them to funding increased law enforcement in that neighbourhood. This, of course, is not exactly the same situation as that of inhabitants of affluent countries. However, it does illustrate how being a beneficiary of injustice can be sufficient to generate a duty of compensation. Inhabitants of affluent countries[48] benefit from current trade and other arrangements that favour the wealthier countries in which they live. They owe compensation as a result.

Another way in which the affluent tend to benefit unfairly at the expense of the poor is via the externalities of activities undertaken disproportionately by the developed world. (Externalities, in this context, are indirect costs not born exclusively by a consumer, but rather shared by others not benefiting from the activities.) For example, global climate is disproportionately influenced by the high-level producers and consumers among the world's affluent, but the effects are felt disproportionately by the world's poorest people.[49]

Thus, there are at least some good grounds for thinking that the world's affluent have duties of compensation to the world's poor. How extensive are these duties? If we were speaking about the duties of rich *countries*, then the duties would be substantial. Ample compensation is owed not only for the various forms of injustice and unfairness mentioned above but also for the past theft of land and resources, colonization and dispossession, enslavement, and violence.

My focus here, however, is on the duties of individual affluent people. What each of them owes is not as large a share of what their country owes as he or she can possibly bear, but rather a fair share of that debt. A *fair* share is typically not the same as an *equal* share. One's fair share will be influenced by the total compensation debt of one's country or region, by the ability of one's compatriots to contribute to paying this debt, the extent to which one has personally benefited unfairly, and the extent to which one has personally been complicit.

Peter Singer explicitly rejects the idea that each person's duty is limited to his or her fair share. However, he rejects that limitation in the context of his own argument. He asks us to imagine a variant on his drowning child case. Instead of a single child, there are ten children drowning.[50] You and nine other adults are all able to wade in and save a child. You save one child, expecting each of the other adults to do likewise. However, you notice that while four of them have done so, five have walked on without saving any children. Having done your fair share, may you now allow five children to die?

Peter Singer's answer—and mine—is that you may not. It is a separate question, as I hope that I have shown, whether we should generalize from this to the case of world poverty. Either way, the suggestion that a fair share is the full extent of one's duty to the world's poor has greater force in the context of a compensation argument than it does in the context of Peter Singer's argument.

It is easy to see what difference these contexts make. Peter Singer's argument is based on the needs of the poor and the ability of the affluent to help (without sacrificing anything of comparable importance). If others are not assisting the poor, their needs do not thereby evaporate. Nor is one's own ability to assist diminished. Thus, we can see how we might, at least in passing emergencies, be expected to exceed our fair share. However, insofar as one's duties are those of compensation, based on one's complicity or unjust enrichment, one's duty is to compensate the amount one owes—rather than the amount others owe. That amount is not (typically) going to change if others who owe compensation are not paying what they owe. This is especially true if one's duties of compensation are generated, as they are in the case of world poverty, by very indirect or imperceptible contributions to or benefits from global ills.

Conclusions

What do you and I owe the world's poor? Peter Singer's (ideal, even if not his fall-back) answer is 'as much as we can without sacrificing anything of comparable moral importance'. Because he thinks that very little is of comparable moral importance, his own conclusion results in very extensive duties. However, if we accept his view of what constitutes 'comparable moral importance' our duties may be more extensive than even he recognizes. We would be required to give up all of our personal projects and pleasures, unless these were congruent with preventing things as bad as extreme poverty. This could include satisfying work, and having and rearing children.

Giving up this much, amounts to a form of (voluntary) servitude, I have argued. But accepting servitude is a plausible candidate for a sacrifice that compares in moral importance to extreme poverty. If that is the case, then Peter Singer's argument leads to a conclusion that is at least quite a bit less demanding than he thinks. Although a life of lavish consumption would still be precluded, one would be permitted to pursue at least some projects and pleasures that enrich life—including a satisfying profession and family life, hobbies, sport, reading, gastronomy, theatre, cinema, and travel, albeit all in moderation. One would also be permitted to save as a personal insurance policy against future threats to the life and essential well-being of oneself and of those who one holds dear.

This all applies even if we accept the first premise of Peter Singer's argument. However, I argued that there is good reason not to accept it. If we substitute that premise for a more reasonable one, we find that while we still have a duty to assist the poor, the extent of that duty is again not as great as Peter Singer suggests.

Whether we opt for an alternative to the first premise, or count voluntary servitude as a bad of 'comparable moral importance', the revised standard of giving is considerably vaguer than is Peter Singer's. The greater vagueness may count in its favour. It would be odd if the boundary between reasonable pursuit of one's own projects over the course of one's life, and assisting others in dire need, were not very fuzzy.

Vagueness also has its disadvantages, however. Without a relatively precise indication of how much affluent people should give, it's more likely that people will delude themselves that they need not sacrifice (much) more than they already are giving. This may be one reason why Peter Singer, in offering a 'fall-back' position on how much affluent people should contribute, mentions very specific proportions of one's income. It is not unreasonable, as a practical rather than theoretical matter, to stipulate precise amounts if they are in the correct range.

However, the actual reason Peter Singer provides for his 'fall-back' sliding scale of required contributions is that he does not want to turn off those who feel that they cannot meet the demanding standards he thinks his arguments require, and therefore give only paltry amounts.[51] He does not consider the possibility that he might be turning people off by indicating that this level of giving is only the beginning of their duty. This would be especially tragic if, as I think, morality does not require as much as he says it does.

According to Peter Singer's argument, we have a duty to prevent bad things from happening. Extreme poverty is bad, but it is not the only bad. Among other evils are those of repressive regimes (including ones not especially marked by extreme poverty), anthropogenic climate change, and the maltreatment of animals. The upshot of Professor Singer's argument is that one could discharge all one's duties if one contributed all one's spare resources to causes other than extreme poverty, at least if those other causes were as effective in preventing evils that are at least as bad.

Compensation arguments, however, would probably not permit this. If compensation is owed to the world's poor, then one must pay one's fair share of that. Similarly, if it is the case that one is complicit in or benefits from the maltreatment of animals or from political repression, for example, one would have to direct at least some of one's giving, as compensation, to causes that relieve those problems. Thus, compensation arguments, either alone or in combination with needs-ability arguments, require a more diverse programme of giving.[52] Such a programme of giving, might also produce conflicts between the different components. For example, saving humans lives might lead to the loss of more animal lives (because so many of the humans saved would then eat animals). Such considerations make the already complex decisions about our duties to give aid even more complicated.

6

Consuming Animals

Humans have been eating animals and using their products for as long as there have been humans. Members of our species eat the flesh of animals, wear their fur, use their hides, eat their eggs, drink their milk, and use various parts of their bodies in myriad products. The number of animals killed and used (even per human capita), was originally much smaller than it became, about ten or fifteen thousand years ago, when humans domesticated certain species and reared them for human use. The numbers increased exponentially with the emergence and growth of intensive animal farming (or what is often known as 'factory farming')[1] over the past two centuries, and with the massive increase in fishing.

Death and suffering

Humans now kill many billions of animals every year in the meat, egg, and dairy industries.[2] This includes over 302 million cows,[3] in excess of 450 million goats,[4] more than 573 million sheep,[5] nearly 1.5 billion pigs,[6] and close to 69 billion chickens.[7] The last of these figures excludes the billions of male chicks who are killed soon after hatching because they cannot produce eggs. More than 127 billion aquatic animals are killed annually.[8] At least some of these numbers are underestimates.[9] To these gargantuan numbers, we need to add the killings of ducks, turkeys, geese, other birds, as well as rabbits, rodents, buffalo, dogs, cats, horses, donkeys, and camels.[10]

The trend has been for the number of animals killed to increase with each passing year, not least because the growth in the human population has increased the overall demand for animal flesh and products, even though some people are reducing their own consumption of animals. The deaths, and in many cases also the lives, of these animals are marked by significant pain and suffering. The facts should be familiar.

Very Practical Ethics. David Benatar, Oxford University Press. © Oxford University Press 2024.
DOI: 10.1093/9780197780831.003.0006

Chickens

Consider chickens first. Almost no chickens live for the three to seven years that constitute their natural lifespan.[11] Because male chicks will never lay eggs and do not grow large enough to become broilers (chickens specifically reared to provide meat), most are killed within days of hatching.[12] The methods by which they are killed include maceration (that is shredding), gassing, electrocution, and suffocation. Female chicks generally live only a little longer—between one and two months—if they are broilers. Those used as layer hens are not killed until their cohort's egg production declines, which is usually between one and two years.

It is not clear that the additional quantity of life is an advantage, given its appalling quality under intensive farming conditions. These stressful conditions lead to aggressive behaviour. To prevent the injuries that would result from the birds pecking one another, the chicks are debeaked, often using a high-temperature guillotine, usually without anaesthetic. Most egg-laying hens are housed in 'batteries'—cramped wire cages in which the birds live their lives. These conditions prevent them from engaging in natural chicken behaviour, including wing flapping, feather ruffling, preening, ground scratching, and dust bathing. Hens experience many health problems. These include foot problems from standing on wire, feather loss from stress, osteoporosis, and, as a result of high levels of ammonia and other toxic gases from excretions, various infections.

In the United States, but not in the European Union, layer hens are subjected to forced moulting by means of food and sometimes even water deprivation. When the hens are 'spent' and can no longer lay eggs, they are sent for slaughter. They are roughly removed from their cages, stuffed in cramped crates, and transported by trucks to the place of slaughter.

Broiler hens, those bred to provide meat rather than eggs, while not housed in battery cages, suffer overlapping fates with layer hens. They are bred to reach slaughter weight as quickly as possible. This may be good for farmers and those who consume chickens, but it is not good for the chickens who suffer many welfare problems as a result. These include cardiovascular problems, which can result in relatively sudden or prolonged and painful deaths. Their disproportionate breast muscle puts strain on their skeletal system, which makes walking painful. The space to walk diminishes as they grow and find themselves 'beak[13] by fowl' (the avian equivalent of 'cheek by jowl') in the rearing shed. They too suffer the adverse health effects of exposure to high levels of ammonia from the accumulating excreta.

The method of slaughtering chickens varies, but the most common mass slaughter method is to shackle the birds upside down by their feet on a conveyer belt that then moves the birds' heads through an electrified stun bath. In theory, this is meant to render them unconscious before their throats are slit by spinning blades further down the conveyer system, from whence they are taken to a scalding tank to defeather them. In practice, some birds are not unconscious when their throats are slit or when they enter the scalding tank.

While billions of chickens are being killed, billions more are produced, in order to continue the supply of flesh and eggs. The new generations are not produced the old-fashioned way—chicken sex. Instead, select males are masturbated by human handlers, who collect the semen and then insert it, via plastic syringes, into the vaginas of hens.

Pigs

While pigs are sometimes allowed to mate, it is much more common for porcine conception in intensive farming to be the combined result of masturbating boars and then artificially inseminating sows. Except for the limited number of jurisdictions in which gestation crates are partially or completely banned, pregnant sows are kept in these highly confined stalls, which are so small that the sows cannot even turn around. Shortly before giving birth, the sows are moved to farrowing crates, which are only slightly larger. The sows remain immobilized in these crates, which have adjacent troughs from which the piglets can suckle. Sows spend almost the entire duration of their short lives in such confined circumstances, before they are sent for slaughter.

Piglets are subjected to such procedures as castration, tail docking, and teeth clipping—usually without anaesthetic. These procedures, like debeaking in chickens, are aimed at countering the effects of aggressive behaviour that results from the stresses of living in very confined spaces with their conspecifics. Pigs are brought to slaughter weight within about six months, far short of the twenty-seven-year lifespan they could otherwise have.[14] Many of them live their truncated lives in environments devoid of stimulation.

Pigs, like other animals, are often transported, without adequate hydration, in cramped conditions over long distances to slaughterhouses. In some places there is no requirement to stun them before they are hoisted by a hind leg and have their throats cut. In other places stunning—by electric current, captive bolts, or carbon dioxide—is required before the animal is exsanguinated. However, given the large number of animals being 'processed', there are cases where a conscious pig has its throat slit or is even dropped into the scalding tank to loosen its bristles.

Cattle

Cattle are most commonly bred for their milk (dairy), and for their flesh (beef and veal). Tail docking, dehorning, branding, castration, all without anaesthesia, are common.

In the dairy industry, calves are removed from their mothers at birth, because the milk they would consume would be milk not available to the dairy industry. These separations of mother and calf cause great emotional distress to both. Because male calves are 'useless', they are typically either killed at birth or sent to veal crates.

Veal crates confine calves in such a way that they are hardly able to move. Running and walking would develop their muscles (otherwise known as their meat), making them tougher, and thus less tender than veal consumers want. The pale colour of the meat is achieved by depriving the calves of crucial nutrients, including iron. The resultant health effects for the calves, such as 'anemia, reduced growth, and increased occurrence of diseases',[15] are not regarded as important because the calves are slaughtered while they are still only a few months old.

Dairy cows live longer (up to about five years), but far from a full bovine lifespan (which is approximately twenty years). Most are kept indoors, often in crowded conditions, although some have access to limited outdoor areas. They are often tethered and unable to roam, which deprives them of mental stimulation. To renew a cow's lactation, she must regularly be impregnated, most commonly by artificial insemination. Dairy cows spend almost all their lives either pregnant or lactating. To boost milk production many are injected with growth hormone, which can have painful, adverse health effects, such as mastitis, for the cows. When their milk production wanes, they are sent for slaughter.

Beef cattle spend the early part of their lives on the range, but between about six months and a year are moved to feedlots, where they are reared intensively in a barren, unstimulating environment, and often standing in their own excrement. They are fed foods, such as corn, which are less than ideal for ruminants. They often suffer ill-health as a result of the conditions in which they are kept.

As is the case with many other kinds of animals, cattle are often shipped long distances for slaughter. During the long trips they are kept in cramped conditions, at temperature extremes, and often without adequate hydration and nutrition. Many are injured *en route*. Some die.

In slaughterhouses, cattle are typically shot in the head with a captive bolt pistol, the purpose of which is to stun the animals before they are hoisted up by their hind legs and have their throats slit. It is not uncommon for stunning to fail or be incomplete, in which cases the animals are still conscious when their throats are slit and sometimes even when they are being dismembered.

Sheep and goats

Sheep and goats can typically graze at pasture (rather than being raised under intensive conditions). However, they too suffer considerably.

Some lambs are subjected not only to castration, tail-docking, and ear-tagging, but also to mulesing, a process in which skin is removed from the buttocks in order to prevent urine and faeces sticking to the wool in that area, and attracting flies. Goats are castrated, ear-tagged, and either disbudded or de-horned, typically without anaesthetic.

Sheep are shorn annually for their wool. While shearing is not in itself painful, it is not uncommon for sheep to suffer nicks and cuts, especially when unqualified or inexperienced shearers are operating at great speed, which they are incentivized to do. Moreover, shearing can be stressful for the sheared animal.

When sheep's wool yield declines, they are sent for slaughter. Lambs are killed before they are a year old, depriving them of about a dozen years of life. These animals, along with goats, are often transported long distances in cramped conditions to slaughterhouses, where they too are subjected to captive bolt stunning before being hoisted upside down and having their throats slit. As with other animals, the stunning is not always effective.

Aquatic animals

Aquatic animals often receive the least attention because many of them are assumed to be less capable of suffering. In the case of such beings as fish, this assumption is without merit. The more that is learned about these animals, the more evidence there is of their capacity to feel and to think.[16] This is also true of cephalopods[17] (such as octopuses and squid), and even more so of marine mammals (namely, cetaceans, such as whales and dolphins).

The *lives* of aquatic animals caught from rivers, seas, and oceans are not typically as bad as those farmed intensively. However, there are many ways in which humans do make the lives of even wild aquatic animals worse—typically by polluting their environment.

Humans cause aquatic animals a vast amount of suffering when they kill them. In small scale fishing, a fish can be pulled out of the water with a hook in its mouth. In larger-scale fishing, they are hauled in nets, which trap other marine animals as 'by-catch'. When they are hauled from great depths, fish can suffer barometric trauma. They then 'drown' on land or ship deck, unless they are first decapitated or disembowelled.

Speciesism

While the foregoing facts are horrifying, they do not settle the ethical question. This is because we must still determine whether such treatment of animals can be *justified*. What should be clear is that most people would be quick to condemn such treatment of at least one kind of animal—the human animal.[18] This is not to deny, of course, that humans often treat other humans in abominable ways. However, when they do, such behaviour is widely condemned.

Can those who criticize such treatment of humans consistently think that treating other animals in these ways is permissible? Put another way, are there relevant differences between humans and animals that can justify treating animals in these ways, if treating humans in the same ways is impermissible?

There is a distinction between relevant differences and irrelevant ones. Irrelevant differences are easy to find. For example, a person's 'race' or sex is not relevant to whether they feel pain or whether their pain is morally considerable. There are some differences between people of different sexes and purported 'races', but none of these are relevant to whether their pains should count. Of course, there have been all too many examples of people's pain being discounted on the basis of their 'race' or sex, but these are instances of wrongful discrimination, known as racism and sexism.

This is not to say that 'race' and sex are never relevant.[19] For example, there is a relevant difference between human males and females that could warrant a health insurance company covering *routine* mammograms for women, but not men, over a certain age. In such cases it is not sex *per se* that justifies the differential treatment, but rather some other associated attribute, such as the presence or absence of breasts and concomitant risk for breast cancer. Once one recognizes what the relevant basis is for differential treatment, one will recognize that it would be sexist (and stupid) to screen five-year-old girls for breast cancer and not to screen those specific men in whom a mammogram is medically indicated.

If we want to know whether humans are justified in treating animals in the ways they do, we cannot simply assert that whereas humans are human, other animals are not human. That would be 'speciesist'[20]—a species analogue of 'racist' and 'sexist'. The fact of species difference cannot *by itself* be of any relevance, just as the fact of 'racial' or sex differences between humans cannot by itself be of any relevance. We need to point to relevant differences (even though those may well be associated with species differences).

It was once purported that a relevant difference is that whereas humans are conscious or sentient, animals are not. The problem with this claim is that there is overwhelming evidence that all mammals (including cattle, sheep, goats, and pigs) as well as birds and fish are all conscious and capable of feeling pleasure and pain. There are some animals, such as crustaceans, regarding whom there is still *some* doubt about whether they are sentient. In those cases, the weight of evidence suggests that they are indeed sentient. Given what is at stake, they should be given the benefit of any doubt, especially in the light of the long track record of underestimating the sentient capacities of other animals.

Even if there are *some* animals who are not sentient, that fact cannot support treating those animals who are sentient as though they were not. It is not the case that *all* non-human animals must be sentient in order for those animals who *are* sentient to be treated as such.

Given that sentience cannot be used to distinguish humans from other animals, a more commonly cited criterion is either the elevated level of cognition typical of humans or some associated capacity, such as linguistic ability or self-awareness. Philosophers use the term 'person' to refer to beings who have such capacities. Whereas 'human' is a biological (and more specifically, a species) category, 'person' is not. At least in principle, some non-humans could be persons. There are certainly many fictional examples (such as Vulcans). There may also actually be, or have been, other persons who are (or were) not members of the species *Homo sapiens*. Earlier hominids, relicts of which species *may* still exist,[21] are one kind of example.

The personhood criterion has been central, one way or another, to many arguments that seek either to deny that animals need to be considered in our moral deliberations or at least to reduce the moral weight of their interests in those deliberations. While some of these particular arguments will be considered, it is unnecessary to examine all of them. They are all liable to some widely recognized problems.

First, it is not at all clear why a being must have elevated levels of cognition in order for his or her pain (or pleasure) to count, or to count significantly. If we distinguish between pain and suffering, then it is true that cognition can sometimes enhance the suffering associated with pain. If, for example, one knows that the pain one is experiencing is part of a terminal illness, one might suffer more than if one lacked such knowledge. However, it is also true that cognition can sometimes *reduce* suffering. If one understands, for example, that the post-operative pain one is experiencing is the result of a procedure that will advance one's interests, one might suffer less than one would if one did not have such understanding. This is why, for example, suffering that is taken to be meaningful can be easier to bear than suffering that is taken to be meaningless.

Thus, while a being's level of cognition can be relevant to how we treat that being, there is no good reason to think that just because he or she lacks sophisticated cognition, we should not give due attention to his or her pain and suffering.

Second, sophisticated cognition is not a criterion that separates all and only humans from all other animals. There are many humans—including babies, and those who are cognitively profoundly impaired—who have less sophisticated cognition than many other animals.

Figure 6.1 depicts a sample of different species. These are arranged in descending order of the cognitive capacity of the *most sophisticated members* of each species.[22] In other words, each arrow represents the maximum cognitive capacity of each species. It is obviously not the case that every *member* of each species has the highest level for that species. Many members of each

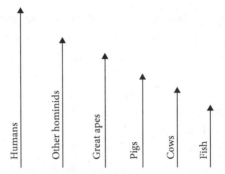

Figure 6.1 Degrees of cognitive capacity.

species have no cognitive capacity at all. This is true, for example, of zygotes of all the species. Normal members of each species will gradually develop *some* cognitive capacity, but they will not all develop the same amount. Normal humans will develop more cognitive capacity than normal cows, for example, but this does not mean that *all* humans will develop more cognitive capacity than *all* cows.

It should also be obvious that even those humans who do develop more cognitive capacity than any other (present or extinct) species, will not have the same level of cognitive capacity. Some of these humans will have more cognitive capacity than others. (A further complication is that 'cognitive capacity' may not refer to a single capacity, but to a range of capacities. As a result, one individual can have a higher level of one cognitive capacity but a lower level of another cognitive capacity than another individual.)

If the absence of higher-level cognition made it permissible to treat animals in the ways in which they are currently being treated, then it would also be permissible to treat many humans in the same ways.

That conclusion is so horrific, that many people (most especially those seeking to defend the current treatment of animals), have resorted to an array of often sophistical arguments to justify such treatment without extending such permission to equivalent treatment of humans who are cognitively less sophisticated than many animals.

A more sophisticated version of such an argument, that seeks to avoid the charge of speciesism, suggests that those deserving special moral consideration must meet either one of two conditions: (a) be a person; or (b) be a 'modal person', where a modal person is a being that although not a person could have been a person.[23] This view, dubbed 'modal personism', purportedly avoids speciesism because it allows the (logical, and perhaps even empirical) possibility that some non-humans could be either persons or modal persons. It has also been said that it captures widespread intuitions about degrees of moral considerability. More specifically, it gives special moral status to all humans, even those who are not persons because (almost all[24]) of those humans who are not persons are still modal persons. That is to say, they 'could have been persons'.

Claims about which non-persons could have been persons raise complex metaphysical questions that can be set aside for our purposes. Instead, two points can be made. First, modal personism does not explain some important speciesist features of ordinary views. Speciesism is not limited to favouring humans over non-humans. It is also manifest in the favouring of some animal species over others. For example, most people in the West (and many in the East) are outraged if pain is inflicted on dogs or they are killed and eaten, but show no such outrage if the same treatment is inflicted on pigs, who are at least as intelligent as dogs. Similarly, there is a widespread failure to recognize that some animals may in fact be persons. (Whether they are, does depend in part on how high one sets the bar for personhood.)

Second, and more important, it is really not clear why we should attach greater weight to the interests of modal persons than we do to other non-persons. To see why, consider the application of modal personism not to moral status, but instead to moral responsibility. According to this application, a being is more (or, on another version, fully) morally responsible for his or her actions, if they meet one of two conditions: (a) be a person; or (b) be a 'modal person'. What this means is that human babies, demented humans, and humans with profound intellectual disability are at least more responsible for their actions than other non-persons with equivalent capacities, and their greater responsibility is on account of their being modal persons.

This view is not only absurd but also unfair. If a being lacks the properties (of personhood) that would heighten their moral responsibility, their responsibility for their actions does not increase merely because they 'could have been a person'. You are responsible if you have the capacity for responsibility, and not if you merely could have had the capacity for responsibility.

The same is true of the extent to which your interests count morally. Although we cannot *prove* that sentience is a sufficient condition for one's interests to count morally, and that sapience is relevant to how those interests should be weighed, there are quite compelling reasons for thinking that this is the case.

Consider sentience first. Although insentient entities, such as plants, can have interests, there is nothing that it feels like to be a plant. Plants cannot care about their well-being. There is, however, something that it feels like to be a fish, chicken, pig, sheep, or cow. That is why beings such as these can feel pain and pleasure. Because pain feels bad, and pleasure feels good, these feelings are relevant to which actions are bad, and which are good.

Sapient beings—or persons—have the capacity to think. That capacity, I have suggested, can make some occurrences bad or worse for the beings that have it, and make other occurrences good or better for them. In other words, sapience can make a difference to a sapient being in a way that affects what we may and may not do to them.

If sentience and sapience are the capacities that make one's interests count, then your interests count to the extent that you have the requisite properties, and not to the extent that you *could have had* them. If that is the case, then views like modal personism and modal sentientism are mistaken.

Moral equality?

In rejecting views that discriminate between species or between modal persons and (other) non-persons, we are not committed to the view that everybody's interests are equal—in the sense of having the same weight.

If characteristics like sentience and sapience influence the extent to which interests count, and if sentience and sapience are a matter of degree, then the extent to which interests of different beings will count is also a matter of degree. For example, a being with only minimal levels of consciousness may have aversive subjective states, but these may feel much less bad than the pain experienced by beings with much higher levels of sentience. If the pains are unequal, they should count unequally (but only to the extent that they are unequal).

A further complication is that consciousness and sentience vary along different axes. We may be able to see things that dogs cannot, but they may smell and hear things that we cannot. Bats and whales can sense through echolocation, and honeybees can sense the earth's magnetic field. We humans have neither of these capacities. We may thus be insensate to some stimuli to which other animals are keenly attuned.[25] There can thus be sensations that adversely affect them, but not us. This complicates the picture of which beings have 'greater sentience'. The term might have to be relativized to particular sentience modalities. There are problems even if we bracket this complexity.

While greater sentience will typically result in one's worst pains being worse and thus counting more than the worst pains of much less-sentient beings, it obviously is not the case that every pain of a more sentient being is worse than every pain of a less sentient being. Similarly, as explained earlier, greater sapience does not *always* result in one's interests counting more, although it may often be the case that a person's interests will be more developed and count more than those of a non-person.

There are, of course, practical problems that arise. First, none of us can ever be sure of how the pains of other humans feel to them. How much more opaque to us are the pains of radically different kinds of beings. Given both this and the long-standing problem of underestimating the extent to which beings—even human beings—who are different from us are capable of feeling or thinking, we should exercise great caution when we are inclined to minimize the capacities of others.

Second, it may be very difficult in practice to make precise comparisons in the degree of sentience or sapience, and thus it may help to employ heuristics that, although not precisely mapping reality, help us to navigate it in cautious ways. For example, comparisons of the relative intelligence of each individual may be invidious, self-serving, and open to abuse. Thus, it may be the case that it is wise to establish some thresholds whereby, for example, the interests of all 'competent' adult humans are treated equally, notwithstanding the actual inequalities between them. Human infants and children, as well as those adult humans with clearly limited cognitive capacities would probably cross the same thresholds as normal adult humans for sentience, but certainly not for sapience. To avoid speciesism, the interests of other species would need to be weighted like those of humans with capacities comparable to competent members of those other species.

Once we recognize that equivalent interests should be treated equivalently, irrespective of the being whose interests they are, it immediately becomes very difficult to see how the current treatment of animals could be justified, given how much pain is inflicted on them in rearing and slaughtering them. Consider two pains in Figure 6.2.

The height of each bar indicates the severity of each of two pains inflicted on two different beings—A and B. To clarify, these are the intensities of the subjective sensations and thus have already controlled for any differences in action that might be required to generate a pain of each intensity. (For

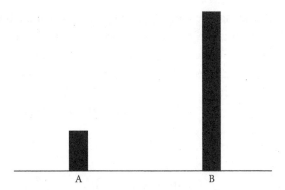

Figure 6.2 Two pains.

example, a slap of particular force might cause much less pain to a rhinoceros than it would to a dog. Thus, the bars do not represent the intensity of any action but rather the intensity of the pain that is felt as a result.)

Now imagine that one had to inflict (or, on a different version, allow) one of the pains. All things being equal, which pain should one inflict (or allow)? The 'all things being equal' condition is necessary in order to control for differences there might be in considerations such as desert. If, for example, A was innocent, but B was not, then it might be thought that one should inflict or allow the greater rather than the lesser pain.

However, in the absence of such considerations, inflicting (or allowing) the lesser pain would be the preferred course of action. This judgement should not change if you discover that A is a pale-skinned person and B a dark-skinned person (or vice versa). In other words, upon being provided with information about the skin colour of A and B, you should not opt for inflicting the greater rather than the lesser pain. Inflicting the greater pain in such a scenario would be racist because the 'race' of the person suffering a pain is irrelevant.

Similarly, one should not think that the more severe pain should be inflicted if one discovered that the lesser pain would be that of a male and the greater pain that of a female (or vice versa). Switching one's judgment in this case would be sexist. This is because the sex of the recipient, like skin colour, is irrelevant.

Just as skin colour and sex are irrelevant, so is species. All things being equal, it is not permissible to inflict (or allow) a greater pain just because it, unlike the lesser pain, is not the pain of a human.

It should be clear that the pains inflicted on animals in the production of meat and other products are immense. In ordinary circumstances, it is near impossible to think that the inflictions of these pains could be justified on the grounds that they are lesser of two evils. It is true that without that meat and other animal products, humans would be deprived of *something*, but it is highly implausible to think that that deprivation is greater than the evils inflicted on animals.

Costs and benefits

To see more clearly why this is the case, we should compare the benefits (primarily to humans) of meat eating, with the costs (primarily but not only to animals). The most notable costs and benefits, not all of which are of equal magnitude, are summarized in Figure 6.3.

Consider first the costs. These include the copious amounts of both acute and chronic pain and suffering, some of which was described at the beginning of this chapter. These may be easy for many people to overlook, not least because they are kept well-hidden. Even many of those people who have been made aware of the costs to animals have a strong inclination to put these costs out of their minds.

Then there are the *billions* of animal deaths caused by human slaughter each year. These deaths are typically painful, but in order to preserve a conceptual distinction between death, on the one hand, and pain and suffering on the other, we can consider death itself rather than the typically painful process of dying. It is possible that an animal's death is not as bad for him as an ordinary adult human's death is bad for that person. That is because killing a person may deprive that person of more than killing a non-person

Costs	Benefits
Pain & Suffering	Taste
Death	Nutrition
Disease	Economic
Environment	Cultural
Inefficient	

Figure 6.3 The benefits and costs of meat eating.

deprives that non-person. However, this is compatible with thinking that death is nonetheless very bad for animals.

In a society that systematically underweights animal interests, it is easy to underestimate just how bad death is for an animal. One helpful heuristic to correct for this is to consider the death of a human being with the same or lower degree of sentience and sapience as the animal whose death we are considering.[26]

Adult non-human mammals have greater cognitive capacity than human infants do. However, most human babies, as they develop, will acquire greater cognitive capacity than adult non-human mammals. Those who accept a simple deprivation account of death's badness could, on this basis, argue that a death of a human baby is typically worse than the death of an adult animal. This is because the human baby will be deprived of more.

The problem with a simple deprivation account of death's badness is that it leads to some very strange implications—including the conclusion that the death of a human baby is worse than the death of a human teenager. This is because a baby, who has a greater remaining life expectancy and is thus deprived of more. It is problems such as these, that lead many people to supplement the deprivation account with what Jeff McMahan has called the 'time-relative interests' account. According to this account, the badness of death must be 'based on the effect that the death has on the victim as he is at the time of death rather than on the effect it has on his life as a whole'.[27] With the addition of this account, the death of a human baby is less bad than the death of a human adolescent, because at the time of death an infant has less interest than the adolescent in the future of which each is deprived.

However, the addition of the time-relative interests account also has the implication that the death of a human baby is less bad than the death of an adult non-human animal. The latter have greater cognitive capacity than human infants do. If death is not very bad for those animals, it is even less bad for human babies. Even if we standardly overestimate how bad death is for human babies, it is still unlikely that death for them is as trivial a harm as most people think that an animal's death is. In other words, even if the death of a human baby is not as bad as many people think, the death of an animal with greater capacities is probably much worse than it is generally taken to be.

Some people may wish to reject the time-relative interests account in order to ward off such an implication. However, they will still face a challenge that is presented by those *cognitively impaired* human babies (and adults) who will never acquire greater cognitive sophistication than the non-human animals who are killed for human consumption. If death is not very bad for those animals, it is no worse for those human babies. Even if we standardly overestimate how bad death is for cognitively impaired human babies, it is still unlikely that death for such a human baby is as trivial a harm as most people think that an animal's death is.

Pain, suffering, and death of animals are the main costs of eating meat and other animal products, and they should be the primary factors we consider. However, they are not the only costs. There are also various adverse health effects for humans. These costs typically result only from *excessive* human consumption of animal products, and would be much less likely to result from more limited consumption of them. Thus, these considerations are not convincingly directed against only occasional consumption of animals.

Some of these health costs are borne by those individuals who consume animals. For example, a diet rich in meat, dairy, and eggs, is much less healthy than a vegan diet. This may be an exclusively prudential consideration. However, other health costs and risks are borne not only by those who themselves eat animals, but also by others.

For example, intensive farming of animals increases the risk of zoonoses—diseases that originate in animals and then jump the species barrier to humans. When mutations of such infectious diseases then allow transmission from human to human, this results in endemic and even pandemic human diseases. Such diseases include avian influenza, swine influenza, variant Creutzfeldt-Jakob disease, acquired immunodeficiency syndrome (AIDS), and severe acute respiratory syndrome (SARS),[28] possibly including its novel manifestation as SARS-CoV-2 (Covid-19).[29] The very conditions—crowding, an environment flowing with excrement, blood, and other bodily fluids, combined with close proximity to humans—that cause so much suffering to animals are also the conditions that make zoonoses more likely.[30]

Another common practice in contemporary animal farming is the use of large quantities of antibiotics. Some of these are used to prevent disease in animals, but large-scale medicinal use would not be necessary even for this purpose if animals were not kept in such crowded conditions. Another use of antibiotics is to bring animals more rapidly to slaughter weight.

The problem with this widespread use of antibiotics in animal agriculture is that it massively increases the risk of antibiotic resistance.[31] We are already seeing some signs of this. It is quite possible that we shall return to a situation in which we no longer have (functional) antibiotic therapies. People will then die in droves from bacterial infections that are currently treatable. That would be a major medical catastrophe.

Industrial levels of animal agriculture also have very serious consequences for the environment—both global and local. Ruminant animals (such as cattle, sheep, and goats) produce a large quantity of methane, a potent greenhouse gas. Meat and dairy combined, account for 74.9% of all greenhouse gases produced in an average diet.[32]

Large-scale animal agriculture also causes local pollution. For example, the waste produced by these animals is not treated in the way that human excreta are. It is initially stored in massive manure lagoons. These often leak, contaminating the groundwater. When the waste is disposed of, it is spread on arable land, but often in quantities that exceed the land's ability to absorb it. There is inevitable runoff into the water sources, with all the resultant adverse sequelae.

Animal-based foods are also responsible for significant local air pollution. For example, rearing animals (and producing food for them) causes the vast majority of particulate matter ($PM_{2.5}$) pollution caused by any food production. Such pollution causes lung and heart disease. In the United States, it has been estimated that animal-based foods are, in this way, responsible for 12 700 premature deaths per year.[33]

One further, and partially related, cost resulting from animal agriculture is its inefficiency. Using land and water to produce feed for animals that will later be killed and eaten is much less efficient than using the same land and water to grow crops to feed humans directly.

These inefficiencies feed into the environmental problems because the environmental costs of food production are unnecessary in part to the extent to which the food production is inefficient.

Consider next the benefits of meat eating, all of which are for humans. Some people like the taste of meat and other animal products and do not derive the same gustatory satisfaction from plant-based alternatives. For them, the gustatorial benefit can be obtained from animals and animals alone. This may change as plant-based products become more sophisticated or if lab cultured animal tissue becomes commercially viable.

How important a benefit is the taste of meat (or milk, cheese, or eggs)? Gastronomes may insist that it is a profound benefit, but any honest weighing of it against the pain and suffering of animals must conclude that it is trivial relative to the costs to animals. Those who think otherwise, should follow Arthur Schopenhauer's advice and 'compare the respective feelings of two animals, one of which is engaged in eating the other'.[34] Those who have difficulty imagining the feelings of two *other* animals, might ask themselves whether they would be willing, in exchange for the taste of the meat they eat, to endure what was endured by the animal they are eating.

Meat and animal products are obviously also nutritious. However, unlike taste, which for some people cannot (yet) be replicated by plant-based alternatives, most people can obtain all their required nutrition from plant-based foods. The claim is not that this is true of all people in all instances. There have been circumstances in which the only way in which somebody could survive was by (killing and) eating an animal. However, there have also been instances in which the only way in which somebody could survive was by (killing and) eating a human. Even if killing and eating a fellow animal or human is justified in such cases, such cases do not provide a generalized permission.

Some people are sceptical that one can meet all one's nutritional requirements without eating animals and their products. It is certainly the case that vegans must give careful attention to their diet. However, that is now much easier than it once was—not for everybody, but certainly for many people, including those most likely to be reading this book. For example, many vegan foods are now enriched with vitamin B12, and such supplements are also available. Omega-3 fatty acids are another kind of nutrient that pose a challenge for vegans. However, the careful vegan can obtain these from chia seeds, brussels sprouts, walnuts, flaxseed powder, and other vegetable sources, as well as in animal-free supplements. Even those with the greatest nutritional requirements—children and pregnant women—can have those requirements met through a careful vegan diet.[35]

If one's nutritional requirements can be met without costs like pain, suffering, and death (for others), then the nutritional benefit from eating animals and their products is not a net benefit relative to an alternative in which one fulfils one's nutritional requirements without those costs. By analogy, if you can get all your nutritional requirements without eating unwanted babies, then whatever nutritional benefit you get from eating such babies is not a net benefit—and you should rather not eat them, even if fulfilling your nutritional requirements from baby meat is *easier*.

Animal agriculture has some economic benefits. Some of these benefits are for consumers—those who purchase and use the animal products. This occurs when meat and animal products are sold more cheaply than plant-based alternatives. However, given the inefficiencies of farming animals, their products are cheaper only when the inefficiencies are subsidized or some of the costs are 'externalized'. This happens, for example, when animal agriculture is subsidized, typically by government, or where the environmental costs of animal agriculture are borne not by producers and consumers, but by everybody. If the costs of animal agriculture were all internalized, the resulting products would be much more expensive for consumers than they currently are.

Where individual consumers can purchase meat and animal products more cheaply than alternatives, they have prudential reasons not to pay the greater price. That may carry *some* moral weight, but typically not enough to justify the practice. Moreover, there are no good moral reasons for keeping those incentive structures in place. It would be better if they were changed.

Other economic benefits of animal products are primarily for those in the business of producing and selling these. They earn their livelihoods from these products. Deriving an economic benefit from an unethical practice is hardly a justification for continuing the practice. However, even if we set this point aside, it is noteworthy that the economic benefits are fungible. If people transformed their diets from ones heavily dependent on animals to ones in which animals played no role, the economy would gradually shift. Those now trading in animal products would come to trade in alternatives, even if the switch sometimes involved some hardship.

One further benefit of using animals for their flesh and products is cultural. Many—arguably most (but not all)—human cultures place some or other value on the use of animals in these ways. Perhaps the most obvious example is the part that animal sacrifice (to God or the gods) plays in many cultures. This may be absent in other cultures, but even then, the use of animal flesh, products, skin, and fur can carry cultural significance. It is no coincidence that one expression we use in English for exuberant celebration is 'killing the fatted calf'. Human celebration not infrequently involves animal flesh.

How much weight should this carry? There are those—normative cultural relativists—who think that a culture's view is morally *decisive*. On this view, if a culture permits or requires some practice, then that practice is, respectively, morally permissible or required. If we were to accept this view, then using animal flesh and other products would be permissible (or required) whenever a culture says it is. Since most cultures do think it is permissible, there would be very little or any scope for criticizing such practices.

However, normative cultural relativism is a difficult view to accept, given its other implications. Eating animals is not all it permits. It also implies, for example, that *human* sacrifice is morally permissible or required in those cultures that take it to be so. Similarly, those cultures that think that genocide is permissible, may permissibly undertake genocide. It is difficult to see why we should grant such moral infallibility to cultures. If individuals can be mistaken about almost everything, why should collective human phenomena, such as cultures not similarly be prone to error?

In rejecting normative cultural relativism, we do not have to conclude that culture has *no* value. Instead, we should recognize that it does have value, but that this value is limited. More specifically, it is insufficient to justify not only human sacrifice and genocide, but also the ways in which most animals are currently treated.

Given the various costs and benefits of consuming animals, and the relative weights of each cost and benefit, it is implausible to think that the benefits outweigh the costs. The force of this conclusion seems true irrespective of which normative theory (other than cultural relativism) one adopts. It is not specifically a utilitarian argument. This is because even non-utilitarians consider costs and benefits.

However, there are some arguments in *favour* of consuming animals that are linked to specific normative theories. Thus, even though I do not think that the best way to approach practical ethical problems is through the application of a specific normative ethical theory, there is reason to consider whether some or other theory can be used in defence of consuming animals. We may begin with utilitarianism because, although the consumption of animals generally fails the utilitarian test, it does not always do so.

Utilitarianism

Utilitarians are of the view that the right action is the one that produces the most utility (on balance). They thus determine the right action by means of a cost-benefit analysis, where the costs and benefits to all affected parties, whether human or not, are considered. Given the great costs and small benefits of consuming animals and their products, utilitarians would typically conclude that animals should not be reared and used to provide food and other products for humans.

One version of the argument would take something like the following form:

1. Sentience is a sufficient condition for moral standing.
2. It would be speciesist (and therefore wrong) to discriminate against a being merely on the basis of her species.
3. Therefore, equal pains (and pleasures) should (morally) count equally, irrespective of the species of the beings whose pains (or pleasures) they are.
4. An action that causes more pain (mainly to animals) than it does pleasure (to humans) is wrong.
5. Rearing and killing animals for food causes (mainly animals) more pain than it brings pleasure (to humans).
6. Therefore, rearing and killing animals for food is wrong.

This version of the argument focuses only on pains and pleasures. It would reduce other costs and benefits to this measure of well-being. (For example, economic costs and benefits would be reduced to the pain and pleasure they cause.) However, it is possible for utilitarians to have a view of well-being that is not (exclusively) hedonistic. Those differences are not material here, because however one interprets 'utility', one is likely to reach the same conclusion.

The utilitarian's conclusion is not a categorical one. That is to say, it is not the conclusion that rearing and killing animals for food is *always* wrong. There are some circumstances, at least in theory, but perhaps also in practice, in which one could produce more benefit than harm by rearing and killing an animal for food. Imagine, for example, that there were hundreds of (temporarily) starving humans and the only way in which one could feed and thus save them, was by killing one large whale (or a genetically engineered mega-bovine). In such a circumstance one animal suffers and dies in order to prevent a much larger number of humans dying.[36] In cases such as this, a utilitarian would think that killing and eating the animal would be permissible. However, these would be relatively rare circumstances. Moreover, the logic that permits the killing of animals in such circumstances, would also permit the killing of humans for food in some exceptional circumstances.

Rights theory

Not everybody agrees with utilitarians that the ends always justify the means. Rights theorists (and deontologists) think that some actions are impermissible even if they would produce the greatest amount of good on balance. In other words, those who think that humans have rights would deny that we may kill one human in order to save a larger number. This, they would say, is because humans have a right not to be killed. The right not to be killed is not the only possible right. Other plausible candidates include a right to bodily integrity and a right not to be subjected to unnecessary pain.

Rights place moral limits on what means may be employed in pursuit of ends. They prohibit some actions that would otherwise be permissible under a utilitarian calculation. They do not typically do the opposite—permit what a utilitarian calculation would prohibit. Given the massive costs of rearing and killing animals and the limited benefits to humans of doing so, one does not have to think that animals are like humans in having rights, in order to think that the current treatment of animals is morally wrong. Given this, what further relevance does consideration of rights theory have for the question of rearing and killing animals for human use?

The most plausible answer to this question is that if animals do have rights, then we may not treat them as we do *even* in those rare circumstances in which the costs of doing so are outweighed by the benefits. That is because such treatment would violate their rights.

There are two other responses to the question. While both of these are, to different degrees, much less plausible, they are expressed sufficiently often that they require attention.

First, some might argue that the only pains and pleasures that are morally considerable are those of beings who have rights. If it is the case that animals do not have rights, then we do not need to consider their pains and pleasures. This view entails a rejection of the first premise in the utilitarian argument outlined above. In other words, the view rejects the claim that sentience is a sufficient condition for moral standing. A further condition must also be met—that the sentient being is a rights-bearer. One problem with this answer is that it is difficult to see why a sentient being must have rights in order for her pains and pleasures to count.

Second, some answer that while animal pains and pleasures *do* matter, painless animal *deaths* do not. The line of reasoning here would be that to have a right not to be killed (painlessly), one has to be the kind of being that can have rights. If animals are not that kind of being, then they can have no right not to be killed.

Even if this latter view were correct, its application to the consumption of animals and their products would be limited. This is because the pain that pervades animal agriculture is so great that almost all rearing and killing of animals for human consumption would be wrong even if animals lacked a right not to be killed.

In any event, the suggestion that animals cannot have rights is problematic. To understand why, it helps to understand a disagreement between rights theorists about the proper function of rights. This is a disagreement between the 'interest' or 'benefit' theory of rights, and the 'choice' theory. According to the interest theory, rights protect interests, whereas according to the choice theory, rights protect choices. Contrary to what some people say, which theory one accepts makes no practical difference to how animals should be treated.

Assume, first, that one adopts the interest theory. Because animals, on account of their sentience (and some degree of sapience), have morally considerable interests, rights can protect those interests. There is thus no reason to think that animals cannot have rights according to the interest theory.

What about the choice theory? Choice here is not understood in the minimal sense in which a cow can choose to graze either here or there. Instead, it is the much richer sense of choice associated with persons—an ability to deliberate in more complex ways about options and to choose between them. It is commonly argued that animals are not capable of making choices of the requisite kind. They cannot have rights because they cannot make the kind of choices that rights protect.

If the choice theory implies that animals do not have rights, because they lack the requisite ability to choose, then it is also the case that many humans—including babies, the profoundly cognitively disabled, and the severely demented—do not have rights. If all that this means is that our treatment of such beings cannot be restricted *by their choices*, then the choice theory seems *reasonable* (whether or not there are reasons to prefer the interest theory). If, however, it means that there are not restrictions *at all* on how we may treat animals and babies, then this implication counts against the choice theory.

However, there is a way for the choice theory to avoid this implication. It could do so by acknowledging that though some beings do not have rights (because they cannot make the choices that rights protect), they can have some analogous claim that protects interests rather than rights. We might call that analogue a 'dright'.[37] If one accepts that sentient non-persons can have such claims, then while it is technically correct that according to the choice theory, animals (and babies) cannot have rights, their lacking rights makes no practical difference to whether we may rear and kill them for our consumption. Drights would protect them against such violations of their interests. To the extent that they have an interest in not being killed, they would have a dright not to be killed.

There is a notable challenge to the idea that animals have rights. This challenge, like a less notable one from which it arises, is rooted in the problem of predation. In the natural world, predatory animals kill and eat their prey. In the less notable challenge, people say that because it is not morally wrong for predators such as lions to kill their prey, it is also not wrong for humans to kill and eat animals.[38]

The problem with this argument is that there are two important differences between the predation by some animals on others, and humans' killing and eating animals.[39] The first of these is that whereas animal predators are not moral agents, ordinary adult humans are. Animals cannot deliberate about whether they should be killing and eating other animals. Ordinary adult humans, however, can engage in such deliberation, both regarding what they eat and regarding what they feed their children. Because animal predators are not moral agents, what they do cannot be termed either right or wrong. It just is.

A second difference is that, whereas humans are able to derive all their nutritional benefits without consuming animals and their products, the same is not true of most predators. Eating animals is thus not a necessity for humans, as it is for some animals.

The more notable challenge to the claim that animals have a right not to be killed can acknowledge both of these differences.[40] This challenge asks us to consider two possible scenarios:

Zebra: In the first scenario, you are in the wild, and you see a lion stalking a zebra.
Baby: In the second scenario, you are in the wild, and you see a lion stalking a human baby.

In both cases you could intervene to prevent the lion from killing her prey. What should you do in each of these cases? A common answer is that while you need not—perhaps even *should not*—stop the lion from hunting the zebra, you would be morally culpable if you failed to prevent the lion from killing the human baby.

Can somebody who attributes rights to animals justify these differential judgements? They cannot defend the non-interference in the first case on the grounds that the lion, because she is not a moral agent, cannot violate the rights of the zebra. This is because the lion similarly cannot violate the rights of the baby.

Perhaps it will be suggested that although the baby's rights would not be violated by the lion, the baby's interests that are important enough to warrant protection by rights, are also sufficiently important to make it the case that his death is something we should prevent—something that is 'prevent-worthy'. The problem is that those who think that animals also have rights would presumably have to think that their interests too are important enough to make their deaths prevent-worthy. Thus, it seems that one should also prevent the death of the zebra.

Critics of animal rights point to the difficulty in explaining the different judgements in *Zebra* and *Baby* and conclude that we should abandon the idea that animals have rights.[41] Others have said that we must either draw that conclusion or we should abandon the idea that the rights of anybody—whether human or animal—are positive.[42] That is to say, humans and animals may have (negative) rights against being treated in ways against which rights protect, but nobody has a (positive) right to others doing anything to protect or advance their interests.

There is, however, another way to reconcile the different judgements in *Zebra* and *Baby*. This third way does not require us to abandon the idea that animals too can have rights. Neither does it commit us to thinking that deaths are never prevent-worthy—that we should never intervene to prevent a death.

According to this third way, humans and animals have rights which protect important interests, including interests in not being killed. The deaths of humans and animals are, *in principle*, prevent-worthy. Whether, in a particular instance, we should prevent a death depends on multiple considerations. One of these is how prevent-worthy a death is. Arguably the death of a person is, all things being equal, more prevent-worthy than the death of a non-person. However, that consideration does not apply to the comparison of *Zebra* and *Baby* because in neither case is the prey a person.

The baby is a *potential* person. Those who think that the deaths of potential persons are worse (and thus more prevent-worthy) than the deaths of those who are neither persons nor potential persons, could use this to explain why the baby but not the zebra should be saved. However, the view that the deaths of potential persons are worse than the deaths of those who will never be persons, is both controversial and, for reasons I shall not explore here, hard to justify.[43]

It is not necessary to appeal to potentiality. This is because there are other factors that *are* relevant. Among these is that prevent-worthy deaths that are the consequence of wrongdoing may have a stronger claim for intervention than those are not. Although the lion does no wrong in either case, it is very likely that a baby finding himself in the wild has been abandoned, neglected, or, at the very least, insufficiently protected by his parents or other adult custodians. The same is not true of the zebra. It would, however, be true of a human's companion animal (or even a zebra who had been reared in a zoo) who was abandoned, neglected, or insufficiently protected by his human guardians.

More importantly, a duty to prevent that which is prevent-worthy must be limited by a duty not to do more harm than good. This applies irrespective of whether the prevent-worthy harm is to animals or to humans. Consider, first, a case of human victims. Even when their rights are violated, it is not necessarily the case that intervention is required. Consider, for example, a foreign regime, such as China, Russia, or North Korea, that is oppressing or persecuting its citizens. The serious human rights violations by these repressive regimes are prevent-worthy in principle. However, it does not follow that other countries always have an all-things-considered duty to prevent those human rights violations. This is because it is often extremely likely that attempting to prevent these rights violations will do more harm than good. Sanctions, and other peaceful means tend not to stop the problem. Military action would very likely lead to millions of (prevent-worthy) deaths and might fail. Even if regime change were brought about, there is a significant danger that what replaces it would be no better.

Wholesale interference with predation is also likely to lead to more harm than good. Predators would die. Prey species population would, unchecked by predators, increase to unsustainable levels. Older and weaker members of prey species might die deaths even more protracted than those brought about by predation—including starvation and disease. The same might not be true of isolated instances of preventing predation, and we need not exclude the possibility that sometimes we should prevent lions from preying on zebra. However, there would need to be something exceptional about such cases because if interference became the norm, the problems of wholesale interference would emerge.

Thus, while one should in principle prevent the death of a zebra in just the same way as one should prevent the death of a human baby, in practice it will more commonly be the case that, all things considered, one should save the human baby even though one should not save the zebra.

Contractarianism

Contractarianism is another way in which some people seek to undermine the conclusion that animals should not be reared and killed in the ways that they are.

Contractarianism is the view that morality consists in the terms of a contract. The general idea is that we each agree to the moral rules that characterize the contract, and we do so in exchange for others similarly agreeing to them. It is a reciprocity agreement. I agree to scratch your back if you agree to scratch mine, and I agree not to stab you in your back if you agree not to stab me in mine.

There are two broad kinds of contractarian theory.[44] Some versions of contractarianism ground morality in *self-interested* reciprocity. According to these versions, each of us enters into the contract because it is in our self-interest to do so. Other versions of contractarianism ground morality in *fair reciprocity*. These versions acknowledge that acting self-interestedly may not always be fair, and we agree to restrict our actions for reasons of fairness, in exchange for other parties to the contract reciprocating that fairness.

According to self-interested contractarianism, the parties to the contract 'include all and only those who those who have *both* of the following characteristics':[45]

1. 'they stand to gain by subscribing' to the contract;
2. 'they are *capable* of entering into (and keeping) an agreement.'[46]

Those who did not stand to gain by entering into the contract would not do so, as it would not serve their self-interest. And one would not enter into an agreement if one were not capable of doing so. If a being is not capable of keeping an agreement, others would not enter into an agreement with that being.

It follows that animals cannot be parties to the contract. While they may stand to gain from the contract, because they are not capable of entering into and keeping it, others have nothing to gain from entering into an agreement with them. While you can decide not to kill sharks, you cannot agree to do so in exchange for sharks not killing you. It would thus not be in your interest to agree to desist from killing sharks.

Because those capable of entering into and keeping agreements are persons, self-interested reciprocity contractarianism implies that only persons are morally considerable.[47] Many advocates of contractarianism are willing to embrace this conclusion with regard to animals. One such advocate has said that animals 'are, by and large, to be dealt with in terms of our self-interest, unconstrained by the terms of . . . agreements with them'.[48] In other words, in our treatment of animals, we need only consider our own interests, not theirs.

Contractarians are understandably reluctant to embrace such implications of their view for those humans who are not persons. It is thus unsurprising that they seek ways to extend moral consideration to human non-persons. Jan Narveson, for example, has offered two reasons for not treating human non-persons in the ways in which he thinks we may treat animals[49] but neither of them is satisfactory.

His first reason is that persons 'generally have little to gain' from treating human non-persons badly.[50] That claim may well be false. Consider medical experimentation, for example. Much of this is currently conducted on animals. However, it is far from clear that animals are good experimental models for human disease.[51] As it happens there is an excellent model for human disease—humans. If we started experimenting on human non-persons (whom we might breed for the purpose), our scientific findings would be much more helpful. If human non-persons do not count in their own right, but only insofar as it is in our interests to treat them well, then there would be nothing wrong with turning human non-persons into the subjects of invasive, painful, and often fatal medical experimentation.

Professor Narveson's second reason for differentiating between human and animal non-persons is that humans who are not persons are 'invariably members of families . . . or other groupings' which makes them the object of love by persons who have interests in their well-being. In this way, he seeks to admit such beings to the contract via (what I shall call) the 'back door'.

Again, it is far from clear that this is an effective way to differentiate human and animal non-persons. First, some *animals* are members of families and other groupings which make them objects of love by persons. The most obvious candidates are companion animals. Perhaps Professor Narveson would be willing to extend indirect moral consideration to such animals. However, it is not clear why close family bonds are necessary for moral consideration via the back door. There is a growing number of persons who are concerned about the welfare of a wide range of animals—not only companion animals but also farmed and wild animals. If having a person care about one's welfare is sufficient to have one's interests count, then animals' interests do count.

Indeed, Professor Narveson's logic can incentivize activists on behalf of animals to make more humans care more about the interests of animals. For example, the activists could make it the case that poor treatment of farmed animals would have negative repercussions for those who treat animals badly.

Second, if Professor Narveson insists that one must be a member of a family or other such grouping in order to enjoy moral protection, then it is an implication of his view that when a human non-person is *not* a member of a family or other such grouping, we may treat that human in the way that animals are currently treated. Consider, for example, an abandoned and unwanted baby.

These considerations in response to Professor Narveson's two reasons suggest that the self-interested reciprocity contractarian may be fundamentally mistaken about what morality is (even though advocates of that view obviously do not think so). The reason why we should consider the interests of sentient beings is not that it advances our own interests, but rather because their interests count.[52]

Can contractarian views grounded in fairness (rather than self-interest) fare any better? John Rawls is the most prominent exponent of such a view. (Technically, he was focused more narrowly on justice rather than on morality, but his view can be applied to morality.) He noted that actual contracts are often entered into by parties with different bargaining power. The terms of the contract are then determined by the different leverage that the respective parties have. To the extent that the bargaining power of different parties is unfair, the terms of the resultant contract will also be unfair.

For this reason, we should ask what the terms of a contract would be if unfair inequalities between the contracting parties were eliminated. To approximate this, Professor Rawls asks us to consider a hypothetical 'original position' in which the contracting parties lack specific knowledge about themselves—such as their sex, sexual orientation, 'race', religion, ethnicity, how healthy they are, and how wealthy or poor they are. Without such knowledge there are no incentives to unfairly favour some demographics over others.

Professor Rawls then asks what principles parties to the original position would choose. Although their choice of these principles from the original position is self-interested, unfairness is avoided because the self-interested choices are made in the absence of knowledge of particularities about oneself.

As a consequence of this, parties in the original position are obviously going to choose principles that will protect them irrespective of their sex, sexual orientation, 'race', religion, ethnicity, whether they are healthy or sick, and whether they are rich or poor. Thus, all people will be protected by a morality grounded in such a contract.

Will animals be protected? John Rawls himself thinks that they are not. This is because the one thing one knows about oneself in the original position is that one is a rational deliberator capable of choosing principles of morality. If you know that, you know that you are not a pig, cow, sheep, chicken, or fish. If you are self-interestedly choosing principles of morality in the original position, you would not choose principles that protect species to which you know you do not belong. For this reason, it is said, one cannot simply stipulate that parties to the original position, in addition to being ignorant of so much else about themselves, are also ignorant about their species.

John Rawls himself seems to have been disturbed by the implication that animals are not protected, but took comfort in noting that his theory is a theory of justice rather than a theory of morality.[53] The implication seems to be that a complete theory of morality would need to incorporate animals (in a direct way). However, if the full theory of morality is modelled on a Rawlsian contract, it is hard to see how it would do any better than a theory of justice at incorporating animals.

While John Rawls did not think that his theory could accommodate animals (other than indirectly), others have argued that his theory does indeed have the resources to have the contract extend to non-human animals.[54] Yet others have rejected such arguments.[55] Rather than plumbing the depths of these debates, a few general comments will suffice.

First, it is not only the moral standing of animals that lies in the balance. If animals are not morally considerable according to Rawlsian contractarianism, then neither are *some* human non-persons. Such a contractarianism can accommodate some human non-persons. For example, it can accommodate those humans who are not *yet* persons—such as babies.[56] This is because all human persons were once children. Parties to the original position would know that they were once were non-persons (not because of specific knowledge about themselves but rather because all known persons were not always persons). They might thus apply principles of morality to 'pre-persons'—beings who are not yet persons but who will become persons.

The same might be true of 'post-persons'—beings who were once persons but no longer are. Human adults with advanced dementia would fit into this category. Parties in the original position would know that they could dement and would thus have grounds for according some moral standing to those who dement.

However, if animal interests cannot be protected by Rawlsian contractarianism, then that theory also cannot protect the interests of those humans who are never persons. If the knowledge that you are a rational deliberator at some point in your life is available to you in the original position, then you know that you are not a 'never person'—a being who is never a person.

If it is an implication of a theory that neither animals nor some human never-persons are morally considerable, then that is a serious mark against that theory. It is much more plausible to think that, for example, the infliction of gratuitous pain on a being is morally wrong than it is to think that a view with the opposite conclusion is correct.

If that is the case, then it makes no difference for our purposes whether Rawlsian contractarianism can accommodate animals and never-persons. Either it cannot, in which case we should reject the theory, or it can, in which case we should not be treating animals in the way in which we are.

The view that animals and human never-persons are not morally considerable seems at odds with a theory predicated on fairness. It is deeply unfair that the pains of a sentient being have no moral claims on us. If the original position is a heuristic for modelling conditions under which a fair contract is generated, then it *should* be modelled in a way that renders sentient non-persons morally considerable.

One way to do that is to insist that while all parties to the original position are rational deliberators capable of choosing moral principles, they know that they could be stripped of this capacity when they exit the original position. The loss of this capacity could be on account of being a human with a congenital, profound intellectual disability, or it could be on account of being a non-human animal.

Causal inefficacy?

The astute reader will note that hitherto the discussion has been about rearing and killing animals for human consumption. It is sometimes objected that the question whether one may permissibly engage in such activities is different from the quotidian question confronting most individuals. That latter question is not whether animals may be reared and killed for human consumption, but rather whether one may purchase and consume meat and other animal products.

These questions are not the same. Farmers rear animals and send them to slaughter. Abattoir workers kill the animals. Ordinary consumers typically neither rear nor slaughter animals.[57] What these consumers ordinarily do is buy meat and other animal products, and consume them.

Some people are of the view that this distinction makes a difference. Whereas rearing and killing animals may wrongfully harm animals, it has been argued that purchasing and, *a fortiori*, eating meat does not harm them. By the time meat is purchased and eaten, the animal's suffering has ended, and he or she is already dead. Although the cows and chickens that produced the milk and eggs one consumes may still be alive when one purchases and consumes their products, not purchasing or eating those items will do nothing to reverse the suffering that those animals have already endured.

The natural response to this argument is to say that while purchasing and consuming these products may not harm the particular animals from whom they were derived, one does contribute to harming animals by sustaining demand for such products through one's purchases and consumption. Thus, while desisting from purchasing and consuming these products will do nothing to reverse the suffering the relevant animals have already endured, it will prevent future suffering.

However, this invites the counter-response that individual purchases and, *a fortiori*, individual instances of consuming animal products typically do *not* contribute to demand. The markets, it is noted, are not so sensitive that somebody desisting from a single purchase will have any impact on demand. It is even less likely, once animal flesh has been purchased, that a decision to eat it, will have any impact on demand. Instead, in contemporary markets, the demand that results in animal suffering is an aggregation of hundreds if not thousands of people's purchasing and consumption activity. If an animal is not harmed by, for example, buying or eating meat, then it cannot be wrong, some people have argued, to buy or eat meat.

There are obvious parallels between this argument and the invocation of causal inefficacy (or so-called inconsequentialism) to argue against individuals having a duty to desist from greenhouse gas emissions, which was discussed in the chapter on the environment.

There are indeed similarities between the two cases, but there are also important differences. Consider the similarities first. In both cases, we are dealing with complex systems. The relationship between actions causing emissions and the harms resulting from climate change is arguably even more complex than the relationship between purchasing animal products from shops and the harm done to animals. However, in both cases the relationship is complex enough that no harm is caused by a single drive or a single meat meal.

Yet it is true, in both cases, that the individual consumer does contribute to the harm, albeit very indirectly and non-linearly. This is summarized in Figure 6.4.

Harm is caused to animals (and others) by intensive farming, transport, slaughter, hunting, fishing, and other practices. Sometimes the harms lead to further treatment of animals that causes other harms (thus creating a feedback loop). For example, because being reared in intensive conditions leads chickens and pigs to peck or bite one another, this leads to debeaking and tail docking, which causes a different harm to the animals.

Obviously, some individual people are directly involved in inflicting the harms on animals. These are the people engaged in farming, transporting, and killing animals. Those people may also be consumers of animal products, but they are not the typical consumer, who is much more removed from the direct infliction of harm.

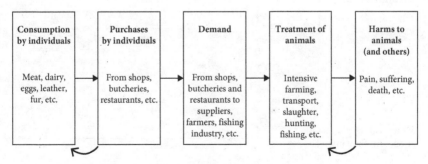

Figure 6.4 From individual meals to harming animals.

204 VERY PRACTICAL ETHICS

The maltreatment of animals is driven by the demand for their flesh and other products. That demand is, in turn, driven by millions of purchases. In most cases people purchase meat and other animal products in order either to consume these themselves or that others can consume them. However, purchases can also, to some extent, drive consumption. Once the meat has already been purchased, some people might eat it even though they would not have bought it to consume it.

In the chapter on our environmental duties, I explained the relevant sense in which an individual's emissions 'contribute' to the harms that result from global warming. Purchasing and consuming animal products contributes to harming animals in a similar sense of 'contribute'—no less harm would be inflicted on animals if the individual purchase or meal did not take place, but the individual act does make some imperceptible difference to the amount of harm.

It does so by contributing to the demand for animal flesh and products, which causes more suffering and death. This can happen in one (or both) of two ways. In many cases, the contribution is that it constitutes one of a string of meals or purchases that aggregate to cause a demand threshold to be passed, triggering further animal suffering and death. This is illustrated, in greatly simplified form, in Figure 6.5.

In this figure, the number of chickens in each column represents individual purchases. The horizontal arrow at the bottom represents the time

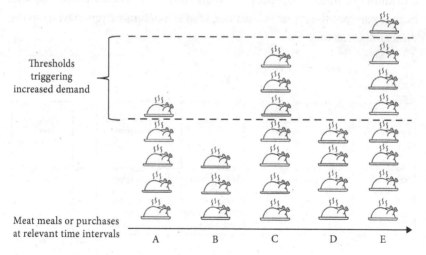

Figure 6.5 Thresholds and contributions.

intervals during which demand can impact on the number of animals who are harmed. The broken horizontal lines are representative of (meal or) purchase thresholds that need to be passed in order to trigger a market impact on the number of animals harmed. (Obviously, the number of purchases actually needed is many orders of magnitude greater than the number represented here, which has been scaled down for illustrative purposes.)

Within the periods represented by columns A and E, no purchase by itself causes any harm, but collectively the purchases pass the threshold that causes additional animals to be harmed. Clearly, in this case, each purchase contributes to harming animals. No purchase is sufficient by itself, but each purchase is necessary for the additional animals to be harmed.

Somewhat more complicated is the period represented by column C. Here one threshold is passed but the second threshold is not. Thus, while it is clear that the first five purchases all contributed to further harm, it might be suggested that the final two did not, because they do not contribute to crossing a further threshold.

Of course, given the complexities of the world, one would likely never know whether one's own purchase was among the first five or the final two. This, in itself, is a reason to desist from making the purchase. However, there *is* a sense in which even the final two purchases contribute to the passing of the first threshold. They make it the case that if any of the first five purchases had not been made, the first threshold would still have been crossed.

Consider an analogous case. Death can be brought about by a thousand cuts. Those who make the 1001st, 1002nd, or 1003rd cuts contribute to the death in the (weak) sense that if, for example, that 266th or 593rd and 1000th cuts had not been made, the death would still have been brought about. The cuts above the threshold contribute to overdetermining the death.

Some will be unsatisfied that this constitutes a contribution (of the right kind) to harm. They will treat purchases above the first threshold that fail to meet the second threshold in the same way as those purchases that fail to reach the first threshold, as is the case in columns B and D. (In these cases, too, those making the purchases will typically not know that their purchases will not be part of a series that crosses a threshold. There is thus reason to desist even from purchases in these cases.)

There is another way in which all meat meals and purchases—including those in B and D, and those above the first threshold in C—contribute indirectly to harming animals. Eating meat and purchasing it, contributes to preserving the social acceptance of eating meat. By contrast, refusing meat, and other animal products, contributes to changing views about acceptable ways to treat animals. These contributions are imperceptible, of course, but here again there is a difference between an imperceptible contribution and no contribution.

Because individual ingestions and purchases of meat products do contribute to causing harm, one has a *reason* to desist from them. However, having a reason to desist is different from having a *duty* to desist.[58] This is because the reason to desist could, in principle, be overridden by reasons to partake. That said, it is more difficult to see how the reason against consuming animals could be outweighed by other reasons, than it is to see how the reason against emitting previously sequestered carbon could be outweighed by other reasons. The benefits of carbon emissions are often (but not always) more substantial than are the benefits of consuming animals.[59]

There is, however, another argument in favour of a duty to desist from consuming animal products. This argument has force even if, as a result of the complexity of the markets, and contrary to what has been argued, some meat meals and purchases do *not* contribute to harming animals.[60] A *fortiori*, it has force if meat meals and purchases make only an imperceptible contribution.

This argument is rooted in a recognition of *why* a meat meal or purchase makes either no or only an imperceptible contribution to animal suffering. The reason is very different from the reason why taking a drive or a flight makes either no or only imperceptible contribution to climate change. If only very few people were driving or flying, there would be no global warming, no climate change, and thus no harms resulting from this. The harms result from an aggregation of billions of emissions. What is harmless on the small scale becomes harmful on the large scale.

In the case of consuming animal products, if individual meals and purchases make very little or no difference, that is only because of the large scale. If the practice were on a small scale, as it once was (and still is in some places), the harms would be obvious. Somebody who wants to eat meat, for example, either has to kill an animal or have somebody else do so on their behalf (and not via as long and complex a causal chain as is the case between emissions and the harms of climate change).

In other words, the difference between emissions and consuming animal products is that in the case of emissions the harm is *caused* by the scale, whereas in the case of consuming animal products the harm is *obscured* (but not eliminated) by the scale.

Some people might think that there is no moral distinction to be made between individual actions that are harmless on the small scale but become very harmful on the large scale, and individual actions that are harmful on the small scale but contribute only imperceptibly to harm when performed on large scale.

We should reject that view, not least because of its implications for a hypothetical case that was raised in the chapter on environmental duties. This is the case of the person who enjoys sipping human tears. They own a slave who is regularly flogged in order to produce tears. There should be no doubt that such a practice would be wrong. Nor would it become permissible if the taste for tears spread and intensive tear farms kept slaves who were flogged for tears that were then sold in shops.

If you were standing in the lachrymal aisle, deciding whether to purchase a vial of tears, you would be correct in thinking that desisting would not prevent any of the suffering generated in producing the tears on the shelves. The pain caused in producing the tears will not be undone. Perhaps you consider whether your purchase might contribute to future demand. You realize that the shop's orders are not sensitive to every single purchase. They do not order an additional vial of tears for every vial that is sold. You are uncertain whether your purchase will cause the relevant sensitivity threshold to be passed.

Should any of these considerations that you ponder in the aisle lead you to think that purchasing an ampoule of tears is permissible? A positive answer sounds like sophistry. You have a duty not to keep slaves and flog them yourself. You have a duty not to engage another person to do the flogging and tear collection on your behalf. The immorality of this practice does not evaporate if tear-production is industrialized, even though the connection between your purchase and the harms is obscured by the complexity of industrialization and supply chains.

This hypothetical case also provides a response to those who would say that much of the suffering inflicted on animals is a result of intensive farming, and that this suffering would be absent in small-scale rearing and slaughter of animals. It is true that the industrialization of animal farming does contribute additional suffering, but it is not clear that this undermines the claim that because small scale rearing and slaughter of animals is wrong, it does not cease to be, if the practice is industrialized (and made worse in the process). Once we consider those with a taste for human tears, we can recognize that industrialization could also add to the suffering of the slaves—perhaps because they are housed in much more confined spaces. The fact that additional suffering would be added through massification would not undermine the conclusion that we should not purchase vials from the vale of tears.

General Carnivore's last stand

The causal inefficacy argument may be the single most sophisticated challenge to the view that it is wrong to purchase and eat meat and other animal products. However, for the reasons just explored, we should not join those who employ this argument to justify an individual's consumption of animal products.

Other arguments in defence of consuming animals have even less to be said in their favour. It may seem odd to consider weaker arguments after having considered a much more sophisticated one. Ordinarily, one dismisses the weaker arguments first and then proceeds to the stronger ones. However, there is a case for considering the weaker arguments after doing the more difficult philosophical work. This is because the weaker arguments are often a last stand for those seeking to defend the consumption of animals. Last stands are typically more desperate than first defences.

Religious arguments

One religious way to try to justify the human use of animals is to revisit the question of animals' moral status, and to claim that there is a morally relevant difference between all (and only) humans, and all other animals. This difference is that while all humans have a soul or are created in the divine image, the same is not true of any other animal. The implication is that it is wrong to treat beings with souls or created in the divine image, in ways in which humans currently treat animals, but that there is no problem with inflicting such treatment to those who are not ensouled or not created in God's image.

We can set aside the obvious questions, such as whether there are souls or a God in whose image he created some beings, as well as questions about which beings have souls and which do not. Some religions have thought that animals *do* have souls. Other people seem to have thought only *some* humans have souls. The possession of a soul or the attribute of being created in God's image is not something that can be verified. To justify manifestly harmful practices by appealing to the (purported) presence or absence of an attribute that can only be asserted and not verified, is deeply problematic. Anybody who doubts this, should ask whether they would countenance such treatment of them by somebody denying that they have a soul, for example.

However, there is an even more fundamental problem with the argument—one that can be directed even to those who *do* think that all and only humans have a soul or were created in God's image. This is that it is unclear why these attributes should make a difference to whether pain and suffering may permissibly be inflicted. Perhaps these attributes make a difference to some ways in which we treat beings. Perhaps, for example, one can only corrupt the souls—whatever that might mean—of those who have souls. Perhaps painlessly taking the life of a being created in the divine image is worse than taking the life of a being not created in that image. That is insufficient to defend the ways in which animals are currently treated, which includes the infliction of considerable pain and suffering.

There is a second religious argument that might be invoked to defend the current use of animals. This is the argument that whereas God permits the use of animals for food and clothing, there is no divine permission to use humans in these ways.

This argument also rests on controversial premises, including that God exists and that texts such as the Bible or Qur'an are the word of God. However, there are further problems with the argument even for those—theists—who accept these premises.

First, even though the Bible seems to suggest that consumption of animals is permissible, it also seems that this permission was a concession. Immediately after God says that humans should have 'dominion over the fish of the sea, and over the birds of the air, and over every living thing that moves on the earth',[61] he says 'I have given you every herb bearing seed, which is upon the face of all the earth, and every tree, on which is the fruit yielding seed; to you it shall be for food'.[62] He then prescribes a similarly vegan diet for all animals.[63] It is only postdiluvian (that is, after the flood), that permission to eat flesh was granted.[64] Prophecies of the messianic era suggest a world in which a vegan diet is again universal—'and the wolf shall dwell with the lamb, and the leopard shall lie down with the kid, and the calf and the young lion, ... and the lion shall eat straw like the ox'.[65]

At this point, some theistic omnivores might respond that while a vegan diet may be the ideal diet in God's eyes, he has nonetheless *permitted* the use of animals, at least for now. In response to this, one might note that this permission is not without restriction. According to many religious traditions, God prohibits cruelty to animals.[66] Much of what humans do to animals *should* be prohibited on these grounds, even though many religious people fail to see that.

Even if we set this aside, and focus on what God does purportedly permit, there is a problem for those who seek to permit whatever the Bible says that God permits. This should be apparent from other practices that, according to the Bible, God permits (or requires). These include slavery,[67] putting sabbath violators to death,[68] and genocide.[69] Most theists do not think that they may now hold slaves, execute sabbath violators, or engage in genocide, divine permission notwithstanding.

There are various strategies aimed at reconciling the biblical permissions with the contemporary rejection of these practices. These include claims that the earlier permission has been superseded or no longer applies, perhaps because the precise conditions are not the same. However, any such strategy provides a route for somebody else saying that the permission to consume animals also no longer applies.

Some theistic omnivores might reply that only some divine permissions no longer apply, and that consuming animals is among those that *are* still in place. The problem with this is that if we accept that only some permissions no longer have applicability, then we are no longer speaking about the plain words of God as reflected in a holy text. Instead, we are speaking about interpretation of that text. It is no longer God saying something, but rather somebody—a fallible human—saying what God is saying. Even if one thinks that God's words are infallible, it does not follow that human interpretation of those words is also infallible. Indeed, given the great variety of conflicting interpretations at least some of them must be wrong.

'Eating meat benefits animals'

Another argument in defence of eating animals, or at least domesticated animals such as cows, sheep, goats, pigs, and chickens, turns on the claim that we benefit *them* by doing so. This, it is said, is because they would not have been brought into existence if they were not going to be eaten. Thus, the practice of eating them, bestows on them the benefit of being brought into existence. The most audacious version of this argument claims that we have not merely a moral *permission*, but a moral *duty* to eat such animals.[70]

At the outset, it should be noted that such an argument *obviously* cannot be applied to some animals. It does not apply to wild animals, including those fish and other aquatic animals who are 'harvested' from the sea and rivers.[71] This is because humans did not bring those animals into existence. It also cannot apply to those domesticated animals whose lives are so miserable that coming into existence cannot, by any stretch of the imagination, be thought to be a benefit to them. This almost certainly applies to the overwhelming majority of intensively farmed animals, whose lives are 'poor, nasty, brutish, and short',[72] but given the crowded conditions in which they live, are the very opposite of solitary. Because all but a very small proportion of commercially available meat comes from animals reared in such conditions, those who wish to appeal to this argument to defend their carnivorism, will have to seek out meat from the small minority of animals not reared in such conditions.

That is, if we assume that the argument works at all. There is good reason to think that it does not, even if we set aside meat that comes from intensively farmed animals and from wild animals. This is because the argument falsely assumes that one is benefited by being brought into existence only to be slaughtered in one's youth, as long as one's short life contains more good than bad. To avoid speciesist biases in such judgements, it is helpful to think of a human analogy. Imagine a couple that decides to bring a child into existence only if they will kill that child after six months of (postnatal) life that contained more good than bad. Would we really think that their baby was benefited by being brought into existence?[73] Who would *act* on a positive answer to such a question, even if they could escape legal repercussions? Thinking about such a human case exposes the absurdity of the idea that we benefit somebody by bringing them into existence only to kill them a short while later. Even if one does not go as far as anti-natalists,[74] who think that coming into existence is always a harm, one can agree that coming into existence is never a benefit.

'More animals are killed in feeding vegans'

There is another argument which claims that concern for animals should lead us to prefer an omnivorous diet involving some limited meat consumption over a strictly vegan diet. According to this argument we do less harm to animals overall through such a diet.[75] The argument applies only to large ruminant animals, especially cattle, and then only to those grazing on grass rather than to those who are fed corn.

According to this argument, vegan diets also involve the deaths of the animals—through the cultivation of crops. For example, mowing of crops kills many small animals, such as mice, rats, gophers, voles, racoons, and rabbits.[76] Many of those not killed by harvesters, are then more exposed to predators.[77]

Eating meat from *corn-fed* cattle would increase rather than decrease the number of animals killed. This is because crops would have to be grown to feed such cattle, and the cultivation and harvesting of those crops would also kill small animals—indeed, many more of them, because a much greater area of land needs to be cultivated to produce feed for cattle over their lifetimes. However, the suggestion is that eating the meat of grass-grazing cattle involves fewer animal deaths. Obviously, the cattle themselves are killed. It is also the case that *some* wild animals are killed in cultivating land for grazing cattle, but the claim is that the number is smaller than when crops are cultivated for crops 'because pasture forage production requires fewer passages through the field with tractors and other farm equipment'.[78] One reason why, according to this argument, beef is to be preferred to the meat of smaller ruminants such as sheep, is that because cows are much larger, each animal death can provide more meat.

Whether this argument works may depend, in part, on the numbers. Does eating a diet that involves large herbivores really result in fewer animal deaths? The number of deaths of intentionally slaughtered animals is much easier to quantify than is the number of unintentional deaths involved in land cultivation, most of which are not readily apparent. Even the most influential proponent of the argument in favour of eating some beef, acknowledges that 'accurate estimates of the total number of animals killed by different agronomic practices from plowing to harvesting are not available'.[79] Nevertheless, he says that 'some studies show that the numbers are quite large'.[80]

He provides a calculation, based on an estimate, and concludes that mixed plant- and forage-production would lead to the deaths of fewer animals. However, even if we think that his per hectare estimate of the number of animals killed is correct,[81] his calculation has nonetheless been criticized for failing to recognize that the number of hectares needed is less if everybody were to be fed a vegan diet than if they were fed a mixed diet. When we calculate the number of animals killed per consumer, the numbers favour a vegan diet.[82]

However, a second problem has also been noted—namely that ethical decisions about whether to eat animals are not reducible to the number of animals killed.[83] We must also consider the amount of suffering. There is good reason to think that the suffering of grazing cattle reared for slaughter is much greater than the suffering of the wild animals who are killed accidentally in the cultivation of crops. The wild animals lead their lives unconfined and engaged in their normal activities until the time they are killed. By contrast, even grazing cattle are confined to some extent. They are also branded, castrated, dehorned, and prevented from sexual activity. When it comes time for slaughter, they are often subjected to the horrors of long-distance transportation and abattoirs that were described at the beginning of this chapter.

To top it all, the wild animals who are accidentally killed already existed, which means that there is no increase in the number of animals dying—only in the timing of those deaths. By contrast, when cattle are killed, these are deaths that could have been entirely avoided by not having bred them in the first place.

Of course, there are other considerations in favour of a vegan diet over one that includes some meat from large ruminant animals. These include the avoidance of certain harms to humans.[84] Some of these are mediated via the mitigation of climate change, which is also to the advantage of those (wild) animals who will exist independent of our breeding herbivores.

Exceptions?

I have argued that eating animals and their products is wrong—or, more accurately, typically or presumptively wrong. It is not a refutation of this position that there may be exceptional cases in which such consumption is not wrong. After all, the claim that we ought not to kill human persons is not undermined by those circumstances, such as self-defence, in which it is permissible to perform such a killing. There may well be some exceptional circumstances in which we would be justified in killing and eating an animal. However, exceptional cases are generally not quotidian. (A possible exception to this claim about exceptional cases, would be that of those people who find themselves in an environment in which the only food source is animal flesh or other products, and who are unable to move to a different environment.)

Eating animals does not *always* involve killing them. Sometimes an animal has already died or been killed—but not in order to provide food. This is true of so-called roadkill. Once an animal has been accidentally killed, may one eat it? One concern one might have about such a practice is that eating an animal accident victim would constitute disrespectfully instrumentalizing the remains of a once sentient being, in the same kind of way that eating a human accident victim would be.[85]

In other situations, it is not even the case that an animal ever has to have died (or been killed), in order for somebody to eat animal flesh. I am not speaking here of the practice of eating (parts of) living animals,[86] which is not uncommon in some places. Instead, I am speaking about a scenario in which no animal needs to die *or suffer* in order for animal flesh to be eaten. More specifically I am speaking about cultured meat—flesh grown in a laboratory from animal cells which were harvested without an animal suffering or dying.[87] Such cultured meat is currently being developed, but it is not yet commercially available. As such, it is not yet a quotidian ethical issue. However, it might someday become one. Are there any moral concerns about eating such flesh?

The moral concern about roadkill—treating the deceased being's remains disrespectfully—would not arise in such a case. This is because cultured meat would not be the remains of any being. If there are any other concerns about cultured meat, they are not the monumental ones that confront the consumption of animal flesh and animal products from animals killed for those purposes. This is exactly why it would be *much* better if all those currently eating meat were instead to eat laboratory-grown flesh. The suffering and deaths of billions of animals could thereby be avoided.

Indeed, the development of competitively priced, readily available meat might be the most effective way of shifting meat-eaters away from consuming dead animals. Those who, despite all the moral problems with eating meat, find the taste irresistible, will have no reason to continue eating the flesh of dead animals if such cultured meat is indistinguishable from it.[88]

This is not to say that there need not be any residual concerns about eating cultured meat. One worry is that the more cultured meat tastes like the 'real thing', the more scope there would be for unscrupulous suppliers and restaurateurs to pass off the flesh of a real animal as cultured meat. Incentives for such practices would diminish the less expensive the cultured product becomes relative to meat from a real animal.

Other concerns about cultured meat may not be instrumentally connected to the infliction of harm, but rather be seen as intrinsic to the practice. However, it is challenging to determine what reasonable basis there might be for such a concern. The prospects for meeting that challenge depend on what kind of concern it is. It is hard to see how the consumption of cultured meat could be strictly impermissible if it involves no chance of harming anybody.

If the concern is not that the practice is, strictly, morally impermissible but rather that it falls short of some ideal way of living, then the prospects for the objection may be more promising. Even then, it is inchoate. The concern may be the same one that many would have with eating cultured *human* flesh. If no humans are harmed in the production of such flesh and if it is unlikely to cause such harm, perhaps by stimulating a taste for human flesh that might then result in murders, it is hard to say exactly *why* the practice falls short of a moral ideal. Must we conclude, as a small number of hard-nosed philosophers do, that in the absence of any harm, there is no moral shortcoming in eating such flesh? Or, is it reasonable to think that the desire to eat human flesh—even if that flesh is cultured rather than derived from a previously living human—suggests something defective about the person harbouring such desires? If so, then perhaps something similar could be said about the desire to eat (even cultured) animal flesh.

The problem is how we determine when a desire does indeed reflect a defect in a person. Although the consumption of human flesh elicits disgust from most people (even when that consumption is unconnected to any harm), disgust is an unreliable marker of moral defect. Even Leon Kass, who has argued for the 'wisdom of repugnance',[89] has acknowledged that 'revulsion is not an argument' and that '*some* of yesterday's repugnances are today calmly accepted'.[90]

However, he provides us with no principled way of differentiating those cases in which repugnance is wise, from those in which it is not. All he says is that in 'crucial cases ... repugnance is the emotional expression of deep wisdom, beyond reason's power fully to articulate it'.[91] He thinks that the widespread repugnance about eating human flesh is one such case.

If the wisdom of some repugnance is 'beyond reason's power fully to articulate it' we obviously cannot expect a *full* account of the wisdom. However, we must be able to provide at least *some* account, for otherwise any attempt to distinguish, in a reasoned way, between wise repugnance and its witless counterpart, will be doomed. I do not plan to pursue this possibility. I have raised it only to indicate that there is a residual question about the eating of animal flesh that is unconnected to the pain, suffering, death, or even use of an animal. I leave this question unanswered because, at least for now, it is not a quotidian one, and must take a backseat to the question whether we may consume animals that have been made to suffer to killed for their flesh and other products.

A practical postscript

The conclusion that we should *not* consume animals and their products can have many more implications than might ordinarily be recognized. It implies that we should not eat meat (including the flesh of fish and other aquatic animals), or consume eggs or dairy, or wear the skins or furs of animals. However, animal products are also to be found in many soaps, shampoos, other cosmetics, in paint, glue, and ink. Indeed, animal products are pervasive. For example, animal fat is used in cooking, and gelatin is found in marshmallows, ice creams, photographic film, sandpaper, and drug capsules. Isinglass, a product derived from dried swim bladders of fish is used in the clarification of some wines and beers.

The list is so long that many people may throw up their hands in despair, wondering whether it is indeed possible to avoid all animal products. If that despair prevents them giving up *any* animal products, then the best will have become the enemy of the good. It is better to make a start and then move closer to the ideal, even if progress towards the ideal is asymptotic—that is, steadily gets closer to the ideal but never reaches it.

There is scope for disagreement about which products one should eschew first. Some people think that we should first forego the flesh and products of the most cognitively advanced of the animals that are typically consumed, on the grounds that they have greater moral standing. Others think that we should first give up the consumption of the smallest animals because we can thereby save the most lives. (The average flesh eater consumes more fish than cows.) Yet others think that we should first abstain from the foods that cause the most suffering. According to this logic one would abstain from chicken and eggs before abstaining from beef, because chickens, on average, suffer more than cows in the production of food for humans.[92]

Much of what divides these views is moot if one's initial steps are big enough—by giving up all animal flesh, for example. That is even more true if one adds eggs and, to a lesser extent, dairy to the list. Removing eggs and dairy from one's diet is a bigger step than giving up flesh, not least because of how many products contain eggs and dairy. However, in many parts of the world it is now much easier than it once was to desist from consuming eggs and dairy, given the wide array of substitutes. Some of these are more expensive than the animal products they replace, which will be relevant to poorer people (who are not the typical readership of this book).[93] One can then move gradually, and where feasible, towards other products that do not include animal products.

There are also questions about how swiftly one moves down the path of removing animals from one's list of consumables. Some people who suddenly go full-vegan—'cold turkey', if one might (exc)use that expression[94]—can relapse. Here individual variation matters. Better to move slowly but surely towards a vegan lifestyle than to rush in and then either rush out or gradually withdraw.

Becoming vegetarian or vegan is not simply a matter of cutting products from one's diet. It also requires attention to what fills those gaps. While vegetarians and vegans can meet all their nutritional needs without consuming animals, and indeed be healthier for doing so, they do have to pay careful attention to their diets, at least until they get into the right dietary habits.

However, the first step to removing animals from the menu and replacing them intelligently, is to recognize just how wrong the current treatment of animals is. Unfortunately, there are powerful psychological disincentives to recognizing this. Not least among these, is resistance to recognizing that one is—or has been—complicit in serious wrongdoing. Many of those who do acknowledge that they should not be consuming animals, often lack the willpower to act accordingly. While these are practical problems of a kind, they are not the practical *philosophical* ones with which this chapter have been concerned.

7
Language

While there is some disagreement about the origin of the expression 'Mind your Ps and Qs', we know that it is an injunction to 'mind your language', 'mind your manners', or to 'be on your best behaviour'. What language we use is sometimes (merely) a matter of manners. On other occasions it is—or, at least, is thought to be—much more than that, namely also a matter of morals.

The subject of this chapter is not all language. Much language does not raise moral issues. Even when it does, they are not always the issues that will be discussed here. Lying, for example, is typically done through language, but the issues it raises are more broadly about deception, which can be done in the absence of language.

Language plays an indispensable role in some conceptions of bullshit, but not in others.[1] Even according to those views that take bullshit to be fundamentally a linguistic matter, it is usually about longer linguistic units—extended phrases, sentences, paragraphs, or longer—than those that constitute the subject matter of the current chapter.

This chapter will be concerned with which words and expressions may not be uttered or written, and whether there are words that should be said in their stead. In some ways morality is now thought to range over more expressions than it once did. Many terms that were previously regarded as acceptable, have ceased to be so regarded. Greater sensitivity—often appropriate, but sometimes crossing into hypersensitivity—about 'race', ethnicity, sex, sexual orientation, and gender identity, for example, has led to new linguistic strictures.

However, we should not lose sight of the fact that at least some language that was previously regarded as morally wrong is no longer regarded as immoral, at least by many people. For example, while there are still those who think that blasphemy and vulgarity or obscenity are morally wrong, the proportion of people espousing this view has reduced—in *some* societies.[2] Thus, instead of saying that conventions of acceptable language have become more restrictive, it would probably be more accurate to say that the conventions of acceptable language have changed.

Very Practical Ethics. David Benatar, Oxford University Press. © Oxford University Press 2024.
DOI: 10.1093/9780197780831.003.0007

Conventions and morality

There is a difference, of course, between:

(i) saying that use of some word or expression is *regarded as* immoral, and
(ii) saying that it *is* immoral.[3]

In the case of (i), a word or expression can be regarded as immoral either by an *individual* or by some grouping, such as a *society*. When applied to a society, the distinction between (i) and (ii) can be understood as the distinction between the usage being:

(i) socially permissible;
and its being
(ii) morally permissible.

When an individual or a society *regards* the use of a word as immoral, they have the *view* that use of that word *is* immoral. They may or may or may not be mistaken about that. The purpose of this chapter is not to engage the empirical question of which words and expressions are regarded as immoral by which individuals and which societies, although sometimes reference will be made to such views. Instead, it is to engage the moral question of which words and expressions are immoral and thus *should* be regarded as such.

Some might object that the distinction between what is regarded as immoral and what is immoral, must collapse in the case of language, because language is unavoidably social and a matter of convention. Although an individual can use terms in idiosyncratic ways or even develop a private language, these will not be understood by others unless they come to recognize the meaning, thereby rendering the words or language social. What words—whether delivered orally or in writing—mean, is dependent on what a linguistic community takes them to mean.

While it is true that language is unavoidably social and conventional, it does not follow from this that what constitutes immoral language is reducible to language that is regarded as wrong. This should be evident from the manifest fact that members of a single linguistic community can disagree about whether the use of certain words or expressions is immoral. We should understand why there can be such disagreement.

To this end, we should distinguish two questions about any word or expression (where words and expressions are understood as particular linguistic vocalizations or written markings):

1. What does X mean?
2. Is saying (or writing, or otherwise communicating) X, morally acceptable?

There are cases where the answer to the first question may be thought to take us very far towards a negative answer to the second question. For example, if the meaning of X is a racial or ethnic slur, it might be thought to follow that uttering X is morally wrong. However, as will become clear, matters are not that simple. In other cases, the distance between establishing the meaning of X and determining whether uttering or writing it is morally impermissible, is even greater.

Before turning to the second question, more needs to be said about the first. In asking what X means, consider first its denotation—its literal or primary meaning,[4] which, as will become clear, is *not* necessarily the same as its etymology.

One common way in which denotation differs is *between* linguistic communities. In most cases, a word that means one thing in one language is meaningless in another. However, there are also some cases in which the same sound or written word mean different things in different languages. In a subset of these cases, the meanings can make the difference between innocuousness and moral or mannerly peril.

For example, if an Afrikaans speaker utters (the admittedly unusual) sentence 'Kies jou kant en vak', which means 'Choose your side and subject', it will sound to an English speaker (who does not understand Afrikaans or who hears the sentence out of context) as 'Kiss yo' cunt 'n fuck'. In Afrikaans the sounds are entirely innocuous, whereas in English some of them are vulgar. To the extent that vulgarity raises ethical issues, the foregoing utterance may be problematic in English but not in Afrikaans—unless the Afrikaans sentence is uttered for the purpose of eliciting the misinterpretation by English speakers, or even merely to create that ambiguity.[5]

Denotation can also vary *within* a language. Sometimes this change occurs over time. A word that means one thing at one time comes to mean another thing at another time. On other occasions, a word can have two different meanings at the same time. A 'table', for example, can refer to a particular piece of furniture, or to a visual display of data, especially in columns and rows. Sometimes one denotation raises moral issues that do not arise in the other denotation. Uttering the word 'cow' with reference to a female human, raises moral issues that do not arise when the word is used with reference to a female bovine.

The meaning of words is not limited to their denotations. A word's connotations are among its meanings. For example, although both the words 'bachelor' and 'spinster' have symmetrical denotations, the former referring to an unmarried man and the latter referring to an unmarried woman,[6] the latter has negative connotations that are absent in the former. Indeed, in some contexts, the connotations of 'bachelor' are actually positive. Such differences in meaning will have obvious relevance to ethical questions about their usage.

However, questions about meaning—whether denotation or connotation, or some mixture of them—do not settle ethical questions about which words we may utter or write. Meaning is relevant, but it is not decisive. There is much else that needs to be said.

The words in question

The categories of words and expressions that have been, are, or might still be brought under moral scrutiny, vary considerably. Some of these categories, and particular examples within them, will be discussed below. Some of the ethical issues arising from them are distinctive of one or other category of words. However, other ethical issues range over a few different categories. Where an ethical issue does span across different categories, it is sometimes the case that people do not notice this, and that they have inconsistent views regarding the different categories of words. These issues are all worthy of examination, in a bid to understand just when particular words and expressions are immoral, and when they are not.

When people raise ethical concerns about language, they typically raise one or more of four kinds of objection, namely that the relevant words:

(a) cause offence;
(b) are disrespectful;
(c) undermine either equality or inclusiveness; or
(d) are vulgar.

These are overlapping objections that cannot always be entirely disentangled. For example, that which causes offence can be perceived as disrespectful, and being disrespected can cause offence. Some words that cause offence are vulgar (that is, obscenities). However, it is possible for the four objections to come apart. It is possible, for example, for some words to cause offence, but because taking offence is inappropriate, the expression of those words is not actually disrespectful. Similarly, words can be disrespectful without being vulgar.

Causing offence, being disrespectful, undermining equality or inclusiveness, or being vulgar *can be* moral lapses. However, not every accusation of such a flaw is a warranted allegation. Sometimes an allegation is without *any* foundation, as is the case when the (innocent, literal) use of the word 'niggardly', which has absolutely nothing at all to do with a racial slur, has caused outrage. There have been a few such incidents,[7] but the most prominent of these was its use in 1999 by David Howard in a budget discussion. Mr Howard, who was then an aide to the mayor of Washington, DC, was pressured to resign. Julian Bond, then chair of the US civil rights organization, the NAACP,[8] appropriately came to Mr Howard's defence, saying 'You hate to think you have to censor your language to meet other people's lack of understanding'.[9]

On other occasions, consideration of one person or group must be weighed against some other factor. One such factor can be consideration of *another* person or group. What, for example, are we to do, when some Hispanic or Latin Americans want people of their ethnicity to be referred to as Latinx(s), while others want members of the same ethnicity to be called Latinos (or perhaps Latinas, in the case of women)?[10] Competing preferences cannot be accommodated simultaneously, at least not without cumbersome repeated disjunctions.

More generally, the fact that a word offends somebody is not a decisive indication that use of that word is morally wrong. To think that it is a decisive indication, would be to give a moral veto to the hypersensitive. That a word offends is a relevant consideration, but we then need to ask (a) whether it is reasonable to be offended by the use of the word, and (b) whether there are other moral considerations that pull in the opposite direction.

When there is nothing morally wrong with a particular word or expression, it may sometimes still be *imprudent* to utter (or write) it. This is the case when the social environment is such that enough people (with power) are outraged, even in the absence of good reason, and could visit some evil upon one in response to one's perceived infraction. While it might be permissible, in such circumstances, to utter the word, it might be unwise to do so. That, itself, is a morally alarming situation, against which some people may wish to take action. Such action might include refusing to be cowed. Sometimes there may be a duty to stand up against the madness, but if the costs are high enough, it will more typically be supererogatory.[11]

To determine which words and expressions are morally impermissible and which ones should replace them, one needs to examine the particular words, or at least categories of words, and evaluate them on their merits. There is presumably a very long list of words that either are or could be contested. They cannot all be examined here. However, some of the main categories, and some examples of specific words within those categories will be scrutinized.

Group slurs

Slurs about racial, ethnic, and other groups, including a sex or a sexual orientation, may seem like a clear-cut case of words that ought not to be uttered. It is clear-cut in some ways, but not in others. A slur, by its very nature, is a kind of insult. Even if we think that individuals may sometimes deserve an insult—'gutless' if cowardly, a 'jerk' (or 'arsehole') if that appellation fits, or a 'bullshitter' if he is one—it is hard to see how levelling typical group slurs can ever be deserved or otherwise justified. For example, 'wop', 'spic', and (when used to refer to a homosexual) 'faggot', are all derogatory and thus, it may be thought, should never be used to refer to entire groups or to members of them. If some individual member of a group is deserving of an insult, it is not on grounds of membership in the group to which the slur is directed.

It is easy to see why using a group slur will typically be wrong. As an insult, there is a moral presumption against levelling it, a presumption that will not typically be defeated. Some are of the view not only that the presumption against *using* a slur can never be defeated but also that it is always wrong to *say* or *write* a slur. That view is hard to justify. The mistake underlying such a view is a failure to distinguish between the 'use' of a word, and its 'mention'.

Use and mention

The failure to distinguish the 'use' and the 'mention' of a word, was cleverly lampooned in Monty Python's 1979 film, *The Life of Brian*. In that case, the word was not a slur, but rather God's name. A man is to be stoned to death for uttering the name of God in vain.[12] The condemned man protests, explaining:

> Look, I'd had a lovely supper and all I said to my wife was 'That piece of halibut was good enough for Jehovah'.

This elicits the fury of the presiding official and the mob gathered to carry out the stoning. The official tells the condemned man not to say the word 'Jehovah' again. With that, one person in the mob then throws a stone at the presiding official. The presiding official calls him out for this, and the stone thrower then justifies his action by saying:

> Well, you did say 'Jehovah'.

A stone is then thrown at *this* person by somebody in the mob. The official attempts to regain control of the stoning by saying:

> Stop that. Stop it, will you stop that. Now look, no-one is to stone anyone until I blow this whistle. *Even* . . . and I want to make this absolutely clear . . . *even* if they *do* say 'Jehovah'.

The official is then immediately stoned to death.

The humour arises from the stoners' inability to distinguish between the 'use' of a word and its 'mention'. One uses the word 'Jehovah' or 'God' if one utters it either in prayer or as a (blasphemous) exclamation—such as 'God damn it!' A mention, however, is different from a use. If John says: 'Do not stone him even if he does say "Jehovah"', John is *mentioning* 'Jehovah' but not *using* the word. In other words, there is a difference between saying:

1. God damn it!

and saying:

2. Don't say 'God damn it!'

The word 'God' is *used* in the first instance, but only *mentioned* in the second. (A complexity is that *I* am not using it in the first instance. When

I refer, as I do here, to somebody saying it, they are using it, but I am merely mentioning it.)

Notice also that 2 is different from:

3. Don't say 'G damn it!' or
3*. Don't say 'G-word damn it!'

Neither 3 nor 3* are injunctions against saying 'God damn it!'. Instead, they are respectively injunctions against saying 'G damn it!' and 'G-word damn it!'. Notice, finally, just how (much more?) obscure this entire explanation would have become if I had eliminated the word 'God' entirely—that is, if every reference to it had to be replaced with 'G' or 'G-word'.

For opponents of traditional blasphemy, emitting the sound of the divine name or making the scratchings that constitute its written form (in whatever language) amounts to blasphemy if those sounds or scratchings are not made in the sacred context—of prayer or religious texts, for example. In any other contexts, those same sounds and scratchings were thought to constitute blasphemy. Although there are still many people who engage in this kind of magical thinking about the word(s) that designate God or his name, many moderns are inclined to see this as primitive thinking.

The irony is that many of those who adopt this smug view towards those religious believers who attribute such magical power to particular scratchings and sounds, are themselves guilty of attributing magical power to words. For these 'moderns', the relevant words are not religious ones but rather racial, ethnic, and other slurs. They think that the mere vocalization of the sound or writing down of the letters is a moral offence, irrespective of whether those vocalizations or writings constitutes a use or a mention.

There have been numerous such cases. Among those who have been targeted are Donald G. McNeil Jr,[13] a *New York Times* journalist, who lost his job at that newspaper, and Professor Adam Habib,[14] who had to stand aside temporarily as director of the School of Oriental and African Studies (SOAS).[15] He managed to retain his position after apologizing, and a 'restorative justice process' was put in place.[16]

Both Mr McNeil and Professor Habib *mentioned* (in perfectly innocuous ways) what the press coyly refers to as the 'N-word'. Mr McNeil was responding to a question from a student about whether a classmate 'should have been suspended for using the N-word in a video from two years ago'. Seeking clarification before answering, he effectively asked, although not in these exact words, whether that classmate had actually used the word or merely mentioned it. In seeking this clarification, he uttered the offending sound.[17]

Professor Habib had similarly responded to a student inquiry, this time about a SOAS staff member who had allegedly used the offending word. Professor Habib responded by saying that if the person used that word—which he mentioned—then it would violate SOAS policy and action would be taken. (Notice how the chilling effect of intolerance has resulted in my own coy description of what Professor Habib said, because the difference between use and a meta-mention—a mention of a mention—is as incomprehensible to intolerant 'progressives' as is the distinction between 'use' and 'mention'.)

Worse than the mob's inability to distinguish use from mention, is (much of) the media's inability to understand such a distinction. Thus, both men were reported by, respectively, the *New York Times*[18] and the *Times Higher Education*,[19] to have *used* the offending word. This is unprofessional reporting because it is inaccurate. It also has massive and unwarranted repercussions for people's reputations. Moreover, it is now routine for many media that make such allegations, not to include in their reports the precise words uttered and the contexts within which they were uttered (perhaps because *that* would raise the ire of the intolerant). Without the provision of those facts, readers are unable to make their own judgments about whether the person really did use the slur or only mentioned it in an innocent way.

There is further similarity between the old and the new intolerance. In the case of God's name, some utterances—those in sacred contexts—are permissible. In the case of slurs, the current intolerance grants certain vocalizations and written expressions of slur words indemnity. These are vocalizations and written expressions of slurs—whether they are merely mentioned or even used—by members of those groups to which they are customarily directed.

This selective indemnity cannot be justified. If a slur is *used* by a member of the group against which the slur is used, it remains a slur. Insulting somebody does not become morally acceptable merely because the same insult is (or could be) used against the person using it. If the slur is merely *mentioned*, then it does not amount to insulting anybody. Again, it should make no difference whether the mention—which is not an insult—is made only by those against whom, when it is used, it is a slur.

Nevertheless, so pervasive and frenzied is the moral panic about the word Mr McNeil and Professor Habib mentioned, it is prudent for me to invoke the purported indemnity here to explain that there is a difference between:

4. calling somebody 'Kike!'

and:

5. saying 'Don't call somebody "Kike"!'

The first is a use, while the second is a mention. (Again, it does not follow that *I* am using the word in the first case. The person who casts the slur is using it. I am referring to them using it.) The second is also different from saying:

6. Don't call somebody 'the K-word'.

and

7. Don't call somebody 'K**e'.

When one utters 5, one is enjoining somebody from calling someone else 'Kike', whereas 6 and 7 could be read as enjoining somebody from, respectively, saying 'K-word' or writing 'K**e'. (Who can actually say or read the word 'K**e' aloud?) Similarly, if somebody were called a 'Kike', it might be inaccurate to say that they had been called a 'K-word'. (There is, after all, more than one K-word.[20])

Those who think it *is* accurate, face a different problem. If 'Kike' and either 'K-word' or 'K**e' are interchangeable, then one has not, in fact, avoided mentioning 'Kike' by means of either of its substitutes. This could open the way to a further intolerance—intolerance for the more oblique references to slurs. Another possible basis for such intolerance would be that the oblique reference invariably conjures up the actual word in the mind of the hearer. References to slurs, much like the tetragrammaton,[21] would then become ineffable.

There are obviously further complexities to the distinction between use and mention. This is because language can have further nuances. There are cases where a clever antisemite might try to hide behind the distinction, by saying something like:

8. If I were not worried about the consequences for me of using the word, I would call you a Kike.

Even if this is technically not an instance of *using* the slur, it is *tantamount* to using it. To clarify, again, when I say it here, I am not using it or saying anything that is tantamount to using it. It is used by the hypothetical person I am quoting. That person is saying something similar to:

9. If I were not worried about the consequence for me of defaming you, I would say that you [insert your chosen false, defamatory statement about the person to whom you are speaking].

Even if such a formulation would get one off the legal hook for defamation in some jurisdictions, it is not a moral exculpation.

In other cases, context will matter. For example, imagine a situation in which somebody says to a Jew:

10. There are those who would call Jews 'kikes'.

This, again, is technically not a use of the word 'Kike'. Whether it is morally equivalent to a use, depends on the context. In some contexts, it will be the case that 10 is being uttered for the same purposes as 8, namely in a (failed) bid to evade moral culpability, even though the speaker is among those who would refer to Jews in precisely this way.

In other contexts, 10 may be entirely innocuous, and not only when it is mentioned here for illustrative purposes. Sometimes the sentence might be uttered simply to state a fact without the speaker thereby endorsing the practice described. Indeed, adjacent sentences might make it clear that the speaker or writer disapproves of the practice. If for example, 10 is followed by: 'I am relieved that social disapproval of such slurs disincentivizes them from speaking in such ways', then, barring any other relevant contextual considerations, the reasonable interpretation is that the speaker is not covertly deploying the slur.

There will be yet other contexts in which it will be entirely unclear from the context whether 10 is innocuous or an attempt to evade moral responsibility.

In such cases the question will arise whether that ambiguity is itself innocuous or an attempt to evade moral responsibility.

Use and use

The distinction between, and discussion of, 'use' and 'mention' reveals that there is often (but not always) nothing morally wrong with mentioning a slur. It does not follow that *using* a slur word is *always* immoral. This is because there are different kinds of usage.[22]

Consider how words become slurs. The fact that a word is now a slur does not mean that it started as one, or at least that it always carried the punch that it now does. For example, the epithet 'dago', that is used to refer derogatively to Spanish, Portuguese, or Italian people, likely arose from the name Diego. Obviously that name is not a slur. Perhaps it then began to be used to refer, generically, to anybody from these countries, in much the way as somebody might speak of a typical Russian (male) as 'Ivan', a typical German (male) as 'Fritz' or 'Hans', and typical (male) Englishman as 'John'.[23] Perhaps at this point, the individual is no longer regarded as an individual, but instead as a generic member of the group. 'Diego' then transforms into 'dago', and the unambiguously derogatory sense emerges.

The same is true for an infamous slur against 'black'[24] human beings. Its etymology is the Latin 'niger', meaning 'black'. That origin very likely carried none of the derogatory content of the slur into which it evolved.

Similarly, terms such as 'retard' (when used as a noun rather than as a verb), 'imbecile', 'idiot', 'moron', and 'cretin' were once standard, non-pejorative medical terms. Such terms are now slurs, if used with reference to those with what are now called either mental or intellectual disabilities. (With reference to others these terms are individual insults rather than group slurs.)

Just as words can become slurs, they can also cease to be. Typically, a word does not cease to become a slur by not using it. However, ceasing to use a slur is *one* way for a slur to fall out of use or, in time, even to become forgotten. That is one entirely reasonable fate for a slur. However, until it has fallen into obsolescence or become forgotten, it continues to pack (often full) punch when it *is* used.

This is the reason why another response to a slur is to use it in a different way to the way in which those intending it as a slur use it. The idea is for those who reject the slur to appropriate it, repurpose it, and then use it in their own way. This was explicitly recommended by the comedian Lenny Bruce.[25] The strategy has had considerable success for the word 'queer', which, although once a terrible slur, has very effectively been reclaimed as a neutral or even positive term.[26]

Many African Americans, not only comedians and rappers, but also ordinary people in everyday language, have attempted something similar for a vile North American slur for 'blacks'.[27] They have used it in ways that undermines it. This has had at least some success, even though it has not (yet?) overtaken the derogatory meaning. At present, the same word has more than one meaning—the slur, but also various non-derogatory meanings, including positive meanings.

The simultaneous existence of derogatory and (even positive) non-derogatory meanings of the same word is not unusual. Two other examples are 'Yid' and 'Jew'. The former is literally Yiddish (or 'Jewish') for 'Jew'. In many contexts both 'Yid' and 'Jew' simply designate a person who is Jewish. Among Ashkenazi Jews, 'Yid' is sometimes used *warmly* as an autonym. However, antisemites have come to use the same words in derogatory ways.[28] In other words, they appropriated a neutral (or positive word) and sought to turn it into a slur.

Sometimes the difference in usage depends on tone or nuance in pronunciation, but not always, at least because these differences are absent in the written form. Sometimes the difference is evident from who is saying the word.[29]

The case of 'Jew' is interesting because its appropriation as a derogatory term by antisemites has caused its original neutral sense to recede to some (limited) extent. There are now many people who, in their own speech and writing, eschew 'Jew' in favour of 'Jewish person'. Well-meaning though that practice is, it may be ill-advised, as it accedes to the antisemite's meaning of 'Jew', instead of reinforcing a meaning that is entirely parallel to 'Christian', 'Kurd', or 'Canadian', for example.

Admittedly, there are differences in how we should respond to:

(a) words that are currently substantially (or exclusively) derogatory, but which some people are—or we could be—appropriating for the purpose of defanging; and
(b) words that are, at present, substantially neutral (or positive) but which have begun being appropriated for derogatory purposes.

This difference is represented diagrammatically in Figure 7.1, where the solid lines indicate the extent to which a shift has already occurred, and the broken lines indicate either the further *possible* changes along each of the same trajectories or the reversal of the changes that have occurred thus far.[30]

The difference is, analogically, between (a) attacking a fortress, and (b) defending one. In (a) one is up against the massive obstacle of derogatory usage. In such cases, it is more difficult (but not impossible) to break through and reclaim the word. Attempts to do so are also more prone to being misunderstood. By contrast, in (b) one has the weight of usage on one's side, or, put differently, the advantage of defence. One seeks to preserve the dominant current usage against an insidious attempt to create a slur and to crowd out the neutral meaning. One's usage is less likely to be misunderstood.

These differences imply that the case for appropriating and undermining a derogatory term is not as strong as the case for defending a neutral one. That, however, does not mean that no case can be made for the former. Any such case would need to take various considerations into account.

For example, just as tone can make a difference to whether the use of a word is a slur or not, so tone can make a difference to how a word can be used with the purpose of undermining its capacity to slur. It can make a difference, for example, whether the word is said in an obviously affectionate tone or in a more ambiguous tone. This is not to say that using the word in even a slurring tone can never be part of an endeavour to undermine the slur.

This is because of a further consideration—context. If, for example, a novel's author has his characters use slurs (as slurs), it makes a big difference whether the book itself endorses or opposes the use of slurs. Many books (and plays, and films) that depict prejudice, do so not to support it, but to show it up and condemn it.[31] Sadly, many people cannot understand that distinction, and the difference it makes.

Another relevant, but again not a decisive, consideration, is the severity of the particular slur at the relevant time. Not all slurs have the same force.

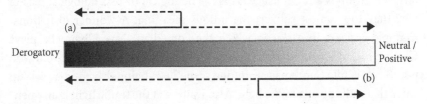

Figure 7.1 Shifting meanings.

Some are milder and others more severe. Slurs that are currently milder might be easier to tame, and less risky to do so.

A further consideration is one that is usually the first to spring to many people's minds—namely the identity of the person using the word. As is the case in considering the ethics of jokes that turn on negative stereotypes,[32] many people oversimplify this consideration. They think that use of a slur can be permissible *only* if the slur word is being repurposed by members of the group to which it is directed. According to this view, only 'blacks' may use anti-'black' epithets in a way that is aimed at eviscerating the slur, and only women may challenge anti-women slurs by using them.

Why would somebody think that only members of the denigrated group have the prerogative to use the word in a different sense? We need an explanation for why this should be the case. It seems odd that a permission to help shift a meaning from a negative one to an innocuous or positive one, should be the preserve of those who are degraded by the negative use. In the case of other wrongs, it is not generally thought that it is only the victims who have a permission to help right the wrong.

Perhaps the explanation is that it is in the mouths, or at the fingers, of members of the denigrated group, that the alternative usage of the word either (i) most likely *is* or (ii) most likely is *seen to be*, an alternative usage of the word. There is something to this rationale, because even if the first of these options is false, the second is certainly true. However, inferring that it is *only* members of the denigrated group who may repurpose the slur oversimplifies matters.

First, we know that it is not uncommon for those on the receiving end of a slur to use it in exactly same way as those who use it as a slur. They may hold prejudices about their own group, or may simply be malicious. For example, when some 'blacks' use the term 'porch negro', and worse, to refer to other 'blacks', they may be using it with as much venom, as an anti-'black' racist.[33]

Second, not every usage of a slur by those who are not members of the targeted group is a racist usage. There is no logical or psychological reason why they too cannot subvert the odious meaning. A wonderful fictional example appears in a skit in which the comedian Dave Chappelle plays Clayton Bigsby—a blind African American who thinks he is 'white' and who is a 'Black White Supremacist'. In one scene he is being driven in a pick-up truck that pulls up at a traffic light. Also waiting at the traffic light is an open-top car, carrying four young 'white' men, whose car radio is blaring hip-hop music. Assuming that they are 'black', Mr Bigsby directs a racial slur at them. The young men are delighted to have been on the receiving end of the word, which they take as a compliment rather than a slur. Two of them 'high five' one another while one says 'Awesome!'.[34]

While that is a fictional example, there are also real-life instances of non-'blacks' who use the same slur word in a non-derogatory sense. This is true of Bill Maher, even though he was forced to apologize for his humorous and obviously non-racist (if not anti-racist) use of the slur word. This should be obvious, in large part because of what we (do or should) know about Bill Maher, but also because of the other contextual considerations.[35]

To reject the view that *only* members of the denigrated group may use slur words in order to subdue those words, is not to deny the more limited view that it may *more often* be permissible for members of the denigrated group to use those slurs in such a way.

Of course, the problem—whether the speaker is a member of the denigrated group or not—is that those hearing or reading the epithet may be justifiably uncertain about how the word is being used. It is *justifiable* uncertainty that is crucial. Whether uncertainty is justifiable will depend, to some extent, on what the listener or reader knows—or should know—about the speaker (or writer). The more reason one's audience has to know that one is using the slur word in a non-derogatory sense, the more reasonable, all other things being equal, it is to use it (in a non-derogatory way, of course).

This condition can be met most easily in private, where 'in private' refers to circumstances in which the only person or people who hear the use, are intimates—family or close friends who know that one would not use a slur word in its derogatory sense.

Public contexts, which are those in which one's audience includes non-intimates, are more complicated. This is for the obvious reason that one's audience then includes people who will know one less well. However, it is not therefore the case that a slur may *only* be repurposed in private contexts. Indeed, repurposing slur words will arguably be more effective when they are used in neutral or affirming ways *in public*. When that happens, one does not have the luxury of being confident that *all* those hearing or reading one's use will know from whom it comes. Here the risks of misinterpretation are greater, but so are the potential benefits.

Public uses, however, are not all of one kind. Indeed, matters become quite complex, as summarized in Figure 7.2, which also compares public uses to private uses.

	Private	Public	
Personal or impersonal use	Personal use	Personal use	Impersonal use
Whether or not the slur is directed at particular person(s)	Slur directed at a particular person (or persons)		Slur not directed at a particular person (or persons), but rather generally.
The *reasonable* interpretation of the person in whose presence it is said is the relevant criterion.	The person to whom the slur is directed is a member of the group to which the slur is typically directed.	The person to whom the slur is directed is not a member of the group to which the slur is typically directed.	The *reasonable* interpretation of all those who will witness the repurposed slur is the relevant criterion.
	The *reasonable* interpretation of the person to whom the slur is directed counts *most*, but the reasonable interpretation of others is also relevant.	The *reasonable* interpretation of the person to whom the slur is directed does count, but often not more than the reasonable interpretation of others.	

Figure 7.2 Defanging slurs through use: Relationship between user and audience.

In the public realm, unlike in private, it makes a difference whether the use is personal or impersonal. A personal use is one directed towards a particular person (or persons), whereas an impersonal usage is not directed towards any particular person, but rather more generally. There is a further distinction between two kinds of personal uses. Some are directed towards a member of the group towards which the slur is usually directed. On other occasions, personal uses are directed towards somebody who is not a member of the group to which the particular slur is usually directed. Somewhat different standards apply in each of these kinds of cases.

Where a slur-word is repurposed publicly and directed at an individual who is a member of the group to whom the slur is usually directed, it is the reasonable interpretation of the person to whom it is directed that is *most* relevant. It is that person to whom the slur is directed and it is thus that person's reasonable interpretation that should carry the most weight (which is not to say that the reasonable interpretation of others does not count at all).

As a result, the rule about the *private* use of repurposed slur-words will have some application to the public realm as well. Directing a reclaimed version of a slur to a stranger is very unlikely to be justified, especially if that stranger is a member of the group usually denigrated by the slur that is used. By contrast, there would be some (but only some) scope for the use of such a word to a close friend, even in some public settings. Obviously vicarious misinterpretation is possible. That possibility is relevant, but not decisive (for reasons I shall outline later).

When a public, personal repurposed use of a slur is directed towards somebody who is not a member of the group to which the slur is usually directed, the slur is still personal, but not to the same extent as it is in the case when the person to whom it is directed *is* a member of the group usually denigrated with that slur. Thus, while that person's reasonable interpretation will count, it will not count quite as much as in the previous kind of case. Here, relatively more weight must be given to the reasonable interpretation of others who witness this use of the slur, and most especially those members of the group to which the slur is usually directed.

Consider, finally, cases of public impersonal repurposed use of a slur-word. In such cases, there is no individual (whether intimate or stranger) whose reasonable interpretation should be privileged. The word is directed toward nobody in particular, but because it is directed generally, it is also not directed *away* from anybody who is part of the group to which it refers.[36]

These are the cases in which it is most difficult to meet the requisite condition—namely, that the most reasonable interpretation of the public is that the slur word is not being used in a derogatory sense. The condition is met when there is good reason for members of the public, or at least those who are willing to familiarize themselves with the relevant considerations, to recognize that the word is not being used in a derogatory sense.

The example of Bill Maher above, is one such example. There was outrage in that case, but that outrage was not reasonable. It should be (and should have been) entirely apparent to anybody who watches or listens to Mr Maher, that he is an opponent of racism—and that he is a comedian, who was very likely joking.

However, even those who wish to dispute this particular case should acknowledge that there are at least some circumstances in which a public impersonal repurposing of the slur word meets the requisite condition. That is to say, there must be *some* circumstances in which it should be clear to any reasonable person that the slur was being used in a way that undermines the slur.

Imagine, for example, a town in which a slur has prominently been used against a few members of a racial or ethnic group. If hundreds of inhabitants of that town who are not themselves members of the targeted group, decide (perhaps with the support of the leaders of the targeted group) to protest this hate by embarking on a solidarity campaign by standing together and carrying a '#WeAreAll[Epithet]s' placard, they may very well be justified in doing so.[37] It is very likely that many people will nonetheless take offence, but their failure to understand the way in which the epithet were being used would be unreasonable.

At this point, it might be asked why the relevant standard, in each case, is whether it is *reasonable* to interpret the use of the slur word as non-derogatory. Why is it not instead whether the slur word is, as a matter of fact, *likely* to be understood in this way? The answer is that it is too much to require a speaker or writer to err so far on the side of 'caution' that even the most unsubtle or obtuse listeners or readers will be left without doubt. If we were morally required to assume the lowest common comprehension denominator when we communicate, we would be hidebound, and not merely with regards to using slur words in non-denigrating ways—and, *a fortiori*, merely mentioning them. Misinterpretation of even the plainest speech is widespread. That would require much more silence—if that too were not prone to misinterpretation.

It could still be that one is ill-advised to use a slur in a non-derogatory way if it will not be understood in that way by a sufficient proportion of the audience. It may be ill-advised partly for prudential reasons, but there could be another reason too. If a large enough proportion of people failed to understand that it were being used in a non-pejorative way, the non-pejorative use might simply not service the goal of eviscerating the slur. Nevertheless, not every uproar in response to an attempt at a non-pejorative use constitutes evidence that the attempt has failed. Uproars are often the work of an undiscerning, vocal few, who may not reflect the views or a somewhat more discerning many.[38]

Group names

Terms used to refer to groups of people are often thought to become offensive even when they have not previously been regarded as slurs. For example, the inoffensive way of referring to Americans with many generations of (sub-Saharan) African ancestry has changed more than once over the years. There was a time when 'Negroes' was entirely inoffensive. It was used with pride by members of the group so designated. In time, 'Colored People' became the preferred term, until that too became dated and offensive.[39] The preferred terms are now 'black' and 'African American'. It is entirely possible that, in time, these terms too will become dated and offensive, and will themselves be replaced.

We know that the earlier terms have not become slurs. They survive in the names of organizations such as the 'United Negro College Fund', and the 'National Association for the Advancement of Colored People'. Although neither organization has changed its name, the emphasis on the now dated words is reduced by typically not pronouncing either name in full. The 'United Negro College Fund' is abbreviated to 'UNCF' or called the 'United Fund'. The 'National Association for the Advancement of Colored People' is—and, probably on account of the length of the full name, always has—typically been referred to as the 'NAACP', which is pronounced 'N, double-A, C, P'.

We need to think differently about such terms than we do about slurs. When a term is clearly a slur, we have good moral reason either to avoid it or to seek to undermine its derogatory meaning. However, when a term is not a slur, but some people prefer a different term, different moral considerations apply.

Here, we need to distinguish between two kinds of cases. In the first, the term, although not (yet?) a slur, has begun to acquire some derogatory connotations, which is what explains why some people want to shift to using a different term. In the second kind of case, the term currently used has not acquired *any* derogatory overtones, and there is merely a preference of some people to switch to a different word.

The first kind of case has some similarities to the case of slurs. The derogatory connotations provide one with a moral reason to avoid them, even if the reason is not as strong as when a term is a slur. However, there is also a difference between slurs and a case of this first kind. Because the term is not (yet) a slur, the case for trying to assert the neutral usage is stronger. We should not abandon a term the moment bad actors attempt to use it disparagingly. If we do so, not only do we capitulate, but they may well then just target the new term that we use as a substitute. For example, we can imagine American racists starting to emphasize the 'African' in 'African American', in order to imply that they are not 'true Americans'. If that starts happening, we are under no obligation to cede use of the term to them, even if there is no widespread usage of the parallel 'European American'. Similarly, if racists start playing up the negative connotations that 'black' has in non-racial contexts—such as 'blackmail', 'black magic', 'blackguard', and 'black market'—and seek to extend these to people who are currently designated as 'black', we will have no duty to follow them. We should instead wrestle (metaphorically, of course) with those who would seek to derogate the term.

Such a struggle may succeed or fail to a lesser or a greater degree. If the derogatory usage becomes sufficiently widespread then we need to start thinking about the word as a slur (or approximating one), and treat it as such. This is what happened to the word 'Chinaman', which became a slur, but previously had an innocent meaning parallel to those which 'Englishman', 'Frenchman', or 'Irishman' still have.[40]

The second kind of case, where a term currently has no derogatory overtones, is yet still different. Let us assume, at least for now, that those preferring to switch terms are a minority even of the group to whom the term applies. (This is the usual case, at least initially, because it is extremely unlikely that most members of a group would suddenly prefer a different term to refer to themselves if the term currently in usage is not derogatory.)

In such a case we have no overriding reason to change our usage. Although doing so might please those people with the novel preference, the pervasive non-derogatory usage of the current term suggests that most people—even most members of the relevant group—do not share that preference. Since we cannot please everybody, there is no duty to please the minority.

However, if, in time, usage shifts substantially to the term that was previously preferred by a minority, and if the earlier usage is now offensive, then we *should* treat the term either like the first kind of case, in which a term has begun to acquire a derogatory meaning, or like a full-blown slur (depending on which characterization is more accurate at the given time). Indeed, even if an earlier term is only dated but not offensive, there may still be a (moral?) presumption to use whatever term is current. It will very likely be clearer and avoid confusion.

If we change assumptions, and speak of a case in which most members of a group currently prefer a different name for their group than the one currently in usage, then we do have a presumptive duty to shift our usage. This applies even if most other people have no such preference to designate the group in the way in which members of that group prefer. In such cases, it is likely that those members of the group preferring the new term would take the current term to be offensive. However, even in the absence of offence, there would be a presumptive duty to comply with the group's preferred designation.

This follows from a broader principle that applies not only to groups but also to individuals—that there is a presumptive duty to call people what they prefer to be called. I say *'presumptive* duty' because there can certainly be situations in which the presumption is defeated. If, for example, some group prefers to be called by a self-aggrandizing term, or a term that already designates another group, then the presumption might be defeated.[41]

Sexist language

Some slurs, such as the use of the word 'bitches' as a synonym for 'women',[42] are sexist slurs. We should respond to them in the same way as we should respond to comparable slurs of other kinds of groups.

Other terms, such as 'history' (which is *not* a contraction of the English 'his story' but is instead derived from the Latin and Greek 'historia'), are certainly not sexist, even though some feminists have preferred to use 'herstory' in order to 'raise consciousness'.[43] The same is true of such terms as 'womenstruation' and 'womenopause'. We need not make any such changes in our language, even if others prefer to do so (or would prefer that *we* do so).

Much more interesting are various words that are neither slurs nor terms that are obviously not sexist. These terms occupy intermediate ground. The first of these is the use of 'man' (or 'mankind') to refer generically to the entire human species, rather than to human males only. The second is a related category—compound words formed from 'man'—words such as 'chairman' or 'postman'. Finally, there is the use of the singular pronoun 'he' (or its possessive or reflexive forms 'his' or 'himself') to refer to people of unstated or indeterminate sex.

The feminist critique

Many feminists have argued that all of these terms are sexist and ought not to be used. They have had considerable success, especially in the academy and government, but in more recent years also beyond these domains, in shifting linguistic conventions. This is especially true of 'man' and its compounds. 'He' (to refer to people of unstated or indeterminate sex) initially proved *somewhat* more resilient. However, it too has been susceptible to changing conventions, especially since calls to consider linguistic reference to 'non-binary' people—those who do not fit, or who do not regard themselves as fitting, exclusively into the category of either 'male' or 'female'—came to the fore. Many journals and academic associations now either prohibit or discourage use of these expressions,[44] other than in exceptional circumstances such as words that are being quoted.

Feminists have argued that the generic use of 'he', 'man' and its compounds, makes women invisible and causes us to overlook them.[45] Such terms also perpetuate the idea that the male is the norm. In support of these claims, they have demonstrated that the gender-specific senses of these terms eclipse the gender-neutral senses, causing people who hear or read them to think of males more than of females.[46] Even where the speaker or writer intends the word in the gender-neutral sense, it is regularly not understood that way.

It has often been inferred from this that using these words to refer to people of unstated or indeterminate sex is sexist and ought to be eschewed. Guidelines for non-sexist language make various suggestions about how these expressions are best avoided. These include using 'human' instead of 'man', replacing 'chairman' with 'chair' or 'chairperson', and using plural formulations and other ways of avoiding the singular pronoun.

Where a singular pronoun *is* used, the guidelines require the disjunctive use of both the male and female pronouns—'he or she' or 'she or he'. Both of these disjunctive formulations exclude 'non-binary' people,[47] but such people can be included via the use of another alternative, namely a singular 'they', which was used long ago,[48] and is coming back into usage.[49]

All instances of 'man' and 'he' that do not refer specifically to males are deemed unacceptable.[50] The use of words like 'chairman' even to refer to males is deemed to be sexist, because, it is said, the same word should be used for male and female incumbents of a position and 'chairman' would be an inappropriate way to refer to females.

It is because they think that the same words should be used to refer to males and females, that authors of guidelines for non-sexist writing urge the use of words such as 'author', 'manager', and 'poet' instead of 'authoress', 'manageress', and 'poetess'.[51] Although the recommended words here were previously used exclusively for males, presumably they are distinguished from words such as 'chairman' in being thought suitable for gender neutral use because they do not include the suffix 'man'.

Exceptions to the rule that the same term be used to refer to males and females seem to be 'congressman' and 'congresswoman'. Although the gender-neutral 'congressperson' and 'representative' are also available, the gender-specific versions have not (yet?) been eliminated to the extent that 'authoress', 'manageress', and 'poetess' have been.

Some of the terms suggested by feminists, although once rarely used and controversial, are now widely used and accepted. The sheer force of (their) current usage carries some moral weight. This is, in part, because there is some value in speaking in ways that are not stilted, and the extent to which the terms have been adopted has undermined the once-stilted sound to many of them.

That a recommended substitute for a word may, at least initially, sound stilted, is clearly not a decisive consideration against making such a change. Whether a word's stiltedness is a decisive consideration against adopting it, depends in part on (i) whether the existing word requires change and (ii) whether there are alternative possible changes that might not sound stilted.

It is indeed the case that many of the erstwhile gendered terms were in need of change. In other words, condition (i) was met. While, in some cases, the changes made were the most reasonable changes to make, in other cases, the problem could have been addressed in more than one way, with the result that while there was a moral imperative to make a change, there was not always a moral imperative to make the precise change that was made. In other words, condition (ii) was not always met. That said, once the particular changes took root and were widely adopted, there is usually no need, and *a fortiori*, no obligation to shift to other terms that could have been substituted for the original problematic terms.

'Man'

Consider first the use of 'man' (and its plural, 'men'). Although 'man' was not genuinely gender-neutral when a change was being sought, it once was. In Old English, 'mann' was used exclusively in the sense of 'human being', and this persisted into the medieval period. Feminists do not dispute this. Casey Miller and Kate Swift cite instances of the word that are manifestly gender neutral. These include a quotation from the clergyman, Aelfric, who wrote (circa 1000 CE):[52] 'His mother was a Christian, named Elen, a very full-of-faith man, and extremely pious.'[53] They also cite a statement from 1597, included in the Oxford English Dictionary, that 'the Lord had but one pair of men in Paradise.'[54]

Clearly the word underwent a change of meaning between then and now. Given that such changes are possible, it seems that an alternative to seeking the replacement of 'man' by 'human' would have been to pursue a return to the original meaning of 'man'. In other words, dissatisfaction with the use of a faux gender-neutral word could have been addressed either by abandoning the word or by shifting its meaning to make it genuinely gender-neutral.

However, it can plausibly be argued that abandoning 'man' in contexts when it is allegedly generic, is easier than shifting the meaning of the word. Thus, although changing the meaning of the word was a logical alternative to abandoning it, it would not have been an efficient alternative. Although it is hard to tell how successful feminists would have been, had they pressed for flagrantly gender-neutral uses of 'man' (by using the word in contexts where the referent was clearly a woman) instead of pushing for the 'human' substitution, there is an intuitive plausibility to the claim that reversing the meaning would have been very difficult (if possible at all). This may be because the true gender-neutralization of 'man' (in its purportedly generic contexts) could likely only be achieved at the cost of its gender-specific meaning in other contexts, at least if confusion were to be avoided.[55] Because there was such an easy and appropriate alternative to 'man', and because the alternative would be quite difficult, the case for the shift to 'human' was compelling.[56]

Compounds of 'man'

Matters were originally different, however, when it comes to *some* compounds of 'man'. Words like 'chairman', 'postman', and 'fireman' (although clearly not 'gentleman') could more readily have acquired a genuine gender-neutral meaning. Given the inroads that the feminist prescriptions regarding sexist language have made, this might be harder for some to see now than it was before. However, there was a time when it did not seem odd, and for many people it is perhaps still not odd, to use some of the 'man'-compounds in specific reference to a woman.

Unlike 'man' simpliciter, where there was reason to preserve a gender-specific sense[57] along with a gender-neutral sense, making the attainment of a genuinely gender-neutral sense more difficult, 'chairman' (for example), is not constrained in this way. It could have come to be used exclusively in a gender-neutral way. If it were used in contexts in which the incumbent were obviously female, as well as in contexts where the incumbents were obviously male,[58] it could have become a truly gender-neutral word. That is to say, its use could have led to no stronger associations with males than females in the minds of the hearers, than do the words that feminists have preferred.

I say 'no *stronger* associations' because shifting to 'chairperson' does not ensure equal association in the minds of hearers. Equal association is likely only when (nearly) as many women as men occupy such positions. The same is true for words such as 'astronaut' and 'prisoner', which are not compounds of 'man', but which may well still be more commonly associated with males, for the simple reason that most astronauts and prisoners are still male.

There was, then, a quite reasonable alternative to replacing 'chairman' with 'chair' (which sounds like a piece of furniture) or 'chairperson'. If a word such as 'chairman' had been gender-neutralized, then it could have been viewed as a contraction (conceptually, not historically or etymologically) of 'chair' and 'human'.[59]

We might then ask how it can be thought to be sexist to have addressed the problem (of gender bias in language) in that way rather than in the way that feminists suggested. It cannot be sexist simply to prefer, and to employ, an alternative, equally good way of dealing with a problem of linguistic bias. In response, it might be suggested that some *coordination* was required to attain the goal. That is to say, if different people were pursuing different strategies, any one strategy would have been weakened. The rejoinder is that the two strategies were not incompatible and thus coordination was not essential. The orthodox feminist view held that there is more than one suitable alternative to 'chairman'—'chair' or 'chairperson'. If enough of those who preferred to gender-neutralize 'chairman' had pursued their strategy, the result could have been yet another gender-neutral alternative to these options.

That is not what has happened. Given current usage, most people are likely to understand 'chairman' as referring to a male. For this reason, it would now be inappropriate to use the term to refer to a female who chairs a committee.

Would it now be acceptable to use the term 'chairman' when referring to a male chairperson, and 'chairwoman' when referring to a female chairperson? That practice, even now, would not cause us to overlook women. However, given that 'chairman' and 'chairwoman' are now clearly gendered terms, it is better to avoid them for the simple reason that the sex of a person is—or should be—irrelevant to their chairing role. We do not have specific words to designate tall from short, or bald from hirsute, or Buddhist from Muslim chairpersons. That is how it should be, but there is similarly no reason to have specific terms to refer to male or female chairpersons. It is thus best to use a gender-neutral term.

In this regard, English has an advantage over those languages that are so highly gendered that, *inter alia*, all nouns, including those that refer to inanimate objects, have a gender. What this shows is that, in these languages, a word's gender need not have anything to do with the sex of the entity to which the word refers—for the simple reason that the entity may have no sex at all. There are even cases where the entity to which a noun refers has a gender that seems to conflict with its sex. (Would such disruptive examples be welcome to the transgendered?) In Hebrew, for example, (almost) all body parts that come in pairs—such as eyes, ears, arms, and legs—are feminine. An exception that is notable for its counter-intuitiveness is that of breasts, which are masculine.

Given how pervasive gender is in languages such as Hebrew, Spanish, French, and Italian, gendered reference is much harder to eradicate from these languages. There is thus a range of challenges that arise in these languages that do not arise in English.[60]

'He'

The third-person singular pronoun is one way in which English *is* grammatically gendered. English speakers have historically distinguished between 'he' and 'she', 'him' and 'her', 'his' and 'hers', and 'himself' and 'herself'. (Other languages draw similar gendered distinctions also in the third-person plural, as well as the first- and second-person singular and plural.)

These expressions are clearly not gender neutral. Is it therefore always wrong to use the male versions when speaking about a generic person?[61] Feminists have argued that it is, and that this is because the male pronoun causes one to overlook women and to treat men as the norm. More recently those advocating for 'non-binary' people have objected that using either a male pronoun or *some* of the feminist alternatives, overlooks those who do not fit neatly into the categories of 'male' or 'female'.

Because females constitute about half of all humans, whereas people who are neither male nor female (or both male and female) constitute an exceptionally small proportion or the human population, females but not those who are neither male nor female, have a claim to be represented linguistically as often as males. Those who are neither male nor female may have a claim to *some* mention, but not to more than their proportion of the population. It is not the case that every linguistic formulation has to accommodate every variation in society. Sometimes the use of statistical norms and majority examples is reasonable.

For example, the contiguous United States contains four time zones. There are even more time zones if one considers Alaska, Hawaii, and various territories and outposts. It would be cumbersome when indicating the time of a national event, for example, to list the time for each of those time zones. It is thus not uncommon to list only Eastern time, and occasionally also Central time, from which other Americans must calculate their time. The reason for using Eastern time as the norm is that that time zone includes the largest single group of people of all time zones in the United States. National events are not occasionally listed under Alaskan, Hawaiian, not to mention Guamanian time, just for the sake of representativity. That practice does not denigrate Americans living outside of the Eastern time zone.

The problem of overlooking women only arises if, as once was the case, it is the norm always to use (only) the male pronoun in contexts where the person's sex is unstated or unknown. If the female pronoun were used sufficiently often in such contexts, then the eclipsing of females would not occur. Although in some cases the male pronoun would be used, on other occasions the female pronoun would be used. We might then view the gendered pronoun (when not used to refer to a person whose sex is known and reflected in that pronoun) as merely an *example* and not as a generic pronoun. Something similar might be said about the occasional use of a gender-neutral singular 'they', in order to include examples of non-binary people. If different gender examples were given on different occasions, neither female nor male would be eclipsed, and no gender would be entirely ignored. This may indeed be the motivation of those opponents of sexist bias in language, who have chosen almost always to use the female pronoun instead of the male one, given that others are almost always using the male pronoun.

Notice, however, that there are a number of possible pronominal (distribution) policies that one might employ in order to avoid a bias against females:

(1) Everybody uses (only some combination of):
   a. 'he or she'; or 'she or he'; or
   b. (singular) 'they'; or
   c. any formulation that avoids singular gendered pronouns—for example, by using either the plural[62] or 'one' (as in 'singular pronouns can be avoided if one speaks about "one" rather than about "he" or "she"').

(2) Everybody alternates between the male and female pronouns, or at least gives equal coverage to each of the two majority genders.

(3) Males use the male pronoun and females use the female pronoun, or vice versa, and non-binary people use a pronoun matching their gender.

(4) Individual speakers and writers choose what pronouns they use. Some would choose the female, some would choose the male, and some would choose (a), (b), or (c) above.

As any one of these policies would undermine the older rule that the male pronoun always be used, and would thereby bring females into the picture, it seems a bit hasty to claim, as many have, that only strategy (1) is acceptable.

(2) and (3) share a problem with (1). They are all unnecessarily prescriptive and coercive. They *require* people to speak and write in ways that are not strictly necessary to avoid the problem of anti-female bias in language. By contrast (4) avoids the problem of prescriptiveness and (moral) coercion. It leaves scope for individual pronominal preference, without tainting, with accusations of sexism, those with different preferences. Pronominal prescription, backed up with moral sanction of those who do not comply, cannot be justified where pronominal liberty can effect the desired diversity of singular pronouns.

Granting this kind of liberty to language users, is like granting authorial liberty to writers of literature and poetry. We do not require such authors to write in different genres, styles, from different perspectives, and so on, in order to attain literary diversity. Instead, such diversity is attained by a range of authors writing as they wish to write. Some authors write scientific fiction, while others write historical non-fiction. Some write about the lives of young women, and some write about the lives of old men. Some write about Tanzanians, some about Parisians, and some about Australians. We do not expect one author to write about the experiences of all.[63]

Now, it might be objected that the fourth option would not lead to an equitable use of gender pronouns—'he' would still prevail. Thus, a more prescriptive policy *is* required. In response to this, it should be noted that the fourth option does not preclude persuasion. Given that feminists have had considerable success in persuading people (particularly in universities and government) that 'he' is sexist, why should we think that they could not have persuaded people that although 'he' is not always sexist, there is a moral argument for more use of 'she'? To the extent that 'she' is indeed under-used in gender-indeterminate contexts, the argument would be compelling. Insofar as people could not be persuaded that more use of 'she' was valuable, they could not be persuaded that any use of 'he' (in the specified contexts) is sexist.

The fourth option—allowing individuals a choice of pronouns to refer to people of unstated or indeterminate sex—has yet another advantage. It facilitates more linguistic variety than any of the other options. The use of singular pronouns does not exclude (a), (b), or (c), but can be used in conjunction with them.

Using alternatives to singular pronouns—whether by employing plurals or speaking of 'one' rather than 'he' or 'she'—is part of ordinary variance in the methods of linguistic expression. Singular (non-disjunctive) pronouns offer still more variety. Moreover, there are situations where use of a singular pronoun is either best or easiest. If one is engaged in an extended discussion about 'the individual', for example, it is sometimes confusing to resort to plural nouns (such as 'individuals') and plural pronouns,[64] or to employ the impersonal 'one' or the second person 'you'. There may be other contexts, such as job advertisements, where it is indeed preferable to use a gender-neutral wording, given how much rests on the gender-neutrality of that particular context.

Those who think that this linguistic variety is either not valuable or not sufficiently valuable, might argue that instead of all the other options above, we should employ *only* (b), namely *singular* 'they'.

Singular 'they' has met with resistance from 'prescriptive grammarians' who have insisted that 'they' is plural and may be used only when speaking about more than one person. In response, it has been convincingly argued that 'they' in place of singular nouns was once 'both accepted and widespread'.[65] Even when the dominant and official sense of 'they' was plural, singular use of 'they' was widespread (at least in informal, usually spoken, contexts). Given this, it has been suggested, we should simply abandon the 'rule' against singular 'they' and use it unashamedly. That view has been enjoying increasing acceptance. There is no need, it is argued, to use 'he' and 'she' in contexts where the referent is of indeterminate sex. English is not as impoverished as is commonly thought. It *does* have a gender-neutral singular third-person pronoun—'they'.

Such an approach would have a few advantages. First, it would constitute a satisfactory response to the feminist objection. Second, it would be inclusive of 'non-binary' people, in what is arguably the simplest way.[66] Third, it would help move away from gendered pronouns, which is an advantage to the extent that sex and gender are irrelevant. Since they are *usually* irrelevant,[67] this is a significant advantage. If one were (now) designing a language, it is hard to see why one would make it as attentive to sex and gender as many natural languages are.

That singular 'they' would achieve all three of these, may sound like a decisive consideration in favour of its exclusive use. However, that is not the case. First, as already noted, there are other ways of meeting the feminist objection, and given the small proportion of the population that is non-binary, we are not *required* to include them in *every* pronominal instance.[68]

Second, while singular 'they' often does not jar, there are other circumstances in which it does still jar, at least to some ears. That it does jar for some is not a reason to join prescriptive grammarians in proscribing such use. The same reasons for not following feminist and other prescriptive grammarians in *requiring* singular 'they' in place of 'he' or 'he or she' are also reasons not to accede to those prescriptive grammarians who would prohibit singular 'they'.

With increasing use, singular 'they' has come to sound less jarring in those contexts where it previously sounded odd, and that trajectory may well continue. To the extent that, at any given time, it sounds strange to a substantial number of people, we have a reason not to require its use when reasonable alternatives exist.[69] Thus, we should not currently *require* the *exclusive* use of 'they' (and other ways of always avoiding gendered pronouns).

Those feminists who would argue that we ought to use singular 'they' notwithstanding its sounding odd to some, in order to force it to sound acceptable, would put themselves in an awkward position regarding the earlier suggestion about the use of 'chairman'. If we must force singular 'they' into acceptability, then there would have been less reason not to have forced gender-neutral 'chairman' into acceptability.[70]

The use of gendered pronouns when referring to people of unstated sex, has proved more resilient than the other gendered terms that were discussed earlier in this section. While that is not surprising, it might still change. If it does, then the new norms might acquire a force of their own. If, by contrast, gendered pronouns persist, their continued use need not necessarily be morally prohibited.

Preferred pronouns

The discussion of pronouns thus far has been in reference to 'generic' people—an unidentified person. Matters are currently more controversial when we are speaking about which pronouns to use in reference to specific people.

It was once, in the vast majority of cases, a straightforward decision to refer to a particular person either as 'he' or as 'she'. This has now become a social minefield. So many people now have a preference for a different pronoun, that many have resorted to signalling their preferred pronouns even when they are 'he' or 'she', and where *which* of those pronouns is preferred is the one that would likely have been inferred in the absence of a declaration of a preference.

It may seem obvious that we should refer to people by their preferred pronouns. There should indeed be a presumption to do so. That presumption would be an instance of a broader presumption that we should call people what they want to be called. However, such a presumption is sometimes defeasible. If your adolescent's or my student's declared preferred pronoun is 'Her Royal Highness', you or I are under no moral obligation to comply with that preference. That may be an extreme example, but it does reveal that the reasonableness of a declared preference is not only a relevant consideration, but also one that could, in some circumstances, defeat the presumption.

There are those who think that complying with *some* requests to use preferred pronouns has something in common with the preference for 'Her Royal Highness'. According to this view, which we might call the 'biological' view, 'he' refers to males, and 'she' to females. Perhaps this view could make allowances for some other pronoun for intersex people, who occupy middle ground between male and female. However, adherents of the biological view claim that referring to a male as 'she' or a female as 'he' is detached from reality and that we have no obligation to indulge people's delusions, whether they be about their royal status or their sex.

Sex is more complicated than this rendition of the biological view suggests. In rare cases, genotypic sex is not equivalent to phenotypic sex, even though both genotype and anatomical phenotype are biological. However, even if we set aside this complexity, one obvious problem with the biological view is that it is far from clear that *gendered* pronouns must agree with a person's biological sex rather than with that person's *gender*.

Whereas somebody's sex is male or female (or, in rare cases, intersex), one's gender is 'masculine' or 'feminine' or something on the spectrum between (or beyond) them. Males can be feminine, and females can be masculine. If pronouns should track gender rather than sex, then there might be nothing delusional about a male who wants to be referred to as 'she'.

There are considerations both in favour of and against, linking pronouns to gender rather than to sex. The case *for* linking them to gender is that the relevant pronouns, along with other words in highly gendered languages are *gendered* rather than *sexed*. As indicated above, the gender of a word need not have anything to do with the sex of the entity to which the word refers. In some cases, as was noted, the gender of a word can even be the opposite of its sex (where, by 'its sex' I mean the sex of the entity it denotes).

The case *against* linking pronouns to gender is that a person's gender is typically harder to determine than their sex. This is partly because gender is a psychological rather than a physical state (even if the psychological state is sometimes manifested behaviourally). It is also partly because, while the vast majority of people are unambiguously one of the two main sexes, gender is much less bifurcated. So-called masculine and feminine attributes exist on a continuum with a much more even distribution. Those attributes can also combine in different ways in different individuals. This might explain the recent proliferation of gender designators. At a recent count, there were over seventy of them.[71] Indeed, at the level of greatest granularity, there may be as many genders as there are individuals, and thus we should not expect the list to end where it currently does, if the present trend of gender classification continues.

For these reasons, linking pronouns to gender rather than to sex is likely to introduce more erroneous pronominal references—both in cases where somebody forgets another's pronouns, which becomes increasingly likely as the number of pronoun preferences increases, and where one has not been told what those pronouns are.

Thus, while we cannot be *certain* that pronouns should be linked to gender rather than to sex, there is at least some reason for thinking that it should be. As a result, there is scope to doubt that requests for pronouns that are at odds with a person's sex are delusional in the way that claims to being a royal often are.[72] Where there is doubt, it is generally advisable to give the benefit of that doubt to the person in reference to whom one is deploying a pronoun.

It is possible to imagine circumstances in which such a benefit of a doubt might reasonably be withheld or overridden. If, for example, somebody repeatedly changes their pronoun preferences, or if one otherwise has reason to think that the preferences are being declared in order to exercise social power rather than more sincerely, then it may be reasonable (even if sometimes imprudent) not to comply.

LANGUAGE 251

However, even if we set these issues aside, there are a few factors to be considered in determining how reasonable a request to use a particular pronoun is. For example, it can make a difference what the preferred pronoun is. 'He', 'she', and 'they' are easier to remember than 'thon', 'e', 'xe', 'tey', 'ey', or 'hu',[73] and at least a dozen other 'artificial' or proposed pronouns, for the simple reason that these latter pronouns are so unusual and plentiful. In some cases, people may even be unsure about how to pronounce them.

How easy it is to remember somebody's pronoun is not only a function of what the pronoun is, but also of how many people's pronouns one needs to remember. Some people have difficulty even remembering the *names* of people who they do not know well. It will be even more difficult for them to remember idiosyncratic pronouns in addition to names. This may be especially true in highly populous settings, such as large conferences and university classes. (The solution to this, it might be said, is to have name or pronoun tags, with preferred pronouns listed on them. However, these may not always be visible from a distance, and it is not clear how many other preferences would then need to be listed on them too.[74])

In summary, there is a presumption in favour of referring to somebody using that person's preferred pronouns. However, people's preferences for particular pronouns can be either more or less reasonable, and either more or less sincere. When they are less reasonable or there is evidence that they are less sincere, we might either have less or no reason to comply, or at least greater excuse for not doing so.

Impertinences

In stark contrast to the growing concerns for respecting people's preferred pronouns is a shift towards casual ways of addressing and referring to people who would previously have been addressed more respectfully.

One way in which this can manifest is in languages, unlike contemporary English, which distinguish more deferential and more familiar second person pronouns. Francophones distinguish between formal 'vous' and informal 'tu', German speakers use the respectful 'sie' or the casual 'du', while Afrikaans speakers use 'u' when more respect is appropriate, and 'jy' when more casual address is apt. English once had a similar distinction—between 'you' and 'thou'—but now 'you' is used almost exclusively (although the more intimate connotations of 'thou' survive in addressing God). When such distinctions are drawn, questions arise about whether it is appropriate to use the more familiar pronouns in circumstances in which this might (reasonably) be regarded as too familiar.

While this problem does not currently occur in English with regard to a choice of second-person pronouns, it does arise in another way, namely in whether to address (or refer to) somebody by their title, or instead to use their first name.

There are obviously some situations in which it is, and perhaps always has been, clear that the use of a first name is reasonable. For example, parents may call their children, and teachers may call their pupils, by their first names. Those are not the situations to be discussed here. Instead, the focus is on situations in which there is at least some convention for one person to address another with a title of some kind—including affectionate pronouns such 'Mother', 'Dad', 'Uncle', or 'Aunty'.

Where there are such conventions, they typically turn on any one or more of the following factors:

a. How well one knows the other person;
b. age (differences);
c. status (differences); and
d. context.

To know somebody well is to be familiar with him (in one sense of familiar). Familiarity in that sense has sometimes, but not always, been a license for familiarity, or informality, in how one addresses that person. Strangers might be addressed by title, but once one comes to know them, there might be a shift to a 'first-name basis'. This is not always the case. In more formal times, even people who knew one another reasonably well might refer to one another as 'Mr A' or 'Miss B'.

Even when a convention sometimes permits the familiar to address one another in a casual way, the other factors often block some informality. A child addressing an adult, or even an adult addressing a significantly older adult might be required, according to the convention, to address them with a title even if the older person is familiar to them. This is why children typically call their parents some version of 'Mom' and 'Dad'. Similar points could be made about status and context, both of which can also block familiarity with somebody manifesting in familiar address.

Although age may be seen as itself a kind of status consideration, it is useful to distinguish it from other status differentials,[75] such as those between boss and employee, commanding officer and subordinate, head of state and civil servant, and teacher and pupil.

Context also matters. For example, friends who are on a first-name (or even nickname) basis with one another, might use more formal address (and reference) in their professional context.

Should the convention be changed?

To describe these conventions is not equivalent to endorsing them. The suggestion that we should abandon them is typically (and most compellingly) justified in the name of equality. It is said that because children and adults, subordinates and leaders are equal, the convention of honorific titles in one direction but not the other should be abandoned. There are a few things to be said about this proposal.

First, one can concede that children and adults, and subordinates and those in authority have *moral* equality—that their equal interests have equal moral weight. The convention of honorific address does not deny this. Insofar as those who subscribe to the convention of honorific address do dispute this, it is because they think that in at least some circumstances the interests of children should count *more*. This suggests that the kind of equality relevant to the convention is not moral equality.

Second, once we turn to other senses of equality, we find that children are *not* equal to adults. Children are much younger, typically have less understanding, less experience, less wisdom, and less power, for example. Adult subordinates are *sometimes* also unequal in all or many of these ways to those adults in positions of authority. When they are not, there is indeed a case (with some exceptions) for moving to more egalitarian forms of address, if that is not already the norm.

Third, if it is suggested that dropping honorific address is a way to counter those inequalities that exist, then we can note that more informal means of address do not remove the differentials. At most they mask them—they create a veneer of equality when none exists. People are quick to recognize these differentials in other contexts. Adults who sexually proposition children, or those in authority who have sexual encounters with those who are subordinate to them, are quickly said to have exploited a power differential. But if such power differentials exist, it is not unreasonable to mark them. If, for example, we do not want adults to treat children as they would equals, we should not encourage children to talk to them as though they were equals. Preserving the honorific address is, of course, no guarantee that appropriate boundaries will be respected, but that does not mean that those boundaries are not worth marking.

Finally, if the convention of honorific address were something that ought to be changed—and changed in the name of equality—then the change should begin somewhere other than where it has begun. To understand why this is the case, one must recognize the moral force of a convention.

The (limited) force of convention

As with the other linguistic practices that have been discussed, it makes a difference what the current convention is. Even if it is the case that, *ab initio*, it would have been better if there were no differentials in the way in which people addressed one another, perhaps by *everybody* calling everybody else by their first name, it does not follow that one can simply ignore an extant convention, in which not everybody is on a first-name basis with everybody else.

This is because when there is a convention of what constitutes polite address, deviations from it can reasonably be interpreted as impolite. There is a presumption against being impolite or impertinent. Again, such a presumption could be defeated if the convention were morally odious, as it would be if there were a convention that people of only one sex, 'race', or religion should address people of another sex, 'race', or religion deferentially. In such cases, there are no morally relevant differences to warrant the asymmetric deference. To the extent that a given societal convention makes these irrelevant features relevant to who owes whom a more deferential address, the convention is morally indefensible. The same is not true—or at least not obviously true—of the differences between adults and children, and higher and lower military ranks, for example.

Now, it may be objected that the convention of more formal address has already begun to be eroded, in the sense that many fewer people follow the convention now than was once the case. As a result, it may be argued that any

Figure 7.3 Shifting to greater informality of address.

instances of more informal address are not as clearly manifestations of impertinence than they once were. There is something to this objection, but not enough to succeed.

Figure 7.3 points to a phenomenon that bears resemblance to one aspect of Figure 7.1. Whereas Figure 7.1 referred to shifting meanings, between derogatory and either positive or neutral meanings of a word, Figure 7.3 refers to a shift from formality to informality of address.

In Figure 7.3, the solid line indicates the extent to which a shift to greater informality has already occurred, and the broken lines indicate either the remainder of the possible trajectory or its reversal.[76]

There can be disagreement about whether the solid line *accurately* represents the point we have reached. Obviously, this cannot be determined with any precision. In any event, the precise point is not important. By contrast, the *approximate* point is important. If the convention had largely been abandoned already, then the erstwhile convention would exert relatively little force. There is good reason to think that that has not (yet?) happened, even in societies that are much more casual than others.

Among the evidence for this is the fact that most children still address their parents and grandparents with affectionate pronouns that refer to their relationship rather than simply using their first names. Most pupils and, at least undergraduate, but sometimes also postgraduate students still address their teachers by title or some other honorific. The same is true of (some) subordinates addressing those in (some) positions of authority, including heads of state and other senior members of government.

Inconsistencies

There are, however, a number of inexplicable inconsistencies in the way in which the convention is being eroded. For example, because children often learn how to address people by the way their parents refer to those people *when speaking to children*, we find a curious asymmetry. Most (but not all) parents refer to themselves and their spouse as 'Mommy' and 'Daddy' (or some variant of that). Yet, when speaking to children about other adults, many of those same parents refer to these other adults by their first names, thus training their children to do so. This is the case even when the adult to whom they are referring is significantly older than the parent. In other words, the message many parents convey to their children is that they, the parents, are to be addressed honorifically as 'mother' and 'father', but other adults may be addressed by their first names only.

It is hard to reconcile this inconsistency. Perhaps it will be suggested that a child's parents are due more respect than other adults by that child. This might explain why a child's teachers are often also still addressed in a more deferential manner, because of the special authority relationship they have with the child. However, even if it is true that some adults are due *more* respect than other adults by particular children, it does not follow that those other adults are due no more respect than the child's friends with whom the child is on a first-name basis. And if it is suggested that an honorific form of address is necessary only if the adult is owed a level of respect above some threshold, it is curious that some parents have presumed to lower the threshold to the precise point they have—below the level of respect owed to parents (and perhaps the child's teachers and doctors) but above almost all other adults.

Another attempt to explain away the apparent inconsistency is to claim that words like 'Mommy' and 'Daddy' are a mark of intimacy and that it is comforting for parents and children to hear and say such words when communicating with one another.[77] One problem with this suggestion is that while parents sometimes address their children in an intimacy-marking manner as 'my child' (or 'my son' or 'my daughter') they more often do not. This suggests that if the use of 'Mommy' and 'Daddy' served only as a marker of intimacy, it would similarly be used on only some occasions, with children addressing their parents by their first names at other times. Yet this is typically not the case. Thus, even if 'Mommy' and 'Daddy' mark intimacy they also serve as honorific forms of address.

A second problem with the suggestion about marking intimacy is that we would then expect that other adults who are not strangers to a child should be addressed in a way that marks a degree of intimacy less than that of parents but greater than that of strangers. Yet, the once common practice of children addressing such adults as 'Aunt' or 'Uncle' (when the adults were not their parents' siblings or siblings-in-law) has been eroded to about the same extent as the use of titles in addressing other adults.

The children of those parents who are leading the trend towards greater informality should be on a first-name basis with *them* before (and not after) they are on a first-name basis with other adults. Even those parents who prefer that their children refer to them by their first names should not presume that other adults are comfortable with such familiarity, given the still existent (even if attenuated) convention that use of a first name indicates greater familiarity. In other words, as long as the convention of honorific address persists to some substantial degree, the failure to use it indicates greater familiarity. Such familiarity, according to the convention, is inappropriate in some cases.

The inconsistencies do not end with the differences between how some children address their parents and how they address other adults. There are similar inconsistencies between how some children address their teachers and how they address other adults. In one stark case that I witnessed, a child's teacher was the wife of a professorial colleague of the child's father. The child addressed her teacher as Mrs So-and-So, but called her husband by his first name! Indeed, she would sometimes refer to them thus in the same sentence, thereby (unintentionally) highlighting the contrast.

Similarly, for all the purported informality in the United States, it is not uncommon for journalists, for example, to address elected officials by their title: 'Mr President', 'Madame Secretary', 'Senator', or 'Mayor', for example. The same courtesy is sometimes extended to medical doctors, and to religious leaders, but not to innumerable others, including people of great distinction. Those others, using a memorable Yiddish idiom, might be warranted in asking of the interviewer: 'What am I, chopped liver?'[78]

While conventions *can* be, and often are, eroded inconsistently, it does not follow that one *may* do so. While honorifics are being preserved for some, assuming a first-name basis for others who are relevantly indistinguishable, one runs the risk of being unduly forward.

Those who would like to see the convention change should follow a particular path. Instead of addressing others in ways that violate the convention, or encouraging children to do so, they should request that others address them in a way that erodes the convention. That includes having their own children address them by their first names.

Complexities

The etiquette or ethics of address is undoubtedly complicated. Among the clearest cases are those of children addressing adults. In such cases, the presumption should be in favour of a more formal address unless they are invited by the adult to address him or her more informally, or unless there is other good reason to think that this particular adult prefers to be addressed in the more casual manner. The presumption is especially strong when there is good reason to think that an adult would be offended by being addressed in a more informal manner.

The case of younger adults addressing significantly older adults is more complicated. The age differential persists. Often the older person is also in a position of greater authority, or once was. Thus, barring special circumstances, it may be preferable to err on the side of formality, at least until the older person has said or otherwise indicated that the first name basis is acceptable. There are also questions about how much of an age differential requires the more formal approach.

Other complexities arise when the age and authority differentials cut in opposite directions. That this can happen is one reason for earlier distinguishing age from other kinds of status considerations. For example, a younger person might occupy a more senior position than an older person. In some such cases, the convention will require the younger, higher-status person (such as the head of state) to be addressed more respectfully by the older, lower-status person (such as a general). On other occasions, the convention might require the opposite—if, for example, the son is the boss, and the father is the employee. These, however, are all more complex than cases in which age and status difference reinforce one another.

Finally, there are questions about which relationships (both hierarchical and equal) between adults necessitate a more formal mode of address, because it is surely the case that not all of them do.

Responding to the 'casual critique'

Those of a more informal bent will be impatient with deliberation about these complexities and will recommend informality. But such people forget that informality is a matter of degree and even they, presumably, have their limits. If one meets an adult by the name of Robert, one does not immediately start addressing him as 'Bob' or 'Bobby' without some indication that this is his preference, and especially if he is considerably older than oneself. And one certainly would not begin calling him by some endearing nickname—perhaps 'Shmoopie'[79]—with which his wife addresses him.

Indeed, we should generally address people the way they prefer to be addressed, irrespective of age or authority. There are exceptions of course. None of us was ever under a moral duty to address Idi Amin as 'His Excellency, President for Life, Field Marshal Al Hadji Doctor Idi Amin Dada, VC, DSO, MC, Lord of all the Beasts of the Earth and Fishes of the Sea, and Conqueror of the British Empire in Africa in General and Uganda in Particular', his preference for that title notwithstanding. Similarly, if a child insisted that we call him 'Sir' or 'Mr Bloggs', we would be under no obligation to do so.

The same does not seem to be true where an adult prefers that children not be on a first-name basis with her or him. Defenders of informality of address might ask of such an adult: 'Who does she think she is?' or 'How pompous must he be to have that preference?' While an inflated ego is one possible reason why somebody might prefer to be addressed more formally, it is not the only possible reason. Another is that the adult is putting himself in the shoes of the child. Because that adult would not dream, as a child, of addressing an adult by his or her first name, he wonders why this child takes these liberties. In other words, the adult might be wondering about the child: 'Who does he think she is to presume to address an adult—not me in particular, but any adult—in that way?'

The perception that adults who prefer that children not be on a first-name basis with them have an inflated ego creates a disincentive to expressing dissatisfaction when they are addressed in this way. It is much easier to ask somebody to address one less formally than it is to ask somebody to address one more formally. This provides an added reason why children should be taught not to presume that they are on a first-name basis with every adult they encounter. Even asking an older person whether they mind being addressed by their first name, puts them in a difficult position, with the result that the 'consent' obtained may not be genuine. It is better to await either an explicit invitation to be on a first-name basis or some implicit but clear indication that the person would be comfortable with that.

Speciesist language

Impertinences are not the only features of language that, unlike slurs, group names, and sexist and gendered language, have not received much attention.

There are too many categories to explore them all, but one significant one is how we speak about non-human animals.

Insults and slurs

Consider, for example, how many insults refer to animals. At the most general level, when somebody calls another human an 'animal'—'What an animal!'—they are offering the opposite of a compliment. Similarly, the word 'brutal', which is derived from 'brute' (meaning 'animal'), is used to refer to an action that, or someone who, is savagely violent. By contrast, we speak about 'humane' (from 'human') treatment or attitudes to designate compassion and benevolence.

There certainly are many non-human animals who engage in savagely violent behaviour, but that is not true of many other animals. Moreover, even the most violent non-human animal species are, by most metrics, far less savagely violent than humans. The contrasting uses of 'brutal' and 'humane' may be partly a prejudice against animals, but they are likely also attributable in part to human self-satisfaction. Humans tend to look down on animals and thus, with some exceptions, it is not surprising that referring to a human as a (non-human) animal will be insulting.

Moving from the general to the particular, there are innumerable examples of animals who feature in insults. Some of these have been recognized more commonly for their sexist rather than their speciesist character. This is true of 'bitch', 'shrew', and 'catty', for example.[80] The insult of such terms to women is widely recognized, but much less attention is given to what such insults say about human attitude to animals. Why should 'bitch', a female dog, be the insult that it is, rather than a compliment? Dogs' nature has led to them being referred to as (hu)'man's best friend' and yet we regularly deploy words like 'bitch' and 'dog' as insults.

Among the many other animal-referencing insults are ox, mule, snake, toad, sheep, lemming, cockroach, donkey, ass, pig, swine, porker, parrot, rat, wolf, louse, ape, frog, jackass, vulture, mongrel, badger, and chicken.

To be sure, references to animals are sometimes positive, as in 'eagle-eyed' and 'busy as a bee', but the existence of such terms does not eliminate the very prominent phenomenon of animal-referencing insults.

Should we abandon the use of such terms? It is unlikely that a single answer will fit all of them, given the various nuances of each that must be considered. However, some general comments, with particular illustrations, can be provided.

First, when animal-referencing epithets are used against a human, it is an *insult* to that human, but a *slur* to the kind of animal referenced (or to animals in general, if the term references all non-human animals). Thus, one set of questions concerns whether an insult—any insult—is permissibly directed to the person who is insulted. That depends on the insult, the insulter, and the insulted.

Another set of questions concerns the implicit slur against animals. Much of what was said above about slurs against human groups would also apply to these questions. There are clearly also differences between slurs against humans and slurs against other animals. Humans, at least beyond infancy, and absent serious cognitive impairment, can *feel* offended by a slur, unlike other animals who would typically not understand it.

However, the negative effects of slurs do not consist only, or even most importantly, in the felt offence that they can cause. The attitudes from which they arise and which they can cause or reinforce can result in (non-verbal) actions that can harm. Just as prejudicial attitudes can result in wrongfully discriminatory treatment of humans, so prejudicial attitudes can result in wrongful treatment of animals.

Thus, we need to ask (a) whether use of a given term reflects an ongoing prejudice, and (b) whether it is likely to implant or entrench such prejudice. The answers are not straightforward. One reason is that neither question can be answered merely by examining etymology. Merely because a term might have arisen from prejudice does not mean either that it is still associated with such prejudice or that it will cause it.

In the human realm, the terms 'sinister' and 'gauche', both of which refer to 'left', originate in prejudice against left-handed people. Yet many people who use these terms today have no inkling of that etymology and do not, in any event, harbour any prejudice against left-handed people. Nor is it plausible to think that using these words is likely to cause such prejudice or to result in any mistreatment of the left-handed. It would thus be difficult to support the claim that we should eschew use of the words 'sinister' and 'gauche'.

Despite the connection, visible on its surface, between 'badger' as a verb and as a noun, it is quite possible that many people simply do not notice that connection. It is even less likely that most users of the verb know that it derives from the 'sport' of badger baiting. It is thus unlikely that most people's use of the verb emerges from any prejudice towards badgers, or that it would cause any such prejudice. To the extent that this is the case, there is similarly no compelling case to be made for dropping the use of this verb.

Similarly, when a term *accurately* picks out some attribute of a species, there may be no harm in using such a term as a metaphor. Thus, we refer to (human) 'hawks' and 'doves'. The former are those who, especially in foreign affairs, advocate aggressive policies, whereas 'doves' are those who advocate peaceful policies. These terms presumably derive from the predatory activity of hawks and the (primarily) herbivorous and granivorous doves (although doves do supplement their diet with some animal protein).

It is true that 'hawks' and 'doves', when used in reference to humans are not *always* insults. Sometimes these terms are used in neutral, descriptive ways, and sometimes they are used as terms of pride. However, even when they are used as insults, they may involve no slur against the animals they mention. The same is not true of the vast majority of animal-referencing insults, which certainly are slurs.

When they are slurs, the permissible options are either to use the slur word in a way that aims at undermining it or to abandon the slur. With regard to the former strategy, one notable difference from slurs against human groups, is that members of the impugned animal species obviously cannot participate in such repurposing.

Companion animals

In recent years, some people have sought to refer to those animals who live with us in our homes, not as 'pets' but as 'companion animals'. The former term is said to be less respectful than the latter. There is something to be said for that. The noun 'pet' seems to be linked to the same word in one of its senses as a verb—namely a being that is stroked or patted.[81] That description of a cat and especially a dog, seems not to do justice to the role that such animals have in the lives of the humans with whom they live. They are not merely recipients of our patting.

'Pet' also has another meaning as a noun, namely one who is treated with special favour or affection. That comes closer to reflecting their relationship with their humans. However, this sense too focuses only on what we do for those animals. It does not attend to what those animals do for their humans.

'Companion animal' does a better job of conveying the reciprocal nature of the relationship, because companionship is typically a two-way street (even if not an entirely symmetrical one). 'Companion animal' is probably also a more accurate description for those animals—such as fish—who (hopefully) one does not spend any time stroking or patting.

There is, thus, some reason to prefer 'companion animal' to 'pet', although 'pet' is hardly an egregiously inappropriate term. By contrast, there is typically something deeply wrong with speaking about an animal's 'owner'. Such a term implies that animals are the property of the 'owner'. Animals are sentient beings, not property to be owned.

Even when it is true, under the law, that humans own their companion animals, there is some value in resisting that mindset, as part of a strategy to change the law. In slave-owning societies, slaves might legally be 'owned'. However, blithely referring to their enslavers as their 'owners' (and certainly without the scare quotes) only normalizes what should be undone. We should similarly move away from viewing animals as our property.

This does not necessarily taint the use of phrases such as 'my dog' or 'my cat'. This is because the possessive pronoun here (as elsewhere) does not have to designate ownership. When one refers to 'my daughter' or 'my father', one is not designating an ownership relationship. Just as you can refer to your dog as 'my dog', so we can say of you, that you are that dog's human. 'Fido's human' is much preferable to 'Fido's owner'.

Animal pronouns

Because animals are not objects but rather sentient beings often with their own personalities, it is also preferable to refer to them as 'he', 'she', 'they', and 'who' rather than 'it'. It is true that some *humans* prefer to be referred to with the pronoun 'it'. This is not entirely without precedent. Babies, perhaps because, genitals aside, are so hard to identify as belonging to a particular sex, are sometimes referred to as 'it'. However, when a human capable of expressing preferences, declares 'it' to be 'its' preferred pronoun, the preference is an unusual one. Moreover, 'it' is much more commonly used in reference to objects. Because animals are, all too often, treated as objects, there is good reason to refer to them in ways that undermine rather than reinforce such attitudes.

Profanity

Having considered language that has recently been and is currently highly contested, as well as some examples of language that *should* be more contested than it has been, some (limited) consideration will now be given to language that was once much more disapproved than it now is—profanity.

The etymology of the word 'profanity' is 'profane', which is the opposite of the sacred. 'Profanity' was originally used exclusively to refer to disrespect for the sacred, but the term has since extended to include obscenities too.

Blasphemy, at least in the view of those who complain about it, is an offence against God. It is also, evidently, an offence against some of God's earthly defenders. Whether blasphemy is an offence against God depends, of course, on whether God actually exists. That is a subject of disagreement that cannot be settled here. However, even if God does exist, it does not follow that blasphemy is a *moral* violation. Many biblically and other religiously prohibited actions seem to fall, even by religious standards, under the rubric of ritual rather than moral prohibitions. Prohibitions on eating leaven on Passover, and on sex with or by a menstruant women, seem to be prohibitions of a ritual kind. Perhaps blasphemy falls into this category too.

Whereas the claim that blasphemy offends God is controversial, it is obviously true that blasphemy offends some humans. However, as noted earlier, that words cause offence is not sufficient to render the uttering of them wrong. The intensity of offence does not change that. The same is true for any offence caused by uttering obscenities.

Of course, the fact that blasphemy or obscenities offend, is *a* consideration against uttering profanities. If there are no considerations pulling in the opposite direction, then the offence one causes is gratuitous. There is then a good case for saying that uttering the profanity is wrong (which is entirely different from saying that it should be without legal protection).

However, offence is gratuitous much less often than is often thought to be the case. This is because there are typically countervailing considerations, and these are often sufficient to justify the profanity. At the very least, the words that offend the hearer typically also have some value to the speaker. If the value to the speaker consists entirely of causing offence, then questions arise about whether the hearer deserves to be offended. Sometimes that is the case, and sometimes it is not.

If we set aside cases in which a profanity is uttered for the purposes of offending, a speaker might want to blaspheme or utter an obscenity for emphasis, for humorous purposes,[82] to cope,[83] to improve performance,[84] or for some other personal expression.[85] These are all examples of value to the speaker—value that should be weighed up against the disvalue to the hearer.

How strong the competing claims of the offended and the offender are, depends on the same kinds of considerations that apply to offence in other contexts.[86] These include (a) how intrusive the offending words are; (b) how easily the offended person can avoid the offensive words without undue cost; (c) how important expressing the offending words is to the person expressing them, and whether they have alternative opportunities to derive this value; and (d) how much social value expressing the offending words has.

These considerations can feature to different degrees and in different combinations in different circumstances. Partly as a consequence of this, they cannot be applied mechanically to yield a verdict in particular cases. Instead, a nuanced discussion of particular cases, that draws on the various considerations, is required. However, there are some general principles that do follow from the various relevant considerations.

For example, it can make a difference whether the profanity is directed towards the person who is offended. All things being equal, you have a stronger claim that somebody not call you 'a God-damned motherfucker' than you have against him describing himself or some indeterminate person in that way.[87] It is the difference between a personal claim not to be insulted and an impersonal claim that others not use words that have nothing to do with you (other, perhaps, than the fact that you might hear them). While you may have a moral claim not to be spoken to in rude, insulting ways, you do not have the same moral claim that somebody not speak *at all* in blasphemous or obscene ways.

When profanities are combined with group slurs (for example, 'fucking Micks') or when they amount to slurs through the addition of a profanity to a non-pejorative group name (for example, 'fucking Irishmen'), they do have a certain directedness—against all members of the relevant group. They should be evaluated primarily as group slurs, even if the profanity element adds *something* to the moral evaluation.

However, it is not only directed profanities that can be wrong. There will be other circumstances in which the offending words are (a) intrusive; (b) could not reasonably be avoided by the offended party; (c) are either not that important to the person expressing them or where the benefit could be derived in some other forum; and (d) there is little social value in expressing them there and then.

Where and when profanities are uttered can make a moral difference. Profanity in a house of worship is quite different from profanity in the pub. Obscenity at a funeral is generally very different from obscenity as part of a stand-up comedy performance. (There are rare exceptions, of course, where funeral and stand-up comedy merge.[88]) An obscenity uttered in a university class is similarly different from one uttered in a kindergarten class.

There are those who think that the use of profanities is indicative of a character flaw. That flaw would be vulgarity, coarseness, boorishness, or at the very least a lack of refinement. This critique has considerable force against those who use profanities unsparingly (or insufficiently sparingly) and without regard to contextual considerations such as place, time, and audience. However, the critique is implausible when directed against those who express profanities more discerningly, which would typically (but not in all cases[89]) also be more sparingly. There is enough value in profanity, and perhaps especially obscenity, for it to have an important role to play in the linguistic repertoire of many people. Moderate profanity does not exhibit the character flaws that unrestrained profanity does.

Those who think that even limited use of profanities demonstrates a character-flaw both ignore the value of profanity and attribute the kind of magically tainting powers to words that were discussed earlier. According to this view, if you say 'Jesus Christ' in the midst of your prayers then no harm is done, but if you shout it out when you bang your thumb with a hammer you are immediately tainted. Alternatively, there is no defect in referring to 'excrement', but uttering the word 'shit' or 'crap', no matter the context, is meant to indicate a character flaw.

Those people who prefer to eschew profanity entirely, are certainly morally free to do so, but that does not mean that the moderate use of profanity indicates a character flaw any more than the moderate use of alcohol does.

Some have suggested that the excessive use of vulgar expressions is indicative of a limited linguistic capacity. The idea is that people use obscenities because they have a limited vocabulary. That view, however, has been empirically debunked.[90]

However, while profanities have their place, there is good reason to use them *relatively* sparingly. The positive effects of swearing enumerated above—emphasis, humour, coping, performance improvement, and other personal expression—do not arise magically from the particular words. Instead, they derive from the words retaining some status as taboo. Obviously, taboo is a matter of degree. The more frequently taboo words are used (overall rather than by a single individual), the less taboo they are likely to be, but then they also lose whatever value arises from being taboo.

If we focus only on emphasis, for example, we might consider the analogy of a highlighter applied to a text. The less you highlight, the more emphasised is that which you do highlight. If, by contrast, you highlight every second word, the result is to reduce the effective highlighting. The same is true of profanity-induced emphasis. If your speech is laden with profanities, uttering another one has less of an emphatic effect than if one generally avoids profanities, but deploys the occasional one.[91]

Similar points can be made about the other benefits of swearing. For example, it may be funny when Dave Chappelle deploys yet another 'fuck', but all things being equal, it will be still funnier if your ordinarily straightlaced grandmother drops an 'f-bomb'.[92]

Responding to (perceived) breaches of language ethics

The ethics of language spans not only what words and expressions we should avoid (and which, if any, we should use in their place) but also how we respond when others say things that we think they should not say. Given how draconian many people's reactions are to (perceived) breaches of language ethics, it is especially important to recognize that our (verbal) reactions (whether oral or written), are themselves liable to ethical evaluation.

Not all *perceived* breaches of language ethics are actual breaches. As has been argued, for example, the *mention* of slurs is typically not wrong. The apoplectic responses we see all too often to such mentions are themselves unethical, even though recognition of this typically has very little social traction.

Similarly, if prejudicial speech can be avoided in more than one way, it is not wrong for somebody to avoid it in the way that they prefer rather than in the way that you prefer. Given the stigma now associated with being accused of racism, sexism, or antisemitism (for example), such accusations should not be levelled inappropriately. When they are levelled without warrant, they are themselves wrong.

Even when somebody has said something that they should not have said, those who would take issue with them, need to consider whether to respond and, if so, what an appropriate response would be. In deliberating about these matters, we should bear a few matters in mind.

First, many well-meaning people may simply lack awareness of the linguistic issues. Their use of the wrong words may reflect no deeper moral problem. For example, many of those who refer to companion animals' 'owners' are not indifferent to animal interests. Similarly, people almost always speak about '*committing* suicide', a term that is clearly a relic of the time in which taking one's own life was a crime or viewed as a sin. Not everybody who uses that term today views suicide as a legal or moral wrong. However, there are still enough people who do think that suicide is wrong for there to be value in not offering implicit support to that view by using a verb so closely related, in one of its senses, to wrongdoing.[93] However, many people may simply not have given the matter any thought and not had the matter drawn to their attention. It is quite normal to use terms that are in common usage, and to do so without thinking about the implications of those terms.

Second, even where people are aware of the problem with a particular word, it is often easy to slip into use of that word. For example, it is all too easy, even if one wants to refer to an animal as 'who' rather than 'it', to slip into the latter, more commonly used pronoun. It can similarly be easy to revert instinctively to referring to somebody who looks like a male as 'he', even though that person might already have declared a preference for a different pronoun.

Third, some demands for particular use of language are 'big asks'. For example, they might require formulations that sound awkward. Try avoiding the word 'commit' before 'suicide'. It is possible, but it does not come naturally. Some words that we are asked to use are hard to pronounce, such as some idiosyncratic preferred pronouns. And sometimes the linguistic demands made on us require unusual feats of memory for some people, such as hundreds of people's particular pronoun preferences.

Fourth, many—perhaps even most—breaches of language ethics are minor relative to other kinds of moral failings. The use of slurs may be among the worst breaches of language ethics, but even these are minor *relative* to physical rather than verbal assaults. The use of sexist language may well contribute to overlooking women (or men[94]), but sexist language is typically much less harmful than sexist actions. Referring to a 'pet' rather than 'companion animal' may be less than ideal, but it is utterly trivial in comparison with the abhorrent treatment to which animals are subjected in order to produce the meat, eggs, and milk that most humans consume. Impertinences may be rude, but they are not assault or theft.

This is not to suggest that we may never challenge somebody regarding a breach of linguistic ethics. However, the case for doing so is strongest when the wrong is clearest, the words are worst, there is an identifiable individual victim of the breach, and a challenge is the best way of responding to the breach. The case for doing so weakens as fewer of these conditions apply.

In other situations, it is often best to seek linguistic change not through reprimand, but rather via personal example, as well as prophylactic and generally (rather than personally) directed explanations of one's linguistic recommendations. Such approaches are less likely to be taken personally, and may thus be more productive than rebukes, which are often (although not always) counterproductive.

Conclusion

According to the nursery rhyme, 'sticks and stones may break my bones, but words shall never hurt me'. This may be a rhetorically powerful move against the verbal bully. However, whether it is *true* depends on what one means by 'hurt' and by how direct a causal chain one has in mind. Words do not usually cause direct physical harm. There are exceptions, at least if one allows at least one intermediate factor in a causal change. For example, words of incitement can lead to actions that do cause physical harm. Group slurs can contribute to a milieu that encourages violence.

Even when words do not (directly) cause physical hurt, they regularly cause psychological harm. Because psychological harm is 'in one's head', does not mean that one should strive to be entirely impervious to it. An insult is an insult and treating it as something other than that is a kind of denial. However, just as one should not attribute less significance to words than is reasonable, neither should one attribute more significance than is appropriate. Words are rarely as harmful as physical assaults. That is the kernel of truth in the nursery rhyme. From this we should not conclude that words do not matter. They often do matter—sometimes more and sometimes less than people think.

8

Humour

Although humour[1] is the very opposite of seriousness, perceived breaches of humour ethics are often taken very seriously. Some people go so far as to think that purportedly errant humourists should be killed. This was the reaction, for example, of some people to the Danish cartoonists whose cartoons depicted the prophet, Mohammed.[2] Various regimes, including Nazis and the Soviets, have severely punished humour directed towards them.[3]

The humourless reaction to humour is not restricted, however, to fundamentalist Muslims, Fascists, Marxists, and other tyrannical regimes. Even in liberal democracies many citizens are outraged at what they take to be breaches of humour ethics, even if their reactions are not as severe.

For example, a philosopher at the University of Wales, Swansea, resigned from that university in response to a barrage of criticism after he told jokes 'with sexual overtones' at a Department Christmas party.[4] A US National Security Advisor, James L. Jones, was taken to task for telling a joke, at an anniversary gala of the Washington Institute for Near East Policy, about a Taliban militant and two Jewish businessmen.[5] There were calls for the resignation of David Letterman after he joked about Sarah Palin's daughter, who advocates premarital abstinence but is herself an unwed mother.[6] A professor at the US Merchant Marine Academy faced the prospect of being fired for a humorous quip that referenced the Colorado movie theatre shooting.[7] In the end he was instead given a forty-five-day suspension and was required to undergo five hours of 'sensitivity training'.[8] And a comedian in New Zealand had to resign from his radio and television jobs after he made a joke about homosexuals and Jews being expendable.[9]

Problematic categories of humour

Not all humour is thought to be morally problematic. Much humour is taken to be innocent and beyond reproach. Ethical questions are typically thought to arise in certain predictable categories of humour.

One such category consists of racial, ethnic, and gender humour—including jokes about 'blacks', Jews, Poles, and women. Another is humour about God, religious figures (such as Mohammed), and other sacred matters. We might refer to this as blasphemous humour. Scatalogical humour is a third category, which includes jokes about genitalia, sex, urination, defecation, menstruation, and other bodily effluvia. Humour about death and suffering—what we might call morbid or tragic humour—includes dead baby jokes, and making light of the Holocaust, famine, and disease. Another category of humour that raises ethical concerns is humour about people's personal attributes—such as their big ears or noses, their short or tall stature, or their mental or physical disabilities. Finally, there are so-called practical jokes (such as the 'candid camera' variety) in which the victims are 'set-up' without their knowledge for the purposes of providing entertainment for others, and the related phenomenon of comic pleasure from people's (unengineered) misfortunes.

Although humour can be and sometimes is morally wrong, it is not wrong as often as popular wisdom suggests.[10] And when it is wrong, it often is not as seriously wrong as many people would have us believe. In arguing for this conclusion, I shall evaluate various views that people seem to hold about the ethics of humour.

The argument will make mention of various jokes that some people may take to be offensive. This is unavoidable without compromising the quality of the argument. A proper discussion of the ethics of humour cannot avoid all reference to the very jokes that some people take to be unethical. In other words, I am not telling the jokes but mentioning them for the purposes of discussing them.[11] Readers who are prone to offense at the mere mention of a joke are advised not to read any further. *Caveat lector!*

Humour is subject to ethical criticism on at least two grounds. First, it is often thought to arise from a moral defect either in the person purveying the humour or in the person who enjoys it. The focus here is on an agent, whether it be the person telling or appreciating a joke.

The other main way of criticizing humour is by focusing on the joke rather than on those telling or laughing at it. Those who fault humour in this way usually do so because of the (wrongfully inflicted) deleterious effects of the humour in question. However, in some select cases, a piece of humour is faulted not because of its effects but rather because of some inherent feature of it.[12]

It is worth noting that the stated flaws are not mutually exclusive. For example, a joke could reflect some moral failing in its teller while also having negative effects. In fact, one flaw might often lead to or explain the other. Thus, if a particular telling of a joke expresses a vice of the joke teller, the joke might, on that basis, have deleterious effects it would not otherwise have. For instance, a joke prompted by malice might cause harm that the same joke offered without any malice would not. Alternatively, the fact that a joke can be expected to have harmful effects on those who do not deserve those harms might sometimes lead us to think that the telling of the joke is an expression of either indifference or malevolence on the part of the joke's teller.

Another way to classify the moral criticisms of humour is to distinguish between contextual and non-contextual criticisms. Non-contextual criticisms take issue with a joke irrespective of its context. The criticism is of a type of joke, which is thought to be wrong irrespective of its context. Contextual criticisms, by contrast, are those that criticize not the joke itself but rather a contextualized instance (or token[13]) of it. One such contextual consideration, as will be discussed later, is the identity of the person telling the joke. Thus, somebody offering a contextual criticism of a man telling a joke about women, might have no objection to a woman telling the same joke.

In what follows, I shall discuss both non-contextual and contextual evaluations of humour and will show how the earlier distinction between different grounds for criticizing humour maps onto this distinction. The various relationships are graphically represented in Figure 8.1.

Non-contextual criticisms

Criticizing humour because of a moral defect in the people purveying or appreciating it can be either contextual or non-contextual. It should be obvious that humour is at least *sometimes* the product of a character defect. Sometimes jokes about racial or ethnic groups or about one or other sex are told or enjoyed because the teller or the audience is prejudiced towards the group that is the butt of the joke. Blasphemous, scatological, tragic, and personal humour as well as practical jokes are sometimes delivered or enjoyed because of insensitivity, maliciousness, or cruelty.

The key question is how often these kinds of jokes are the product of character defects. Some of those writing on the ethics of humour have held the

Two grounds for assessing the ethics of humour				
Agent (Humourist or appreciator)		**Humour**	
1. Some categories of humour always express a defect in the agent.	2. Some instances of humour express a defect in the agent, but others do not.	3. Humour itself	4. Effects
Non-contextual	Contextual	Non-contextual	Contextual

Figure 8.1 Two grounds for assessing the ethics of humour.

extreme view that in the case of some kinds of humour, the answer is 'always'. (Category 1 in Figure 8.1.) With respect to these kinds of humour, their critique is non-contextual. It is not that one of these kinds of jokes is acceptable in some circumstances but morally wrong in others. Instead, it is, on this view, always a product of some or other vice.

For example, some people have argued that jokes that turn on negative racial, ethnic, or gender stereotypes *always* reflect badly on those who enjoy them. The suggestion is that one cannot enjoy a joke that turns on a stereotype without actually endorsing the stereotype.[14] It is not possible, on this view, to adopt the prejudicial attitude hypothetically. To laugh at a joke about women, Jews, or 'blacks', is to show you up as, respectively a sexist, antisemite, or racist.

Arguments for this conclusion ask us to introspect. They suggest that if we do, we will find that 'we intuitively know that sharing [the joke's assumptions] is what would enable us to find the joke funny'.[15] This claim is problematic. If we assume, for the moment, that introspection is a reasonable methodology, we find that many honest introspectors simply do not find that they share the prejudicial assumptions of the jokes they enjoy. They find instead that they can enjoy a joke that employs a stereotype of a particular group of people without actually endorsing that stereotype. Consider, for example, the following joke:

A Jew, a Scot, and an Englishman have dinner together at a restaurant. After the meal, the waiter approaches them and asks to whom he should present the bill. The Scot says: 'I'll pay'. The headline in the newspaper the next morning reads: 'Jewish ventriloquist found dead in alley'.

Stereotypes about Englishmen are inert in this joke, but the joke does turn on stereotypes about Jews and Scots. According to the stereotypes both groups are tightfisted. But this purported attribute is combined with canniness in the Jew and a propensity to violence in the Scot. The wily Jew, intent on avoiding payment for the dinner, cleverly tries to get the Scot to pay. The Scot, equally unwilling to pay, (over-) reacts by killing the Jew.

At least some people say that they can enjoy a joke of this kind even though they are as confident as possible that they do not endorse the underlying stereotypes. To this it might be objected that the joke would be less funny if it had been an Englishman who said he would pay and an American ventriloquist who had been found dead in an alley. In that version one might see the point of the joke, but one would not find it as funny, even if the relevant stereotypes were stipulated in advance of telling the joke. The suggestion is that this shows that we do indeed need to endorse the underlying stereotypes to find the joke funny.

However, this objection overlooks the fact that actually *endorsing* the stereotypes is not the only alternative to merely *stipulating* them. Intermediate between these is *recognizing* stereotypes and this may well be sufficient to enjoy the joke.[16] This is not to deny the possibility that there are those who find the joke funny because they do endorse the underlying stereotypes. Instead, it is to say that endorsing the stereotypes is not necessary for enjoying the humour—or even *fully* enjoying it. Introspection suggests that one can, and some people do, (fully) enjoy such jokes without endorsing the stereotypes,[17] in which case jokes turning on a racial, ethnic, or gender stereotype are not *always* tainted by flaws in the person recounting or enjoying the joke.

So far, I have been assuming that introspection is a reasonable methodology for determining whether endorsing a stereotype is necessary for appreciating humour that turns on that stereotype. Against this assumption it might well be suggested that introspections are unreliable because even honest introspectors may be unaware of their implicit biases. However, if the introspective method is unreliable then those claiming that one cannot enjoy a joke that turns on a stereotype without actually endorsing the stereotype cannot appeal to introspections to make their case. Nor is it sufficient for them to point to the numerous studies that have shown that implicit biases are widespread. They need to show that it is the presence of an implicit bias that causes the relevant humour to be appreciated. For if it were the case that somebody had an unconscious prejudice, but this played no role in appreciating a particular piece of humour, it would not be the case that the humour appreciation were an *expression* of the prejudice. In short, those who claim that appreciating humour that turns on a stereotype is always an expression of prejudice cannot simply make that claim. They need to provide evidence.

Just as jokes that turn on stereotypes do not seem always to be an expression of a defect in those who appreciate the jokes, so jokes about the ugly or the disabled, or about violence, rape, or death, do not seem *always* to arise from insensitivity or cruelty in the person telling or enjoying such jokes. Such vices may explain why some people like jokes of these kinds, but for others the appreciation of such jokes is explained in other ways.

For some people it can arise from the opposite character traits. It is precisely because of their sensitivities or anxieties about the sufferings and misfortunes that they seek relief in lightheartedness about these serious matters. Think, for example, of the old man who says, 'When I awake in the morning, the first thing I do is spread my arms. If I don't hit wood, I get up'. Such a quip does not indicate that the old man regards his death as a trivial matter. Instead, it is his anxiety about death (and interment) that gives rise to his humour. While this is a case of self-directed humour, there is no reason to think that something similar is not sometimes occurring when people joke about the tragedies that befall others. Such tragedies can cause us anxiety, and humour is one way in which we can deal with them.

Thus, we see that to joke about something is, contrary to what some people think, not necessarily to trivialize it. When jokes are told about serious matters, we are not necessarily treating these matters as though they were not serious. We can laugh at the serious, and sometimes we do so precisely because we recognize it to be serious.

However, saying something in jest is not the same thing as saying it seriously. Indeed, sometimes a joke or a skit or some other piece of humour is found to be funny precisely because it could never be said in seriousness (without exceeding the bounds of civility). Consider the following joke:

A little boy says to his older brother: 'Mommy and Daddy bought me a bicycle, but they didn't buy you one. Mommy and Daddy bought me a television for my bedroom, and they didn't buy you one. Mommy and Daddy took me on an overseas holiday, but they didn't take you'.

The brother replies: 'Yes, but at least I don't have cancer'.

That retort would be grotesquely cruel, even in response to the gloating that preceded and precipitated it. If it were said in seriousness,[18] in real life, it would be inexcusable. It is the knowledge of that, combined with the knowledge that the joke is *not* real life that partly explains the joke's funniness. In the hypothetical scenario of the joke, we contemplate the possibility of such transgressive behaviour, while realizing that it is not actual. The contemplation of it is funny to many people in a way in which the actual witnessing of it would not be.

It is not merely the contemplation of the transgressive that explains why some people find some jokes about nasty subjects funny. Consider the following two closely related rape jokes:

> A young nun is taking a walk one evening. A man forces her to the ground and rapes her. Afterwards he asks her what she is going to tell Mother Superior. The young nun replies: 'I'll tell her that it was a beautiful evening and thus I decided to take a walk. While I was out, a terrible man attacked me and raped me.... Twice, if you're not too tired'.

> Two young nuns are taking a walk. They are attacked by two men, who proceed to rape them. In the midst of the rape, the one nun cries out: 'Forgive them, Lord, for they know not what they do'. Thereupon the other nun cries out: 'Mine does!'

Part of the humour here is again the contemplation of reactions from the hypothetical nuns that we could never imagine in real life. The scenario is incongruous with our expectations of reality. But there are also surprising incongruities internal to the jokes. We think that the nun in the first joke is speaking in the past tense but then the punch line implicitly shifts the tense, and we realize that she is speaking about not only the past but also the immediate future, which will then be incorporated into her past tense account to Mother Superior.

In the second of the jokes, part of the humour lies in the incongruous interpretation, by the second nun, of her colleague's invocation of Jesus's words. Thus, the humour is partly a function of amusing incongruities and their apperception. It is a kind of mental calisthenic. Enjoying this mental exercise does not necessarily mean that one has defective attitudes towards rape.

Another non-contextual moral critique alleges that some kinds of humour are always tainted, not because of a defect in those spreading or enjoying it, but instead because of a defect in the humour itself. (Category 3 in Figure 8.1.) It seems to be the case that this claim is made about very few types of humour. Perhaps the clearest example is (purportedly) blasphemous humour. Although those concerned about such humour might take blasphemers to be morally defective, their basis for objecting to the humour lies not in the blasphemer but in the blasphemy. Humour that 'takes the Lord's name in vain' or that irreverently depicts the sacred, or, in some cases, depicts God or a prophet in any way, is thought to be wrong.[19]

Arguments that a particular type of humour is always wrong because it is blasphemous are deeply controversial. This is because they rest on highly contested premises. They assume not only that God exists but also that blasphemy is morally wrong (as distinct from being prohibited on non-moral grounds) and that a particular piece of humour constitutes blasphemy. Atheists, of course, will deny the basic assumption of God's existence and the other assumptions fall like dominos in consequence. However, even theists, who agree about God's existence, can disagree about the other assumptions and especially the final one. There is wide variation in the views of religious people about what constitutes blasphemy and blasphemous humour. Some are much more permissive than others. For these reasons, the non-contextual moral critique of blasphemous humour is hard to defend.

Contextual criticisms

It should not be surprising that non-contextual criticisms of humour are harder to defend. They make more expansive claims than contextual criticisms do. More specifically, they say that *all* humour of a particular kind is morally wrong. Such claims are hard to believe. Much more plausible is the view that various kinds of humour can be morally acceptable in some contexts but wrong in others. On this view, we should not be evaluating types of jokes but rather particular instances of a joke to determine whether they are morally permissible.

The thought that humour can be wrong when it stems from a defect in the person telling or appreciating a joke, is a contextual critique when a particular instance of a joke is faulted not because all jokes of that type are thought to stem from a personal defect but rather because that particular instance of it is thought to do so. (Category 2 in Figure 8.1.) In other words, telling a particular joke, J, could be wrong for one person, P (because J would reflect a defect in P), even though it would not be wrong for another person, Q (because J would not reflect a defect in Q).

A defect in the joke teller is not the only basis for a contextual criticism of humour. The other basis arises when an instance of humour is thought to inflict a wrongful harm. (Category 4 in Figure 8.1.) Because a given joke can be harmful in some situations but not in others, and because where it is harmful the harm is permissibly inflicted in some circumstances but not in others, a contextual critique makes reference to the particular circumstances in which a joke is told.

Humour only rarely causes physical harm, at least directly. Some kinds of practical jokes would be the most likely of the various types of humour to cause such harm. They are also the kind of joke most easy to fault. Imagine, for example, the practical joker who contrives to cause somebody to slip or fall for the amusement of others. Such actions could be physically injurious, and the infliction of such harm, or the risk of it, will typically be unjustified.

It is arguably somewhat more common for humour to cause physical harm *indirectly*. Consider, for example, a case of somebody who responds violently to a piece of humour that he finds offensive. The violent reaction to the Mohammed cartoons in the Danish *Jyllands-Posten* newspaper is a possible example.[20] Of course, it is not uncontroversial in such cases to say that the humour *caused* the violence.

This is because the intolerant, violent reactor has a choice about how to react to the humour. He is not caused or forced to react violently. He chooses to do so. However, this does not settle the issue. Even if we deny that the humour causes the violence, the humour could still be faulted on the grounds of the violent reaction to it. Some may be willing to concede that the person who reacts violently to humour is indeed responsible, and yet want to say that the humourist bears some responsibility too.

The force of this line of argument depends, in part, on how likely, and thus reasonably foreseeable, the resultant violence is. If one knows that people are very likely to respond violently, then there are moral reasons to desist. These reasons may very often override the reasons to express the humour (given that the benefits of humour would typically be outweighed by the harms of the violent reaction). Even here, it may make a moral difference whether the violence will likely be directed against oneself or against others. It may also make a difference how long one must desist from the humour. The case for desisting temporarily while the threat can be neutralized is stronger than the case for desisting permanently. The longer people must censor themselves for fear of violence, the more corrosive are the effects of remaining silent.

However, it is implausible to suggest that the violence resulting from the Danish cartoons was reasonably foreseeable. In retrospect, this may seem like a ludicrous claim. However, there was a complex chain of events that separated the publication of the cartoons at the end of September 2005, and the resultant violence in late January and February 2006. This includes the compilation of a dossier by two Muslim leaders, that they then hawked around the Muslim world, drumming up the violent reaction.[21]

Furthermore, the publication of the cartoons cannot be deemed immoral merely because the cartoons, via a long and complex causal change, did actually result in violence. If we deny this, then *any* humour—or anything else—could become morally wrong merely because some ignorant or intolerant person responds to it violently.[22] Those who call for violence bear significant responsibility for the violence that then ensues, even if that call is only answered much later. However, calling for violence—incitement—is quite different from violent responses to utterings that the violent reactor mistakenly takes as a justification for violence.

The most common harmful effects of humour are not physical. When humour harms, the harms are typically psychological, including offence, embarrassment, shock, disgust, and the feeling of being demeaned or insulted. Humour is sometimes also thought to inculcate, spread, or reinforce negative attitudes about those individuals or groups that are the butt of the humour.[23] Such attitudes might themselves be thought to be harmful. At the very least, they might be thought to pose the risk of causing harm to those toward whom the attitudes are held.

Common mistakes in humour ethics

In assessing the effects of humour, common thinking about the ethics of humour is prone to a number of mistakes.

The benefits are ignored

First, the focus tends to be (almost) exclusively on the *negative* effects. Of the positive effects that are overlooked, the most obvious is the pleasure that humour brings. Where critics of humour do consider the pleasure, this often forms part of the critique. The suggestion is that there is something wicked about taking pleasure in humour that also has the negative effects. Such a critique is obviously sometimes apt. Sometimes it is wicked to laugh at the expense of another. However, it is not *always* wrong. One can better see why this is the case if one considers some of the other benefits of humour.

For example, humour is a powerful tool that can be wielded against those who abuse power.[24] Tyrants have no moral complaint when others, and especially those they oppress, laugh at them. It is because of humour's subversive power that many a despot has sought to prohibit humour that mocks him or his associates. For example, in Zimbabwe it was a criminal offence to ridicule the President, Robert Mugabe.[25]

Sometimes the oppressed begin to joke about the risks of joking. Here is one example from the Third Reich:

> What is fratricide?
> If Hermann Goering slaughters a pig.
> What is suicide?
> If someone tells this joke in public.[26]

Other repressive regimes have been a little less sensitive about satire. In such cases humour can serve the function of conveying (sometimes scathing) criticism in a form that is more palatable to those being satirized. It is often the case that a true and critical word spoken in jest is tolerated more readily than a true and critical word spoken in seriousness would be. South African comedian, Pieter Dirk Uys, lampooned Apartheid and Apartheid-era politicians (as he does post-Apartheid politicians) with relative impunity.[27]

This phenomenon does not occur only at the political level. Even in inter-personal relationships, criticisms offered in jest are often more agreeable than criticisms offered in earnestness. And it is because we all have our foibles that others may sometimes joke about us. Thus, it is not only tyrants who have no justified complaint about being the butt of a joke.

Humour has other benefits too. It can puncture pretentiousness, and lighten mood. It can help people cope with their anxieties—about disease, disability, and death, for example. It is often the case that when people joke about these things it is not because they are failing to take them seriously, but instead precisely because they do take them so seriously.

Tragedies often breed dark humour. Think, for example, of the flurry of jokes that were generated in response to the Ethiopian famine, the space shuttle disasters, the death of Diana Spencer, and the O.J. Simpson murder trial following the killing of Nicole Brown Simpson and Ron Goldman.

Humour also flourishes in circumstances of adversity, enabling people to battle the ill-effects of being victimized, oppressed, or persecuted. Soviet citizens joked about the USSR, mocking the repression, the inefficiencies, the drabness, and the shortages. Jews joke about antisemitism, and 'blacks' joke about racism.

The dynamics vary. Sometimes a group that is stereotyped employs jokes embodying the stereotype in an attempt to neutralize the potency of the stereotype. More rarely, the stereotype becomes the butt of the joke. Consider the following joke, which has both a Jewish and a 'black' variant:

> Two Jews are walking down a street and see a sign on a church saying: 'Become a Christian and earn $100'. They don't know what to make of this, but they decide that one will convert and will share the money with the other. The prospective convert enters the church. After a while he emerges. His friend says to him:
> 'Where's my $50?'.
> The new Christian replies: 'Is that all you people think about?'

> Two 'blacks' are walking down a street and see a sign on a building saying: 'Become white and earn $100'. They don't know what to make of this, but they decide that one will become 'white' and will share the money with the other. The prospective 'white' enters the building. After a while he emerges. His friend says to him:
> 'Where's my $50?'.
> The new 'white' replies: 'Get yourself a job!'

These versions of the joke rest on a recognition of stereotypes about Jews and 'blacks', but the butt of the joke is not the Jew or the 'black'. Instead, it is those who hold the stereotypes about them.[28]

Contextual considerations are oversimplified

Many people recognize that context is crucial for determining when a joke expresses a defect in the joke teller, but a common view about humour ethics tends to oversimplify the contextual considerations. For example, it is often thought that jokes about 'blacks', Jews, women, Poles, or the disabled, for example, are morally tainted unless they are told by members of the group that is the butt of the joke. Some go so far as to say that unless one is a member of the group about which one is joking, telling the joke is wrong.

This view is correct in asserting that the identity of the joke teller is relevant to a moral assessment of a given telling of a joke. Depending on who is telling a joke, the joke either is or is not an expression of a defect in the joke teller. However, where the view is wrong is in claiming that only group-insiders may tell jokes about the group. What it seems to assume is that all and only group-insiders can tell the joke without either (a) the joke being an expression of a defective attitude or (b) the joke being *viewed* as the expression of such an attitude.

However, neither of these assumptions can be supported. First, it is possible for group-insiders to share defective attitudes about the group. It is not uncommon for people to internalize prejudices or other negative attitudes towards a group of which they are members. When such group-insiders tell jokes about their group they may well be exhibiting the same attitudes as prejudiced people outside the group. If a joke is morally problematic because it expresses some defect in the joke teller, then the telling of a joke about 'blacks', for example, is wrong if the person telling it is a 'black' who shares that defect.

Second, because of this phenomenon we cannot assume that group-insiders will not be viewed (at least by those with a more nuanced view of human psychology) as expressing the problematic attitudes.

Third, there are situations in which we can be confident that the joke teller does *not* share the negative attitudes even though he or she is *not* a member of the group about which the joke is being told. Sometimes we know somebody sufficiently well—or we know that those to whom we tell a joke know us sufficiently well—that the telling of the joke will not be viewed as an expression of a bad attitude.

Thus, while the identity of the person purveying some piece of humour is clearly a relevant contextual consideration, it should not be reduced to the crude principle that all and only group-insiders may joke about the group.

Another contextual consideration is the identity of those to whom the humour is directed, namely its audience. This consideration too is oversimplified—and in a way that connects with the identity of the humourist. Thus, it is often thought that if a group-insider tells a joke to fellow group-insiders, the humour is innocent. If, however, the same joke is told to those outside the group being joked about, then the joke telling is morally suspect, whether or not the teller is a member of the group. The thought seems to be that telling a joke about 'blacks', for example, is not likely to inculcate or reinforce anti-'black' attitudes in 'blacks', or that there is something less troubling about a disabled person laughing at disability than there is about an able-bodied person laughing at the same joke.

While this view contains some truth, it too is insufficiently refined. It probably is true that group-insiders, although not immune, are often less prone to adopting negative attitudes towards the group. Moreover, it does seem true that self-deprecatory humour is less worrying than humour that deprecates others. Nevertheless, because people can enjoy jokes about others without having or coming to have negative attitudes towards those people, we cannot assume that it is always impermissible to tell a joke about a group to those not in the group.

A third contextual consideration is the identity of the group *about which* (rather than *to which*) the joke is told. The conventional wisdom here is that there is no problem telling jokes that are critical of men but that there is a presumption against telling jokes that are critical of women. Similarly, while it is acceptable for 'whites' to be the butt of a joke, telling jokes about 'blacks' is presumptively wrong. The rationale seems to be that subordinate groups are more vulnerable than dominant ones and that laughing at the 'underdog' is morally problematic in a way that laughing at dominant groups is not.

Again, there is an element of truth to this view. Telling jokes about some groups is more likely to cause (wrongful) harm than telling jokes about others. But this does not mean that telling jokes about historically disadvantaged groups always (wrongfully) harms, or that telling jokes about historically advantaged groups never (wrongfully) harms. For example, jokes about 'whites' might be more dangerous in Zimbabwe than they are in Sweden, and jokes about male nurses may be more damaging than jokes about female doctors.

Offence is given too much weight

Possibly the most common mistake made in thinking about the ethics of humour is to treat offence either as a decisive moral consideration or, at the very least, as a very strong moral consideration. It is often thought that because a piece of humour offends somebody it is therefore wrong, or is at least presumptively so. Variants on this view claim that offence must either reach a certain level of intensity, or be sufficiently widespread, or must result from a violation of particular sensibilities—such as religious or racial ones—in order for the humour that gives rise to the offence to be judged wrong.

When this view is stated bluntly, as I have just stated it, it sounds untenable. It might be wondered, therefore, whether anybody really makes the mistake of thinking it true. Because the argument is rarely stated explicitly it is hard to *prove*, at least without probing people, whether they are in fact espousing such a view. However, it does seem reasonable to attribute the view to those who, in criticizing an instance of humour, refer to its offensiveness and say nothing more.[29] There are many examples of this.[30]

What tends to happen is that people express their outrage at a piece of humour (or people note that others are outraged about it) and they infer that the humour must be wrong. Alternatively, it is noted how many people are outraged or how intensely outraged people are, and it is assumed that there must be a good reason either why so many people are upset or why people are so upset.

However, in the absence of a justification for the outrage, it is the outrage itself that is doing the work of (purportedly) justifying the claim that humour is wrong. In other words, it is one thing to say that humour is wrong for such and such reasons, and people are outraged because it is the sort of wrong that elicits justified offence. It is another thing to say that the humour is wrong because people are outraged by it.

All versions of the view that humour is wrong because it causes offence are problematic. If the view were correct, then it would grant a moral veto to the hypersensitive.[31] Those easily offended or outraged would be able to render instances of humour immoral. That, in turn, would imply that there is no difference between warranted and unwarranted outrage—or at least that the distinction is irrelevant to our assessment of the ethics of humour. It would assume that people always have a moral right not be offended. It would also ignore the fact that humour that offends some people can bring more important benefits to others.

Finally, offence arguments can be two-edged swords that produce judgements that if not contradictory are certainly in tension with one another. Thus, A might be offended by B's joke, but B might be offended by A's offence—that is, by his humourlessness. If offence is a sufficient condition for rendering immoral the conduct that generates the offence, then although B's joke is immoral, so is the very reaction of A that makes the joke immoral.

Although offence is not a very weighty moral consideration against telling a joke, this does not mean that it is irrelevant. The fact that one's humour would cause others offence is often something we must consider. That consideration will regularly be overridden, but there are times when it will not be outweighed by other considerations. The clearest scenario is where the offence is gratuitous—where the offending humour produces no benefit to redeem it. It would be wrong, for example, to tell crude jokes to prudes if *all* that this achieved was the mortification of the prudes.

Judging jokes

How can we judge (prospectively) when we may tell a joke and when we may not? How can we judge (retrospectively) whether some humour that has been disseminated should instead have been withheld?

It should be obvious that no formula can be provided. If, as I have suggested, the non-contextual criticisms of humour are defective, we cannot even say that some kinds of jokes should never be told. Instead, any judgment will need to take into account the specifics of a given joke in a given context. Drawing on the earlier discussion, a few general guidelines can be provided.

We obviously need to ask, in a specific context, whether the humour expresses some defect in those purveying or appreciating the humour. We also need to consider the effects of telling a joke. That involves considering the expected harms of telling the joke, but it also requires us to consider the joke's expected benefits. The harms and benefits will be influenced by facts about the humourist, the audience, and the butt of the joke, but not in the crude ways that are often assumed.

However, these are not the only determinants of the quality and quantity of the harms and benefits. The location and the timing, for example, can also be relevant. Sometimes a joke is 'too soon' after a tragedy. And some jokes may be acceptably told in one place but not in another. Consider here the difference between telling a profanity-laden, deeply disgusting joke in a bar and telling it in a church or a cemetery.

We need to weigh up the harms against the benefits. This does not mean that our determination must be a utilitarian one or, if it is a utilitarian one, that it must be a simplistic utilitarian calculation. For example, if a joke will offend, we should ask whether the offence is deserved or not, and whether it is warranted or unwarranted. If it is deserved or unwarranted, it should be discounted in our weighing up of the harms and benefits. If it is undeserved or warranted it should weigh more heavily.

Considering and weighing all these factors will enable us to make more nuanced judgments about humour than are typically made. It is possible to think intelligently and carefully about the ethics of humour. This does not mean that in some cases there will not be scope for reasonable disagreement. For example, it will sometimes be unclear what the consequences of a joke will be, how important it is to tell it, or how warranted the resultant offence will be. In such uncertainties, humour ethics is no different from the ethics of other practices.

Another way in which humour ethics is the same as the ethics of other practices, is that whereas some humour that is not morally impermissible, may nonetheless be morally undesirable or deficient. That it is say, it might be morally better that one does not purvey that humour. In other cases, humour that is morally permissible carries no negative moral valence at all.

Conclusion

Humour is often about serious subjects and the ethics of humour is, of course, no laughing matter. It deserves our serious consideration. It is possible, however, to take humour too seriously. In conclusion, consider one deeply ironic example.

Nando's, the South African chicken restaurant chain, is well known for its witty, irreverent advertisements. In one of its advertisements, a blind old lady is led into a pole by her guide dog, who then snatches her take-out Nando's chicken after she lies concussed on the pavement. The advertisement was greeted with outrage by protesters who claimed that it made light of the blind. Some protesters thought that the advertisement 'was more offensive to the reputation of guide dogs'.[32] The Advertising Standards Association of South Africa ruled that the advertisement was offensive to the blind (but not to the guide dogs) and that it had to be withdrawn.[33]

The irony here is that the chickens consumed in Nando's outlets are, during their lifetimes, made to suffer in all the appalling ways in which chickens are reared and killed.[34] Yet those objecting to the advertisement completely ignored this very serious moral problem and took the most important moral issues to be the reputation of guide dogs and the sensibilities of the blind.[35] That distortion is indicative of how unreliable popular views about the ethics of humour can be.

In a famous example of 'anti-humour' we are asked: 'Why did the chicken cross the road?' This looks like the set-up for a joke, but when the 'punch line' is delivered—'Because she wanted to get to the other side'—we realize that it is in fact not a joke at all (although that might make it a kind of joke).[36] Asking questions about Nando's advertisements may look like a case of humour ethics, but when the answers badly distort the relative weight of different moral considerations, it may, in fact, be a case of 'humour anti-ethics'. Taking humour ethics seriously involves not taking it more seriously than it should be taken.

9
Bullshit

In one scene in his *History of the World, Part I*, Mel Brooks plays Comicus presenting himself at a Roman unemployment agency. Asked to state his occupation, he says: 'Stand-up philosopher'. The official at the window replies: 'What?' Comicus repeats and explains: 'A stand-up philosopher! I coalesce the vapour of human experience into a viable and logical comprehension'. The official replies knowingly (and not inappropriately in this particular case): 'Oh, a bullshit artist!'

According to one stereotype, manifest in this skit,[1] philosophers are bullshit artists. No doubt this is true of some philosophers, but not all philosophers are bullshitters, and those who are, constitute only a small proportion of all bullshit producers. Bullshit is ubiquitous. Harry Frankfurt, the philosopher who has most prominently written *about* bullshit,[2] began his essay on this topic with the claim: 'One of the most salient features of our culture is that there is so much bullshit'.[3] Unless the culture to which Professor Frankfurt was referring was human culture as a whole, the implication here seems to be that bullshit is prevalent only in some cultures. If that is indeed an implication of what he was saying, then he must be mistaken. It would be surprising if humans have not been bullshitting, at least in some form, in all cultures and for at least as long as humans have had language.[4]

This fact, if it is a fact, does not bode well for those who would like to see the end of bullshit. In this regard, bullshit is no different from so many other human faults. It will last as long as humanity. That does not mean that we should resign ourselves to bullshit. While bullshit is inevitable, its quantity is not. Each one of us has most control over whether one generates bullshit oneself, but we can also have some influence on the quantity of bullshit produced by others. We exercise this influence through the way we respond to their bullshit. However, before examining what we ought to do about bullshit, we should first have a clearer idea of what it is, why there is so much of it, and what its dangers are.

What is bullshit?

While we can get a *clearer* idea of what bullshit is, we do need to recognize, as Harry Frankfurt himself does, that 'the phenomenon... is so vast and amorphous that no crisp and perspicacious analysis of its concept can avoid being procrustean'.[5]

Max Black made an excellent start in sharpening our understanding of bullshit, although his focus was on 'humbug',[6] a more delicate term, and which he notes is closely associated with 'balderdash, claptrap, rubbish, cliché, hokum, drivel, buncombe, nonsense, gibberish, or tautology'.[7] Professor Black understands 'humbug' as 'deceptive misrepresentation, short of lying, especially by pretentious word or deed, of somebody's own thoughts, feelings, or attitudes'.[8] Varying threads here have been picked up by subsequent theorizers of bullshit,[9] most notably Harry Frankfurt and Gerald (Jerry) Cohen.

Like Max Black, Harry Frankfurt distinguishes between bullshit and lies, although Professor Frankfurt does not think that they are different only in degree. Instead, he thinks that whereas the liar is interested in misrepresenting the facts, the bullshitter is not interested in the facts at all. The bullshitter just talks (or writes) without regard to whether or not what he is saying is true. The bullshitter is trying to 'convey a certain impression of himself'.[10] Thus, the 'essence of bullshit is not that it is *false* but that it is *phony*'.[11]

Jerry Cohen says that he and Harry Frankfurt are interested in different kinds of bullshit[12]—that whereas Harry Frankfurt is interested in 'a bullshit of ordinary life', he, Jerry Cohen, is interested in 'a bullshit that appears in academic works'.[13] He calls the first 'Frankfurt's bullshit' and the second 'Cohen's bullshit'. These (roughly) correspond, he notes, with two senses of 'bullshit' provided in the Oxford English Dictionary—'trivial or insincere talk or writing', and 'nonsense, rubbish' respectively.

Jerry Cohen is primarily interested in a particular kind of nonsense, namely what he calls 'unclarifiable unclarity'.[14] These are collections of words that are unclear and which cannot be made clear. This, arguably, is a prime (and justly infamous) example:

> The move from a structuralist account in which capital is understood to structure social relations in relatively homologous ways to a view of

hegemony in which power relations are subject to repetition, convergence, and rearticulation brought the question of temporality into the thinking of structure, and marked a shift from a form of Althusserian theory that takes structural totalities as theoretical objects to one in which the insights into the contingent possibility of structure inaugurate a renewed conception of hegemony as bound up with the contingent sites and strategies of the rearticulation of power.[15]

Jerry Cohen recognizes that there are other kinds of nonsense. These include what he calls rubbish—'arguments that are grossly deficient either in logic or in sensitivity to empirical evidence'[16]—as well as 'irretrievably speculative comment which is neither unclear nor wanting in logic'.[17] Perhaps there are other forms of nonsense too.

There are some important differences between 'Frankfurt's bullshit' and 'Cohen's bullshit'. Because the former is characterized by an indifference to the truth, and because indifference is an attitude, we identify the product via the agent and his or her activity. Bullshit is the product of bullshitting. 'Cohen's bullshit', by contrast, is a particular kind of output, irrespective of the attitude of the person who produced it. Thus, in the case of 'Cohen's bullshit' the bullshit is basic and the bullshitting derivative. In other words, bullshitting is that which produces bullshit.

It is not clear that these two kinds of bullshit are taxonomically exhaustive, or whether there are other species of bullshit. One possibility is a form of 'obscurantism'.[18] Although Filip Buekens and Maarten Boudry wish to distinguish obscurantism from bullshit,[19] this is because they have only 'Frankurt's bullshit' in mind and they correctly see that it is not the same as that (even though obscurantism might sometimes result from indifference towards the truth).

Obscurantism is similar to Jerry Cohen's 'unclarifiable unclarity'. However, it is not identical with it either. Obscurantist expression could sometimes—often with much effort—be made clear, but doing so would reveal that the expression is shallow rather than deep, trite rather than novel, or silly rather than clever. This does not mean that obscurantism of this sort is not bullshit. Making shallow or trite or stupid comments in high-sounding language is surely a kind of bullshit. In other words, *clarifiable* unclarity may very well also be one kind of bullshit.

It is harder to know what to think about other phenomena, however. Part of the difficulty here is determining the boundaries of the concept. For example, should we see (some) 'spin'[20] as a form of bullshit or merely as an adjacent or related concept? Spin, in the relevant sense, is a 'bias or slant on information, intended to create a favourable impression when it is presented to the public'.[21]

Spin in this sense can sometimes have features in common with paradigmatic forms of bullshit. It can involve nonsense, often in the form of unsupported or jargon-laden claims. It may be obscurantist. The spin-doctor is usually attempting to convey a particular impression of himself or of those for whom he is spinning. When spin is deceptive, it typically does not amount to outright lying. But there are also differences between spin and the paradigmatic kinds of bullshit. The reason why spin typically does not include overt lies is that the spin-doctor is often *not* indifferent to the truth. He seeks to create the desired impression without being untruthful. And sometimes spin is perfectly intelligible. Thus, we can either view some spin as an independent form of bullshit or we can view it as merely sharing some features in common with bullshit.

Other cases may be even more complicated. Can only words, whether spoken or written, be bullshit or, following Max Black, should we count some deeds (and related phenomena) as bullshit? If empty words are bullshit words, then perhaps empty deeds are bullshit deeds.

The phenomenon of a 'bullshit job'—a job that 'could be eliminated with no downside'[22]—has certainly been described.[23] Closely related are phenomena such as 'bullshit work' and 'bullshit tasks'. Consider some real examples:[24]

1. A bullshit email: A government department sends out emails letting employees know that the internet connection is down—emails that only reach those employees once the internet connection is working again.
2. A bullshit request: Government employees receive an email with a link to an online cyber-security training course they are required to take. They are then sent a reminder to complete the task. The link does not work. When one of the employees reports this malfunctioning link, it is not corrected and no further requests to complete the training are sent.
3. A bullshit task: Employees in an organization are requested, annually, to complete an electronic form in which they must indicate what proportion of their time they spent on each of a few different kinds of

activity. The form can be completed only by guessing the proportions. Worse still, because the form is prepopulated with the previous year's guesses, which can then be altered for the current year, employees can see that the guesses they provided the previous year were not even accurately recorded.

4. Bullshit patient service satisfaction survey: At a medical clinic, patients are asked to give a score (from 1, the worst, to 10, the best) reflecting their level of satisfaction with the care they receive in the clinic. At a management meeting, somebody proposes putting up signs suggesting that patients provide a score of 9 or 10. One bullshit-detector at the meeting proposes that the clinic instead improve the level of care so that patients are sufficiently satisfied that they give a better score. He offers some practical suggestions, which are not accepted.

Bullshit of this kind does share some features in common with the more paradigmatic senses of 'bullshit'. For example, they are 'nonsense' of a kind—not *linguistically* unintelligible, but rather rationally unintelligible. Moreover, to keep funding or performing such work or tasks one needs to be indifferent to whether they are doing any good. Finally, creating, sustaining, or holding such positions *sometimes* involves presenting a pretentious image of oneself or of the incumbent. While bullshit work has these features, it also does not fit neatly into the paradigmatic versions. Thus, there is *a* case to be made for seeing it as a different species of bullshit. On the other hand, it could be seen as a bullshit-derivative rather than the real thing.

Figure 9.1 contains a summary outline of the varieties of bullshit just discussed. It is not intended to be definitive, but only to provide a clear summary of the taxonomy, to indicate possible gaps, and to suggest where we *might* draw a divide—at the bold circle—between paradigmatic cases of bullshit and more peripheral cases.

It seems unlikely that one could definitively resolve the foregoing matters and determine precise boundaries to the concept of 'bullshit'. Nor is it obvious that we need to in order to discuss the ethics of producing and responding to bullshit. We can focus on paradigmatic cases. To the extent that the conclusions are also relevant to those bullshitty features of non-paradigmatic bullshit, they can be applied to them. First, however, we need to ask two further preliminary questions—why is there so much bullshit, and what are its dangers?

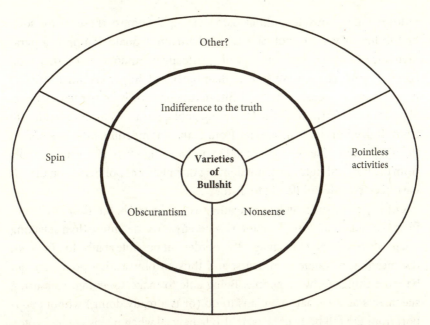

Figure 9.1 The varieties of bullshit.

The prevalence and dangers of bullshit

It is easy to understand why there is so much bullshit. First, it is simply easier than the alternative. This is clearest in the case of 'Frankfurt's bullshit'. This sort of bullshitter does not have to worry about whether she is speaking truthfully. She simply expresses herself without regard to the truth. She does not have to inquire, investigate, or grapple with the complexity and nuance of the world. She simply 'mouths off'. Having and expressing opinions is so much easier than forming and expressing *informed* opinions. Uncritical thinking is easier than critical thinking. It is similarly easier to speak nonsense than sense, and easier to obscure than to clarify. To be sure, speaking either nonsense or platitudes in hifalutin jargon may take either effort or the perverse (either natural or cultivated) talent of the bullshit *artist*. Nevertheless, it surely takes less effort and talent than it does to express interesting and important ideas in plain language.

Bullshit also *works*. Bullshitters typically get ahead, not least because most people are either gullible or, if they do recognize the bullshit, very indulgent of it. Consider politicians, for example. Some of these are the sorts of bullshitters who do not care about the truth. Donald Trump is a paradigmatic example.[25] Perhaps he will eventually be undone, but if that is on account of his bullshitting (rather than outright lying or criminal activity) it will likely be because his bullshitting under oath is construed as lying. Significant proportions of the US voting public rewarded his indifference to truth. Indeed his bullshitting, far from being an impediment to election to the highest office, seems to have aided his campaign.[26] In citing an example from the political right, I am not denying that plenty of politicians on the left have been equally indifferent to truth.

Other politicians may be more attentive to the truth, but they either obfuscate or talk nonsense. That too is generally rewarded more than speaking nuanced ideas in plain language. It is harder—if possible at all—to pin down the meaning of vague comments, and thus an obfuscating politician can be more things to more people. Being able to make sweeping, reassuring statements about what one plans to do (or is already doing) without support from the full body of facts, is also beneficial when one is seeking votes. Electorates are taken in by such talk.

Although they can be more conspicuous, politicians are far from the only examples of bullshitters getting ahead. Bullshitters in all walks of life can sound confident, knowledgeable, and intelligent. They are in the business of presenting a favourable, even if inaccurate, view of themselves. They inspire confidence, and win jobs, sales, contracts, awards, grants, and other opportunities.

Nor does bullshit only work with others. It often works its magic on the bullshitter himself. Those who believe their own bullshit can feel better about and more confident in themselves, with all the benefit that brings. Sometimes the self-deception is the cause rather than (or in addition to) the effect of bullshitting. In such cases, the fact that one has deceived oneself enables one to spew bullshit in the first place.[27]

Understanding why bullshit is so prevalent also enables us to see why it is so dangerous. One way or another, it involves deception—sometimes of self, but more importantly of others. If one speaks without regard to the truth but people take one to be talking with due attention to the truth, they can be deceived. Similarly, if one is speaking nonsense, but this fact is disguised, as it typically is in bullshit, then the uncritical may incorrectly think that one is, in fact, speaking sense and should be taken seriously. Even if one is obfuscating and presenting some banality as a profundity, one's audience might be deceived into thinking that one is saying something of importance.

Bullshit also wastes time and resources. Some of this waste takes place when the bullshit is believed. For example, decisions might be made on the basis of bullshit rather than a reliable, coherent statement of the way the world is. That can cause no end of trouble. Because bullshit prevents matters from being clearly understood, stupidity can run rampant. Instead of problems being properly addressed, people can continue to posture and pontificate about them, often producing one bullshit 'solution' after another. Alternatively, time and energy are spent trying to understand that which cannot be understood, or which once understood turns out not to have been worth all the effort.

Bullshit can waste time and resources even when it is not believed (initially by some and later by others). Alberto Brandolini's Bullshit Asymmetry Principle, also known as Brandolini's Law states: 'The amount of energy necessary to refute bullshit is an order of magnitude bigger than to produce it'.[28] It might have been better named the Bullshit *Radical* Asymmetry Principle. Bullshit, as we have seen, is easy to produce. It is immensely difficult to refute or to expose. One has to bother to establish what the facts are, to attempt to clarify what has been obfuscated, and carefully to show that the reason why other unclarity cannot be clarified is because it is nonsense. One often has to do this in the face of the bullshitter defending his bullshit by bullshitting more—further bullshit that requires still more time and energy to confront. The bullshitter keeps blocking the sewer that the bullshit-buster is trying to unblock. Because bullshitting is so much easier than bullshit-busting, the bullshit-buster cannot hope for more than the occasional breakthrough.

Are some kinds of bullshit more dangerous than others? Harry Frankfurt thinks that indifference to truth (bullshit common in everyday life) is more dangerous than unclarifiable unclarity (the sort of bullshit prevalent in academia). He provides three reasons. First, he says that 'while what goes on in the academic world may sometimes have considerable influence elsewhere, it very often does not'.[29] Second, 'texts that are genuinely unintelligible will very likely not be read, and it is even less likely that much will for very long be based on them'.[30] Finally, he says that 'unintelligibility bears its fault on its face',[31] and is thus more readily discernible than indifference to truth.

While these reasons are all true to some extent, an overly optimistic reading of them will leave us too complacent about unclarifiable unclarity.

We can only hope that those sectors of the humanities where unclarifiable unclarity (as well as obscurantism) prevails have only limited influence. However, students of such work do graduate, and then work in 'the real world'. Perhaps the academic bullshit to which they have been exposed at university ceases to exert any influence, but we should not count on that. In any event, their time at university would have been better spent acquiring actual skills, including the critical ones that would enable them to 'spot buncombe at a hundred paces'.[32]

The last two reasons are arguably even more optimistic. Unintelligible texts seem to have an allure to a certain sort of person, who presumes that they are unintelligible only because they are so profound, and that years of engagement with them will bring enlightenment. Once considerable time and energy has been invested, there are incentives not to admit that this emperor has no clothes.[33] Whether or not the 'unintelligibility bears its fault on its face', they do not see it.

Even if unclarifiable unclarity is less dangerous than indifference to truth, it does not follow that the former is not dangerous at all, and for that reason alone it merits our attention and concern. Moreover, Harry Frankfurt's argument compares indifference to truth with only unclarifiable unclarity. While the latter is Jerry Cohen's chief concern, it does not, as we have seen, exhaust the category of 'Cohen's bullshit'. There are forms of nonsense that are not restricted to the academy and that do not bear their faults upon their faces. The same is true for much spin. Our concerns about bullshit should thus not be restricted to 'Frankfurt's bullshit', very dangerous though that bullshit certainly is.

Responding to bullshit

Given the prevalence and dangers of bullshit, how should we respond to it when we smell its presence? It is tempting to answer that we should always respond in exactly the opposite way that most people do respond. Most people, if they detect bullshit at all, simply accept it, or excuse it. Indeed, that is another reason why there is so much of it. There is usually no resistance when it is dumped before—or on—people. The opposite reaction would be to be deeply intolerant of it. It would be, at every opportunity, to 'call bullshit',[34] denounce it, and attempt to get others to do likewise. While that is the tempting answer, matters are unfortunately not that simple.

Tolerating bullshit

To see why this is the case, we should begin by examining various attempts to excuse or tolerate bullshit. While none of them are convincing responses to all bullshit, they are reasonable responses to some of it.

One way to respond to those who *detect* bullshit is to say that they are mistaken—that their bullshit detector has yielded a false positive. This response is itself sometimes pure bullshit, but it is not always so—or at least not always *obviously* so. There can sometimes be reasonable disagreement about whether something is bullshit. Indeed, Harry Frankfurt, in his response to Jerry Cohen, suggested that the latter's sole example of unclarifiable unclarity—a text from Etienne Balibar—may actually be clarifiable.[35] Professor Frankfurt's attempt to clarify this text does seem like a strain, and he himself admits that his own interpretation is 'vague'. However, the point does not rest on this specific example.

For example, Jonathan Lear has accused Lawrence Summers of bullshit when Professor Summers, then President of Harvard University and talking about the relative paucity of women at the highest levels of mathematics and the sciences, gave a series of explanations that he said were 'my best guess'.[36] According to Professor Lear, those 'three little words indicate that—at least at the time of utterance—the issue did not really matter that much to' Professor Summers.[37]

My own view is that this is deeply unfair. We do not *fully* understand why women are unrepresented in some areas (and men in others).[38] It is those who pretend that they do have a full understanding who are the bullshitters. The rest of us need to grapple with existing data, and formulate (or take note of) hypotheses that can then be tested. That is exactly what Professor Summers was doing—pointing to available evidence, and proposing hypotheses that he himself said needed to be tested.[39] Instead of bullshitting that he knew it all, he admitted his—and our—ignorance and was clearly presenting lines of inquiry. Thus, I would argue, this is a case in which bullshit has been called erroneously.

A second response to bullshit is to claim that it is harmless and thus something that should be tolerated. Clearly this is not true of much bullshit, but this does not mean that it is never true. One possible example is the case of manners. In a bid to be polite we often say things without regard to whether they are true. As Thomas Nagel notes, we routinely say things like 'How nice to see you', irrespective of whether we are pleased to see the person in question.[40] Yet this is harmless, says Professor Nagel, because 'you know perfectly well that this is not meant as a report of my true feelings'.

Moreover, polite expressions such as these play an important social role. If we were completely unfiltered and said whatever was on our minds—such as 'It is not at all nice to see you'—we would all hurt and be hurt much more than we already are. If that is not already clear, then consider this example:

> People gabble away about their children and their children's children, who are not of the slightest interest to me. I have to put on the tight and exceedingly painful mask of cordiality, firmly fixed over my inward rage. I smile, I nod, I blink. And so I have to swim in the pool of idiocy with all the family flat-fish. I cannot say, as a doctor once did, 'Pray, ma'am, go to hell and take your demmed (sic) boy with you'. Decency requires humbug, but, my God!—it's a wearisome trial.[41]

It is not clear, of course, that manners are bullshit, even though they may bear some resemblance to it. (They certainly have a more appealing scent.) Here is another case that, if bullshit, seems to be benign.[42] It concerns an anecdote about Ludwig Wittgenstein recalled by Fania Pascal:

> I had my tonsils out and was in the Evelyn Nursing Home feeling sorry for myself. Wittgenstein called. I croaked: 'I feel just like a dog that has been run over'. He was disgusted: 'You don't know what a dog that has been run over feels like'.[43]

Again, it is not obvious that Fania Pascal was indeed bullshitting. Not every metaphorical or imprecise use of language amounts to bullshit. However, Harry Frankfurt considers how it might be an instance of bullshit. He is careful to note that the event might not have happened as Fania Pascal recalls. More specifically, he considers the possibility that Ludwig Wittgenstein 'was trying to make a small joke, and it misfired'. However, if we assume that Fania Pascal's comment was bullshit and that Ludwig Wittgenstein was not joking, then the latter seems priggish for having responded as he (purportedly) did. Fania Pascal's suggestion that she felt like a dog that had been run over is utterly inconsequential and thereby benign. It is the sort of bullshit we should ignore. The fact that it is not even clearly bullshit is another reason why it should not have been called as such. Ludwig Wittgenstein should have given

Fania Pascal the benefit of the doubt. He should not have rushed to judgment and, *a fortiori*, not rushed to *express* judgement.

Perhaps the clearest example of harmless bullshit is that which is generated in jest (and which is recognized as having been produced for that purpose). Consider, for example, the Bullshit Generator,[44] which generates bullshit phrases, and the vastly more impressive Postmodernism Generator,[45] which generates (bullshit[46]) postmodernist academic papers. (Dare we call the latter Fake Poos?)

A third response to bullshit is that we do not need to call out or condemn bullshit if everybody knows it is bullshit. This argument overlaps with the 'benign bullshit' argument because one way in which bullshit might be thought to be benign is that it is seen for what it is. The idea is that if everybody knows that something is bullshit then nobody will be taken in by it, and it can therefore do no harm.

Where the two arguments might be thought to be distinct is that whereas some bullshit may be benign in itself, because it is about trivial matters, other bullshit might be benign *only* because it will be identified as bullshit. In other words, it might be about serious matters that potentially could do great damage, save for the (purported) fact that everybody recognizes it as bullshit, thereby neutralizing its otherwise dangerous capacity.

If the suggestion is that all bullshit is seen for what it is, then it is far too optimistic and extensive an excuse. Much bullshit goes unrecognized, and even when it is identified, it is indulged. Recognizing bullshit is thus no guarantee against noxious effects.

Jonathan Lear has sought to distinguish between ordinary bullshit and bullshit artistry. He says that whereas the 'run-of-the-mill bullshitter goes through the motions of hiding his indifference to truth or the falsity of what he is saying ... the bullshit artist revels in the fact that he can put his indifference on display'.[47] Professor Lear says that because of this the bullshit artist, unlike the ordinary bullshitter, 'demands our complicity'. However, Professor Lear then notes that 'once we recognize that the bullshit artist flaunts his indifference' and gets away with it 'we have reason to go back to the ordinary bullshitter and ask whether it really is true, as [Harry] Frankfurt asserts, that he must hide it'.[48]

We do not have to accept Professor Lear's particular distinction between the ordinary bullshitter and the bullshit artist—I, for one, do not[49]—in order to accept his point that there are bullshitters who flaunt rather than conceal the fact that they are bullshitting, and that they get away with this as a result of widespread complicity. That complicity is only enhanced by complacency about bullshit. Thus, even if it is true that bullshit works best when it is not recognized as bullshit, it works really well even if it is so recognized. As a result, we should go beyond recognizing it to actually doing something about it.

A final argument for not confronting bullshit is an argument from resignation (or despair). According to this argument, bullshit is inevitable, inescapable, and unstoppable, and thus there is simply no point in trying to stop it.

The premise of this argument is true, at least in the sense that bullshit will never be entirely eradicated (for as long as there are humans).[50] However, merely because we cannot stop all bullshit does not mean that we cannot stop some of it. Indeed, offering the argument from resignation is the best way of securing a self-fulfilling prophecy. By contrast, the first step to limiting bullshit is recognizing that we can reduce its overall quantity.

There is surely wisdom in knowing which bullshit one can and which one cannot either stop or limit, although the epistemic challenges here are often so great that even the wisest cannot know. We have to deal with uncertainty here, as in so many other areas of life.

In responding to bullshit we should focus, all things being equal, on that bullshit we have some chance of preventing, limiting, or reversing. We should recognize that often our chance of success depends on whether others join us in confronting the same bullshit. We typically *cannot* count on such help, but sometimes this is because the bullshit is more dangerous (because it is more widely believed or tolerated). In such cases, the lesser chance of success may be partially counterbalanced by the importance of trying. Sometimes one must take a lead, either because it may encourage others to follow or merely because there is symbolic value in somebody refusing to be complicit.

The resilience of bullshit is thus not a blanket excuse for not confronting it. Nevertheless, we are not obliged to confront all bullshit everywhere. There are some instances where our inability to curtail bullshit, combined with other factors, releases us from a bullshit-busting duty.

Challenging bullshit

While there are circumstances in which we need not—and sometimes even should not—challenge bullshit, there are many others where we should do so.

It is not the case that everybody is equally duty-bound to confront bullshit. Some people have a special duty to confront it. That duty may arise from their job—perhaps a journalist or a public official (such as a member of the parliamentary opposition, or a police detective). Alternatively, it might arise from some other way in which one is specially placed. One might, for example, be the only person or one of a very few with access to information that, if released, would expose the bullshit. In such cases there is greater reason to call the bullshit.

Before one can literally call bullshit, one needs to be reasonably confident in the proposed call—confident that what one plans to call bullshit is indeed that. Sometimes it will be quite clear. Other times, it will take some work to check that what seems like bullshit is indeed the real thing.[51] This is obviously very important because peremptory accusations of bullshit may themselves be bullshit.[52]

Sometimes the investigation can be continuous with the call. Indeed, one possible way to call bullshit is not to do so explicitly, but rather to ask questions that expose it: 'What exactly do you mean by that?'; 'But how is that compatible with this?'; 'How would you respond if somebody were to say such and such?'.

On rare occasions, a bullshitter may fold in the face of such questioning. This is most likely in the case of bullshitters who have both of two features. First, they are innocent bullshitters—that is, they are not indifferent to the truth and they are repeating or even generating other forms of bullshit (such as nonsense) unwittingly. Second, they are corrigible bullshitters—that is, gently showing them that they are bullshitting will lead to them bullshitting less. They can be led to understand that they are bullshitting and they have the capacity to respond appropriately.

It seems, however, that most bullshitters lack one or both of these characteristics. They are very unlikely to fold in the face of questions that expose their bullshit. Such questions are much more likely to lead to more bullshit. This does not mean that the questioning or explicit calling of bullshit is in vain. This is because even if the bullshitter will not admit to bullshitting, it may become apparent to others who hear the call (or the questioning) that they are in the presence of bullshit. Given that most bullshitters do not easily confess to their 'tauro-copro-verbia', and that they can bamboozle those who are more gullible, exposing bullshit can take perseverance.

Challenging bullshit does not end with the literal act of calling it. It is not enough that one brings the bullshit to the attention of others. Something has to be *done* about it. Its effects need to be neutralized. If, for example, one's university proposes to adopt a (new) 'strategic plan' or 'mission and vision statement', laden with bullshit, as these documents typically are, it is not enough that everybody winks knowingly while the administrators present it, but then proceed to vote in support it. The ultimate purpose of calling bullshit is, if not to prevent it, then at least to render it inert.

Sadly, this is all immensely difficult. People are very reluctant to confront bullshit even when it is made manifest to them. Indeed, they are so reluctant to do anything about it that there are strong psychological impulses to resist admitting its presence. Even when it is acknowledged, this acknowledgement is often compartmentalized in order to obviate having to do something about it.

This means that calling and confronting bullshit can impose significant costs on those intolerant of bullshit. We need to understand such costs because they are morally relevant. If we are going to say that people have a duty to confront bullshit, we need to consider not only the harms of the bullshit but also the harms to those who perform the ascribed duty.

There is considerable social pressure on people to be polite—that is, to comport themselves in ways that are considerate and respectful of others. Calling bullshit or even subjecting bullshitters to persistent questioning to expose their bullshit will *appear* to many as a breach of these norms. This is partly because our politeness norms are deeply inconsistent. If, for example, you dominate a conversation, you are being inconsiderate and disrespectful of others, but much more disapproval will be directed to the person who tells you that you are dominating the conversation than will be directed to you. Similarly with the bullshitter. He is inconsiderate and disrespectful, but this is met with a conspiracy of silence. Those who refuse to be part of that conspiracy and speak up will often experience more opprobrium than the bullshitter.

Not only will the anti-bullshitter lose friends, he often also will not influence people. This is because of the human tendency to a herd mentality. Many people might see the bullshit, but they do not want to break rank for fear of group disapproval. They will do so if they see enough others doing so, but it is not the case that one rank-breaker immediately leads to others breaking rank (notwithstanding Hollywood's regular representations to the contrary).

Instead, what typically happens in this context and in so many others, is this. If one person breaks rank—in this context, by calling bullshit—the rest of the herd will then wait to see what happens. More often than not, an enforcer of the herd will say something to isolate the person calling bullshit. In the mildest cases, it will be a pious defence of the bullshit (typically involving more bullshit). In more serious cases the bullshit caller will be reprimanded, explicitly or implicitly, for his breach of etiquette. In the most extreme circumstances, he will be persecuted to some degree or another. Onlookers, fearful of being subjected to the same disapproval or persecution, will either remain silent or will actively side with the enforcer.

Even the mildest of these costs is sufficiently psychologically serious to deter most people from speaking up, which is one important reason why we are surrounded by so much bullshit. We should thus not underestimate the seriousness of these costs to people. Matters are still much worse where calling bullshit results in your being sent to a concentration camp or gulag, or in your being executed. There has been no shortage of regimes where this happens.

Clearly we cannot tell North Koreans under the Kim regime, and could not tell Europeans under the Nazis, and Soviet citizens under Stalinism, and so forth, that they have or had a duty to call bullshit on their oppressors. The price they would have to pay, as well as the likelihood of making absolutely no difference, would be so high that we cannot reasonably say they have a duty to call the bullshit of these regimes.

However, it also cannot be the case that there must be *zero* cost to somebody before he or she can be said to have a duty to speak up. Here we confront an unfortunate truth: If people do have a duty to speak up even at some cost to themselves, and if only a small number of people are going to fulfil that duty, a price will be paid by those doing what they should be doing. In other words we have a kind of moral paradox (that arises too in innumerable other contexts). I call this the 'paradox of desert'.[53] Those least deserving of paying a price, on account of their acting rightly, are the most likely to pay it, whereas those most deserving of paying a price, on account of failing to act rightly, are the least likely to pay it.

This is, of course, deeply unfair, and it does generate secondary duties (especially) on the part of those not discharging the primary ones. If they are not going to speak up, then there are other things they should and should not do. Most importantly, they should not join those who impose the costs on the bullshit-buster. That is to say, they should not join in with those who ostracize or marginalize that brave person. Where possible, they should also quietly act in ways that support the bullshit-buster. This might include offering a kind, even if private, word of support, or voting against the bullshit, especially if there is a secret ballot. Those who violate not only their primary duties to neutralize bullshit, but also their secondary ones, have much to answer for (even though they are almost never called upon to do so).

Much bullshit is entrenched either structurally or through popular support. Uprooting it requires collective action. Regrettably, such action is typically absent. This absence does not absolve each individual of *all* responsibility. Put another way, individuals have some responsibility to resist bullshit. However, given the costs of resisting, it is unreasonable to insist that any individual has a duty, in the absence of others doing likewise, no matter how much harm fulfilling that duty may cause him. It is difficult to say precisely where duty ends and supererogation (or going beyond the call of duty) begins, but it is helpful to recognize that some resistance to bullshit is supererogatory rather than a matter of strict duty.

There is a spectrum of moral praise and blame. Those who exercise heroic levels of opposition to bullshit are better than those who merely play their part. Those who play their part are better than those who stand by. Worse than those who stand by, are those who actively help thwart those who are either doing their part or acting heroically. Those who thwart the heroes and those complying with their duty, are not merely free-riders. Instead they are collaborators, enablers, or perpetrators.

Producing bullshit

It is not unreasonable to think that our duty to desist from producing bullshit is even clearer and stronger than a duty to confront the bullshit produced by others. First, the duty not to produce is so much easier to execute than the duty to confront. Not producing bullshit does not require one to do anything. One must simply desist from doing something. By contrast, confronting bullshit requires time and energy, not to mention courage. Second, desisting from bullshit requires the collaboration of others less often than confronting bullshit does.

However, desisting from bullshitting often does entail costs for the bullshit-abstainer. These costs are typically not as high as those of the bullshit-buster. The latter, as we have seen, runs into conflict with the bullshitter and with those complicit in the bullshit. The result is typically some or other degree of hostility towards the bullshit-buster. The bullshit-abstainer, by contrast, is not a direct threat to the bullshitter. The price that the bullshit-abstainer pays is not reaping the rewards of bullshitting. As we saw earlier, there are many such rewards. Bullshitting is so much easier than bullshit-free communication, and thus it saves time and energy, at least for those who have no compunction against bullshitting.

Bullshit also influences people, usually to the advantage of the bullshitter. Those who puff up their products, as bullshitters do, are better at selling them. The salesman who 'sells you *on* the product' is more likely to get you to buy it. Indeed, the fact that the word 'selling' means not only 'exchanging for money', but also 'promoting', 'plugging', or 'pushing' is no accident. Sometimes the product is the salesman himself. He is *selling* himself in the last three senses just mentioned. That is why bullshitters are more likely to get jobs, win scholarships, obtain grants, and secure other opportunities. Here is what Alan Richardson says, only partially tongue in cheek, about grant proposals:

> These require a sort of breathless discussion of how ground-breaking and exciting your research is, how it requires a hundred thousand dollars to do, how fabulous it will be to have research assistants (who will do your photocopying and be paid fifteen thousand a year for the privilege) ... Proposal writers know that this is all bullshit ... proposal readers know it, too ... and ignore exactly what the writers put in as the bullshit component. But no one will succeed if she does not put in the bullshit.[54]

When bullshitters do wrong, they are also more likely than non-bullshitters to evade responsibility. They *speak* evasively, by obfuscating or spinning. Speaking evasively is a much better way of successfully evading than speaking directly is. At the University of Cape Town, for example, Flemming Rose had been invited by the university's Academic Freedom Committee to deliver the annual TB Davie Academic Freedom lecture in 2016. He was subsequently disinvited by the University Executive. One reason offered by the University's then Vice-Chancellor in defence of that decision, was that bringing Mr Rose to campus 'might retard rather than advance academic freedom on campus'.[55] This is full-throttle bullshit: One violates academic freedom and then says that one is in fact advancing academic freedom.[56]

At the same institution, numerous artworks were covered up—some by the university authorities but at least one by offended individuals—and later removed in response to objections.[57] Those defending these actions denied that the artworks were being censored, claiming first that they were being 'curated',[58] and later that the artworks were removed 'not in an act of censorship ... but rather to open a dialogue regarding the place of artworks on campus'.[59] This sort of bullshit[60] enables one to save face (at least amongst dupes and fellow bullshitters).

Evasiveness is valuable not only when one has done wrong, but also when one has acted rightly but unpopularly—that is acted in a way that is perceived to be, but is not actually, wrong. Admitting that one has acted in ways that are unpopular will elicit no sympathy from those subscribing to the popular view against which one has offended. Consider, for example, the university librarian who uncovered one of the aforementioned censored art works.[61] As it happened, the librarian voluntarily revealed his identity (and was then roundly criticized by those endorsing the censorship).[62] However, we can imagine a scenario in which he had not disclosed his identity, but somebody had asked him whether he had performed the act. By bullshitting he could have created either some uncertainty or some fog in which to hide.

Thus, there are numerous advantages to bullshitting that the non-bullshitter forgoes. That there are disadvantages to desisting from bullshitting does not entail that we may bullshit. Doing the right thing—and not doing the wrong thing—regularly has costs. The mere presence of costs cannot void a duty. However, we do need to be sensitive to those costs, along with other variables, in determining the extent and strength of our duties.

When more people are bearing the costs of acting rightly, it is less unfair to ask any individual to bear them. There will still be free-riders, but it is easier to target those free-riders than it is to target the non-compliant when non-compliance is the norm. When there is widespread non-compliance the unfairness to the compliant is greater. It is obviously impossible to quantify exactly how much bullshit there is, but it does seem to be so prevalent that it is the norm, at least in some domains.

Given this, it would be unreasonable to insist that producing bullshit is always strictly prohibited. We need a more nuanced approach that takes account of the costs that non-bullshitters incur, as well as other considerations. Obviously there can be no formula to determine when we may bullshit, and then how much we may do so. Nevertheless, it is possible to offer some general guidance.

The strong presumption must be against bullshitting. Desisting from bullshit production is the default position. If that presumption is to be defeated in a given case (or kind of case) one has to be able to make a compelling argument that it is defeated. More specifically, it should be compelling to a reasonable person without a vested interest. Since one typically has an interest in one's own bullshitting, convincing oneself is thus not the standard. This does not mean that one must always consult others before one bullshits. This is often impractical, as much bullshit is impromptu. Even when one could consult, one would typically consult those closest to one—family and friends—and they are not without bias about one's interests either. Thus the test of convincing a reasonable person without a vested interest may often be a hypothetical one—a theoretical benchmark with which one's conduct may or may not accord.

We should, to the extent that we can, avoid putting ourselves in situations where the costs of not bullshitting would be high. For example, avoid the extramarital affairs, nefarious business practices, drunkenness, or censorial behaviour, that will invite the later 'need' for bullshitting. Similarly, if you have options,[63] avoid those lines of work in which it is especially difficult to succeed without bullshitting. Arguably these include motivational speaking, spokesperson jobs, and *some* kinds of sales positions.[64]

In the real, messy world, there are important jobs and tasks that sometimes require one to bullshit. Medical research, for example, requires vast amounts of funding for which researchers have to apply. Of course, not all medical research has important goals. Even when it does, sometimes the research itself is unlikely to attain those goals, most commonly because of defective methodology. Nevertheless, there is at least some medical (and other) research that, if undertaken, could attain important goals. What this shows is that it is not always possible to avoid bullshitting—at least not without giving up important, attainable goals. The fact that bullshitting is still required to secure grants to do such research, is not a sufficient reason to desist from becoming a researcher of this kind.

Thus, we should ask ourselves how important the goal is, whether the bullshit is actually a means to it, and whether there are alternative—less bullshitty and otherwise noxious—means to the same goal. Grants to do philosophical work are not necessary to the extent that grants to do medical work are, not least because so much philosophical work can be done without extensive funding even if ample funding is pleasing for philosophers to have.[65]

To the extent that the bullshit is necessary to attaining an important goal, we should consider how harmful (or harmless) it is. The more harmful the bullshit the stronger the case against it even if it does advance an important goal. In addition to the dangers explored earlier, we should also consider the likelihood that bullshitting on one occasion or in one context will foster more bullshit in others—whether by oneself or others. For example, bullshitting in writing research grants is arguably more compartmentalized than is bullshitting in politics. While there are counter-examples, the bullshitting in grants does not overflow into bullshitting in science to the extent that bullshitting in one political moment metastasizes into bullshitting into other moments. This may be because grant writing is a discrete kind of academic activity, quite distinct from other academic activities. By contrast, political speeches, deals, votes, and so forth are far more integrated. Once a politician begins to bullshit, bullshitting is likely to pervade his political behaviour.

In summary, each one of us should be aiming to minimize the amount of bullshit we produce. The problem with general guidelines such as the ones above is that they leave much scope for self-deception. People are inclined to underestimate how much bullshit their desired job will require, overestimate the importance of their bullshit's goals and the likelihood of attaining them, and underestimate how dangerous their bullshit is. In short, they are inclined to think that the presumption against bullshitting is defeated when it is in their interests to bullshit.

There is no escaping this danger. Certainly, a categorical opposition to bullshit would be no more successful, not least because it would be more likely to be dismissed. It would also be unduly burdensome on those few who did not dismiss such categorical opposition. The more nuanced recommendation is thus appropriate both for principled and pragmatic reasons. We thus have to deal with the messiness. The conscientious individual will be mindful of the proclivity for self-deception and will vigorously scrutinize his or her own judgements in a bid to minimize, even if not entirely eradicate, such deception. Those who minimize their bullshit more than can strictly be required of them, deserve praise for doing so.

Other people can help us to minimize our bullshit, just as we can help them to minimize theirs. In addition to calling one another's bullshit—delicately where that manner would suffice—we can reward those who do not bullshit and we can refuse to reward (and sometimes even penalize) those who do bullshit. If that were done on a sufficiently large scale, the incentive structures would change. Recognizing this is not the same as thinking that it *will* be done on a sufficiently large scale to change the incentive structures. Nevertheless, every instance in which a bullshit-abstainer is rewarded for desisting from bullshit is a small victory.[66]

Conclusion

Bullshit is pervasive, and causes much more damage than most people realize. The world would be a much better place if there were not so much of it. Yet the deck is stacked against reducing its volume, because individuals are incentivized to produce it, and disincentivized to block production. Bullshitters get ahead. They tend to 'win friends and influence people'. The opposite fate typically befalls bullshit-busters, while those who desist from producing bullshit forgo the benefits of bullshitting. Thus, we have a Tragedy of the Bullshit Commons. Everybody is incentivized to bullshit, but the consequence of so many people bullshitting is pollution of the discursive environment.

The best response would be a coordinated one designed to minimize it. However, this is unlikely (even though we do have some institutions, such as a free press, that do have some role to play in reducing bullshit, at least in public life). In any event, the individual has moral decisions to make about bullshit even in the absence of a coordinated public response. I have outlined what we should do about our own bullshit and that of others. Ideally, one should 'neither a producer nor a consumer be'. In practice, matters are more complex, but that should not be an excuse for abandoning ourselves to it. Our presumption should be to resist it except where there is a compelling case to be made for overriding that presumption in limited ways. That, I hope, is not bullshit.

10
Forgiveness

We have all been wronged and we have all wronged others. Alexander Pope was thus entirely correct in saying that 'to err is human'.[1] But is it the case, as he also proffered, that 'to forgive [is] divine'? Of course, he did not mean that forgiveness is the sole preserve of God—that *only* God can or may forgive. Instead, the claim is that forgiveness is God-like, in the sense of being righteous, worthy, or noble. Being forgiving is widely regarded as a virtue, but is it *always* virtuous? If not, when is it and when is it not? Are there circumstances in which we should not forgive, and are there others in which it would be wrong not to?

To answer these questions, we need to know exactly what forgiveness is. However, we immediately face a problem—namely that the definitional questions are difficult to disentangle from the moral questions. This is partly because some interpretations of what forgiveness is pre-judge moral questions. For example, if we understand forgiving as something that only victims do, then we have pre-empted the moral question whether only the victim has the moral standing to forgive a wrongdoer or whether others also do. In order words, if forgiving is something that by definition only victims can do, then one cannot even ask the moral question 'May non-victims forgive?'

The wisest response to this problem is to acknowledge it, to develop a tentative understanding of forgiveness, but then to be willing to revise components of that understanding if one's subsequent moral deliberations suggest that such revisions would be appropriate.

The willingness to provide a tentative, revisable understanding of forgiveness also enables us to respond to another reason why definitional and moral questions about forgiveness are difficult to disentangle from one another—namely, that some people have a moralized understanding of what forgiveness is. That is to say, among their criteria for whether something counts as forgiveness are moral ones. According to such a view, the label 'forgiveness' only applies to something virtuous or otherwise good. Thus, we *first* need to know when something resembling forgiveness is good before we can say definitively whether it really counts as forgiveness.

However, if we are willing to outline a tentative understanding of forgiveness then we can lay down the non-moral criteria before proceeding to examine the moral questions. Those who think that our understanding of forgiveness should be moralized, can then adapt the basic understanding of forgiveness to take account of the moral conclusions. The rest of us need not revise our understanding of what forgiveness is on the basis of the moral deliberations. Instead, the latter will inform us only about when we should forgive and when we should not.[2]

Some cases

Discussions about the nature and ethics of forgiveness often make the mistake of ignoring the wide range of cases in which questions about forgiveness can arise. Two important variables are the severity of the wrong and the (prior) relationship between the victim and wrongdoer. Some wrongs are utterly trivial, many are more serious, and some are monumental. Sometimes those who wrong us are strangers. We may become aware of them through the harm they cause us, but sometimes they harm us without their identity ever becoming known to us. In other cases, the perpetrator is an acquaintance, a friend, a close friend, or a family member.

Before trying to understand what forgiveness is and to consider the ethical questions concerning it, it may help to have some sample cases before us.

1. A stranger accidently knocks you as he walks past you on a sidewalk. It's a minor bump. Nobody is injured. In some versions of this scenario the stranger expresses regret, either more or less profusely, at having bumped you. In other versions, he is oblivious or indifferent to having knocked you.
2. An acquaintance or friend has made an appointment to meet you somewhere. She keeps you waiting thirty minutes. In varying versions, you receive either no apology, a perfunctory apology, or a heart-felt one.
3. Upon returning to the lot where you parked your car, you find that somebody has dented it, but has not left a note of apology or contact details. If you decide to have the dent repaired, that will cost a few hundred dollars (and some inconvenience).

4. Somebody steals your backpack, which contains your laptop, wallet, driver's licence, and credit card. Replacing the computer involves a significant cost. You are also severely inconvenienced by having to cancel and replace your credit card, obtain a new driver's licence, and by having to do without your computer until you can get it replaced.
5. You are defamed by an acquaintance who calls you a liar and impugns your integrity in other ways. What the acquaintance claims is a lie is in fact the truth, and demonstrably so. The other slurs, although false are difficult to prove so, at least in the kangaroo court of public opinion. She spreads the defamatory remarks via social media. They are picked up by the local press, and by an international blog regularly read by your colleagues abroad.
6. You discover that your spouse has been unfaithful. In some versions it was a single indiscretion. In other versions, he or she has been having sex with other men or women over an extended period. In some but not other versions you have contracted a sexually transmitted disease as a result. In one version that disease is HIV.
7. You are raped or otherwise sexually assaulted. In some versions your assailant is a stranger, in some he is an acquaintance, while in others he is a family member.
8. Somebody murders your child. In one version the murderer is never found. Alternatively, the murderer is a stranger whose identity you subsequently learn. Or the murderer is your spouse.

What is forgiveness?

In attempting to understand a complex and widely used concept such as forgiveness, we have to be attentive to how the word is used, while also recognizing that the best account of what it is, may have to depart in some ways from ordinary usage. Both of these conflicting considerations are important. If we define a term in a way that is utterly unmoored from ordinary usage, we will have done a very poor job of defining the term that people are actually using. For example, if one stipulated a definition of forgiveness as 'the relief of hunger', nothing one then said about (the morality of) forgiveness would be at all helpful to those interested in that to which 'forgiveness' usually refers. On the other side, a definition that did not depart at all from ordinary usage would likely be more imprecise and confused than it need be.

This is because there is often a messiness and confusion in ordinary usage. Philosophical accounts are meant to clear up some of that, so that we are left with greater clarity about the concept.

If we consult ordinary usage, it would seem that forgiveness is *fundamentally* (albeit not entirely) about overcoming[3] those negative attitudes and feelings[4] toward a wrongdoer that arose as a result of the wrong perpetrated by the wrongdoer. In other words, forgiveness involves what has sometimes been called a 'change of heart'. What we fundamentally want when we want forgiveness is that the victims of our wrongs cease to view us negatively on account of the wrongs that we did to them.[5]

There certainly are other ways in which the word 'forgive' is used. Some of these are clearly non-moral, non-literal, or even ironic.[6] Other usages are closer to standard usage but seem to be derivative or secondary usages. Before considering any of these, however, the initial formulation of what forgiveness is requires further explication.

Who can forgive?

According to the dominant view of what forgiveness is, the foregoing formulation is insufficiently restrictive in that it includes within the scope of 'forgiveness' instances of third parties overcoming negative attitudes and feelings towards the wrongdoer for what he did to the victim. Those who favour a more restrictive view[7] think that forgiveness involves overcoming those negative attitudes and feelings toward a wrongdoer that arose as a result of *being wronged*. In other words, only victims *can* forgive. (A reminder: The conceptual question whether only victims *can* forgive is different from the moral question whether only victims *may* forgive—that is, whether victims are the only ones morally permitted to forgive. This moral question will be considered later.)

The more restrictive interpretation of forgiveness is not quite as restrictive as it may at first appear to be. If, for example, somebody rapes your child, your child is the primary victim. However, you too can be a victim. In raping your child, the assailant can[8] cause you untold trauma, grief, anger, and resentment, for example. If one holds the view that one can only forgive for wrongs done to oneself, then you *can* still forgive the rapist—but only for the wrongs done to you in raping your child. *You* cannot overcome the negative attitudes and feelings that your child has against the assailant, and thus you cannot forgive for your child.[9]

But can one only forgive for wrongs done to oneself? It is clear that you cannot overcome your child's negative attitudes and feelings towards the perpetrator. However, this does not settle the question. This is because one's own negative attitudes and feelings towards the rapist are multifaceted. As a secondary victim, you can obviously bear ill-will toward your child's rapist for what he did to you. It may be the case that, given the right conditions, you can overcome that ill-will. However, you can also be outraged at what the rapist has done *to your child*. Indeed, that will be the focus of good parents. They are going to be much angrier about what was done to the child than about what was done to themselves though the rape of their child. Yet, it may be the case, in the right circumstances that you *can* overcome that outrage too. In other words, while you cannot overcome your *child's* negative attitudes and feelings towards the sexual assailant, you can overcome *your* negative attitudes and feelings towards the assailant for what he did to your child. Given this, there seems to be no *conceptual* bar to forgiving wrongs done to others, as long as we do not confuse forgiving for wrongs done to others and forgiving *on behalf* of others.[10]

Of course, it remains open to advocates of the more restrictive understanding of forgiveness to insist that the concept is applicable only when one is overcoming negative attitudes and feelings toward a wrongdoer that arose as a result of being wronged. However, this does seem to be mere stipulation, as neither ordinary usage nor the concept itself seem to necessitate it. For this reason, we should favour the broader understanding of what forgiveness is.

It is obvious that the dead (as well as the permanently unconscious) cannot forgive. This is because they do not have *any*—not merely negative—attitudes and feelings, and thus none to overcome. Therefore, a murderer can ordinarily not be forgiven by his (primary) victim.[11] It is usually a conceptual impossibility. Some wrongs are unforgivable in this particular (descriptive rather than normative) way. If a victim of a non-lethal wrong dies before he or she has forgiven, forgiveness from that victim ceases to be possible even though it once was.[12]

Which negative attitudes and feelings?

Much philosophical ink has been spilled in trying to determine exactly which kinds of attitudes and feelings must be overcome in order for somebody to have forgiven. Proposals have been made by some, and counter-examples have been provided by others. For example, Jeffrie Murphy suggests that forgiveness involves overcoming 'the vindictive passions of resentment, anger, hatred, and the desire for revenge',[13] while Norvin Richards has provided a counter-example, in which all these particular passions are overcome but we would not agree that forgiveness had taken place.[14]

Rather than attempting to provide a full list of the attitudes and feelings that forgiveness overcomes, we should recognize that the wide variability of items on the list is entirely consistent with the range of reasonable responses that people can have to being wronged.

Being wronged typically (and appropriately) occasions negative attitudes and feelings towards the person who committed the wrong. Which precise attitudes and feelings are reasonable will depend in part on the nature and severity of the wrong. It will also depend on who committed it and against whom it was committed. We do not have to specify all these possible attitudes and feelings. Instead, we can say that forgiveness involves overcoming whichever of them are present in a particular case.

Spectrum or threshold?

There is an ambiguity in the idea of 'overcoming' negative attitudes and feelings. To count as forgiveness, is the overcoming of negative attitudes and feelings to be understood as a matter of degree or as a binary matter? On the former view, one can forgive to a greater or lesser extent, whereas according to the latter view, one either forgives or one does not.

Consider the case in which you discover that your spouse has been unfaithful to you. This elicits very serious negative attitudes and feelings towards your spouse. You feel betrayed, and are outraged by the infidelity of your spouse, whom you no longer trust.

In due course, and given the appropriate conditions, your negative attitude and feelings toward your spouse may soften and lessen. According to the spectral view of forgiveness, the further you move along that path towards the attitudes and feelings you had before the infidelity (was discovered), the more you have forgiven, but you will not have *entirely* forgiven until you reach the attitudes and feelings you had *ex ante*.[15]

The threshold view is less demanding. It does not require a restoration of the attitudinal and emotional situation that preceded the infidelity. According to this view, a *substantial* overcoming of negative attitudes and feelings is sufficient to count as forgiveness. One has forgiven once one passes the threshold, even though the relationship has not returned to what it was before the infidelity. The threshold view need not deny that there are degrees of overcoming. However, it would deny that any degree beneath the threshold counts as forgiveness.

The emergence of the negative attitudes and feelings, the subsequent improvement, and the competing views are represented in Figure 10.1.

Those who accept the threshold view can disagree about just where the threshold should be set. However, not all such disagreement would be reasonable. It seems implausible—because incompatible with our ordinary usage—to peg the threshold too close to the immediate post-wrong attitudes and feelings. In that area of the spectrum, one has simply not overcome enough. Nor does it seem reasonable to peg the threshold at the midpoint. Instead it seems that the threshold must be closer to the *ex ante* position, but just how close it must be, can be the subject of reasonable disagreement. It might also vary depending, for example, on the nature of the wrong.

It is conceptually possible for the threshold to be set *at* the *ex ante* position, in which case, forgiveness occurs at the same point as complete forgiveness does on the spectrum view. It would then share that feature with the spectrum view. It would still differ from the spectrum view in not allowing degrees of forgiveness—as distinct from degrees of overcoming, which it can and must allow—prior to complete forgiveness.

My illustration so far is a case where there was a prior relationship between the wrongdoer (the adulterer) and the victim (the betrayed spouse). However, cases where the victim had no relationship with the wrongdoer prior to the wrong can be accommodated as easily. In such cases the attitudes and feelings *ex ante* are none or neutral. You don't know her, and you have no attitudes or feelings towards her. If she then wrongs you, you come to resent her. Returning to the *ex ante* position would (roughly) be getting to the

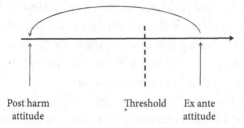

Figure 10.1 Spectrum versus threshold views of forgiveness.

position where you are neutral towards her. A threshold earlier than the end of the spectrum would be where one had overcome enough of the negative to count as having forgiven even though some residual negative attitudes and feelings remain.

Which view of forgiveness should we adopt—the spectrum or the threshold? On a balance of considerations, it seems that the threshold view is better—so long as we add the following nuance to this view: the shorter the 'distance' between the *ex ante* and (appropriate) *post hoc* attitudes and feelings, the closer the threshold should be to the *ex ante* position. The distance is shortest in the case of the most minor wrongs, when only mildly negative attitudes and feelings are warranted. In such cases the threshold should be at, or at least extremely close to, the *ex ante* position. Anything short of a return to that position does not seem to count as forgiveness, at least in ordinary usage.

Consider the case where your friend keeps you waiting for half an hour. Let us assume that this delay does not have catastrophic consequences, that the tardiness is not part of a pattern of your friend's behaviour, and so forth. Some resentment would be apt for this single lapse, but unless you return to—or perhaps *very* close to—the *ex ante* view of your friend, it does not seem as though you have forgiven her. Overcoming just part of your mild resentment is simply not enough.

However, in the case of more significant wrongs, the threshold should be placed earlier on the spectrum. In such cases, we do not typically require a return all the way to the *ex ante* position—the situation in which, attitudinally and emotionally, it is as if the wrong never occurred—to say that somebody has forgiven.

If we adopt the threshold view, with the threshold's position varying depending on the severity of the wrong, then all we are required to give up in rejecting the spectrum is that one can partially forgive. One can still partially *overcome* negative attitudes and feelings. However, we are precluded from calling that a degree *of* forgiveness. It might still be a degree *towards* forgiveness. That seems like a tolerable sacrifice.

What forgiveness is not

Much more needs to be said to delineate what does not and what does count as forgiveness.

Pharmaceuticals and forgetting

First, as many philosophers have noted, not all means and reasons for overcoming the relevant attitudes and feelings counts as forgiveness. If, for example, one took a 'chill pill' to calm one's moral anger, one would not normally be thought to have forgiven the wrongdoer. Similarly, if one simply forgot the wrong (perhaps because of a blow to the head or the onset of dementia), this would not count as forgiveness even though one no longer harboured negative attitudes or feelings towards the wrongdoer.

This has led some people to suggest that forgiveness involves some kind of 'self-activity or effort'.[16] However, depending on how we understand this phrase, it may be too restrictive. It is easy to see how forgiving severe wrongs would require significant self-activity or effort. However, in the case of minor wrongs, it may not take much effort at all to overcome the negative attitudes or feelings. Those with a forgiving personality might, even after more severe wrongs, overcome these sentiments quite naturally without having to work on themselves or expend effort.[17] However, if self-activity is understood also to include an inner inclination or disposition to overcome the negative sentiments, then the phrase 'self-activity or effort' is not unduly restrictive. It can accommodate cases in which the negative sentiments are overcome as a result of a forgiving temperament.

If so, then there might be *some* instances of forgetting that could count as forgiveness. These clearly would not be instances that resulted from brain injury or disease. Nor does it seem that forgetting a serious wrong—if that is even possible in the absence of injury, disease, or some other aberration—could constitute forgiveness. However, what about forgetting a minor wrong, and forgetting it precisely because it is minor? It really is unclear whether or not we should count such instances of forgetting as forgiveness. This is where the imprecision of the concept makes a definitive answer difficult, if not impossible.[18] One could argue that in the case of minor wrongs, forgetting is one way to forgive. Perhaps somebody with a forgiving temperament is disposed to forget such minor wrongs as somebody accidently bumping one's arm as one passes on the sidewalk. Alternatively, one might insist that though forgetting and forgiving are functionally equivalent, they are not the same even in the case of minor wrongs. According to this view, the way we classify forgetting in the case of minor wrongs should be consistent with the way we classify it in the case of serious wrongs.

Whichever view one takes about this, everybody can agree that forgetting can *follow* forgiving. If you forgive a wrong, your subsequently forgetting that it occurred does not undo the fact that you already forgave it. In other words, everybody can agree that so long as you still remember the wrong when you overcome the negative attitudes and feelings toward the wrongdoer, you have forgiven. Especially with minor wrongs and perhaps even some intermediate ones, one might well then simply forget that the wrong ever occurred.

Justification

In determining the contours of what forgiveness is, it matters not merely *how* the negative attitudes and feelings are overcome, but also *why* they are. Consider, for example, the case (above) of your friend who keeps you waiting for thirty minutes. As you wait you become steadily more indignant about your friend's lack of consideration. Suppose, upon your friend's arrival and the exchange that follows, you realize that *you* had mixed up the time, erroneously thinking that you were meeting half an hour earlier than you had actually agreed. At this point, your negative sentiments about your friend melt away. This, however, is not forgiveness. Instead, you have recognized that your friend did nothing wrong. She was entirely justified in arriving when she did. Negative attitudes and feelings can thus be overcome by recognizing that the act you thought was wrong was in fact justified.[19] Justification is different from forgiveness.

Excuse

Some have suggested that forgiveness is also to be distinguished from excuse.[20] According to this view, to excuse somebody implies that they should not have done what they did, but it is also to recognize that the person was not a fully responsible agent. If, for example, the friend who kept you waiting thirty minutes was indeed late, but you learn that this was only because her hearing impairment had led her to mis-hear the appointment time, then you might excuse her for not being on time. You recognize that she was not fully responsible for the error. This too will involve overcoming your negative attitudes and feelings towards her, but it would be because you realize that they are inapt. That recognition and the consequent adjustment of one's attitudes and feelings constitute excusing rather than forgiving.

Because responsibility can be a matter of degree, it is possible to excuse a wrongdoing to the extent to which it was not within the control of the wrongdoer, but also forgive it to the extent that it was within the wrongdoer's control. This can sometimes make it difficult in practice to differentiate precisely the extent to which one is forgiving and the extent to which one is excusing, but it might also not matter, given that the outcome—overcoming the negative attitudes and feelings—is the same.

It is possible, of course, for you to be mistaken about whether a wrongdoer is (fully) responsible. You may believe that the person who steals your backpack is fully responsible when he or she is in fact a kleptomaniac, or you might believe that the thief is a kleptomaniac when in fact he or she is entirely responsible. What matters in determining whether you *are* forgiving or excusing is whether you *believe* that the wrongdoer is responsible, because that is what provides the reason *why* you are overcoming the negative attitudes and beliefs. Obviously, it is better for your beliefs to be accurate, but whether you *are* excusing or forgiving depends on whether you believe that the wrongdoer was responsible. (By contrast, whether you *should* be forgiving or instead excusing depends not on what you believe but on whether the wrongdoer is or is not responsible.)

Condoning

Forgiveness should also be distinguished from condoning. Condonation is a more ambiguous concept than either justification or excuse. Those writing on this topic have recognized that there can be different kinds of condonation.[21] When condonation involves approving of wrongdoing it cannot be forgiveness because in order to forgive, you must recognize that the action that elicited the negative attitudes and feelings was wrong.

However, sometimes those who condone an action *do* acknowledge that it was wrong. Their condonation consists in not (adequately) condemning (even inwardly) the action that they, at least notionally, take to be wrong. Usually condoning does not follow an initial period of negative attitudes and feelings towards the offender.[22] Instead, the condonation begins with the first awareness of the wrong. As such it involves no 'overcoming' of negative attitudes or feelings and thus no forgiveness.

Perhaps there are some cases of condonation where there are initially negative responses to the wrongdoer, but even then, the condoning involves taking the wrong insufficiently seriously. In other words, it is an under-reaction to the wrong. Under-reactions no more count as forgiveness than the downward adjustment of over-reaction counts as forgiveness. In other words, it is not forgiveness if one initially over-reacts to a wrong and then moderates one's response to an appropriate level. If, for example, you are more indignant and resentful than you should be in response to your friend who arrives late for an appointment, and you then recognize this and succeed in adjusting your indignation and resentment to an appropriate level, you have not forgiven your friend. You have overcome negative attitudes and feelings, but ones that were inappropriate in the first place. That is 'getting a grip on oneself'. It is not forgiveness. It is similarly not forgiveness to feel (or come to feel) less indignation (etc.) than one should have.

Mercy

Forgiveness is also routinely, and appropriately, distinguished from mercy. To 'accord a wrongdoer mercy is to inflict a less harsh consequence on that person than allowed' or deserved.[23] For those who think that one can only forgive for wrongs done to oneself, mercy differs from forgiveness in that one can be merciful to a wrongdoer for what he or she did to a third party—as when a judge is merciful in imposing a lesser sentence.

Another suggested difference is that whereas 'I can forgive a person simply in my heart of hearts... I cannot show mercy simply in my heart of hearts'.[24] We must be careful here not to overstate this difference by comparing forgiving with *showing* mercy. The difference lessens when we compare showing forgiveness with showing mercy (or when we compare forgiving with *feeling* merciful). However, it remains true that forgiveness is fundamentally a change of heart, even though it can manifest in action, and that mercy is fundamentally something that is shown and only derivatively something that is felt.

Arguably the most basic difference between forgiveness and mercy is that the powerless can forgive, but to bestow mercy it has to be the case that one has the power to treat the wrongdoer more severely than one mercifully elects to. For example, it is *possible* to forgive the unknown person who dented your car.[25] You can overcome your negative attitudes and feelings toward that unknown person. However, you cannot accord that person mercy—you cannot treat him or her less severely than allowed or deserved unless you not only know who that person is but also have the power to treat him or her more severely than you do.[26]

Reconciliation

Forgiveness is also often distinguished from reconciliation. One way in which this is done is by describing a serious wrong, noting that in time the victim could substantially overcome the negative attitudes and feelings towards the perpetrator but also not want to resume the prior relationship.[27] This way of distinguishing forgiveness from reconciliation correctly assumes a threshold view of forgiveness, and compares it with a spectrum view of (complete) reconciliation. It is thus unsurprising that they are prised apart.[28]

There are other ways to distinguish forgiveness from reconciliation. One such way would be by claiming that while forgiveness can be unilateral, reconciliation must be bilateral. This is not implausible. Forgiveness can be unilateral in the sense that you *can* overcome your negative attitudes and feelings toward the wrongdoer without any connection to, let alone any contribution from, the wrongdoer. For example, you might give up the negative feelings towards the unknown person who stole your backpack. Reconciliation, by contrast, seems to require two parties. To be reconciled with somebody requires something not only from you but also from that other person. Thus, as is the case with tango, it takes two to reconcile.[29]

Finally, the concept of reconciliation seems to imply there was a prior relationship, which is restored. After all, it is *re*conciliation. If that is the case, then this is another way in which forgiveness can differ from reconciliation. One can forgive those with whom one had no relationship before they wronged you, whereas you cannot reconcile with such people.

Performatives and behaviour

If forgiveness is fundamentally a change of attitude and feelings, then forgiving is not a performative.[30] A performative is an utterance whereby one alters social reality. One does not describe the way things are but rather makes them a particular way through the utterance. For example, if one utters the words 'I promise' in the right conditions then the uttering of those words has made it the case that one has promised. Similarly, if the marriage officer utters the words 'I now pronounce you husband and wife' in the right circumstances, then his uttering those words makes it the case that the relevant man and woman are married.

Forgiveness is not like this. Uttering the words 'I forgive you' does not amount to forgiving.[31] This is because merely uttering the words does not cause the attitudes and feelings to change. The words 'I forgive you' should thus be understood either as a description of a mental change that has already taken place[32] or possibly as the expression of an intention to try to bring about such a change.[33]

If one understands utterances of the words 'I forgive you' in the second of these ways—namely, as expressions of an intention to try to bring about a mental change—then one might, as Geoffrey Scarre does, understand such utterances as performatives. That is, one might understand them as a kind of promise to overcome the negative attitudes and feelings.[34] However, even if we understand 'I forgive you' as a promise (rather than as merely the expression of an intention), this does not mean that forgiveness (unlike promising) is a performative. This is because there is a difference between a promise to forgive and actually forgiving.[35]

This is no different from any other promise. If you promise to meet me at the bookshop, you have not thereby met me at the bookshop. It is true that, given your promise, I have a complaint against you if you do not meet me at the appointed place and time. However, that is precisely because the promise and the meeting are not the same. If they were the same, the mere promise would require no follow-up—no ('further') meeting.

Forgiveness should also not be confused with the behaviour that typically results from overcoming negative attitudes and feelings towards the wrongdoer. How people act can provide some evidence of whether they have or have not overcome those attitudes and feelings, but it is that internal change rather than the behavioural expressions of it that constitutes forgiveness.

Alteration of the normative situation

Although it is the dominant view, not everybody agrees that forgiveness is fundamentally about overcoming negative attitudes and feelings.

Christopher Bennett has suggested that 'forgiveness is primarily a normative rather than a psychological phenomenon'.[36]

According to his 'Alteration Thesis', forgiveness is the alteration of 'the normative situation created by wrongdoing'. This requires some explanation. Wrongdoing, he says, occurs when people violate *primary* obligations. The wrongdoing then creates *secondary* obligations. Some of these secondary obligations are those of the wrongdoer. They include obligations *directed* to the victim (such as apologizing for the wrong, and taking action to rectify the harm done), as well as *nondirected* obligations (such as cultivating guilt and remorse).[37]

Professor Bennett notes that one way to alter secondary obligations is by discharging them. If the perpetrator apologizes and makes restitution, then he has discharged those obligations. Forgiveness is a different way to alter secondary obligations—namely, by the victim, through the exercise of his or her normative powers.[38] The victim has the normative power to alter only the directed obligations.

According to the Alteration Thesis, there are two kinds of forgiveness: 'rights-waiving forgiveness' and 'redemptive forgiveness'.[39] The first kind is when the victim waives the wrongdoer's obligations. In other words, the victim can relieve a wrongdoer of the obligation to apologize or to rectify the harm. Redemptive forgiveness, by contrast, is possible when the wrongdoer has already discharged his secondary obligations. The victim, recognizing this, can make 'a commitment to the wrongdoer no longer to treat him as standing under the previous secondary obligations'.[40]

There is an element of truth in the Alteration Thesis. Forgiveness *can* sometimes alter the normative situation. If, for example, a repentant wrongdoer is forgiven, and released from a duty to compensate the victim, perhaps because the wrongdoer is destitute, then the victim will have altered the normative situation by forgiving the perpetrator.

Forgiveness can also be a *response* to an alteration in the normative situation, which the account of redemptive forgiveness only partly acknowledges. When a wrongdoer is remorseful and makes restitution, the wrongdoer has altered the normative situation, which can in turn render forgiveness reasonable. However, remorse and restitution does not always *have* to precipitate a commitment to the wrongdoer. A rapist might be remorseful and even make some kind or restitution, but this does not require the victim to forgive the rapist.

Moreover, all this is entirely compatible with forgiveness being a change of heart. After all, a change of heart can result from, warrant, or lead to a change in the normative situation. For example, a change of heart can *result* from and be *warranted* by a change in normative situation that is brought about by the perpetrator's repentance. A change of heart can *lead to* a change in the normative situation. If, for example, I forgive you for forgetting our appointment, you are no longer in the normative situation of needing to seek forgiveness.

Professor Bennett believes that the Alteration Thesis has greater explanatory power than the 'change of heart' view. For example, he says that it is difficult to explain why, on the latter view, special standing is required to forgive, whereas according to the Alteration Thesis, one can forgive only if one has the relevant normative powers—powers that the victim does, and others do not have.[41]

We have already seen that a 'change of heart' view can explain why only the victim can overcome his own negative attitudes and feelings, but that there is no reason why third parties overcoming their negative attitudes and feelings towards the wrongdoer should not also be called 'forgiveness'. We are not yet in a position to say whether, according to a 'change of heart' view, only victims should have the moral standing to forgive. However, the Alteration Thesis does not have the explanatory power it is said to have. We might ask the advocate of the Alteration Thesis *why* the victim has the relevant normative powers.

In the case of rights-waiving forgiveness, presumably the answer is that the secondary obligations are owed to the victim and thus only the victim may waive these (undischarged) obligations. The answer is less clear in the case of redemptive forgiveness. While it is true that the victim can both recognize that the wrongdoer's secondary obligations have been discharged and make a commitment to treat the wrongdoer as though this is the case, there is no reason why third parties cannot have the same recognition and make the same commitment. There is no in-principle reason why I cannot recognize that somebody has made amends to you, or why I cannot commit to acting as though that is the case. In other words, it is not clear why third parties cannot be said to bestow redemption forgiveness on wrongdoers.

Another purported advantage of the Alteration Thesis is that, unlike the 'change of heart' view, which suggests that the obstacles to restoring relationships are psychological, it claims that it is the normative situation that is the barrier to the normal relationship.[42] According to the Alteration Thesis, while 'forgiveness may involve a change of heart, what *enables* the forgiver to change their emotions towards the wrongdoer is that there is a . . . new normative relationship, for those relations to be about.'[43] While the Alteration Thesis 'can explain the change of heart ... it is hard to see how the Change of Heart approach can explain the normative effects of forgiveness.'[44]

If it is true that 'what enables the forgiver to change their emotions ... is a new normative relationship', then the victim changes the normative situation in order to change his heart. Yet, this is entirely wrong in many cases.

Consider a scenario in which you are sexually assaulted. Negative attitudes and feelings arise within you toward the perpetrator. Your assailant acquires various obligations as a result of this assault—but may or may not recognize this. You would not ordinarily waive the assailant's obligations to apologize and make restitution to you in order that you can overcome your negative attitudes and feelings. Given the way human psychology works, it seems like a very bad way to change your attitudes and feelings towards your assailant. Indeed, rights-waiving forgiveness, as it is understood here, seems to be very distant both from the psychology of forgiveness and from our ordinary usage of 'forgiveness'.

Even in most cases of *trivial* harms—such as being knocked gently by a passerby—one typically does not volunteer the words 'I forgive you' or 'there's no need to apologize' *before* that person has at least gestured an apology. Yet, it is conceivable that there are *some* cases of trivial wrongs in which we can imagine one waiving one's rights to an apology or restitution. However, this would be because the wrong is so minor that one does not have the negative attitudes and feelings to start with, or one overcomes them even before the wrongdoer has had the opportunity to apologize. Thus, even in these cases, one is not waiving one's rights in order to bring about a change of heart.

What about redemptive forgiveness? Here it is true that 'what enables the forgiver to change their emotions ... is a new normative relationship'. However, the most plausible candidate for the 'new normative relationship' here is that brought about by the perpetrator's remorse and restitution— rather than the forgiver's commitment to the perpetrator. The perpetrator's remorse and restitution can facilitate the change of heart in the victim, which in turn facilitates treating the wrongdoer as forgiven. This is not to deny that there might be cases in which the perpetrator repents, and the victim, although not experiencing a change of heart, recognizes that such a change would be appropriate. The victim might then seek—with or without making a commitment—to treat the perpetrator as though he had been forgiven. The behavioural alteration is then implemented in the hope of bringing about the change of heart, but none of this suggests that forgiveness does not consist in the change of heart.

This discussion also shows why it is, in fact, not at all 'hard to see how the Change of Heart approach can explain the normative effects of forgiveness'. Changes in the perpetrator's heart can make other changes in the victim's heart apt. Those changes in turn render certain actions appropriate. Put another way, changes of heart (just like actions) can alter the normative situation and call for different attitudes, feelings, and actions.

Perhaps the fundamental reason why the Alteration Thesis does a much worse job than the 'change of heart' view does of capturing what we mean by forgiving is that it is much worse at explaining why we want to be forgiven—at least when we are truly repentant. We do not 'want forgiveness because we want the normative situation to be altered in ways that only the victim can alter it'.[45] Instead, we want it because we want the victim to overcome his or her negative attitudes and feelings towards us.

What a repentant wrongdoer wants when she seeks forgiveness is not (merely) the words 'I forgive you', or even words that signal the victim's commitment to change her attitudes and feelings. What is wanted is the actual change of attitudes and feelings. The words, even if expressive of a commitment, have only derivative appeal. They are not what is fundamentally sought. Consider a situation in which a victim says that he forgives the repentant wrongdoer, but the victim's behaviour suggests otherwise. Perhaps the victim still refuses to speak to the wrongdoer or speaks only in frosty tones. The wrongdoer would rightly conclude that she has not *actually* been forgiven.

Wrongdoers may be more interested in being *treated* as though they were forgiven than they are in merely being *told* that they have been forgiven. However, even the behavioural correlates of forgiveness do not constitute forgiveness. What the truly repentant wrongdoer wants is for the victim's attitudes and feelings to change, and for the victim's behaviour to result from that. The internal changes are what constitute forgiveness.

To forgive or not to forgive?

If forgiveness involves overcoming negative attitudes and feelings towards a wrongdoer, then forgiveness is not within one's control in the way that one's actions are. One can choose whether or not to act—for example, whether to shun or speak to somebody, whether or not to *say* that one has forgiven them, or whether or not to help them. Attitudes and feelings, however, are much less subject to control. One cannot simply choose to have different attitudes and feelings towards somebody and thereby bring them about. This is not to deny that one has *some* control over them—by, for example, directing one's focus, making relevant associations, attempting to persuade oneself, and, even more indirectly, by cultivating some but not other dispositions.

However, just because one has only limited and indirect control over one's attitudes and feelings does not mean that some of them are, and others are not, appropriate. Your jealousy, or resentment, or anger, or trust, or affection for somebody could be appropriate or inappropriate. Similarly, some attitudes or feelings could be appropriate but not to the degree you have them. Perhaps somebody merits some trust but not as much as you have placed in them. It is when one's attitudes and feelings do not track what they should be, that we should exercise our limited and indirect powers in an attempt to bring them in line. No doubt, this will be easier for some than for others. Indeed, some people routinely (even if not unerringly) respond appropriately to the relevant circumstances, whereas others struggle not to overreact or underreact.

When we ask whether or not one should forgive, we are asking whether it is appropriate to overcome the negative attitudes and feelings towards the wrongdoer, and to what extent it is appropriate to overcome them. The word 'appropriate' is suitably ambiguous. Sometimes overcoming attitudes and feelings is appropriate in the sense that *not overcoming* them would be unreasonable. On other occasions, it is reasonable in the sense that *overcoming* them is *not* unreasonable. In the latter case, not overcoming them—or not to the same degree—would also be reasonable. This ambiguity is important because forgiveness can be reasonable in either of these senses. In other words, sometimes we *should*—where the 'should' can have varying degrees of force—overcome our negative attitudes and feelings towards the wrongdoer, and sometimes it is merely not unreasonable that we do so.

Where forgiveness is not unreasonable, we might say, for the sake of convenience, that it is 'permissible'. Where we 'should' forgive, forgiveness is either 'required' or 'recommended', depending on the strength of the 'should'. Where forgiveness is unreasonable, we might say that it is either 'morally defective' or even 'prohibited'. Using such terms—and especially 'required' and 'prohibited'—is not without some difficulty, given the limits of the control we have over whether we forgive. Can you be required to do, or prohibited from doing something that may not be within your control? Nevertheless, there is some value in distinguishing between cases in which forgiveness is required, recommended, permissible, and impermissible. They tell us what out attitudinal and emotional responses should (and should not) be. However, the limited control people have in this domain is certainly relevant to whether and how much we blame those who are unable to align their attitudes and feelings with what is appropriate.

Negative reactive attitudes and feelings

In seeking understanding about when—and to what degree—overcoming negative attitudes and feelings is appropriate, it is helpful to think about why those attitudes and feelings were appropriate in the first place.

How we react, even internally through our attitudes and feelings, to those who harm us, should depend (at least partly) on the extent to which that harm is a product of either their indifference or maliciousness toward us.[46] As Peter Strawson famously noted, I feel the same pain if somebody 'treads on my hand accidentally, while trying to help me' and when he 'treads on it in contemptuous disregard' for me.[47] However, my attitudes and feelings towards the person who treads on my hand differ—and appropriately so—in these two cases. Where the pain is caused as a result of indifference or ill-will, it is quite reasonable for this to give rise to negative attitudes and feelings towards the person who has hurt me.

One common way to explain why it is reasonable is that my failure to respond in this way seems to indicate a lack of self-respect[48]—I do not see myself as somebody worthy of decent treatment.[49] I am, in effect, endorsing the wrongdoer's inappropriate view of me. Those who have difficulty seeing this when the victim is oneself, should consider instead a case where others are wronged. If you know about somebody being wronged and do not develop negative attitudes and feelings towards the wrongdoer, you are not respecting the victims as beings who should not be treated that way. There is also an important sense in which you are not treating the wrongdoer with respect. You are not acknowledging that the perpetrator is a moral agent. You should not respond to an assault on a sentient being by a moral agent in the same way you would to an 'assault' on an insentient object or by one. If, for these reasons, you become ill-disposed towards a wrongdoer for what he does to others, you should have the same sort of response when *you* are the victim.

The justifiability of negative reactive attitudes and feelings towards wrongdoers does not *have to* make reference to self-respect (or respect for other victims). The idea that we should have negative attitudes and feelings towards responsible agents for their wrongdoing is arguably more basic than the concept of respect. There are three broad attitudinal and emotional responses that one could have towards wrongdoing: (a) negative; (b) positive; (c) neutral. If you truly recognize something as wrongdoing, you could not respond to it in either of the latter two ways. The only reasonable response is the first. Wrongdoing, unlike a genuinely natural tragedy, is attributable to a person (or a group of people). The wrongdoer is the author of the wrongdoing. It is his indifference or maliciousness towards the victim that brings about the wrong. It is thus entirely appropriate that the negative attitudes and feelings that one has towards the wrong be carried over to the wrongdoer (in the same way that we are not only favourably disposed towards 'rightdoing' but also hold in esteem those who act rightly).

This does not mean, of course, that the negative attitudes or feelings one has towards the wrongdoer must be unqualified. You are not committed to thinking that the wrongdoer is all bad. First, the negative attitudes and feelings, to be appropriate, must be proportional to the wrong that person has generated. Minor wrongs warrant only similarly minor negative attitudes and feelings. Second, it is often appropriate to have both positive and negative attitudes and feelings towards somebody. If somebody has done both good and bad (whether to you or to others), both positive and negative attitudes towards that person can be appropriate. However, the negative response to *serious* wrongs can *reasonably* crowd out any positive response there might otherwise have been to the wrongdoer's positive traits.[50]

Repentance

Like forgiveness, repentance is primarily a change of heart. One regrets or is remorseful for what one did. However, again like forgiveness, repentance typically has external manifestations. The repentant person seeks to convey the change of heart to others, and most especially the victim where this is possible.

What counts as true repentance and as an appropriate external manifestation of this, varies, depending on the severity of the wrong. In the most minor cases, as where one gently and accidentally knocks somebody, a momentary realization, regret, and apology are sufficient. In more serious cases much more is required, both in terms of time and energy. If you have slandered somebody or been unfaithful to your spouse, deep remorse (and not mere regret) is appropriate. A genuinely repentant person will make whatever restitution is possible. The slanderer, for example, will seek to undo or counteract the damage done by the slander. Where trust has been breached, as in the case of the adulterer, the wrongdoer might seek to rebuild it (if possible).

When a wrongdoer repents, she distances herself from the wrongful act. She makes clear that if she were able to relive the moment, she would not commit the wrong. In other words, she no longer has the attitude (of indifference or ill-will) toward the victim that gave rise to the wrong. She thereby renders forgiveness reasonable.[51] The victim has a basis for overcoming the negative attitudes and feelings that arose following the wrong. Those attitudes and feelings were appropriate at the time, because they were appropriately reactive to the mental states of the wrongdoer who committed the wrong. Once the wrongdoer repents, the mental states to which the victim reacted have changed, perhaps warranting a change in the mental states of the victim.

Because repentance is primarily a change of heart, victims confront an epistemological question: How do they know that the wrongdoer has undergone a genuine change of heart? This problem is most acute when the wrongdoer and victim do not know one another's identity (even after the wrong). Somebody dented your parked car without leaving a note. You do not know his identity and he has lost the opportunity to know yours. In such situations you have no way of knowing whether the wrongdoer ever repented.

There are epistemological problems even when one does know—and interacts with—the wrongdoer. After all, insincere apologies are neither impossible nor uncommon. We can never get into the minds of others and thus can never be sure that somebody has repented. The best evidence we have is the behaviour of the wrongdoer. Sometimes that evidence is limited (a simple apology), but other times it is significant (profuse and repeated apologies, ample restitution or rectification, and sometimes non-repetition of the wrong despite having the opportunity to repeat it). The evidence is often more limited in the case of minor wrongs, but these are also cases in which the epistemic bar should be lower. In the case of more serious wrongs, we require more evidence, but because true repentance requires so much more in these cases, there can be more evidence if the perpetrator really is repentant.

It is one thing to say that true (and full) repentance makes forgiveness reasonable or appropriate—that is, in the sense of not unreasonable. It is quite a different matter to say that repentance makes forgiveness appropriate in the sense of 'recommended' or 'required'. Is the further claim also true?

While the wrongdoer distances herself from her earlier attitudes towards the victim, it remains the case that she had those attitudes at the time of the wrong. That fact, and the wrong itself, can never be undone. This is true across the spectrum of wrongs, from minor to serious. However, its relevance is very different across that spectrum. In the case of serious wrongs, there is likely to be irreversible or ongoing damage done by the wrong. This might include lost opportunities, traumatic memories, other psychological disturbance, physical injury or disease, and bereavement. It is not unreasonable for the victim to continue to have ongoing negative attitudes and feelings towards the perpetrator for this. The victim might recognize that the perpetrator is repentant and may derive some comfort from that. The perpetrator's repentance may (or may not) enable the victim to overcome some of the negative attitudes and feelings towards the perpetrator, but perhaps not enough to count as forgiveness. The victim might think that it is all very well that the perpetrator has now had a change of heart, but the victim continues to live with sequelae of the wrong and thus cannot forgive. That seems entirely reasonable, even if another victim of a similar wrong can forgive. If forgiving and not forgiving are both reasonable, then it cannot be said that forgiving is required.[52]

We should give a different answer at the other end of the spectrum. Although here too, the wrong is not undone by the wrongdoer's repentance, there are none of the enduring effects.[53] At least in the absence of a pattern of such behaviour by the perpetrator (which would put into doubt the authenticity of the repentance), it would be unreasonable for the victim not to forgive. In such cases, there is an obligation to forgive. This does not mean that the victim has a right to be forgiven. There can be an obligation to forgive without that obligation being owed *to* the victim.

Matters are understandably more complicated between the two ends of the spectrum. However, two comments are in order. First, the closer a wrong is to each end of the spectrum, the more it should be treated like one of the extremes. Second, greater uncertainty in the middle of the spectrum is to be expected.

Forgiving the unrepentant?

Repentance renders forgiveness reasonable. Can forgiveness be reasonable in the absence of repentance? Put another way, is repentance necessary for morally appropriate forgiveness, or can it be appropriate to overcome one's negative attitudes and feelings toward a wrongdoer who has not distanced himself from the wrong he committed? The challenge for those who would offer an affirmative answer is to explain how attitudes and feelings towards the wrongdoer that seem appropriate at the time the wrong is committed can cease to be appropriate without any change (of the right kind) in the wrongdoer.[54] If *he* has not changed, how could it be appropriate to change *our* attitudes towards him? How can so-called 'unconditional forgiveness' be warranted?

A related but secondary (and weaker) argument against forgiveness in the absence of repentance is that it is patronizing toward the wrongdoer. One can only forgive those who have done wrong. Thus, forgiving somebody implies that he did something wrong. Yet the unrepentant wrongdoer might reject that characterization of what he did. Imagine, for example, that your friend arrives what you take to be late for your meeting, but that he says is the actual time you agreed to meet. If, despite knowing of this disagreement, you insist on forgiving your friend, he might be indignant. He might say: 'You are not in a position to forgive me because I have done nothing wrong!' Perhaps this is why Oscar Wilde is purported to have said 'Always forgive your enemies; nothing annoys them so much.'[55]

In response to this, it might be suggested that there is nothing wrong with patronizing those who (actually) wrong us. It is sufficient that the victim recognizes the wrong; the wrongdoer does not have to recognize it too. It might be granted that in cases where reasonable people can disagree about whether a wrong was done, we should desist from forgiving those who do not acknowledge their wrongdoing—or at least to desist from *telling* them that we have forgiven or plan to forgive them. However, it might be suggested that with more serious wrongs, the wrongdoer has no claim on the victim not to be patronizing about this matter. The problem with this argument, however, is that it embodies an awkward tension: One is justifying the overcoming of negative attitudes by appealing to one of those attitudes (namely, a patronizing attitude).

One kind of argument for the permissibility of forgiving the unrepentant arises from concern for the victim. The worry is that if the appropriateness of forgiveness were dependent on the perpetrator repenting, then the victim is reliant on the perpetrator in order for the victim to permissibly overcome negative attitudes and feelings that can be destructive to the victim. The perpetrator has already wronged the victim. It would be unfair to require the victim to endure the ongoing burdens of negative attitudes and feelings toward the unrepentant perpetrator. Such attitudes and feelings can consume the victim. Even when they do not, they cause psychic distress.

This is a well-meaning argument, but it is both flawed and unnecessary. It is flawed because it does not tell us why negative attitudes and feelings towards the perpetrator are no longer appropriate. It does not tell us why the perpetrator no longer merits a negative assessment for the wrong. Instead, it tells us that there are prudential reasons why victims should (be permitted to) overcome appropriately negative attitudes and feelings. The argument is also unnecessary, because there is a way to avoid much (even if not all) of the burdens of negative attitudes and feelings towards the wrongdoer, but without actually forgiving him.

This is because one alternative to forgiving is 'not dwelling upon' the wrong.[56] One can desist from dwelling upon a wrong without forgiving the wrongdoer. To understand the difference, consider a different phenomenon: bereavement. If a close relative or friend dies, you are overwhelmed by sadness and the sense of loss. In time, you adapt to this loss and it will not preoccupy your mind in every waking minute and many a dormant one too. You do not cease to regret the death or to miss the person. If asked 'Do you still miss the person?' or 'Do you still regret the death of the person?', you will answer with a resounding 'Yes!'. There may also be times—anniversaries of the death, or poignant reminders of the deceased—when the intensity of feeling surges. These constitute further evidence that you have not ceased to mourn or to regret the loss. However, you have, following the initial period of most intense mourning, ceased to dwell on the death in your daily life. You are getting on with your life, but you are still sad that the person died.

Something similar is possible when somebody wrongs you. If it is a serious wrong, your feelings, both about what has been done to you and towards the person who has done it, may well overwhelm you. In time, you may adapt and acquire the ability no longer to dwell on the wrong, even if the perpetrator does not repent. If asked 'Have you forgiven the perpetrator?' you may answer that you have not. There may also be moments—perhaps upon seeing the perpetrator or encountering some other reminders—when the intensity of the negative feelings and attitudes will surge (and then subside again). These constitute further evidence that you have not forgiven. Yet your daily life, at least following the period of adaptation, is not consumed by those feelings. You are not dwelling upon the wrong or the wrongdoer.

It is true that you have not entirely escaped the negative attitudes and feelings and that these may even cause some distress. That, sadly, is the cost of reacting appropriately to an unrepented wrong. It is a further reason why wrongdoers are obligated to repent and make amends. Nevertheless, in not dwelling on the wrong, to the extent that this is possible, you are able to avoid the worst effects of the perpetrator's dereliction. The extent to which it is not possible to avoid dwelling on it, is also the extent to which forgiveness would not be possible—even if were permissible.

It is clear that in a normal person, the passage of time enables some adaptation—in response to being bereaved, wronged, or any number of other fates. One typically does not feel as intensely years afterwards as one does at the time. Perhaps it will be suggested that the adaptation in response to a wrong is at least part of forgiveness. However, there is a good reason to reject that position. The surges of emotion at key points, support the view that one has not in fact forgiven.

The second of these points does not apply to the most minor wrongs. There are typically no surges of intensity later. This is partly because in cases of minor wrongs there are often not intense responses even initially. Even when we do respond intensely in the moment, hindsight gives us some perspective—often we have overreacted. The upshot is that we often *completely* overcome all negative attitudes and feelings towards those who have inflicted a minor wrong on us—even if they never even apologized.

However, this need not be forgiveness. Instead, a combination of adaptation, memory limitations, and other psychological phenomena, operating on a response to a very minor wrong, can lead to an outcome that simulates but is not the same as forgiveness (followed by forgetting). Thus, anybody who thinks that repentance is a necessary condition for forgiveness, need not think that we must hang onto the negative attitudes and feelings we initially have against those who inflict minor wrongs on us.

The well-being of the victim is not the only argument that has been offered for forgiveness in the absence of repentance. For example, Eve Garrard and David McNaughton have argued that 'our common (and morally frail) humanity provides us with a reason for unconditional forgiveness. We are all in this boat together and our common condition gives us a reason to be forbearing about each other's weaknesses and indeed wickednesses, a reason stemming from our awareness of our own'.[57]

One problem with this argument is that it is not clear why our *common* moral frailty supports (unconditional) forgiveness. Surely the moral frailty of the wrongdoer is what is relevant, whether or not the victim shares such frailty? Consider, for example, some (as yet) imaginary, morally enhanced, super-human species. Members of this species would not share our moral frailty—or, at least, not to the same degree. It is not clear why that should be an impediment to their understanding *our* moral weakness and 'cutting us some slack'. They would recognize that *we* are morally frail creatures (just as we might forgive a child who has not yet developed the impulse control of ordinary adults).

However, perhaps the suggestion is that if we have comparable levels of moral weakness, we are in no position to point fingers. We are no better than those who wrong us, and thus we should not hold onto negative attitudes and feelings towards them. At best, such an argument would apply in only some cases, for sometimes the victim *is* better than the perpetrator. While we all have moral flaws, we are not all equally morally flawed. There are people who will do things that their victims would never do. Of course, one could respond with some kind of counter-factual—if I had had your background, then I too would have been capable of what you are capable of—but that is not an argument from common moral frailty. Instead it is an argument from *hypothetically* common moral frailty.

However, there is a more basic problem with the shared humanity argument—one that applies even when the victim is as prone to wrongs comparable to those of the wrongdoer. There is a crucial difference between (a) those who have moral failings and repent, and (b) those who have moral failings but do not repent. The former but not the latter have the insight and humility to recognize and regret their failings and to make amends. The moral failings may be common to all, but recognizing and regretting those failings is not. It is one thing to grant latitude to those who err and then seek our forgiveness. It is quite a different matter to forgive those who wrong us and see absolutely nothing wrong with having done so. The initial and appropriate negative attitudes and beliefs we have towards them continue to be appropriate at least until they repent.

Michele Moody-Adams offers a different defence of forgiveness in the absence of repentance. She says that neither 'the wrongdoer nor . . . the victim ... should be permanently or essentially defined by the wrongdoing and its effects'.[58] She says that 'the core task of forgiveness is to reject the narratives that give rise to this predicament, and to replace them with more helpful narratives', but cautions that 'hopeful narratives count as expressions of forgiveness only when they remain embedded in a particular view of humanity: a view that simultaneously acknowledges both the human capacity for wrongdoing and the human capacity for change and moral renewal'.[59]

Whether a wrongdoer 'should be permanently or essentially defined by the wrongdoing and its effects' depends in large part on the seriousness of a wrong. A murderer, for example, *should* permanently, although not essentially, be recognized as a murderer, at least if he never repents. (This does not preclude our simultaneously recognizing other features of his.)

It is quite different in the case of minor wrongs. Somebody who once spoke an unkind word should not be classified as 'unkind' even if he does not repent. However, forgiveness is not necessary to avoid such a narrative. It is possible to recognize an unrepented misdeed, to desist from forgiving it, but also to recognize that humans are complex beings with both flaws and excellences and to have a correspondingly nuanced view of the human being. Thus, it does not seem that forgiveness is really necessary to reject oversimplified narratives.

In any event, it is not clear how Professor Moody-Adams's conception of forgiveness can allow for unconditional forgiveness. If forgiveness 'simultaneously acknowledges both the human capacity for wrongdoing and the human capacity for change and moral renewal',[60] and the wrongdoer has not changed or undertaken any renewal, then the more 'hopeful' narrative is detached from reality. It is misplaced hope.

Similar problems confront Margaret Holmgren's argument for unconditional forgiveness. While she does not think we should blame victims for the negative attitudes and feelings that arise in response to being wronged,[61] she believes that these attitudes and feelings involve a conflation of the offender with his actions and attitudes and 'thereby fail to respect the offender both as a sentient being and as a moral agent who retains his basic moral capacities in spite of his wrongdoing'.[62] As a result, we ought to overcome them through a process of forgiveness.

Why should we think that in having negative attitudes and feelings towards the wrongdoer we 'conflate him with his actions and attitudes'?[63] Margaret Holmgren says[64] that Stephen Darwall's distinction between evaluative and recognition respect is crucial here. Evaluative respect for somebody depends on their actions, attitudes, or traits. Recognition respect, by contrast, is owed equally to all persons. It is recognition respect, Professor Holmgren says,[65] that is involved in forgiveness. Presumably we overcome our negative evaluations in order to recognize the equal worth of the wrongdoer. In adopting and retaining our negative attitudes and feelings toward the wrongdoer we 'slide from the reasonable belief that the unrepentant offender is responsible for the offense and his current lack of remorse for it to the vague claim that he is "identified with" them. We then judge the conglomerate to be "bad", "unworthy", "wholly and utterly bad".'[66]

There are problems with this line of argument. First, it is entirely possible to evaluate negatively a person's actions and attitudes without thinking that the wrongdoer should cease to be recognized as a person. This does not mean that in evaluating a person's actions and attitudes, we are making *no* judgement about the person whose actions and attitudes they are. Our actions and attitudes are either products or parts of who we are, and evaluations of them have implications for evaluations of us. However, to evaluate a person negatively is not (necessarily) to cease to recognize that person as a person.

Second, when negative evaluations either of actions or of the people who author them are appropriate, it is rarely if ever appropriate to judge the person as 'wholly and utterly bad'. Most people are partly good and partly bad, and act both well and badly. The proportions of good and bad vary from person to person, but most people are not 'wholly and utterly bad', even though some people (such as Adolf Hitler and Joseph Stalin) are so bad and do so much wrong that any good is utterly obscured. In most cases, however, our judgements of people and their actions should be more nuanced. There might be a temptation to evaluate those who wrong us more negatively than the wrong warrants, but overcoming such overestimations is not forgiveness, at least on the view of forgiveness I have outlined.

Is it ever wrong not to forgive?

It is commonly thought that victims do not owe forgiveness to those who wrong them and that wrongdoers certainly have no right to be forgiven. Even if that view is correct, it does not follow that it is never wrong not to forgive. In those circumstances in which the weight of moral reasons indicate that it would be appropriate to overcome one's negative attitudes and feelings and there are few or no reasons to retain them, then it would be wrong not to forgive.

Consider a case of a minor wrong, such as the minor bump by a passerby, or the friend who arrives late to meet you. If the relevant conditions are then met—the minor wrong did not have major sequelae, the wrongdoer sincerely apologizes, and, in the case of your friend, there is no pattern of such behaviour—it would be unreasonable to continue to harbour negative attitudes and feelings. Only a petty, overly indignant person would continue to bear a grudge. While the wrongdoer might have no right to being forgiven, when forgiveness is not forthcoming when it should be, the wrongdoer may recognize this as a failing on the part of the unforgiving person.

If we consider very serious wrongs, it seems unlikely that it could ever be wrong not to forgive (even if, in the right circumstances, it would also not be wrong *to* forgive). Even if the wrongdoer repents for having raped you or killed your child, those actions will have produced massive harm, some of it lasting the rest of your life. While genuine remorse and substantial restitution may make it reasonable to forgive, the weight of those reasons cannot so obviously outweigh the harms that it would be wrong to desist from forgiving. It may be reasonable either to forgive or not to do so.

Similar principles would apply to wrongs intermediate between the very mild and the severe. The greater the enduring harm, the deeper the remorse and the more complete the restitution required for forgiveness to be appropriate and for the absence of forgiveness to be wrong. Yet some harms will be sufficiently serious or enduring that we cannot say it would be wrong for the victim not to forgive.

Taking back forgiveness

It is possible for negative attitudes and feelings that we had towards a wrongdoer and that we overcame, to arise again. Is this phenomenon morally inappropriate? There are certainly conditions in which it is not. If, for example, one initially overcame these mental states because one reasonably but mistakenly believed that the wrongdoer was genuinely remorseful, and one subsequently discovers that the remorse was feigned, it would be entirely appropriate for the negative attitudes and beliefs to re-emerge.

Similarly, imagine that you forgive your remorseful spouse for his or her infidelity, but that he or she is once again unfaithful, perhaps after some time has elapsed. One possibility here is that your spouse was not sufficiently remorseful to avoid this further lapse, in which case this may be like the previous example. However, it is also possible that your spouse's remorse was no match for his or her lust—the remorse was genuine, but the weakness greater. In such a case one might reasonably develop negative attitudes and feelings towards your adulterous spouse. Some of that will be attributable to the latest instance of infidelity, but it would not be unreasonable for this offence to be seen in the context of the first one. 'This is not the first time you have cheated on me!' In other words, the new breach may rightfully occasion new negative attitudes and feelings about the initial one.

Yet there will be other cases in which it would indeed be morally inappropriate to harbour negative attitudes and feelings that one had overcome. More specifically, if one had appropriately overcome those mental states and there was no good reason for them to re-emerge—such as no new evidence or additional breach—then resurrecting them would be wrong.[67]

When (not) to say 'I forgive you'

If the earlier discussion about the nature of forgiveness is correct, then forgiveness, at least in its core sense, is not a performative. The words 'I forgive you' either indicate that a change of heart has already occurred or that the speaker intends to attempt to bring about such a change. If that is so, then one should only say 'I forgive you' when either of these is true. In the latter case it would actually be better to say 'I shall try to forgive you' so as to avoid the possibility that in uttering 'I forgive you' you are misinterpreted as saying that you have already forgiven. 'I shall *try to* forgive you' is also better than 'I *shall* forgive you', given that one's attitudes and feelings are not within one's control to the degree that one's actions are. One cannot guarantee that one will indeed forgive. At the most one can undertake to try to do so.

There are further conditions. If, for example, you had overcome the negative attitudes and feelings toward the wrongdoer, but it was inappropriate for you to have done so, perhaps because the wrongdoer had not repented, then it would typically be better not to disclose this, especially to the wrongdoer. We can certainly imagine exceptions to this general rule, but it would be a presumption that would need to be defeated if uttering the words were to be permissible.

Who may forgive?

I have suggested that forgiveness involves overcoming those negative attitudes and feelings toward a wrongdoer that arose as a result of the wrong perpetrated by the wrongdoer, and that given this understanding of what forgiveness is, it is possible not only for the (direct) victim of the wrong but also for others to forgive the wrongdoer. Those others can forgive for the indirect wrongs done to them, but they can also overcome the negative attitudes and feelings that they harbour towards the wrongdoer for what he did to the direct victim. That too is a form of forgiveness. What is not possible is for third parties to overcome the victim's negative attitudes towards the wrongdoer. In this way it is conceptually impossible for one person to forgive for another person. In other words, it is not possible to forgive for (or on behalf of) another person, even though it is possible to forgive for wrongs done to somebody else.

However, asking who can forgive is different from asking who may forgive. The first is a conceptual question, whereas the second is a moral one—a question about who is morally permitted or has the moral standing to forgive. This is not to say that the two questions are unconnected. If it is conceptually impossible for me to forgive your assailant on your behalf (in the sense of my overcoming your negative attitudes and feelings), then the question whether I am morally permitted to forgive on your behalf, simply does not arise. There is no point in asking whether I may overcome your negative attitudes and feelings towards your assailant if that is an impossibility.[68]

Instead the questions about what is permissible arise in the realm of what is possible. The least controversial of these questions concerns your moral standing to forgive wrongs done indirectly to you. If, for example, your child is murdered then your child is the primary victim, but you are a secondary or indirect victim in that your child's death has various negative effects on you. Let us imagine that in time you can forgive the murderer for what he did to you in murdering your child. There is widespread agreement that you are also permitted to forgive the murderer for what he did to you in killing your child (assuming that the relevant conditions for morally permissible forgiveness are met). The indirect wrong is done to you and thus you clearly are permitted to forgive that wrong.

The difficult cases are those in which you can overcome your negative attitudes and feelings towards a wrongdoer for what he did to the (primary) victim. Assuming that other conditions for morally permissible forgiveness are met, may you overcome those attitudes and feelings towards your child's murderer for what he did to your child (rather than to you)? In this particular case the primary victim no longer exists and thus you cannot reference his or her actual attitudes and feelings in considering the appropriateness of your forgiving. If your child was murdered as an infant or toddler, you cannot even ask what she would have wanted you to do. Instead you have to be guided by the same considerations you would use for wrongs done to you and to determine whether forgiveness would have been morally appropriate.

If your child was murdered as an adult or even as an older child, then you can at least ask what your child would have wanted you to do, and then take the answer to that question into account. However, the preferences of even a previously competent person are not determinative of whether you may forgive. If their preference either to forgive or not forgive would have been morally inappropriate, then you should not concur in that error.

The same is true in the case of primary victims who still exist as competent persons. If, for example, your spouse inappropriately forgives her defamer, you should desist from making the same moral mistake. Similarly, if your friend inappropriately fails to forgive minor and repented wrongs you should not similarly refuse to forgive the wrongdoer for what he did to your friend.

These deliberations about forgiving wrongdoers for what they have done to others are outlined in Figure 10.2.

It might be wondered why we should attend at all to whether the victim forgives or would have wanted us to forgive the wrongdoer. If the victim's preferences concerning forgiveness are subjected to the test of moral appropriateness, why should we not rather bypass the victim and decide purely on the basis of whether forgiveness is morally appropriate?

The answer is that the views of the victim, where available, are relevant even if not decisive. It has already been noted that sometimes reasonable people can differ on whether they forgive a wrong. Sometimes it is both morally permissible to forgive but also morally permissible to withhold forgiveness. In such cases there is something to be said for following the victim's wishes. Those wishes add a further consideration either in favour of or against forgiveness. Sometimes that additional consideration will sufficiently outweigh others such that we should rather than merely may follow the victim's preferences. That complexity is not captured in Figure 10.2.

Those who think that the concept of forgiveness applies only to wrongs done to oneself need not dismiss all these considerations. They will deny

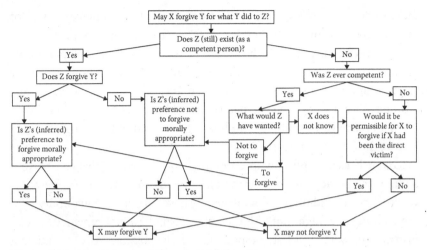

Figure 10.2 May X forgive Y for what Y did to Z?

that overcoming one's negative attitudes and feelings towards wrongdoers for what they do to others counts as forgiveness. However, they will not deny that there are moral questions pertaining to whether it is morally permissible to overcome our negative attitudes and feelings towards wrongdoers for what they do to others. Even if such overcomings do not count as forgiveness, they may constitute some other phenomenon such as 'schmorgiveness'. Just as there is an ethics of forgiveness, so there is also an ethics of schmorgiveness.

Conclusion

Wrongdoing is rife. We are regularly wronged and we regularly wrong others. There is thus much to forgive and to be forgiven. However, forgiveness is far from the only possible response to wrongdoing. Indeed, it is probably not the most important response. Far more important are the various forms of rectifying wrongdoing—regret, remorse, repentance, restitution, as well as resolve to resist similar transgression. Wrongdoing can never be undone. What has been done will forever have been done. In this sense, at least, forgiveness should not be viewed as 'wiping the slate clean'.[69]

Nevertheless, some of the negative effects can be arrested or ameliorated. This is done only rarely. Most wrongs are unrepented and un-restituted. Addressing this should take priority over forgiveness, not only because it is more important but also because, as I have argued, it is a precondition for forgiveness. Once that condition is met, forgiveness becomes appropriate.

The conclusion that forgiveness is not always morally appropriate seems to be at odds with the widespread admiration for those who have forgiven unrepentant perpetrators of even unspeakable evil. These include Gordon Wilson who, lying trapped in the rubble caused by the Enniskillen Remembrance Day bombing, and holding the hand of his dying daughter, forgave the (IRA) bombers.[70]

Are such cases sufficient to show that forgiveness is always a virtue? Should we instead take the admiration to be misguided? Alternatively, can we reconcile the admiration many people have for such magnanimity with the view that we ought not to forgive those who have not repented? An affirmative answer to this last question may well be possible. We can think that forgiving the unrepentant is wrong and yet admire those capable of forgiving great evils in the absence of repentance. Our admiration can be for their exceptional ability to overcome—or never feel—ill will against the perpetrators because of how difficult this would be for ordinary people. For example, I might admire the tenacious faith of believers in the face of their Job-like trials, even though I take their faith to be misguided. There is something to admire, even in the error. The same is true of those who forgive when they should not. However wrong that may be, it is always a lesser wrong than the one to which they have been subjected.

11
Conclusion

In this book, I have considered nine ethical issues that confront ordinary individuals in their everyday lives. I have asked what we should do or not do in each case, and I have sought to answer those questions.

I examined the ethics of humour, sex, language, bullshit, forgiveness, consuming animals, smoking (especially in the presence of non-smokers), the treatment of the environment, and aiding those in dire need. Although each of these issues are distinct, there is some overlap between some of them.

For example, consuming animals has a significant carbon footprint. Cigarette smoking, which also contributes to global warming, albeit to a much lesser degree, is also responsible for some other environmental pollution. Saving the lives of humans (and some animals) can result in the consumption of more animals, because those saved will usually eat meat. Humour sometimes includes the use of slurs and taboo language, and questions arise about whether the humorous context affects the morality of deploying such terms. Questions about forgiveness arise for ethical breaches in any of the other areas discussed.

These overlaps are not the only ways in which the chapters connect. While I have treated each topic separately, cross-referencing other topics only occasionally, it is important also to consider the relationship between the arguments advanced and conclusions defended in each chapter.

It would be a problem, for example, if arguments advanced in one chapter were inconsistent with arguments advanced in another. Inconsistencies between a person's different views are often not obvious, but they are problematic even if they are subtle. Thus, in thinking about any one topic, I have also thought about possible implications for other topics, seeking a coherent set of views across the various topics.

In this concluding chapter, the plan is to consider some of the threads running through my treatment of the different topics, and to consider some final issues arising from earlier parts of the book.

Causal inefficacy

One issue that recurs in a number of topics is 'causal inefficacy' or 'inconsequentialism'. The general issue is that some actions (or omissions) make either no, or only imperceptible, difference to whether somebody is harmed, yet an aggregation of hundreds, thousands, or sometimes millions of such actions or omissions does cause or avoid harm.

Some people view causal inefficacy as an *argument* against an individual having any reason, and *a fortiori* any duty, to desist from actions that themselves are causally inefficacious, even if an aggregation of such actions is harmful. Others take causal inefficacy to be a problem to be resolved, rather than a justification for the permissibility of such actions. I have argued that we should take the latter view—that there is a problem to be resolved, rather than a justification to be invoked.

Some people might be inclined to treat all cases of causal inefficacy alike. However, I have argued that notwithstanding the commonalities between different instances of the causal inefficacy problem, there are also important differences between them. Although these were mentioned in separate chapters, there is some value in drawing those threads together in a sample comparison between the cases of consuming animals, environmental impact, and smoking. These are summarized in Figure 11.1.

Although each of the kinds of actions can be compared with regard to different factors, the practical differences between them—whether and, if so,

	Consuming animals	Environment	Smoking
Contribution	Contributing to harm (or risk)		
Exemplar	Setting an example that may have ripple effects		
Need?	No need to eat animals	Sometimes a need to emit.	No need to smoke (in presence of non-smokers)
Scale?	Harm *obscured* as one scales up	Harm *arises* only once one scales up	Risk of harm *increases* with scale
Right to act?	No	To some extent	No
Duty to desist?	Extensive	Partial	Extensive

Figure 11.1 Causal inefficacy comparisons.

when, we may perform the action in question—depends not on any single factor. Instead, it depends on the particular constellation of factors operative in each case.

Consider, first, the similarities between the different cases. In each of the sample cases, an action—whether purchasing or eating a meat meal, taking a flight, or smoking in the presence of non-smokers—contributes either to harm or to the risk thereof. In the respective chapters, I explained what the relevant sense of 'contributes' is. Our actions either make some imperceptible difference (rather than no difference) or, at the very least, the expected disutility of the action is not zero. That is to say, even if some instances of these actions may make no difference, because we cannot typically know which those instances are, we should treat them as actions that make some difference to harm or risk or harm. Meat purchases contribute to demand for animal flesh, emissions contribute to global warming, and smoking contributes to the risk of those non-smokers in whose presence a cigarette is smoked.

In addition to these arguably more obvious ways in which individual actions contribute to harm or risk, there is also the example that one can set in acting or omitting. Performing each of these actions contributes, even if only imperceptibly, to normalizing such activities. By contrast, (conspicuously) desisting from such actions can do the opposite.

These are the ways in which the three cases are alike. However, there are also important differences between them. Whereas, in ordinary contexts, there is no need to consume animals, or to smoke in the presence of non-smokers, there is *sometimes* (but only sometimes) a need to emit carbon and other environmentally damaging gases.

Another way of thinking about the 'need' to perform an action, is to ask what would be sacrificed by desisting from the action in question. There may be a gustatory sacrifice in foregoing meat, but that is the sacrifice of a pleasure rather than anything more significant. (I make the reasonable assumption here that the nutrition can, in ordinary circumstances, be obtained from alternative, plant-based sources.)

Because smokers can smoke out of range of non-smokers, the sacrifice of not smoking in the presence of non-smokers is usually a sacrifice of convenience. There are circumstances, such as lengthy flights, in which it is impossible to smoke beyond the range of non-smokers. In those circumstances, the sacrifice might be greater, although even then there can be nicotine delivery mechanisms that do not affect non-smokers and which could minimize the sacrifice of smokers desisting from smoking in the presence of non-smokers.

The situation is more mixed in the case of carbon emissions. Often sacrificing an emissions activity, such as a joy ride, is the sacrifice of a mere pleasure. However, on other occasions, the sacrifice is of greater significance—foregoing a rare family reunion, or an educational or business opportunity.

Another difference between the various cases, and one which has typically been overlooked, is *how* the problem of causal inefficacy arises in each case. In the case of consuming animals, there is no problem of causal inefficacy when the scale is small. In such cases, the harm (such as killing an animal) is closely connected to the activity of eating meat. In such cases an identifiable animal is killed in order to be eaten. There can be no meat eating without an animal being killed. The problem of causal inefficacy arises as a result of scaling up to industrial levels of meat production. In other words, the harm is *obscured* by the scale.

The situation is quite different in the case of greenhouse gas emissions. Here, the individual actions are harmless in the absence of millions of other emissions. In other words, if there were not the volume of other emissions, one's own individual emitting act would not be harmful at all. The problem *arises* only with scale. The fact that the emissions become harmful only when the scale is increased does not mean, as I argued in the chapter on the environment, that we may emit with abandon. However, it does mean that emissions are different from consuming animals, for example.

The case of smoking in the presence of non-smokers is different from both the previous cases (if, for the moment, we set aside the carbon-footprint of smoking, which applies even when the smoking is not in the presence of non-smokers). Here, we have something approaching a linear scale. Smoking a single cigarette in the presence of a non-smoker very marginally increases the risk of harm to the non-smoker. The risk increases with each additional cigarette smoked in that non-smoker's presence.

When we combine the fact that there is no need to eat animals, with the fact that, on the small scale, there is a close connection between consuming animals and the harm done to them, we should reach the conclusion that there is no right to consume animals. The fact that the connection between action and harm is obscured when we scale up to industrial levels, does not change the fact that there is no right to eat animals. Those who doubt this, should consider what they would say about the case of the industrial production of human tears for consumption by other humans—a case that I raised, first in the environmental chapter, and then again in the chapter on consuming animals. The correct conclusion, I argued, is that we have an extensive duty to desist from consuming animals. (There may be rare exceptions, just as there may be rare exceptions to our duty not to consume humans.)

The situation is different in the case of carbon emissions. In *some* such cases there is a significant need to emit, or at least a significant sacrifice in not emitting. If we combine this with the fact that these emissions would be harmless if there were not as many other people emitting as much as is being emitted, then we should conclude that there is a right to *some* emitting activities. As a result, the duty to desist is partial. Just how limited or extensive it is, is a matter that was discussed in the relevant chapter. The point here is that the duty is not as categorical as the duty not to consume animals.

The case of smoking, while not identical to the case of consuming animals, is closer to that case than to the case of global emissions (even if we consider only the harm argument and set aside the offence argument, which was also discussed in the chapter on smoking). This is because the combination of there being no need to smoke in the presence of non-smokers, and the fact that the risk to non-smokers exists even at the small scale, should lead us to conclude that there is no right to smoke in the presence of non-smokers. That is true on the small scale, and becomes even more significant as the scale increases.

The problem of causal inefficacy does not apply only to the three cases just considered. They are merely prominent examples. The problem also arises in other topics that have been examined in this book. For example, how much difference does one's own calling out of others' bullshit affect the total amount of bullshit? What sacrifice would calling out such bullshit involve? Similarly, how much difference will one's own attempts to defang a slur make, and what sort of sacrifice would such an attempt involve? How much evil would be prevented by the aid one provides, and how much of a sacrifice does this involve? These, and related questions, were considered in the relevant chapters.

How demanding is duty?

In the Introduction, I pointed to disagreement about how demanding—or extensive—an individual's duty is. Some philosophers, I noted, require us to do as much as we possibly can (without sacrificing anything of comparable moral significance). Such views allow very little scope for the supererogatory (and other components of the permissible) realm, which is effectively crowded out by the expansive domain of duty. Although no plausible views of morality require *nothing* of us, there are some views that require very little of us.

I suggested in the Introduction that such views at the extremes are less likely to be correct. This is because morality involves weighing up competing considerations in a reasonable way. If, for example, one can do a great deal of good at no cost, or almost no cost, it is not reasonable to think that one has no duty to do the good. However, the greater the cost that must be incurred to do the good, the less reasonable it is to say that one has a duty to do that good.

It should thus be unsurprising that, in defending views about the respective practices, I have often reached conclusions that, while imposing considerable duties on us, also allow significant space for permissible as well as supererogatory actions—the latter being morally creditworthy actions (or omissions) that sacrifice more than one can be morally required to sacrifice.

For example, I argued, contrary to some, that individuals *do* have duties regarding the environment. These include a significant duty both to minimize their own greenhouse gas emissions and to support policies and laws that would be needed to respond appropriately to the problem of global warming. However, contrary to others, I also argued that each individual person's duty is limited in the absence of an effective co-operative scheme.

I also argued that while individuals do have a duty to aid those in dire need, that duty is more limited than some philosophers have suggested. Those who contribute more are acting in morally credit-worthy ways, but beyond what is strictly required of them.

Those who think that we have very extensive duties to the world's poor argue that the amount of good we can do for them far outweighs the benefit to us of keeping the resources that we could use to help them. I suggested that while this is the case for more limited giving by each individual person, it can become less plausible as the proportion of one's income that one might give away increases. It is not uncommon, for example, for the additional resources to be needed to protect oneself or one's family from later evils.

Those defending extensive duties will likely argue that even in such cases, the resources can do much more good for others than for oneself, not least because the choice is between helping many others and helping oneself. The suggestion is that the greater good would be served by expending the resources on a greater number of impoverished people than on oneself. But this view implies that sacrifice of the self is a duty. That, I suggested, is unreasonable rather than reasonable. Sacrificing oneself in such circumstances is more plausibly thought of as supererogatory.

Similar reasoning was manifest in my discussion of bullshit. Although fully cognizant of, and alarmed about, the dangers of bullshit, I argued that there is a limit on an individual's duty to counter the bullshit of others. This is because of just how costly it can be to 'call bullshit'. Once the costs are great enough, calling bullshit is no longer a duty but becomes supererogatory.

I argued that there is a stronger duty to desist oneself from bullshitting, but that even then, bullshitting may sometimes be permissible within tightly constrained limits. One example I provided is that of a medical scientist who must bullshit in grant-writing, in order to obtain funding for important research. There are certainly limits on how much bullshitting is permissible even in such a case, but weighing up the benefits and costs, should lead us to conclude that 'playing the game' of grant-writing may be permissible within limits.

None of the foregoing is to suggest that our duties are *always* limited. Because the extent of our duty is determined by a range of competing considerations, it is sometimes the case that a duty *is* much more extensive.[1]

This, I argued, is true in the case of eating animals, and smoking in the presence of non-smokers. The trivial human interests in gustatory pleasures, and the consequent minimal sacrifice in abstaining from animal products, simply cannot outweigh the important interests that animals have in not being killed and subjected to pain and suffering.

The risk to a non-smoker of being exposed to a single cigarette is much less than the harm to animals from being raised and killed for food, but other considerations are nonetheless sufficient to support a duty not to smoke in the presence of non-smokers.

First, the risk from second-hand smoke is not the sole consideration. The immediate discomfort (outlined in the offence argument) would be sufficient to render smoking in the presence of non-smokers impermissible.

Second, even if we consider only the risk of harm, smokers do not have to desist entirely from smoking to avoid smoking in the presence of non-smokers. They must merely shift the location of their smoking. That is the most reasonable way to balance the interests of smokers and non-smokers.

Third, it would have been better for the smoker if the smoker had never started smoking, and a smoker must bear the responsibility of having become a smoker.[2] Once the smoker chooses to become dependent on nicotine, the smoker cannot expect the non-smoker to pay even a minimal price for the smoker's choosing that dependency.

Although the problem of causal inefficacy arises in both the case of eating animals and in the case of smoking in the presence of non-smokers, I argued that this problem can be resolved, and that that resolution supports robust duties not to eat meat or smoke in the presence of non-smokers.

Although I discussed, separately, how extensive our various quotidian ethical duties are, it may well be the case that how extensive one of one's duties is, depends to some extent on what one is doing in connection with other problems. For example, a high carbon emitter may have more extensive (restitution-based) duties to the global poor than a low carbon emitter, given that the high carbon emitter is contributing more to climate change harms that affect the world's poor disproportionately. Alternatively, a bullshit-buster in danger of losing her job may have less extensive duty to give away resources that she might need if she does indeed lose her job.

I have not explicitly argued that our negative duties to avoid inflicting (unjustified) harm are stronger than at least those of our positive duties (whether to bestow benefits or to rescue from harm) that we have not assumed through our voluntary actions or negligence. However, I do think that that is the case. I cannot provide an extensive argument here for that conclusion, but I can gesture at a few considerations in support of it.

As I noted in the Introduction, positive duties, all things being equal, are more demanding than negative ones. The more demanding a duty is, the less reasonable it is to think that it outweighs other moral considerations. Thus, positive duties—and *a fortiori* the more extensive they are—are less likely, all things being equal, to pass the test of reasonableness.

Yet another often unnoticed reason for thinking that our duties are limited in scope arises from the relationship between a person's duties and that person's authority.[3] If we have positive duties, then, at least in some situations, these can include duties (and thus the authority) to *interfere* with the freedom of others. For example, one way to prevent somebody from suffering the evils of absolute poverty is to prevent that person from being brought into existence. That in turn, might sometimes require interference with the reproductive freedom of those who would bring her into existence. Either interference with this freedom would constitute a sacrifice of 'comparable moral significance' or it would not. This gives rise to a dilemma for many advocates of extensive duties.

The first horn of the dilemma is that if interfering with somebody's reproductive freedom would constitute a sacrifice of 'comparable moral significance', then the cost of a positive duty's interference with one's *own* freedom will often also be a sacrifice of comparable moral significance. If one is not entitled to prevent the existence of a child but is then morally required to expend the resources to save that child from poverty, one lacks the freedom to expend those resources in the way one would prefer to expend them. The more extensive the duty the greater the moral significance of the cost. If that sacrifice is of comparable moral significance, then one does not, after all, have an all-things-considered duty to save the child.

One complexity here is that 'interference' is not identical in the two cases. If I successfully interfere with somebody's reproductive freedom, they literally have no choice. By contrast, if I act on a duty that interferes with *my* freedom, I did at least have a choice about whether to do my duty. In other words, the first kind of interference is a literal constraint, whereas the second is a constraint (purportedly) imposed by morality.

We can acknowledge that there is *some* difference between these two kinds of constraint, and that the former might be somewhat worse than the second. However, it can only be *somewhat* worse because, given that those acting within the constraints of morality are said to have no moral discretion, they must do what they might not want to do. Thus, there must still be cases where the interference by a purported duty does amount to a sacrifice of comparable moral significance.

Consider next the second horn of the dilemma, namely the possibility that one's duty to interfere with the reproductive freedom of the absolute poor is a cost that is *not* of comparable moral significance to the harm that one thereby prevents. This is a conclusion that may well not sit well with those who typically endorse more extensive duties. They want to claim that we must help those who are in need, but also that we do not have the authority to prevent the need. According to this view, we have minimal authority but maximal duty. That does not seem reasonable. If you are (held) responsible for solving a problem, it is unreasonable to deny you the authority to prevent it from arising in the first place.

The paradox of desert

There is another problem that I explicitly mentioned first in the chapter on bullshit, but which manifests in a few of the topics I have covered, as well as in many other ethical contexts. This problem adds some further support to a non-maximalist view of duty, but that further support is limited because it is a problem that also arises for less demanding views about the extent of duty.

Introducing the paradox

This problem is what I call the 'paradox of desert'. It arises from the fact that doing the right thing can come at a (sometimes substantial) cost to the person who is acting rightly.[4] The paradox is that those who, on account of acting rightly, are least deserving of paying the price of acting rightly, are the very people who pay it. To the extent that paying the price is deserved by anybody, those who, on account of failing to act rightly, are most deserving of paying it, are the very people who do not pay it.

The paradox does not claim that somebody not paying a price *always* deserves to pay it. As a non-quotidian ethical example, consider the case of a person who, though not complicit with an oppressive regime, also does not engage in the kind of resistance that can result in one's being executed. Although those who do engage in such resistance are especially undeserving of the price some of them pay, those who do not engage in resistance are not themselves deserving of death.

In other cases, those who do not act rightly may indeed deserve to pay the price that is instead paid by those who do act rightly. Consider, for example, two judges operating within a system in which independence from political forces is punished, and compliance with political forces is rewarded. The judge who provides a politically compliant, but judicially flawed, judgement (thereby retaining his job or the chance of further professional advancement) does indeed deserve to pay the price that he does not pay, namely losing his job).

The paradox is not that 'bad things happen to good people', a phenomenon that is paradoxical only to the extent that one thinks that we live in a just world (perhaps because there is a just deity ensuring justice). Instead, the paradox is that the *very* thing—acting rightly—that incurs the cost, also makes the cost (especially) undeserved.

The paradox does not arise in *every* circumstance in which somebody acts rightly. The paradox need only arise *sometimes*. I would go further and claim that it arises *often*. Even when it does arise, it does not always do so with the same force. I shall soon say more about when it arises, but only after some further introduction of the problem.

Consider, first, a terminological issue. There are those who will resist the term 'paradox' in this context. This is because they think that there can be a paradox only when there is strict logical contradiction. Given that the problem I shall explore does not depend on understanding it as a *paradox*, those who are resistant to the term 'paradox of desert' may replace it with their preferred alternative—'conundrum of desert' or 'problem of desert', for example.

That said, I shall stick with the phrase 'paradox of desert', because the problem that I am presenting *does* constitute a paradox in at least some standard senses of that term. Some of those senses are colloquial rather than technical. In a colloquial sense something is paradoxical if it embodies some conflict or absurdity, or something unexpected (that may or may not be reconcilable or explicable). Thus, we have terms such as 'the paradox of hedonism',[5] 'Peto's paradox',[6] and the 'French paradox'.[7]

The 'paradox of desert' is also a paradox in at least some less colloquial senses (even though it does not involve logical contradiction). Saul Smilansky, for example, understands 'paradox' to include 'an absurd conclusion derived by acceptable reasoning from acceptable premises', and absurdity as a 'fundamentally alien relationship between . . . [a] state of affairs and human reason, human nature, or our basic expectations about the moral order'.[8] The paradox of desert arguably meets this definition of a paradox. There are various ways of characterizing the 'absurd conclusion' that is generated by 'acceptable reasoning from acceptable premises', but one of these is that 'one ought to do that which, if one does it, will incur a cost that one does not deserve (or, in one sense, one ought not) to incur'.

Consider, next, two kinds of *cost* of doing the right thing. Such costs can be what I shall call either 'internal' or 'external' (or some mixture of the two). Internal costs are those that are inherent in acting rightly. If, for example, one owes a financial debt, then the cost of paying that debt is inherent in acting rightly. Paying the debt incurs the relevant cost quite independent of external considerations.[9]

External costs, by contrast, are ones that are the result of the particular environment within which doing the right thing is located. If, for example, you will be ostracized for acting rightly, then the cost is not internal to acting rightly. Instead, it is a product of acting rightly within an environment in which doing so results in ostracism.

There are also two kinds of *unfairness*—intrinsic and (extrinsic or) comparative. Something is intrinsically unfair when it is unfair in itself. If you owe a debt and you fail to pay it, then that is intrinsically unfair. If you are part of a group that owes a debt, and you default while other members of the group pay their debt, then there is both the intrinsic unfairness of your not paying your debt as well as the comparative unfairness of your not paying your debt while others are paying theirs.

In some situations, comparative unfairness can make the costs of acting rightly be not only internal but also external. Consider, for example, a situation in which your failing to pay your share of a group debt results in others having to pay a greater share than they would have paid if you had acted rightly. In such a case, some of the costs incurred by those acting rightly, by paying their debt, are internal. That is true of the costs that they would have had to bear if you had paid your debt. However, the incremental cost that they bear as a result of your defaulting is an external cost.

Application of the paradox

The problem generated by the paradox of desert becomes steadily more pronounced as we regress through three kinds of cases on a spectrum, as seen in Figure 11.2.

In cases of the first kind, in which everybody is acting rightly,[10] the fact that each person is paying the price for acting rightly might be thought to be *entirely* fair. This, it might be argued, is because it is not intrinsically unfair to bear costs that it is right to bear, and because there is nobody who is unfairly evading the costs and thereby generating any comparative or intrinsic unfairness.

To evaluate this argument, we need to distinguish between two senses of 'acting rightly'. This phrase is neutral between 'acting in accordance with one's duty' and 'acting in a supererogatory way'. The argument that there is no unfairness in situations in which everybody is 'acting rightly' has greatest

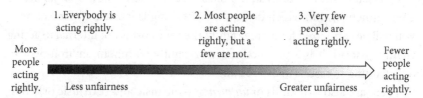

Figure 11.2 The emergence of the paradox of desert, as fewer people act rightly.

force in situations in which by 'acting rightly' we mean 'acting in accordance with one's duty'. However, when we mean 'acting in a supererogatory way', then the paradox of desert has some application. If the costs are not required, then there may well be some intrinsic unfairness in the costs being paid by people who, because they are acting in a supererogatory way, are least deserving of paying them. Although everybody, in this scenario, is acting in a supererogatory way, there would be comparative unfairness to the extent that the *degree* of supererogation differed.[11]

There is more unfairness in cases of the second kind, irrespective of which sense of 'acting rightly' we employ. More specifically, it is intrinsically unfair that some people are not bearing the costs that it would be right for them to bear, and comparatively unfair that they are not bearing those costs while others *are* bearing the costs of acting rightly. Those few who, on account of not acting rightly, are the most deserving of bearing the costs, but are also the few who are not bearing them. The unfairness is enhanced to the extent that the defaulting by some creates external costs for the many who are acting rightly.

The full force of the paradox emerges in cases of the third kind. Because very few people are doing the right thing, the unfairness is greatest in two ways. First there is the widespread intrinsic unfairness of (so many) people not bearing the costs that they should be bearing. Second, there is also the comparative unfairness of a few people bearing the costs of acting rightly while so many others do not do so. The problem is heightened when the costs of acting rightly become external, as a result of so many others' not acting rightly.

The problem generated by the paradox of desert has both *retrospective* and *prospective* manifestations. Retrospectively, we simply note that those who acted rightly paid a price they least deserved to pay. In some cases, those who acted wrongly were, on that account, spared paying a price that, because they acted wrongly, they were (more) deserving of paying.

Prospectively, the paradox presents a moral *dilemma* to the person who is considering whether or not to act rightly. She knows that if she acts rightly, she will thereby be least deserving of having paid the very price that she will have paid. If, for this reason, she does not pay the price, she will, in some circumstances, thereby be more deserving of paying the price. This paradox presents a dilemma about how to act. What you deserve is not fixed until you act, but however you act, you will get what you least deserve. Should you act rightly and thereby incur undeserved cost, or should you avoid that outcome by not acting rightly, in which case you will have avoided incurring a cost you did not deserve to incur, but in some circumstances you will do so by coming to deserve (more), a cost that you avoided incurring?

The example I provided in the chapter on bullshit is that those who do the right thing by speaking up against instances of bullshit pay the price while those who remain silent do not. These costs are largely external because if the majority were speaking up against bullshit, the costs of doing so would either be eliminated or significantly reduced. Yet it is those who do the right thing who are less deserving of paying a price.

Similarly, those who do the right thing and reduce their emissions are those who least deserve to incur the costs that such reductions involve. Indeed, the more diligent the person is in reducing emissions, the greater the cost to that person. Some of these costs are internal, but some are external because they are necessitated by the fact that so few others are acting rightly. By contrast, the more a person falls short of doing the right thing, the less of a price that person pays. At the bottom end, they pay no price at all.

The case of giving aid is somewhat more complicated. On its face, we might say of those who give away more rather than less to help those in dire need, that they are least deserving of incurring the costs of giving. However, some of those who do give more, do not take the costs to be *real* costs. According to this view, helping those in need can be seen as a net benefit to the person providing the help.

One plausible way in which it might be thought to be a net benefit, is that the satisfaction from helping others might well outweigh the costs of giving. This is an important observation, but it needs to be qualified in two ways.

First, at least some of those who give to those in dire need, do so because they think that it is the right thing to do rather than because they find it rewarding. Even if they experience a net positive return on a certain level of giving, any donations beyond that level would amount to a net cost.

Second, there may be questions about the extent to which subjective judgements about net benefit can be trusted. For example, a generous giver might, at a later stage, find herself unable to fund a vital personal cost, and only then recognize that an earlier claim about net benefit was mistaken. It is not possible for that later assessment and the earlier one both to be correct.

Giving aid is not the only case in which the costs might be thought (sometimes) to be outweighed by the benefits of acting rightly (or virtuously). One can imagine similar claims being made about the environmental and bullshit-calling duties. In other words, it might be said that acting rightly, even if that comes at great cost, may nonetheless be a net benefit.

It is reasonable to concede that acting rightly carries *some* reward, and that *sometimes* this reward will outweigh the costs of acting rightly. To the extent that a cost of acting rightly is indeed not a net cost in a given case, the paradox of desert would not apply in that case.

However, the paradox of desert does not need to arise in *every* case in which acting rightly comes at some cost. It need only arise in *some* cases, namely in those situations in which acting rightly comes at a net cost. (My own view is that there are *many* such cases.) Thus, my fundamental claim about the paradox of desert stands in opposition only to the view that acting rightly (or virtuously) is *always* a net benefit to the person who acts rightly. However, such a view is highly implausible.

There is much more to be said about its implausibility than can be said here. However, some comments can be offered. In general, the view that acting rightly is always a net benefit requires some contrivance. One such contrivance is simply to stipulate that the value of acting rightly is so great that it always defeats any cost, no matter how great the cost.

Even when the stipulation is dressed up in an argument of some kind, it remains a stipulation. If, for example, one says that acting rightly is so greatly rewarded in the afterlife that it outweighs any cost in this life, the argument is actually an embellished stipulation. If we are to accept such a claim, we need evidence that there is an afterlife, and that right is not only rewarded there but sufficiently rewarded to outweigh the costs that it is said to outweigh. While some comfort is to be derived from such wishful thinking, we have no evidence to support it.

If we reject the view that acting rightly is *always* a net reward, there remains an open question about how often it is. The answer must recognize that the greater the costs, the less likely that acting rightly is a net reward. With this recognition, we would need to examine the costs in any particular case, a task I shall not undertake here.

Implications for the extent of duty

The paradox of desert is disturbing in its own right. However, it is arguably also relevant to debates about the extent, or demandingness, of duty. More specifically, it adds support to non-maximalist views of duty—that is, to views that limit the scope of duty, thereby allowing more moral space for supererogation. To see why this is so, we need to distinguish between the two senses of 'acting rightly' that were discerned earlier. That is, we need to distinguish between 'acting in accordance with one's duty' and 'acting in a supererogatory way'.

My view that the paradox of desert lends support to non-maximalist views of duty is not obviously correct, because there are two ways of looking at the matter. On the one hand, we might say that when some people do, and others do not do what they are required to do, the unfairness is greater because those who do the right thing had no moral option. In other words, they were constrained by the requirements of morality. The fact that they then bear the costs of duty while many others do not, is more unfair. Thus, the greater the extent of duty, the *more* unfairness there is.

However, there is also a case to be made for the view that the unfairness is greater when somebody acting in a supererogatory manner thereby pays a price that others are not paying. According to this view, the fact that the action was not required, means that the person who acted in a supererogatory manner was even more virtuous than somebody doing only what they are required to do, and no more. Because they are more virtuous, they are even less deserving of paying the price of virtue. Put another way, bearing the costs of duty is less unfair than bearing the costs of supererogation. Thus, the greater the scope of duty, the *less* unfairness there is.

Both of these accounts have an initial plausibility. However, if we probe further, we should reach the conclusion that the paradox of desert shows that there is more unfairness when the scope of duty is greater. In beginning that probe, we should notice that the two accounts are making different comparisons.

The first view examines a moral-choice differential. It says that where somebody, acting within moral constraints, has less choice, the unfairness to the person acting rightly is greater than when they have more choice within those constraints. There are more constraints when one is duty-bound than when one is acting in a supererogatory manner.

The second view examines a (purported) virtue differential. It says that the person acting in a supererogatory way is more virtuous than somebody who is doing their duty. Paying a particular price for supererogation is thus more unfair than paying the same price for a person fulfilling their duty.

The problem for the second view is that while supererogatory actions may be more virtuous than actions that fulfil duties, this is only true within a

CONCLUSION 361

single view about where duty ends and where supererogation begins. It does not apply when comparing different views about the extent of duty.

In Figure 11.3, the vertical arrows represent the increasing demandingness of an action or omission. Examples include the proportion of one's income that one gives away, the extent to which one desists from greenhouse gas emissions, or the extent of the sacrifice one makes to 'call bullshit'. The two broken horizontal lines represent the limit of duty, according to each of two different views about the extent of a duty. Actions below the horizontal line are duties, whereas those above the horizontal line are supererogatory.

The first thing to notice is that even within the realm of duty, some actions are more demanding than others. Thus, Action B is more demanding than Action A. If it is more virtuous to perform more demanding actions, then fulfilling some duties is more virtuous than fulfilling others.

Action C is more demanding than Action B. Action C is beyond the requirements of duty on the first view, and thus supererogatory on that view, but is a requirement of duty on the second, more expansive view of duty. However, it is the same action in both cases. How demanding Action C is, does not depend on where we set the limit of duty. Instead, it depends on where on the scale of demandingness it sits. Thus, while on any particular view about the limits of duty, supererogatory actions will be more demanding than what one is duty-bound to do, we cannot extrapolate from this

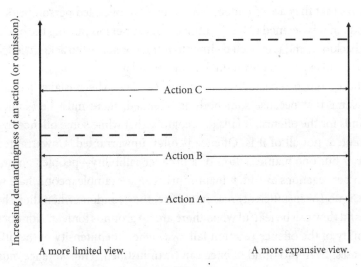

Figure 11.3 Two views on the limits of duty.

that an action required by duty on one view is less demanding than the same action that is viewed as supererogatory by another view.

Our question is whether the paradox of desert presents more of a challenge to limited views of duty or to extensive views of duty. That an action falls beyond the bounds of duty on one view, does not mean that it is more virtuous than the same action when that action falls within the bounds of duty on another view. Thus, we cannot cite degree of virtuousness as a reason for thinking that more extensive views of duty limit the unfairness highlighted by the paradox of desert. By contrast, we *can* cite the absence of moral option as a reason for heightening the unfairness illuminated by the paradox of desert.

Thus, while the paradox of desert arises for all views of right action, it is especially problematic for those views that expand the realm of duty and thereby shrink the realm of supererogation. This is certainly not a decisive consideration against maximalist views of duty, but it is one factor that counts against such views.

Offence

Offence is another issue that arises in a few of the topics covered in this book. In contemporary lay (that is, non-philosophical) moral discourse, offence is often treated as very powerful or decisive moral consideration. If somebody declares that they are offended, especially if the offended person belongs to a group that is deemed to be a 'victim class', the person causing the offence is on a backfoot, and is expected either to retract or at least to acknowledge the offence and express regret about having caused it.

I have argued repeatedly against such a view. The mistake it makes is to assume that because somebody is offended, there must be (sufficient) grounds for the offence. It fails to recognize that while some offence may be warranted, not all of it is. Offence is often unwarranted. Unwarranted offence is but one manifestation of a broader fallibility—people's emotional and other reactions are often inappropriate. For example, people hate when there is no (or insufficient) reason to hate, they condone when they should not, and they can be fearful when there are no grounds for fear. Nor does the fallibility of the offence reaction fall away when the intensity of the offence increases. Even profound offence can be unjustified. Thus, offence must be evaluated to determine whether it is reasonable.

Those who fail to recognize this, give a veto to the hypersensitive. They also, I have noted, wield a two-edged sword. If some action offends and is therefore taken to be wrong, then if others are offended by the offence, the initial offence is also wrong. (That could precipitate an offence-race, in which each new line of offence is regarded as offensive.)

Some of those seeking to preserve the veto of (some) offence, might argue that it is only the offence of some people that counts. When, for example, 'cisgendered, straight, white, Christian males' are offended by the offence of other groups, the offence of the 'cisgendered, straight, white, Christian males' does not count. There is much to be said against such thinking, but here it need only be noted that this is not sufficient to take one edge off all two-edged offence swords. If some trans people, gays, 'blacks', Jews, or females are offended by an action, and other trans people, gays, 'blacks', Jews, or females are offended by this offence, the relevant sword remains double edged.

What is offence?

Although offence is not a decisive consideration, it may nonetheless have some force. How much force it has, can vary. One of the variables is what is meant by 'offence'. This is a word with more than one meaning, and its multiple ambiguity is a source of confusion. We thus require some disambiguation. One meaning we can immediately set aside is 'a breach of law'. That is not the relevant sense of the word when we are speaking about what is, and what is not, *ethical*.

However, we should also exclude 'offence' understood as a 'moral breach', not because it has nothing to do with morality, but rather because to label something an 'offence' in this sense is already to have reached a moral conclusion. When people advance an offence argument against some action, they are providing an argument why that action is immoral. They are saying that it is immoral because it offends. That would be a circular argument if by 'offends' one simply means 'wrongs'.

Instead, 'offence' is being used to refer to a reactive condition in one person that results from an action performed by another (where 'action' is broadly understood to include linguistic and other expressions, as well as omissions). The suggestion is that causing that condition is what makes (or contributes to making) the action immoral. However, just what the relevant condition is, is the source of further ambiguity. It would be ideal if we could settle on different terms to refer to the different reactive conditions. However, as we have seen, especially in the chapter on smoking, no particular words—such as 'offence', 'nuisance', 'irritation', 'annoyance', or 'disgust'—pick out the precise distinctions we need. Thus, we may need to stick with 'offence' and then differentiate different kinds of offence.

What is common to all the relevant senses of 'offence' is that they do not, in themselves, amount to 'harm', although some kinds of offence, if multiplied sufficiently, could cause harm. Noise, for example, is one kind of offence. It may not be harmful in itself, but if there is enough of it, or if it prevents one from sleeping for an extended period, it could indeed cause harm.

It is offences of this kind that tend to provide a stronger basis for judging the actions that cause them to be immoral. This is true even when they do not amount to harm. One distinguishing feature of this kind of offence is that it is (or includes) a physiological response that is not mediated by a psychological state. Eye irritants, noise, and olfactory pollution, are examples. There may be some variation in how members of a particular species respond to such stimuli, but where there is a physiological response that is not mediated by psychological states, they have something relevant in common. We might call this 'physiological offence'.[12]

It differs from cases in which for an action to cause offence, the offended person must have a particular attitude or belief. Being offended by the sight, or mere awareness, of religious practices (merely on account of their being religious practices), or by blasphemy, are examples of somebody being offended on account of an attitude or belief. We might call this 'attitudinal offence'.

Attitudinal offence can have physiological effects. For example, somebody's antipathy for inter-racial or homosexual sex may be so deep that the sight of it causes a negative physiological offence in that person. However, in such cases, the attitudes and beliefs *do* mediate the physiological response, which is why even when there are physiological effects, we do not have an instance of physiological offence, as I have defined it.

It is also possible for what I have called physiological offence to give rise to certain attitudes. For example, a non-smoker might cough in response to second-hand smoke and thereby develop a negative attitude towards the act of smoking in the presence of non-smokers. Despite that attitudinal consequence, the offence in question remains physiological in the sense I have suggested. This is because the attitude follows the physiological response rather than being necessary for it.

Evaluating offence

The distinction between physiological offence and attitudinal offence, although morally relevant, is *not* a distinction between impermissible and permissible offence. Actions that cause physiological offence will be *harder* to justify than actions that cause attitudinal offence, but the distinction, by itself, does not settle the ethical question. We must look not only at the kind of offence but also at a range of other considerations, some of which explain why the distinction between physiological and attitudinal offence is a helpful one. This was done in the fullest way in the chapter on smoking, where the offence in question was physiological.

In that chapter, drawing on Joel Feinberg, but also adapting his analysis, I noted a few relevant considerations. One is the extent to which the offending conduct is intrusive. The more intrusive, the harder, all other things being equal, it is to justify the offending action.

Related to this is the extent to which the offended person can reasonably avoid exposure to the offending conduct. The qualification imposed by 'reasonably' is necessary to exclude cases in which the offending conduct can be avoided only at significant cost to the person who is offended. The more difficult it is for the offended person to reasonably avoid the offence, the harder, all other things being equal, it is to justify the offending action.

We also need to consider how important the offending conduct is to the person engaging in it, and the extent to which they can secure that good without exposing those who are offended to that offending conduct. The more important the action and the more difficult it is for them to secure that good without causing offence, the easier it is, all other things being equal, to defend engaging in the offending conduct.

The social value of the offending conduct is also a relevant consideration. The greater the social value, the easier it is, all other things being equal, to justify the offending conduct.

The considerations about intrusiveness, avoidability, importance to the person performing the act, and alternative opportunities for securing that good, can be bundled into a distinction between actions that are *primarily* self-regarding and those that are *substantially* other-regarding. The closer an action is to being primarily self-regarding, the less moral reason that the person performing that action has to desist from it. By contrast, the more substantially other-regarding an action is (and assuming the other-regarding effect is *negative*), the more moral reason the person performing the action has to desist from performing it.

The foregoing might be thought to imply that while we may cause offence if we have good reason for doing so, causing gratuitous offence is impermissible. Whether that is true depends on just how we understand 'gratuitous offence'. If one means offence that literally has no point, then it may be trivially true. One causes the offence and nothing at all is gained. However, what if we raise the bar only marginally, and consider a case when the point of causing offence is to cause offence? Some people might take that to be gratuitous, while others might suggest that it cannot be gratuitous because there is at least some point to giving offence.

Whether or not this is regarded as gratuitous, we should not automatically conclude that giving offence in order to give offence is always wrong. At least sometimes the offended person may have behaved in ways that deprive them of any moral claim not to be offended.

Applications

When we apply the foregoing considerations, I argued, we should reach the conclusion that the relevant offence caused to non-smokers is sufficient to impose at least a very strong presumption against smoking in their presence—a presumption that is not easily defeated. By contrast, if the mere knowledge (or 'bare knowledge' as it is often called) that smokers were smoking in a designated smoking area, caused offence to some non-smokers, that would be a different kind of offence, and would not be sufficient to impose a duty on smokers not to smoke in those areas.

Similarly, offence resulting from the mere knowledge that some people are engaging in sexual practices of a particular kind, would provide no reason for those engaging in such practices to desist. Arguments for or against such sexual practices in private would have to turn on issues other than offence.

However, offence may play a role in decisions about *where* people may have sex.[13] Although such offence would typically be attitudinal rather than physiological offence, a constellation of other considerations would, at least in some contexts, militate against having sex in the presence of non-consenting onlookers. Although having sex is important to many people, and very likely has social value, at least some sex in public—on a crowded bus, to use Joel Feinberg's example—would be intrusive and not reasonably avoidable by onlookers. Moreover, the individual and social benefit can be obtained by having sex in private, or at least less conspicuously. The application of this analysis is not restricted to only some kinds of sexual practices. It applies to *all* sex, even to the least controversial kind—heterosexual sex between loving spouses. They too should 'get a room'.

The public-private distinction has *some*, albeit more limited, application also to offence caused by humour and language. Sometimes, I argued, one may tell in private a joke that one should not tell in some public settings, if by 'in private' we mean a situation in which the audience knows one well enough to know that the joke is not an expression of prejudice, insensitivity, or some other vice. And sometimes, I also argued, one may say things in private that one should not say in some public settings. However, the constraints that offence imposes on humour and language, are likely to be less restrictive than those it imposes on smoking and sex. This is because much (but not all) of the social and individual value of humour and language is dependent on its being expressed in some public way.

Non-quotidian views about quotidian ethics

The views I have defended in this book are unusual in two ways. First, many of them differ from the views of the vast majority of humanity. Second, while some of the views I have defended enjoy much more support from philosophers than from non-philosophers, my *set* of views is unusual even among philosophers. I do not have (definitive) quantitative data to prove that my views do differ from these respective comparative classes. Nevertheless, the claims are not entirely speculative, because there is at least *some* evidence for them. Both of the variances are worthy of some explication and explanation.

Uncommon views

Perhaps the clearest case of my views differing from those of most people, is the consumption of animals and their products. If we take practice to be an approximation of people's views, then it would seem that most people support the consumption of animals. This is because only a small (even though growing) fraction of humanity is vegetarian and, *a fortiori*, vegan.[14] It is possible, of course, that most people think that eating animals is wrong, but do it anyway. While there are *some* such people, it seems that most people think that it is morally entirely acceptable to eat animals. Thus, my views on this topic are both more revisionary and restrictive than ordinary views.

In this regard, though, my views are much closer to the views of most philosophers writing on this topic.[15] There may be more omnivorous philosophers than vegetarian or vegan ones, but the proportion of philosophers who are vegetarian or vegan seems higher than the rest of humanity.[16] More significantly, of the philosophers working on questions about the treatment of animals, the vast majority are those opposed to the consumption of animals.[17]

If asked, more people would likely be opposed to bullshit, but this is very probably a case where people's views are even less likely to match their actions. Moreover, the opposition to bullshit may well be of a very general, notional kind. I suspect that most people are not very good at detecting bullshit, and perhaps especially their own. Evidence for the claim that people are bad at detecting the bullshit of others is to be found in the millions of people in many countries who fall for the bullshit of those politicians they support. When those supporters start spouting the same bullshit, we have evidence of their internalizing it and thus believing their own bullshit. It is certainly the case, again inferring (approximately) from action, that very few people think that they have even a limited duty to desist from bullshitting, or to call out the bullshit of others. The same is true of academics in general, and of philosophers in particular.[18]

Ordinary people's views about sex are vastly divergent. There are still many places in the world where people espouse highly conservative views about sex, even when their own actions fall short of their declared views. There are other places, where views about sex have shifted substantially. These changes have included both dropping some taboos and adopting others.

My views on sexual ethics are the least settled of all the topics considered in the book, and I think that there is reasonable disagreement between some kind of conservative view and some kind of permissive view. However, the particularities of neither these conservative nor permissive views matches the views of most actual sexual conservatives and liberals. For example, many sexual conservatives oppose homosexuality (and other non-procreative sex), whereas I think that there are no good grounds for opposing homosexuality. I also think, although I did not argue in *this* book,[19] that it is procreative rather than non-procreative sex that is morally wrong.

The alternative, more permissive view is at odds with the views of most sexual liberals. The latter, while happy to endorse promiscuity, premarital sex, and sometimes even extramarital sex, are nonetheless resistant to *all* paedophilia, bestiality, and necrophilia. I have argued that this resistance is difficult to reconcile with the rationale underlying a defence of promiscuity. At least some philosophers have been willing to accept the logical implications of the casual view of sex. However, those philosophers do not seem to give any credence to the conservative view of sex that I think may have some truth to it. (That truth might be merely that significant sex is morally *better* than casual sex, even if casual sex is also permissible.) Moreover, almost all philosophers would reject my particular views about procreative sex.

My views on humour and language ethics are, in some ways more permissive, and in other ways more restrictive than other peoples' views. I argued that humour can be morally wrong and that there are some linguistic expressions from which we ought to desist. However, I also argued that many instances of humour and many linguistic expressions that are morally condemned, should not be. My views are nuanced and unusual in another way—they do not track either conservative or 'progressive' views. Instead, they intersect with both. Contrary to many conservatives, I do not think that there is anything morally wrong with much of what is taken as blasphemy. While I agree with progressives, against many conservatives, that language ought to be more inclusive in some ways, I reject other ways in which self-identified progressives tell us language should be more inclusive. In these ways, my views overlap with those of some conservatives. In summary, conservatives, I think, are too sensitive about some jokes and some linguistic expressions, and progressives are too sensitive about others. This is true of both philosophers and non-philosophers alike, even if the precise profile of each groups' hypersensitivity differs.

There is a growing consensus that smoking in the presence of non-smokers is morally wrong, a consensus perhaps even more pronounced among philosophers. In this regard, my view as a philosopher is not exceptional. However, if we judge by the social acceptability of smoking in the presence of non-smokers, there are parts of the world, home to a disproportionate number of all humans, where such smoking is still thought acceptable.

There is also a growing concern about humanity's greenhouse gas emissions and other environmental pollution. However, here the disjunct between views and actions is likely to be greater. It is also likely to be more enduring, until effective ways can be found to reduce emissions without significant sacrifice. This is because short-term self-interest is easier than long-term altruism. For these reasons, I am concerned that my conclusions about the duties of individual people toward the environment are likely to be understood as a justification for 'business as usual', and thus be seen as entirely congenial to the current practice. That would be a misinterpretation of my position. I do think that each person's duty is limited, and that there is some discretion about how it should be discharged. However, the limits on the duty are themselves limited. The duty may be limited, but it is neither eviscerated nor eliminated.

That position will put me at odds, not only with anthropogenic climate change denialists, and those more sophisticated people who advance the causal inefficacy argument, but also with those environmentalists who will take my view to be insufficiently revolutionary. To them, I say that we agree on the need to reduce emissions to 'net zero', but we disagree on the *extent*— and only on the extent—of an *individual* person's duty to contribute to that goal. I do not think that the arguments support a more extensive duty than I have suggested, even though I am fearful that the nuance of my conclusion will be lost on those who wish to rationalize current levels of emissions and other pollution.

I have similar concerns about my conclusion that while individual people have duties to contribute to saving others from dire conditions, those duties are not as extensive as (and their limits fuzzier than) Peter Singer, his followers, and others have suggested. However, it is an open question whether my view or theirs is more likely to backfire. Peter Singer has acknowledged that asking more than people can bring themselves to give, could result in people simply giving up giving, or at least giving up the idea of giving more than they are currently giving. That is why he proposes a fall-back position. I noted that the claim that the fall-back position is only the beginning of duty, rather than its end, might itself have some of the effect that he fears.

It is an open question whether such a problem will materialize, and how it compares with a feared complacency-inducing effect of my argument. However, arguments are not games designed to interact with human psychology. Both those arguing for extensive duties towards the world's poor and I are interested in which conclusions are supported by the weight of argument.

Consequentialists may sometimes be required to temper that with concern about the effects of an argument when it interacts with other features of human psychology, while simultaneously keeping up a pretence that it is only about the force of the arguments themselves. I am not suggesting, however, that that is what consequentialists are all doing in the case of duties to the world's poor. While I have fears about how my arguments and conclusions will be interpreted, I do not alter my conclusions on this basis—save to add on reference to my fears.

One encouraging feature of my view about the duties to give aid and to desist from emissions and pollution is that, if understood correctly—a big 'if'—it could be more conducive to either fulfilment or approximation. This is not only because less demanding standards are easier to meet but also because people may be more likely to aim at more achievable goals. My view also gives credit for supererogatory action, which can be an incentive to such action without having to claim, wrongly I believe, that that degree of sacrifice is morally required.

In summary then, my views on our duties regarding the environment and to those in dire need, will be congenial to many who misinterpret them, and rejected by those who recognize but disagree with the nuances. The correct response to this is neither to lose the nuance nor to reach a conclusion that, in my view, it would be incorrect to reach.

On the final topic, forgiveness, I am also at odds with many philosophers and non-philosophers. I think that forgiveness is sometimes apt, but other times not. A common view is to valorize forgiveness—always, or almost always. According to some views, the less wrongdoers deserve forgiveness, the more virtuous the victim's forgiveness is. Those advocating such views, might not claim that forgiveness in such circumstances is a *duty*, but they do think that it is supererogatory. I have the opposite view. I think that many, but not all, instances of forgiveness that others take to be supererogatory are actually morally defective or even morally impermissible. That may sound like a harder-line view than it really is. I have much to say about how the counterintuitiveness of my position can be mitigated. My view is, nevertheless, theoretically divergent from the views of many people.

Thus, I have defended an unusual constellation of views on nine different topics (with implications for other topics too). It is difficult to box the full set of my views. Some of my arguments call for radically new views and practices. Others call for more modest changes. Where my arguments do call for changes, those changes are not all in the same direction. Sometimes the change is towards something new, and sometimes it is towards views and practices that are being abandoned. Will those few views be called 'reactionary'? If so, then, with two qualifications, my set of conclusions is part reactionary, part conservative, part liberal, and part revolutionary.

The first qualification is that when my views are, in some sense, 'reactionary', 'conservative', or 'revolutionary', the relevant sense is not political, in which realm my commitments are liberal. I support a liberal political order in which, for example, armed insurrection in support of reactionary, conservative, or revolutionary ends is not justified. Where my views are reactionary, conservative, or revolutionary, it is in a moral sense—that we ought, morally, to return to some earlier value, preserve some value, or adopt radically new views.

The second qualification is that when I say that my views are part reactionary, part conservative, part liberal, and part revolutionary, I do not mean that all these are equal parts. Indeed, there is something disturbing about those whose views on one or two topics enable one to predict their views on more topics than consistency would require. This is what happens when people think in ideological lockstep.

Neither reactionaries, conservatives, liberals, nor revolutionaries have exclusive claim to the truth. There is some good sense on the right, the left, and the centre, even though that good sense is not equally distributed. Indeed, it is very likely that, in general, those at the extremes are less likely to be correct overall, even though they may be correct about *something*. Moderates are more likely to be correct on average, but they too will be wrong sometimes—namely on those occasions when the correct view is towards one of the extremes. (No plausible view about genocide or other mass murder, for example, could be a moderate one. The correct view is that it is always wrong.)

The unreliability of many common views

The fact that my conclusions deviate as they do from common views is not a reason to be concerned about my conclusions. This is because of how unreliable common views about ethical matters are. Consider, for example, the public uproar that, with great frequency, arises when somebody makes a joke or uses a word that is considered a breach of humour or language ethics. The 'righteous indignation' and social traction of these responses stand in stark contrast to the silent indifference to the suffering and death that humans inflict on billions of animals each year. As I noted in the chapter on humour, one can receive more criticism, from some quarters, for joking about animals than one will for killing or eating them.[20] While humour ethics is a subject worthy of our attention, any view that takes joking to be worse than the industrial farming and killing of animals, must be a perversion of morality.

In addition to such distortions of what is of moral importance, common views are often unduly simplistic. Nuance is, of course, difficult, and thus it is unsurprising that people will commonly succumb to oversimplification. Yet, nuance is exactly what is needed in thinking about ethical issues, just as it is needed in thinking about so much else. Things are complicated, and any thinking that erases that complexity is likely to be flawed.

Simplistic thinking results not only from the difficulty of thinking in more nuanced ways but also from the tendency of people to have opinions before they have made the necessary investigations and done the necessary thinking. Many people have opinions on matters on which they are not qualified to have opinions—or, at least, *informed* opinions. This is true with regard to scientific questions (such as climate change, and vaccine safety and effectiveness), and is even more true with regard to moral questions (which are often predicated to some extent on scientific questions, but which also raise complex normative issues).

Where one has not adequately investigated a matter, one should have either no opinion or, at least, an explicitly tentative opinion. Even when one has investigated a matter, sometimes the correct conclusion, given the available evidence and arguments, is either agnosticism or a conclusion that is either limited in its scope or tentative in its confidence level. One way in which the scope of a conclusion can be limited is circumstantial. That is to say, sometimes applying an argument to one context can lead to a different conclusion than applying the same argument to a different context. One thus needs to be sensitive to altering contexts.

I have reached conclusions of all these types at various points in this book. I am happy to acknowledge that on some topics (many of those not covered in this book, but also on a few in it), I have either no opinion or only a limited or tentative one.

Human fallibility

Such agnosticism and tentativeness are among the appropriate responses to human fallibility and other limitations. However, such fallibility has other relevance too.

Moral knowledge and moral action

Even when one reaches the correct (and non-agnostic) conclusion about what one ought to do, it does not follow that one will do it. This is because people often fail to do what we think we ought to do (or to abstain from doing what we think it is wrong to do). One's judgement about what one ought to do is overwhelmed by one or more psychological dynamics. These include rationalization that one's judgement does not apply in a given circumstance, overwhelming desire to act against one's judgement, felt social pressure, fear of the costs of acting rightly, and distraction or confusion, especially in highly pressured circumstances.

While we are all flawed, and while we likely do not have equal degrees of control over our shortcomings, we are also not utterly powerless in the face of them. There are things we can do to minimize departures from our moral judgements. Those techniques have not been the focus of this book, which has been concerned with how we ought to act, rather than with how we can get ourselves to do what we ought to do.

While little has been said about the latter matter, it is not difficult to *think* of the sorts of things one could do in this regard. It is much more difficult to *do* those things than to think what they are. Nevertheless, it is worth identifying some of them.

One can determine where one's interests diverge from doing the right thing. This can require searing honesty with oneself. Such honesty is itself not easy, but one of the few tools for advancing it is to abstract from oneself and to consider the issue as though it were a third party's interests that one were examining. For example, if somebody else's bullshitting would be unacceptable, then one's own bullshit in the same circumstances is also unacceptable.

Another tool is to work towards changing the incentive structures, in order more closely to align one's incentives with doing the right thing. While there cannot be complete alignment because acting rightly will sometimes require sacrificing some of one's own interests, it is possible to narrow the gap. If, for example, there were a sufficiently green infrastructure, then turning on lights, taking a drive, or perhaps someday even purchasing an airplane ticket, would not pit these activities against one's environmental duties.

Yet another tool is to consider, in advance of facing high pressure circumstances, what it is one ought to do under such circumstances. If one deliberates under more leisurely conditions about what one should do under highly pressured conditions, one will be better equipped to respond appropriately in the high-pressured situation. This cannot be foolproof, but it is a way to minimize errors that are likely to arise under harried conditions.

Where acting rightly is difficult, one technique is to adapt oneself gradually to acting rightly. If, for example, one cannot give up all animal products immediately, then one might move gradually towards vegetarianism and then veganism. For example, one might reduce the amount of meat one eats, and then eliminate it. One might seek out free-range eggs and milk, and then later eliminate them from one's diet. While any of the steps along the way to veganism may be insufficient, taking those steps rather than attempting to leap directly to the ideal might make it more likely that one achieves one's goal without relapsing. Just as the best should not be the enemy of the good, so the less bad should not be the enemy of the worse.

This is not an uncontroversial position because it might be thought to countenance wrongful action (in the interim). It is easy to see the force of that critique, especially when the steps on the way to doing one's duty involve either participation or complicity in considerable evils. Imagine a slave 'owner' who frees 90 percent of his slaves, but keeps 10 percent of them. Even if he treats his residual slaves better, he remains an 'owner' of slaves, and we should not condone that.

However, no condoning or countenancing need be implicit in recommending gradualism to those who would otherwise not be able to bring themselves to do their duty. There is no condonation in the recognition that it is less bad to hold fewer rather than more slaves. If the (not too) gradual reduction enables somebody to abandon all slave owning within a reasonable time and without relapsing into further slave purchases, that must surely be less bad than retaining all one's slaves. Recognizing that something is less bad is not the same as claiming that it is not bad at all. If you merely reduce the amount of meat you eat, you are not doing your duty, but you are at least doing less wrong.

Gradualism is even easier to defend when somebody is discharging her duties and is adapting to steadily more supererogation. In such cases, the person is doing no wrong, and is striving for non-required improvements.

Judging others

It is typically much easier to judge others for their shortcomings than it is to judge oneself for one's own failings. This is partly because it is often easier to see the faults of others and to overlook any mitigating considerations.[21]

The foregoing example of slave-owning is a good illustration. We look back (or elsewhere in our own times) at slave owners and wonder how they could possibly not have seen the wrongfulness of their actions. We wonder why other members of those societies, who benefited in some, even unintentional and unwilling ways, could not have protested.

Yet, it is very likely that future people will look back on our own generation and wonder how so many people could not have seen the wrongfulness of much that is utterly normal today.[22] This includes not only the massive maltreatment of animals, but also our ongoing carbon emissions in the face of demonstrable evidence of anthropogenic global warming and resultant climate change. (Perhaps the 'woke' among them will start removing statues of Nelson Mandela because he ate animals, or of Al Gore because he flew around the world delivering his environmental message.[23]) The future people might wonder why those reducing their meat consumption and reducing their carbon emissions did not reduce to zero, and why so many people have not protested more vocally.

There will be considerable force to any future critiques of these kinds. They suggest that we should not be smug in our own retrospective judgements. Even though we are correct in condemning slavery, we may be guilty of comparable moral failures. Our own failures may be more difficult to see now, precisely because we occupy a context in which animals are consumed on a massive scale, animal products are pervasive and difficult to avoid entirely, and the economy is still a high-carbon one.

In such contexts, even conscientious people cannot disentangle themselves from the current evils in the way that those in a remote future might be able to. In some possible future world in which animal products have yielded almost entirely (or even merely more substantially) to plant-based alternatives, and where the economy is either low-carbon or carbon-neutral, it will be easy to avoid the consumption of animals and emission of greenhouse gases. When it is easy enough to avoid those evils, it also becomes hard to understand how people for whom avoiding those evils was more difficult, were unable to dissociate from them.

The suggestion that our generation should not be smug in our retrospective moral judgements has even more force when we consider our condemnation, not of such serious evils as slavery, but of the lesser flaws (or 'flaws') of our forebears (and our contemporaries). The smug condemnation of slave owners and slavery beneficiaries, while one nonchalantly eats one's chicken burger, is outdone by the smug condemnation of those using terms such as 'chairman', 'Miss', 'actress', *mentioning* a slur, or not using somebody's preferred pronoun, while one dines on bacon and eggs. This is certainly a case of the pot calling the kettle black.

This is not to say that we may not criticize wrongful actions, whether they are severely or only mildly wrong. It is only to say that in offering such criticisms, a little more introspection is also warranted. That might lead us to be more *understanding* of past (and present) wrongdoing, which is not the same as *condoning* or *justifying* it. If everybody around you is keeping slaves, or eating meat, or unremittingly emitting carbon, those actions do not cease to be wrong. However, it is easier to understand why people either might not see (the severity of) the wrong or might perform the wrongful action despite the recognition that it is wrong.

A concluding, but not a final word

Mindful of the power of the 'retrospectoscope', and what it might, in the future, reveal about the conclusions for which I have argued in this book, I cannot pretend to offer a final word on any of the topics I have covered. However, I have grappled with them as best I can.

Some of my conclusions, especially some of those about the ethics of language, apply to our time (or to the past), and the arguments for them could lead to different conclusions at some future time, depending, for example, on what particular words and expressions connote then.

It is also possible that some of the issues will become moot in due course. Perhaps very few future people will smoke at all, and thus will not confront the question about whether to smoke in the presence of non-smokers. Perhaps animals will fade from human diets to the extent that eating animals is regarded in the same way that we now regard cannibalism (or adults consuming human milk). Perhaps our economy will become so green that daily life will not present the environmental ethical challenges it now does. Issues that are currently quotidian ethical ones may well cease to be so.

Alternatively, perhaps the worst fears of environmentalists will materialize, crucial tipping points will be passed, humans (and other animals) will face catastrophic effects of global warming, and it will become too late to stop global warming. In such a scenario, a book on cataclysmic (if not apocalyptic) ethics might be more necessary than one on quotidian ethics.

It is also possible that many, or all, of the issues in this book will remain live ones, but there will be future insights that reveal flaws in the arguments I have advanced. It does not follow from this that *any* disagreement between my views and future sentiments will constitute grounds for dismissing my arguments or conclusions. Change sometimes brings improvement, but it does not always to do so. Humanity very regularly takes morally regressive steps.

For example, some contemporary sensitivity, I have argued, is *hyper*sensitivity. Insofar as negative judgements of past practices are the result of hypersensitivity, the problem lies with the hypersensitivity rather than with the past practice. We should not assume that future humans will be without faults of their own—faults that cause them to condemn some of my (or our) views that should not be condemned. Just as our descendants might be critical of us, they might be criticized by *their* descendants. Some things do not change!

All this calls for a delicate balance between the courage of one's convictions and the humility to recognize that one's convictions could be mistaken. One crucial way of maintaining this balance is via a genuine willingness to engage with the (best) *arguments* for opposing views.[24] It is only through such engagement that one can either justify one's convictions or discover the flaws in them (and, in the latter case, either adjusting or abandoning them). It is not easy to maintain the balance between conviction and humility. Nor is it easy to engage dispassionately and honestly with opposing views. However, that does not diminish importance of these virtues in all areas of life, but not least in thinking about quotidian ethics.

Notes

Intro

1. Those books are, in chronological order: Henry Sidgwick, *Practical Ethics: A Collection of Addresses and Essays* (London: Swan Sonnenschein & Co., 1898); Herbert Samuel, *Practical Ethics* (London: Thornton Butterworth Ltd., 1935); Peter Singer, *Practical Ethics* (Cambridge: Cambridge University Press, 1979), with two further editions in 1993 and 2011. There is also a book with that title by Thomas Reid, but in that case, *Practical Ethics* was a modern title given to a collection of essays (edited by Knud Haakonssen, Princeton University Press, 1990; Edinburgh University Press, 2007) that was originally titled *Essays on the Active Powers of Man* (Edinburgh: J. Bell; London: G.G.J. & J. Robinson, 1788).
2. I have said more about this neglect in the introduction to David Benatar, ed., *Ethics for Everyday* (Boston: McGraw-Hill, 2002).
3. Those instructors using this book as a class text, may want to read David Benatar, 'Teaching Ethics for Everyday', *American Philosophical Association Newsletter on Teaching Philosophy*, Vol. 5, No. 2, Spring 2006, pp. 8–12.
4. For a longer argument in defence of my, admittedly unusual, practice, see David Benatar, 'Why don't academics address each other politely?', *Times Higher Education*, 31 January 2019, https://www.timeshighereducation.com/opinion/why-dont-academics-address-each-other-politely. A longer version can be found here: David Benatar, 'Toward more respectful academic reference practices', *What's Wrong*, 4 February 2019, https://whatswrongcvsp.com/2019/02/04/toward-more-respectful-academic-reference-practices/.
5. I recognize that there are other group categorizations (such as 'male', 'female', and 'Jew') that also have fuzzy boundaries, and yet I do not use scare quotes in these cases. However, there is much more clustering of people on the spectrum of biological sex than there is of people on the spectrum of 'race'. Moreover, sex is relevant more often than 'race' is. (There could be unprejudiced reasons to want a doctor of the same sex as oneself, but ordinarily a preference for a doctor of the same 'race' as oneself would be the result of prejudice.) Unless one adopts a racialized view of 'Jew', even this category and its contrast, 'non-Jew', has (even proportionally) fewer ambiguous cases than is true with regard to 'race'.
6. See, for example, Karen Brodkin Sacks, 'How did Jews become white folks?', in *Race*, edited by Steven Gregory and Roger Sanjek (New Brunswick: Rutgers University Press, 1994).
7. This does not preclude people self-identifying along racial lines, but to the extent that one's self-identification determines one's 'race', Rachel Dolezal is who she says she is, which shows the limits of self-identification as a standard.
8. K.K. Rebecca Lai and Jennifer Medina, 'An American puzzle: Fitting race in a box', *New York Times*, 16 October 2023, https://www.nytimes.com/interactive/2023/10/16/us/census-race-ethnicity.html (accessed 17 October 2023).
9. Available here: https://www.politicsweb.co.za/opinion/the-new-blasphemy.

Chapter 1

1. I believe that I first used the term publicly when I organized a conference under the title 'Quotidian Ethics: Moral Deliberations about Everyday Life' at the University of Cape Town, South Africa, in August 1999. James Rachels was the keynote speaker. I subsequently published an edited collection of essays (not from the conference). That collection (David Benatar, ed., *Ethics for Everyday* [Boston: McGraw-Hill, 2002]) did not have the term 'quotidian ethics' in the title, but it did discuss the term and the area of inquiry to which it referred. More recently,

I contributed an entry on quotidian ethics to the first and third editions of the *International Encyclopedia of Ethics* ('Quotidian ethics', in *International Encyclopedia of Ethics*, edited by Hugh LaFollette [Hoboken, NJ: Wiley-Blackwell, 2013], pp. 4281–85. Revision published in 3rd edition, 2022).
2. See the *Shorter Oxford English Dictionary* (Oxford: Clarendon Press, 1973), p. 1734.
3. Among the topics *not* covered in *this* book are gossip, tipping, gambling, photographing people without their consent, taking recreational drugs, infringing copyright, bullying and shaming people, parental and filial duties, lying, the keeping of companion animals, as well as such virtues as modesty and gratitude, and such vices as jealousy and envy. Many, but not all, of these, were covered in David Benatar, ed., *Ethics for Everyday*.
4. Peter Singer, *Practical Ethics*, 3rd ed. (New York: Cambridge University Press, 2011), p. 1.
5. Ibid, p. 2.
6. This reminds me of a joke:

> Little boy: 'Dad, where did I come from'?
> Father: 'The stork brought you'.
> Little boy: 'I see. And where did you come from'?
> Father: 'The stork brought me too'.
> Little boy: 'Okay. And where did grandpa come from'?
> Father: 'The stork brought him too'.
> Little boy: 'That's very strange. It seems that, for at least three generations, there has been no sex in our family'.

7. I shall add some complexities to this below.
8. Rights and duties, as will be explained later in this introduction, are related to one another, but there is a difference between a view that derives rights from duties (a duty-based view), and one that derives duties from rights (a rights-based view).
9. They might disagree about how bad an outcome must be in order to count as 'catastrophic'.
10. I first wrote about this methodology in a short essay for a competition sponsored by eight bioethics journals. Contributors were asked to write on the topic 'What are the methods of theoretical bioethics?' I take those methods to be the same as the methods of practical ethics more generally. That essay was never published, not because it was rejected, but rather because nothing came of the competition, despite repeated requests. I *did* publish a letter about the failure to complete that competition. See David Benatar, 'There's No Method in the Badness', *Bioethics*, Vol. 27, No. 3, 2013, p. 174.
11. To clarify, these normative claims need not be—and, as I have argued—are best not high-level claims characterizing a particular theory. Instead, they are lower-level normative claims.
12. The adverbial senses would be 'acting in a morally preferable, praiseworthy, desirable, or supererogatory way'.
13. See David Benatar, 'Bioethics and Health and Human Rights: A Critical View', *Journal of Medical Ethics*, Vol. 32, No. 1, January 2006, pp. 17–20.
14. These are the different sense of 'a right' distinguished by Wesley N. Hohfeld, *Fundamental Legal Conceptions*, edited by Walter Wheeler Cook (New Haven: Yale University Press, 1919).
15. That is, cases of necrophilia where the ante-mortem person whose corpse is involved gave consent to this use prior to death.
16. While it is possible to draw distinctions between manners and etiquette, and between morals and ethics, I shall here use each word in both pairs as a synonym for the other word of the same pair.
17. For further discussion, by way of example, of the scope and strength of a *right* to reproductive freedom (which gives rise to a correlative duty) see, David Benatar, 'The limits of reproductive freedom', in *Procreation and Parenthood*, edited by David Archard and David Benatar (Oxford: Oxford University Press, 2010), pp. 78–102.
18. This is something of an oversimplification. For example, there may sometimes be utilitarian reasons for demanding less of people than utilitarianism would otherwise require. For example, Peter Singer, concerned that his conclusion about the scope of our duty to give to the world's poor, might cause people to despair and give less rather than more, suggests a fall-back position. (See the chapter 'Giving Aid'.) Those who then give more, might be acting in a supererogatory way relative to the fall-back position. However, to the extent that exceeding the fall-back level of giving does not meet the level dictated by his basic argument, it is not actually supererogatory.

19. In some taxonomies, positive requirements arising from our voluntary actions are called *obligations* rather than *duties*, with the word 'duties' reserved for those requirements that arise 'naturally'. See, for example, John Rawls, *A Theory of Justice*, rev. ed. (Cambridge, MA: Belknap Press of Harvard University Press, 1999), p. 96.
20. *Enforcing* negative duties, by contrast, can require considerable time and effort.
21. Such conditions—under Nazism and Stalinism, for example—pose impossible ethical dilemmas.
22. This is not to deny that there are many contemporary religious people who still endorse child marriages, and some who still endorse slavery, but these constitute a much smaller proportion of the relevant religion than was once the case.
23. The same applies even if we are talking about not law, but 'law', where the latter refers to that which, on the natural law view, falls short of being law on account of violating morality.

Chapter 2

1. I refer to paedophilia and necrophilia as sexual *practices* but they (like zoophilia) could also be understood as sexual orientations. I shall say more about orientations later, but my focus will be primarily on what people do rather than what they feel.
2. See Burton Leiser, 'Homosexuality, morals, and the law of nature' in *Ethics in Practice*, edited by Hugh LaFollette (Cambridge, MA: Blackwell, 1997), pp. 242–53.
3. David P. Barash and Judith Eve Lipton, *The Myth of Monogamy: Fidelity and Infidelity in Animals and People* (New York: Henry Holt and Company, 2001).
4. Bruce Bagemihl, *Biological Exuberance: Animal Homosexuality and Natural Diversity* (New York: St Martin's Press, 1999).
5. Douglas G.D. Russell, William J.L. Sladen, and David G. Ainley, 'Dr George Murray Levick (1876–1956): Unpublished Notes on the Sexual Habits of the Adélie Penguin', *Polar Record*, Vol. 48, No. 4, 2012, pp. 387–93.
6. See, for example, William A. Haddad, Ryan Reisinger, Tristan Scott, Marthán Bester, and P.J. Nico de Bruyn, 'Multiple Occurrences of King Penguin (*Aptenodytes patagonicus*) Sexual Harassment by Antarctic Fur Seals (*Arctocephalus gazella*)', *Polar Biology*, Vol. 38, No. 5, 2015, pp. 741–46.
7. C.W. Moeliker, 'The First Case of Homosexual Necrophilia in the Mallard *Anas platyrhynchos* (Aves: Anatidae)', *Deinsea*, Vol. 8, 2001, pp. 243–47.
8. Exodus, 20:13, Deuteronomy, 5:17.
9. These and other points of interpretation are discussed by Sanford Levinson, 'On Interpretation: The Adultery Clause of the Ten Commandments', *Southern California Law Review*, Vol. 58, 1985, pp. 719–25.
10. Leviticus 15:19–30; 18:19; 20:18.
11. Exodus, 13:3; 20:12, Deuteronomy, 16:3.
12. Tanners and skin-lighteners aside.
13. As distinct from the kind of love that usually exists between family members other than spouses. (Of course, romantic love between siblings, or between parents and children, might be possible. I shall say more about this below.) The addition of 'romantic' might seem like an *ad hoc* condition to rule out much (even if not all) incest. However, it may be reasonable to think that sex is a suitable expression of one kind of love but not of another.
14. Vincent Punzo, *Reflective Naturalism: An Introduction to Moral Philosophy* (New York: Macmillan, 1969), p. 198.
15. I am not denying that some people might have equal romantic love for more than one person. However, this phenomenon seems rare and it is difficult to imagine that undiminished love for increasing romantic partners could stretch as far as undiminished love for increasing numbers of children. It is easy to understand equal love for six or seven children but not for an equivalent number of romantic partners. Perhaps that is attributable to a failure of imagination. On the other hand, because of the dangers of self-deception, we cannot simply take at face value the self-reports of those who claim to be able to romantically love six or seven people equally.
16. It is interesting that many of those who take paedophilia to be harmful do not have the same reprobation for sex between two people both of whom are (in the relevant sense) children.

17. Alfred Kinsey, Wardell B. Pomeroy, Clyde E. Martin, and Paul H. Gebhard, *Sexual Behavior in the Human Female* (Philadelphia: W.B. Saunders Co., 1953), pp. 120–21; Robert Ehman, 'Adult–child sex', in *Philosophy and Sex*, new rev. ed., edited by Robert Baker and Frederick Elliston (Buffalo, NY: Prometheus Books, 1984), p. 436; Igor Primoratz, *Ethics and Sex* (London: Routledge, 1999), p. 138. When I presented this argument at a conference, one commentator claimed that there is much evidence to suggest that the harm does not result from the taboo. In support of this claim, she cited Anna Luise Kirkengen's *Inscribed Bodies: Health Impact of Childhood Sexual Abuse* (Dordrecht: Kluwer, 2001). I, however, am unable to find any support for her claim in this work. The book does deal with the adverse effects of sexual interactions with children. However, the question whether it is the sexual interactions themselves or the taboos against them that cause harm, is a specialized question that, as far as I can tell, is not addressed in this book. I mention the source in fairness to my commentator and for the benefit of those readers who wish to examine it for themselves.

18. Allen Buchanan has argued, in the context of a different debate, that the 'morality of inclusion' requires that cooperative frameworks be made more inclusive where this is possible without unreasonable cost. (See his 'The Morality of Inclusion', *Social Philosophy and Policy*, Vol. 10, No. 2, 1993, pp. 233–57.) Notice that even those ways of satisfying paedophilic preferences that do not involve actual children—such as child pornography that is either synthesized (that is, without using real models or actors) or is produced by adults being represented as children—are also abhorred, even where adult pornography is not. This suggests that the common abhorrence of paedophilia is not fully explained by the harm it is believed to do to the children involved.

19. That is, until the taboos can be eliminated.

20. T.G.M. Sandfort, 'The argument for adult–child sexual contact: A critical appraisal and new data', in *The Sexual Abuse of Children: Theory and Research*, Vol. 1, edited by William O'Donohue and James H. Geer (Hillsdale, NJ: Lawrence Erlbaum Associates, 1992), pp. 38–48; Bruce Rind, Philip Tromovitch, and Robert Bauserman, 'A Meta-Analytic Examination of Assumed Properties of Child Sexual Abuse Using College Samples', *Psychological Bulletin*, Vol. 124, No. 1, 1998, pp. 22–53.

21. See, for example, David Finkelhor, 'What's Wrong with Sex between Adults and Children: Ethics and the Problem of Sexual Abuse', *American Journal of Orthopsychiatry*, Vol. 49, No. 4, 1979, pp. 692–97.

22. This objection was raised by an anonymous reviewer for *Public Affairs Quarterly*, in which journal I published a paper on the significance and casual views.

23. Child liberationist views reject paternalistic interference with children (beyond the very earliest years) in just the way that liberals reject paternalistic interference with competent adults.

24. In an earlier paper on this topic, I used the example of a tomato rather than an orange. In a response to that paper Fiona Woollard wondered 'why a tomato has been chosen'. She says that it conjures up images of dissatisfied theatre audiences throwing rotten tomatoes at incompetent performers, and suggests there is an 'apparent lightheartedness' to the example. I was dumbfounded by this response to the example, as I had no humorous intent and never thought of rotten tomatoes. In fact, I was trying to choose an innocuous example. I can only hope that oranges do not trigger other associations I do not have in mind. If they do trigger such associations, choose any fruit, vegetable, or other food that you do take to be innocuous.

25. That person may not know that the party with whom they are having sex is married. When sex is casual that ignorance is more likely.

26. Or *all* parties if there are more than two parties to a marriage.

27. Diogenes Laertius, *Lives of Eminent Philosophers*, Book VI: 69, edited and translated by Stephen White (Cambridge: Cambridge University Press, 2020), p. 250.

28. It is not uncommon these days to use the term 'masturbation' more generally to include the manual stimulation of another's genitals—hence the phrase 'mutual masturbation'. Once a second party is involved, then the significance view's implications seem clear (at least if we assume that mutual masturbation counts as 'sex'—masturbation is permissible only if it is an expression of mutual romantic love.

29. Perhaps this is the source of the humour behind Woody Allen's quip as Alvy in *Annie Hall*: 'Hey, don't knock masturbation. It's sex with someone I love'.

30. Peter Singer, for example, has defended bestiality. See his 'Heavy petting', *Prospect Magazine*, 20 April 2001, https://www.prospectmagazine.co.uk/magazine/heavypetting (accessed 29 April 2019).

31. Of course, such benefits would have to be offset against the risks of sexually transmitted diseases, or steps would have to be taken within a sexual life governed by the casual view to minimize such risks.
32. In this context, 'like' cannot mean 'sexually attracted to' because that would be too weak to differentiate it from the pure hedonist view. Instead it would have to mean something like 'have psychological affections-less-than-love for'.
33. I am grateful to Raja Halwani for putting this to me, and for suggesting that I raise and respond to the possibility of a non-hybrid intermediate view.
34. This appears not to be true of the promiscuous, unless one stipulates that anybody with whom one has sex is thereby an intimate.
35. This view was suggested to me by an anonymous reviewer for *Public Affairs Quarterly*, the journal in which I first wrote about these matters.
36. Fiona Woollard, 'Promiscuity, Pedophilia, Rape and the Significance of the Sexual', *Public Affairs Quarterly*, Vol. 33, No. 2, April 2019, pp. 137–58. In this article she responds to an earlier article of mine in which I first presented the significance and casual views. See David Benatar, 'Promiscuity, Pedophilia, and Rape: Two Views of Sexual Ethics', *Public Affairs Quarterly*, Vol. 16, No. 3, 2002, pp. 191–201.
37. Fiona Woollard, 'Promiscuity, Pedophilia, Rape and the Significance of the Sexual', p. 150.
38. Ibid, p. 152.
39. Ibid, p. 153.
40. Ibid.
41. Ibid.
42. Ibid.
43. There are complexities here. Sometimes force-feeding may have a benevolent motive even if it is also disrespectful in violating somebody's autonomy. Shimon Glick makes an argument for force-feeding on the basis of a benevolent motive. See Shimon M. Glick, 'Unlimited Human Autonomy—A Cultural Bias?', *New England Journal of Medicine*, Vol. 336, No. 13, 27 March 1997, pp. 954–56.
44. Fiona Woollard, 'Promiscuity, Pedophilia, Rape and the Significance of the Sexual', p. 150.
45. She does not comment on bestiality and necrophilia, probably because I had not discussed these practices in the earlier paper to which she was responding.
46. Fiona Woollard, 'Promiscuity, Pedophilia, Rape and the Significance of the Sexual', p. 148.
47. Some versions of the anti-reproductive view would be more demanding than this.
48. I have defended the anti-natalist view at length, mainly in *Better Never to Have Been: The Harm of Coming into Existence* (Oxford: Oxford University Press, 2006), but also in various articles and in *The Human Predicament: A Candid Guide to Life's Biggest Questions* (New York: Oxford University Press, 2017). There I defend what I call 'philanthropic' arguments for anti-natalism. I've also advanced a misanthropic version in 'The misanthropic argument for anti-natalism', in *Permissible Progeny?* edited by Sarah Hannan, Samantha Brennan, and Richard Vernon (New York: Oxford University Press, 2015), pp. 34–64.
49. There is also *almost* no chance of a pregnant woman who has sex becoming pregnant again, although there are some very rare cases of what is called 'superfetation'. The reproductive view also rules out sexual activity other than penile-vaginal intercourse, but that implication will be less worrying for at least some advocates of the reproductive view.
50. Michael Levin borrows this conception of a function from Larry Wright. Michael Levin, 'Homosexuality, Abnormality, and Civil Rights', *Public Affairs Quarterly*, Vol. 10, No. 1, 1996, p. 32.
51. Michael Levin, 'Why Homosexuality Is Abnormal', *Monist*, Vol. 67, No, 2, April 1984, p. 261.
52. When I say that women *can* 'gain fulfilment from procreation because there is typically something that it feels like for a woman to gestate a child', I am not claiming that women always gain fulfilment from procreation. A woman who has some of her ova harvested, ova that are then (especially without her knowledge) fertilized and implanted in another woman, does not have any gestational or procreational experience (that a man could not also have).
53. Although it is unclear what desire Michael Levin had in mind, there is some reason to think that it is the desire for sexual satisfaction. This is because he compares the exclusive homosexual with the celibate priest, but not with other (voluntarily or involuntarily) childless people. Curiously, he says that his view is compatible with celibate priests not being unhappy. This, he says is because they 'deny themselves as part of a higher calling which yields compensating satisfactions'. ('Why Homosexuality Is Abnormal', p. 271.)

54. It could also be advanced against sex exclusively with pre-pubescent children, but I shall focus on bestiality and necrophilia in this discussion.
55. For example, this argument was advanced in an amicus brief by the states of Alabama, South Carolina, and Utah to the United States Supreme Court in the case of *Lawrence v Texas*. The authors of the brief were writing in support of a Texas anti-sodomy law. There are also many jurisdictions that include prohibitions on bestiality and sodomy in the same sections of the penal code, thereby suggesting some kind of equivalence. See Lucas Paoli Itaborahy and Jingshu Zhu, *State-Sponsored Homophobia: A World Survey of Laws: Criminalisation, Protection and Recognition of Same-Sex Love*, 8th ed. (N.p.: International Lesbian Gay Bisexual Trans and Intersex Association, May 2013).
56. See David Benatar, 'Homosexuality, bestiality, and necrophilia', in *Palgrave Handbook of Sexual Ethics*, edited by David Boonin (Cham, Switzerland: Palgrave Macmillan, 2022), pp. 223-31.
57. According to one quip, the 'ethics of incest is all relative'. According to another quip, 'incest is a game for the whole family'. The word 'incest', like the word 'family', is ambiguous. Just how distant must a biological relationship be before it ceases to count as incest? Some think that sex between cousins counts as incest, but others do not. These issues need not be resolved here. For the purposes of this discussion we can focus on paradigmatic cases, which arguably include sex between siblings, and between parents and children.
58. See Jonathan Haidt, *The Righteous Mind: Why Good People Are Divided by Politics and Religion* (New York: Vintage Books, 2012), pp. 45-47.
59. I say 'in most cases' because even those who take the neutral view can accept that there are some circumstances in which sex ought not to be reproductive. These would be cases in which the offspring would suffer or be at risk of suffering an unusually severe harm.
60. The corresponding casual views would a denial that casual sex is either (a) moral defect, or (b) less than ideal.

Chapter 3

1. Jonathan Franzen, 'Carbon capture', *New Yorker*, Vol. 91, No. 7, 6 April 2015, p. 61.
2. I am not claiming that prudential considerations cannot also happen to be moral ones. However, moral considerations extend well beyond prudential considerations to the impact that one's actions have on others.
3. J.R. McNeill, *Something New under the Sun* (New York: W.W. Norton and Company, 2000).
4. My focus will be on the global environment, but some of what I shall say will also apply to (merely) local pollution.
5. They may also have environmental duties not to create too many (even low-level) carbon emitters, but I shall say more about this below.
6. I am not saying that the absence of these beings would be bad. Indeed, I think the opposite. It would better if there were no sentient life on earth (David Benatar, *Better Never to Have Been* [Oxford: Oxford University Press, 2006]). When I say that there would be no life on earth without CO_2, I am merely making a descriptive claim.
7. The term 'biosphere' can be used in somewhat different senses, but this literal sense is reasonable. It is also the sense in which Tyler Volk uses the term. See CO_2 *Rising* (Cambridge: MIT Press, 2008), p. 208n2.
8. For more on the carbon cycle, see Tyler Volk, CO_2 *Rising*.
9. Holli Riebeek, 'The carbon cycle', Earth Observatory, 16 June 2011, https://earthobservatory.nasa.gov/features/CarbonCycle/page1.php (accessed 24 December 2020).
10. Hundreds of millions of years ago, the levels of atmospheric CO_2 were much higher than they are today. These gradually reduced. They were at their lowest levels during the Ice Age.
11. IPCC Core Writing Team, R.K. Pachauri, and L.A. Meyer, eds., *Climate Change 2014: Synthesis Report: Contribution of Working Groups I, II and III to the Fifth Assessment Report of the Intergovernmental Panel on Climate Change* (Geneva, Switzerland, 2014), pp. 3, 45.
12. A.J. McMichael, *Planetary Overload* (Cambridge: Cambridge University Press, 1993), p. 136; 'Carbon dioxide in Earth's atmosphere', Wikipedia, https://en.wikipedia.org/wiki/Carbon_dioxide_in_Earth's_atmosphere (accessed 23 December 2020).
13. Daily updated levels can be found here: https://www.co2.earth (accessed 12 September 2023).
14. Erle Ellis, *Anthropocene* (Oxford: Oxford University Press, 2018), p. 66.

NOTES 385

15. A.J. McMichael, *Planetary Overload*, p. 138.
16. Mike Berners-Lee, *How Bad Are Bananas? The Carbon Footprint of Everything* (London: Profile Books, 2010), p. 2.
17. More precisely 1.2 degree centigrade. '2020 tied for warmest year on record, NASA analysis shows', Goddard Institute for Space Studies, National Aeronautics and Space Administration, 14 January 2021, https://www.giss.nasa.gov/research/news/20210114/ (accessed 17 January 2021).
18. IPCC Core Writing Team, R.K. Pachauri, and L.A. Meyer, eds., *Climate Change 2014: Synthesis Report*, p. 63. The prognosis according to the Sixth Assessment Report is not better. See V. Masson-Delmotte et al, eds., IPCC: Summary for Policymakers. In: *Climate Change 2021: The Physical Science Basis: Contribution of Working Group I to the Sixth Assessment Report of the Intergovernmental Panel on Climate Change* (Cambridge: Cambridge University Press, 2021), p. 17.
19. Malte Meinshausen et al, 'The RCP Greenhouse Gas Concentrations and Their Extensions from 1765 to 2300', *Climate Change*, Vol. 109, 2011, p. 233.
20. Tyler Volk, CO_2 *Rising*, p. 159.
21. Henry Fountain, Blacki Migliozzi, and Nadja Popovich, 'Where 2020's record heat was felt the most', *New York Times*, 14 January 2021, https://www.nytimes.com/interactive/2021/01/14/climate/hottest-year-2020-global-map.html (accessed 15 January 2021); 'Verkhoyansk', *Wikipedia*, https://en.wikipedia.org/wiki/Verkhoyansk#Climate (accessed 17 January 2021).
22. This is already happening. See IPCC Core Writing Team, R.K. Pachauri, and L.A. Meyer, eds., *Climate Change 2014: Synthesis Report*, pp. 16, 62, 74.
23. 'Tropical cyclones and climate change', *Wikipedia*, https://en.wikipedia.org/wiki/Tropical_cyclones_and_climate_change (accessed 27 December 2020).
24. Mark Maslin, *A Very Short Introduction to Global Warming*, 2nd ed. (Oxford: Oxford University Press, 2009), pp. 86–87.
25. Ibid, p. 90.
26. Ibid, p. 96.
27. Ibid, p. 90. The 2014 Intergovernmental Panel on Climate Change report says that it 'is very likely that human influence has [already] contributed to the observed global scale changes in frequency and intensity of daily temperature extremes since the mid-20th century'. IPCC Core Writing Team, R.K. Pachauri, and L.A. Meyer, eds., *Climate Change 2014: Synthesis Report*, pp. 7–8.
28. This is already happening and is projected to continue. See IPCC Core Writing Team, R.K. Pachauri, and L.A. Meyer, eds., *Climate Change 2014: Synthesis Report*, pp. 41, 12 respectively.
29. Ibid, p. 12.
30. Mark Maslin, *A Very Short Introduction to Global Warming*, pp. 116–18.
31. Barbara Neumann, Athanasios T. Vafeidis, Juliane Zimmermann, and Robert J. Nicholls, 'Future Coastal Population Growth and Exposure to Sea-Level Rise and Coastal Flooding—A Global Assessment', *PLoS One*, Vol. 10, No. 3, 11 March 2015, e0118571. https://doi.org.10.1371/journal.pone.0118571, pp. 10–11.
32. A.J. McMichael, *Planetary Overload*, pp. 144–49.
33. Ibid, pp. 152–59; Tony McMichael, *Human Frontiers, Environments and Disease*, (Cambridge: Cambridge University Press, 2001), pp. 300–303.
34. A.J. McMichael, *Planetary Overload*, p. 159.
35. IPCC Core Writing Team, R.K. Pachauri, and L.A. Meyer, eds., *Climate Change 2014: Synthesis Report*, p. 69.
36. Qi Zhao et al, 'Global, Regional, and National Burden of Mortality Associated with Non-Optimal Ambient Temperatures from 2000 to 2019: A Three-Stage Modelling Study', *Lancet Planetary Health*, Vol. 5, No. 7, July 2021, pp. e415–25.
37. Antonio Gasparrini et al, 'Projections of Temperature-Related Excess Mortality under Climate Change Scenarios', *Lancet Planetary Health*, Vol. 1, No. 9, 2017, pp. e360–67.
38. Moreover, the world's poorer people, who emit carbon at low levels *per capita* and who lack the resources to respond to temperature extremes, live disproportionately in hotter parts of the world, which will become even hotter.
39. IPCC Core Writing Team, R.K. Pachauri, and L.A. Meyer, eds., *Climate Change 2014: Synthesis Report*, p. 69.
40. Tony McMichael, *Human Frontiers, Environments and Disease*, pp. 303–4.
41. 'Carbon dioxide in the Earth's atmosphere', *Wikipedia*.

42. See, for example, John Cook, Naomi Oreskes, Peter T. Doran, et al, 'Consensus on Consensus: A Synthesis of Consensus Estimates on Human-Caused Global Warming', *Environmental Research Letters*, Vol. 11, 2006, 048002.
43. William R.L. Anderegg, James W. Prall, Jacob Harold, and Stephen H. Schneider, 'Expert Credibility in Climate Change', *Proceedings of the National Academy of Sciences*, Vol. 107, No. 27, 6 July 2010, pp. 12107–9.
44. IPCC Core Writing Team, R.K. Pachauri, and L.A. Meyer, eds., *Climate Change 2014: Synthesis Report*, p. 37.
45. Ibid, p. 5.
46. Ibid, p. 8.
47. H.-O. Pörtner et al, eds., *Climate Change 2022: Impacts, Adaptation and Vulnerability: Contribution of Working Group II to the Sixth Assessment Report of the Intergovernmental Panel on Climate Change* (Cambridge; New York: Cambridge University Press, 2022), p. 148.
48. David Michaels, *Doubt Is Their Product: How Industry's Assault on Science Damages Your Health* (New York: Oxford University Press, 2008), pp. 197–202.
49. There would also be implications for incest, discussed in Chapter 2. If one accepts both the metaphysical and conceptual claims then incest could *never* harm the resulting child, even if it causes that child to have serious birth defects that some different child would not have had.
50. I have said more about these lines of argument in *Better Never to Have Been*, pp. 20–22.
51. Simo Kyllönen makes this point. 'Climate Change, No-Harm Principle, and Moral Responsibility of Individual Emitters', *Journal of Applied Philosophy*, Vol. 35, No. 4, November 2018, p. 739. However, he attributes the point to John Broome, *Climate Matters: Ethics in a Warming World* (New York: W.W. Norton & Company, 2012).
52. Nick Watts et al, 'The 2020 Report of the *Lancet* Countdown on Health and Climate Change: Responding to Converging Crises', *Lancet*, Vol. 397, 9 January 2021, pp. 129–70.
53. It does seem to be true, however, that the *worst* effects of global warming and climate change will only be experienced in the further future to people who do not yet exist.
54. This argument has been advanced most famously by Walter Sinnott-Armstrong, 'It's not my fault: Global warming and individual moral obligations', in *Perspectives on Climate Change*, edited by W. Sinnott-Armstrong and R. Howarth (Amsterdam: Elsevier, 2005), pp. 221–53. See also Ewan Kingston and Walter Sinnott-Armstrong, 'What's Wrong with Joyguzzling?', *Ethical Theory and Moral Practice*, Vol. 21, 2018, pp. 169–86.
55. Derek Parfit, *Reasons and Persons* (Oxford: Clarendon Press, 1984), pp. 78–82.
56. Dale Jamieson notes, correctly, that '[c]ontributing to an outcome is not the same as causing it'. *Reason in a Dark Time* (New York: Oxford University Press, 2014), p. 181.
57. Tyler Volk, CO_2 *Rising*, pp. 30, 33–43.
58. Dale Jamieson, 'When Utilitarians Should Be Virtue Theorists', *Utilitas*, Vol. 19, No. 2, 2007, pp. 160–83.
59. Stan Eales, *Earthtoons: The First Book of Eco-Humor* (New York: Warner Books, 1991). (No page number.)
60. Ibid.
61. One way to neutralize the slurs that others direct towards one, is to employ them oneself.
62. It is not even possible by killing oneself, because one's subsequent decomposition—and worse still, cremation—involve greenhouse gas emissions. To be sure, those emissions would certainly be offset by the prevention of one's subsequent emissions if one had continued living. However, attaining zero emissions is also not necessary or even desirable—as I shall now explain in the main text.
63. As noted earlier, some emissions of previously sequestered carbon—via volcanic activity, for example—are not anthropogenic. However, the rate at which is this occurs has not led to overall accumulation of atmospheric greenhouse gases to anything like the extent that anthropogenic emissions have.
64. Donald J. DePaolo, 'Sustainable Carbon Emissions: The Geologic Perspective', *MRS Energy and Sustainability: A Review Journal*, Vol. 2, 2015, p. 10.
65. Sequestering is a matter of degree. If, for example, one burns a tree, the carbon released had been sequestered in the wood. That level of sequestering is not nearly as secure and enduring as carbon in deep earth and marine sediment.
66. John Nolt, 'The Individual's Obligation to Relinquish Unnecessary Greenhouse-Gas-Emitting Devices', *Philosophy and Public Issues* (New Series), Vol. 3, No. 1, 2013, pp. 139–65; Simo Kyllönen, 'Climate Change, No-Harm Principle, and Moral Responsibility of Individual Emitters', pp. 737–58.

67. John Nolt, 'The Individual's Obligation to Relinquish Unnecessary Greenhouse-Gas-Emitting Devices'.
68. In some circumstances 'necessary emissions' and 'sustainable emissions' might be equivalent, but they are not necessarily so. Necessary emissions may be lower than sustainable ones. There is also a possible world—much more heavily populated than ours—in which the sustainable level of emission is lower than the level that is 'necessary'. This is the situation in which the population exceeds the earth's carrying capacity. In such a circumstance it would be implausible to say that individuals were duty bound to reduce their emissions to 'sub-necessary' levels.
69. Walter Sinnott-Armstrong, 'It's not my fault: Global warming and individual moral obligations'. See also Ewan Kingston and Walter Sinnott-Armstrong, 'What's wrong with joyguzzling?'.
70. Derek Parfit, *Reasons and Persons*, pp. 78–82.
71. Jonathan Glover, 'It Makes No Difference Whether or Not I Do It', *Proceedings of the Aristotelian Society, Supplementary Volumes*, Vol. 49, 1975, pp. 171–90.
72. Ibid, pp. 174–75.
73. There are cases in which you might bring about somebody's death entirely innocently. (For example, without your knowledge, somebody wires up your light switch to a remote explosive device. You turn on the light and somebody is killed by the resultant explosion.) In such cases, you are not morally responsible for the death even if you were the proximate cause of it.
74. In the case of the bandits, their fair share of the villagers' beans is zero.
75. In addition to the difference to which I point in the main text, there are some others too: (a) the bandits are a coordinated group acting in concert, whereas the damage caused to the environment is typically the result of a large number of individuals acting alone rather than in concert; (b) the contribution that each bandit makes to the resultant harm is part of a straightforward causal chain and linear process, whereas the contribution made by each emitter to the environment is part of a highly complex set of systems—even if emissions are linear, the effects are not.
76. To the extent that they do not all *willingly* accept the proposal, but are under the influence of coercive pressures, they are not all equally responsible.
77. The officer who gives the order to fire would also bear responsibility, as would those who ordered the execution.
78. Mike Berners-Lee, *How Bad Are Bananas?*, pp. 131–32.
79. Ryan Darr argues that common-sense morality can account for the climate-related duties of individuals better than others have recognized. ('Climate Change and Common-Sense Moral Responsibility', *Environmental Ethics*, Vol. 39, Spring 2017, pp. 21–38.) He uses the case of tax evasion and argues that even if one's own evasion of taxes would make only a miniscule difference, one still has a moral duty to pay one's taxes. However, what he fails to recognize is that tax evasion is a case of free-riding rather than what I shall be calling 'rare-fare-riding'. It is thus not analogous to whatever duties individuals may have regarding their emissions in the absence of a cooperative scheme.
80. Anja Karnein has argued that we can sometimes even have a duty to 'take up the slack' created by others not doing their fair share. ('Putting Fairness in Its Place', *Journal of Philosophy*, Vol. 111, No. 11, 2014, pp. 593–607.) However, even she does not think that we are *always* required to take up the slack. I have said why I think an individual's duties are limited in the absence of a cooperative scheme, but I shall not render explicit why these reasons make an individual's environmental duties fall outside Professor Karnein's account of when we are required to take up the slack created by others not doing their duties.
81. All data in this paragraph are for 2018 and are drawn from the Global Carbon Atlas, http://www.globalcarbonatlas.org/en/CO2-emissions (accessed 19 January 2021). I have cited the consumption rates rather than the production rates, because the former better captures the carbon footprint of individuals in each of the countries.
82. IPCC Core Writing Team, R.K. Pachauri, and L.A. Meyer, eds., *Climate Change 2014: Synthesis Report*, p. 63.
83. https://trillionthtonne.org (accessed 15 January 2021). Website no longer available.
84. Bastien Girod, Detlef Peter van Vuuren, and Edgar Hertwich, 'Global Climate Targets and Future Consumption Level: An Evaluation of the Required GHG Intensity', *Environmental Research Letters*, Vol. 8, No. 2, 2013, pp. 1–10.
85. Data in this paragraph are for 2018 and are drawn from the Global Carbon Atlas, http://www.globalcarbonatlas.org/en/CO2-emissions (accessed 19 January 2021).

86. Seth Wynes and Kimberly A. Nicholas, 'The Climate Mitigation Gap: Education and Government Recommendations Miss the Most Effective Individual Actions', *Environmental Research Letters*, Vol. 12, 2017, pp. 1–9.
87. Assuming that a '500-milliliter ... plastic bottle of water has a total carbon footprint equal to 82.8 grams ... of carbon dioxide'. Marie-Luise Blue, 'What is the carbon footprint of a plastic bottle?', Updated 11 June 2018, https://sciencing.com/carbon-footprint-plastic-bottle-12307187.html (accessed 20 January 2021).
88. Mike Berners-Lee, *How Bad Are Bananas?*, p. 18.
89. Different flight carbon calculators provide somewhat different estimates of the emission levels of the same route. My calculation is based on the estimate of Carbon Footprint's Carbon Calculator https://www.carbonfootprint.com/calculator.aspx (accessed 20 January 2021).
90. Valentina Bisinella, Paola Federica Albizzati, Thomas Fruergaard Astrup, and Anders Damgaard, eds., *Life Cycle Assessment of Grocery Carrier Bags* (Copenhagen: The Danish Environmental Protection Agency, 2018).
91. John Tierney, 'Recycling is garbage', *New York Times*, 30 June 1996, https://www.nytimes.com/1996/06/30/magazine/recycling-is-garbage.html (accessed 20 January 2021); John Tierney, 'The reign of recycling', *New York Times*, 3 October 2015, https://www.nytimes.com/2015/10/04/opinion/sunday/the-reign-of-recycling.html (accessed 6 October 2015); Geraldine Sealey, 'Is recycling worth the trouble, cost?', *ABC News*, 7 January 2006, https://abcnews.go.com/US/story?id=91824&page=1 (accessed 19 January 2021); Earth Talk, 'Is recycling worth it?', *Scientific American*, 5 October 2015, https://www.scientificamerican.com/article/is-recycling-worth-it/ (accessed 19 January 2021).
92. Ibid.
93. See, for example, Anthony J. McMichael, John W Powles, Colin D Butler, and Ricardo Uauy, 'Food, Livestock Production, Energy, Climate Change, and Health', *Lancet*, Vol. 370, 6 October 2007, pp. 1253–63. See especially p. 1258.
94. Center for Sustainable Systems, University of Michigan. 'Carbon footprint factsheet'. Pub. No. CSS09-05, 2020.
95. Peter Scarborough et al, 'Dietary Greenhouse Gas Emissions of Meat-Eaters, Fish-Eaters, Vegetarians and Vegans in the UK', *Climate Change*, Vol. 125, 2014, pp. 179–92. The mean daily greenhouse gas emissions are adjusted for age and sex. The annual figures are my calculations from the daily data, with rounding to the first decimal point.
96. Cited by Peter Scarborough et al, 'Dietary Greenhouse Gas Emissions of Meat-Eaters, Fish-Eaters, Vegetarians and Vegans in the UK', p. 186.
97. William Todts, ed., 'CO_2 Emissions from Cars: The Facts', European Federation for Transportation and Environment, 2018, p. 31. The larger size of cars can be (partially) offset by greater fuel efficiency technology. However, if car size had not increased while fuel-efficiency improved, the carbon impact would have been lower. Larger cars also pose a greater risk to pedestrians and cyclists, and exacerbate congestion. (Ibid, p. 34.)
98. 'UK briefing: The plug-in hybrid con', September 2020, https://te-cdn.ams3.digitaloceanspaces.com/files/2020_09_UK_briefing_The_plug-in_hybrid_con.pdf (accessed 20 May 2024), p. 2. This source cites 164 gCO_2 per kilometre for diesel-powered car and 167 gCO_2 per kilometre for a petrol-powered car.
99. Stacy C. Davis, Susan W. Diegel, and Robert G. Boundy, *Transportation Energy Data Book*, Edition 34 (Oak Ridge, TN: Oak Ridge National Laboratory, August 2015), pp. 11–13. The United States Environmental Protection Agency provides the figure of about 404g CO_2 per mile. https://www.epa.gov/greenvehicles/greenhouse-gas-emissions-typical-passenger-vehicle#pane-2 (accessed 25 January 2021). I have converted the *per mile* figures to *per kilometre*. This is explicitly a 'wheel to wheel' assessment. In other words, it counts not only tailpipe emissions but all emissions, including those associated with manufacture and repair. The UK report does not indicate whether it's assessment is 'wheel to wheel'. The US figure includes CO_2 from renewable sources, which is another confounder of the comparison.
100. In the following figure, the data for vehicle kilometres travelled per capita in each of the countries is estimated from Figure 3.4 in Liisa Ecola, Charlene Rohr, Johanna Zmud, Tobias Kuhnimhof, and Peter Phleps, *The Future of Driving in Developing Countries* (Santa Monica, CA: Institute for Mobility Research, Rand Corporation, 2014), p. 19. In some cases, this data differs from other sources. See, for example, 'Sectoral profile—transport', Odyssee-Mure, https://www.odyssee-mure.eu/publications/efficiency-by-sector/transport/distance-travelled-by-car.html (accessed 25 January 2021).

NOTES 389

101. Lindsay Wilson, 'Shades of green: Electric cars' carbon emissions around the globe', Shrink That Footprint, February 2013, p. 5.
102. Lindsay Wilson, 'Shades of green: Electric cars' carbon emissions around the globe', p. 11.
103. Ryuji Kawamoto et al, 'Estimation of CO_2 Emissions of Internal Combustion Engine Vehicle and Battery Electric Vehicle Using LCA', *Sustainability*, Vol. 11, 2019, p. 9.
104. Ibid, pp. 1–15.
105. Lindsay Wilson, 'Shades of green: Electric cars' carbon emissions around the globe', pp. 6–7.
106. Ibid, p. 14.
107. Ibid. Mr. Wilson makes this claim specifically only about the United Kingdom and Germany, but based on his figures, the same can be inferred about the other countries I have mentioned.
108. Ibid, pp. 6–7.
109. William Todts, ed., 'CO_2 Emissions from Cars: The Facts', p. 19; Patrick Plötz et al, 'Empirical Fuel Consumption and CO2 Emissions of Plug-In Hybrid Electric Vehicles', *Journal of Industrial Ecology*, Vol. 22, No. 4, 2017, pp. 773–84; 'UK briefing: The plug-in hybrid con', September 2020, https://www.transportenvironment.org/sites/te/files/publications/2020_09_UK_briefing_The_plug-in_hybrid_con.pdf (accessed 21 January 2021) p. 1.
110. Hannah Ritchie, 'Climate change and flying: What share of global CO_2 emissions come from aviation?', *Our World in Data*, 22 October 2020, https://ourworldindata.org/co2-emissions-from-aviation (accessed 26 January 2021).
111. Ibid.
112. Center for Sustainable Systems, University of Michigan. 'Carbon footprint factsheet'. Pub. No. CSS09-05, 2020.
113. Different flight carbon calculators provide somewhat different estimates of the emission levels of the same route. My calculations are based on the estimates of Carbon Footprint's Carbon Calculator https://www.carbonfootprint.com/calculator.aspx (accessed 26 January 2021).
114. Hannah Ritchie, 'Which form of transport has the smallest carbon footprint', *Our World in Data*, 13 October 2020, https://ourworldindata.org/travel-carbon-footprint (accessed 25 January 2021).
115. Hannah Ritchie, 'Climate change and flying: What share of global CO_2 emissions come from aviation?'.
116. Robbert Kivits, Michael Charles, and Neal Ryan, 'A Post-Carbon Aviation Future: Airports and the Transition to a Cleaner Aviation Sector', *Futures*, Vol. 42, 2010, pp. 199–211.
117. Maggie Astor, 'Do airline climate offsets really work? Here's the good news, and the bad', *New York Times*, 18 May 2022, https://www.nytimes.com/2022/05/18/climate/offset-carbon-footprint-air-travel.html (accessed 19 May 2022).
118. Zeke Hausfather, 'Let's not pretend planting trees is a permanent climate solution', *New York Times*, 4 June 2022, https://www.nytimes.com/2022/06/04/opinion/environment/climate-change-trees-carbon-removal.html (accessed, 6 June 2022).
119. Seth Wynes and Kimberly A. Nicholas, 'The Climate Mitigation Gap: Education and Government Recommendations Miss the Most Effective Individual Actions', pp. 1–9.
120. Mike Berners-Lee, *How Bad Are Bananas?*, pp. 151–52.
121. Even if we apply a reasonable discount rate to each successive year of the created person's life, the impact will nonetheless be greater than any other greenhouse gas–emitting activity an ordinary individual would undertake. Moreover, it is not clear that any discounting is reasonable. We do not know whether emissions mitigation capacity will increase over the course of one's offspring's lifetime, or whether the emissions problem will instead become exacerbated.
122. Data are for 2018 and are drawn from the Global Carbon Atlas, http://www.globalcarbonatlas.org/en/CO2-emissions (accessed 27 January 2021).
123. But not entirely unproblematic, as I shall explain later.
124. For example, Mike Berners-Lee, whose estimates I have been considering in the previous few paragraphs. See *How Bad Are Bananas?*, pp. 151–52.
125. The same does not apply to adopted children.
126. More accurately, it 'typically takes at least two to procreate'. See below.
127. Paul A. Murtaugh and Michael G. Schlax, 'Reproduction and the Carbon Legacies of Individuals', *Global Environmental Change*, Vol. 19, 2009, pp. 14–20.
128. See David Benatar, *The Second Sexism: Discrimination against Men and Boys* (Malden, MA: Wiley-Blackwell, 2012), p. 140.
129. Paul A. Murtaugh and Michael G. Schlax, 'Reproduction and the Carbon Legacies of Individuals', pp. 14–20.

130. Ibid.
131. The terms 'subsistence' and 'luxury' emissions are Henry Shue's. ('Subsistence Emissions and Luxury Emissions', *Law and Policy*, Vol. 15, No. 1, January 1993, pp. 39–60.)
132. A similar point can be made about past procreation. If there were now only four billion people on the planet instead of nearly double that, the level to which an individual would need to reduce his emissions would be double what it currently is.
133. However, see below.
134. David Benatar, *Better Never to Have Been*; David Benatar, *The Human Predicament: A Candid Guide to Life's Biggest Questions* (New York: Oxford University Press, 2017).
135. See Chapter 6.
136. Those who think that the non-identity is insurmountable may have to acknowledge that the suffering, caused in thousands of years' time, may not harm anybody.
137. D. Kinley III, ed., *Chernobyl's Legacy: Health, Environmental and Socio-Economic Impacts*, 2nd rev. ed. (Vienna, Austria: International Atomic Energy Agency, April 2006).
138. Under some circumstances, having a companion animal can also have an impact on global emissions. This is especially true if one breeds the animal or purchases the animal from a breeder, and if one feeds the animal meat.

Chapter 4

1. IARC Monographs on the Evaluation of Carcinogenic Risks to Humans, *Vol 83: Tobacco Smoke and Involuntary Smoking* (Lyon, France: World Health Organization, 2004). This document differentiates different levels of evidence—sufficient evidence of carcinogenicity, limited evidence of carcinogenicity, inadequate evidence of carcinogenicity, and evidence suggesting a lack of carcinogenicity. I cite examples only of the first level.
2. The US Surgeon General's recent reports on the health consequences of smoking differentiate four different levels of strength of inference of a causal connection between smoking and a particular disease. Level 1 is evidence that is *sufficient* to infer a causal relationship. Level 2 is evidence that is *suggestive but not sufficient* to infer a causal relationship. Level 3 is evidence that is *inadequate* to infer the presence or absence of a causal relationship. Level 4 is evidence that is *suggestive of no causal relationship*. In what follows I only cite instances that meet Level 1.
3. U.S. Department of Health and Human Services, *The Health Consequences of Smoking: A Report of the Surgeon General* (Atlanta, GA: U.S. Department of Health and Human Services, Centers for Disease Control and Prevention, National Center for Chronic Disease Prevention and Health Promotion, Office on Smoking and Health, 2004), Chapter 3.
4. Ibid.
5. Ibid.
6. U.S. Department of Health and Human Services, *The Health Consequences of Smoking:50 Years of Progress: A Report of the Surgeon General* (Rockville, MD: Office of the Surgeon General, 2014), Chapter 7.
7. Ibid, Chapter 10.
8. U.S. Department of Health and Human Services, *The Health Consequences of Smoking: A Report of the Surgeon General*, Chapter 6.
9. U.S. Department of Health and Human Services, *The Health Consequences of Smoking: 50 Years of Progress: A Report of the Surgeon General*, Chapter 9.
10. Ibid.
11. Ibid, Chapter 7.
12. Ibid, Chapter 11.
13. Smoking is also often associated with sex, as this joke illustrates:

    Q: Do you smoke after sex?
    A: I don't know, I have never looked.

14. This condition is important but genuine consent is often very difficult to obtain. I say more about this later.
15. There may be exceptions, but those further rare complexities will not be discussed here.
16. I said more about this in the introduction to this book.

17. Maria Zafeiridou, Nicholas S Hopkinson, and Nikolas Voulvoulis, 'Cigarette Smoking: An Assessment of Tobacco's Global Environmental Footprint across Its Entire Supply Chain', *Environmental Science and Technology*, Vol. 52, No. 15, 2018, pp. 8087–94.
18. Helmut J. Geist, 'Global Assessment of Deforestation Related to Tobacco Farming', *Tobacco Control*, Vol. 8, No. 1, March 1999, pp. 18–28.
19. The discussions about causal inefficacy in Chapter 3, and about minor increases in risk, later in this chapter, are relevant here too.
20. The qualification 'just' is important. Perhaps those who want to see you squandering your money on cigarettes and then see you suffer and die have an interest in your taking up smoking. The tobacco companies certainly have an interest in your becoming a smoker. However, none of these seem to be moral reasons in favour of taking up smoking.
21. IARC Monographs on the Evaluation of Carcinogenic Risks to Humans, *Vol 83: Tobacco Smoke and Involuntary Smoking*, pp. 165, 167, 360, 363, 367, 557, 682, 876, 1181, 1182.
22. Prabhat Jha and Richard Peto, 'Global Effects of Smoking, of Quitting, and of Taxing Tobacco', *New England Journal of Medicine*, Vol. 370, No. 1, 2 January 2014, p. 63. This is not an argument for starting smoking but then quitting before one turns 40. This is because of how difficult it is to quit. It is far better never to begin in the first place.
23. What constitutes 'in the presence of non-smokers' can vary. I shall focus here on second-hand smoke—smoke that is breathed in by non-smokers. However, there is also the concept of third-hand smoke—'the invisible yet toxic brew of gases and particles clinging to smokers' hair and clothing, not to mention cushions and carpeting, that lingers long after second-hand smoke has cleared from a room', Roni Caryn Rabin, 'A new cigarette hazard: "Third-hand smoke"', *New York Times*, 3 January 2009, https://www.nytimes.com/2009/01/03/health/research/03smoke.html (accessed 10 February 2010).
24. Exhaled mainstream smoke is also filtered, for the passive smoker, by the smoker's lungs.
25. Mattias Öberg, Maritta S. Jaakkola, Alistair Woodward, Armando Perugga, and Annette Prüss-Ustün, 'Worldwide Burden of Disease from Exposure to Second-Hand Smoke: A Retrospective Analysis of Data', *Lancet*, Vol. 377, No. 9760, 8 January 2011, p. 139.
26. IARC Monographs on the Evaluation of Carcinogenic Risks to Humans, *Vol 83: Tobacco Smoke and Involuntary Smoking*, p. 1410.
27. Ibid.
28. Ibid, p. 1411.
29. U.S. Department of Health and Human Services, *The Health Consequences of Smoking: 50 Years of Progress: A Report of the Surgeon General*, Chapter 8.
30. A.J. Sasco, M.B. Secretan, and K. Straif, 'Tobacco Smoking and Cancer: A Brief Review of Recent Epidemiological Evidence', *Lung Cancer*, Vol. 45, S2, 2004, pp. S3–9. These authors indicate that smokers have a 15–30 times greater increase in risk. (See p. S4.) That amounts to a 1400% to 2900% increase.
31. James L. Repace, 'Risks of passive smoking', in *To Breath Freely: Risk, Consent, and Air*, edited by Mary Gibson (Totowa, NJ: Rowman & Allanheld, 1985), p. 23.
32. Giselle Salmasi, Rosheen Grady, Jennifer Jones, and Sarah D. McDonald, 'Environmental Tobacco Smoke Exposure and Perinatal Outcomes: A Systematic Review and Meta-analysis', *Acta Obstetricia et Gynecologica*, Vol. 89, 2010, pp. 423–41; Jo Leonardi-Bee, John Britton, and Andrea Venn, 'Second Smoke and Adverse Fetal Outcomes in Nonsmoking Pregnant Women: A Meta-analysis', *Pediatrics*, Vol. 127, No. 4, April 2011, pp. 734–41.
33. U.S. Department of Health and Human Services, *How Tobacco Smoke Causes Disease: The Biology and Behavioral Basis for Smoking-Attributable Disease: A Report of the Surgeon General* (Atlanta, GA: U.S. Department of Health and Human Services, Centers for Disease Control and Prevention, National Center for Chronic Disease Prevention and Health Promotion, Office on Smoking and Health, 2010), Chapter 8; U.S. Department of Health and Human Services, *A Report of the Surgeon General: How Tobacco Smoke Causes Disease: What It Means to You* (U.S. Department of Health and Human Services, Centers for Disease Control and Prevention, National Center for Chronic Disease Prevention and Health Promotion, Office on Smoking and Health, 2010), p. 13.
34. U.S. Department of Health and Human Services, *The Health Consequences of Smoking: 50 Years of Progress: A Report of the Surgeon General*, Chapter 9.
35. U.S. Department of Health and Human Services, *The Health Consequences of Smoking: A Report of the Surgeon General*, Chapter 4.
36. Ibid, Chapter 5.

37. The situation is a little different to the extent that a pregnant woman's smoking leads to a miscarriage. Whether this is a harm to the foetus does depend on whether it is morally considerable at the time of the miscarriage (or at the time of death, if that is prior to miscarriage). However, this is moot, given that one cannot tell in advance whether smoking will lead to miscarriage or instead to a defect in the child that develops from the foetus.
38. See, for example, Kevin Puzychki et al, 'Tobacco Smoke Exposure and Household Pets: A Systematic Literature Review Examining the Health Risk to Household Pets and New Indications of Exposed Pets Affecting Human Health', *International Public Health Journal*, Vol. 10, No. 1, 2018, pp. 11–24; Marchello Rodrigues Roza and Carlos Alberto Assis Viegas, 'The Dog as Passive Smoker: Effects of Exposure to Environmental Cigarette Smoke on Domestic Dogs', *Nicotine and Tobacco Research*, Vol. 9, No. 11, November 2007, pp. 1171–76; Elizabeth R. Bertone, Laura A. Snyder, and Antony S. Moore, 'Environmental Tobacco Smoke and Risk of Malignant Lymphoma in Pet Cats', *American Journal of Epidemiology*, Vol. 156, No. 3, 2002, pp. 268–73; Laura A. Snyder et al, 'p53 Expression and Environmental Tobacco Smoke Exposure in Feline Oral Squamous Cell Carcinoma', *Veterinary Pathology*, Vol. 41, 2004, pp. 209–41; Helen Roberts and Brian S. Palmeiro, 'Toxicology of Aquarium Fish', *Veterinary Clinics: Exotic Animal Practice*, Vol. 11, No. 2, 2008, p. 370; 'Be Smoke-Free and Help Your Pets Live Longer, Healthier Lives', US Food and Drug Administration, https://www.fda.gov/animal-veterinary/animal-health-literacy/be-smoke-free-and-help-your-pets-live-longer-healthier-lives#dog (accessed 17 July 2023).
39. See Chapter 6.
40. See the discussion of this in Chapter 3, about our environmental duties.
41. For more on this, see Chapter 3 on our environmental duties.
42. I acknowledge that cigarettes that are not smoked in proximity to non-smokers do nonetheless contribute toxic substances to the broader environment. However, their impact on the non-immediate environment is miniscule in comparison with the impact of cars on the broader environment.
43. Joel Feinberg, *Offense to Others* (New York: Oxford University Press, 1985), p. 58.
44. Ibid, pp. 57–60.
45. These are terms that Keith Butler uses to describe two kinds of unwanted effect of smoke on non-smokers. He says that the malodours are an 'annoyance' and that the 'short term physiological irritation of the eyes, nose, mouth, throat, and lungs caused by the inhalation of smoke' are an 'irritation'. (Keith Butler, 'The Moral Status of Smoking', *Social Theory and Practice*, Vol. 19, No. 1, Spring 1993, p. 6.)
46. Joel Feinberg, *Offense to Others*. Professor Feinberg's interest was in legal regulation of offensive conduct, but the considerations he adduces are also relevant to individuals considering what morality requires of them. He might not have agreed with everything I say about these considerations, but the broad thrust of what I say is, I think, congenial to his position.
47. Of course, some substantially other-regarding actions are beneficial to others. Those are typically not ones that cause offence. There are exceptions, but then all things are not equal.
48. 'Malice' or 'spite', according to Professor Feinberg.
49. John Stuart Mill, 'Of the liberty of thought and discussion', in *On Liberty and Other Essays* (Oxford: Oxford University Press, 1991).
50. Ibid, p. 40.
51. There may be scenarios in which things get 'worse'. Perhaps another of your companion animals is called 'Camilla' and you can occasionally be heard shouting at King Charles to 'stop humping Camilla'. My own recommendation in this case would be to let King Charles and Camilla enjoy themselves.
52. Perhaps some ways of naming animals—most likely as numbers—can negatively affect how we or others treat them. However, that sort of consideration aside, animals are unlikely to be affected by a name in the way that an ordinary human will be.
53. The conservative philosopher, Roger Scruton, named one of his pigs 'Singer' after the animal liberationist philosopher, Peter Singer. Professor Scruton served sausage made from 'Singer' to a journalist visiting his farm. See Sholto Byrnes, 'Roger Scruton: The patron saint of lost causes', *Independent*, 3 July 2005, https://www.independent.co.uk/arts-entertainment/books/features/roger-scruton-the-patron-saint-of-lost-causes-296509.html (accessed 1 April 2019). It is hard to say whether this was out of malice or humour (or malicious humour). Either way, it is unlikely that this would cause offence to Peter Singer, who would appropriately be more concerned about how the pig was treated.
54. Let us assume that in the dim light, one cannot reliably fish out ash-free punch.

55. For some people, it would make a difference whether they were wearing shoes. Others would prefer not to step in saliva even if they were wearing shoes, given that this could then be traipsed into the home.
56. Those who think it is, might want to consider spitting outdoors and farting, at least if both are done in the presence of others. In many societies, farting in the presence of others, even outdoors, is socially taboo to a degree that outdoor spitting in the presence of others is not. It is hard to justify that differential response, not least because spitting outdoors leaves a more enduring residue than outdoor farting.
57. It would not be fair to complain that including this particular social disvalue is double counting, given that we have already considered the health effects on individual smokers and those individual non-smokers in whose presence they smoke. This complaint would not be fair because those same facts are relevant both to the harm argument and to the offence argument.
58. See, for example, Thomas A. Hodgson, 'Cigarette Smoking and Lifetime Medical Expenditures', *Milbank Quarterly*, Vol. 70, No. 1, 1992, pp. 81–125 (which found that smokers account for greater healthcare costs over their lifetimes than do non-smokers) and Jan J. Barendregt, Luc Bonneux, and Paul J. van der Maas, 'The Health Care Costs of Smoking', *New England Journal of Medicine*, Vol. 337, No. 15, 9 October 1997, pp. 1052–57 (which found the opposite).
59. In a larger space with fewer people, non-smokers can move further away.
60. The fewer others who are smoking, the more likely the recusal of one smoker will be to influence the remaining ones.
61. *WHO Global Report on Trends in Prevalence of Tobacco Smoking 2000–2025*, 2nd ed. (Geneva: World Health Organization, 2018), p. 11.
62. Lora Jones, 'Vaping: The rise in five charts', BBC, 31 May 2018, https://www.bbc.com/news/business-44295336 (Accessed 4 April 2019).
63. They are also known as e-cigs, vapes, vape pens, e-hookahs, and either Electronic Nicotine Delivery Systems (ENDS) or Electronic Non-Nicotine Delivery Systems (ENNDS).
64. Oren Rom, Alessandra Pecorelli, Giuseppe Valacchi, and Abraham Z. Reznick, 'Are E-Cigarettes a Safe and Good Alternative to Cigarette Smoking?', *Annals of the New York Academy of Sciences*, Vol. 1340, 2014, p. 70.
65. Chitra Dinakar and George T. O'Connor, 'The Health Effects of Electronic Cigarettes', *New England Journal of Medicine*, Vol. 375, No. 14, 6 October 2016, p. 1374.
66. Ibid, p. 1379.
67. Ibid, p. 1375.
68. Ibid, p. 1374.
69. Ibid, p. 1378.
70. Jennifer Unger, 'E-Cigarettes: Introducing New Complexities and Controversies to the Field of Nicotine and Tobacco Research', *Nicotine and Tobacco Research*, Vol. 17, No. 10, 2015, pp. 1185–86; Stanton A. Glantz, 'Do Not Recommend Trying E-Cigarettes for Smoking Cessation', *New England Journal of Medicine*, Vol. 374, No. 22, 2 June 2016, pp. 2173–74.
71. Chitra Dinakar and George T. O'Connor, 'The Health Effects of Electronic Cigarettes', pp. 1373–74; Oren Rom et al, 'Are E-Cigarettes a Safe and Good Alternative to Cigarette Smoking?', pp. 68–69.
72. Sara Kalkhoran and Stanton A Glantz, 'E-Cigarettes and Smoking Cessation in Real-World and Clinical Settings: A Systematic Review and Meta-Analysis', *Lancet Respiratory Medicine*, Vol. 4, February 2016, pp. 116–28.
73. Steven L. Bernstein, 'Electronic Cigarettes: More Light, Less Heat Needed', *Lancet Respiratory Medicine*, Vol. 4, February 2016, p. 86.
74. Jan Czogala et al, 'Secondhand Exposure to Vapors from Electronic Cigarettes', *Nicotine and Tobacco Research*, Vol. 16, No. 6, June 2014, pp. 655–62.
75. Andreas D. Flouris et al, 'Acute Impact of Active and Passive Electronic Cigarette Smoking on Serum Cotinine and Lung Function', *Inhalation Toxicology*, Vol. 25, No. 2, 2013, pp. 91–101.
76. See, for example, Maciej Lukasz Goniewicz et al, 'Levels of Selected Carcinogens and Toxicants in Vapour from Electronic Cigarettes', *Tobacco Control*, Vol. 23, 2014, pp. 133–39.
77. World Health Organization, 'Electronic Nicotine Delivery Systems and Electronic Non-Nicotine Delivery Systems (ENDS/ENNDS), August 2016, p. 4, https://www.who.int/fctc/cop/cop7/FCTC_COP_7_11_EN.pdf (accessed 8 April 2019).
78. In the aptly titled *Miss Manners' Guide to Excruciatingly Correct Behavior*, Judith Martin cautions smokers: 'If you wish to smoke in the presence of clean people, you must ask their permission and be prepared to accept their refusal to grant it' (New York: Atheneum, 1982), p. 637.
79. See note 23 above about third-hand smoking.

80. Health Canada, *Tobacco Control Programme: Regulatory Proposal for Reducing Fire Risks from Cigarettes*, December 2002, p. 2.
81. David T. Butry, Jeffrey P. Prestemon, and Douglas S. Thomas, 'Investigation of the Decline in Reported Smoking-Caused Wildfires in the USA from 2000 to 2011', *International Journal of Wildland Fire*, Vol. 23, 2014, pp. 790–98.
82. Bruce N. Leistikow, Daniel C. Martin, and Christina E. Milano, 'Fire Injuries, Disasters, and Costs from Cigarettes and Cigarette Lights: A Global Overview', *Preventative Medicine*, Vol. 31, 2000, p. 91.
83. Health Canada, *Tobacco Control Programme: Regulatory Proposal for Reducing Fire Risks from Cigarettes*, p. 3.
84. Thomas E. Novotny, Kristen Lum, Elizabeth Smith, Vivian Wang, and Richard Barnes, 'Cigarette Butts and the Case for an Environmental Policy on Hazardous Cigarette Waste', *International Journal of Environmental Research and Public Health*, Vol. 6, 2009, p. 1693.
85. This is not ideal either, but at least it is better than littering.
86. Kathleen Register, 'Cigarette Butts as Litter—Toxic as Well as Ugly?', *Underwater Naturalist*, Vol. 25, No. 2, August 2000, p. 24.
87. Ocean Conservancy, *Building a Clean Swell: 2018 Report* (Washington, DC: Ocean Conservancy, 2018), p. 13.
88. Thomas E. Novotny et al, 'Cigarette Butts and the Case for an Environmental Policy on Hazardous Cigarette Waste', p. 1694; James Rainey, 'Plastic straw ban? Cigarette butts are the single greatest source of ocean trash', NBC News, 27 August 2018, https://www.nbcnews.com/news/us-news/plastic-straw-ban-cigarette-butts-are-single-greatest-source-ocean-n903661 (accessed 9 April 2019).
89. Kathleen Register, 'Cigarette Butts as Litter—Toxic as Well as Ugly?', p. 25.
90. J.P. Vakkalanka, L.S. Hardison Jr, and C.P. Holstege, 'Epidemiological Trends in Electronic Cigarette Exposures Reported to U.S. Poison Centers', *Clinical Toxicology*, Vol. 52, 2014, pp. 542–48.
91. Ji Won Kim and Carl R Baum, 'Liquid Nicotine Toxicity', *Pediatric Emergency Care*, Vol. 31, No. 7, July 2015, pp. 517–21.
92. King James I of England, 'A Counterblaste to Tobacco' (London: R. Barker, 1604), http://www.laits.utexas.edu/poltheory/james/blaste/blaste.html (accessed 4 February 2019).
93. The reasons for this should be obvious. They include the poorer-quality roads, road signals, the less safe cars, and the lesser enforcement of rules of the road, in the poorer countries.
94. International Traffic Safety and Data and Analysis Group, 'Road Safely Annual Report, 2018', Organization for Economic Co-operation and Development/International Transport Forum, 2018.
95. Ibid, p. 24.
96. That is 5 700 000 000 000 cigarettes.
97. Jeffrey Drope and Neil W. Schluger, eds., *The Tobacco Atlas*, 6th ed. (Atlanta: American Cancer Society, 2018), p. 22.
98. It is not obvious that the comparative metric should be kilometres driven compared to number of cigarettes smoked. Why must one kilometre be compared to one cigarette? However, no other comparison seems more obvious. Thus, it might be that we are attempting to compare risks that are not entirely commensurable.
99. Spencer L. James et al, 'Morbidity and Mortality from Road Injuries: Results from the Global Burden of Disease Study 2017', *Injury Prevention*, Vol. 26, 2020, pp. i46–i56.
100. Committee on Passive Smoking, Board on Environmental Studies and Toxicology, National Research Council, *Environmental Tobacco Smoke: Measuring Exposure and Assessing Health Effects* (Washington, DC: National Academy Press, 1986), p. 296. The variability is to be expected, given the differences in how much the smoker smokes, how much time the spouse spends with the smoker, how much ventilation there is, and so forth.
101. Mark J. Utell, Jane Warren, and Robert Sawyer, 'Public Health Risks from Motor Vehicle Emissions', *Annual Review of Public Health*, Vol. 15, 1994, pp. 157–78; Michal Krzyzanowski, Birgit Kuna-Dibbert, and Jurgen Schneider, eds., *Health Effects of Transport-Related Air Pollution* (Copenhagen: World Health Organization, 2005).
102. Richard A. Muller and Elizabeth A. Muller, 'Air Pollution and Cigarette Equivalence', *Berkley Earth*, 2019. http://berkeleyearth.org/air-pollution-and-cigarette-equivalence/ (accessed 14 February 2019).
103. Some of *that* pollution is the result of the production and consumption of tobacco products.

Chapter 5

1. This assumes a restrictive definition of the poor as those who live on less than $2 per day (based on 2011 purchasing power parities), a figure calculated with reference to the cost of the required daily caloric intake as well as other necessary expenses. Rakesh Kochhar, 'What it means to be poor by global standards', Pew Research Center, 22 July 2015, http://www.pewresearch.org/fact-tank/2015/07/22/what-it-means-to-be-poor-by-global-standards/ (accessed 2 August 2017).
2. They live on $10 or less per day. Rakesh Kochhar, 'Seven-in-ten people globally live on $10 or less per day', Pew Research Center, 23 September 2015, http://www.pewresearch.org/fact-tank/2015/09/23/seven-in-ten-people-globally-live-on-10-or-less-per-day/ (accessed 2 August 2017).
3. Some go so far as to say that focusing on an individual's duties is actually counterproductive. See Paul Gomberg, 'The Fallacy of Philanthropy', *Canadian Journal of Philosophy*, Vol. 32, No. 1, 2002, pp. 29–65.
4. What individuals (and states) owe may not have to consist—or consist alone—of financial contributions. However, my focus here is on financial contributions because, for many people, this is one way, and sometimes the best way, to help alleviate the problem.
5. See Rakesh Kochhar, 'A global middle class is more promise than reality', Pew Research Center, 8 July 2015, http://www.pewglobal.org/2015/07/08/a-global-middle-class-is-more-promise-than-reality/ (accessed 2 August 2017).
6. Jan Narveson, 'We Don't Owe Them a Thing! A Tough-Minded but Soft-Hearted View of Aid to the Faraway Needy', *Monist*, Vol. 86, No. 3, July 2003, pp. 419–33.
7. Ibid.
8. Later I shall discuss the relevance of this difference.
9. Peter Singer, *The Life You Can Save* (New York: Random House, 2009), p. 3; Peter Singer, *Practical Ethics*, 3rd ed. (New York: Cambridge University Press, 2011), p. 199.
10. Peter Singer, 'Famine, Affluence, and Morality', *Philosophy and Public Affairs*, Vol. 1, No. 3, Spring 1972, pp. 229–43. However, in this article he notes that he does not need as demanding a principle to require saving the child from drowning in the pond. He says that even the following weaker principle would suffice to produce that conclusion: 'if it is in our power to prevent something very bad from happening, without thereby sacrificing anything *morally significant*, we ought, morally, to do it' (p. 231, my emphasis).
11. His argument was first presented in 'Famine, Affluence, and Morality', pp. 229–43. There are slight variations on the argument in his various formulations of it. The one listed here is from *Practical Ethics*, 3rd ed., p. 200.
12. *Practical Ethics*, 3rd ed., p. 202.
13. Indeed, it is so demanding that it is not met even by people as generous as he is.
14. Peter Singer, *Practical Ethics*, 2nd ed. (New York: Cambridge University Press, 1993), p. 246.
15. Peter Singer, *The Life You Can Save*, p. 164.
16. Peter Singers says that 'we may need to set our standards lower [than the very demanding conclusion] in order to draw more people to meet them'. *The Life You Can Save*, p. 137.
17. Michael Maren, *The Road to Hell: The Ravaging Effects of Foreign Aid and International Charity* (New York: The Free Press, 1997).
18. Ibid.
19. That is, at least one *for now*. If too many people gave to the one charity that fitted these conditions, the resources at the disposal of the charity might outstrip the needs of—or its ability to meet the needs of—its beneficiaries.
20. https://www.givewell.org.
21. Garrett Cullity asks us to imagine this. See 'The life-saving analogy', in *World Hunger and Morality*, 2nd ed., edited by William Aiken and Hugh LaFollette (Upper Saddle River, NJ: Prentice-Hall, 1996), p. 61. He also asks us to imagine that there are others on the beach who could help with the saving, but only a few are doing so. He takes this to be a complete analogy, but I think that there are missing elements, which I add here.
22. I grant that the phrase 'undue moral or personal sacrifice' is vaguer than Peter Singer's. That has both strengths and weaknesses as I shall discuss later.
23. More extreme property rights views would claim that a right to private property entails not having to give *any* of it away. Peter Singer raises the question whether people do indeed have property rights (*Practical Ethics*, 3rd ed., p. 204). However, more moderate private property

views are not incompatible with some redistribution, and thus the property rights objection has its greatest force against more demanding views about the extent of our duties. This is an objection not to the first premise by itself, but rather to the conclusion of Peter Singer's argument, as he understands it.

24. A moral right to retain one's property is, here, obviously not a moral right to a legal right to retain one's property for it would then be indistinguishable from the previous possibility I mentioned.

25. John Arthur, 'World hunger and moral obligation: The case against Singer', in *Vice and Virtue in Everyday Life*, 3rd ed., edited by Christina Sommers and Fred Sommers (Fort Worth: Harcourt Brace Jovanovich, 1993), p. 848.

26. Peter Singer, *The Life You Can Save*, pp. 130–37; Peter Singer, 'What should a billionaire give—and what should you give?', *New York Times*, 17 December 2006, http://www.nytimes.com/2006/12/17/magazine/17charity.t.html (accessed 23 December 2006).

27. Peter Singer addresses this latter claim. *The Life You Can Save*, pp. 28–29.

28. Peter Singer advances exactly this view in his discussion of our duties to the world's poor. *Practical Ethics*, 3rd ed., pp. 196–98.

29. He does consider a non-consequentialist view of moral responsibility. However, his response is to reject it rather than to show that it is compatible with the first premise of his argument. His rejection is (too) quick. He points to one 'way of making sense of the non-consequentialist view of responsibility' (*Practical Ethics*, 3rd ed., p. 197), namely by basing it on a view that the only rights are negative ones (to non-interference). He suggests that this view of rights makes sense only if one takes humans to be isolated individuals. This, he says, is mistaken because humans are in fact social beings. One problem with this argument is that it treats 'isolated individual' and 'social being' as mutually exclusive. In fact, humans are, in general, social individuals. Different humans combine these in different degrees. Some are more individualistic, and some are more social. A view that recognized such combination of the individual and the social might give much more scope to the individual than Peter Singer allows, even if it also gave much more scope for social responsibilities than would be allowed by those who think we have no positive duties to others.

30. Unless doing so would prevent you from spending the resources on preventing an even greater evil.

31. While there might be some poor who are responsible for their situation, this is not true of the overwhelming majority of the world's poor, and especially the world's absolute poor.

32. John Arthur, 'Rights and the duty to bring aid', in *World Hunger and Morality*, 2nd ed., edited by William Aiken and Hugh LaFollette (Upper Saddle River, NJ: Prentice-Hall, 1996), p. 48. John Arthur speaks about 'preventing the death of an innocent' rather than 'preventing something bad from happening to an innocent'. I've chosen the latter formulation because it is not restricted to the prevention of death but also covers the prevention of other very bad fates. Also, John Arthur seems to be speaking only of the sacrifices of the rescuers and their families, whereas I think we should also include other sacrifices that have substantial moral importance. These include sacrificing of third-party interests.

33. Peter Singer, *The Life You Can Save*, pp. 38–39.

34. Stuart Rachels, 'The Immorality of Having Children', *Ethical Theory and Moral Practice*, Vol. 7, 2014, pp. 567–82.

35. I argue for this at greater length in David Benatar, 'Famine, Affluence, and Procreation: Peter Singer and Anti-Natalism Lite', *Ethical Theory and Moral Practice*, Vol. 23, No. 2, 2020, pp. 415–31.

36. See Chapter 3.

37. David Benatar, *Better Never to Have Been: The Harm of Coming into Existence* (Oxford: Oxford University Press, 2006).

38. Consider the following real but anonymized case: 'SA' left her family in Izmir, in 1935 when she was twenty, to travel to a distant corner of the world to get married. She saw her parents only once more before their deaths thirty years later. Forgoing that one trip back to Turkey would have been a much greater sacrifice than many less costly luxuries.

39. *Practical Ethics*, 3rd ed., pp. 212–13.

40. Ibid, p. 213.

41. In outlining Peter Singer's argument, I noted his view that non-utilitarians could, consistent with his argument, permit us some luxuries in life. However, it is unclear *how* he can think this if he thinks that not only utilitarians, but also non-utilitarians should reject the servitude argument (and related arguments). In other words, if non-utilitarians cannot appeal to something like the servitude argument, then it is not clear why Peter Singer can think that the conclusion of

his argument is any less demanding for non-utilitarians than it is for utilitarians. If the conclusion is not (or not much) less demanding for non-utilitarians then we have (further) reason for doubting that the first or third premises, or both, enjoy the broad support Peter Singer claims they do.

42. Even in temporary emergencies, it may be the case that those best placed to save, have only *immediate* responsibility to bear the costs but should be compensated by others later. See David Miller, 'Distributing Responsibilities', *Journal of Political Philosophy*, Vol. 9, No. 4, 2001, p. 468.
43. This is a play on the 'Lockean proviso'. See John Locke, *Second Treatise of Government*, edited by C.B. Macpherson (Indianapolis: Hackett Publishing Company, 1980), Chapter V, paragraph 27.
44. Unless, perhaps, one had to protect nephews, nieces, or other people of the next generation with whom one had close bonds.
45. Thomas Pogge is a prominent exponent of such an argument. *World Poverty and Human Rights* (Cambridge: Polity Press, 2002).
46. Ibid, p. 20.
47. Ibid, p. 22.
48. This can include migrants, and especially immigrants, from poorer countries.
49. And by non-human animals.
50. Peter Singer, *The Life You Can Save*, p. 144.
51. Ibid, p. 151.
52. An advocate of a compensation argument might argue that compensation to different parties could be aggregated and then shared in such a way that some people contribute to some compensatory payments while other people contribute to others. However, this requires a high level of collaboration. Individuals needing to discharge their duties of compensation without the guarantee of others collaborating, will need a more diverse compensation portfolio.

Chapter 6

1. Another term used is CAFO: concentrated animal feeding operation.
2. The data presented here for cows, sheep, pigs, and chickens are for 2018, the latest year for which there was data at the time of writing. See Bas Sanders, 'Global animal slaughter statistics and charts: 2020 update', *Faunalytics*, 29 July 2020, https://faunalytics.org/global-animal-slaughter-statistics-and-charts-2020-update/ (accessed 5 May 2021). Mr Sanders drew his data from the United Nations Food and Agricultural Organization.
3. Approximately 302 128 113 cows.
4. These data are for 2016. See Bas Sanders, 'Global goat slaughter statistics and charts', *Faunalytics*, 10 October 2018, https://faunalytics.org/global-goat-slaughter-statistics-and-charts/.
5. Approximately 573 781 178 sheep.
6. Approximately 1 484 492 840 pigs.
7. Approximately 68 785 221 000 chickens.
8. Nobody counts the number of aquatic animals killed. These animals are measured in tonnes, which is an apt indication that they are not regarded as individuals but rather as biomass. My figure here is for 2018 and is based on the United Nations Food and Agricultural Organization's estimate that 178.5 million tonnes of fish were 'produced' or 'captured' that year (*The State of the World Fisheries and Aquaculture: Sustainability in Action* [Rome: Food and Agricultural Organization, 2020], p. 2) and assumes that the 'average marine animal's weight' is about 1.4 kg. See https://www.adaptt.org/about/the-kill-counter.html (accessed 13 May 2024).
9. In some cases, this is because animals killed privately may not register in official figures. In the case of aquatic animals, the numbers may well be higher given the vast number of fish weighing a lot less than the 1.4 kg average weight of marine animals on which the calculated number is based.
10. For a vivid impression of the number of animals killed every *second*, see ADAPTT's 'kill counter', which is available here: http://www.adaptt.org/about/the-kill-counter.html.
11. Christian Cotroneo, 'How long do chickens live?', *Treehugger*, 31 January 2022, https://www.treehugger.com/how-long-do-chickens-live-4859423 (accessed 13 January 2023). They can live even longer if protected from predators.
12. The exceptions are those used in breeding more chickens.
13. That's an *amputated* beak.

14. Jessica M. Hoffman and Teresa G. Valencak, 'A Short Life on the Farm: Aging and Longevity in Agricultural, Large-Bodied Mammals', *GeroScience*, Vol. 42, 2020, pp. 909–22.
15. Mehrdad Mohri, Shahrokh Poorsina, and Reza Sedaghat, 'Effects of Parenteral Supply of Iron on RBC Parameters, Performance, and Health in Neonatal Dairy Calves', *Biological Trace Element Research*, Vol. 136, 2010, pp. 33–39.
16. See, for example, Victoria Braithwaite, *Do Fish Feel Pain?* (Oxford: Oxford University Press, 2010).
17. Peter Godfrey-Smith, *Other Minds: The Octopus, the Sea, and the Deep Origins of Consciousness* (New York: Farrar, Straus and Giroux, 2016).
18. Although many people lose sight of the fact that we too are animals, it can be tedious to refer continually to human animals and non-human animals. As a shorthand, I shall refer to humans and animals, but I do not thereby mean to deny that humans too are animals.
19. There is sometimes disagreement about when 'race' and sex are relevant. For example, there is a debate about whether they are relevant for affirmative action.
20. This term was coined by Richard Ryder. He first used it in a leaflet, circulated in Oxford in 1970. This is recounted in Richard D. Ryder, 'Speciesism Revisited', *Think*, Vol. 2, No. 6, Spring 2004, pp. 83–92. The term was subsequently popularized by Peter Singer, *Animal Liberation*, 2nd ed. (New York: The New York Review/Random House, 1990).
21. See, for example, Gareth Patterson, *Beyond the Secret Elephants* (Bryanston: Tracey McDonald Publishers, 2020).
22. This is constructed on the basis of the available evidence. There may, somewhere, be a species, the normal adult members of which are more cognitively sophisticated than humans.
23. Shelly Kagan, 'What's Wrong with Speciesism?', *Journal of Applied Philosophy*, Vol. 33, No. 1, February 2016, pp. 1–21.
24. Shelly Kagan recognizes that there could be some exceptions. See his discussion of anencephaly on page 18 (Shelly Kagan, 'What's Wrong with Speciesism?').
25. Ed Yong, *An Immense World: How Animal Senses Reveal the Hidden Realms around Us* (New York: Random House, 2022).
26. This is a test that Ned Hettinger recommends in a different context—that of animal experimentation. See Edwin Converse Hettinger, 'The Responsible Use of Animals in Biomedical Research', *Between the Species*, Vol. 5, No. 3, Summer 1989, pp. 123–31.
27. Jeff McMahan, *The Ethics of Killing* (New York: Oxford University Press, 2002), p. 170.
28. David Benatar, 'The Chickens Come Home to Roost', *American Journal of Public Health*, Vol. 97, No. 9, September 2007, pp. 1545–46.
29. Scientific opinion on this is still divided, with some people favouring a laboratory-leak hypothesis. However, as far as I can see, the wet-market or other zoonotic thesis is still the dominant scientific one.
30. David Benatar, 'Our cruel treatment of animals led to the Coronavirus', *New York Times*, 13 April 2020, https://www.nytimes.com/2020/04/13/opinion/animal-cruelty-coronavirus.html (accessed 20 November 2023).
31. Michael J. Martin, Sapna E. Thottathil, and Thomas B. Newman, 'Antibiotics Overuse in Animal Agriculture: A Call to Action for Health Care Providers', *American Journal of Public Health*, Vol. 105, No. 12, pp. 2409–10.
32. Center for Sustainable Systems, University of Michigan, 2020, 'Carbon footprint factsheet', Pub. No. CSS09-05. For more on the environmental impact of meat and dairy production, see the chapter on the environment in this book.
33. Nina G.G. Domingo et al, 'Air Quality-Related Health Damages of Food', *Proceedings of the National Academy of Sciences*, Vol. 118, No. 20, 2021, e2013637118.
34. Arthur Schopenhauer, 'On the sufferings of the world', in *Complete Essays of Schopenhauer*, translated by T. Bailey Saunders (New York: Wiley Book Company, 1942), Book 5, p. 2.
35. Johanna Dwyer and Franklin M. Loew, 'Nutritional Risks of Vegan Diets to Women and Children', *Journal of Agricultural and Environmental Ethics*, Vol. 7, No. 1, 1994, pp. 87–109; Ann Reed Mangels and Suzanne Havala, 'Vegan Diets for Women, Infants and Children', *Journal of Agricultural and Environmental Ethics*, Vol. 7, No. 1, 1994, pp. 111–22.
36. I added the condition that the humans are 'temporarily' starving. This is important because if killing the animal would only delay the deaths of the humans by a few days, then the utility calculation may well not work in favour of killing the animal.
37. This is obviously a play on 'right' but also alludes to the French word for a 'right', namely 'droit'.

38. Peter Alward, who defends this argument, calls it the 'naïve argument against moral vegetarianism'. See 'The Naïve Argument against Moral Vegetarianism', *Environmental Values*, Vol. 9, 2000, pp. 81–89.
39. David Benatar, 'Why the Naïve Argument against Moral Vegetarianism Really Is Naïve', *Environmental Values*, Vol. 10, No. 1, 2001, pp. 103–12.
40. See, for example, Carl Cohen, 'Do Animals Have Rights?', *Ethics and Behavior*, Vol. 7, No. 2, 1997, pp. 91–102; Rainer Ebert and Tibor Machan, 'Innocent Threats and the Moral Problem of Carnivorous Animals', *Journal of Applied Philosophy*, Vol. 29, No. 2, 2012, pp. 146–59. (The latter authors use the example of a wildebeest rather than a zebra, but that is not a material difference.)
41. Carl Cohen, 'Do Animals Have Rights?'.
42. Rainer Ebert and Tibor Machan, 'Innocent Threats and the Moral Problem of Carnivorous Animals'.
43. The purported moral significance of potentiality would require extensive discussion. Although I bypass it here, I note that taking the death of potential persons to be worse than the death of those who are never persons would be at odds with the 'time-relative interests' account referred to above.
44. The difference between them has been characterized in somewhat different ways. I find Allen Buchanan's taxonomy, which I follow here, to be the most helpful. (Allen Buchanan, 'Justice as Reciprocity versus Subject-Centred Justice', *Philosophy and Public Affairs*, Vol. 19, No. 3, Summer 1990, pp. 227–52.) As this reference suggests, his primary focus is on differing views of 'justice', but he notes that what he says also applies to contractarian views of morality.
45. Jan Narveson, 'A defense of meat eating', in *Animal Rights and Human Obligations*, 2nd ed., edited by Tom Regan and Peter Singer (Englewood Cliffs, NJ: Prentice-Hall, 1989), p. 193.
46. Ibid.
47. While only persons are morally considerable on this view, it does not follow that *all* persons are morally considerable. Any persons who can be so dominated that other persons have nothing to gain by entering into an agreement with them, will not be parties to the contract, and will thus not be morally considerable.
48. Jan Narveson, 'A defense of meat eating', p. 194.
49. Ibid, p. 195. Professor Narveson offers a third consideration, but this is not a reason for distinguishing animals from human non-persons. Instead, it is a reason for sometimes treating human non-persons *more like* animals. He says that 'there is a genuine question about the morality of, for instance, euthanasia, and that infanticide has been approved of in various human communities at various times' (Jan Narveson, 'A defense of meat eating', p. 195). The suggestion seems to be that it may not, after all, be wrong to practise infanticide on babies or euthanasia on profoundly cognitively impaired humans. This comment is a reasonable response to those who think that while euthanasia of animals is permitted, euthanasia of humans is not. However, while it seeks to defend treating human non-persons more like animals, it does not show that we may treat human non-persons in all the cruel ways in which farmed animals are treated. Indeed, because euthanasia, when it really is euthanasia (and not a euphemism for something else) is a kindness, it defends the extension to humans the rare kindness often withheld from humans but shown to animals.
50. Ibid.
51. See, for example, Hugh LaFollette and Niall Shanks, *Brute Science: Dilemmas in Animal Experimentation* (London: Routledge, 1996).
52. In Allen Buchanan's language, morality is 'subject-centred' rather than a matter of reciprocity. 'According to subject-centered conceptions, basic rights . . . are grounded not in the individual's strategic capacities but rather in other features of the individual herself—her needs or nonstrategic capacities' (Allen Buchanan, 'Justice as Reciprocity versus Subject-Centred Justice', p. 231).
53. John Rawls, *A Theory of Justice* (Oxford: Oxford University Press, 1973), p. 17 and p. 512.
54. See, for example, Mark Rowlands, 'Contractarianism and Animal Rights', *Journal of Applied Philosophy*, Vol. 14, No. 3, 1996, pp. 235–47.
55. Robert Garner, 'Rawls, Animals and Justice: New Literature, Same Response', *Res Publica*, Vol. 18, 2012, pp. 159–72.
56. For reasons I shall not discuss here, this might not also apply to pre-sentient foetuses.
57. The meat of wild animals is consumed by those hunters who do themselves kill (but not rear) what they eat.
58. As I noted in the chapter on our environmental duties.

59. Again, I am not speaking about those circumstances in which consumption of animals is really required to meet the nutritional needs of the people consuming them.
60. I am not speaking here about other circumstances in which eating or purchasing meat does not cause harm for other reasons. For example, what I say here would not apply to eating roadkill.
61. Genesis 1:28.
62. Genesis 1:29.
63. Genesis 1:30.
64. Genesis 9:3.
65. Isaiah 11:6–7.
66. In Judaism, for example, there is a principle of צער בעלי חיים (the 'suffering of living beings'), a principle which prohibits the infliction of such suffering.
67. For example, Leviticus 25:44–46, Numbers 31:18.
68. Exodus 31:15.
69. Deuteronomy 7:2.
70. Nick Zangwill, 'Our Moral Duty to Eat Meat', *Journal of the American Philosophical Association*, Vol. 7, No. 3, 2021, pp. 1–7.
71. A small minority of fish and other aquatic animals are brought into existence by humans and farmed.
72. A phrase borrowed from Thomas Hobbes, who used it to describe the 'state of nature'. *Leviathan*, i.xiii.9.
73. Nick Zangwill ('Our Moral Duty to Eat Meat') has a response to such cases, but that response is inadequate. See David Benatar, 'We Have No Moral Duty to Eat Meat: A Reply to Nick Zangwill', *Public Affairs Quarterly*, Vol. 36, No. 4, October 2022, pp. 331–43.
74. David Benatar, *Better Never to Have Been: The Harm of Coming into Existence* (Oxford: Oxford University Press, 2006).
75. Steven L. Davis, 'The Least Harm Principle May Require that Humans Consume a Diet Containing Large Herbivores, Not a Vegan Diet', *Journal of Agricultural and Environmental Ethics*, Vol. 16, 2003, pp. 387–94.
76. For a fuller list see Steven L. Davis, 'The Least Harm Principle May Require that Humans Consume a Diet Containing Large Herbivores, Not a Vegan Diet'.
77. Andy Lamey, 'Food Fight! Davis versus Regan on the Ethics of Eating Beef', *Journal of Social Philosophy*, Vol. 38, No. 2, Summer 2007, pp. 331–48.
78. Steven L. Davis, 'The Least Harm Principle May Require that Humans Consume a Diet Containing Large Herbivores, Not a Vegan Diet', p. 390.
79. Ibid, p. 389.
80. Ibid.
81. There are reasons to question it. See Andy Lamey, 'Food Fight! Davis versus Regan on the Ethics of Eating Beef'.
82. This is the view of Gaverick Matheny, 'Least Harm: A Defense of Vegetarianism from Steven Davis's Omnivorous Proposal', *Journal of Agricultural and Environmental Ethics*, Vol. 16, 2003, pp. 505–11.
83. Ibid.
84. Andy Lamey, 'Food Fight! Davis versus Regan on the Ethics of Eating Beef'.
85. There may typically also be further concerns about eating a human, most notably, the psychological effects this might have on relatives and friends of the eaten.
86. This practice must be an ancient one because it was prohibited by one of the so-called Noahide Laws:
אבר מן החי, the prohibition on eating the limb of a living animal.
87. Of course, some cultured meat may not meet this requirement. However, I am considering the case where the pedigree of the cells is not morally problematic.
88. I set aside here, the possibility that somebody might have a perverse reason—specifically wanting to eat the flesh of a once living animal.
89. Leon Kass, 'The Wisdom of Repugnance', *New Republic*, Vol. 216, No. 22, 2 June 1997, pp. 17–26.
90. Ibid, p. 20.
91. Ibid. He does say something about why he thinks that repugnance for cloning is wise, but he does not provide a general account of when repugnance is and when it is not a manifestation of wisdom.
92. However, given the environmental impact of cows, others would prioritize abstention from both beef and milk.

NOTES 401

93. To the extent that animal products are cheaper, this is, as mentioned earlier, because some of the actual costs, over and above those to the animals themselves, have been 'externalized'. That is to say, not all the costs are not being passed on to the individual consumers. Among those costs that are not, are the environmental ones, but also government subsidies that are effectively borne by all taxpayers, whether or not they are consumers of animals. This does not help the individual purchaser and thus, rather than being a quotidian ethical issue, is an ethical issue in public policy.
94. Perhaps 'cold tofurkey' would be better.

Chapter 7

1. It does in Cohen-style bullshit, but not in Frankfurt-style bullshit. See Chapter 9.
2. In other societies, intolerance of blasphemy is rampant, and one can still face severe punishment for blasphemy, and what counts as blasphemy is expansive.
3. Moral relativists make no such distinction, and regard (ii) as reducible to (i). In other words, for them, something is immoral if it is regarded as immoral. Such a view allows no scope for moral error—somebody thinking that something is (or is not) immoral, and yet being mistaken. For some indication of why I reject this view, see the introduction to this book.
4. Or meanings.
5. Misunderstandings between languages can be more innocuous, and more entertaining. My maternal grandfather, an attorney, once quoted the Persian mathematician, philosopher, and poet Omar Khayyam, in court. The Afrikaans magistrate, not quite understanding to whom my grandfather had referred, interjected: 'Ekskus, Meneer Goldberg, wie se ouma is dit?' which, in English means 'Excuse me, Mr Goldberg, who's grandmother (ouma) is that?'
6. Arguably, 'spinster' has an additional denotative feature lacking in 'bachelor', namely that the person is not merely at but *beyond* the usual age for marriage.
7. See 'Controversies about the word *niggardly*', *Wikipedia*, https://en.wikipedia.org/wiki/Controversies_about_the_word_niggardly (accessed 19 July 2022).
8. 'National Association for the Advancement of Colored People'. More on that name later.
9. 'About niggardly', *Washington Post*, 29 January 1999, https://www.washingtonpost.com/archive/opinions/1999/01/29/about-niggardly/2204430b-376f-4d1d-91f5-b1b950e37932/ (accessed 19 July 2022).
10. Only 23% of Latino adults have even heard of the term 'Latinx'. Of those who have heard the term 33% think that it should be used. Only 3% of all Latino adults—both those who have and have not heard the term—use it themselves. See 'About one-in-four U.S. Hispanics have heard of Latinx, but just 3% use it', Pew Research Center, 11 August 2020, https://www.pewresearch.org/hispanic/2020/08/11/about-one-in-four-u-s-hispanics-have-heard-of-latinx-but-just-3-use-it/#fn-29384-1 (accessed 21 July 2022).
11. In very rare cases, when the prudential costs of infringing the social norm are sufficiently great, and the value of taking a moral stand insufficient to outweigh this, the imprudence of uttering the word could even make uttering the word either morally impermissible or at least less than morally ideal. These must be very rare cases, for otherwise the powerful intolerant can too easily make the utterance of some words morally impermissible or defective, which would be to grant a kind of moral veto to them.
12. The scene can be viewed here: https://www.youtube.com/watch?v = Cnn2aGVcCEc (accessed 14 July 2022).
13. Donald G. McNeil Jr, 'NYTimes Peru N-word, Part one: Introduction', *Medium*, 1 March 2021, https://donaldgmcneiljr1954.medium.com/nytimes-peru-n-word-part-one-introduction-57eb6a3e0d95 (accessed 14 July 2022).
14. Unathi Nkanjeni, 'Adam Habib and the N-word: A wrap of what happened', *TimesLive*, 15 March 2021, https://www.timeslive.co.za/news/south-africa/2021-03-15-adam-habib-and-the-n-word-a-wrap-of-what-happened/ (accessed 14 July 2022).
15. As an aside, it is worth noting that at least some people now regard the word 'Oriental' with reference to people from Asian or Pacific ancestry, as offensive. See '"Oriental": Rugs, not people', *NPR*, 2 September 2009, https://www.npr.org/2009/09/02/112465167/oriental-rugs-not-people (accessed 19 July 2023).

16. 'SOAS Board accepts recommendations of independent external investigation in full: Director to stay on with restorative justice process in place', 5 May 2021, https://www.soas.ac.uk/news/newsitem153016.html (accessed 14 July 2022).
17. Donald G. McNeil Jr, 'NYTimes Peru N-word, part three: What happened in the 2019 investigation?', *Medium*, 1 March 2021, https://donaldgmcneiljr1954.medium.com/nytimes-peru-n-word-part-three-what-happened-in-the-2019-investigation-6f8e9939a385 (accessed 14 July 2022).
18. Marc Tracy, 'Ex-Times reporter who used racial slur publishes a lengthy defense', *New York Times*, 1 March 2021, https://www.nytimes.com/2021/03/01/business/donald-mcneil-new-york-times-racial-slur.html (accessed 14 July 2022).
19. Chris Havergal, 'Adam Habib to 'step aside' as SOAS director during racism probe', *Times Higher Education*, 18 March 2021, https://www.timeshighereducation.com/news/adam-habib-step-aside-soas-director-during-racism-probe (accessed 14 July 2022).
20. 'K-word', *Wikipedia*, https://en.wikipedia.org/wiki/K-word (accessed 14 July 2022).
21. The tetragrammaton is the four-letter name for God that, in English, is represented as YHWH or JHVH.
22. See, for example, Randall Kennedy, *Nigger: The Strange Career of a Troublesome Word* (New York: Vintage Books, 2003), pp. xv, xvi, xvii, 37, 43.
23. Feminists may complain that it is no accident that the typical member of each linguistic group is male. I shall return to this issue later.
24. See the Preface for an explanation of why I use scare quotes.
25. John Cohen, *The Essential Lenny Bruce: His Original Unexpurgated Satirical Routines* (St Albans: Granada, 1975), p. 84. While it is still an open question whether particular slurs can be appropriated to a sufficient degree to positive ends, it is clear that Lenny Bruce himself had some success in shifting the bounds of (legally) acceptable language by assaulting a different fortress—that of 'obscenity'. His use of 'ass', 'balls', 'cock-sucker', 'cunt', 'fuck', 'mother-fucker', 'piss', 'screw', 'shit', and 'tits' were ruled obscene by the court, as were various of his monologues ('Legal opinions relating to obscenity prosecutions of comedian Lenny Bruce', *Famous Trials*, https://www.famous-trials.com/lennybruce/559-legalopinions#people, accessed 18 July 2022). Although many of these words are still not fit for polite society, the pioneering use by Lenny Bruce and others, has had the fortunate result that comedians and others no longer face prosecution for using them, at least in some countries. For more on obscenity, see below.
26. Elana Michelle Nachman, a Jewish lesbian feminist, changed her surname, first to 'Dykewoman' and then to 'Dykewomon', in a clear and good-humoured attempt to reclaim an anti-lesbian slur. The last part of her adopted surnames, we are told, involved 'jettisoning the 'man' in both her old and new names'. See Alex Williams, 'Elana Dykewomon, author who explored lesbian lives, dies at 72', *New York Times*, 14 August 2022, https://www.nytimes.com/2022/08/14/books/elana-dykewomon-dead.html (accessed 18 August 2022). However, 'Nachman' is only related to the word 'man' if it is derived from the German name 'Nachmann'. If, instead, it is a transliteration of the Hebrew name נחמן, then it has no connection to the English word 'man'.
27. Although racial categories are not the only ones with fuzzy boundaries, I use scare quotes for all instances of such terms only. For other categories, I use quotation marks to mark the word (rather than the members of the set), but not more generally. This is because racial categories are both more vague and *generally* more odious than categories such as 'woman', 'Jew', or Italian, for example. (The use of 'Jew' becomes more odious when it is used as a racial, or similar, term. I shall soon say more about this.)
28. For 'Yid', see 'The Daily Stormer's Jew-hating style guide revealed', *Times of Israel*, 16 December 2017, https://www.timesofisrael.com/the-daily-stormers-jew-hating-style-guide-revealed/ (accessed 18 July 2022).
29. The football club, Tottenham Hotspur, has been associated with its significant Jewish fanbase. This has led supporters of opposing teams to subject them to antisemitic verbal abuse. In response, Tottenham Hotspur fans have chanted 'Yid' and 'Yiddo' as a term of pride. However, to indicate how contested these matters are, even this usage has been controversial. See, for example, 'Dictionary includes Spurs fans in Yid definition', *BBC*, 12 February 2020, https://www.bbc.com/news/uk-51479810 (accessed 18 July 2022).
30. This is obviously an oversimplification of the possibilities. Other possibilities include the current trajectory continuing for some variable length of time before being reversed. The time frame for each of these possibilities can also vary.
31. Another possibility is simply to describe or depict the prejudice, without explicitly opposing it.

32. For more on this, see Chapter 8.
33. See, for example, cases that I describe in *The Fall of the University of Cape Town: Africa's Leading University in Decline* (N.p.: Politicsweb Publishing, 2021), pp. 117, 308, 339, 361, 412.
34. See https://www.youtube.com/watch?v = BLNDqxrUUwQ (accessed 19 July 2022).
35. See https://www.youtube.com/watch?v = 5Xdx5XQkA2g (accessed 15 August 2022). Interestingly, YouTube requires viewers to 'sign in to confirm your age' before watching this clip.
36. Where a slur-word is being repurposed, the group to which it is directed will often not be the group to which the slur usage is usually applied, but rather an even more general group.
37. The inspiration for this imaginary case is the true case of Billings, Montana, where a cinderblock was thrown through the bedroom window of a Jewish child who had taped a cut-out menorah to his window. The police advised the parents of that child to remove symbols identifying their home as Jewish. Some Christians in Billings had a different idea. They began printing images of menorahs and putting them up in their windows. Instead of Jews having to hide their Jewish identity, thousands of families identified themselves with the Jewish inhabitants of their city. At first, that led to attacks on Christian homes, but this led to even more Christians putting up pictures of menorahs. Eventually the haters had to retreat. See 'Not in our town', *Facing History and Ourselves*, https://www.facinghistory.org/resource-library/not-our-town-0 (accessed 25 July 2022). Admittedly a menorah is not a slur, although it may be very close to that for those who throw cinderblocks through windows bearing menorahs.
38. I say 'somewhat' because I am pessimistic about the degree of discernment characteristic of most people.
39. Not in South Africa, however, where 'Coloured', although a term used by the Apartheid regime to refer to so-called mixed race people, is embraced, even in the post-Apartheid period, as a cultural identity by one group of South Africans.
40. 'Dutchman' is interesting in that its different senses run the gamut from innocuous, to dated, to noxious. Two of its meanings are 'a native or inhabitant of the Netherlands' and 'a person of Dutch descent'. These senses are parallel to 'Englishman'. Another sense is 'a member of any of the Germanic peoples of Germany, Austria, Switzerland, and the Low Countries'. That usage is listed by Merriam Webster as 'archaic', but not as derogatory. (See https://www.merriam-webster.com/dictionary/dutchman, [accessed 21 July 2022].) When used in yet another way, in South Africa, it is a derogatory term for Afrikaners (*Dictionary of South African English*, https://dsae.co.za/entry/dutchman/e02182 [, accessed 21 July 2022]).
41. I shall say more about this later in this chapter.
42. That this is also speciesist is rarely noted. I shall say more about this below.
43. Casey Miller and Kate Swift, *Words and Women: New Language in New Times*, updated (New York: HarperCollins, 1991), p. 146. See also: https://en.wikipedia.org/wiki/Herstory (accessed 26 July 2022). For an example, see the (US) National Organization for Women's website: http://erights4all.com/now/valdostanow/herstory.htm (accessed 8 December 2003, but no longer available).
44. See, for example, the American Philosophical Association's 'Guidelines for non-sexist use of language': https://www.apaonline.org/page/nonsexist (accessed 20 November 2023).
45. See, for example, Janice Moulton, 'The myth of the neutral "man"', in *Feminism and Philosophy*, edited by Mary Vetterling-Braggin, Frederick A. Elliston, and Jane English (Totowa, NJ: Littlefield, Adams & Co., 1978), pp. 124–37; Casey Miller and Kate Swift, *Words and Women*, pp. 21–42.
46. For example: Joseph W. Schneider and Sally L. Hacker, 'Sex Role Imagery and Use of the Generic "Man" in Introductory Texts', *American Sociologist*, Vol. 8, No. 1, February 1973, pp. 12–18; Linda Harrison, 'Cro-Magnon Woman—In Eclipse', *Science Teacher*, Vol. 42, No. 4, April 1975, pp. 8–11. It would be interesting to see whether similar results would be produced now, given the (incomplete, but nonetheless significant) extent to which gender stereotypes have been undone in the last few decades.
47. At least if the disjunction is an exclusive or strong one. On an inclusive or weak disjunction 'he or she' or 'she or he' would be true for those who are both 'he' and 'she', which is one kind of non-binary. However, neither 'he or she' nor 'she or he' would include those non-binary people who occupy the 'neither he nor she' category.
48. Dennis Baron, 'A brief history of singular "they"', *The Web of Language*, 30 July 2018, https://blogs.illinois.edu/view/25/677177 (accessed 5 August 2018).

49. André Wheeler, 'Merriam-Webster dictionary adds 'they' as non-binary pronoun', *Guardian*, 18 September 2019, https://www.theguardian.com/science/2019/sep/17/merriam-webster-they-nonbinary-pronoun (accessed 23 September 2019).
50. This is so even if one is referring to an astronaut, pilot, soldier, or some other role in which males still predominate. The idea is that our language should break down stereotypes. To this end, the recommendation is that our language should *not* reflect reality, but should instead help form a new reality. We are enjoined to engage in a kind of linguistic affirmative action. Curiously there seems to be less concern about undermining stereotypes when one is speaking about 'perpetrators' or 'victims'. In such cases, the preponderance of males among perpetrators (and the alleged overrepresentation of females among victims) is sometimes seen as grounds to refer to perpetrators as 'he' (and victims as 'she'). For example, see Sharon Lamb, 'Note on terminology' in *The Trouble with Blame* (Cambridge, MA: Harvard University Press, 1996). I say the *alleged* overrepresentation of females among victims, because males are actually the main victims of non-sexual physical abuse. See David Benatar, 'The second sexism', *Social Theory and Practice*, Vol. 29, No. 2, April 2003, pp. 179–80. I see the value in undermining stereotypes. I also see the value in reflecting reality. I am not sure which value ought to prevail when the two conflict.
51. Casey Miller and Kate Swift, *The Handbook of Non-Sexist Writing*, 2nd ed. (London: The Women's Press, 1989).
52. While on the subject of avoiding bias in language, we might note that whereas some would understand this as AD 1000 (Anno Domini, Year of our Lord), others prefer to speak of 1000 CE (Common Era), referring to the era common to Jews and Christians. However, this era is not common to Muslims too. (Alternatively, 'CE' *could* be understood to stand for 'Christian Era'.) Of course, the very designation of the referent year as 1000 is Christo-centric. The same year is designated differently in the Jewish, Chinese, Islamic, and other calendars. I mention this not to prescribe linguistic changes in this area, but instead to highlight an example of how far consistently inclusive language would have to reach. I cannot see how we could employ any common counting of the years that would not be biased to some or other group. As a result, we might as well just accept the dominant counting for common purposes (even if non-dominant groups preserve their own counting for group-specific purposes). It is easier to shift from 'AD' to 'CE', but I'm not convinced that Christians should be morally prohibited from employing 'AD'—such a requirement might unjustifiably restrict freedom of religious expression—although I do think that they should be aware of many Jews' preference to use 'CE' themselves. Thinking about these sorts of terms, which are not about women, might help feminists to overcome biases in judging which allegedly sexist words they can, and which words they cannot, *require* others to change.
53. Cited by Casey Miller and Kate Swift, *Words and Women*, p. 31.
54. Ibid.
55. When 'man' was genuinely gender-neutral, it did not simultaneously have a gender-specific meaning. The gender specific terms were 'waepman' and 'carlman' for males and 'wifman' for females. Professor Roger Lass has informed me that 'wifman' took the pronoun 'he', and that 'wif' was neuter and thus took 'hit', the forerunner of 'it'.
56. This assumes, of course, that we are using the term in contexts in which it is not inappropriate to overlook non-humans. In such cases, 'man' in a gender-neutral sense would not have been the solution. Instead, we would need to choose whatever broader term was appropriate—such as 'sentient being'.
57. That is, unless, in shifting the meaning of 'man' back to the gender neutral, one also reinstated 'waepman' or 'carlman', which would have been more a stretch.
58. And in contexts in which the incumbent was not obviously either male or female.
59. Alternatively, it could be viewed (conceptually again) as a contraction of 'chair' and either 'woman' ('wifman') or 'waepman' (or 'carlman'). Indeed, Roger Lass informed me that some compounds of 'man'—yeoman, bondman, chapman, freeman, goodman, herdsman, hiredman, kinsman, leofman, mootman, and so on—were in use when 'man' was still genuinely gender neutral (as evidenced by the fact that they were in use when a male 'man' was still referred to as a 'carlman'.
60. If this book is ever translated into a more gendered language than English, I offer apologies to readers for not discussing the particularities of those challenges.
61. The preferred pronouns of specific individuals will be considered later.
62. This strategy is more difficult in those languages where the plural is also gendered, thus excluding use of the plural in place of the singular pronoun.

63. Indeed, those inclined to 'progressive' or 'inclusive' prescription tend to offer literary prescriptions that run in the opposite direction to (but which do not contradict) the prescriptions in (1) to (3) and in the 'vice versa' version of (4). In recent years, there have been objections to authors writing from the perspective of characters that do not share the authors' racial, ethnic, gendered, or other such identity. According to this view, 'white' men may not write about 'black' women, for example. The purported explanation is that a person from one identity category cannot really put themselves in the shoes of somebody from a different identity category. The claim that people of one identity group cannot know what it is like to be a member of another identity group is an empirical claim. If it is presented as an exceptionless claim, it is almost certainly false in any meaningful way. (In a literal way, the only person whom one can know what it is like to be, is oneself. Others who share some or other category—such as 'race', ethnicity, sex, or sexual orientation—will have some features in common with oneself, but not everybody in each of these groups thinks in the same way.) How well anybody writing about somebody else can construct the perspective of that person is to be determined by the nature of the literary product, rather than the identity of the author. Readers can decide how convincing a character is.
64. For a humorous account of the confusion that singular 'they' can cause, see Rafi Bastos, 'They/Them', https://www.youtube.com/watch?v=iB_qpiq-WiI (accessed 19 July 2023).
65. Ann Bodine, 'Androcentrism in Prescriptive Grammar: Singular "They", Sex-Indefinite "He", and "'He or She"', *Language in Society*, Vol. 4, 1975, pp. 129–46.
66. Perhaps there would be objections from those with more idiosyncratic pronouns, more about which will be said below.
67. There are some contexts in which it is not irrelevant. For example, it is relevant for some people to know the sex of a doctor they might consult, or the sex or gender of a potential romantic partner.
68. It has been suggested to me that perhaps we *are* required to include them in every instance because: (a) we can do so easily (unlike including everybody in the time-zone case above); and (b) they are marginalized in other ways. While these considerations have some force, and do suggest that we should *sometimes* include them, I do not think that these considerations show that we are required to use singular 'they' in *every* case. So universal a requirement is not necessary for countering marginalization. Moreover, as I explain in the text above and below, singular 'they' has some shortcomings that make it unsuitable in some cases. Sometimes the use of 'they' will cause confusion in listeners, who might think that it is being used to designate plural, and when it is not confusing it may sometimes be jarring.
69. Nor can those to whom it sounds odd simply be dismissed as insensitive to feminist concerns. In one study, it was found that of the 'seven people closest to the women's movement, only one was willing to say she would be comfortable using "a person ... they" as an alternative' (Barbara Bate, 'Nonsexist Language Use in Transition', *Journal of Communication*, Vol. 28, 1978, p. 146). I suspect it is likely that if such a study were done now, one would find such formulations would sound less odd, but the fundamental point remains true—what sounds odd cannot be dismissed as insensitivity to feminist concerns. What sounds odd will very likely be linked to dominant usage, even among those who would like usage to be different.
70. The criticism cannot be reversed against those who do not *require* the use of gender-neutral 'chairman', but who instead suggest it as an alternative, *permissible* way of addressing feminist concerns.
71. Shaziya Allarakha, 'What are the 72 other genders?', 2 February 2022, https://www.medicinenet.com/what_are_the_72_other_genders/article.htm (accessed 15 August 2022).
72. I leave aside the republican thought that *all* claims to being royal are delusional.
73. See 'Table of standard and non-standard third-person singular pronouns' in 'Gender neutrality in languages with gendered third-person pronouns', *Wikipedia*, https://en.wikipedia.org/wiki/Gender_neutrality_in_languages_with_gendered_third-person_pronouns#Table_of_standard_and_non-standard_third-person_singular_pronouns (accessed 2 July 2022).
74. Examples include one's spouse's preferred pronouns (for references to one's spouse), which holidays one celebrates (for which holiday greetings would be welcomed and which would not be), and one's dietary preferences (so that one is not repeatedly bothered with offers of hors d'oeuvres one will not eat).
75. I say more below about why it is helpful to distinguish age from other status differentials.

76. This is (again) an oversimplification of the options. For example, the trajectory towards informality might continue a while before being reversed. The degree of the reversal can also vary. Another variable is the time period over which this all happens.
77. I am grateful to Greg Fried for raising this possible argument.
78. 'Chopped liver as an expression', *Wikipedia*, https://en.wikipedia.org/wiki/Chopped_liver#Chopped_liver_as_an_expression (accessed 10 August 2022).
79. This is a reference to the television situation comedy, *Seinfeld*. See 'Shmoopie', https://www.youtube.com/watch?v = MNW6CFdjMo8 (accessed 31 October 2023).
80. While there may be more gendered animal-based insults directed towards women, there are also some that are directed towards men. For example, a woman may be called a 'cow', while a male might be referred to as a 'bull'. 'Bitch' is much more common than 'cur', but that latter term, when it is used, is used in reference to men.
81. 'Patted' is a synonym for 'petted'.
82. Innumerable contemporary comedians, many of whose performances are replete with obscenities, provide ample evidence of this. However, the phenomenon is not restricted to comedians.
83. For example, swearing increases people's ability to withstand pain. See Richard Stephens, John Atkins, and Andrew Kingston, 'Swearing as a Response to Pain', *NeuroReport*, Vol. 20, No. 12, 5 August 2009, pp. 1056–60.
84. For example, swearing has been found to increase muscular performance. See Richard Stephens, David K. Spierer, and Emmanuel Katehis, 'Effect of Swearing on Strength and Power of Performance', *Psychology of Sport and Exercise*, Vol. 35, March 2018, pp. 111–17.
85. Rachel Braier, 'In praise of the C-word', *Guardian*, 11 July 2016, https://www.theguardian.com/media/mind-your-language/2016/jul/11/in-praise-of-the-c-word (accessed 17 July 2016); Jamie Rann, 'How swearing became a weapon of resistance for Ukrainians', *Guardian*, 13 April 2022, https://www.theguardian.com/books/2022/apr/13/putin-ukraine-war-russian-language (accessed 17 April 2022).
86. For a somewhat expanded treatment of these issues, see the discussions in Chapter 4.
87. As in 'Which God-damned mother-fucker stole my pen?'
88. See, for example, 'Graham Chapman's memorial service', https://www.youtube.com/watch?v = Bm2XPkqENaw (accessed 21 August 2022). Referring to the Graham Chapman as a 'freeloading bastard', John Cleese noted that he felt he should say this of Graham because Graham 'would never forgive me if I didn't'. John Cleese then took the opportunity to be 'the very first person at a British memorial service' to say 'fuck'.
89. For some comedians, there may be value in expletive-laden monologues. They might swear regularly while on the job, but this would not be incompatible with a discerning use of profanities, especially if they did not speak the same way in all other aspects of their lives.
90. Kristin L. Jay and Timothy B. Jay, 'Taboo Word Fluency and Knowledge of Slurs and General Pejoratives: Deconstructing the Poverty-of-Vocabulary Myth', *Language Sciences*, Vol. 57, 2015, pp. 251–59.
91. In other words, the use of profanities is liable to the principle of diminishing marginal utility.
92. This reminds me of the following joke:

    Question: How does one get one hundred old ladies to shout out 'fuck' in unison?
    Answer: Get one old lady to shout out 'Bingo!'

93. Obviously, there are other senses of 'commit' as a verb. For example, one can commit in the sense of making a commitment. However, this is obviously not the sense in which one speaks about 'committing suicide'.
94. Consider, for example, the common practice of referring to the number of victims, of a terrorist attack, for example, as including 'women and children'. Use of such a phrase is a way of overlooking men.

Chapter 8

1. Humour includes not only jokes but also comedy, cartoons, satire, quips, puns, comic impersonations, and so forth. I shall sometimes refer to 'jokes' or one of the other forms of humour without always meaning to restrict my comments to that particular form of humour. I do not propose to provide a definition of humour. Defending one definition over rivals would be a

massive undertaking, well beyond the scope of this chapter. Even stipulating a definition would be ill advised and make little or no difference to what I have to say. The word 'humour' can be used in different senses. A definition covering all reasonable senses would either have to be so general as to cover all senses or it would have to be a disjunction of all (reasonable) meanings. That said, it should be clear from the context of what I shall say that when I use words like 'humour' or 'joke' I am excluding bizarre cases where people find humour in something that fails to meet the (minimal) aesthetic conditions to count as humour. One such bizarre case would be somebody opening up a mathematics textbook, seeing an equation and laughing, where there are no contextual considerations that would explain why the equation met the relevant aesthetic conditions. While we can say that this person 'found the equation humorous', when I use the word 'humour' (and 'joke') in this chapter, I am not using the term so broadly as to include the equation that this strange person finds humorous. I am not denying that the word *can* be used in this way. It is just that I am not using it that way here. I shall not stipulate what the aesthetic conditions are for something to count as humour. That too would take me beyond the scope of the current chapter and would unnecessarily tie my analysis to a particular view. My analysis of humour ethics is compatible with a wide range of views about what the relevant conditions are.
2. For a discussion on the ethics of the Mohammed cartoons, see David Benatar, 'A Storm in a Turban', *Think*, No. 13, Summer 2006, pp. 17–22.
3. Detleve J.K. Peukert, *Inside Nazi Germany: Conformity, Opposition and Racism in Everyday Life* (London: Penguin, 1993), p. 198; Ben Lewis, 'Hammer & tickle', *Prospect Magazine*, 20 May 2006, http://www.prospectmagazine.co.uk/magazine/communist-jokes/ (accessed 15 November 2012); Mark Nesbit, 'Dead Funny', *Index on Censorship*, Vol. 29, No. 6, December 2000, pp. 118–20.
4. Laurence Goldstein, 'Only Joking?', *Philosophy Now*, No. 34, December 2001–January 2002, p. 26.
5. Nathan Guttman, 'James Jones' Jewish joke—funny or inappropriate?', *Haaretz*, 25 April 2010, https://www.haaretz.com/2010-04-25/ty-article/james-jones-jewish-joke-funny-or-inappropriate/0000017f-eb70-d3be-ad7f-fb7bc5d10001 (accessed 23 July 2023).
6. Randy Cohen, 'The ethics of Letterman's Palin joke', *New York Times*, 22 June 2009, http://ethicist.blogs.nytimes.com/2009/06/22/the-ethics-of-lettermans-palin-joke/ (accessed 14 October 2012).
7. While showing a film during a class, eleven days after the shooting, he said 'If someone with orange hair appears in the corner of the room, run for the exit'. See Dan Berrett, 'Fired for a joke? Professor's quip is no laughing matter at the Merchant Marine Academy', *Chronicle of Higher Education*, 16 August 2012, http://chronicle.com/article/Professors-Joke-Is-No/133759/ (accessed 13 September 2012).
8. Ariel Kaminer, 'Professor suspended over Colorado shootings joke', *New York Times*, 12 September 2012, http://www.nytimes.com/2012/09/13/nyregion/merchant-marine-academy-professor-wont-be-fired-for-colorado-shooting-joke.html (accessed 9 November 2012).
9. 'New Zealand comic resigns over Hitler joke', *Haaretz*, 27 June 2010, https://www.haaretz.com/2010-06-27/ty-article/new-zealand-comic-resigns-over-hitler-joke/0000017f-e7a8-d97e-a37f-f7edfa090000 (accessed 21 May 2014).
10. When I say 'popular wisdom' I am referring, as the above examples should make clear, not to the views of philosophers or other theorists about the ethics of humour but to the views of the broader population. Some philosophers also have (what I take to be) overly restrictive views on the ethics of humour, and I shall make reference to them too, but my interest is not limited to what philosophers say about humour ethics. I seek to address views that are held much more widely. Of course, what constitutes 'popular wisdom' varies, both geographically and temporally. I am referring to views that are held widely in some or other part of the world in our own times.
11. Philosophers distinguish between the 'use' of a term and the 'mention' of it. If you call me a moron, you are using the using the word 'moron'. If, by contrast, you say 'Bob called you a moron' you are mentioning the word 'moron'. I am mentioning rather than using (or telling)

jokes. For more on the use-mention distinction see Chapter 7.
12. This last distinction is not the distinction between consequentialist and deontological assessments of humour. This is because a deontological assessment can cut across these two kinds of faults. Criticizing a joke because of some inherent feature of it does appear to be a deontological assessment. However, because a determination of whether deleterious effects are

wrongfully inflicted can be made in a deontological way, faulting humour on account of its effects isn't always a consequentialist matter.
13. The type-token distinction is a technical philosophical one. Those unfamiliar with it may, without cost, ignore the reference to a token.
14. Ronald de Sousa, 'When is it wrong to laugh?', in *The Philosophy of Laughter and Humor*, edited by John Morreall (Albany: State University of New York Press, 1987), pp. 226–49. Ronald de Sousa's view is endorsed by Merrie Bergman, 'How many feminists does it take to make a joke? Sexist humor and what's wrong with it', *Hypatia*, Vol. 1, No. 1, Spring 1986, pp. 63–82. Claudia Mills also seems to endorse this view. See her 'Racist and Sexist Jokes: How Bad Are They (Really)?, *Report from the Center for Philosophy and Public Policy*, Vol. 7, No. 2/3, Spring/Summer 1987, pp. 9–12.
15. Ronald de Sousa, 'When is it wrong to laugh?', p. 240. The particular joke that he uses as an illustrative example is a very weak rape joke. I have elsewhere (David Benatar, 'Prejudice in Jest: When Racial and Gender Humor Harms', *Public Affairs Quarterly*, Vol. 13, No. 2, April 1999, pp. 191–202) provided a detailed response to his musings about that joke and I shall not repeat them here.
16. I make this distinction and discuss the issues further in David Benatar, 'Prejudice in Jest: When Racial and Gender Humor Harms'.
17. I provide some anecdotal evidence of this in David Benatar, 'Prejudice in Jest: When Racial and Gender Humor Harms', p. 202.
18. The qualification 'in seriousness' because it is possible to imagine a circumstances in which brothers might be joking with one another. Indeed, two brothers that knew this particular joke might re-enact it in jest.
19. There are many examples of people taking humour to be wrong on the grounds of it being (purportedly) blasphemous. The *Jyllands-Posten* publication of the Mohammed cartoons is one infamous case. Millions of people around the world took the cartoons to be wrong for this reason. Nor were all these people themselves Muslims. Journalist Charlene Smith claimed that 'never, ever, should we blaspheme a person's God or goddess' ('Freedom of the press also requires respect for religion and culture', *Cape Times*, Friday, 10 February 2006). In another, less well-known case some Christians in South Africa objected to what they took to be blasphemous humour in a University of Cape Town student humour magazine. See Errol Naidoo, 'Blasphemy in the media', *Joy Magazine*, 2009, https://joymag.co.za/article/blasphemy-in-the-media/ (last accessed 23 July 2023). These complaints led to the magazine being withdrawn from the shelves of a major chain of shops, and to an apology from the University of Cape Town.
20. For more on this, see David Benatar, 'Cartoons and Consequences', *Think*, No. 17/18, Spring 2008, pp. 53–57.
21. Flemming Rose, *The Tyranny of Silence: How One Cartoon Ignited a Global Debate on the Future of Free Speech* (Washington, DC: Cato Institute, 2014), pp. 90–103.
22. Those responses do not always have to be disapproving responses. Merely printing or innocently quoting the Bible or the Qur'an, for example, could become wrong if, irrespective of one's own intentions, somebody takes the words of the religious text as a justification for violence.
23. For example, South African President Jacob Zuma believes that he was demeaned by cartoonist Jonathan Shapiro (aka Zapiro), and jokes about racial or ethnic groups have been said to exacerbate stereotypes about those groups.
24. There are many people, of course, who do not overlook *this* benefit. However, there are many others who do. This includes not only those who abuse power but also their many supporters.
25. Here is an example of one anti-Mugabe joke:

> A man is caught in a traffic jam when someone taps on the car window. The driver lowers the window and asks what he wants. The other man says, 'President Mugabe has been kidnapped and the ransom is $50-million. If the ransom is not paid, the kidnappers are threatening to douse the president with petrol and set him on fire. We are making a collection. Do you wish to contribute?'
>
> The man in the car asks, 'On average, what are people donating?'
> The other replies, 'About two or three gallons'.
> (*The Herald*, Wednesday, 10 May 2006, p. 6)

26. Steve Lipman, *Laughter in Hell: The Use of Humor during the Holocaust* (Northvale, NJ: Jason Aronson, 1991), p. 52.
27. If my memory serves me correctly, one cabinet member, Piet Koornhof, even (knowingly and freely) participated in one of Mr Uys's films.

28. The joke (in its two forms) is instructive in a variety of ways. First, it provides further support for the point I made earlier that one does not have to endorse a stereotype to find funny a joke that turns on that stereotype. Second, the fact that a joke incorporates a stereotype does not mean that it reinforces or spreads that stereotype. It could instead subvert the stereotype. Third, although the butt of the joke is, respectively, those who hold stereotypes about Jews and 'blacks', this does not mean that Christians and 'whites' are being stereotyped as stereotypers. One does not have to think all (or even almost all) Christians or 'whites' have these attitudes in order to find the joke funny. One need only be aware that there are (or have been) many Christians and 'whites' who have held these views.
29. Where they do add something but all they add is about the intensity of the offense or about religious or racial sensibilities having been offended, they seem to be advocating one of the variants of the offence argument to which I referred in the previous paragraph.
30. Here are just a few: Afzal Ahmad, Chairman of the American Islamic Association, in a letter to the *New York Times* said he found the *Jyllands-Posten* cartoons 'both hurtful and offensive'. The only other thing he said in criticism of the cartoons was: 'In my view, freedom of speech in a public arena carries with it a huge responsibility not to malign people's deeply held religious belief systems'. See 'Violent reactions to offensive images (4 letters), *New York Times*, 7 February 2006, https://www.nytimes.com/2006/02/07/opinion/violent-reactions-to-offensive-images-718270.html (last accessed 1 November 2023). This suggests that he is advancing the version of the offence argument that objects to offending people's religious beliefs. Criticizing the same cartoons, Kofi Annan, then Secretary General of the United Nations, said 'I share the distress of the Muslim friends who feel that the cartoon offends their religion'. See Joel Brinkley and Ian Fisher, 'U.S. says it also finds cartoons of Muhammad offensive', *New York Times*, 4 February 2006, https://www.nytimes.com/2006/02/04/politics/us-says-it-also-finds-cartoons-of-muhammad-offensive.html (last accessed 1 November 2023). If Mr Annan said more, it was not quoted by the *New York Times*, suggesting that either he or the newspaper took the point about offence to be the heart of the criticism. At a performance in Johannesburg, comedian John Cleese told a joke about a tour group to the Dachau concentration camp that arrived too late in the day to be admitted. The joke's punch line was that somebody in the group, hearing that they had been refused entry, said: 'Tell them we are Jewish'. Some Jewish members of Mr Cleese's audience took exception. One said that it 'is truly offensive and (Cleese) should know how we feel'. See 'Cleese at fawlt with tasteless Holocaust joke', *South African Jewish Report*, 28 June to 5 July 2013, p. 2. That was the only criticism attributed to that complainant. Again, either the complainant said no more, or the reporter was of the view that this captured the essence of the complaint.
31. See, for example, David Benatar, 'Should we grant moral veto to the hypersensitive?', *Cape Times*, Monday, 2 March 2009, p. 9.
32. Melanie-Ann Feris, 'Blind object to Nando's guide dog advert', IOL News, 28 February 2000, http://www.iol.co.za/news/south-africa/blind-object-to-nando-s-guide-dog-advert-1.29600#.UKpIu0Lvbww (accessed 19 November 2012).
33. Sapa, 'Nando's ad falls foul—ASA', IOL, 1 March 2000, http://www.iol.co.za/news/south-africa/nando-s-ad-falls-foul-asa-1.29788#.UKpIu0Lvbww (accessed 19 November 2012).
34. For more on the ethics of eating animals, see Chapter 6.
35. Because they cannot see the advertisement, those blind people who objected to it are offended by the bare knowledge of its existence.
36. This 'anti-joke' has spurred many real jokes that are humorous variants on the original.

Chapter 9

1. It is also found in C.E. Vulliamy's *Little Arthur's Guide to Humbug* (London: Michael Joseph, 1960), pp. 23, 79.
2. Which is not the same as saying that he is either (a) the philosopher who has most prominently written bullshit or (b) the philosopher who written the most prominent bullshit.
3. Harry Frankfurt, 'On bullshit', in *On the Importance of What We Care About* (New York: Cambridge University Press, 1988), p. 117.
4. We should not exclude the possibility of non-linguistic bullshit.
5. Harry Frankfurt, 'On bullshit', p. 117.

6. Max Black, 'The Prevalence of Humbug', *Philosophical Exchange*, Vol. 13, No. 1, Article 4, 1982, pp. 1–23.
7. Ibid, p. 5.
8. Ibid, p. 23.
9. A 'theorizer of bullshit' is, of course, different from a 'bullshit theorizer'.
10. Harry Frankfurt, 'On bullshit', p. 121.
11. Ibid, p. 128.
12. G.A. Cohen, 'Deeper into bullshit', in *Contours of Agency: Essays on Themes from Harry Frankfurt*, edited by Sarah Buss and Lee Overton (Cambridge, MA: MIT Press, 2002), p. 323.
13. Ibid.
14. Ibid, pp. 332–33.
15. Judith Butler, 'Further Reflections on Conversations of Our Time', *Diacritics*, Vol. 27, No. 1, Spring 1997, p. 13.
16. G.A. Cohen, 'Deeper into bullshit', p. 333. One also finds some of this kind of nonsense in the academic world. Indeed, this is the sort of bullshit Brian Earp has in mind when he says:

> There is a veritable truckload of bullshit in science. When I say bullshit, I mean arguments, data, publications, or even the official policies of scientific organizations that give every impression of being perfectly reasonable—of being well-supported by the highest quality of evidence, and so forth—but which don't hold up when you scrutinize the details. Bullshit has the veneer of truth-like plausibility. It looks good. It sounds right. But when you get right down to it, it stinks. (Brian Earp, 'The unbearable asymmetry of bullshit', *Healthwatch Newsletter*, Vol. 101, 2016, p. 4)

17. G.A. Cohen, 'Deeper into bullshit', p. 333. He cites David Miller's example: 'Of course, everyone spends much more time thinking about sex now than people did a hundred years ago'.
18. Filip Buekens and Maarten Boudry, 'The Dark Side of the Loon: Explaining the Temptations of Obscurantism', *Theoria*, Vol. 81, 2015, pp. 126–42.
19. Ibid, p. 127.
20. For more on spin, see Neil C. Manson, 'Making Sense of Spin', *Journal of Applied Philosophy*, Vol. 29, No. 3, 2012, pp. 200–213.
21. *Oxford English Dictionary*, Draft additions, 1993.
22. Sometimes there is not only no downside, but there are unmitigated benefits to eliminating the job.
23. David Graeber, 'Are you in a BS job? In academe, you're hardly alone', *Chronicle of Higher Education*, 6 May 2018, https://www.chronicle.com/article/are-you-in-a-bs-job-in-academe-youre-hardly-alone/ (accessed 9 June 2018); David Graeber, *Bullshit Jobs: A Theory* (New York: Simon & Schuster, 2018).
24. Identifying details have been omitted to protect my sources.
25. An academic citation is certainly not necessary, but here is one anyway: Lars J. Kristiansen and Bernd Kaussler, 'The Bullshit Doctrine: Fabrications, Lies, and Nonsense in the Age of Trump', *Informal Logic*, Vol. 38, No. 1, 2018, p. 13–52.
26. It is true that he did not win a second term in 2020, but in the absence of bullshit he would almost certainly not have won a first term, and he may have lost the 2020 election by more.
27. 'Know thy Humbug' is Eumenes Panoptikos's advice to young Arthur. C.E. Vulliamy's *Little Arthur's Guide to Humbug*, p. 89.
28. 'Brandolini's Law', *Wikipedia*, https://en.wikipedia.org/wiki/Brandolini%27s_law (accessed 7 November 2023).
29. Harry Frankfurt, 'Reply to G.A. Cohen', in *Contours of Agency: Essays on Themes from Harry Frankfurt*, edited by Sarah Buss and Lee Overton (Cambridge, MA: MIT Press, 2002), p. 343.
30. Ibid.
31. Ibid.
32. Sir Isaiah Berlin recalled the following:

> The late Harold Macmillan told me that when he was a student at Oxford, before the First World War, he went to the lectures of a philosopher called J. A. Smith, a Hegelian metaphysician. In his first lecture to his audience of students, this professor spoke as follows: 'All of you, gentlemen, will have different careers—some of you will be lawyers, some of you will be soldiers, some will be doctors or engineers, some will be government servants, some will be landowners or politicians. Let me tell you at once that nothing I say during these lectures will be of the slightest use to you in any of the fields in which you will attempt to exercise

your skills. But one thing I can promise you: if you continue with this course of lectures to the end, you will always be able to know when men are talking rot'.

(Ramin Jahanbegloo, *Conversations with Isaiah Berlin* [New York: Charles Scribner's Sons, Maxwell Macmillan International, 1991], p. 29)

My friend, the late Peter Collins, recalled Sir Isaiah relating this story somewhat differently, in which the final line was the more colourful 'spot buncombe at a hundred paces'. Dr Collins was unsure whether his recollection was accurate, but this alternative possible version is worth recording.

33. Jerry Cohen himself describes this sort of dynamic. See 'Deeper into bullshit', pp. 321–22.
34. To 'call bullshit' is to publicly identify something as bullshit—that is by calling it 'bullshit'.
35. Harry Frankfurt, 'Reply to G.A. Cohen', pp. 341–42.
36. Jonathan Lear, 'Whatever', *New Republic*, 21 March 2005, https://newrepublic.com/article/68113/whatever (accessed 30 October 2018).
37. Ibid.
38. Those who are not convinced should read David Benatar, *The Second Sexism: Discrimination against Men and Boys* (Malden, MA: Wiley-Blackwell, 2012).
39. For more on this, see David Benatar, *The Second Sexism*, pp. 225–28.
40. Thomas Nagel, 'Concealment and Exposure', *Philosophy and Public Affairs*, Vol. 27, No. 1, 1998, p. 6.
41. C.E. Vulliamy's *Little Arthur's Guide to Humbug*, pp. 113–14.
42. This case is also discussed by Harry Frankfurt ('On bullshit', p. 123) although not as an example of benign bullshit.
43. Fania Pascal, 'Wittgenstein: A personal memoir', in *Recollections of Wittgenstein*, edited by Rush Rhees (Oxford: Oxford University Press, 1984), pp. 28–29, cited in Harry Frankfurt, 'On bullshit', p. 123.
44. Which can be found here: http://www.bullshitgenerator.com.
45. Which can be found here: http://www.elsewhere.org/pomo/.
46. Both bullshit generators mentioned here generate Cohen-style bullshit. Here is a joke about Frankfurt-style bullshit:

    A monkey is sitting on a tree branch. A giraffe comes by.

    Giraffe: Good morning, Mr Monkey. What are you doing today?
    Monkey: Not much. Just eating some fruit, enjoying the sun, and picking fleas off my balls. However, do you see that lioness over there? Later I'm going to make passionate love to her.
    Giraffe: Okay, have a good day.
    The giraffe moves on. A short while later an elephant comes by.
    Elephant: Good morning, Mr Monkey. What are you doing today?
    Monkey: Not much. Just eating some fruit, enjoying the sun, and picking fleas off my balls. However, do you see that lioness over there? Later I'm going to pleasure her until she screams with joy.
    Elephant: Okay, have a good day.
    The elephant leaves. A short while later a lion with a large mane arrives.
    Lion: Good morning, Mr Monkey. What are you doing today?
    Monkey: Not much. Just eating some fruit, enjoying the sun, picking fleas off my balls... and talking shit with my friends.

47. Jonathan Lear, 'Whatever'.
48. Ibid.
49. My own way of drawing the distinction is between those who show great skill in producing their bullshit and those who produce more pedestrian bullshit. It is the difference between carefully crafted bullshit and that which is simply dumped.
50. I do not exclude the possibility that some non-human animals may also be capable of bullshitting. Whether that is the case will depend in part on various empirical questions that we *may* currently be unable to answer.
51. C.E. Vulliamy has the character Mr Eumenes Panoptikos claim that the 'knowledge of humbug is the beginning of wisdom'. See *Little Arthur's Guide to Humbug*, p. 21.
52. David Egan says:

    A lot of bullshit-calling exhibits neither patience nor imagination. There can be a smug and even arrogant attitude with which people dismiss ideas that resist easy assimilation. Calling bullshit puts an abrupt stop to the conversation: like bullshitting itself, it can encourage us to stop thinking rather than to think further. This strategy is rhetorically seductive: it makes you feel that, if you agree with the bullshit-caller, you're in on the joke, you're not being hoodwinked. This kind of seductive speech, the kind that makes its hearers feel virtuous without actually making them virtuous, is part of what Plato described as sophistry. Calling bullshit might be one of the most insidious forms of bullshit.

'Calling bullshit', *The Point*, 2018, https://thepointmag.com/2018/examined-life/calling-bullshit (accessed 3 November 2018).

53. More will be said about this in Chapter 11.
54. Alan Richardson, 'Performing bullshit and the post-sincere condition', in *Bullshit and Philosophy*, edited by Gary L. Hardcastle and George A. Reisch (Chicago: Open Court, 2006), p. 87.
55. Max Price, 'Letter to the Academic Freedom Committee', University of Cape Town, 12 July 2016. In early 2017, the same Dr Price signed the statement, jointly sponsored by Robert P. George and Cornel West, 'Truth seeking, democracy, and freedom of thought and expression', 14 March 2017, https://jmp.princeton.edu/statement (accessed 5 May 2017).
56. David Benatar, 'A violation of academic freedom by any other name smells as sour', *Politicsweb*, 22 July 2016, http://www.politicsweb.co.za/opinion/uct-a-blow-against-academic-freedom (accessed 14 January 2019).
57. See David Benatar, *The Fall of the University of Cape Town* (N.p.: Politicsweb Publishing, 2021), pp. 346–53.
58. Jay Pather, 'UCT is not a closed and controlled gallery', *Daily Maverick*, 11 August 2017, https://www.dailymaverick.co.za/article/2017-08-11-right-of-reply-uct-is-not-a-closed-and-controlled-gallery/ (accessed 14 January 2019).
59. Elijah Moholola, 'UCT Response on inaccurate claims of censorship of artworks', *Politicsweb*, 4 October 2018, http://www.politicsweb.co.za/opinion/censorship-of-artworks-ucts-response (accessed, 14 January 2019).
60. This particular bullshit was called out by Elisa Galgut and William Daniels, 'Coverings and cover-ups: The art of bullshit', *Politicsweb*, 1 November 2018, https://www.politicsweb.co.za/opinion/the-art-of-bullshit-at-uct (accessed 14 January 2019).
61. Natalie Pertsovksy and GroundUp Staff, 'Quarrel over Sarah Baartman sculpture at UCT', *GroundUp*, 2 March 2018, https://www.groundup.org.za/article/quarrel-over-sarah-baartman-sculpture-uct/ (accessed 15 January 2019).
62. See, for example, Black Academic Caucus, 'The place of Sarah Baartman at UCT', 26 March 2018, https://thoughtleader.co.za/blackacademiccaucus/2018/03/26/the-place-of-sara-baartman-at-uct/ (accessed 15 January 2019).
63. I recognize, of course, that many people have limited options.
64. The claim here is not that every member of these professions is a bullshitter. Instead, the claim is that these are professions especially prone to bullshit and in which it is very difficult to succeed without bullshitting.
65. I am reminded of the following joke:

> Mathematicians do not have to budget for much in their research grant applications. They need only paper, a pencil, and a wastepaper basket into which they can deposit their errors. Philosophers need even less money. They do not need the wastepaper baskets.

66. Sometimes the reward may simply be a lesser penalty. Consider, for example, somebody who has committed a punishable offence. If, instead of trying to bullshit her way out of punishment, she confesses to the wrongdoing and pleads guilty, a lesser penalty may be appropriate.

Chapter 10

1. Alexander Pope, *An Essay on Criticism*, line 525.
2. It is also possible for somebody to have a *partially* moralized account, whereby what forgiveness is includes some moral criteria, while still allowing that an instance of forgiveness could be wrong.

3. Or 'abandoning' or 'withdrawing', but 'overcoming' seems best.
4. Peter Strawson correctly mentions feelings as well as attitudes, but then uses '(reactive) attitudes' as shorthand for '(reactive) attitudes and feelings'. Peter Strawson, 'Freedom and resentment', in *Free Will*, edited by Gary Watson (Oxford: Oxford University Press, 1982), p. 63.
5. It has been suggested to me that, according to ordinary usage, 'forgive' *also* denotes a change in status of the person who is forgiven—that that person is released from owing the forgiver what would otherwise have been owed. I do not deny that the word also has this meaning, and I shall say more about this shortly and then again later in the chapter. However, it is entirely possible to think that the word *also* has this second meaning, while thinking that the meaning I have stated is the most *fundamental* one. Those genuinely interested in forgiveness, even if they are (also) interested in being released from debt, want this release *because* the forgiver has had a change of heart. If they are primarily interested in being released from debt and do not really care whether the forgiver has had a change of heart, it does not look as though it is forgiveness that they really want. Moreover, those who are really remorseful and want forgiveness may be very willing to remain in some kind of debt to the forgiver.
6. David Novitz mentions the following examples: 'an older sister may be said never to have forgiven her brother for being the favourite of her parents, for being good-looking, graceful, or athletic' or 'I may fail ... to forgive you for trouncing me at tennis' ('Forgiveness and Self-Respect', *Philosophy and Phenomenological Research*, Vol. 58, No. 2, June 1998, p. 303). For another example, see the title of Geoffrey C. Ward's *Unforgivable Blackness: The Rise and Fall of Jack Johnson* (New York: Alfred Knopf, 2005).
7. For a long time, I was among those who held this view.
8. One situation in which it would not, is if the parent never learns that the child has been raped.
9. Even if you enable your child to overcome her negative reactive attitudes, it is still the child, rather than you, who is forgiving the perpetrator.
10. Glenn Pettigrove makes this point, although with regard to the moral rather than conceptual question. 'The Standing to Forgive', *Monist*, Vol. 92, No. 4, 2009, pp. 586–91.
11. A possible exception is where the murder is not instantaneous. Perhaps the victim is shot but languishes for a few days before dying and knowing that he will die. It is *possible* in such circumstances for the victim to forgive the murderer.
12. People sometimes speak of 'forgiving' (monetary) debts. Whereas such debts and the associated credits can be inherited, that is not the case with forgiveness in its paradigmatic sense. In other words, if A owes a monetary debt to B (including one arising from a wrong A did to B), and B dies, then B's child, C, can inherit the entitlement. C may then demand or waive ('forgive') the payment of that debt. However, it is different with negative attitudes and feelings, which die with the victim. They are not inherited in any literal way.
13. Jeffrie G. Murphy, 'Forgiveness, Reconciliation, and Responding to Evil', *Fordham Urban Law Journal*, Vol. 27, 2000, p. 1355; John Kekes adds 'bitterness' ('Blame versus Forgiveness', *Monist*, Vol. 92, No. 4, 2009, p. 499); and Howard Wettstein adds 'revulsion, sadness, depression with the state of things, annoyance, even relative indifference' to the possible list ('Forgiveness and Moral Reckoning', *Philosophia*, Vol. 38, 2010, p. 446).
14. Norvin Richards, 'Forgiveness', in *Ethics*, Vol. 99, No. 1, October 1988, p. 78.
15. Although Norvin Richards does not speak about a spectrum, he does seem to think that one has only (fully) forgiven once one has overcome all the negative attitudes and feelings ('Forgiveness', p. 79). Macalester Bell has an alternative view, according to which one does not have to purge oneself of all negative attitudes and feelings. All that is required is that one 'must no longer be led or dominated by' them. See 'Forgiving Someone for Who They Are (and Not Just What They Have Done)', *Philosophy and Phenomenological Research*, Vol. 77, No. 3, November 2008, pp. 636–37.
16. Paul M. Hughes, 'Moral Anger, Forgiving, and Condoning', *Journal of Social Philosophy*, Vol. 25, No. 1, Spring 1995, p. 107.
17. Some may wonder whether it would make a difference whether a person's personality was forgiving only because of medication they were taking. I shall not engage this question, which takes us well beyond questions about forgiveness, and which does not need to be resolved in order to make the more general claim I am making here. Put another way, there will be hard cases when it is unclear whether a given case is a case of 'forgiving' or a case of 'pharmaceuticals'. The existence of hard cases does not undermine the claim that there are also easy cases.

18. David Novitz thinks that it is 'less appropriate to speak of forgiveness where minor wrongs are concerned' ('Forgiveness and Self-Respect', pp. 300–301).
19. Jeffrie G. Murphy, 'Forgiveness, Reconciliation, and Responding to Evil', pp. 1355–56.
20. Ibid., p. 1356.
21. For example, Paul M. Hughes distinguishes between (a) 'overlooking and thereby approving' and (b) 'overlooking while nevertheless disapproving' ('Moral Anger, Forgiving, and Condoning', p. 111); and Charles Griswold distinguishes between (a) 'accepting while not disapproving' and (b) 'tolerating while disapproving' (*Forgiveness: A Philosophical Exploration* [New York: Cambridge University Press, 2007], p. 46).
22. This is true of both senses of condoning I am discussing.
23. This is adapted from Jeffrie Murphy ('Forgiveness, Reconciliation, and Responding to Evil', p. 1356), who says that 'to accord a wrongdoer mercy is to inflict a less harsh consequence on that person than allowed *by institutional (usually legal) rules*' (my emphasis). I have dropped the italicized words because I think that one can show mercy outside of institutional rules; and I have added 'or deserved' because at least sometimes that seems to be the appropriate benchmark.
24. Jeffrie Murphy, 'Forgiveness, Reconciliation, and Responding to Evil', p. 1356.
25. I shall return later to the *morality* of forgiving the person who dented your car.
26. Does it matter if, as I argued years ago, one way of 'treating' people is by thinking ill (or well) of them? (David Benatar, 'Prejudice in Jest: When Racial and Gender Humor Harms', *Public Affairs Quarterly*, Vol. 13, No. 2, April 1999, pp. 191–203.) I doubt that a definitive answer can be provided, but my own sense is that even those who agree that merely regarding people in a particular way is a *kind* of harm, it is a *different* kind of harm, and that mercy does not extend to this kind of case. When we speak about the power to show mercy, we are speaking about legal, social, or economic power, rather than power merely over one's own thoughts. If the attribution of 'mercy' could be made to those whose only power is over their own thoughts, then the class of who counts as 'powerless' would be unreasonably diminished.
27. Jeffrie Murphy provides the following example ('Forgiveness, Reconciliation, and Responding to Evil', p. 1357.):

    Imagine a battered woman who has been repeatedly beaten and raped by her husband or boyfriend. This woman—after a religious conversion, perhaps—might well come to forgive her batterer (i.e., stop hating him) without a willingness to resume her relationship with him. 'I forgive you and wish you well' can, in my view, sit quite consistently with 'I never want you in this house again'. In short, the fact that one has forgiven does not mean that one must also trust or live again with a person.

28. If one adopted the spectrum view of both forgiveness and reconciliation, then examples such as this could not be used to distinguish them. Then both forgiveness and reconciliation would admit of degrees, and they would track one another more closely.
29. More accurately, and unlike tango, it takes *at least* two to reconcile.
30. J.L. Austin, *How to Do Things with Words*, 2nd ed. (Cambridge, MA: Harvard University Press, 1975).
31. David Novitz makes this point ('Forgiveness and Self-Respect', pp. 301–2).
32. Geoffrey Scarre ('On Taking Back Forgiveness', *Ethical Theory and Moral Practice*, Vol. 19, No. 4, 2016, p. 937) suggests that declaring 'I forgive you' implies this. Therefore, he says that where 'that change has not occurred, or is incomplete, the words ought not to be spoken, on pain of being misunderstood'. His view differs from mine in that I do not think that this is the only possible interpretation of what somebody is saying in uttering the words 'I forgive you', although I do concede that it is the more plausible meaning.
33. David Novitz suggests instead that all uttering those words 'can do is renounce the claims that I have on you' ('Forgiveness and Self-Respect', pp. 301–2). However, as he notes, 'forgive' is being used a different sense here, namely to 'pardon' (at least in one sense of *that* term).
34. 'The words express a commitment to move on and to act in future in a non-resentful manner, and (as in the case of any promise) one should not say them unless one is sure that one can live up to them'. Geoffrey Scarre, 'On Taking Back Forgiveness', pp. 936–37. Margaret Holmgren seems to hold the same view. *Forgiveness and Retribution* (New York: Cambridge University Press, 2012), pp. 43–44.

35. I am grateful to Jessica du Toit for suggesting this.
36. Christopher Bennett, 'The Alteration Thesis: Forgiveness as a Normative Power', *Philosophy and Public Affairs*, Vol. 46, No. 2, 2018, p. 207.
37. Ibid, pp. 214–15. Wrongdoing also generates (defeasible) secondary obligations for others. These include obligations to condemn the wrong and support the victim.
38. Ibid, pp. 215–16.
39. Ibid, p. 217.
40. Ibid, 218–19. The same commitment can also be part of rights-waiving forgiveness, except that then it is not made in recognition of the wrongdoer having discharged his obligations.
41. Ibid, p. 225.
42. Ibid. p. 225.
43. Ibid, p. 225.
44. Ibid, p. 226. (It is far from clear what is being said here, or even whether a single claim or multiple claims are being made. However, in the following I shall respond to what I take to be the most plausible understanding of it.)
45. Ibid, p. 211.
46. I say 'at least partly' because where negative reactive attitudes are warranted, their severity will also depend on the severity of the wrong. While I am now considering the aptness of negative reactive attitudes, I shall later say something about the aptness of their severity.
47. Peter Strawson, 'Freedom and resentment', p. 63.
48. S.J. Perelman, playing on the words from Alexander Pope cited at the beginning of this chapter, quipped that 'To err is human, to forgive, supine' ('To err is human, to forgive supine', *New Yorker*, 4 October 1969, pp. 36–38.)
49. Jeffrie Murphy is one who thinks that forgiving too readily *may* result from a lack of self-respect. 'Forgiveness in counseling: A philosophical perspective', in *Character, Liberty, and Law: Kantian Essays in Theory and Practice* (Dordrecht: Kluwer, 1998), pp. 227–28.
50. I am reminded, tangentially, of the joke about the man sitting in a bar. The bartender says to him:

    'You see this bar? I built it with my own bare hands, brick by brick, working through rain and cold. Do they call me McDonald the bar builder? No!'

    'You see that church across the street? I built that church with my two hands, laying one stone at a time, through foul weather. Do, they call me, McDonald the church builder? No, they do not!'

    'You see that pier on the lake? I built that myself, driving in all the pilings and laying and hammering in all the planks. Do they call me McDonald the pier-builder? No!'

    'But you fuck *one* sheep...'

    Whether bestiality is a serious wrong depends, of course, on issues discussed in Chapter 2. One does not have to assume that bestiality is a serious wrong to find this joke funny. It might be sufficient to recognize that it is regarded as a serious wrong—or even only that many people often fixate on a single action that somebody performs, even when there is more complexity to that person. The joke is not intended to illustrate when one action *reasonably* crowds out all other features of a person.
51. Jeffrie G. Murphy, 'Forgiveness and resentment', in Jeffrie G. Murphy and Jean Hampton, *Forgiveness and Mercy* (New York: Cambridge University Press, 1998), p. 26.
52. Contra Cheshire Calhoun, who says that 'to stop my hard response after you have repented ... is to do nothing more than I ought ... Reason requires changing one's heart, and forgiveness thus ceases to be elective' ('Changing One's Heart', *Ethics*, Vol. 103, October 1992, p. 79). My arguments in this paragraph also counter the claim that when the perpetrator repents, forgiveness become *redundant* on the grounds that given the repentance there is nothing to forgive. For an outline of an argument that forgiveness *is* redundant once the wrongdoer repents, see Aurel Kolnai, 'Forgiveness', *Proceedings of the Aristotelian Society* (New Series), Vol. 74, 1973–1974, p. 98.
53. More accurately, if there are any ongoing effects, it is because the victim has overacted, and while that overreaction needs to be moderated, that overcoming does not count as forgiveness, for reasons outlined earlier.
54. Alternatively, the challenge is to show why the negative attitudes and feelings towards the wrongdoer were not appropriate in the first place. Margaret Holmgren (in *Forgiveness and Retribution*) seems to adopt this view, and I respond to it below.

55. Although this quip is widely attributed to Oscar Wilde, including in several anthologies of quotations, I have been unable to find an original source. Oscar Wilde did say something similar: 'I find that forgiving one's enemies is a most curious morbid pleasure; perhaps I should check it out'. Oscar Wilde, 'To Lord Alfred Douglas', 20 April 1894, *The Complete Letters of Oscar Wilde*, edited by Merlin Holland and Rupert Hart-Davies (New York: Henry Holt and Company, 2000), p. 590.
56. Geoffrey Scarre confuses forgiving and not dwelling on ('On Taking Back Forgiveness', p. 935).
57. Eve Garrard and David McNaughton, 'In Defence of Unconditional Forgiveness', *Proceedings of the Aristotelian Society*, Vol. 103, 2003, p. 59.
58. Michele Moody-Adams, 'The Enigma of Forgiveness', *Journal of Value Inquiry*, Vol. 49, 2015, p. 164.
59. Ibid, p. 166.
60. Ibid.
61. Margaret Holmgren, *Forgiveness and Retribution*, p. 62.
62. Ibid, p. 11.
63. Ibid, p. 87.
64. Ibid, p. 34.
65. Ibid. p. 35.
66. Ibid, p. 87.
67. Even if both forgiving and not forgiving would have been appropriate, once one has forgiven, it can be inappropriate to reverse it.
68. One could still ask a hypothetical moral question: If I could overcome your negative attitudes and feelings, would it be morally permissible for me to do so?
69. This is not the same sense of wiping the slate clean as that used by Lucy Allais, 'Wiping the Slate Clean: The Heart of Forgiveness', *Philosophy and Public Affairs*, Vol. 36, No. 1, 2008, pp. 33–68.
70. Cited by Eve Garrard and David McNaughton, 'In Defence of Unconditional Forgiveness', p. 39.

Chapter 11

1. In some cases, doing one's duty may require considerable sacrifice. Consider, for example, a duty not to betray an innocent when such betrayal would result in the torture of death of the person you would betray. Not betraying that person might come at great cost to you. Opinions are divided in such cases. Some think that given how great the cost is to you, you are permitted to betray the other person—that the *pro tanto* duty is not a duty *tout court*. Others say that, notwithstanding the massive cost to you, you are not permitted to betray the other person. On this view, your negative duty is an all things considered duty that is not defeated by your own important interests. I shall not settle such disagreements here, not least because I do not need to do so for the purposes of this book, given that such cases are typically not quotidian ones (unless one's quotidian circumstances are those of a repressive totalitarian regime).
2. I recognize that the responsibility for becoming a smoker is often not *full* responsibility. If, for example, a person becomes a smoker as a child, and children are not fully responsible, then the smoker is not fully responsible for having become a smoker. However, it remains the case both that the smoker is substantially responsible and that the non-smoker is typically not at all responsible for the smoker having taken up smoking.
3. I say more about this in David Benatar, 'Famine, Affluence, and Procreation: Peter Singer and Anti-Natalism Lite', *Ethical Theory and Moral Practice*, Vol. 23, No. 2, 2020, pp. 415–31.
4. When I speak about 'doing the right thing' or 'acting rightly', I include omissions, for sometimes acting rightly amounts to desisting from doing certain things.
5. This is the paradox that pleasure is best obtained without directly pursing it. See Henry Sidgwick, *The Methods of Ethics*, 7th ed. (London: Macmillan and Company, 1907), p. 48.
6. This paradox arises from the hypothesis that the incidence of cancers arising from somatic mutations should be greater among larger animals than among smaller animals, given that there are more cell divisions in larger animals (because they have more cells). Paradoxically, the expected incidence is very different from the actual incidence. The paradox was first described by Richard Peto, 'Epidemiology, multistage models, and short-term mutagenicity tests', in *The Origins of Human Cancer*, edited by H.H. Hiatt, J.D. Watson, and J.A. Winstein (Cold Spring Harbor, NY: Cold Spring Harbor Conferences on Cell Proliferation, 1977), pp. 1403–28. It was,

to the best of my knowledge, named 'Peto's Paradox' by Leonard Nunney, 'Lineage Selection and the Evolution of Multistage Carcinogenesis', *Proceedings of the Royal Society of London B*, Vol. 266, 1999, pp. 493–98.

7. This is the paradox that the French have lower rates of coronary heart disease than one would expect given that their diet is high in saturated fat. See S. Renaud and M. de Lorgeril, 'Wine, Alcohol, Platelets, and the French Paradox for Coronary Heart Disease', *Lancet*, Vol. 339, 20 June 1992, pp. 1523–26.
8. Saul Smilansky, *10 Moral Paradoxes* (Malden, MA: Blackwell, 2007), p. 5.
9. I am *not* claiming here that repaying a debt is always the right thing to do. One can imagine circumstances in which paying a debt will enable the creditor to act wrongly, in which case some might maintain that there is no duty to pay the debt. Instead, my claim is that when acting rightly involves paying a debt, the cost to the debtor of paying the debt is internal to acting rightly.
10. If 'everybody' is taken literally, then such cases are either fictional or refer to highly restricted scenarios in which 'everybody' refers to a small number of people.
11. Some may want a case to illustrate this. The problem with providing an illustration is that there is so much disagreement about where duty ends, and supererogation begins. Thus, any illustration of universal supererogation would likely be controversially characterized as such.
12. How common or typical a given physiological response is among those subjected to the stimulus can impact on the moral permissibility of the action (although not as much as it impacts on whether the action should be legally permissible). However, because ethical assessments should be more responsive to particular circumstances than laws need be, it is possible for even an idiosyncratic physiological response to provide a good reason, all else being equal, not to perform the action that triggers that response.
13. I leave open the question of what constitutes '(having) sex'. It obviously does not include hand-holding or a quick kiss. However, between such practices and coitus lie a full spectrum of activities, at least some of which will count as sex. To simplify the current discussion, I focus only on practices that do indeed amount to having sex.
14. About 5% of people worldwide describe themselves as vegetarian, and a further 3% describe themselves as vegan. 'An exploration into diets around the world', Ipsos MORI Global Advisor Survey, August 2018.
15. There are many dozens of philosophical defenders of better treatment of animals. There are relatively few (such as Raymond Frey, Peter Carruthers, Carl Cohen, Michael Allen Fox, and Nick Zangwill) who defend the consumption of animals, and even some of them concede that *some* of the ways in which we treat animals are unjustified.
16. In one poll, with over two thousand respondents, 25% reported as vegetarians, and 8% as vegans. See 'Philosophers, Eating, Ethics—a Discussion of the Poll Results', *Leiter Reports*, 10 October 2012, https://leiterreports.typepad.com/blog/2012/10/philosophers-eating-ethics-a-discussion-of-the-poll-results.html (accessed 2 January 2023). Even if we acknowledge that these self-reports may exceed actual levels of vegetarianism and veganism among philosophers (Eric Schwitzgebel and Joshua Rust, 'The Moral Behavior of Ethics Professors: Relationships among Self-Reported Behavior, Expressed Normative Attitude, and Directly Observed Behavior', *Philosophical Psychology*, Vol. 27, No. 3, 2014, pp. 293–327), we nonetheless have reason for thinking that vegetarianism and veganism are more common among philosophers than in the general population (not least because self-reporting may also exaggerate the prevalence of vegetarianism and veganism among all people).
17. There may be some selection bias here—those more interested in animal well-being might be more likely to enter into the field. Alternatively, or in addition, the explanation might be that the overwhelming weight of evidence and arguments supports vegetarianism and veganism. Whatever the explanation, it remains true that among those philosophers writing on the topic, I share views with the majority rather than the minority.
18. For some examples, see Alan Sokal and Jean Bricmont, *Fashionable Nonsense: Postmodern Intellectuals' Abuse of Science* (New York: Picador, 1998); David Benatar, *The Fall of the University of Cape Town: Africa's Leading University in Decline* (N.p.: Politicsweb Publishing, 2021).
19. I have argued for this in other books, including David Benatar, *Better Never to Have Been: The Harm of Coming into Existence* (Oxford: Oxford University Press, 2006); and David Benatar, *The Human Predicament: A Candid Guide to Life's Biggest Questions* (New York: Oxford University Press, 2017).
20. See Chapter 8. I provide another example in David Benatar, *The Fall of the University of Cape Town*, p. 73.

21. I say 'often' because there clearly are people who are much harder on themselves than they are on others.
22. Those future people sitting in judgement of our generation will very likely be susceptible to similar judgements from people in the still later future.
23. For the record, I would oppose both of those statue removals. Nelson Mandela was a great man, worthy of memorial, despite his flaws, and Al Gore's air travel might well be justified if his air travel has indeed succeeded in reducing net emissions.
24. Those arguments might come from others. Alternatively, they might result from putting oneself in the shoes of those with opposing views and attempting to construct the best arguments one can in support of those views.

Bibliography

'2020 tied for warmest year on record, NASA analysis shows', Goddard Institute for Space Studies, National Aeronautics and Space Administration, 14 January 2021, https://www.giss.nasa.gov/research/news/20210114/.

'About niggardly', *Washington Post*, 29 January 1999, https://www.washingtonpost.com/archive/opinions/1999/01/29/about-niggardly/2204430b-376f-4d1d-91f5-b1b950e37932/.

'About one-in-four U.S. Hispanics have heard of Latinx, but just 3% use it', Pew Research Center, 11 August 2020, https://www.pewresearch.org/hispanic/2020/08/11/about-one-in-four-u-s-hispanics-have-heard-of-latinx-but-just-3-use-it/#fn-29384-1.

ADAPTT (Animals Deserve Absolute Protection Today and Tomorrow), 'Kill counter', http://www.adaptt.org/about/the-kill-counter.html.

Ahmad, Afzal, 'Violent reactions to offensive images', *New York Times*, 7 February 2006, https://www.nytimes.com/2006/02/07/opinion/violent-reactions-to-offensive-images-718270.html.

Allais, Lucy, 'Wiping the Slate Clean: The Heart of Forgiveness', *Philosophy and Public Affairs*, Vol. 36, No. 1, 2008, pp. 33–68.

Allarakha, Shaziya, 'What are the 72 other genders?', 2 February 2022, https://www.medicinenet.com/what_are_the_72_other_genders/article.htm.

Alward, Peter, 'The Naïve Argument against Moral Vegetarianism', *Environmental Values*, Vol. 9, 2000, pp. 81–89.

American Philosophical Association, 'Guidelines for non-sexist use of language', https://www.apaonline.org/page/nonsexist.

Anderegg, William R.L., James W. Prall, Jacob Harold, and Stephen H. Schneider, 'Expert Credibility in Climate Change', *Proceedings of the National Academy of Sciences*, Vol. 107, No. 27, 6 July 2010, pp. 12107–9.

Arthur, John, 'World hunger and moral obligation: The case against Singer', in *Vice and Virtue in Everyday Life*, 3rd ed., edited by Christina Sommers and Fred Sommers (Fort Worth: Harcourt Brace Jovanovich, 1993), pp. 845–52.

Arthur, John, 'Rights and the duty to bring aid', in *World Hunger and Morality*, 2nd ed., edited by William Aiken and Hugh LaFollette (Upper Saddle River, NJ: Prentice-Hall, 1996), pp. 39–50.

Astor, Maggie, 'Do airline climate offsets really work? Here's the good news, and the bad', *New York Times*, 18 May 2022, https://www.nytimes.com/2022/05/18/climate/offset-carbon-footprint-air-travel.html.

Austin, J.L., *How to Do Things with Words*, 2nd ed. (Cambridge, MA: Harvard University Press, 1975).

Bagemihl, Bruce, *Biological Exuberance: Animal Homosexuality and Natural Diversity* (New York: St Martin's Press, 1999).

Barash, David P., and Judith Eve Lipton, *The Myth of Monogamy: Fidelity and Infidelity in Animals and People* (New York: Henry Holt and Company, 2001).

Barendregt, Jan J., Luc Bonneux, and Paul J. van der Maas, 'The Health Care Costs of Smoking', *New England Journal of Medicine*, Vol. 337, No. 15, 9 October 1997, pp. 1052–57.

Baron, Dennis, 'A brief history of singular "they"', *The Web of Language*, 30 July 2018, https://blogs.illinois.edu/view/25/677177.

Bastos, Rafi, 'They/Them', https://www.youtube.com/shorts/iB_qpiq-WiI.

Bate, Barbara, 'Nonsexist Language Use in Transition', *Journal of Communication*, Vol. 28, 1978, pp. 139–49.

Bell, Macalester, 'Forgiving Someone for Who They Are (and Not Just What They Have Done)', *Philosophy and Phenomenological Research*, Vol. 77, No. 3, November 2008, pp. 625–58.

Benatar, David, 'Prejudice in Jest: When Racial and Gender Humor Harms', *Public Affairs Quarterly*, Vol. 13, No. 2, April 1999, pp. 191–202.

Benatar, David, 'Why the Naïve Argument against Moral Vegetarianism Really Is Naïve', *Environmental Values*, Vol. 10, No. 1, 2001, pp. 103–12.

Benatar, David, ed., *Ethics for Everyday* (Boston: McGraw-Hill, 2002).

Benatar, David, 'Promiscuity, Pedophilia, and Rape: Two Views of Sexual Ethics', *Public Affairs Quarterly*, Vol. 16, No. 3, 2002, pp. 191–201.

Benatar, David, 'The Second Sexism', *Social Theory and Practice*, Vol. 29, No. 2, April 2003, pp. 177–210.

Benatar, David, 'Sexist Language: Alternatives to the Alternatives', *Public Affairs Quarterly*, Vol. 19, No. 1, January 2005, pp. 1–9.

Benatar, David, *Better Never to Have Been: The Harm of Coming into Existence* (Oxford: Oxford University Press, 2006).

Benatar, David, 'Bioethics and Health and Human Rights: A Critical View', *Journal of Medical Ethics*, Vol. 32, No. 1, January 2006, pp. 17–20.

Benatar, David, 'A Storm in a Turban', *Think*, Vol. 5, No. 13, Summer 2006, pp. 17–22.

Benatar, David, 'Teaching ethics for everyday', *American Philosophical Association Newsletter on Teaching Philosophy*, Vol. 5, No. 2, Spring 2006, pp. 8–12.

Benatar, David, 'The Chickens Come Home to Roost', *American Journal of Public Health*, Vol. 97, No. 9, September 2007, pp. 1545–46.

Benatar, David, 'Cartoons and Consequences', *Think*, Vol. 6, No. 17/18, Spring 2008, pp. 53–57.

Benatar, David, 'Should we grant moral veto to the hypersensitive?', *Cape Times*, Monday 2 March 2009, p. 9.

Benatar, David, 'The limits of reproductive freedom', in *Procreation and Parenthood*, edited by David Archard and David Benatar (Oxford: Oxford University Press, 2010), pp. 78–102.

Benatar, David, 'A First Name Basis?', *Think*, Vol. 10, No. 29, Autumn 2011, pp. 51–57.

Benatar, David, *The Second Sexism: Discrimination against Men and Boys* (Malden, MA: Wiley-Blackwell, 2012).

Benatar, David, 'Quotidian ethics', in *International Encyclopedia of Ethics*, edited by Hugh LaFollette (Hoboken, NJ: Wiley-Blackwell, 2013), pp. 4281–85. Revision published in 3rd ed., 2022.

Benatar, David, 'There's No Method in the Badness', *Bioethics*, Vol. 27, No. 3, 2013, p. 174.

Benatar, David, 'The misanthropic argument for anti-natalism', in *Permissible Progeny?*, edited by Sarah Hannan, Samantha Brennan, and Richard Vernon (New York: Oxford University Press, 2015), pp. 34–64.

Benatar, David, 'A violation of academic freedom by any other name smells as sour', *Politicsweb*, 22 July 2016, http://www.politicsweb.co.za/opinion/uct-a-blow-against-academic-freedom.

Benatar, David, *The Human Predicament: A Candid Guide to Life's Biggest Questions* (New York: Oxford University Press, 2017).

Benatar, David, 'Toward more respectful academic reference practices', *What's Wrong*, 4 February 2019, https://whatswrongcvsp.com/2019/02/04/toward-more-respectful-academic-reference-practices/.

Benatar, David, 'Why don't academics address each other politely?', *Times Higher Education*, 31 January 2019, https://www.timeshighereducation.com/opinion/why-dont-academics-address-each-other-politely.

Benatar, David, 'Famine, Affluence, and Procreation: Peter Singer and Anti-Natalism Lite', *Ethical Theory and Moral Practice*, Vol. 23, No. 2, 2020, pp. 415–31.

Benatar, David, 'Our cruel treatment of animals led to the coronavirus', *New York Times*, 13 April 2020, https://www.nytimes.com/2020/04/13/opinion/animal-cruelty-coronavirus.html.

Benatar, David, *The Fall of the University of Cape Town: Africa's Leading University in Decline* (N.p.: Politicsweb Publishing, 2021).
Benatar, David, 'The new blasphemy', *Politicsweb*, 30 March 2021, https://www.politicsweb.co.za/opinion/the-new-blasphemy.
Benatar, David, 'Homosexuality, bestiality, and necrophilia', in *Palgrave Handbook of Sexual Ethics*, edited by David Boonin (Cham, Switzerland: Palgrave Macmillan, 2022), pp. 223–31.
Benatar, David, 'We Have No Moral Duty to Eat Meat: A Reply to Nick Zangwill', *Public Affairs Quarterly*, Vol. 36, No. 4, October 2022, pp. 331–43.
Benatar, David, 'The Paradox of Desert', *Journal of Applied Philosophy*, doi: 10.1111/japp.12721
Bennett, Christopher, 'The Alteration Thesis: Forgiveness as a Normative Power', *Philosophy and Public Affairs*, Vol. 46, No. 2, 2018, pp. 207–33.
Bergman, Merrie, 'How Many Feminists Does It Take to Make a Joke? Sexist Humor and What's Wrong with It', *Hypatia*, Vol. 1, No. 1, Spring 1986, pp. 63–82.
Berners-Lee, Mike, *How Bad Are Bananas? The Carbon Footprint of Everything* (London: Profile Books, 2010).
Bernstein, Steven L., 'Electronic Cigarettes: More Light, Less Heat Needed', *Lancet Respiratory Medicine*, Vol. 4, February 2016, pp. 85–87.
Berrett, Dan, 'Fired for a joke? Professor's quip is no laughing matter at the Merchant Marine Academy', *Chronicle of Higher Education*, 16 August 2012, https://www.chronicle.com/article/fired-for-a-joke-professors-quip-is-no-laughing-matter-at-the-merchant-marine-academy/.
Bertone, Elizabeth R., Laura A. Snyder, and Antony S. Moore, 'Environmental Tobacco Smoke and Risk of Malignant Lymphoma in Pet Cats', *American Journal of Epidemiology*, Vol. 156, No. 3, 2002, pp. 268–73.
Bisinella, Valentina, Paola Federica Albizzati, Thomas Fruergaard Astrup, and Anders Damgaard, eds., *Life Cycle Assessment of Grocery Carrier Bags* (Copenhagen: The Danish Environmental Protection Agency, 2018).
Black, Max, 'The Prevalence of Humbug', *Philosophical Exchange*, Vol. 13, No. 1, Article 4, 1982, pp. 1–23.
Black Academic Caucus, 'The place of Sarah Baartman at UCT', 26 March 2018, https://thoughtleader.co.za/blackacademiccaucus/2018/03/26/the-place-of-sara-baartman-at-uct/.
Blue, Marie-Luise, 'What is the carbon footprint of a plastic bottle?', Updated 11 June 2018, https://sciencing.com/carbon-footprint-plastic-bottle-12307187.html.
Bodine, Ann, 'Androcentrism in Prescriptive Grammar: Singular "They", Sex-Indefinite "He", and "He or She"', *Language in Society*, Vol. 4, 1975, pp. 129–46.
Braier, Rachel, 'In praise of the C-word', *Guardian*, 11 July 2016, https://www.theguardian.com/media/mind-your-language/2016/jul/11/in-praise-of-the-c-word.
Braithwaite, Victoria, *Do Fish Feel Pain?* (Oxford: Oxford University Press, 2010).
'Brandolini's law', *Wikipedia*, https://en.wikipedia.org/wiki/Brandolini's_law.
Brinkley, Joel, and Ian Fisher, 'U.S. says it also finds cartoons of Muhammad offensive', *New York Times*, 4 February 2006, https://www.nytimes.com/2006/02/04/politics/us-says-it-also-finds-cartoons-of-muhammad-offensive.html.
Brodkin Sacks, Karen, 'How did Jews become white folks?', in *Race*, edited by Steven Gregory and Roger Sanjek (New Brunswick: Rutgers University Press, 1994), pp. 78–102.
Broome, John, *Climate Matters: Ethics in a Warming World* (New York: W.W. Norton & Company, 2012).
Buchanan, Allen, 'Justice as Reciprocity versus Subject-Centered Justice', *Philosophy and Public Affairs*, Vol. 19, No. 3, Summer 1990, pp. 227–52.
Buchanan, Allen, 'The Morality of Inclusion', *Social Philosophy and Policy*, Vol. 10, No. 2, 1993, pp. 233–57.
Buekens, Filip, and Maarten Boudry, 'The Dark Side of the Loon: Explaining the Temptations of Obscurantism', *Theoria*, Vol. 81, 2015, pp. 126–42.

'Bullshit generator', https://www.bullshitgenerator.com.
Butler, Judith, 'Further Reflections on Conversations of Our Time', *Diacritics*, Vol. 27, No. 1, Spring 1997, pp. 13–15.
Butler, Keith, 'The Moral Status of Smoking', *Social Theory and Practice*, Vol. 19, No. 1, Spring 1993, pp. 1–26.
Butry, David T., Jeffrey P. Prestemon, and Douglas S. Thomas, 'Investigation of the Decline in Reported Smoking-Caused Wildfires in the USA from 2000 to 2011', *International Journal of Wildland Fire*, Vol. 23, 2014, pp. 790–98.
Byrnes, Sholto, 'Roger Scruton: The patron saint of lost causes', *Independent*, 3 July 2005, https://www.independent.co.uk/arts-entertainment/books/features/roger-scruton-the-patron-saint-of-lost-causes-296509.html.
Calhoun, Cheshire, 'Changing One's Heart', *Ethics*, Vol. 103, No. 1, October 1992, pp. 76–96.
'Carbon dioxide in Earth's atmosphere', *Wikipedia*, https://en.wikipedia.org/wiki/Carbon_dioxide_in_Earth's_atmosphere.
Carbon Footprint, Carbon Calculator, https://www.carbonfootprint.com/calculator.aspx.
Center for Sustainable Systems, University of Michigan, 'Carbon footprint factsheet', Pub. No. CSS09-05, 2020.
'Chopped liver as an expression', *Wikipedia*, https://en.wikipedia.org/wiki/Chopped_liver#Chopped_liver_as_an_expression.
'Cleese at fawlt with tasteless Holocaust joke', *South African Jewish Report*, Vol. 17, No. 22, 28 June to 5 July 2013, p. 2.
CO_2 Earth, https://www.co2.earth.
Cohen, Carl, 'Do Animals Have Rights?', *Ethics and Behavior*, Vol. 7, No. 2, 1997, pp. 91–102.
Cohen, G.A., 'Deeper into bullshit', in *Contours of Agency: Essays on Themes from Harry Frankfurt*, edited by Sarah Buss and Lee Overton (Cambridge, MA: MIT Press, 2002), pp. 321–39.
Cohen, John, *The Essential Lenny Bruce: His Original Unexpurgated Satirical Routines* (St Albans: Granada, 1975).
Cohen, Randy, 'The ethics of Letterman's Palin joke', *New York Times*, 22 June 2009, http://ethicist.blogs.nytimes.com/2009/06/22/the-ethics-of-lettermans-palin-joke/.
Committee on Passive Smoking, Board on Environmental Studies and Toxicology, National Research Council, *Environmental Tobacco Smoke: Measuring Exposure and Assessing Health Effects* (Washington, DC: National Academy Press, 1986).
'Communications from Elsewhere' (Postmodernism Generator), https://www.elsewhere.org/pomo/.
'Controversies about the word *niggardly*', *Wikipedia*, https://en.wikipedia.org/wiki/Controversies_about_the_word_niggardly.
Cook, John, Naomi Oreskes, Peter T. Doran, et al, 'Consensus on Consensus: A Synthesis of Consensus Estimates on Human-Caused Global Warming', *Environmental Research Letters*, Vol. 11, 2006, 048002.
Cotroneo, Christian, 'How long do chickens live?', *Treehugger*, 31 January 2022, https://www.treehugger.com/how-long-do-chickens-live-4859423.
Cullity, Garrett, 'The life-saving analogy', in *World Hunger and Morality*, 2nd ed., edited by William Aiken and Hugh LaFollette (Upper Saddle River, NJ: Prentice-Hall, 1996), pp. 51–69.
Czogala, Jan, Maciej L. Goniewicz, Bartlomiej Fidelus, Wioleta Zielinska-Danch, Mark J. Travers, and Andrzej Sobczak, 'Secondhand Exposure to Vapors from Electronic Cigarettes', *Nicotine and Tobacco Research*, Vol. 16, No. 6, June 2014, pp. 655–62.
Darr, Ryan, 'Climate Change and Common-Sense Moral Responsibility', *Environmental Ethics*, Vol. 39, Spring 2017, pp. 21–38.
Davis, Stacy C., Susan W. Diegel, and Robert G. Boundy, *Transportation Energy Data Book*, Edition 34 (Oak Ridge, TN: Oak Ridge National Laboratory, August 2015).

Davis, Steven L., 'The Least Harm Principle May Require That Humans Consume a Diet Containing Large Herbivores, Not a Vegan Diet', *Journal of Agricultural and Environmental Ethics*, Vol. 16, 2003, pp. 387–94.

DePaolo, Donald J., 'Sustainable Carbon Emissions: The Geologic Perspective', *MRS Energy and Sustainability: A Review Journal*, Vol. 2, 2015, pp. 1–16.

de Sousa, Ronald, 'When is it wrong to laugh?', in *The Philosophy of Laughter and Humor*, edited by John Morreall (Albany: State University of New York Press, 1987), pp. 226–49.

'Dictionary includes Spurs fans in Yid definition', *BBC*, 12 February 2020, https://www.bbc.com/news/uk-51479810.

Dinakar, Chitra, and George T. O'Connor, 'The Health Effects of Electronic Cigarettes', *New England Journal of Medicine*, Vol. 375, No. 14, 6 October 2016, pp. 1372–81.

Domingo, Nina G.G., et al, 'Air Quality-Related Health Damages of Food', *Proceedings of the National Academy of Sciences*, Vol. 118, No. 20, 2021, e2013637118.

Drope, Jeffrey, and Neil W. Schluger, eds., *The Tobacco Atlas*, 6th ed. (Atlanta: American Cancer Society, 2018).

'Dutchman', *Dictionary of South African English*, https://dsae.co.za/entry/dutchman/e02182.

'Dutchman', *Merriam Webster Dictionary*, https://www.merriam-webster.com/dictionary/dutchman.

Dwyer, Johanna, and Franklin M. Loew, 'Nutritional Risks of Vegan Diets to Women and Children', *Journal of Agricultural and Environmental Ethics*, Vol. 7, No. 1, 1994, pp. 87–109.

Eales, Stan, *Earthtoons: The First Book of Eco-Humor* (New York: Warner Books, 1991).

Earp, Brian, 'The unbearable asymmetry of bullshit', *Healthwatch Newsletter*, Vol. 101, 2016, pp. 4–5.

Earth Talk, 'Is recycling worth it?', *Scientific American*, 5 October 2015, https://www.scientificamerican.com/article/is-recycling-worth-it/.

Ebert, Rainer, and Tibor Machan, 'Innocent Threats and the Moral Problem of Carnivorous Animals', *Journal of Applied Philosophy*, Vol. 29, No. 2, 2012, pp. 146–59.

Ecola, Liisa, Charlene Rohr, Johanna Zmud, Tobias Kuhnimhof, and Peter Phleps, *The Future of Driving in Developing Countries* (Santa Monica, CA: Institute for Mobility Research, Rand Corporation, 2014).

Egan, David, 'Calling bullshit', *The Point*, 31 October 2018, https://thepointmag.com/2018/examined-life/calling-bullshit.

Ehman, Robert, 'Adult–child sex', in *Philosophy and Sex*, new revised ed., edited by Robert Baker and Frederick Elliston (Buffalo, NY: Prometheus Books, 1984), pp. 431–46.

Ellis, Erle, *Anthropocene* (Oxford: Oxford University Press, 2018).

Feinberg, Joel, *Offense to Others* (New York: Oxford University Press, 1985).

Feris, Melanie-Ann, 'Blind object to Nando's guide dog advert', *IOL News*, 28 February 2000, http://www.iol.co.za/news/south-africa/blind-object-to-nando-s-guide-dog-advert-1.29600#.UKpIu0Lvbww.

Finkelhor, David, 'What's Wrong with Sex between Adults and Children: Ethics and the Problem of Sexual Abuse', *American Journal of Orthopsychiatry*, Vol. 49, No. 4, 1979, pp. 692–97.

Flouris, Andreas D., et al, 'Acute Impact of Active and Passive Electronic Cigarette Smoking on Serum Cotinine and Lung Function', *Inhalation Toxicology*, Vol. 25, No. 2, 2013, pp. 91–101.

Fountain, Henry, Blacki Migliozzi, and Nadja Popovich, 'Where 2020's record heat was felt the most', *New York Times*, 14 January 2021, https://www.nytimes.com/interactive/2021/01/14/climate/hottest-year-2020-global-map.html.

Food and Agricultural Organization, *The State of the World Fisheries and Aquaculture: Sustainability in Action* (Rome: Food and Agricultural Organization, 2020).

Frankfurt, Harry, 'On bullshit', in *On the Importance of What We Care About* (New York: Cambridge University Press, 1988), pp. 117–33.

Frankfurt, Harry, 'Reply to G.A. Cohen', in *Contours of Agency: Essays on Themes from Harry Frankfurt*, edited by Sarah Buss and Lee Overton (Cambridge, MA: MIT Press, 2002), pp. 340–44.

Franzen, Jonathan, 'Carbon capture', *New Yorker*, Vol. 91, No. 7, 6 April 2015, pp. 56–65.

Galgut, Elisa, and William Daniels, 'Coverings and cover-ups: The art of bullshit', *Politicsweb*, 1 November 2018, https://www.politicsweb.co.za/opinion/the-art-of-bullshit-at-uct.

Garner, Robert, 'Rawls, Animals and Justice: New Literature, Same Response', *Res Publica*, Vol. 18, 2012, pp. 159–72.

Garrard, Eve, and David McNaughton, 'In Defence of Unconditional Forgiveness', *Proceedings of the Aristotelian Society*, Vol. 103, 2003, pp. 39–60.

Gasparrini, Antonio, et al, 'Projections of Temperature-Related Excess Mortality under Climate Change Scenarios', *Lancet Planetary Health*, Vol. 1, No. 9, 2017, pp. e360–67.

Geist, Helmut J., 'Global Assessment of Deforestation Related to Tobacco Farming', *Tobacco Control*, Vol. 8, No. 1, March 1999, pp. 18–28.

George, Robert P., and Cornel West, 'Truth seeking, democracy, and freedom of thought and expression', 14 March 2017, https://jmp.princeton.edu/statement.

Girod, Bastien, Detlef Peter van Vuuren, and Edgar Hertwich, 'Global Climate Targets and Future Consumption Level: An Evaluation of the Required GHG Intensity', *Environmental Research Letters*, Vol. 8, No. 2, 2013, pp. 1–10.

Give Well, https://www.givewell.org.

Glantz, Stanton A., 'Do Not Recommend Trying E-Cigarettes for Smoking Cessation', *New England Journal of Medicine*, Vol. 374, No. 22, 2 June 2016, pp. 2173–74.

Glick, Shimon, 'Unlimited Human Autonomy—A Cultural Bias?', *New England Journal of Medicine*, Vol. 336, No. 13, 27 March 1997, pp. 954–56.

Global Carbon Atlas, http://www.globalcarbonatlas.org/en/CO2-emissions.

Glover, Jonathan, 'It Makes No Difference Whether or Not I Do It', *Proceedings of the Aristotelian Society, Supplementary Volumes*, Vol. 49, 1975, pp. 171–90.

Godfrey-Smith, Peter, *Other Minds: The Octopus, the Sea, and the Deep Origins of Consciousness* (New York: Farrar, Straus and Giroux, 2016).

Goldstein, Laurence, 'Only Joking?', *Philosophy Now*, No. 34, December 2001–January 2002, pp. 25–26.

Gomberg, Paul, 'The Fallacy of Philanthropy', *Canadian Journal of Philosophy*, Vol. 32, No. 1, 2002, pp. 29–65.

Goniewicz, Maciej Lukasz, et al, 'Levels of Selected Carcinogens and Toxicants in Vapour from Electronic Cigarettes', *Tobacco Control*, Vol. 23, 2014, pp. 133–39.

Graeber, David, 'Are you in a BS job? In academe, you're hardly alone', *Chronicle of Higher Education*, 6 May 2018, https://www.chronicle.com/article/are-you-in-a-bs-job-in-academe-youre-hardly-alone/.

Graeber, David, *Bullshit Jobs: A Theory* (New York: Simon & Schuster, 2018).

Griswold, Charles, *Forgiveness: A Philosophical Exploration* (New York: Cambridge University Press, 2007).

Guttman, Nathan, 'James Jones' Jewish joke—funny or inappropriate?', *Haaretz*, 25 April 2010, https://www.haaretz.com/2010-04-25/ty-article/james-jones-jewish-joke-funny-or-inappropriate/0000017f-eb70-d3be-ad7f-fb7bc5d10001.

Haddad, William A., Ryan Reisinger, Tristan Scott, Marthán Bester, and P.J. Nico de Bruyn, 'Multiple Occurrences of King Penguin (*Aptenodytes patagonicus*) Sexual Harassment by Antarctic Fur Seals (*Arctocephalus gazella*)', *Polar Biology*, Vol. 38, No. 5, 2015, pp. 741–46.

Haidt, Jonathan, *The Righteous Mind: Why Good People Are Divided by Politics and Religion* (New York: Vintage Books, 2012).

Harrison, Linda, 'Cro-Magnon Woman—In Eclipse', *Science Teacher*, Vol. 42, No. 4, April 1975, pp. 8–11.

Hausfather, Zeke, 'Let's not pretend planting trees is a permanent climate solution', *New York Times*, 4 June 2022, https://www.nytimes.com/2022/06/04/opinion/environment/climate-change-trees-carbon-removal.html.
Havergal, Chris, 'Adam Habib to "step aside" as SOAS director during racism probe', *Times Higher Education*, 18 March 2021, https://www.timeshighereducation.com/news/adam-habib-step-aside-soas-director-during-racism-probe.
Health Canada, *Tobacco Control Programme: Regulatory Proposal for Reducing Fire Risks from Cigarettes*, December 2002.
Hettinger, Edwin Converse, 'The Responsible Use of Animals in Biomedical Research', *Between the Species*, Vol. 5, No. 3, Summer 1989, pp. 123–31.
Hodgson, Thomas A., 'Cigarette Smoking and Lifetime Medical Expenditures', *Milbank Quarterly*, Vol. 70, No. 1, 1992, pp. 81–125.
Hoffman, Jessica M., and Teresa G. Valencak, 'A Short Life on the Farm: Aging and Longevity in Agricultural, Large-Bodied Mammals', *GeroScience*, Vol. 42, 2020, pp. 909–22.
Hohfeld, Wesley N., *Fundamental Legal Conceptions*, edited by Walter Wheeler Cook (New Haven: Yale University Press, 1919).
Holmgren, Margaret, *Forgiveness and Retribution* (New York: Cambridge University Press, 2012).
Hughes, Paul M., 'Moral Anger, Forgiving, and Condoning', *Journal of Social Philosophy*, Vol. 25, No. 1, Spring 1995, pp. 103–18.
IARC Monographs on the Evaluation of Carcinogenic Risks to Humans, *Vol. 83: Tobacco Smoke and Involuntary Smoking* (Lyon, France: World Health Organization, 2004).
International Traffic Safety and Data and Analysis Group, 'Road Safety Annual Report, 2018', Organization for Economic Co-operation and Development/International Transport Forum, 2018.
IPCC Core Writing Team, R.K. Pachauri, and L.A. Meyer, eds., *Climate Change 2014: Synthesis Report. Contribution of Working Groups I, II and III to the Fifth Assessment Report of the Intergovernmental Panel on Climate Change* (Geneva, Switzerland, 2014).
Itaborahy, Lucas Paoli, and Jingshu Zhu, *State-Sponsored Homophobia: A World Survey of Laws: Criminalisation, Protection and Recognition of Same-Sex Love*, 8th ed. (International Lesbian Gay Bisexual Trans and Intersex Association, May 2013).
Jahanbegloo, Ramin, *Conversations with Isaiah Berlin* (New York: Charles Scribner's Sons, Maxwell Macmillan International, 1991).
James I, King of England, 'A Counterblaste to Tobacco' (London: R. Barker, 1604).
James, Spencer L., et al. 'Morbidity and Mortality from Road Injuries: Results from the Global Burden of Disease Study 2017', *Injury Prevention*, Vol. 26, 2020, pp. i46–56.
Jamieson, Dale, 'When Utilitarians Should Be Virtue Theorists', *Utilitas*, Vol. 19, No. 2, 2007, pp. 160–83.
Jamieson, Dale, *Reason in a Dark Time* (New York: Oxford University Press, 2014).
Jay, Kristin L., and Timothy B. Jay, 'Taboo Word Fluency and Knowledge of Slurs and General Pejoratives: Deconstructing the Poverty-of-Vocabulary Myth', *Language Sciences*, Vol. 57, 2015, pp. 251–59.
Jha, Prabhat, and Richard Peto, 'Global Effects of Smoking, of Quitting, and of Taxing Tobacco', *New England Journal of Medicine*, Vol. 370, No. 1, 2 January 2014, pp. 60–68.
Jones, Lora, 'Vaping: The rise in five charts', BBC, 31 May 2018, https://www.bbc.com/news/business-44295336.
Kagan, Shelly, 'What's Wrong with Speciesism?', *Journal of Applied Philosophy*, Vol. 33, No. 1, February 2016, pp. 1–21.
Kalkhoran, Sara, and Stanton A Glantz, 'E-Cigarettes and Smoking Cessation in Real-World and Clinical Settings: A Systematic Review and Meta-Analysis', *Lancet Respiratory Medicine*, Vol. 4, February 2016, pp. 116–28.

Kaminer, Ariel, 'Professor suspended over Colorado shootings joke', *New York Times*, 12 September 2012, http://www.nytimes.com/2012/09/13/nyregion/merchant-marine-academy-professor-wont-be-fired-for-colorado-shooting-joke.html.

Karnein, Anja, 'Putting Fairness in Its Place', *Journal of Philosophy*, Vol. 111, No. 11, 2014, pp. 593–607.

Kass, Leon, 'The Wisdom of Repugnance', *New Republic*, Vol. 216, No. 22, 2 June 1997, pp. 17–26.

Kawamoto, Ryuji, et al, 'Estimation of CO_2 Emissions of Internal Combustion Engine Vehicle and Battery Electric Vehicle Using LCA', *Sustainability*, Vol. 11, 2019, pp. 1–15.

Kekes, John, 'Blame versus Forgiveness', *Monist*, Vol. 92, No. 4, 2009, pp. 488–506.

Kennedy, Randall, *Nigger: The Strange Career of a Troublesome Word* (New York: Vintage Books, 2003).

Kim, Ji Won, and Carl R. Baum, 'Liquid Nicotine Toxicity', *Pediatric Emergency Care*, Vol. 31, No. 7, July 2015, pp. 517–21.

Kingston, Ewan, and Walter Sinnott-Armstrong, 'What's Wrong with Joyguzzling?', *Ethical Theory and Moral Practice*, Vol. 21, 2018, pp. 169–86.

Kinley, D., ed., *Chernobyl's Legacy: Health, Environmental and Socio-Economic Impacts*, 2nd revised ed. (Vienna, Austria: International Atomic Energy Agency, April 2006).

Kinsey, Alfred, Wardell B. Pomeroy, Clyde E. Martin, and Paul H. Gebhard, *Sexual Behavior in the Human Female* (Philadelphia: W.B. Saunders Co, 1953).

Kirkengen, Anna Luise, *Inscribed Bodies: Health Impact of Childhood Sexual Abuse* (Dordrecht: Kluwer, 2001).

Kivits, Robbert, Michael Charles, and Neal Ryan, 'A Post-Carbon Aviation Future: Airports and the Transition to a Cleaner Aviation Sector', *Futures*, Vol. 42, 2010, pp. 199–211.

Kochhar, Rakesh, 'A global middle class is more promise than reality', Pew Research Center, 8 July 2015, http://www.pewglobal.org/2015/07/08/a-global-middle-class-is-more-promise-than-reality/.

Kochhar, Rakesh, 'Seven-in-ten people globally live on $10 or less per day', Pew Research Center, 23 September 2015, http://www.pewresearch.org/fact-tank/2015/09/23/seven-in-ten-people-globally-live-on-10-or-less-per-day/.

Kochhar, Rakesh, 'What it means to be poor by global standards', Pew Research Center, 22 July 2015, http://www.pewresearch.org/fact-tank/2015/07/22/what-it-means-to-be-poor-by-global-standards/.

Kolnai, Aurel, 'Forgiveness', *Proceedings of the Aristotelian Society* (New Series), Vol. 74, 1973–1974, pp. 91–106.

Kristiansen, Lars J., and Bernd Kaussler, 'The Bullshit Doctrine: Fabrications, Lies, and Nonsense in the Age of Trump', *Informal Logic*, Vol. 38, No. 1, 2018, pp. 13–52.

Krzyzanowski, Michal, Birgit Kuna-Dibbert, and Jurgen Schneider, eds., *Health Effects of Transport-Related Air Pollution* (Copenhagen: World Health Organization, 2005).

'K-word', *Wikipedia*, https://en.wikipedia.org/wiki/K-word.

Kyllönen, Simo, 'Climate Change, No-Harm Principle, and Moral Responsibility of Individual Emitters', *Journal of Applied Philosophy*, Vol. 35, No. 4, November 2018, pp. 737–58.

Laertius, Diogenes, *Lives of Eminent Philosophers*, Book VI: 69, edited and translated by Stephen White (Cambridge: Cambridge University Press, 2020).

Lai, K.K. Rebecca, and Jennifer Medina, 'An American puzzle: Fitting race in a box', *New York Times*, 16 October 2023, https://www.nytimes.com/interactive/2023/10/16/us/census-race-ethnicity.html.

Lamb, Sharon, 'Note on terminology', in *The Trouble with Blame* (Cambridge, MA: Harvard University Press, 1996), p. viii.

Lamey, Andy, 'Food Fight! Davis versus Regan on the Ethics of Eating Beef', *Journal of Social Philosophy*, Vol. 38, No. 2, Summer 2007, pp. 331–48.

Lear, Jonathan, 'Whatever', *New Republic*, 21 March 2005, https://newrepublic.com/article/68113/whatever.

'Legal opinions relating to obscenity prosecutions of comedian Lenny Bruce', *Famous Trials*, https://www.famous-trials.com/lennybruce/559-legalopinions#people.

Leiser, Burton, 'Homosexuality, morals, and the law of nature', in *Ethics in Practice*, edited by Hugh LaFollette (Cambridge, MA: Blackwell, 1997), pp. 242–53.

Leistikow, Bruce N., Daniel C. Martin, and Christina E. Milano, 'Fire Injuries, Disasters, and Costs from Cigarettes and Cigarette Lights: A Global Overview', *Preventative Medicine*, Vol. 31, 2000, pp. 91–99.

Leonardi-Bee, Jo, John Britton, and Andrea Venn, 'Secondhand Smoke and Adverse Fetal Outcomes in Nonsmoking Pregnant Women: A Meta-Analysis', *Pediatrics*, Vol. 127, No. 4, April 2011, pp. 734–41.

Levin, Michael, 'Why Homosexuality Is Abnormal', *Monist*, Vol. 67, No. 2, April 1984, pp. 251–83.

Levin, Michael, 'Homosexuality, Abnormality, and Civil Rights', *Public Affairs Quarterly*, Vol. 10, No. 1, 1996, pp. 31–48.

Levinson, Sanford, 'On Interpretation: The Adultery Clause of the Ten Commandments', *Southern California Law Review*, Vol. 58, 1985, pp. 719–25.

Lewis, Ben, 'Hammer and tickle', *Prospect Magazine*, 20 May 2006, http://www.prospectmagazine.co.uk/magazine/communist-jokes/.

Lipman, Steve, *Laughter in Hell: The Use of Humor during the Holocaust* (Northvale, NJ: Jason Aronson, 1991).

Locke, John, *Second Treatise of Government*, edited by C.B. Macpherson (Indianapolis: Hackett Publishing Company, 1980).

Mangels, Ann Reed, and Suzanne Havala, 'Vegan Diets for Women, Infants and Children', *Journal of Agricultural and Environmental Ethics*, Vol. 7, No. 1, 1994, pp. 111–22.

Manson, Neil C., 'Making Sense of Spin', *Journal of Applied Philosophy*, Vol. 29, No. 3, 2012, pp. 200–213.

Maren, Michael, *The Road to Hell: The Ravaging Effects of Foreign Aid and International Charity* (New York: The Free Press, 1997).

Martin, Judith, *Miss Manners' Guide to Excruciatingly Correct Behavior* (New York: Atheneum, 1982).

Martin, Michael J., Sapna E. Thottathil, and Thomas B. Newman, 'Antibiotics Overuse in Animal Agriculture: A Call to Action for Health Care Providers', *American Journal of Public Health*, Vol. 105, No. 12, 2015, pp. 2409–10.

Maslin, Mark, *A Very Short Introduction to Global Warming*, 2nd ed. (Oxford: Oxford University Press, 2009).

Masson-Delmotte, V., et al, eds., *Climate Change 2021: The Physical Science Basis. Contribution of Working Group I to the Sixth Assessment Report of the Intergovernmental Panel on Climate Change* (N.p.: Cambridge University Press, 2021).

Matheny, Gaverick, 'Least Harm: A Defense of Vegetarianism from Steven Davis's Omnivorous Proposal', *Journal of Agricultural and Environmental Ethics*, Vol. 16, 2003, pp. 505–11.

McMahan, Jeff, *The Ethics of Killing* (New York: Oxford University Press, 2002).

McMichael, A.J., *Planetary Overload* (Cambridge: Cambridge University Press, 1993).

McMichael, Anthony J., John W. Powles, Colin D. Butler, and Ricardo Uauy, 'Food, Livestock Production, Energy, Climate Change, and Health', *Lancet*, Vol. 370, 6 October 2007, pp. 1253–63.

McMichael, Tony, *Human Frontiers, Environments and Disease* (Cambridge: Cambridge University Press, 2001).

McNeil, Donald G., Jr, 'NYTimes Peru N-word, Part one: Introduction', *Medium*, 1 March 2021, https://medium.com/@donaldgmcneiljr1954/nytimes-peru-n-word-part-one-introduction-57eb6a3e0d95.

McNeil, Donald G., Jr, 'NYTimes Peru N-word, Part three: What happened in the 2019 investigation?', *Medium*, 1 March 2021, https://donaldgmcneiljr1954.medium.com/nytimes-peru-n-word-part-three-what-happened-in-the-2019-investigation-6f8e9939a385.

McNeill, J.R., *Something New under the Sun* (New York: W.W. Norton and Company, 2000).
Meinshausen, Malte, et al, 'The RCP Greenhouse Gas Concentrations and Their Extensions from 1765 to 2300', *Climate Change*, Vol. 109, 2011, pp. 213–41.
Michaels, David, *Doubt Is Their Product: How Industry's Assault on Science Damages Your Health* (New York: Oxford University Press, 2008).
Mill, John Stuart, 'Of the liberty of thought and discussion', in *On Liberty and Other Essays* (Oxford: Oxford University Press 1991), pp. 20–61.
Miller, Casey, and Kate Swift, *The Handbook of Non-Sexist Writing*, 2nd ed. (London: The Women's Press, 1989).
Miller, Casey, and Kate Swift, *Words and Women: New Language in New Times*, updated (New York: HarperCollins, 1991).
Miller, David, 'Distributing Responsibilities', *Journal of Political Philosophy*, Vol. 9, No. 4, 2001, pp. 453–71.
Mills, Claudia, 'Racist and Sexist Jokes: How Bad Are They (Really)?, *Report from the Center for Philosophy and Public Policy*, Vol. 7, No. 2/3, Spring/Summer 1987, pp. 9–12.
Moeliker, C.W., 'The First Case of Homosexual Necrophilia in the Mallard *Anas platyrhynchos* (Aves: Anatidae)', *Deinsea*, Vol. 8, 2001, pp. 243–47.
Moholola, Elijah, 'UCT Response on inaccurate claims of censorship of artworks', *Politicsweb*, 4 October 2018, http://www.politicsweb.co.za/opinion/censorship-of-artworks-ucts-response.
Mohri, Mehrdad, Shahrokh Poorsina, and Reza Sedaghat, 'Effects of Parenteral Supply of Iron on RBC Parameters, Performance, and Health in Neonatal Dairy Calves', *Biological Trace Element Research*, Vol. 136, 2010, pp. 33–39.
Moody-Adams, Michele, 'The Enigma of Forgiveness', *Journal of Value Inquiry*, Vol. 49, 2015, pp. 161–80.
Moulton, Janice, 'The myth of the neutral "man"', in *Feminism and Philosophy*, edited by Mary Vetterling-Braggin, Frederick A. Elliston, and Jane English (Totowa, NJ: Littlefield, Adams & Co., 1978), pp. 124–37.
Muller, Richard A., and Elizabeth A. Muller, 'Air pollution and cigarette equivalence', *Berkeley Earth*, 2019, http://berkeleyearth.org/air-pollution-and-cigarette-equivalence/.
Murphy, Jeffrie G., 'Forgiveness and resentment', in *Forgiveness and Mercy*, edited by Jeffrie G. Murphy and Jean Hampton (New York: Cambridge University Press, 1998), pp. 14–34.
Murphy, Jeffrie G., 'Forgiveness in counseling: A philosophical perspective', in *Character, Liberty, and Law: Kantian Essays in Theory and Practice* (Dordrecht: Kluwer, 1998), pp. 223–38.
Murphy, Jeffrie G., 'Forgiveness, Reconciliation, and Responding to Evil', *Fordham Urban Law Journal*, Vol. 27, 2000, pp. 1353–66.
Murtaugh, Paul A., and Michael G. Schlax, 'Reproduction and the Carbon Legacies of Individuals', *Global Environmental Change*, Vol. 19, No. 1, 2009, pp. 14–20.
Nagel, Thomas, 'Concealment and Exposure', *Philosophy and Public Affairs*, Vol. 27, No. 1, 1998, pp. 3–30.
Naidoo, Errol, 'Blasphemy in the media', *Joy Magazine*, 2009, https://joymag.co.za/article/blasphemy-in-the-media/.
Narveson, Jan, 'A defense of meat eating', in *Animal Rights and Human Obligations*, 2nd ed., edited by Tom Regan and Peter Singer (Englewood Cliffs, NJ: Prentice-Hall, 1989), pp. 192–95.
Narveson, Jan, 'We Don't Owe Them a Thing! A Tough-Minded but Soft-Hearted View of Aid to the Faraway Needy', *Monist*, Vol. 86, No. 3, July 2003, pp. 419–33.
National Organization for Women, 'The herstory of the National Organization for Women', accessed 8 December 2003, http://erights4all.com/now/valdostanow/herstory.htm.
Nesbit, Mark, 'Dead Funny', *Index on Censorship*, Vol. 29, No. 6, December 2000, pp. 118–20.

Neumann, Barbara, Athanasios T. Vafeidis, Juliane Zimmermann, and Robert J. Nicholls, 'Future Coastal Population Growth and Exposure to Sea-Level Rise and Coastal Flooding—A Global Assessment', *PLoS One*, Vol. 10, No. 3, 11 March 2015, e0118571.

'New Zealand comic resigns over Hitler joke', *Haaretz*, 27 June 2010, https://www.haaretz.com/2010-06-27/ty-article/new-zealand-comic-resigns-over-hitler-joke/0000017f-e7a8-d97e-a37f-f7edfa090000.

Nkanjeni, Unathi, 'Adam Habib and the N-word: A wrap of what happened', *TimesLive*, 15 March 2021, https://www.timeslive.co.za/news/south-africa/2021-03-15-adam-habib-and-the-n-word-a-wrap-of-what-happened/.

Nolt, John, 'The Individual's Obligation to Relinquish Unnecessary Greenhouse-Gas-Emitting Devices', *Philosophy and Public Issues* (New Series), Vol. 3, No. 1, 2013, pp. 139–65.

'Not in our town', *Facing History and Ourselves*, https://www.facinghistory.org/resource-library/not-our-town-0.

Novitz, David, 'Forgiveness and Self-Respect', *Philosophy and Phenomenological Research*, Vol. 58, No. 2, June 1998, pp. 299–315.

Novotny, Thomas E., Kristen Lum, Elizabeth Smith, Vivian Wang, and Richard Barnes, 'Cigarette Butts and the Case for an Environmental Policy on Hazardous Cigarette Waste', *International Journal of Environmental Research and Public Health*, Vol. 6, No. 5, 2009, pp. 1691–705.

Nunney, Leonard, 'Lineage Selection and the Evolution of Multistage Carcinogenesis', *Proceedings of the Royal Society of London B*, Vol. 266, No. 1418, 1999, pp. 493–98.

Öberg, Mattias, Maritta S. Jaakkola, Alistair Woodward, Armando Perugga, and Annette Prüss-Ustün, 'Worldwide Burden of Disease from Exposure to Second-Hand Smoke: A Retrospective Analysis of Data', *Lancet*, Vol. 377, No. 9760, 8 January 2011, pp. 139–46.

Ocean Conservancy, *Building a Clean Swell: 2018 Report* (Washington, DC: Ocean Conservancy, 2018).

'"Oriental": Rugs, not people', *NPR*, 2 September 2009, https://www.npr.org/2009/09/02/112465167/oriental-rugs-not-people.

Parfit, Derek, *Reasons and Persons* (Oxford: Clarendon Press, 1984).

Pascal, Fania, 'Wittgenstein: A personal memoir', in *Recollections of Wittgenstein*, edited by Rush Rhees (Oxford: Oxford University Press, 1984), pp. 28–29.

Pather, Jay, 'UCT is not a closed and controlled gallery', *Daily Maverick*, 11 August 2017, https://www.dailymaverick.co.za/article/2017-08-11-right-of-reply-uct-is-not-a-closed-and-controlled-gallery/.

Patterson, Gareth, *Beyond the Secret Elephants* (Bryanston: Tracey McDonald Publishers, 2020).

Perelman, S.J., 'To err is human, to forgive, supine', *New Yorker*, 4 October 1969, pp. 36–38.

Pertsovksy, Natalie, and *GroundUp* Staff, 'Quarrel over Sarah Baartman sculpture at UCT', *GroundUp*, 2 March 2018, https://www.groundup.org.za/article/quarrel-over-sarah-baartman-sculpture-uct/.

Peto, Richard, 'Epidemiology, multistage models, and short-term mutagenicity tests', in *The Origins of Human Cancer*, edited by H.H. Hiatt, J.D. Watson, and J.A. Winstein (Cold Spring Harbor, NY: Cold Spring Harbor Conferences on Cell Proliferation, 1977), pp. 621–37.

Pettigrove, Glenn, 'The Standing to Forgive', *Monist*, Vol. 92, No. 4, 2009, pp. 586–91.

Peukert, Detleve J.K., *Inside Nazi Germany: Conformity, Opposition and Racism in Everyday Life* (London: Penguin, 1993).

'Philosophers, eating, ethics—A discussion of the poll results', *Leiter Reports*, 10 October 2012, https://leiterreports.typepad.com/blog/2012/10/philosophers-eating-ethics-a-discussion-of-the-poll-results.html.

Plötz, Patrick, et al, 'Empirical Fuel Consumption and CO_2 Emissions of Plug-in Hybrid Electric Vehicles', *Journal of Industrial Ecology*, Vol. 22, No. 4, 2017, pp. 773–84.

Pogge, Thomas, *World Poverty and Human Rights* (Cambridge: Polity Press, 2002).

Pope, Alexander, *An Essay on Criticism* (London, 1758).

Pörtner, H.-O., et al, eds., *Climate Change 2022: Impacts, Adaptation and Vulnerability. Contribution of Working Group II to the Sixth Assessment Report of the Intergovernmental Panel on Climate Change* (Cambridge; New York: Cambridge University Press, 2022).

Price, Max, 'Letter to the Academic Freedom Committee', University of Cape Town, 12 July 2016.

Primoratz, Igor, *Ethics and Sex* (London: Routledge, 1999).

Punzo, Vincent, *Reflective Naturalism: An Introduction to Moral Philosophy* (New York: Macmillan, 1969).

Puzychki, Kevin, et al, 'Tobacco Smoke Exposure and Household Pets: A Systematic Literature Review Examining the Health Risk to Household Pets and New Indications of Exposed Pets Affecting Human Health', *International Public Health Journal*, Vol. 10, No. 1, 2018, pp. 11–24.

Rabin, Roni Caryn, 'A new cigarette hazard: "Third-hand smoke"', *New York Times*, 3 January 2009, https://www.nytimes.com/2009/01/03/health/research/03smoke.html.

Rachels, Stuart, 'The Immorality of Having Children', *Ethical Theory and Moral Practice*, 2014, Vol. 7, pp. 567–82.

Rainey, James, 'Plastic straw ban? Cigarette butts are the single greatest source of ocean trash', NBC News, 27 August 2018, https://www.nbcnews.com/news/us-news/plastic-straw-ban-cigarette-butts-are-single-greatest-source-ocean-n903661.

Rann, Jamie, 'How swearing became a weapon of resistance for Ukrainians', *Guardian*, 13 April 2022, https://www.theguardian.com/books/2022/apr/13/putin-ukraine-war-russian-language.

Rawls, John, *A Theory of Justice* (Oxford: Oxford University Press, 1973).

Rawls, John, *A Theory of Justice*, revised ed. (Cambridge, MA: Belknap Press of Harvard University Press, 1999).

Register, Kathleen, 'Cigarette Butts as Litter—Toxic as Well as Ugly?', *Underwater Naturalist*, Vol. 25, No. 2, August 2000, pp. 23–29.

Reid, Thomas, *Essays on the Active Powers of Man* (Edinburgh: J. Bell; London: G.G.J. & J. Robinson, 1788).

Reid, Thomas, *Practical Ethics*, edited by Knud Haakonssen (Princeton, NJ: Princeton University Press, 1990; Edinburgh: Edinburgh University Press, 2007).

Renaud, S., and M. de Lorgeril, 'Wine, Alcohol, Platelets, and the French Paradox for Coronary Heart Disease', *Lancet*, Vol. 339, No. 8808, 20 June 1992, pp. 1523–26.

Repace, James L., 'Risks of passive smoking', in *To Breath Freely: Risk, Consent, and Air*, edited by Mary Gibson (Totowa, NJ: Rowman & Allanheld, 1985), pp. 3–30.

Richards, Norvin, 'Forgiveness', in *Ethics*, Vol. 99, No. 1, October 1988, pp. 77–97.

Richardson, Alan, 'Performing bullshit and the post-sincere condition', in *Bullshit and Philosophy*, edited by Gary L. Hardcastle and George A. Reisch (Chicago: Open Court, 2006), pp. 83–97.

Riebeek, Holli, 'The carbon cycle', Earth Observatory, 16 June 2011, https://earthobservatory.nasa.gov/features/CarbonCycle/page1.php.

Rind, Bruce, Philip Tromovitch, and Robert Bauserman, 'A Meta-Analytic Examination of Assumed Properties of Child Sexual Abuse Using College Samples', *Psychological Bulletin*, Vol. 124, No.1, 1998, pp. 22–53.

Ritchie, Hannah, 'Climate change and flying: What share of global CO_2 emissions come from aviation?', *Our World in Data*, 22 October 2020, https://ourworldindata.org/co2-emissions-from-aviation.

Ritchie, Hannah, 'Which form of transport has the smallest carbon footprint', *Our World in Data*, 13 October 2020, https://ourworldindata.org/travel-carbon-footprint.

Roberts, Helen, and Brian S. Palmeiro, 'Toxicology of Aquarium Fish', *Veterinary Clinics: Exotic Animal Practice*, Vol. 11, No. 2, 2008, pp. 359–74.

Rom, Oren, Alessandra Pecorelli, Giuseppe Valacchi, and Abraham Z. Reznick, 'Are E-Cigarettes a Safe and Good Alternative to Cigarette Smoking?', *Annals of the New York Academy of Sciences*, Vol. 1340, 2014, pp. 65–74.

Rose, Flemming, *The Tyranny of Silence: How One Cartoon Ignited a Global Debate on the Future of Free Speech* (Washington, DC: Cato Institute, 2014).

Rowlands, Mark, 'Contractarianism and Animal Rights', *Journal of Applied Philosophy*, Vol. 14, No. 3, 1996, pp. 235–47.

Roza, Marchello Rodrigues, and Carlos Alberto Assis Viegas, 'The Dog as Passive Smoker: Effects of Exposure to Environmental Cigarette Smoke on Domestic Dogs', *Nicotine and Tobacco Research*, Vol. 9, No. 11, November 2007, pp. 1171–76.

Russell, Douglas G.D., William J.L. Sladen, and David G. Ainley, 'Dr. George Murray Levick (1876–1956): Unpublished Notes on the Sexual Habits of the Adélie Penguin', *Polar Record*, Vol. 48, No. 4, 2012, pp. 387–93.

Ryder, Richard D., 'Speciesism Revisited', *Think*, Vol. 2, No. 6, Spring 2004, pp. 83–92.

Salmasi, Giselle, Rosheen Grady, Jennifer Jones, and Sarah D. McDonald, 'Environmental Tobacco Smoke Exposure and Perinatal Outcomes: A Systematic Review and Meta-Analysis', *Acta Obstetricia et Gynecologica*, Vol. 89, 2010, pp. 423–41.

Samuel, Herbert, *Practical Ethics* (London: Thornton Butterworth Ltd., 1935).

Sanders, Bas, 'Global goat slaughter statistics and charts', *Faunalytics*, 10 October 2018, https://faunalytics.org/global-goat-slaughter-statistics-and-charts/.

Sanders, Bas, 'Global animal slaughter statistics and charts: 2020 update', *Faunalytics*, 29 July 2020. https://faunalytics.org/global-animal-slaughter-statistics-and-charts-2020-update/.

Sandfort, T.G.M., 'The argument for adult–child sexual contact: A critical appraisal and new data', in *The Sexual Abuse of Children: Theory and Research*, Volume 1, edited by William O'Donohue and James H. Geer (Hillsdale, NJ: Lawrence Erlbaum Associates, 1992) pp. 38–48.

Sapa, 'Nando's ad falls foul—ASA', IOL, 1 March 2000, http://www.iol.co.za/news/south-africa/nando-s-ad-falls-foul-asa-1.29788#.UKpIu0Lvbww.

Sasco, A.J., M.B. Secretan, and K. Straif, 'Tobacco Smoking and Cancer: A Brief Review of Recent Epidemiological Evidence', *Lung Cancer*, Vol. 45, S2, 2004, pp. S3–9.

Scarborough, Peter, et al, 'Dietary Greenhouse Gas Emissions of Meat-Eaters, Fish-Eaters, Vegetarians and Vegans in the UK', *Climate Change*, Vol. 125, 2014, pp. 179–92.

Scarre, Geoffrey, 'On Taking Back Forgiveness', *Ethical Theory and Moral Practice*, Vol. 19, No. 4, 2016, pp. 931–44.

Schneider, Joseph W., and Sally L. Hacker, 'Sex Role Imagery and Use of the Generic "Man" in Introductory Texts', *American Sociologist*, Vol. 8, No. 1, February 1973, pp. 12–18.

Schopenhauer, Arthur, 'On the sufferings of the world', in *Complete Essays of Schopenhauer*, translated by T. Bailey Saunders (New York: Wiley Book Company, 1942), pp. 1–18.

Schwitzgebel, Eric, and Joshua Rust, 'The Moral Behavior of Ethics Professors: Relationships among Self-Reported Behavior, Expressed Normative Attitude, and Directly Observed Behavior', *Philosophical Psychology*, Vol. 27, No. 3, 2014, pp. 293–327.

Sealey, Geraldine, 'Is recycling worth the trouble, cost?', *ABC News*, 7 January 2006, https://abcnews.go.com/US/story?id=91824&page=1.

'Sectoral profile—Transport', Odyssee-Mure, https://www.odyssee-mure.eu/publications/EFFICIENCY-by-sector/transport/distance-travelled-by-car.html (accessed 25 January 2021).

Shue, Henry, 'Subsistence Emissions and Luxury Emissions', *Law and Policy*, Vol. 15, No. 1, January 1993, pp. 39–60.

Sidgwick, Henry, *Practical Ethics: A Collection of Addresses and Essays* (London: Swan Sonnenschein & Co., 1898).

Sidgwick, Henry, *The Methods of Ethics*, 7th ed. (London: Macmillan and Company, 1907).

Singer, Peter, 'Famine, Affluence, and Morality', *Philosophy and Public Affairs*, Vol. 1, No. 3, Spring 1972, pp. 229–43.

Singer, Peter, *Practical Ethics* (Cambridge: Cambridge University Press, 1979).

Singer, Peter, *Animal Liberation*, 2nd ed. (New York: The New York Review/Random House, 1990).

Singer, Peter *Practical Ethics*, 2nd ed. (New York: Cambridge University Press, 1993).
Singer, Peter, 'Heavy petting', *Prospect Magazine*, 20 April 2001, https://www.prospectmagazine.co.uk/magazine/heavypetting.
Singer, Peter, 'What should a billionaire give—and what should you give?', *New York Times*, 17 December 2006, http://www.nytimes.com/2006/12/17/magazine/17charity.t.html.
Singer, Peter, *The Life You Can Save* (New York: Random House, 2009).
Singer, Peter, *Practical Ethics*, 3rd ed. (New York: Cambridge University Press, 2011).
Sinnott-Armstrong, Walter, 'It's not my fault: Global warming and individual moral obligations', in *Perspectives on Climate Change*, edited by W. Sinnott-Armstrong and R. Howarth (Amsterdam: Elsevier, 2005), pp. 221–53.
Smilansky, Saul, *10 Moral Paradoxes* (Malden, MA: Blackwell, 2007).
Smith, Charlene, 'Freedom of the press also requires respect for religion and culture', *Cape Times*, Friday, 10 February 2006.
Snyder, Laura A., et al, 'p53 Expression and Environmental Tobacco Smoke Exposure in Feline Oral Squamous Cell Carcinoma', *Veterinary Pathology*, Vol. 41, 2004, pp. 209–41.
'SOAS Board accepts recommendations of independent external investigation in full: Director to stay on with restorative justice process in place', 5 May 2021, https://www.soas.ac.uk/news/newsitem153016.html.
Sokal, Alan, and Jean Bricmont, *Fashionable Nonsense: Postmodern Intellectuals' Abuse of Science* (New York: Picador, 1998).
Stephens, Richard, John Atkins, and Andrew Kingston, 'Swearing as a Response to Pain', *NeuroReport*, Vol. 20, No. 12, 5 August 2009, pp. 1056–60.
Stephens, Richard, David K. Spierer, and Emmanuel Katehis, 'Effect of Swearing on Strength and Power of Performance', *Psychology of Sport and Exercise*, Vol. 35, March 2018, pp. 111–17.
Strawson, Peter, 'Freedom and resentment', in *Free Will*, edited by Gary Watson (Oxford: Oxford University Press, 1982), pp. 59–80.
'Table of standard and non-standard third-person singular pronouns' in 'Gender neutrality in languages with gendered third-person pronouns', *Wikipedia*, https://en.wikipedia.org/wiki/Gender_neutrality_in_languages_with_gendered_third-person_pronouns#Table_of_standard_and_non-standard_third-person_singular_pronouns.
The Daily Stormer's Jew-hating style guide revealed', *Times of Israel*, 16 December 2017, https://www.timesofisrael.com/the-daily-stormers-jew-hating-style-guide-revealed/.
Tierney, John, 'Recycling is garbage', *New York Times*, 30 June 1996, https://www.nytimes.com/1996/06/30/magazine/recycling-is-garbage.html.
Tierney, John, 'The reign of recycling', *New York Times*, 3 October 2015, https://www.nytimes.com/2015/10/04/opinion/sunday/the-reign-of-recycling.html.
Todts, William, ed., CO_2 *Emissions from Cars: The Facts* (Brussels: European Federation for Transportation and Environment, 2018).
Tracy, Marc, 'Ex-Times reporter who used racial slur publishes a lengthy defense', *New York Times*, 1 March 2021, https://www.nytimes.com/2021/03/01/business/donald-mcneil-new-york-times-racial-slur.html.
'UK briefing: The plug-in hybrid con', September 2020, https://te-cdn.ams3.digitaloceanspaces.com/files/2020_09_UK_briefing_The_plug-in_hybrid_con.pdf.
Unger, Jennifer, 'E-Cigarettes: Introducing New Complexities and Controversies to the Field of Nicotine and Tobacco Research', *Nicotine and Tobacco Research*, Vol. 17, No. 10, 2015, pp. 1185–86.
U.S. Department of Health and Human Services, *The Health Consequences of Smoking: A Report of the Surgeon General* (Atlanta, GA: U.S. Department of Health and Human Services, Centers for Disease Control and Prevention, National Center for Chronic Disease Prevention and Health Promotion, Office on Smoking and Health, 2004).

U.S. Department of Health and Human Services, *How Tobacco Smoke Causes Disease: The Biology and Behavioral Basis for Smoking-Attributable Disease: A Report of the Surgeon General* (Atlanta, GA: U.S. Department of Health and Human Services, Centers for Disease Control and Prevention, National Center for Chronic Disease Prevention and Health Promotion, Office on Smoking and Health, 2010).

U.S. Department of Health and Human Services, *A Report of the Surgeon General: How Tobacco Smoke Causes Disease: What It Means to You* (Atlanta, GA: US Department of Health and Human Services, Centers for Disease Control and Prevention, National Center for Chronic Disease Prevention and Health Promotion, Office on Smoking and Health, 2010).

U.S. Department of Health and Human Services, *The Health Consequences of Smoking: 50 Years of Progress: A Report of the Surgeon General* (Rockville, MD: Office of the Surgeon General, 2014).

U.S. Food and Drug Administration, 'Be smoke-free and help your pets live longer, healthier lives', https://www.fda.gov/animal-veterinary/animal-health-literacy/be-smoke-free-and-help-your-pets-live-longer-healthier-lives#dog.

Utell, Mark J., Jane Warren, and Robert Sawyer, 'Public Health Risks from Motor Vehicle Emissions', *Annual Review of Public Health*, Vol. 15, 1994, pp. 157–78.

Vakkalanka, J.P., L.S. Hardison Jr, and C.P. Holstege, 'Epidemiological Trends in Electronic Cigarette Exposures Reported to U.S. Poison Centers', *Clinical Toxicology*, Vol. 52, 2014, pp. 542–48.

'Verkhoyansk', *Wikipedia*, https://en.wikipedia.org/wiki/Verkhoyansk#Climate.

Volk, Tyler, *CO2 Rising* (Cambridge, MA: MIT Press, 2008).

Vulliamy, C.E., *Little Arthur's Guide to Humbug* (London: Michael Joseph, 1960).

Ward, Geoffrey C., *Unforgivable Blackness: The Rise and Fall of Jack Johnson* (New York: Alfred Knopf, 2005).

Watts, Nick, et al, 'The 2020 Report of The *Lancet* Countdown on Health and Climate Change: Responding to Converging Crises', *Lancet*, Vol. 397, 9 January 2021, pp. 129–70.

Wettstein, Howard, 'Forgiveness and Moral Reckoning', *Philosophia*, Vol. 38, No. 3, 2010, pp. 445–55.

Wheeler, André, 'Merriam-Webster dictionary adds 'they' as non-binary pronoun', *Guardian*, 18 September 2019, https://www.theguardian.com/science/2019/sep/17/merriam-webster-they-nonbinary-pronoun.

Wilde, Oscar, 'To Lord Alfred Douglas', 20 April 1894, *The Complete Letters of Oscar Wilde*, edited by Merlin Holland and Rupert Hart-Davies (New York: Henry Holt and Company, 2000), p. 590.

WHO Global Report on Trends in Prevalence of Tobacco Smoking 2000–2025, 2nd ed. (Geneva: World Health Organization, 2018).

World Health Organization, 'Electronic nicotine delivery systems and electronic non-nicotine delivery systems (ENDS/ENNDS), August 2016.

Williams, Alex, 'Elana Dykewomon, author who explored lesbian lives, dies at 72', *New York Times*, 14 August 2022, https://www.nytimes.com/2022/08/14/books/elana-dykewomon-dead.html.

Wilson, Lindsay, 'Shades of green: Electric cars' carbon emissions around the globe', *Shrink That Footprint*, February 2013.

Woollard, Fiona, 'Promiscuity, Pedophilia, Rape and the Significance of the Sexual', *Public Affairs Quarterly*, Vol. 33, No. 2, April 2019, pp. 137–58.

Wynes, Seth, and Kimberly A. Nicholas, 'The Climate Mitigation Gap: Education and Government Recommendations Miss the Most Effective Individual Actions', *Environmental Research Letters*, Vol. 12, 2017, pp. 1–9.

Yong, Ed, *An Immense World: How Animal Senses Reveal the Hidden Realms around Us* (New York: Random House, 2022).

Zafeiridou, Maria, Nicholas S Hopkinson, and Nikolas Voulvoulis, 'Cigarette Smoking: An Assessment of Tobacco's Global Environmental Footprint across Its Entire Supply Chain', *Environmental Science and Technology*, Vol. 52, No. 15, 2018, pp. 8087–94.

Zangwill, Nick, 'Our Moral Duty to Eat Meat', *Journal of the American Philosophical Association*, Vol. 7, No. 3, 2021, pp. 1–7.

Zhao, Qi, et al, 'Global, Regional, and National Burden of Mortality Associated with Non-Optimal Ambient Temperatures from 2000 to 2019: A Three-Stage Modelling Study', *Lancet Planetary Health*, Vol. 5, No. 7, July 2021, pp. e415–25.

Index

For the benefit of digital users, indexed terms that span two pages (e.g., 52–53) may, on occasion, appear on only one of those pages.

Figures are indicated by an italic *f* following the page number.

actions
   primarily self-regarding, 115–16, 127, 128, 131, 365–66
   substantially other-regarding, 127, 129–31, 365–66
addiction, 112, 116, 135–36
addressing and referring to people by
   first name only, 251
   group name, 236, 265
   surname only xiv
   See also pronouns, preferred
adultery, 28, 31, 41, 49–50, 316–17, 330–31, 339–40
aesthetic response. *See* disgust
affluence, 145–46, 148–49, 156–57, 158, 164–65, 166–67, 168, 169
antibiotics, 186–87
apology, 225, 233
   forgiveness and, 311, 324, 326, 335, 339
   repentance and, 330–32, 339
applied ethics, distinguished from practical ethics, 10, 12
Aristotelianism, 148
Arthur, John, 154–56

Bennett, Christopher, 323–24, 325
bereavement, 332, 334, 335
Black, Max, 289, 291
blasphemy, 218, 223–25, 264–65, 266, 364, 369
   in humour, 271, 272, 277
Brandolini, Alberto, Bullshit Asymmetry Principle, 295

cars. *See* driving
causal inefficacy, 346, 352
   consuming animals and, 202, 208
   environment and, 73, 81–82, 108, 370
   smoking and, 119, 133
character traits, 11, 17, 266, 272, 275. *See also* virtue; virtue ethics
children, 182, 298, 336
   addressing adults, 252, 253, 255–57, 258, 259
   favouring one's own, 148, 164–65
   forgiving for wrongs against, 313, 341–42
   poverty and, 145
   smoking and, 112, 118, 138, 140
   vegan diet and, 188, 194
civility, 3, 275
Cohen, Gerald (Jerry), 289–90, 296, 297
companion animals
   cleaning up faeces of, 111
   linguistic reference to, 262, 268
   naming of, 129
   second-hand smoke and, 118
   special duties to, 196, 198–99
connotation, 221, 237, 251–52, 313, 377. *See also* denotation
consent, 17
   first-name basis and, 259
   offence and, 366–67
   sex and, 18–19, 38–39, 46, 48–49
   smoking and, 113, 118, 124, 137
consequentialism, 10–11, 77–78, 114–15, 370–71
   scope of duty and, 21–22
convention, 1, 218, 219, 239–40
   manners and, 19–21, 251
cosmetics, 216
dairy, consumption of
   animal suffering and, 171, 174, 187–88, 202, 216, 217, 268, 375
   global warming and, 95, 187
   human health and, 186

death
   animals' 171, 184–86, 192–93, 195–97, 204, 211
   car accidents, caused by, 142, 143*f*
   deprivation account of, 184–85
   human, 75, 187
   humour about, 271, 275, 281
   smoking-related, 118, 133, 142, 143*f*
   time-relative interests account of, 185–86
deforestation, 65, 94–95, 115

denotation, 220–21, 222, 230, 250. *See also* connotation
deontology, 10–11, 77–78, 114–15, 121, 147, 148, 191–92
desert, 127, 128, 183, 223, 264, 272, 286, 308, 321, 371. *See also* paradox of desert
disgust, 29–30, 56, 215, 279, 298, 363–64
disrespect, 9, 214, 221, 222, 251, 264, 302. *See also* respect
driving
    environment and, 3, 85, 86, 93, 96, 98, 102, 106, 107
    smoking compared to, 115, 122, 141
    See also causal inefficacy; pollution, driving as a cause of
duty
    -based view, 10–11 (*see also* deontology)
    correlated to rights, 16
    natural, 22–23, 24
    oneself, to, 114–15, 137
    positive and negative, 22–24
    scope (or extent) of, 7, 16, 21, 146, 152–54, 156, 349, 359, 369–71 (*see also* morality, demandingness of)

eggs, consumption of, 171, 172, 187–88, 216, 376–77. *See also* causal inefficacy; veganism
egoism, 10
ethics, applied. *See* applied ethics
etiquette. *See* manners
extra-marital sex. *See* adultery

fairness
    environmental, 79, 82, 87, 89, 91
    giving aid and, 156–57, 167–68, 170
    reciprocity and, 197, 199–201
    See also unfairness
fair share, 82, 88f, 91, 156–57, 167–68, 170. *See also* free-rider
fallibility, 8–9, 69–70, 176, 362, 373–75, 378
farting. *See* spitting compared to farting
Feinberg, Joel, 126, 127, 365, 366–67
fish, 118, 176, 177, 181, 200, 209, 216, 263
fishing, 171, 176, 203, 211
forced insemination of animals, 173, 174
Frankfurt, Harry, 288, 289, 290, 293, 295, 296, 297, 298–99
free-riding, 79, 87, 89, 110, 304, 306. *See also* unfairness
fur, 171, 189, 216

Glover, Jonathan, 81–82, 83–84
God. *See* religion

Habib, Adam, 225–26, 227
harm, 17, 71, 85, 86–87, 117, 119. *See also* causal inefficacy
health insurance, 163, 164, 177
health risks resulting from
    climate change, 67–68
    maltreatment of animals, 186–87, 217
    nuclear energy, 110–11
    pollution, local, 67–68, 111, 142–44
    poverty, 145
    sex, 38, 40, 57–58
    smoking, 112, 115–16, 117, 133, 135, 136–37
Holmgren, Margaret, 337–38
humility, 28, 336, 378

ignorance, 20, 200, 279, 297
impoliteness. *See* manners
inconsequentialism. *See* causal inefficacy
inheritance, 164–65
insemination. *See* forced insemination of animals
insults, 223, 226, 229, 260, 265, 269, 279. *See also* slurs
insurance, 133, 163, 168–69, 177
intolerance, 226, 227, 278, 279, 296, 302. *See also* tolerance/toleration
introspection, 273, 274–75, 377

judgementalism, 298–99, 372–73, 375 *See also* moral judgements

law
    causal inefficacy and the, 73–74, 81, 107, 119, 350
    dead-letter, 88–89
    duty to obey the, 113
    ethics, distinguished from, 25–27, 118, 263
    natural, 4, 30, 52, 54
    offence as breach of the, 363
    quotidian ethics, distinguished from, 1, 2–3, 72–74
leather, 171, 189, 216
Levin, Michael, 53–54, 55
life-and-death issues, 1, 3–4
litter, 111, 139–40
love
    contractarianism and the role of, 198
    liking, distinguished from, 45
    mutual romantic, 33, 36, 37, 39–40, 42, 44, 57, 60, 61–62
    parental, 36
    unidirectional, 48
    See also marriage, loveless

Maher, Bill, 233, 235
manners, 218, 220, 251–58
    bullshit and, 297–98, 302–3
    morality, relationship to, 19
    smoking and, 138
marriage
    ceremony, 35–36, 322–23
    child-, 25, 50
    incestuous, 57
    loveless, 36, 49–50
    open, 42–43, 50
    sex and, 36, 41, 49–51, 60
masturbation, 43, 44, 58–60
    of animals, 173
McMahan, Jeff, 185
McNeil, Donald G. Jr, 225–26, 227
meat, 216, 268, 345
    animal suffering and, 171, 184–86 (*see also* causal inefficacy)
    cultural benefits of, 189
    cultured (laboratory grown), 214–16
    economic costs and benefits of, 188–89, 191
    global warming and, 95, 96, 107, 187
    reduced consumption of, 375, 376
    religious significance of, 189
    roadkill, 214
    See also veganism
mention-use distinction. *See* use-mention distinction
method, philosophical, 7, 190, 273, 274–75
milk. *See* dairy, consumption of
Moody-Adams, Michele, 336–37
morality, 16
    demandingness of, 349, 370
    domain of (*see* scope of)
    law and (*see* law, ethics, distinguished from)
    moral judgements, 13–14, 134 (*see also* fallibility)
    perversion of, 372–73
    retrospective, 285, 357, 376–77, 378
    scope of, 17–19, 114–16
moral mathematics, mistake of. *See* causal inefficacy
moral panic, 227
moral relativism. *See* relativism, moral

name
    God's, 223–25, 226, 277 (*see also* blasphemy)
    remembering a, 251
    See also addressing and referring to people by; companion animals, naming of
natural law. *See* law, natural
non-utilitarians, 148, 157–58, 160, 165, 190. *See also* Aristotelianism; deontology; rights

obligations. *See* duty
obscenity, 218, 222, 264–65, 266. *See also* profanity
offence, 17, 20, 362–66
    bullshit and, 305–6
    humour and, 271, 278, 279, 284, 286–87, 367
    language induced, 221–22, 367 (*see also* sexism, language; slurs)
    smoking and, 124, 131, 133–34, 137, 139, 349, 351
    See also manners

paradox of desert, 303, 353
    bullshit and, 358–59, 361
    carbon emissions and, 358–59, 361
    giving aid and, 358
Parfit, Derek, 74
politeness. *See* manners
pollution, 364, 369–70, 371
    animal agriculture as a cause of, 187
    driving as a cause of, 87, 97, 123, 141–44
    local environmental, 63, 64, 87, 111, 131, 176
    noise, 9, 111, 125, 130, 131, 132, 364
    smoking as a cause of, 117–18
    See also spitting
poverty
    duty to assist those in, 145
    suffering of those in, 145
precautionary argument, 61, 136–37
privacy, respect for, 3
private
    humour in, 367
    -public distinction, 366
    sexual and other intimacy in, 44–45, 46, 128, 366–67
    slurs in, 233–34, 367
    smoking in, 4–5, 115–16, 139
procreation, 55, 211
    climate change and, 73, 100, 106–7
    duties of aid and, 150, 158–60, 164–65, 352–53
    sex and, 4, 50, 52, 53–54, 55, 56–57, 58, 60, 368, 369
profanity, 63, 264, 286. *See also* blasphemy; obscenity
promises
    obligations generated by, 22–23, 41–42
    performative nature of, 322–23
    sexual exclusivity and, 41–43
pronouns
    affectionate, 252, 255
    animal, 263
    familiarity and, 251–52
    generic, 239, 240, 244
    preferred, 248, 376–77

public-private distinction. *See* private-public distinction

quotidian ethics, 1, 2, 36–37, 63–64, 73–74, 202, 214, 215–16, 367, 377
  extreme cases, differentiated from, 12, 23–24, 213–14, 354
  very practical ethics and, 27

race xiv–xv, 176–77, 183, 199, 218, 254
  original position and, 199–200
racism
  accusations of, 233, 235, 267
  humour and, 273, 281
  language, manifestation in, 232–33, 237
  speciesism compared to, 176–77, 183
  See also slurs
rape, 28–29, 30–31
  abortion and, 102
  badness of, 28–29, 40, 44, 45–47, 49
  forgiveness and, 277, 313, 314, 339
  jokes about, 275, 276–77
  marital, 28–29
  relativism and, 8
  See also forced insemination of animals
referring to people. *See* addressing and referring to people by
relativism, moral, 7, 189–90
religion
  consuming animals and, 208
  humour and, 271
  law distinguished from, 24–25
  offence, 124, 128–29, 271, 284, 364
  original position and, 199–200
  sex and, 30–31, 52, 53
  See also blasphemy
repentance, 324–25, 327, 330, 343–44
reproductive freedom, 352–53. *See also* procreation
repugnance. *See* disgust
respect, 125, 251, 262, 302
  duty to treat people with, 9, 20
  self- 329, 330
  wrongdoers, for, 337–38
  See also disrespect
responsibility, 22–23
  emissions, for, 79, 82–85, 100
  moral and causal, 82
  voters' 83
  See also duty, scope (or extent) of
rights
  animal, 191
  concept (or theory) of, 10–11, 16–17, 147, 191–92, 193–94
  duty to aid, and a, 147, 148, 151–52, 160

forgiveness, and, 324, 325–26
smoking, and, 121, 137
roadkill. *See* meat, roadkill
Rose, Flemming, 305

sexism
  accusations of, 267
  humour and, 273
  language and, 239–44, 268
  speciesism compared to, 176–77, 183
  See also slurs
shampoo. *See* cosmetics
Singer, Peter
  duties to those in need, on, 146–68, 370
  sexual morality, on, 3
slurs, 220, 222, 345
  blasphemy, compared with, 225–26
  defanging of, 229–36, 349
  group, 223–29, 265
  responding to others' use of, 267, 376–77
  speciesist, 260
  words becoming, 229, 237–38
  See also sexism, language, in
Smilansky, Saul, 355
soap. *See* cosmetics
sorites, 162
speciesism, 176, 182–84, 191, 211, 259
spitting, 125, 126, 131
  compared to farting, 393n.56
stereotypes, 279, 288
  humour and, 232, 273–75, 281–82
suffering. *See also* harm
  animal, 145, 184–85, 186, 187–88, 191, 209, 213, 214, 215–16
  climate change, caused by, 63, 67–68, 71
  humour about, 271, 275
  poverty, caused by, 145, 352
  procreation, caused by, 51, 58–60, 352
supererogation, 14–16, 18, 21–22, 23, 349–51, 375
  bullshit and, 304, 351
  duty, imprecise boundary with, 16, 91–92, 162–63, 304
  environment and, 91–92
  forgiveness and, 371
  giving aid and, 162–63, 350, 371
  language and, 222–23
  paradox of desert and, 356–57, 359–62

tolerance/toleration, 28, 280, 297

unfairness
  animals, to, 180, 199–200, 201
  bullshit and, 303–4, 306
  comparative or intrinsic, 355–57

environmental, 87, 89, 110
forgiveness and, 333–34
paradox of desert and, 353
rich and poor, between, 165
See also fairness; free-riding
"Unlockean proviso" 163–64
unnaturalness. *See* duty, natural; law, natural
use-mention distinction, 223, 236, 267, 271, 376–77
utilitarianism. *See* consequentialism

veal, 174
veganism, 217, 367–68, 375
   animal suffering and, 211 (*see also* causal inefficacy)
   environment and, 95, 96, 187
   health and, 186–87, 188, 217
   religion and, 209–10
   See also meat
virtue, 16, 378
   forgiveness as a, 310–11, 344, 371
   paradox of desert and, 358–59, 360–62
virtue ethics, 1, 11, 78, 114–15
vulgarity. *See* profanity

Wilson, Gordon, 344
wool, 175
Woollard, Fiona, 47–49

zoonoses, 186